BADGE OF COURAGE

◆

BADGE OF COURAGE

THE LIFE OF STEPHEN CRANE

LINDA H. DAVIS

HOUGHTON MIFFLIN COMPANY

Boston   New York   1998

For information about permission to reproduce selections from
this book, write to Permissions, Houghton Mifflin Company,
215 Park Avenue South, New York, New York 10003.

Library of Congress Cataloging-in-Publication Data
Davis, Linda H.
    Badge of courage : the life of Stephen Crane / Linda H. Davis.
        p.   cm.
    Includes bibliographical references and index.
    ISBN 0-89919-934-8
    1. Crane, Stephen, 1871–1900 — Biography. 2. Authors, American —
19th century — Biography.   I. Title.
PS1449.C85Z5793   1998
813'.4 — dc21
[B]   98-11870   CIP

Printed in the United States of America

QUM 10 9 8 7 6 5 4 3 2 1

Book design by Melodie Wertelet

Frontispiece: Photograph of Stephen Crane in 1894 by Corwin Knapp Linson.
Stephen Crane Collection, Department of Special Collections, Syracuse University Library

The author is grateful for permission to reprint the following: Excerpts
from *Correspondence of Stephen Crane Set,* Stanley Wertheim and Paul Sorrentino, eds. Copyright © 1988 Columbia University Press. Reprinted with
permission of the publisher. Poems #I, II, IX, and X from vol. 10 of *Collected Works of Stephen Crane,* edited by Fredson Bowers (Charlottesville, Va.,
University Press of Virginia, 1975), reprinted with permission of the University Press of Virginia. Excerpts from the letters of Jonathan Townley
Crane and Mary Helen Peck Crane, reprinted with permission from the
Stephen Crane Collection (#5505), Clifton Waller Barrett Library, Special
Collections Department, University of Virginia Library. Excerpts from the
correspondence of Stephen and the Cora Crane, reprinted with permission from the Stephen Crane Papers and the Cora Crane Papers, Rare
Book and Manuscript Library, Columbia University. Excerpts from the
letters of Thomas Beer and Sylvester Scovel, reprinted with permission of
the University of Minnesota Libraries and Ms. Kate Donahue.

For Chuck
Beloved and friend,
researcher *par excellence*

CONTENTS

Preface   *ix*

I ✦ THE PARSONAGE

1   How Do You Spell "O"?   *3*

2   Great Bugs at Onondaga   *21*

3   The Girl Who Blossomed in
a Mud Puddle   *38*

4   The Noise of Rumors   *58*

5   The Commanding Power of Genius   *76*

II ✦ THE BATTLEFIELD

6   Yellow Sky   *99*

7   The Coming Man   *116*

8   Red Hair   *141*

9   God Save Crane   *168*

10   They Say Smolenski Wept   *190*

11   Living Tally   *211*

III ✦ THE MANOR

12 Warm and Endless Friendship   229

13 The Best Moment of Anybody's Life   246

14 The Ashes of Love   272

15 Lord Tholepin of Mango Chutney   291

16 The Red Room   311

Epilogue: Interpreters   331

Notes   341

Selected Bibliography   381

Index   397

PREFACE

My introduction to Stephen Crane came late, in 1988, when I read his great novella *The Monster* while researching an idea for a book that I never wrote. Somehow Crane and I had missed each other through all my long years of schooling. I was thirty-five years old when I read *The Monster*, and it stunned me. Such was the power of Crane's prose and of the subject matter, which eerily evoked the death of my father in a house fire when I was eight years old, in 1961. My twenty-nine-year-old father died while trying to save my life, and for years afterward I was haunted by dreams in which I could never see his face. What had my handsome young father looked like after the fire? *The Monster* focuses on the aftermath of a house fire, in which a young man is burned nearly to death while rescuing a child. Thereafter he lives as a man without a face — a monster. From the quiet outbreak of the fire, which moves "in silvery waves over the grass" and silently drifts into the branches of a cherry tree wisp by wisp, as sneakily as if "a troop of dim and silent gray monkeys had been climbing a grapevine into the clouds," to the moment of young Jimmie Trescott's rescue — the boy too stricken with fear to move or speak, his eyes fixed on the bedroom door his savior will enter — and then to the unforgettable scene in which Henry Johnson is defaced by exploding chemicals in Dr. Trescott's home laboratory, I was riveted. Who was Stephen Crane? What shaped the man and the writer, what happened to him that he came to write this story in this way?

In the century since Crane's death, five books on his life have appeared: Thomas Beer's *Stephen Crane: A Study in American Letters,* published in 1923; John Berryman's *Stephen Crane: A Critical Biography,* originally published in 1950 and in a revised edition in 1977; R. W. Stallman's *Stephen Crane: A Biography,* in 1968; James B. Colvert's 1984 *Stephen Crane;* and Christopher Benfey's *The Double Life of Stephen Crane,* 1992. Of these books, each of which has contributed importantly to the huge body of criticism, reminiscence, and other writing on Crane and his work, only Stallman's is a conventional full-length biography. In the thirty years since that book was published, hundreds of new Crane letters have become available, and all have been published in the excellent two-volume *Correspondence of Stephen Crane,* edited by Stanley Wertheim and Paul Sorrentino. In 1994 Wertheim and Sorrentino published *The Crane Log: A Documentary Life of Stephen Crane 1871–1900,* another invaluable source. Thanks to Sorrentino and the widow of Melvin H. Schoberlin, Commander Schoberlin's unpublished biography of Crane, "Flagon of Despair," along with revealing letters and other documents gathered in the course of his exhaustive research, also became available at the Crane Collection at Syracuse University.

More excavation work has separated fiction about Crane from fact. John Clendenning showed that Thomas Beer, who was a novelist, apparently fabricated letters of Crane's and even invented stories and romances — including one with a woman named Helen Trent — which were for years picked up as fact by subsequent scholars, writers, and biographers. Scholars such as Thomas A. Gullason, Joseph Katz, and Michael Robertson have turned up new details on Crane's early life and schooling. Altogether, the painstaking work of the last few decades has greatly enriched — and clarified — the portrait of Crane, who has long been shrouded in myth and rumor, in the fantastic tales that began to form around him when he became world-famous at the age of twenty-five.

Memorable in his time as a personality as well as a writer, Stephen Crane is remembered today primarily as the author of a classic Civil War novel, *The Red Badge of Courage.* But he deserves to be as well known for a handful of great short stories. A prolific writer, he cranked out stories, novels, newspaper articles, war dispatches, semifictional war tales, and poetry, moving with ease from one genre to the next. Though much of the ten volumes' worth of professional writing is hackwork and forgettable, at his best Crane broke new literary ground. With his unconventional style — impressionistic, ironic, often dazzling — his prose delved below the surface to expose painful psychological truths. He was a superb technician. His finest reporting pieces — particularly one on a journey into a Pennsylvania coal mine — were forerunners of the brilliant and subjective literary journalism that would distinguish *The New Yorker* and other publications in this century. As scholar J. C. Levenson has pointed out, Crane's short short story "The Upturned Face" is written in the laconic prose style Hemingway is said to have invented. His poetry, what he called his "lines," though seriously limited and flawed, seem to prefigure Pound and the Imagists, still twenty years in the future.

Both in *The Red Badge* and in his superlative short stories written after the Spanish-American War, Crane pioneered a new way of writing about war. Michael Shaara, in his own great Civil War novel, *The Killer Angels*, acknowledged writing his book for "much the same reason" that Stephen Crane wrote *The Red Badge:* because he wanted to know what it felt like to be in that war. Writers as diverse as Shelby Foote, Amy Lowell, H. L. Mencken, Edmund Wilson, Willa Cather, Eudora Welty, H. E. Bates, A. J. Liebling, Henry James, and H. G. Wells have acknowledged Crane's importance to literature. As Sherwood Anderson wrote, "Stephen Crane was a craftsman. The stones he put in the wall are still there."

He wanted to be "unmistakable," and he was. His work was as intensely personal — and troubled — as Van Gogh's, his brush stroke as revolutionary and alive. He was an explosion of color in a gray age. Both in his writing and in his living, he was something of an outlaw — a rebel whose cause was truth, the real thing. His prose was charged with raw energy and nervous daring, a quality Crane himself best expressed in a phrase in "The Upturned Face": "the singing of the nerves." There was something dangerous about such writing, about such a man. He was a literary Elvis, and he left the William Dean Howells generation all shook up.

In his life and in his brilliant work, Stephen Crane embodied the best of his country's spirit: that of the trailblazer, the gutsy, independent-minded individual. He was a product of his Victorian era, yet he seems a very contemporary figure — a man of the 1990s more than of the 1890s. He was as American as jazz, as the cowboy, as baseball. As complex and compelling a personality as any fictional character, Crane provided more than his share of lively copy to the reviewers and reporters who wrote and wrote and wrote about him. Whatever one's opinion of him, he was never a bore. I am reminded of something Robert Duvall said about Au-

gustus McCrae, the character he played in the miniseries of Larry Mc-
Murtry's *Lonesome Dove:* he was *at least* as great a character as Hamlet. So
was Stephen Crane, and I considered it a privilege to play my part as his
biographer. I loved the years with Crane. It's been one helluva ride.

◆

Many people shared in my long and often bumpy eight-year journey with
Stephen Crane, offering personal and professional support along the way.
Without them — and without the astonishing amount of Crane scholarship that preceded my own work — I could never have stayed in the
saddle.

Two wonderful friends unselfishly served as readers. Stephen B.
Oates, a biographer and Civil War historian I greatly admire, first encouraged me to take on Crane. His steady faith helped sustain me over
the long haul. I will always be indebted to him for his honest and perceptive comments on a late draft of the manuscript, for catching me in errors, and for the many times he went out of his way to tell me what he
liked in the work and how much he believed in it. Like all great teachers,
Stephen knows the value of positive reinforcement. His praise was better
than bouquets of gardenias.

James B. Colvert was no less generous with his time and his encouragement. Himself the author of an excellent short life of Crane, and of
some of the most brilliant and graceful critical writing about him, Jim actually shared notes and other source material with me. Like Stephen
Oates, he caught me in errors and pointed out deficiencies — perhaps far
too gently. To have the support and counsel of someone whose own writing on Crane has informed my own reading has meant more than I
can say.

Without the groundbreaking work of others, I would never have
got out of the starting gate. Biographers Thomas Beer, John Berryman,
Melvin H. Schoberlin, R. W. Stallman, James B. Colvert, Christopher
Benfey, and Lillian Gilkes, the biographer of Cora Crane, paved the way.
The work of Stanley Wertheim and Paul Sorrentino has corrected most
of the errors that have plagued Crane scholarship and brought lucid, elegant harmony to the written record. Along with editing Crane's *Correspondence* and producing the Crane *Log,* Wertheim and Sorrentino have
written a number of scholarly pieces on Crane's life and work that have
also been extremely helpful. Stanley Wertheim generously shared ideas

and information with me, notably his research on Amy Leslie. Though we did not agree about everything, I benefited from our discussions and our correspondence. I have the highest respect for Stan's major work on Stephen Crane, and for Paul's.

I am also indebted to the perceptive and fiercely intelligent writing and scholarship of J. C. Levenson, whose first-rate introductions to many of the volumes of *The Works of Stephen Crane,* edited by Fredson Bowers, added much to my understanding of Crane's life and work.

The encouragement and interest of friends, family members, and others have meant more to me than they know. I particularly thank Bob Ward, who gamely helped with my research in England and in Baden- weiler, Germany; helped my husband, Chuck, with his research on Amy Leslie; and served as my poetry adviser. Our talks about Crane's poetry are echoed in my writing. Ann and Leon Fielding graciously opened the doors of their incomparable Brede Place to me and my entourage, shar- ing information and photographs and giving us all an unforgettable day. My friends Anne and Alan Jones drove the Crane sleuths all over Eng- land to see the places where he lived and passed through.

My darling daughter, Allie Yanikoski, spent many hours typing source notes into the computer for her computer-shaky mom; her friend Eleanor Monserud cheerfully helped with the bibliography. My beloved mother, Patricia H. Davis, kindly helped care for my house and children during the homestretch of this book and paid for some of the pho- tographs. My dear friend Harrison Kinney, a prolific and wonderful writer, urged me on and helped keep my spirits up with his faith in me, as did my good friend Sandy Blanton of the Peter Lampack Agency, who sent me writings about Crane over the years.

Stephen Crane's great-nephew, Dr. Robert Crane, generously shared photographs and memories of the Crane family. Dr. Rudolph Bauert of Badenweiler talked with me about Crane over refreshments in the garden of his home and sent me a copy of the German death certificate and other helpful materials. Dr. Charles Millstein of the Department of En- dodontics, Tufts University School of Dental Medicine, told me about dentistry in the late nineteenth century. Dr. Frank Ryan patiently an- swered my questions about tuberculosis, providing crucial insights about Crane's health. My bright and amusing friend Dr. Fred Landes good-na- turedly let me pick his brain on other medical issues. The gifted Jill Wein- stein helped me empathize with Crane's love of horses and riding by reawakening my own love of the ride. And through their constant interest in my work year after year, my precious friends kept me going, most notably Ann Jones, Gary Monserud, Martha and Bob O'Brien, Helen Sheehy, Fran Kiernan, my father-in-law, Dick Yanikoski, my aunt and uncle, Larry and Connie Lister, and my sweet mother-in-law, Julie Yanikoski, who died before this book, which she was impatiently waiting to read, was finished.

My agent, Max Gartenberg, hung in throughout the years without ever making me feel bad about taking so long. I thank him for that and for the grace, intelligence, and meticulousness with which he has worked on my behalf.

I have been extremely fortunate in my publisher. I particularly thank my editor, Janet Silver, a model of judicious editorial judgment, patience, and tact, who believed in my Stephen Crane and supported the book when I needed it most. My manuscript editor, Peg Anderson, did a masterful job of improving my copy and was a pleasure to work with. I also thank Janet Silver's assistant, Heidi Pitlor, and her former assistant, Wendy Holt, now a Houghton Mifflin editor, for their hard work and cheerful support.

For permission to quote from their Stephen Crane collections and to reproduce photographs and illustrations, I thank the Clifton Waller Barret Library, Special Collections Department, University of Virginia Library, with special thanks to Michael Plunkett, Christina M. Deane, and Pauline Page. I thank the University Press of Virginia for permission to publish poems from the *Collected Works of Stephen Crane*, edited by Fredson Bowers; also the Stephen Crane Papers and Cora Crane Papers, Rare Books and Manuscripts Library, Columbia University, with particular thanks to Jean W. Ashton and Ellen Scaruffe; the Dartmouth College Library, especially Philip N. Cronenwett; the University of Minnesota Libraries, and Alan K. Lathrop; and the Stephen Crane Collection, Department of Special Collections, Syracuse University Library, with extra thanks to Carolyn A. Davis. For permission to publish photographs of Amy Leslie, I am most grateful to the Harvard University Theatre Collection and Brian Benoit and to the *Chicago Sun Times*, particularly Richard Cahan and Jim Strong.

Sincerest thanks also to Jeff Adams, Sally Alderdice (Claverack Free Library), Paul Ardler (Port Jervis Free Library), the Asbury Park Free Library, the Baker Library (Dartmouth College), Betty Beck (Des Moines County Historical Society), Alma Jean Bennett, George A. Biastre (Ever-

green Cemetary Association), the Boston Public Library, Jana Bovino
(Downers Grove, Illinois, Public Library), the Haydon Burns Library
(Jacksonville, Florida), Sister Kathryn Callahan (Congregational Ar-
chives and Records, Congregation of Sisters of the Holy Cross, South
Bend, Indiana), John Clendenning, the Cook County (Illinois) recorder of
deeds, Margaret Vasey Dixon, Leo Dolenski, Kate Donahue, Sister M.
Rosaleen Dunleavy, C.S.C. (Cushwa-Leighton Library, St. Mary's Col-
lege), Kristy Eldridge, Burgermeister Engler (Badenweiler, Germany),
Joseph Epstein, Sylvia Stark Farrington, Tara Fellini, Dr. John Foss, the
Free Public Library of Philadelphia, Elizabeth Friedmann, Richard C.
Fyffe (Special Collections, University of Connecticut Library), Susie
Guest (Burlington, Iowa, County Library), Diana Haskell and Margaret
Kulic (Newberry Library, Chicago), the Houghton, Widener, and Nathan
Marsh Pusey libraries at Harvard University, Joseph Kanon, Laurel and
Katie Kirke, Lafayette College (especially Jan S. Ballard); the Library of
Congress, Arthur Lubow, Charles Michaud (Turner Free Library), Di
Newton, Ingrid Nyholm (Chicago Historical Society), Mary Rose West
Osborne, Liz Prevett (Harvard Law Library), the Mugar Memorial
Library at Boston University, the National Archives (Waltham, Mas-
sachusetts, and Washington, D.C.), the Newark Public Library, the
New York Public Library, Michael Robertson, Ronile Rubino, Helen
Q. Shroyer (Special Collections Library, Purdue University), Mary Ann
Shaw, Jane Siegel and Patrick Lawlor (Rare Books and Manuscripts
Library, Columbia University), the Skillman Library (Lafayette Col-
lege), John J. Slonaker, Corliss Smith, Louis Stableford, the Tippecanoe
County (Indiana) Public Library, the UCLA University Research Library,
the University of Pennsylvania Library, the U.S. Army Military History
Institute (Carlisle, Pennsylvania), the Van Pelt–Dietrich Library Center
(University of Pennsylvania), the Volusia County (Florida) Library Cen-
ter, the Harold Washington Library Center (Chicago Public Library),
Ray Wenlinger (The Players Library), James W. West, M.D., Clenise
and Alex White, Phyllis Wright, Jim Woodman (Boston Atheneum),
Laura Yanikoski, Richard Yanikoski, and Suzanne Zack (Stowe-Day
Foundation Library, William H. Gillette Collection).

Last — but first in importance, and first in my heart — I thank
my husband, Chuck Yanikoski, though I hardly know how. For eight
years he shared his marriage with Stephen Crane, without jealousy and
with awe-inspiring generosity. He dug a ton of material out of the library

for me, served as my first reader on the manuscript, and spent countless hours discussing Crane with me. He was my psychiatrist, pep squad, minister, and best friend. He urged me on when I felt overwhelmed and discouraged and believed in me when my faith in myself faltered. He was indispensable to the writing of this book, and its dedication to him is but a meager repayment for all that I owe him and for all that he is.

I

THE
PARSONAGE

1

HOW DO YOU
SPELL "O"?

In the fall of 1890, a group of Delta Upsilon fraternity brothers at Lafayette College in Easton, Pennsylvania, stormed one of the college dormitories in search of their next hazing victim. East Hall was set far from the other college buildings, down a hill, so the hazers had to go out of their way to get him. Lafayette's dangerous hazing practices had recently come to the attention of the local press. Just two weeks earlier the *Easton Sunday Call* had reported that a group of sophomores had surprised a freshman baseball player, who attacked the leader of the group with a bat, critically injuring him.

The new pledge, who lived alone in a single room, had recently arrived from a school up north. When the sophomores reached Room 170 at the rear of the building, they issued a "loud summons," remembered Ernest G. Smith, who was one of the group, and pounded on the door. There was no answer. The brothers and freshman pledges lighted a lamp and burst into the room. They were startled to see the pledge quivering in a corner, holding a loaded revolver. He was unimpressive looking — small and thin, with pale hair and large, shadowed eyes. He was dressed, improbably, in "a grotesque nightgown." His skin had turned a "ghastly white" and he was "extremely nervous." By the time Smith saw the pledge, the revolver was aimed at the floor. Then the boy's body went limp, and the gun dropped from his hand. According to Smith, cooler heads prevailed, preventing further hazing of the new boy.

It was the last time anyone would record seeing Stephen Crane afraid.

Years later, seeming to draw on this experience in a work of fiction, he would write: "he was suddenly smitten with the terror. It came upon his heart like the grasp of claws. All the power faded from his muscles. For an instant he was no more than a dead man."

◆

The image of Stephen Crane pale and quivering, backed into a corner with a loaded revolver in his hand, is at odds with other pictures of the scrappy, scrawny kid, who was usually remembered for his pluck. His brother Edmund (Ed) — one of eight older brothers and sisters — offered a picture of three-year-old Stevie, as his family called him, struggling to keep up with his brothers when they went bathing in the Raritan River near Bound Brook, New Jersey. Not yet able to swim, Stevie had nevertheless ventured in over his head, extending his arms out over the water like a preacher at a baptism, calling out to his brothers that he was "fimming." One summer day in 1875, when he was not yet four, Stevie got in so far over his head that Edmund finally "plucked him out, gasping but unscared, just as his yellow hair was going under," remembered his brother. "We boys were naturally delighted with his grit."

And yet water — taken in a religious context that would seem quite literal to a young child — figured in an episode that had terrified Stephen a year earlier. On August 10, 1874, the two-year-old accompanied his middle-aged parents and his grown sister Agnes to a Methodist revival meeting at Camp Tabor, near Denville, New Jersey. There, according to a witness, the preacher thundered on about "the final conflagration" awaiting them. Stamping his feet, raising and smashing down his fist, he asked the sinners whether they were prepared "to take hell by storm? Are your bones iron, and your flesh brass, that you plunge headlong into the lake of fire?" And as the sinners responded with a chorus of "fervent supplication," baby Stevie "clung to his sister's skirt, and wept."

Stephen Crane's childhood as the son of the Reverend Jonathan Townley Crane, a Methodist minister, and Mary Helen Peck Crane, a clergyman's daughter and a member of the Woman's Christian Temperance Union, had its share of psychological terrors — the worst of the religious rhetoric flying out at the sensitive young boy, it seems, like furies or black riders coming from the sea, as he would later write. In *Holiness, the Birthright of All God's Children*, Stephen's father described man's condition as "one of inexpressible evil. He is guilty, condemned, corrupt, helpless, the wrath of God resting on him, and hell waiting his coming, with its eternal darkness and despair." The maternal side of Stephen's family was stocked with ministers, even including a Methodist Episcopal bishop, Jesse Truesdale Peck, author of the chilling *What Must I Do to Be Saved?* "Upon my mother's side, everybody as soon as he could walk, became a Methodist clergyman — of the old ambling-nag, saddlebag, exhorting kind," Stephen wrote a friend years later.

Family legend maintains that Stephen was descended from both a Stephen Crane of Elizabethtown, New Jersey, who was married to a woman with red hair, and a Revolutionary War patriot, also named Stephen Crane, who was bayoneted to death by British troops just before the battle of Springfield in June 1780. The novelist, who was named for both Stephens, would embrace the story as part of his inheritance, though it is not certain that he was descended from the second man. Writing about the patriot Crane's courageous death, Stephen would say, "In those old times the family did it's duty." Of his immediate forebears, who had traded their guns for Bibles, he would write with disappointed affection. His father "was a great, fine, simple mind" who had written "numerous" tracts on theology. As for his mother, Stephen is said to have marveled that such a well-educated, talented woman "could have wrapped herself so completely in the 'vacuous, futile, psalm-singing that passed for worship' in those days."

Stephen Crane's parents were not, in fact, the one-dimensional people that such comments would indicate. The frizzy-bearded, bespectacled father, who was "without an evil habit," as his wife put it, was also courageous in his convictions. He was not afraid to express even the more unwelcome parts of Methodist ideology or to disagree with the church hierarchy, including his own father-in-law. Remembered in later years as an "eloquent" preacher, "a pleasant, genial personage, always dignified, yet cheerful and companionable," he was beloved for his sense of humor. Some of his admirers even tried to get "a book of his witticisms" published, said a granddaughter. In family diaries, letters, and reminiscences, Jonathan Townley Crane emerges as a noble, scholarly, kind man who was modest about his own preaching, a physically affectionate and sympathetic father who was keenly interested in his children and proud of his wife. "The baby is a miracle, as all babies are, & to be appreciated, must be seen," he once wrote his father-in-law. He was patient — even amused, it seems — with his numerous children, who were apt to interrupt him in the midst of a sermon. Bursting into a Sunday service with a rattrap in hand, two of them once called out, "Here it is, Father. You said to bring it to you as soon as we found it." During another service he shook out what he thought was his pocket handkerchief and found himself holding a child's undershirt. He liked to work in his garden and was once so distracted by the beauties of nature while trolling for pickerel that he "almost forgot the fish."

Jonathan Townley Crane was born on June 19, 1819. Raised in Connecticut Farms (Union), New Jersey, he had lost both of his parents by the time he was thirteen. Forced to make his own way in the world, he became apprenticed to a trunk maker, who helped him go to college, and at eighteen he made the decision that would direct the course of his life thereafter, leaving the Presbyterian Church in which he had been raised for the Methodist Episcopal Church. Having rejected the "repulsive" Calvinist teachings of his youth, which included such "deformities" as predestination and infant damnation, he now embraced a kindlier church that preached salvation through individual faith but was scarcely less severe in the narrowness of its doctrine. Jonathan's rigid set of beliefs seemed calculated to keep him toeing the moral line by rejecting all pleasures that threatened one's virtuousness, including dancing, drinking, smoking, novel reading, and gambling. After graduating from the College of New Jersey (later Princeton University) in 1843 with a prize in English composition, he became an itinerant preacher on circuits in New Jersey, Pennsylvania, and New York. Early in 1848, at the age of twenty-eight, he married twenty-one-year-old Mary Helen Peck — a love match, it seems — the only daughter of Methodist clergyman George Peck, editor of the *Methodist Quarterly Review*.

Mary Helen Peck Crane looks out from the only known photograph of her, taken in middle age, with a kind, softly smiling face distinguished by a prominent nose. A boyhood friend of Stephen's would remember that she "dressed in dark colors, somewhat suggesting the quakeress without the poke-bonnet." Born on April 20, 1827, she graduated from Rutgers Female Institute in New York the year before she married. The letters she wrote home to her parents give a picture of a woman who is duty-bound, reconciled to life as a minister's wife and the mother of a large brood, and yet frustrated, feeling that she should be doing something more than tending her children and sewing.

Writing to her parents soon after her wedding, she talked of the difficulties of being apart from her husband when he left in the mornings on his pastoral calls. "I find that I am yet something of a *baby* — I can hardly help feeling lonely when left alone but of course I cannot always go with him, or always have him stay with me, however I think I am improving, and I trust that the sage lectures of my dear mother were not altogether lost upon me." Sensing that her husband's parishioners were "a little shy of me at first" — an attitude she attributed to her city origins — she was making an effort to draw them out and was succeeding. "Pray for me," she wrote in closing. Her husband felt the separations, too. In a letter to his mother- and father-in-law, written as he was about to go away on business a year after his marriage, he confided his feelings about leaving his wife and their first child. The baby was sick, and Mary Helen apparently pregnant again. "I had hoped to take my little world with me: but this now seems quite doubtful," he wrote. His wife, he wrote in another letter, was "my better half."

Being married to a clergyman meant frequent moves, and for Helen it also meant unending pregnancies — fourteen in all. Following a relatively long settling-in period at Pennington Seminary in New Jersey, where Jonathan served as president from 1849 to 1858, the Cranes moved with their rapidly growing brood from one church to the next in New Jersey and New York, living in each place from one to three years.

The letters to Helen's parents were soon dominated by accounts of sick children, children suffering accidents and mishaps, children outwearing and outgrowing their clothes. There was always a new baby in the house. The lonely young bride of the first year was quickly replaced in these letters by a figure barely discernible beneath a mountain of sewing. She was "getting weary of quite so much of it," she wrote in one letter. "I have plenty of work, enough for two or three pairs of hands," she wrote in 1857, nine years after her marriage. Her husband — "Mr. Crane," she called him in her letters — assumed a large part of the letter-writing duties. He sent his in-laws cheerful, newsy accounts of "Mrs. Crane" or "Helen," of their children, and of church business. He dutifully repeated the children's funny remarks and worried about their health, filling the letters with more details than his overburdened wife could get into hers. In one letter dated "Sunday Evening, Feb. 18th / 20 minutes past 10 o'clock," he records the birth of a baby girl.

> Dear Father,
>   All is well. While deeply engaged in reading the life of John Nelson, I was interrupted by sounds not to be mistaken. They were nothing more nor less than the crying of a genu-

ine baby, which mother pronounced, in her report, 'a great big girl.' I am writing (and *was reading*) in the front room, or parlour, while the Committee on Posterity are in session in the back room *upstairs*, Ergo, the said crying was a pretty fair performance for the first attempt, showing that the young lady in question is well provided for in the matter of lungs.

While keeping an ear lovingly tuned to the clamor of his swelling household, Jonathan was deeply engaged in his ministerial work and related interests, to which he applied himself with seemingly boundless energy. Awarded a doctorate of divinity from Dickinson College in Carlisle, Pennsylvania, in 1856, he turned out articles and books declaiming the evils of dancing, novel reading, and intoxication. He lectured on astronomy and pondered the flammable question of slavery as the country moved toward civil war. Though he was against slavery, he proposed a system modeled on Russia's serfdom as a compromise to avoid war. By late January 1865, Jonathan had preached at or attended seven funeral services for soldiers, the last one for a former prisoner at Andersonville. From his post in Morristown, New Jersey, Jonathan noted the fall of Richmond and Petersburg, as well as Lee's surrender, which left the town "full of joy." He offered a brief entry for Lincoln's assassination, which had not yet been confirmed: "The whole place rings with the startling rumor," he wrote on April 15, 1865. "How cheering the thought that God lives." There followed "a day of gloom, and excitement," during which he preached to a full house, though he "felt wholly unfitted to preach at all."

Consumed by the demands of her large family, Helen Crane managed only a fleeting mention of the war in the letters she hastily wrote her parents. "I hope Sherman will get through safely and do great things," she wrote on November 20, 1864. Even religious matters were only lightly touched on. Whatever great or small things Helen wanted to accomplish for herself would have to wait. Although she wrote her father that she had not inherited her mother's "failing" — a tendency to "work too hard" — she sewed and mended clothes and linens by the bushel, making quilts, new jackets, overcoats, and pants out of old jackets and trousers.

She loved to paint but was usually compelled to lay aside her brushes for the sewing needle. One year, however, she produced a picture of autumnal Virginia in crayon. "Mr. C. thinks [it] finer than an oil painting," she wrote her parents. "I have an ardent admirer of my genius in my husband, he is very proud of my paintings and flowers." Stealing some time to write to her parents, she confessed that she was seeing "visions of pantaloons with rents before & behind with troops of unfinished and unmended garments, coming to haunt me as I write but I must send them to the rear." Her husband helped with the children, "taking care of Sissy at night which is a great relief to me," she wrote when her household was ringing with whooping cough, but the burden fell on her. By 1869, after more than twenty years of marriage and child-rearing, she expressed amazement about a complimentary mention of her in a Methodist paper. "I guess the accomplishments have long since disappeared — been burried out of sight by stern realities and duties," she wrote her parents.

By then, stern reality had brought illness and death into the large household. The energetic Jonathan suffered from what he called sick headaches — "the enemy of my peace in the days of my youth." Five of the Crane children died in infancy or childhood, a high mortality rate even in those pre-vaccine days. Lizzie and Blanche died of scarlet fever in October 1866, within three days of each other, thus breaking the family circle, noted Jonathan, and beginning "our colony on the other shore." The following January Jonathan's fifty-eight-year-old sister, Agnes — "my beloved sister" and "a faithful conscientious christian," he wrote in his journal — died at the Crane home three days after she suddenly began "bleeding at the lungs," perhaps of tuberculosis. A month later the eleventh Crane child, a boy named Jesse Peck, was born. He died at the age of five months, of cholera infantum. Two more children died of unknown causes.

The letters to Helen's parents tell of a baby girl who suffered from "fits," she says only, and later died; of Sis (Nellie) taking iron one summer "to strengthen her"; and of children who seemed to their mother "debilitated" even when healthy. Having contracted dysentery as a toddler, Georgie continued to be a worry, looking "emaciated," in his father's eyes, long after the illness had passed. He suffered from convulsions, attributed to a bad cough, and was a slow learner whose speech also developed slowly. "Nellie," Mary Helen, was overtaken at seventeen or eighteen by something her mother referred to vaguely as "difficulties" and was sent away for some weeks. Though the doctor had not seemed alarmed, Helen worried that her eldest daughter was "destined to a life of disease and suffering."

In his journal, at least, Jonathan seemed borne aloft by his faith. "Well, God reigns, and in his hands we are all safe, whatever awaits us," he wrote on the first expected death of a child. Another baby had gone "from our arms, to those of the Good Shepherd," yet another "to the better home above." In her letters home, Helen wrote of missing her dead babies, who were buried under a rose bush in Elizabeth, New Jersey.

In the fall of 1871 the family was living in a three-story red brick house at 14 Mulberry Street, a quiet, tree-shaded street in Newark, where Jonathan had been the church's presiding elder since 1868. At 5:30 in the morning of November 1, Helen gave birth to her fourteenth and last child, a boy they named Stephen. The new baby — "our precious baby," Helen called him — arrived less than two years after the birth of an apparently healthy baby boy, who had died. Helen was now forty-five years old; Jonathan, fifty-two. Stephen joined eight surviving brothers and sisters, Mary Helen, George Peck, Jonathan Townley, William Howe, Agnes Elizabeth, Edmund Bryan, Wilbur Fiske, and Luther, ranging in age from eight to twenty-one.

On a summer day nearly four years later, a small yellow-haired boy stretched out on the back of a large Newfoundland dog named Solomon, who was paddling in the Raritan River. By holding on to the big dog's collar, Stevie was able to swim along while his older brothers bathed.

As the baby of the family, Stephen was always holding on — to an older sister's hand, to the dog's collar — struggling to keep up, to stay afloat. Cherubic-looking, with huge blue eyes and blond curls brushed with gold, he was physically fragile. At five months the baby seemed to his father "uncommonly strong," but by eight months the Cranes were worried enough to take him to the country. The move revived him; the infant appeared "much improved by the change from the city to the woods." At not quite two, he seemed "fat and flourishing"; a month later, however, Jonathan described him as "so sick that we are anxious about him." Though he was a faithful diarist of Stephen's health, Jonathan offered no precise information about the nature of these illnesses, which in time frequently kept the boy home from school.

Like the two creased and grainy photographs of Stephen Crane that survive from this time, the few known facts about his childhood form a hazy picture. After Newark, the family moved to Bloomington when his father became presiding elder of the Elizabeth District. He was a plucky, precocious boy who taught himself to read before the age of four and was attempting to write by age three, when he offered his own letters to "Ganma" to be included in one of his father's letters to George Peck. "I suppose that he will expect her to reply in regard to every topic introduced," Jonathan wrote his father-in-law with obvious delight. Stephen's older brothers and sisters, urged along by his proficiency with language, read to him and challenged him with large vocabulary words. Edmund, finding the baby "bright and very teachable," "amused myself by having him pronounce five and six syllable words," he wrote later. "After a few laughable failures, [Stephen] would accomplish a correct pronunciation by spelling the word after me syllable by syllable, resolving them into their sound."

Within the confines of a strict Methodist upbringing, Stephen did the normal boy things, playing for hours at toy soldiers, using buttons in place of real figures as he patiently maneuvered his troops across the floor. He had a trick pony, an old, white circus animal "he loved devotedly," said Edmund. Stevie was sure that the "B" branded on the pony's shoulder stood for P. T. Barnum. The family spent summers at Ocean Grove, a burgeoning Methodist enclave on the New Jersey shore, and made excursions to the Methodist campground at Denville.

If anything set Stephen Crane apart from other children, it was his mother. After nearly twenty-three years of marriage, Helen had finally escaped the sewing pile to make her contribution to the world outside. Taking Uncle Jesse Peck's dictum to heart — that a woman must "be able to bring her quiet but potent influence to bear against public dangers" — she now joined the temperance cause with zeal, attending meetings locally and out of town. She gave public lectures about the eroding effects of alcohol on the human body, and joined the newly founded Woman's Christian Temperance Union, her sense of mission undoubtedly propelled by the experience of her own brother, Wilbur F. Peck, whose life had been shattered by alcoholism. In June of 1873, Wilbur Peck took a temperance pledge in Newark in the presence of his father and Jonathan.

As his wife was finding her wings, Jonathan's were becoming less powerful. He had taken on the conservative Holiness Movement, which required a second conversion experience called "entire sanctification." The movement was gaining strength within the church hierarchy, and, having written against it in *Holiness* in 1874, Jonathan found himself under siege by some Holiness advocates, who conspired to ruin his reputation and drive him down in the church ranks. *Holiness* was endorsed by some church leaders but was reviled in print as a "poisonous reptile" by a reviewer who exulted in having burned the book in his stove after reading it. "That brethren should so differ was painful to him," Helen would write later. George Peck's prominence may have prevented church officials from taking further action against Jonathan, but in 1876, following Peck's death, the church sent Jonathan back to the itinerant ministry, like an angel expelled from heaven. He was assigned to the Cross Street Church in Paterson, New Jersey, in 1876, then was compelled to move his family again just two years later, when the presiding elder of the Newark Conference decided to reduce expenses by hiring a pastor at a smaller salary. (Jonathan had been paid only $1,250, he noted in his diary, and was "promised at least $150 more.") On April 6, 1878, when Stephen was six, the Cranes moved to Port Jervis, New York, where Jonathan became pastor of the Drew Methodist Church. But the attacks on his book continued to wound him. While going on with his ministry with all his usual energy, he began revising the book with the hope of changing some minds.

A pretty place nestled amid softly rolling, pine-covered hills in the Delaware Valley at the juncture of New York, New Jersey, and Pennsylvania, Port Jervis was an Erie Railroad town. Most of its 10,000 residents worked for the railroad or in jobs related to it. Before long the wife of the new minister began to make her mark, drawing large audiences and favorable press from the *Port Jervis Gazette* for her lectures on alcoholism. (The town boasted as many as eighty saloons at one time.) Some of these talks were enhanced by crayon illustrations and live demonstrations. At one memorable lecture, Mrs. Crane cracked an egg into a glass, then poured alcohol over it to show how the mass hardened. Helen also lectured "on the false religions of India" and on "China and Its People" — the latter enlivened by children dressed in native costume, including Helen's own blond, six-year-old Stephen, according to one story, dressed as a coolie. With her husband, she cofounded a Sunday school for the town's black children, and she would later help organize an industrial school to provide work and training for local black women and children. Helen's housekeeping suffered; the church ladies clucked their disapproval and advised her to stay home and care for her family.

In the summer of 1878, when he was seven, Stephen was introduced to a slightly older boy, Post (George) Wheeler. The two boys were attending a WCTU rally with their mothers, and afterward Stephen and his mother accompanied the Wheelers to their town in Pennsylvania for a short visit. "The day coach was full," said Post, so he and Stevie sat apart from their mothers in the smoking car. Stevie, a blond, pale, "hungry-looking" boy, lit up a Sweet Caporal cigarette, gave one to Post, and proceeded to smoke it while occasionally glancing over his shoulder toward his mother.

The next day the boys attended a centenary celebration commemorating the British and Indian attack on Forty Fort. Their mothers gave each boy a quarter "to spend as we liked." Stevie boldly approached a street vendor selling beer for ten cents and plunked down a dime.

"Gimme one," he said.

"Hey?" said the vendor.

"I said gimme a beer."

The fat Dutchman took the dime.

"You gimme a beer or gimme back my dime!" said Stevie, his voice "a shrill falsetto."

The vendor offered him a token amount that was mostly foam.

"That ain't half full!" he said. "You fill it up."

Later, the wide-eyed Post Wheeler watched Stevie drink the beer.

"Stevie . . . how'd you dast do it?" said Post.

"Pshaw!" said Stevie. "Beer ain't nothing at all." Then he added, "How was I going to know what it tasted like less'n I tasted it? How you going to know about things at all less'n you *do* 'em?"

Speaking at a children's day festival held at the Methodist Church in June, the Reverend Crane had talked about "the great difficulties through which the young mind passes before it is properly moulded and prepared to meet the world in its many phases of sin and folly." If the tenor of the Crane household was predominantly religious, it was also word-driven. Words, Stephen soon learned, were power. Delivered in a thundering voice at an open-air revival meeting, words could terrify; there was drama in such preaching. In the Bible's grand sweep and poetry were fiery colors and vivid imagery: the lake of fire, the four horsemen of the Apocalypse, the riders and horses arrayed for battle, the serpent and the eagle and the dragon, a beast rising from the sea — such images were repeated like waves throughout the Book of Revelation. The words washed over Stephen and entered him. As a speaker, Jonathan had a flair for ad-libbing and was able to hold an audience spellbound. People praised his uncompromising rhetoric for its tenderness and style. His sermons were distinguished by allusions to fables and the writings of Homer. Every day before young Stephen was the example of a father putting words on paper; excluding letters and diaries, he wrote ten pages a day. The subject matter and literary quality perhaps mattered less as an example to his children than the act of writing itself. "Did nothing all day worth mentioning," Jonathan once confided to his journal, putting words down anyway.

Before Stephen was in school, Jonathan wrote a series of slight, charming tales for children that offered a gentle moral or lesson. Two of the pieces purported to be letters from a cat and a dog; another, written as a fable, showed the metamorphosis of a potato worm into a silver-winged moth. In the years to come, Stephen's sister Agnes wrote fiction for women's magazines. His brother Townley became a cub reporter for the *New York Tribune*. Even Uncle Wilbur Peck wrote poetry, which he sent to Jonathan for his opinion. Of all the writing Cranes before Stephen, however, it was his mother, the indefatigable temperance lecturer, who showed real talent. Her folksy, humorous, heavily colloquial tales drew on her own long years of household drudgery; two of her stories appeared in the *New Jersey Tribune and Advertiser* and the *Monmouth Tribune*.

Edmund retained a memory of Stephen, scarcely past babyhood, trying to write his own compositions at a table, the words represented by "weird marks." Townley, a fledgling reporter by then, would often ask their mother for the spelling of a word. Imitating his older brother's tone of voice, Stevie looked up from his paper and said, "Ma, how do you spell 'O'?"

Uncle Jesse Peck had long ago decreed that "novel reading is a crime," an activity that "murders the heart, the intellect and the body." Father himself had warned of the perils of reading "trashy literature." But Stephen's brothers got hold of dime novels, which they fed to the baby like candy. By the time he was four, Stephen was reading James Fenimore Cooper, apparently without fear of eternal damnation — and also without fear of his father, who would probably have forgiven his youngest child. In 1866 Jonathan himself had read *Vanity Fair*, or part of it, in order to form an objective opinion of the novel, which was being praised as "a true picture of English 'Society,'" he noted in his journal.*

At the age of eight, Stephen took a shine to Little Goody Brighteyes and wrote a story about the character, which has not survived. Following an erratic first year of school, which began on September 2, 1878, when he was just shy of his seventh birthday, he wrote his first known poem:

---

* He disapproved of the book: "If the picture is true, 'Society' needs reforming," he wrote.

I'd Rather Have —

Last Christmas they gave me a sweater,
    And a nice warm suit of wool
But I'd rather be cold and have a dog,
    To watch when I come from school.

Father gave me a bicycle,
    But that isn't much of a treat,
Unless you have a dog at your heels
    Racing away down the street

They bought me a camping outfit,
    But a bonfire by a log,
Is all the outfit I would ask
    If I only had a dog.

They seem to think a little dog
    Is a killer of all earth's joys;
But oh, that "pesky little dog"
    Means hours of joy to the boys.

Though he was on the honor roll of Miss E. Reeve's class in the Main Street School, by August Stephen's health was again a worry. Jonathan wrote about it with some frequency. Noting in his diary on August 8 that "Stevie is not well," Jonathan reported an improvement the next day. Helen had taken the train out to neighboring Hartwood to get medicine, and by the eleventh Stephen seemed "very much better." But months later he was spending school days at home. Writing to Agnes on November 17, Jonathan said only that "Stevie is well, and is getting some flesh on his bones, but is not at school."

February 16, 1880, began much like any other day. Having preached a vigorous sermon on infidelity the night before "to an unusually large congregation," Jonathan climbed the stairs of his parsonage to write the sermon he was to give that evening and was seized by chest pains. Helen flew into action, applying a mustard plaster to her husband's chest and feet, then giving him brandy and morphine in rapid succession. But Jonathan died before the doctor arrived, about a half-hour after the pain began. He was sixty years old.

Some fourteen hundred mourners — more than double the size of the congregation — poured through the church to pay their respects. "The audience was one of the largest, if not the largest, ever assembled in the church," said the *Port Jervis Daily Union*. Ministers streamed in from the district; clerics arrived from other churches. A memorial was held in place of a local temperance meeting. Accompanied by the Crane family and local ministers, Jonathan's body was taken by train to Elizabeth, for a still larger funeral at St. James's Methodist Episcopal Church. The service was conducted by a dozen ministers, and some one hundred clergymen attended. Jonathan was buried in the family plot in Elizabeth's Evergreen Cemetery, "as a flood of golden sunshine burst upon the scene," Helen wrote later. For nearly a month after Jonathan's death, the *Daily Union* wrote about the loss of the Reverend J. T. Crane, which had greatly affected the town.

Amid the public outpouring of sympathy and grief, Helen and her children were required to leave the parsonage. For reasons that are unclear, she moved to Roseville, near Newark, apparently leaving Stephen in the care of twenty-two-year-old Edmund, who, along with Wilbur and Luther, had dropped out of Centenary Collegiate Institute after their father died. Edmund secured a teaching job in Sussex County, New Jersey, and he and Stephen boarded at the home of some Crane cousins, Mr. H. W. Van Sycle and his wife and four sons.

Stephen was forever silent on the subject of his father's death and the months of rootlessness following it, saying only, in years to come, that he had been seven years old when Jonathan died. He was actually eight.

✦

Agnes was heartbroken by her father's death. "Oh. my Father! Here is my greatest heartache," she confided to her diary nine months later. "Sometimes. often. I cannot seem to believe that he is gone beyond where he can hear the cries of his children and see their tears."

In spite of her grief, Agnes stayed in school and graduated from Centenary in June as class valedictorian. As revealed by her diary entries and the testimony of those who knew her, Agnes was the selfless daughter, always striving to be perfect and paying a personal price for it. She "was perfect in *all* my lessons *all* this week," she had written at seventeen or eighteen; "Have been perfect all day this week." Feeling that she was a "horrid creature" and wondering "if it is too late for improvement," her greatest ambition had been to be "a better Christian" and "a lady in the fullest sense of the word." She became well educated in both the classics and in science and was thoroughly familiar with "the best literature." She wanted to be accomplished in the arts of drawing, painting, and writing — above all, she wanted to *"write,"* she had confided to her diary long before. Her family was so "oyster-like . . . there are few to whom I can speak freely and I have learned, too, that people will talk to me with great vivacity about their own troubles but grow inattentive when a reciprocal confidation — ever so slight, is attempted."

William graduated from Albany Law School and was admitted to the bar in May. In mid-June, Helen and Stephen went to live with him at 21 Brooklyn Street, near the Delaware and Hudson Canal, in Port Jervis. Then, three years after Jonathan's sudden death, Stephen and Helen moved again, to the resort town of Asbury Park, 120 miles from Port Jervis on the New Jersey coast.

At a time when he needed continuity and rootedness, Stephen had come to a transient community that seemed to underscore his sense of being orphaned and adrift. Described by the *American Baedeker* as an "extraordinary settlement, possible only in America," where "thousands of persons young and old, voluntarily elect to spend their summer vacations under a religious autocracy, which is severe both in its positive and negative regulations," Asbury Park, along with its sister town, Ocean Grove, offered a contradictory mix of regulation and escape. Asbury Park was primarily a pleasure resort of great wooden hotels, boarding houses and cottages, with well-fed guests promenading along the mile-long plank boardwalk fronting the ocean. Called "Ocean Grave" by its youth, Ocean Grove was a prohibition town that advertised itself as "the Summer Mecca of American Methodists" and offered a refuge from life's "temptation and dissipations." Holiness meetings, Bible lessons, temperance discussions, and evening entertainments such as a lecture on the "proper normal pose" when walking were the order of the day. One might attend a performance by a whistler or a musical recital by "graduates of the blind asylum."

Townley and his wife, Fannie, lived in Asbury Park, as did Nellie, now Mrs. Van Nortwick, and her husband. Agnes, who had resigned a teaching job at Port Jervis's Mountain House School when she was unable to control her class, took a position at Asbury Park's intermediate school. When Helen purchased a clapboard and shingle house called Arbutus Cottage at 508 Fourth Avenue, Agnes apparently moved in with her to help care for Stephen. Agnes was now a tall, slender young woman of twenty-seven, with large brown eyes and spinsterish pince-nez. "Mother has hope that her ugly duckling may turn out a swan," she liked to say. Whatever Agnes lacked in physical allure was more than compensated by her cynical, keen mind, which was of a literary, intellectual bent, and by her sweet nature, her "radiant personality," and her "spirit of fun," said two of Stephen's friends. A woman of "magnetic charm," "she was Stephen Crane's good angel, brightening his boyhood as an older sister can sometimes do."

To another childhood friend, however, Agnes seemed overwhelmed with duties and unequal to the task of caring for her adventurous little brother, then scarcely out of knee pants. Small and undernourished-looking at twelve and thirteen years old, Stephen would come home from school or ice skating on the lake to find no supper on the table. He would set off again to "range the neighborhood for food and companionship," remembered an anonymous friend, "telling tales to the children of the various mothers — mine was one — who often sewed on his buttons."

While Agnes taught school and helped care for Stephen, Helen immersed herself in the temperance cause. Promptly elected president of the WCTU for Asbury Park and Ocean Grove, she was soon giving lectures, holding a temperance meeting for juveniles, and worrying about "the growing taste for worldly amusements which keeps the young from the house of God." A small, "bird-like" woman, in the eyes of a family friend, she went about it all with energy and efficiency. The temperance people were impressed with her knowledge, her ladylike demeanor, "her intelligence and culture, and [her] marked administrative ability." In the words of a granddaughter, Helen "planned her work and campaigns like a general marshaling his forces in review before the battle, and in her planning said she was trying to 'catch Time by the fetlock'" — an inaccuracy that amused her horse-loving youngest child. "Stephen solemnly assured her several times that she would get her head kicked off if she were not more careful."

For the most part, Stephen's brothers and sisters were well settled. Townley, who was all newspaperman, had quickly advanced at the local office of the *New York Tribune*. He headed the Long Branch departments of both the *Tribune* and the Associated Press and served as the editor of the *Asbury Park Shore Press*. Having established a law practice in Port Jervis, William purchased a home with a wide porch and expansive lawns at 270 Main Street. This now served as the family's home base in that town. As civic-minded as both of his parents, though in a different way, William seemed to have a hand in everything. He ran as the Republican candidate for town clerk and lost, but he won positions on the Board of Education and the Water Works. He served as special judge for Orange County, debated at the Young Men's Literary Society against the notion that women are the intellectual equals of men, and gave a lecture on "The Mississippi Pig." Brothers George and Luther, virtually empty ovals in the family portrait gallery, were presumably working in mundane jobs; when one picks up their trails later, George is found working for the post office, Luther for the railroad. Wilbur, known as "Bert," struggled through medical school at the College of Physicians and Surgeons in New York, getting failing grades for two years.

The move to Asbury Park marked the beginning of a chain of losses that would alter the Crane family and affect Stephen in ways we can only guess at. On November 26, 1883, Townley's wife, Fannie, whom he had known since childhood, died of Bright's disease. Her death apparently followed the deaths of their two young children. Then Agnes became ill and had to resign her teaching job. Just twenty-eight years old, she died on June 10, 1884, of cerebrospinal meningitis. Weeks later, the family almost lost Luther when he took an overdose of laudanum while sick with flulike symptoms; he was found unconscious at Arbutus Cottage. It took the doctor and several unnamed others five hours to revive him.

There is no record of Stephen's reaction to these family crises; the Crane family seems to have made some effort to protect him. Agnes died at Ed's home, which was then in Rutherford, New Jersey, about sixty miles from Asbury Park. Whether it was thought best that Agnes be removed from Arbutus Cottage during her illness, so as to prevent upsetting thirteen-year-old Stephen, or there was another reason for her being there is unknown. Although she died at the start of her teaching career, she was so admired in the community that the Asbury Park Board of Education issued a formal preamble and resolution expressing their sorrow at the loss. She was blessed with "many rare graces of character," was "faithful . . . efficient," a teacher of "tireless industry, skill and tact." Two of her stories had been published in *Frank Leslie's Illustrated Newspaper*, one of them just a month before she died.

Stevie was still "delicate," said Edmund. Though he was stronger than he looked "and could outwalk nearly everyone," said Post Wheeler, he lacked the stamina for active sports, which he loved. "Sensitive about his health," but possessing the grit and determination that had marked him since earliest childhood, "he would box until he dropped exhausted to prove his strength." He had proved a good, if not brilliant, student during his first year, 1883–84, in the new school system, maintaining an average of "85 or above" at the Asbury Park grammar school.

Stephen wrote his first known story, "Uncle Jake and the Bell Handle," the year after Agnes died, when he was about fourteen. "Uncle Jake," the tale of two country bumpkins who drive their wagon into the big city for a day's trading and shopping and abruptly flee when Uncle Jake pulls a bell handle at the precise moment that a gong sounds in the hotel where they are waiting to have dinner, is a deft, highly accomplished piece of writing. Even in early adolescence Stephen could manage an effective comic tone. Along with a finely tuned ear and an eye for the telling detail, he showed a mature perception of human character and behavior. And he understood city squalor and the hardness of tenement life, where animals and dirty children forage together against a backdrop of tin cans, clotheslines, and "grimy, smoky factories" where merchants haggle over goods, cheat one another, and lie about market prices. Stephen was already writing well enough to be published. And the printer's symbols in his hand on the "Uncle Jake" manuscript further show that he was aiming at publication.

2

GREAT BUGS AT ONONDAGA

On September 14, 1885, Stephen's years of public schooling and living year-round at home ended. Not quite fourteen, he enrolled at his father's old school, Pennington Seminary, a rigid, coeducational boarding school seven miles north of Trenton, designed mainly to prepare young men for the ministry.

Shaped by Jonathan Townley Crane and tied to Ocean Grove and Asbury Park through three of its trustees, Pennington dispensed religion in heavy doses. Chapel was compulsory twice daily. Bible class met on Sunday afternoon, and prayer meeting was held on Wednesday night. Students learned the Scriptures and the Apostles' Creed. Sundays were especially solemn, with mandatory church attendance; all secular activities — even walking for pleasure — were forbidden. If there was a saving grace for Stephen, it was the school's strong athletic department, which emphasized football and baseball. Less pleasurable but more important, Pennington also stressed proficiency in both the written and the spoken word. Students were drilled in composition and required to read essays aloud.

Soon after Stephen left for Pennington, Helen fell critically ill in Asbury Park of something described in the *Asbury Park Shore Press* as "a temporary aberration of mind," "mental troubles" that left her mind "feeble." By spring she had evidently recovered. But Stephen and his family were about to suffer one of their most grotesque losses. On September 26, 1886, cheerful twenty-three-year-old Luther, now a flagman for the

Erie Railroad, fell in front of an oncoming train, which mutilated his left arm and leg and severed two fingers. Taken unconscious to William's home in Port Jervis, he lay in a state of shock until he died, almost twenty-four hours later. Luther was the third member of Stephen's immediate family to die within six years.

"Master Stephen Crane has returned home from Pennington Seminary where he has been studying for the past two years, and will spend his vacation at his mother's pleasant home on 4th Avenue," reported the *Asbury Park Tribune* the following summer. His mother was now reporting for Townley's *New York Tribune* on the summer sessions of the Seaside Summer School of Pedagogy, held at Avon-by-the-Sea, while continuing her work for the WCTU. Stephen seems to have spent the summer of 1887 honing his own writing skills. While he was home on vacation, an Asbury Park newspaper called the *Daily Spray* published an unsigned three-hundred-word sketch.* Titled "Asbury's New Move," it depicted a man with the fictional-sounding name of Superintendent Snedeker ordering a pair of lovers off the public beach at Asbury Park. The spectacle is broken up "with a cloud of blushes"; the lovers — "a pair of those tender seaside doves" — are seen under "a very loud-striped parasol." Obviously written by someone who knew the ways of Asbury Park, understood its contradictions, and regarded it all with detached amusement, the piece radiated wit, humor, and talent. Seemingly the work of a mature person, it was probably written by fifteen-year-old Stephen Crane.

About a month before the Christmas holidays that year, a teacher at Pennington Seminary accused Stephen of hazing another student. He denied the charge, but the teacher did not believe him, so he went to his room, packed his trunk, and left. Back home with his family, Stephen said, "As the Professor called me a liar there was not room in Pennington for us both, so I came home." "Nothing would induce him to return to the seminary," said Wilbur later, explaining that "Stephen's most marked characteristic was his absolute truthfulness. He was in many minor scrapes but no consideration of consequences would induce him to lie out of them, and the imputation that he was a liar, made the imputer *persona non grata* with Stephen thereafter."

Apparently in deference to Stephen's wishes, Helen decided to send him to Claverack College and Hudson River Institute in New York State.

---

* It was simultaneously published in the *Philadelphia Press*.

Stephen wanted a military career, and Claverack, a quasi-military school, was to prepare him for West Point. On December 23, Helen wrote to the school's president, the Reverend Arthur H. Flack, inquiring about tuition. Flack replied that as a Methodist minister's son, Stephen was entitled to a lower price — "$160.00 per year, instead of the standard $225.00" — for tuition, board, and incidentals. The price tag was steep at a time when Harvard charged $150 for tuition and small private colleges cost about $50. Furthermore, as the son of Pennington's esteemed former principal, Stephen may have been paying a much lower tuition at that school. Flack assured Mrs. Crane that "we would do our best to give [Stephen] a thorough college preparation and at the same time make for him a pleasant Christian school home."

✦

He would look back on his time at Claverack as "the happiest period of my life although I was not aware of it." Claverack, he said, was "simply pie." Reputed to be one of the state's leading preparatory schools, it was coeducational and drew students from fourteen states and several foreign countries. Set in the Hudson River Valley some four miles east of the river, Claverack seemed as ideal as its picturesque setting and as solid as the mountain stone foundations on which it was built.

Along with close academic and personal supervision, the school placed a strong emphasis on religion — "morning prayers daily and religious services every Sabbath evening in the Chapel which all are required to attend; also bible classes every Sabbath afternoon for the study of the Scriptures," said the catalogue. There were optional "social religious meetings," along with regular exercise: daily calisthenics for the young ladies, military drill in uniform and with antique rifles for the gentlemen. Claverack offered weekly student recitals and annual concerts by prominent New York City musicians and singers. Students could choose among four literary societies, attend frequent lectures on topics ranging from history to etiquette, and receive special instruction if they were "very backward in Common English in consequence of ill-health or other unfortunate circumstances in early youth."

But according to a classmate of Stephen's named Harvey Wickham, Claverack's "high reputation" was a sham. The once rigorous old school had loosened its tie under softer leadership after merging with the Hudson River Institute, which drew "much of its patronage from parents cursed with backward or semi-incorrigible offspring." Enrollment had dwindled; discipline had given way to "a certain devilish, carefree spirit." The girls in their long dresses and the cadets in their blue and gold military uniforms wandered the country roads and lanes "as [if] in a terrestrial paradise like packs of cheerful wolves out of bounds, out of hours and very much out of hand." Stephen was unpunctual and often skipped class.

After beginning in midyear, in January 1888, the lean, blond sixteen-year-old soon established himself as someone who both craved and flouted convention. Signing his name "Stephen T. Crane" because everyone else had a middle name, he tried "to win recognition as a regular fellow," said classmate Armistead "Tommie" Borland. From the beginning, the school allowed him to follow his own course of study rather than adhere to the required curriculum. He enrolled in the classical department, then transferred to the academic program, taking physiology, English literature, English history, and grammar, his worst subject. In April, at Helen's request, the Reverend Flack reluctantly excused Stephen from declaiming, a required course, though "we . . . don't like to do so," he wrote her.

Classmate A. Lincoln Travis would remember Stephen as a highly literate but erratic student, lucky to pass examinations in math and science, and yet "far in advance of his fellow students in his knowledge of History and Literature," his favorite subjects. "He was a voracious reader of all the nineteenth century English writers and reveled in the classics of Greece and Rome," said Travis. "Plutarch's lives was his constant companion and even at this age he was familiar with the English and American poets. He would frequently quote from Tennyson's 'In Memoriam' and William Cullen Bryant's 'Thanatopsis,'" poems whose combined themes — death, the loss of religious faith, skepticism, the search for truth, and comfort in the "healing sympathy" of nature, as Bryant wrote in "Thanatopsis" — offered clues to Stephen's personality and anticipated some of the major themes of his own fiction and poetry.

He was at his most conventional in uniform, possessing what Harvey Wickham called a "perfectly hen-like attitude toward the rank and file." From the beginning of the school year, the cadets practiced for Prize Drill, which determined the best company in the regiment and the most worthy candidates for promotion. Held on Washington's Birthday, the drill was second only to Commencement in importance. On Memorial Day the battalion marched to the cemetery at the Claverack Reformed

Church, where more than sixty soldiers from the Revolutionary War, the War of 1812, the Mexican War, and the Civil War were buried, and covered the graves with flowers. Stephen took to the military exercises with the humorlessness of a real soldier and quickly moved up in rank to corporal. He directed his squad around the Claverack Drill Hall with "nasal orders," said Wickham. After Wickham dropped his rifle during a Prize Drill, Stephen, who was his senior officer, exploded, calling him an "idiot" and an "imbecile."

"You were fairly decent up to the last minute. And then to drop your gun!" he cried. "Such a thing was never heard of. Do you think *order arms* means to drop your gun?"

He went home for the summer of 1888, wearing "the stripes of a corporal on his natty uniform," noted the *Asbury Park Daily Press*. As the summer citizens of Asbury Park bestirred themselves on what the *New York Tribune* called "the bathing suit question," forcing the chief of police to intercept all improperly attired sea bathers before they entered the water, and Ocean Grove banned the sale of novels, Stephen set about gathering resort news for Townley. According to an old friend of Stephen's father, Willis Fletcher Johnson, who was then day editor of the *New York Tribune*, Stephen's first reporting work was so insignificant that Townley "paid him for it out of his own pocket." He "did not inform the office of it, but sent Stephen's news in and collected the space-rate for it as though it were his own." Stephen's pieces were published as unsigned items. One such report, on a religious camp meeting in Ocean Grove, called the event a "love feast" carried off by a magnetic minister who "wins souls to higher things." "Four Christian Chinamen sent up a written testimony that they loved Jesus better and better every day," the anonymous reporter added gleefully.

He returned home to the familiar bustle. His busy mother entertained WCTU national president Frances E. Willard at Arbutus Cottage in early summer. Helen delivered a temperance lecture to a large audience and addressed a mother's group on the topic "Overcome." By now Helen was becoming an active member of the local press corps. She was recognized locally as "the pleasant-faced little lady seldom absent from her seat" at the reporter's table in the Auditorium. But Townley was attracting more attention. Dubbed "the Shore Fiend" for his tenacity as a reporter, he was seen by local residents as the consummate newspaperman who existed only for the *Tribune*, "the veritable incarnation of that great newspaper." Now thirty-six and widowed seven years, he was a broad, bald, seedy-looking man who wore a fore-and-aft cap and a dirty tweed overcoat year-round over a colored muffler that was tucked in and pinned in place of a shirt. Townley himself seemed pinned together, made of old, neglected parts. He drank heavily — he was perhaps already an alcoholic — and his teeth were "yellow and uncared for," said Stephen's friend Post Wheeler. His clothes, health, and works in progress provided regular fodder for the Asbury Park papers. So familiar was Townley's tweed overcoat that when he turned up on the streets wearing a new suit, it was noted in the *Daily Press*. "You all know Townley Crane, don't you? He wears a *very* handsome new suit of summer clothes. It is a pleasure to thus see the material prosperity of our friends."

Meanwhile, Stephen, the insignificant kid brother, seems to have slipped around town unnoticed, taking in the "seething summer city," as he would call it, and the human carnival and storing most of it away for future use.

Back at Claverack that September, Stephen wanted a horse to ride. Though Helen had rented out Arbutus Cottage for part of the summer and was presumably hard pressed by Claverack's tuition and the extra costs for books, uniforms, and miscellaneous items, such as a sixty-seven-cent baseball, she wrote to the Reverend Flack to request that Stephen be allowed horseback rides for exercise. Flack turned down the request, noting that "the livery is connected with the hotel and we do not wish that the students shall have any business there at all." He reassured her that Stephen was getting plenty of exercise playing tennis and baseball, which he particularly enjoyed.

Stephen cut class for baseball and played catcher barehanded until far into the season, lavishing iodine and witch hazel on his sore hands until he began wearing a heavy buckskin glove. "It was his pose in those days to take little interest in anything save poker and baseball, and even in speaking of these great matters there was in his manner a suggestion of noblesse oblige," recalled Harvey Wickham. In their reminiscences, Wickham and a couple of other Claverack classmates remembered Stephen Crane as a contradictory personality — "self-deprecation coupled with arrogance," as Wickham put it. Something of a rebel, he was "extremely irregular in his habits — a law unto himself," said Tommie Borland.

With the exception of baseball, Stephen participated in school activities without really entering them, conforming and yet slipping away. He seemed to be two people, performing cadet rituals with zeal, yet displaying a "slightly sheepish air on the parade ground" which Wickham attri-buted to "fear of ridicule, especially of his own." Chumming around with his roommate, Earl Reeves, reputed to be the "richest boy in school," wearing a dirty sweater to Reeves's fashionable duds, Stephen also sought the company of social outcasts, such as the school's Cuban students, from whom he picked up bits of Spanish. He sang in the Methodist choir in his thin, pleasant tenor voice, but escaped sitting for sermons by volunteering to pump the pipe organ. Like other students, he drank coffee and ate banana cake at Mrs. Myers's pie shop, but he loathed cruel student pranks — such as the time students tied the legs of a sleeping grocer, then locked the man in his shop, or the time a student mob hanged an "unpopular student in effigy." Even harmless adolescent gestures, such as wearing a coat inside out in a St. Patrick's Day parade in mocking tribute to the Irish, invited his scorn. "So! You're a professional damn fool," he drawled to one participant.

He was not among the students who rushed rooms and filled their pillowcases with stolen apples. But he knocked on dormitory doors with Reeves in search of forbidden tobacco; he swore — "Damn you, Wickham!" and "Ho, hell," strong language then — and ignored his mother's warning about staying away from pool and billiard rooms, the training grounds for vice. While Stephen "enjoyed a certain reputation for villainy," said Wickham, "his name was never among those read out at morning chapel."

When a group of cadets formed a short-lived secret misogynist society called S.S.T. Girlum,* Stephen joined — but he fell in love anyway with red-haired Harriet Mattison, Claverack's best pianist, and with Jennie Pierce, "madly, in the headlong way of seventeen," he confessed later. ("Jennie was clever. With only half an effort she made my life so very miserable.") Sounding like a man of the world, he pronounced one young woman "a damn nice girl"; of another he said, "My God, what a lot of harm she is going to do before she dies!" Tommie Borland, who was younger, hero-worshiped Stephen and tagged after him. He "learned many things" from Stephen Crane, he said later, "not all for the good of my immortal soul — the rudiments of the great American game of poker and something more than the rudiments of the ways of a man with a

* The meaning behind the name is long forgotten.

maid." Women, said Borland, were attracted to Stephen — "for he was indeed physically attractive without being handsome." "He had, as a boy, a very high inception of personal honor, but I do not think it was proof against favors thrown at him by women to whom he was attracted."

He was aloof and reserved, without intimates, and not generally popular. "Only women and other hero worshippers ever really liked him," said Wickham. Seemingly indifferent to the opinions of others, yet not shy about offering his own, Stephen was "more or less difficult to approach," said Borland. Dubbed "The Stephen Cranium" by the *Vidette*, Claverack's school paper, Stephen was "a congenital introvert" for whom "intimacy with other men was out of character and went only so far as was necessary to give the appearance of normal behavior," said Borland. Climbing out of bed in the mornings late for drill, scrambling into socks and trousers, he skipped the shirt, buttoning his jacket over his small bare chest.

In February 1890 the *Vidette* ran an articulate but dull piece on the great explorer Henry M. Stanley. It read like a competent class paper, its prose as staid and buttoned-down as the cadet drawn on the magazine's cover. It was Stephen Crane's first signed publication. The unmemorable essay was followed in spring by an item in the "Battalion Notes" column and by a couple of slight but more promising unsigned efforts on student baseball. Reporting on "the long looked for and cherished season," Stephen noted that "Crane, catcher," had been elected captain but had turned it down, no explanation given. The first baseman was elected in his place. Most striking in this little piece is the glimpse it offers of a born writer. He is caught by the vivid detail, such as the school president watching the game with an enthusiasm that sends his plug hat (a bowler) into the air. With sophisticated wit and irony and the same bold self-confidence he showed in "Asbury's New Move," Stephen creates a fine miniature portrait:

> The village dominie, who ordinarily is looked upon with awe
> and reverence, sinks gloomily behind the pall of favoritism
> on these occasions, and may be seen to complacently stand
> for more than an hour beside the worst boy of boarding
> school fame, and look admiringly upon his sin stained brow
> as he explains a new feature of the game.

•

Even before Stephen returned to Asbury Park for the summer, his family had decided that he should not go back to Claverack. William, it was later said, had persuaded Stephen that there was no future in a military career; there would be no war in his lifetime. The family owned shares in some Pennsylvania mines, and the consensus was that Stephen should pursue a mining engineering program at Lafayette. Telling his friends that "he was fed up with school" and "wanted to go into journalism," Stephen affected a mature, nonchalant air about leaving. But by June 15 he was already "longing for some of my old companions at Old Claverack," he wrote his classmate Odell Hathaway.

> I am smoking a cigar after a 10:00 AM breakfast of roast pigeon and gooseberries yet I wish to God I was puffing on a cigarette butt after a 7:00 AM breakfast of dried-beef and oat meal at H.R.I. If you see Tuttle give him my kindest regards and tell him to write. Good-bye, old man, write to me. I don't forget my friends and you will always have my best wishes.

That summer Stephen reported again for the *Tribune*, but now under his name. It was a dull beat. As Townley's assistant, he spent his time writing up humdrum doings at Avon-by-the-Sea, taking note of lectures, classes, instructors, and various prominent visitors. Two local drownings piqued his interest a little, tossing him a character in the form of "bronzed and sturdy Captain Kittell." He amused himself with a mildly funny, brief account of a tenor who once sang before the king of the Zulus in Southern Africa and was presented with four of the king's wives as thanks, "all over six feet four inches in height." But his copy was unmemorable. He seemed merely to be doing his homework — dutifully, unenthusiastically, his interest only occasionally aroused.

Always now he had his mother's example before him. Two of Helen's humorous stories of family life, heavy on dialect, had been published, one under a pseudonym, "Jerusa Ann Stubbs," that left no doubt about her sense of humor, another under "Mrs. M. Helen Crane." That summer of 1890 she produced a historical account of Ocean Grove's oldest cottage, which appeared in leaflet form. Valuing creative writing as she did painting, she had had a short story of Agnes's published in *Frank Leslie's Illustrated Newspaper* two years after her death.

At summer's end Stephen crossed the Delaware and ascended a

steep hill to the Lafayette College campus in Easton, Pennsylvania. Registering on September 12, he surrendered to an intellectually numbing curriculum: chemistry, algebra, industrial drawing, French, theme writing (a technical writing course taught by the engineering faculty), Bible, and elocution — altogether "a very drab course for a man of literary taste such as Crane," a classmate acknowledged later. The school offered no elective courses in any program. Though students could get hold of current newspapers and magazines, books were literally kept under lock and key, in a single room that comprised the college library. Lafayette was controlled by the Presbyterian Synod of Pennsylvania and had an ordained minister as its president. Like Claverack and Pennington, it turned on a religious axis. The prescription for learning was familiar to Stephen: mandatory Bible and morning chapel, the word of God informing and directing the curriculum like a traffic cop.

Lafayette's boys hazed and hazed, "raise[d] more hell than [at] any college in the country," Stephen bragged to a friend. The practice was not restricted to fraternities; "the entire sophomore class" hazed the freshmen, noted a historian, with thirty or forty boys breaking down bedroom doors and dragging the younger students from their beds. Apparently reacting to his loss of nerve on the night hazers came to his dormitory room, Stephen joined the freshman class in a rough event called "banner scrap." It consisted of scrambling for a flag hung twelve feet off the ground from a building; the sophomores were armed with bags hard with flour. "I send you a piece of the banner we took away from the Sophemores last week," Stephen wrote Odell Hathaway. "It dont look like much does it? Only an old rug, ain't it? But just remember I got a *black and blue nose*, a barked shin, skin off my hands and a lame shoulder. . . . So, keep it, and when you look at it think of me scraping about twice a week over some old rag that says 'Fresh '94' on it."

With determined normalcy, he set about doing the usual college things. He joined the largest fraternity, Delta Upsilon, and two rival groups, the Washington Literary Society and the Franklin Literary Society, where he could attend lectures and debates and find his way to current books. Afternoons he played baseball, winning the notice of his teammates, who considered him promising enough to be a candidate for the next spring's varsity team. He hiked with a group of Delta Upsilon brothers to the summit of local Mt. Paxinosa. Small and sallow, a reticent fellow who socialized little beyond his own fraternity, he seemed average to classmate Ernest G. Smith — slightly more sophisticated and cynical than the other boys, but unremarkable. If he stood out at all in the class of ninety-four freshmen, it was as an incessant cigarette smoker at a time when only a minority of students smoked. An upperclassman would remember Stephen walking alone one Sunday, silent and smoking, "gazing at the clear fall sunset across the hills."

Writing to an unidentified friend at Claverack that fall, Stephen sounded lonely. He advised his former schoolmate to start having fun — "mark my words, you will always regret the day you leave old Claverack," he wrote. He himself regretted the loss of Phoebe "Pete" English, a former Claverack student with whom he was corresponding, and the fellows there, "whom I still love as of old." He had "left a big slice of my heart up among the pumpkin seeds and farmers of Columbia Co." He asked his friend not to forget him.

He frequently missed classes at Lafayette. He ended the semester with grades for only four of the seven courses he had taken, receiving a 92 for elocution, an 88 in French, a 60 in algebra ("the third lowest grade in the class," noted a historian), and a zero for theme writing.

Ernest Smith found Stephen in his room quietly packing up. Saying little except that "his family affairs would not permit him to remain at Lafayette," he descended the steep hill, crossed back over the Delaware, and was "dropped from the rolls" — "without censure."

His brief stay at Lafayette had sufficiently impressed his classmates to win him a place in the class yearbook, *Melange.* There had been another Crane there at the same time, and the two men — their characteristics somewhat confused — were recalled in a piece called "Our Departed":

> Funny fowls were these two Cranes,
> Steve had wit and Dwight had brains,
> Dwight was short and Steve was tall,
> One had grit, the other gall.

The family accepted the failure of the mining engineering experiment. Before leaving Lafayette, Stephen had written Edmund and asked him to persuade their mother to let him change his course of study to belles lettres. He had decided on a literary career. To Stephen's "delight," said Edmund, their mother agreed. When the Christmas holidays ended, he left for another Methodist institution, Syracuse University, in upstate New York. Great-uncle Jesse Peck, who had died seven years earlier, had been one of the university's founders, and Helen apparently thought

Stephen might be entitled to a scholarship (it is unclear whether he received one).

One day in January 1891, Stephen emerged from a cab filled with tobacco smoke and walked the long plank walk up to the "dandy" Delta Upsilon chapter house at Syracuse, facing Thornden Park. The fraternity house was "valued at $20,000," Stephen wrote Odell Hathaway. Several of his old Claverack friends were at the college, and "there are some darn pretty girls here, praise be to God," he wrote on January 9. "I expect to see some fun here."

He settled into a spacious second-floor apartment with a bay window and a roommate named Clarence N. Goodwin, from Washington, D.C. He joined several clubs — the Nut-Brown Maiden, a coasting club; an eating group called the Tooth Pick Club, and Delta Upsilon's cricket club, for which he served as captain. He wasted no time trying out for the baseball team and later admitted that he had come to Syracuse "more to play baseball than to study." His legend as a catcher had preceded him, having been announced in the college *Syracusan*.

Standing out from the rest of the team in "a Crimson sweater, buff-colored trousers and a pair of broken patent-leather shoes," as a classmate observed, the new catcher and sometimes shortstop of the varsity nine was an unpromising-looking youth. He gave the appearance of someone who had been skimped on. He was small-chested and droop-shouldered, with unruly white-blond hair, yellow skin, and cool blue-gray eyes. "His skin, hair and eyes appeared to be all of one dull and lifeless hue," said pitcher Mansfield French. "And his legs in their black stockings" looked "like pipe stems." In spite of Stephen's youth and thinness he would arrive on the diamond winded from climbing the hill and invariably cursing. His complaints about the hill were so predictable, said a classmate, that they "soon became a feature of the practice. The men gradually got to wondering, 'what Steve would say about the hill to-day,' and every day he had a new collection of choice epithets." And yet he was agile and gritty, standing up to the plate "like a professional," said classmate Clarence Loomis Peaslee, giving the game everything he had.

He was a good but not strong batter, hitting mostly singles and batting .300 or better in his first six games. Compensating for a weak arm, he threw with his whole body but was still "unable to line the ball down to the base in acceptable form," said French. Throwing off "mask, cap and protector," he would "give a hop and skip and throw with a complete body swing," doubling up afterward from the pain in his shoulder. Even catching seemed to take all his strength. The pitcher was a large fellow, and the impact of his ball caused Stephen "to bounce back with every catch," observed Peaslee. But what he lacked in physical strength he made up for in enthusiasm and sheer force of will. Impatiently slapping his bare hand against his padded glove at a strike, he offered "biting sarcasms when a teammate made a poor play" and generously praised a good play, endearing himself to his teammates. In a middling team — they won three games and lost three — Stephen was considered "the best player on the nine, and one of the best catchers that the university ever had." His teammates elected him captain, a singular honor for a freshman.

Enrolling as a "special student," or nondegree candidate, in the College of Liberal Arts, Stephen registered for only one course, English literature. Though he occasionally sat in on Charles J. Little's class in ancient history, he spent most of his time doing exactly as he pleased. With the single exception of Professor Little, whom Stephen admired wholeheartedly, he felt "a fierce contempt" for Syracuse's faculty, said fraternity brother Frederic Lawrence. He rarely roused himself for class. Even Professor Little could seldom lure him up the accursed hill to campus. Stephen had his own work to do, his own mission, which had nothing to do with listening to lectures.

The *Tribune*'s Willis Fletcher Johnson took a keen interest in the careers of Townley and Stephen. Impressed with Stephen's imaginative gift with words, he hired him as a Syracuse correspondent. Thus Stephen had an excuse, if he needed one, to go his own way at school. "When I ought to have been at recitations," he said later, "I was studying faces on the streets, and when I ought to have been studying my next day's lessons I was watching the trains roll in and out of the Central Station." The police station was another favorite haunt. He watched prisoners brought in for petty crimes, and he talked with "shambling figures who lurked in dark door-ways or deserted slum streets," said a classmate.

It was not book learning that he balked at but "the cut-and-dried curriculum." In this college of 812 students, Stephen Crane was a visiting scholar of a kind that was very much his own invention. "Lounging about his room" while his fraternity brothers went to class, he read newspapers, history, and literary masterpieces, often late into the night —*Faust, Anna Karenina*, and *War and Peace*, books discovered not in class but in a downtown bookshop. Frederic Lawrence discovered that Stephen knew everything about "the organization, equipment and methods of every important war force in Europe. He could mention offhand the numbers of each standing army, the tonnage of each navy and its gunpowder. The place and character of the 'next war' was a perpetual subject of speculation," though he had seemingly abandoned his dreams of a military career. "As to himself, his future was in literature, and never for an instant did he doubt his own success," said Lawrence.

Many afternoons, Lawrence would come upon Stephen with "a bull-dog pipe clenched in his teeth," slowly writing copy for the *Tribune* "in his clear, legible hand." He produced one or two pages a day. When he wasn't reading or writing or playing baseball, he played tennis or walked for hours around the city and the surrounding countryside. The walks fueled him, like a good meal, making him more talkative and enthusiastic about life, said Lawrence. After lunch, Stephen typically disappeared into the city. Nights found him at the forbidden local theater with friends. He struggled to acquire a taste for alcohol. He played poker or sat with a girl at a table in a local music hall, drinking beer and talking about art, as "daringly clad" girls "in low neck waists and skirts just above the knees" sang and danced.

Determined that he "would not be bossed by anyone," Stephen spoke his mind — to an upperclassman or the university chancellor — with a self-assurance that belied his five-foot-six, 125-pound frame. One day a senior entered the library and called out for "a freshie to turn grindstone" (sharpen the carving knives), adding, "Come on, Crane!" Stephen refused, saying, red-faced, that "he 'never had and never would turn grindstone for anybody,' which was voted very bad grace for a fresh-man," noted Peaslee. Another time Stephen disagreed with Chancellor Charles N. Sims in a class he was teaching and provoked the chancellor into an appeal to the Bible.

"Tut, tut — what does St. Paul say, Mr. Crane, what does St. Paul say?" said old Sims.

"I know what St. Paul says, but I disagree with St. Paul," came the reply.

But when his fraternity brothers protested his smoking indoors, the rebel willingly exiled himself to an unfinished cupola on the top of the house, where he served as the grinning captain of the smoking minority. With an old rug, odd pieces of furniture, a Turkish water pipe (Stephen's contribution), and reams of paper, the smokers created a salon where they could talk about art, science, and literature and swap personal stories by the hour. Not even the harsh Syracuse winter deterred them. They put on earflaps, ulsters, and mittens when the weather turned raw.

Stephen could seem ordinary and "unimpressive" — "not possessed of a strong individuality," said Clarence Peaslee. Moody and reserved, he "talked about how hard life was and how unfair it all seemed," remembered one student, and yet he showed what classmate Frank Noxon called "a haunting solicitude for the comforts and welfare of other people, especially those of narrow opportunity. He thought about it as one thinks about an art or a craft, developing a style and inventing original methods." An essay that he read aloud at the chapter house one night was prepared with the immaculate care he would give to professional copy. He always wrote this way because, he explained, "from the outset he had kept in mind the compositor, whose earnings depended upon the amount he could set, and this in turn upon the time it took to read the story."

Stephen kept largely to himself and his fraternity friends, but he was often seen in the company of university girls, toward whom he was respectful and deferential, said Frank Noxon. He formed a close friendship with Frederic Lawrence, "Lorrie," one of the smoking outlaws at the chapter house who had also grown up a minister's son in Port Jervis, though the two had not met then. "Most men" loved him, said a classmate, and his teammates on the varsity nine were "his indulgent friends."

When the middle trimester ended in April, Stephen did not bother to sign up for any more courses. Though he got an A in English literature, he continued with his own pursuits, seeming to Peaslee, at least, "always cool, never worried about anything."

He was writing more seriously now, experimenting with tone and style and trying out different subjects. Even his less impressive literary efforts showed a mature technical skill. "He has sung before crowned heads and before heads in dilapidated old hats; before the gilded, tasseled boots of the German hussar and the ponderous, wooden sabots of the Hollandese peasant," he wrote in "The King's Favor," an expansion of a passage in his *Tribune* piece of the previous summer, about an opera singer who performs for the king of the Zulus and is rewarded with one of the king's wives. It appeared in the May 1891 *University Herald* over the initials "S.C."

With a professionalism beyond his years, he handled rejections gracefully, even showing a friend one he'd received for a dog story submitted to *St. Nicholas Magazine*. Stephen appreciated the "complimentary" style of the rejection, which said that the magazine had too many dog stories. As a writer, he had nothing to hide. He left manuscript pages lying around his room among the books, athletic gear, tobacco cans, papers, newspapers, and clothing that covered his desk and floor. Anyone could pick them up and read them. He even let his friends in on the earliest gestational phase of the creative process, blocking out stories for them and trying out possibilities as though he were modeling a new suit of clothes.

After the *Syracuse Sunday Herald* ran a story about a Minnesota train delayed by caterpillars, Stephen wrote an unsigned spoof for the *Tribune* called "Great Bugs at Onondaga," which told of a train in Syracuse's Onondaga County that had been stopped by a large mass of enormous insects swarming over the tracks. With a reporter's precision, Stephen noted that the incident had occurred in the limestone quarries "southeast of Brighton Corner, between here and Jamesville, on the Delaware Lackawanna & Western Railroad" and that the giant bugs, which were something like lightning bugs, had covered some sixty feet of track. The "turtle-like armor" of the insects' shells had made "a crackling sound like the successive explosions of toy torpedoes" when they were run over. Investigators had found "innumerable small holes" in the nearby limestone quarries, and "traces of a peculiar ovula, some hatched and some apparently blighted." The amused editors of the *Syracuse Daily Standard*, which ran the piece simultaneously with its publication in the *New York Tribune*, took the precaution of framing the "Great Bugs" story with a disclaimer, saying that the story had reached the press by way of an alcoholic in overalls who "had perhaps in his sober moments read or heard the reports of caterpillars and other insects stopping trains in Minnesota and South Carolina." The *Tribune* ran a tongue-in-cheek editorial in apology for the hoax.

With no apologies, Stephen also wrote a shamelessly anti-Semitic sketch called "Greed Rampant." A short, straightforward work presented as a one-act play set in Paradise, New Jersey, at the end of time, its cast consisted of Mr. John P. St. Peter, a Crowd of Gentiles, and a Mob of Jews. The premise is that the Jews will have to stampede the gates of Paradise to get in and the Gentiles will make very effort to keep them out. Served up without a whiff of irony, the Jewish mob consists entirely of clothes dealers and pawnbrokers. In the end, they are outdone by their own greed when the outwardly civilized Gentiles toss them a false sign advertising cheap job lots in Sheol, causing a stampede out of Paradise.

Fast-paced and vivid, "Greed Rampant," which lay unpublished during Crane's lifetime, is perhaps best understood as a comic misfire. It is the work of a nineteen-year-old still in the experimenting stage, an exercise by an adolescent living in an age when racial and religious stereotypes were accepted and considered funny. The Gentiles, in fact, fare little better than the Jews. Paradise, significantly, is in New Jersey, the scene of Stephen's earliest religious training. St. Peter is a doddering old man sleeping on the job, seen ineffectually batting away the Jewish "invaders" with his big key to the gate.

"College life is a waste of time," Stephen told classmate George Chandler as they discussed their plans for the future. Chandler said he was bound for medical school; Stephen said he was going to leave Syracuse "to be a newspaper reporter." Shortly after attending a Delta Upsilon chapter meeting on June 12, 1891, he left, ending his experiment with college.

3

THE GIRL WHO
BLOSSOMED IN A
MUD PUDDLE

In mid-June, Stephen, Frederic Lawrence, and friends Louis "Lew" Senger and Louis Carr went camping in the rugged woods of Sullivan County, New York. It was a hard country of brambles and great boulders, swamps and mossy caves tucked into mountainside thickets, "bunches of scrub oaks as big as a man's wrist," wrote Stephen, the trees "scarred" by bears' claws. A hunter's heaven, its dense, "tangled forests" were alive with game. "This country may have been formed by a very reckless and distracted giant who, observing a tract of tipped-up and impossible ground, stood off and carelessly pelted trees and boulders at it," Stephen wrote.

In these woods, by a blackberry patch near the Mongaup River Falls, the Crane youngsters had once built a shanty from a tangled collection of hemlock boughs, sawed-off trees, stones, slabs, and leaves all woven together, which Agnes dubbed "Saint's Rest." The family had filled every hard, leafy corner, sleeping one on top of the other, and one night Stevie's hammock had broken, sending the six-year-old boy crashing down on Agnes. "His bones were not sufficiently upholstered to make it anything but an unpleasant experience," said Agnes.

Stephen relished the stories he heard from the local folk of Sullivan County — "the old gnarled and weatherbeaten inhabitants," he called them, the "wonderful yarn-spinners." They told tales about bears and bear hounds, about hunting wild hogs, and the time " 'Lew' Boyd chased [a] wounded wild hog for 200 miles." There was a fablelike story of a panther and its "siren voice" that could imitate a child's cry and lure people from their beds into the woods. There was one about the Indian War of 1779, and the true story of the last of the Mohicans. Stephen listened closely to adventure yarns about people named Nelson Crocker, Calvin Bush, and Cyrus Dodge, from places like Callicoon, and he wrote them down.

When the brief idyll in the forest ended, he returned to the crowded streets of the New Jersey shore towns. "Great train-loads of pleasure-seekers and religious worshippers," he wrote, "are arriving at the huge double railway station of Ocean Grove and Asbury Park." The copy he turned out for the *Tribune* was more confident-sounding and satirical than his previous work. Like someone coming out of the dark into a garishly lighted room, he seemed startled by the "wriggling, howling mass of humanity" on the streets of Ocean Grove — the metaphor recalling his ugly depiction of the Jews in "Greed Rampant." In Stephen's prose this human image was more frightening than the wild animals of his later Sullivan County sketches; perhaps because in their context of God worshiping and pleasure seeking, the Asbury Parkers seemed less natural than the animals in their native habitat. Instead of Sullivan County's "virtuous bushwhacker," he found rapacious hackmen; in place of brambles and boulders there were sidewalks cluttered with travelers' trunks. The hunter who lived simply with nature was here replaced by the naturalist who "has made a careful study of the vegetable life of New Jersey." In Asbury Park fishing was a sport, a "heroic" spectacle; in Sullivan County it was a necessity, something unselfconscious. To Stephen, the color of civilization was "bright-hued" and garish, hard on the senses.

Although Stephen preferred the company of bushwhackers to that of the Asbury Park summer people, his writings about the religious worshipers and pleasure seekers were superior to the stories he based on Sullivan County legends. In contrast to his straight-faced, almost reverential treatment of the corncob-pipe-smoking old man telling yarns to his grandson, the trappers and hunters he affectionately called "liars," his view of Asbury Parkers was ironic.

Though his reporting that summer consisted of the usual obligatory mundane local news, notices of lectures and recitations and "devotional exercises," the literary writer sometimes surfaced. "Parties from the hotel go on long pedestrian tours along the banks of the Shark River, and create havoc among the blithesome crabs and the festive oysters," he wrote in one piece. The parties of painters on the riverbank, positioned under white umbrellas, looked to him like "a bunch of extraordinary mushrooms."

Since Stephen's newspaper work was still unsigned, it is unclear how much he published in the *Tribune* and elsewhere that summer. Two items were certainly his. Eleven others, judging by their style, themes, and imagery, were possibly his. Two of the possibles appeared in the *New York Herald* and the *New York Times*. What is certain is that he was always writing.

Because Stephen was too shy to do so, Townley approached Willis Fletcher Johnson with a couple of Stephen's stories. Johnson was greatly impressed with them and told Stephen. Thus reassured, the young writer showed him two of the Sullivan County tales, each about two thousand words in length, and a "big bundle of manuscript," Johnson recalled, about a prostitute named Maggie. Johnson accepted the stories for publication in the *Tribune*'s Sunday supplement, and in February 1892, "Hunting Wild Hogs" and "The Last of the Mohicans" appeared in print.

Johnson found much to admire even in these inferior Sullivan County tales, but the novel about the street girl left him breathless. Though it suffered from an overuse of adjectives and "was in some respects crude," said Johnson, "it was powerful and impressive."

On the morning of August 17, Stephen covered a lecture at Avon-by-the-Sea sponsored by the Seaside Assembly as part of their series on American art and literature. The subject was the novelist William Dean Howells. The speaker, Hamlin Garland, was a bearded, good-looking young Boston teacher, a rising literary star and regular contributor to such important magazines as *Harper's Weekly* and the *Arena*, a radical Boston magazine. His first book, *Main-Travelled Roads*, a collection of stories about life on the western prairies, had recently been published. Of greatest interest to the young writer in the audience that day were Garland's theories about art and literature. A proponent of the new realism, Garland stressed the importance of the *new* — in writing style, subject matter, and form. From his own belief in the theory of evolution and his readings of Herbert Spencer, Hippolyte Taine, and others, Garland had formed the idea that true art must reflect contemporary American life in all its variety and color. Eugène Véron's *Aesthetics* further influenced Garland's thinking. He determined that realism in art must not be simply objective, which is deadly, but must reflect the personality of the observer, for that is what gives art and literature its uniqueness — the point being to depict "reality *as the author sees it*." Praising Howells as "by all odds the most

American and vital of our literary men to-day," a writer who "stands for all that is progressive and humanitarian in our fiction," Garland spoke feelingly about Howells's theories of art, which promoted the truthful and the realistic and required no "special material," just that "the novelist be true to himself."

Stephen listened, enthralled. He was so impressed by Garland's words that his short report for the *Tribune* consisted almost entirely of quotation, the bouquet of a dazzled student. Garland was not only the first significant writer Stephen had ever gotten so close to, he held the same literary ideas, spoke the same language. In the years to come, Hamlin Garland would give different accounts of how he and Stephen Crane met, variously claiming that he had sought Stephen out after reading his concise and accurate report of the lecture — an unlikely scenario, given that Stephen's piece was mundane — and that Stephen had approached *him* after the lecture. Garland was impressed with the young reporter's "laconic" style of talking — "My name is Crane, Stephen Crane," he said, and asked for Garland's lecture notes. They continued to meet afterward, and a friendship of sorts began.

Garland, some ten years older than Stephen, was "a nonsmoking teetotaler," said a biographer, as methodical and self-important as Stephen was irregular and unassuming. "Until the day of his death," Garland "hoarded every scrap of paper with writing upon it, particularly the various versions of his own laboriously copied manuscripts" — the antithesis of Stephen, who left manuscript pages lying about like cigarette paper. But like Crane, Garland was a largely self-educated man who had left school early to embark on his own program of reading. The two writers shared a love of literature and baseball. Garland had been a pitcher in his younger days, and he and Stephen often talked inshoots and outdrops, sometimes getting up a game. To Garland, Stephen was a "wonderful boy" with a "frank" gaze. Stephen would say that "Hamlin Garland was the first to over-whelm me with all manner of extraordinary language."

In mid-August, as the Asbury Park summer season was winding down, Stephen set off for a campsite in Pike County, Pennsylvania, with Senger, Carr, and Lawrence. Life in the woods was a tonic to his health. His pale yellow skin turned the copper brown of an American Indian, said Lawrence, forming a strange contrast to his blond hair. Stephen "loved this life," Lawrence said, "and his health was magnificent." Back in Port Jervis, with the spirit of the camp still in him, he inscribed the register of the nearby Hartwood Park Association on September 30:

Shortly after dusk this evening a flock of Cranes flew upon the property of the Association and alighted near the clubhouse. The mother bird had considerable difficulty in keeping her children quiet and in making them retire for the night. There were in the flock:

Mrs. Helen Peck Crane,	Asbury Park, N.J.
J. Townley Crane,	" "
William Howe Crane,	Port Jervis, N.Y.
E. B. Crane,	Lake View, N.J.
Stephen Crane,	Asbury Park, N.J.

On October 2, in the same register, Stephen noted that "Mother Crane caught seven fine pickerel to her own satisfaction and the astonishment of her brood. The next day she caught three more nice fish in less than an hour."

That fall, Stephen collected his furniture and other possessions and moved into Edmund's house in Lake View, a suburb of Paterson, New Jersey. This became his new home base and official residence. The streets were his university now. He began making trips into New York, wandering into the tenements and exploring the Bowery, the brazen, mile-long strip of saloons and dance halls, brothels, flophouses, and dirty, unlighted alleyways lying east of Broadway, from Worth Street to about East 4th Street. A universe unto itself, the Bowery was a place of lost souls and souls for sale, Manhattan's ragged, gaudy edge, where the show went on dependably each night, "its nightly glitter rak[ing] the eye with raw tones of green and red," as the novelist Thomas Beer said. Theodore Roosevelt called it "one of the great highways of humanity, a highway of seething life, of varied interest, of fun, of work, of sordid and terrible tragedy," a place "haunted by demons as evil as any that stalk through the pages of the Inferno." To Stephen Crane, human nature here "was open and plain, with nothing hidden" — it was "unvarnished," he told a friend, R. G. Vosburgh. In this raw place filled with people, a writer could slip in unnoticed.

Just as Stephen was beginning his life as a full-time writer, death struck the family again. On November 16, after a long illness, Anna (Annie) Crane, Townley's wife of just seventeen months, died. The marriage had seemed doomed almost from the start. Five months after the wedding, the Asbury Park papers had begun reporting on Anna Crane's health problems. First described as suffering from "congestion of the brain," then psychological problems resulting from the grippe, Annie entered the Trenton Asylum as a private patient. There she suffered two attacks of paralysis and died. Just twelve days later, the *Asbury Park Journal* incorrectly reported the death of Mrs. Mary Helen Crane, which Townley swiftly denied. But Helen's health had been failing for some time. In January she had resigned as president of the Asbury Park WCTU. Now she was critically ill from what the papers vaguely reported as the combined effects of a bad cold, a painful carbuncle on her neck, and depression brought on by her daughter-in-law's death, which she had learned of while "confined to her bed." On December 7, Helen died in Paterson, New Jersey. She was sixty-four, four years older than Stephen's father had been when he died. Stephen, just turned twenty, appointed Edmund as his guardian.

"Suddenly it struck each man that he was alone, separated from humanity by impassable gulfs," Stephen wrote in "The Octopush." In this, the best of his Sullivan County tales, four hapless men — called simply the Tall Man, the Little Man, the Quiet Man, and the Pudgy Man — wander and stumble through a mountainous forest. Innocents and social misfits who seem unconnected to the outside world, they are the ultimate orphans, forsaken not only by society but by the universe. Ostensibly representing Stephen and his camping friends — Senger was the Tall Man, Carr was the Pudgy Man, and Stephen both the Quiet Man and the Little Man — the wanderers in the woods are essentially aspects of the author.

Written and published in newspapers in 1892 in the months after his mother's death, the tales have a pervading theme: that man is alone in the universe. Almost as if seen through the eyes of a child, this universe is a place of towering tree trunks and peaked granite mountains, a big red sun and man-eating bears — a nightmare forest of sobbing hemlocks and "listening pines," of "unseen live things," and "black water, in which there were things that wiggled," where vindictive weeds throttle the lilies and drag them to the murky bottom below. Here "in a wilderness sunlight is noise." The tree stumps look spattered with blood. "The music of the wind in the trees is songs of loneliness, hymns of abandonment, and lays of the absence of things congenial and alive," Stephen wrote in "A Ghoul's Accountant." Here the moon watches over you, and the night, even a mountain, follows you. The entrance to a cave suggests a gaping mouth, something that can swallow a man.

As in a fairy tale, Stephen's little men wander in a wood — an ancient symbol for a place of self-discovery — where one might encounter a brown giantess or a lone house inhabited by a ghoul. But here, unlike the fairy-tale wood, there is no resolution of the characters' conflict: man is adrift. The nameless, egocentric child-men see the world only through their own vanity, confusion, and sense of impotence. The landscape is stocked with death's heads — shrunken, gray, "slate-colored" figures with voices that suggest a tomb or "cave-damp," where sleeping men are "mummy-like." Stephen drew himself in the figure of a recluse sitting before an altarlike stone in a cave illuminated by candles — "an infinitely sallow person" with "yellow fingers," he wrote in "Four Men in a Cave," adding religious imagery and sickliness to the picture.

The Sullivan County tales never rise above sketches to become fully developed short stories, but the best of them suggest the subconscious mind at work. The tales have a kind of dream reality: the images are distorted, but the feeling in the writing is psychologically true. Sometimes the little man's fears turn out to be his imagination run amok: the "wild cry" of a black dog is not a harbinger of death but simply the sound of a hungry animal; the ghoul is not out to harm the man but wants his help with some arithmetic — the old school nightmare. There is nothing under the bed after all, Stephen says. But the happy endings tacked on to the stories feel falsely reassuring. He had made a start, he was developing an artistic creed and discovering imagery that expressed his ideas, but he was not there yet.

In these sketches, Stephen used color, metaphor, and imagery to greater effect than he had before. "Troops of blue and silver darning-needles danced over the surface," he wrote in "The Octopush." "Bees bustled about the weeds which grew in the shallow places. Butterflies flickered in the air. Down in the water, millions of fern branches quavered." His use of red was particularly striking: "The sun sank in red silence," "The sun slid down and threw a flare upon the silence, coloring it red," "Dusk came and fought a battle with the flare. . . . Tossing shadows and red beams mingled in combat."

His own war — not "with the world but with myself" — was just beginning.

✦

Life on New York's mean streets was war. In the hardscrabble Bowery, whose fourteen-block universe spread like an infection, the poor preyed upon the poor, said chronicler Thomas Beer. The unlighted alleys were "so seldom cleaned," wrote Beer, "that gypsies often were unearthed in piles of rubbish months after their relatives had given up a hunt for some vanished entity." South of this district was seedy Park Row, where Park Street converged with Nassau and Spruce. This area housed the major newspapers: the *New York Times*, the *Tribune*, the *World*, and the *Sun*. In the winter of 1892, a slight, shabbily dressed figure with "a cigarette dangling from his lower lip" canvassed both areas, looking for subject matter and assignments.

When he was on the street, it was the commonplace things that caught Stephen's eye: a red, horse-drawn furniture van slowly navigating down a narrow street, the lighted gas lamps, the colors of the city — red, blue, and green. A hand-organ man, a girl fiercely chewing gum. A club-wielding policeman, newsboys hawking the latest edition of the paper. He wrote of "a small boy with a pitcher of beer so big that he had to set it down and rest every half block." Barber shops advertised "bay rum and a clean towel to every customer"; liquor stores sold "Hot spiced rum, 6 cents; Sherry with a Big Egg in it, 5 cents"; a restaurant served breakfast for thirteen cents, dinner for fifteen — signs that struck at Stephen's empty pockets and stomach.

In January 1892, Helen's will was probated, providing Stephen with an income of three hundred dollars a year, to be set aside for him until he graduated from college. In the meantime, with an occasional sale to the *Tribune* and the use of Edmund's house in Lake View, which offered sanctuary and food, he was able to get by. When he wasn't scratching up subject matter to work into newspaper pieces, he worked on his street-girl novel. Writing to his old friend from Claverack Tommie Borland, from Port Jervis that February, Stephen called him "a bird, a regular damned bird," and offered some worldly advice.

> So you lack females of the white persuasion, do you? How unfortunate! And how extraordinary! I never thought that the world could come to such a pass that you would lack females, Thomas! You indeed must be in a God forsaken country.
>
> Just read these next few lines in a whisper:— I — I think black is quite good — if — if its yellow and young.

Stephen was apparently back in New York when William became entangled in a lynching in Port Jervis. Having served as judge of Orange County for one year when Stephen was at Syracuse, William was now known locally as "Judge Crane." One day a servant told him about an incident taking place across the street from his house. A black man named Robert Lewis, alleged to have raped a white woman, Lena McMahan, was being taken to jail in a police wagon when a mob appeared and dragged him to a maple tree in front of the Reformed Church on East Main Street. William got dressed and made his way through a crowd of some two thousand people just as Lewis was being hoisted to the tree. Somehow managing to wrest the rope from the mob's hands and free the man, William stood guard over the badly bloodied figure, singlehandedly fending off the crowd and instructing the sole policeman present to use his gun. While the crowd threatened to shoot back and closed in on the victim, menacing him with matches held close to his face, William stood his ground and told him to keep quiet. But despite all his effort, and those of the doctor and the police officer, the crowd finally overwhelmed them and hanged Lewis.

The *Port Jervis Evening Gazette* reported William's testimony at the inquest. Elements of the story would appear later in a work of Stephen's fiction.

✦

While he was on the Asbury Park beat that summer of 1892, covering shore news for Townley, he met a young married woman named Lily Brandon Munroe. Her husband, Hersey Munroe, was a prosperous geologist who had provided her with a home in Washington and another in New York. While he was away on business, Lily was staying at the Lake Avenue Hotel with her mother-in-law and her younger sister, Dorothy. The same hotel housed Townley's press bureau. Stephen was twenty, Lily a little older. The one available photograph of her, taken with her husband, shows a slender, laughing girl leaning against a rail fence, holding her hat in her hand. Described by those who knew her as "very beautiful" and "exquisitely feminine," she had gracefully shaped dark brows like Stephen's and the golden hair he loved on women. His nieces had that hair, and he had said that "if he ever found a woman whose hair was golden like ours, he would marry her," according to Edmund's daughter Edith. Stephen was so captivated by Lily's beauty that he took her to an artist friend in New York, David Ericson, to have her portrait painted.

Little is known about the woman Stephen Crane called "L.B.," conspicuously omitting her married initial. Frequently left alone while her husband was on Geological Survey trips, she had been married only about a year when she met Stephen. She was "very fond of violets," said Ames Williams, who interviewed her years later. She came from a wealthy family. And she loved Stephen, in spite of his abject poverty, his indifference to dress (he even made notes on his shirt cuffs), and his decidedly undashing appearance. "Frail" and "undernourished," suffering from "a hacking cough," which did not prevent him from smoking cigarettes, he "was not a handsome man, but [he] had remarkable almond-shaped eyes," Lily said later. He was "extremely brilliant" and "very idealistic, without a trace of vulgarity." Convinced that he would die young, he wanted only "a few years of real happiness," he told her. He could not bear the sight of people eating heartily — "like animals," he told her — "and he would urge Lily to hurry with the plate of ice cream" he had bought her. She was not put off by his "melancholy" nature, and she seems not to have minded his oddly prudish side. He disapproved of women's bathing suits (Lily simply refrained from swimming), and he did not enjoy hearing her sing in public, for that attracted other admirers. And though he sometimes danced with her, he did not care for dancing. While the "gossiping porch sitters" looked on in disapproval (Stephen delighted in shocking the old ladies), he and Lily passed the summer strolling on the great wooden boardwalk, riding the merry-go-round, and watching the surf roll in. He especially loved watching the ocean, which he felt belonged to them. He told Lily that "whenever she saw the ocean she would think of him."

She was his "dearest, the one of all," Stephen wrote later. He loved the lines of her face, her smile; he enjoyed her company. Unable to give her material things, hard pressed even to buy her an ice cream, he gave her the manuscripts of some of his Sullivan County tales, the best part of himself.

Lily Brandon Munroe would say that she and Stephen Crane "were very much in love" but that both families opposed the romance. Her rich father was presumably not eager to see his daughter leave her husband for a poor writer with no prospects; at dinner with Lily and Mr. Brandon in New York Stephen had a glimpse of the father's attitude toward him. Perhaps trying to impress Mr. Brandon as someone who was not uncultivated and therefore not altogether unworthy of Lily, Stephen began speaking to him in French. Mr. Brandon instantly reproved him. "My daughter does not speak French, Mr. Crane," he said.

According to Lily, Stephen "begged" her "to elope with him and she considered the proposal seriously before declining" — apparently because of his lack of financial security and her family's disapproval. Lily's husband found out about Stephen and at some point destroyed the "many letters and pictures" the writer had given her. He later destroyed the manuscript of Stephen's street-girl novel, which Stephen had also given Lily. But her romance with Stephen was not over.

The Asbury Park summer season was in full swing, with "the sombre-hued gentlemen . . . arriving in solemn procession, with black valises in their hands and rebukes to frivolity in their eyes," Stephen wrote for the *Tribune*. Thousands of city people came to the shore that summer, filling the boarding houses and hotels. The tents of the less affluent went up under the trees. In the evenings everyone spilled onto the boardwalk to parade in fine dress under the glare of electric lights while a brass band played. The city had spent tens of thousands of dollars on athletic facilities and new amusements, such as a toboggan slide. Fifteen thousand dollars was spent on the bicycle track alone, Stephen noted.

He took in the whole human carnival, from the monied summer guests to the seaside fakirs, from women with babies to the ever-present summer girl, "a bit of interesting tinsel flashing near the sombre-hued waves. She gives the zest to life on the great boardwalk. Without her the men would perish from weariness or fall to fighting." Noticing "a young man . . . with a struggling moustache" dancing with a girl, Stephen observed that "he holds her — well, as if he were afraid of losing her."

His melancholy notwithstanding, he tramped miles along the beach, sometimes walking all day. He even worked up a hearty appetite for fish cakes and crabs. That summer, between July 2 and September 11, he published at least ten reports on Asbury Park doings, worked on his novel, according to Lily, and wrote a New York street scene study, "Travels in New York: The Broken-Down Van," published in the *Tribune*.

To another young *Tribune* reporter, Arthur Oliver, Stephen Crane "was not highly distinguished above any other boy of twenty who had gained a reputation for saying and writing bright things." Like Oliver, Stephen wanted "to write something out of the ordinary," but "to hear him talk you would say his passionate ambition was baseball."

"Somehow I can't get down to the real thing," Oliver said. "I know I have something unusual to tell, but I get all tangled up with different notions of how it ought to be told."

Stephen scooped a handful of sand and threw it into the wind.

"Treat your notions like that," he told Oliver. "Forget what you think about it and tell how you feel about it. Make the other fellow realize you are just as human as he is. That's the big secret of story-telling. Away with literary fads and canons. Be yourself!"

His reporting had become more satiric and daring. He took on the religious element — "the cool, shaded Auditorium will soon begin to palpitate with the efforts of famous preachers delivering doctrines to thousands of worshippers" — and even Asbury Park's founder and chief financier, James Bradley, who wore flashy clothes and "fierce and passionate whiskers." Bradley had a penchant for erecting signs and statuary, including a marble bathtub, along the boardwalk, and Stephen imagined in print that instead of "Keep off the grass" a Bradley sign said "Don't go in the water attired merely in a tranquil smile," or "Do not appear on the beach when only enwrapped in reverie."

But when Stephen turned his pen to the American Day parade of the Junior Order of United American Mechanics, he found he'd gone too far. On August 17, while Townley was away, Stephen and Arthur Oliver went into a billiard parlor for a cigar. When they emerged, they found the parade in full swing. There were hundreds of marchers, Stephen observed, "bronzed, slope-shouldered, uncouth" men "begrimed with dust." They wore ill-fitting clothes and "plodded," rather than marched, like beasts of burden. And yet they were "dignified" in their unpretentious way. They marched with "a pace and bearing emblematic of their lives." Leaning against a door with his cigar half extinguished but still clenched between his teeth, Stephen was struck by the irony of the spectacle — the homely, shuffling marchers parading for the leisured, well-heeled spectators dressed in "summer gowns, lace parasols, tennis trousers, straw hats and indifferent smiles." The idea that wealthy Asbury Parkers could appreciate the unaffected honesty of these common workers with dirty fingernails struck him as absurd.

"Well, Stevie, how about it?" said Oliver.

Stephen tossed aside his cigar, let out a few choice words, and rushed off to the *Tribune* office to write his story.

"The bona fide Asbury Parker is a man to whom a dollar, when held close to his eye, often shuts out any impression he may have had that other people possess rights," he wrote in conclusion.

> He is apt to consider that men and women, especially city
> men and women, were created to be mulcted by him: Hence

the tan-colored, sun-beaten honesty in the faces of the members of the Junior Order of United American Mechanics is
expected to have a very staggering effect upon them. The
visitors are men who possess principles.

At least two editors, including Willis Fletcher Johnson, passed the
piece along for publication. William K. Devereux, whom Townley had
asked to check Stephen's copy in his absence, was amused by it but
thought the *Tribune* too humorless to print it. He was wrong. The article
was published, unsigned, on August 21 and, as Devereux said later,
"raised hob all over the country."

People misread it. The JOUAM marchers were outraged; the *Tribune*
article had not only mocked their style of marching, but their very patriotism, said a letter to the editor published on August 23, adding that the
piece was "un-American."

"Personally I do not think The Tribune would publish such a slur on
one of the largest bodies of American-born citizens if it knew the order,
its objects, or its principles," wrote an offended marcher. The JOUAM
was "a national political organization," whose purpose was to keep
America pure by shutting out foreign influences such as immigration,
"foreign competition," and to keep "sectarian interference" out of American schools. They demanded that "the Holy Bible be read in our public
schools." As for the marchers' drilling, it was admittedly not military, but
it was American.

Townley rushed to his brother's defense, firing off a piece for the *Asbury Park Daily Press* in which he lamented the views of readers "who claim
that the correspondents have no right to say anything about the town
excepting in the way of praise." He himself had been "terribly black-
guarded" for some of his articles and "reviled like a pickpocket over an
Associated Press dispatch that was never seen by any person in the em-
ploy of the great news gathering corporation until it was published."
Without identifying Stephen Crane as the writer, on August 24, two days
after the publication of Townley's defense, and the day after the letter to
the editor from the offended JOUAM member, the *Tribune* apologized
to its readers for the piece, calling it "a bit of random correspondence,
passed inadvertently by the copy editor."

The brouhaha had more to do with politics than with rhetoric. The
Tribune was owned and edited by Whitelaw Reid, candidate for vice president of the United States on the Republican ticket with Benjamin Harri-

son. Stephen's bald and provocative portrait of the marchers, which was "susceptible [to] garbling and misrepresentation," said Johnson, provided choice fodder for the newspapers opposed to Reid's candidacy. They deliberately distorted the piece and served it up to the public as a slander on the working man. "The article was in bad taste, unworthy of a reputable reporter, and still more discreditable to a newspaper with the standing of the *New York Tribune*," intoned the *Asbury Park Daily Journal*. Though the paper did not name Crane, it described the author as a "young man" with "a hankering for the razzle-dazzle style," who "has a great future before him, if, like the good, he fails to die young."

Arthur Oliver thought he detected "just a bit of pride" in Stephen's face when he asked what Oliver thought of the piece. Johnson saw "a much agitated" young man who was worried about the consequences of his writing and anxious to fix things.

The talk about Stephen's piece continued, creating "a great sensation" through secondhand accounts. Whitelaw Reid, who had not read the piece when it was published, asked Johnson "for the facts in the case. I gave them," said Johnson, "showing him the item as it was originally published, and that was the end of the case, so far as he was concerned." But Stephen was fired anyway. Word went around that Townley was also to be let go at the end of the season. Townley looked as "glum as a king who had lost his crown," said Arthur Oliver. " 'Stevie' greeted me with a saintly smile he always had ready for every disaster." He told Oliver he was amazed that "a little innocent chap like me could have stirred up such a row in American politics. It shows what innocence can do if it has the opportunity!" he said.

Later it was said that "the parade that made Steve Crane famous" had cost the Republicans the presidential election. Though *Tribune* editors and reporters such as Ralph Paine liked Stephen and were sorry that he'd "toyed with a boomerang," they agreed that by freeing him from mundane reporting, the firing "might be the making of him." Johnson himself thought that "a man who could write 'Four Men in a Cave' ought not to waste his time in reporting that 'The Flunkey-Smiths of Squedunk are at the Gilded Pazaza Hotel for the season.' "

Asked, after some time had passed, whether he regretted writing the piece, Stephen said, "No! You've got to feel the things you write if you want to make an impact on the world."

✦

He used Townley's *Tribune* stationery to write a letter to the manager of the American Press Association, asking for an assignment. He proposed opening "a special article trade" with the APA. "I have written special articles for some years for the Tribune and other papers. Much of my work has been used by the various press associations, and I would like to deal directly with you if possible." Nothing came of it.

Without so much as a part-time reporting job, without any prospects, he moved into a cheap apartment house in New York that fall with a group of medical students, including Frederic Lawrence and Lucius Button.

The new lodgings, located at 1064 Avenue A (formerly Eastern Boulevard) between the Bowery and the East River, stood in one of New York's ghettos. With the optimism of youth, the fellows called the apartment the Pendennis Club, presumably after Thackeray's novel, in which a spoiled young man grows up to write a successful novel and enjoys many love affairs before marrying his true love.

Here, once elegant old Knickerbocker houses were nearly obliterated by overcrowded, sunless tenements built for two families but housing ten. People lived in filthy cellars, on fire escapes, doorstoops, church corners — wherever they could find a suggestion of shelter. "Didn't live nowhere," said two barefoot brothers described in a book that had brought the Lower East Side to national attention just two years earlier, *How the Other Half Lives*, by Jacob Riis.

It was a world of unrelieved degradation and squalor, infecting "family life with deadly moral contagion," wrote Riis. The Lower East Side was clogged with ash barrels and refuse, cheap lodging houses, forlorn-looking shops and tenements, two-cent restaurants, opium joints, and stale beer dives — four thousand saloons below 14th Street, noted Riis. It offered an endless expanse of brick walls and narrow alleys crisscrossed with pulley lines strung with ragged clothes and patched linen. The cobbled streets were jammed with horse-drawn cabs, peddlers' carts, and poor immigrants; Arabs; Italians, many wearing yellow kerchiefs or red bandannas; pigtailed Chinese; Greeks; Russian and Polish Jews, the men bearded and wearing skullcaps. Stephen and his roommates were among the American-born minority, along with Negroes, bohemians, and assorted others.

Women wearing long skirts and shawls, their hair pinned up, stood at the curbs selling stale produce or bread in the shape of long wreaths from bags of "dirty bed-tick," noted Riis. They carried babies in their arms, rotting vegetables in their aprons, or great bundles of firewood on their heads. Old women sat in rows under the almshouse trees, wrote Riis, "some smoking stumpy black clay-pipes, others knitting or idling, all grumbling." There were children everywhere, dirty and ragged. Many died in crowded tenement rooms for lack of fresh air. Urchins pitched pennies in dark halls, slid down wooden cellar doors, or sewed knicker-bockers in the sweater district. Bowlegged, half-naked, shoeless children with bruised faces lived on the street. Child abuse and murder were com-mon; criminals ranging from the groups of thieves known as growler gangs, to professional beggars to "firebugs" who set fire to their homes to collect insurance money on the furniture, were rampant. In Riis's star-tling photographs the expression in the eyes of children and adults of every nationality is always the same: wasted, resigned, and hopeless.

Through this vibrant human wasteland moved the slight figure of Stephen Crane, "in search of the local color that would give life to the great work," said Frederic Lawrence, who often accompanied him. Like Jacob Riis, who had spent countless hours walking the worst streets of the Lower East Side, often alone, Stephen took in his new surroundings "with keen and sympathetic" interest — but with a writer's cool detach-ment, noted Lawrence.

New York's premier police reporter — the "boss reporter," his rivals on Mulberry Street called him — forty-three-year-old Jacob Riis had come to Avon-by-the-Sea in the summer of 1892 to give a lecture, illus-trated with his own photographs, on the plight of tenement dwellers trapped in the city in the summer. The lecture, which Stephen had at-tended, raised money for an organization that provided a two-week holi-day in the country for slum children. In his *Tribune* piece, Stephen gave no sign of having been moved by the talk. But now, as he experienced first-hand how the other half lived, living in poverty himself and soaking up the atmosphere for his novel about a girl of the slums, he was undoubt-edly influenced by Riis's work. Like an actor playing a part, he donned ragged clothes and entered a store on Beekman Street where Edmund was working. He had already told his brother not to give him more than a nickel if he ever came in, and on this day, when he saw Stephen enter the store, Ed obliged, silently dropping the coin into the hand of the hungry-looking beggar who approached him.

Back at the Pendennis Club, his own poverty having become all too real, Stephen continued to work on his novel. Lawrence was struck by how carefully Stephen formed the sentences in his head before his pen touched the paper in his clean script, which he seldom corrected. He was a figure of meticulousness amid the chaos of the world outside his window, which he was so faithfully committing to paper. Each sentence was a triumph. Having set it down, he'd relight his pipe or begin singing a popular tune, take a turn about the room, or look out the window. All the while he concentrated on the next sentence, the light in his face brightening, then extinguishing, said Lawrence. His roommates knew enough to keep away from Stephen while he was working, though he himself would sometimes initiate conversation. Writing perhaps a page a day, three at most, and not writing at all for days at a time, he finished the novel sometime during the winter of 1892–93.

Maggie is set in fictional Rum Alley, whose name suggests actual Bowery streets, which had names like Bottle Alley, Cat Alley, Blind Man's Alley, and Bandit's Roost. The novel is the story of a poor Irish slum girl who is seduced and abandoned by vulgar, swaggering Pete, a bartender friend of her brother's. Disowned by her family, Maggie becomes a prostitute, finally ending her brief life by walking into the river.

Stephen had taken the familiar and the banal as his plot, reworking ideas that social historians and reformers like Jacob Riis and Thomas De Witt Talmage had already advanced about the demoralizing effects of the slums. Since 1890 the *Arena* and *Scribner's* magazine had been running exposés of slum life. Stories and sketches on the subject were common. The plot of *Maggie* — virtuous-young-woman-is-spoiled-by-heartless-seducer — had been used in an 1889 slum novel by Edgar Fawcett, *The Evil That Men Do*. Riis had written of tenement women who remain uncorrupted by their vile atmosphere, "of womanhood pure and undefiled. That it should blossom in such an atmosphere is one of the unfathomable mysteries," he reflected. Stephen's Maggie "blossomed in a mud puddle" and "grew to be a most rare and wonderful product of a tenement district, a pretty girl."

And yet no one would confuse the writing of Stephen Crane with that of anyone else. Ignoring the romantic, sentimental approach of earlier slum fiction, he dared to show that poverty was not only cruel but sordid and unredeeming. Jacob Riis had dared before him in journalism and photographs. Now Stephen broke new ground in fiction. Mingling an unblinking, realistic point of view with highly artful prose, he was fresh and very modern. From the opening paragraph, in which a small boy is seen hurling stones at "howling" urchins on Devil's Row "for the honor of Rum Alley," Stephen announced his arrival on the literary scene with brashness and self-confidence. "No other wrote like that, or would begin a tale with anything like the stride of this one," said one friend. He used the materials at hand: a stone fight he had witnessed one day ("Did you ever see a stone fight?" he'd excitedly asked Lawrence, his face alight), the view from the Pendennis Club, which was close enough to the East River to see the prison yard at Blackwell's Island from an upstairs window.

> From a window of an apartment house that uprose from amid squat, ignorant stables, there leaned a curious woman. Some laborers, unloading a scow at a dock at the river, paused for a moment and regarded the fight. The engineer of a passive tugboat hung lazily over a railing and watched. Over on the Island, a worm of yellow convicts came from the shadow of a grey ominous building and crawled slowly over the river's bank.

Breaking with traditional narrative form for an episodic treatment delivered in short, impressionistic chapters, he hurled metaphors and images at the reader like rocks. From the smarmy Pete, whose "patent-leather shoes looked like weapons," to Maggie's brutal mother, a one-dimensional character who is little more than a Sullivan County giantess prone to drunken rampages, Stephen's vividly drawn characters almost out-shouted their stereotypes. He had absorbed it all — the Bowery's crude dialect and profanity, which he used lavishly; "the darkening chaos of back yards"; the dirty street urchins and dissipated parents; the brazen violence; the degradation and despair of this world where "souls did not insist on being able to smile." He depicted Maggie's world not realistically, as Riis had, but as a "dark region" of "gruesome doorways" that "gave up loads of babies to the street and the gutter," a place where the door of a saloon opened like a mouth. He had transformed his Sullivan County mountains and caves into concrete and mortar. His street girl was a variant of the little man abandoned to an uncaring universe that could turn devouring. But with *Maggie*, Stephen had made a large creative advance over the sketches. Unlike the little men who stumbled through the woods in blind ignorance, whose actions were without consequences in the indifferent universe, the new characters suffered the moral consequences of their actions. With *Maggie*, Stephen had moved from a comic exercise to tragedy and a more sophisticated, developed ironic perspective.

"You can't find preaching on any page of *Maggie*! An artist has no business to preach," he told a young uptown woman during a stimulating conversation about books. "A story must have a reason, but art is — oh, well, not a pulpit." While thinking himself a disinterested and tough observer — the antithesis of a preacher — he had in fact taken a passionately moral stance. With each sentence he blamed everyone but the innocent Maggie for her fall. He condemned Pete, Mrs. Johnson, and society itself for their monstrous, self-serving behavior, for taking the easy way out. Maggie alone was a victim of circumstance.

In writing the novel he had wanted "to show that environment is a tremend[ous] thing in the world and frequently shapes liv[es]." And if he had achieved that, then he would prove to people that "one makes room [in] Heaven for all sorts of souls, notably an occasional street girl, who are not confidently expected to be there by many excellent people."

He was impatient to see his work in print. Willis Fletcher Johnson cautioned him that "it would be difficult to find a reputable publisher who would dare to bring [the novel] out." The subject was marketable, but as written, pockmarked with profanity, *Maggie* was too coarse for the general public. "It would so shock the Podsnaps and Mrs. Grundys as to bring him a storm of condemnation," Johnson told Stephen. Years later the *Tribune* editor would remember Stephen Crane's first novel as a work of "throbbing vitality" — "every line seemed alive and active," he wrote. He marveled at how the youngest Crane had managed to absorb both the speech and manners of the Bowery denizens. The writing had the qualities of "stark brutality and astounding frankness," while lacking "prurience . . . erotic suggestiveness . . . the 'sex motive'" which would later characterize so much of American fiction, said Johnson. Hamlin Garland thought the novel "bitter" but absorbing, filled with the same "vividness and originality of diction and more of the uncompromising truth" that had distinguished Stephen's piece on the JOUAM parade. Garland was so taken with *Maggie* that he wrote a note for Stephen to take to Richard Watson Gilder, editor of the popular magazine the *Century*. The note called the manuscript *"great"* and Stephen Crane "an astonishing fellow."

While *Maggie*'s fate lay undecided, winter arrived with a vengeance. One night Stephen and Phil May, a British artist and illustrator, borrowed a tiger skin belonging to illustrator William Francis "Frank" Ver Beck. A policeman found them under the skin, walking up and down Broadway at 3:30 A.M., and brought them into the Tenderloin station. He released the young men but kept the skin.

During that cold winter, Stephen had a couple of small publications to warm him — "The Cry of a Huckleberry Pudding," a Sullivan County tale, appeared in the *Syracuse Herald* in December, and "A Tent in Agony" was published in the monthly *Cosmopolitan*, his first publication in a popular magazine. But pressed by the "haggard purse," the young man in the shabby rain ulster felt that he'd "sell my steps to the grave at ten cents per foot," he told a new friend.

4

THE NOISE OF

RUMORS

On a white winter day in January 1893, when New York City was cloaked in snow that had turned the whole world white, the gray figure of Stephen Crane entered a red brick apartment building at Broadway and 30th Street. He was tagging along with Lew Senger to meet Senger's cousin, the painter Corwin Knapp Linson. As he stepped from the terra-cotta-colored hall into Linson's studio, he made a memorable picture.

The artist saw that Stephen was fair, with "rumpled" blond hair, and, at twenty-one, only the faint beginnings of a mustache above an engagingly frank smile. The moment he removed the long rain ulster, he seemed to shrink, but Linson noticed that though "slight," Stephen's body was well proportioned and athletic, and his face was "lean but not thin." Seven years older than Stephen, Linson had studied art in Paris in the same class as Paul Gauguin. He was impressed by the clean lines of Stephen's profile, which reminded him "of the young Napoleon" — "but not so hard, Steve," he said later — and by the remarkable eyes, of a "gray-blue intensity." His long fingers, stained yellow from nicotine, played nervously with a cigarette, which he mostly held rather than smoked. The cigarette kept going out in his fingers, and he used match after match relighting it.

Stephen was getting nowhere with the publication of *Maggie*. Willis Fletcher Johnson had sent him to Ripley Hitchcock with the manuscript, and the editor had rejected it but praised the author: "That boy has the real stuff in him," he told Johnson. The *Century* had rejected it as well, and with no other takers in sight, Stephen was impatiently moving toward printing the novel himself. In mid-January he applied for copyright at the Library of Congress, calling his book *A Girl of the Streets / A Story of New York.* He sent the one-dollar fee with a letter written on Pendennis Club stationery. And then, with money paid by William for Stephen's one-seventh share of Arbutus Cottage and from the sale (also to Will) of his shares in the Kingston, Pennsylvania, coal mine — totaling perhaps $1,000 — he and Frederic Lawrence took the manuscript to a printing shop they'd often passed on lower Sixth Avenue. Without haggling over the price, he sold his future for the street girl.

On Johnson's advice, Stephen took a pseudonym, and *Maggie: A Girl of the Streets* (A Story of New York), by Johnston Smith, was born between saffron yellow paper covers, price fifty cents. "Neither Mr. Podsnap nor Mrs. Grundy might suspect him of being the guilty author!" Stephen told Johnson.

He became his own agent and salesman, sending yellow *Maggie*s out into the world with the alacrity of a pitcher on a baseball mound. He sent the book to social reformers and editors, like John D. Barry of the *Forum*, and to Hamlin Garland, anonymously, with the enticing inscription: "The reader of this book must inevitably be shocked, but let him keep on till the end, for in it the writer has put something which is important" — (he wrote much the same words in other copies of the novel). He handed it to Corwin Knapp Linson without identifying himself as the author. Stephen's friends tried to help sales by conspicuously reading copies in the elevated train "so that passengers would think the metropolis was *Maggie*-mad," said his friend from Syracuse, Frank Noxon. As Stephen waited for the "sensation" he was sure the book would cause, his roommates read and reread the novel and threw a book party for the author. On the night of the party, in late February or early March, *Maggie*s lined the wall, held up the wassail punch bowl, filled in the empty spaces where furniture should have been. The author, dressed in jacket and tie, thrummed a banjo and posed for a photograph amid some of the revelers, including two human skeletons smoking corncob pipes. As the party grew rowdier toward midnight, the landlady protested that she couldn't sleep; she rented rooms "to gentlemen, not animals," she added. Waving to the others to keep quiet, Stephen called out: "The animals apologize and will return to their cages at once!"

"Cheese it!" he told the others.

He soon grew angry at the lack of interest in the novel. "No one would see it," he told Linson, "not even the jays who would sell their souls for a nickel. I sent copies to some preachers who were maniacs for reform — not a word from one of 'em."

"I wrote across the cover so they couldn't miss it, that if they read it, they would see the sense. I knew they'd jump at first, but I hoped they were intelligent. You'd think the book came straight from hell and they smelled the smoke. Not one of them gave me a word! Icebergs, CK, flints!"

The kitchen maid used some of the *Maggies* to start the fire.

A month or so after *Maggie* appeared in covers, reactions began trickling in. Garland, who had guessed that Stephen Crane was the author, thought the novel a work of integrity that showcased Stephen's "genius for phrases." The *Forum*'s John Barry took the time to write a thoughtful letter, telling Stephen that he considered the novel too brutal and dark; it had produced "a kind of horror" in him. He found fault with its pitiless realism, the "vulgar and profane" Bowery talk, and the character of Maggie. Stephen had given her no inner life; he had "observed from the outside only." Barry encouraged him to "try something else . . . to study the thoughts as well as the acts of characters" and to come to his office to discuss the novel.

Stephen told Linson he was grateful for Barry's "genuine interest" in his work, but the letter seemed to trouble him. At Garland's suggestion, he had sent William Dean Howells a copy of the novel, and now, weeks later, "having recieved no reply I must decide that you think it a wretched thing?" he wrote Howells.* The older man was moved by the young writer's "heartbreaking note," and he promptly responded that he had not had time to give the book more than a glance, but that glance had given him the impression that Stephen was "working in the right way." He said that he would write again after he had read it.

Soon after the Pendennis Club party, Linson turned up at Stephen's rooms in the early morning to find him sitting by the window in a haze of cigarette smoke with a white towel wrapped around his head, "turban-like." The leavings of his recent activity lay around him — an ink bottle and sheets of foolscap. He had been up all night writing a story, he told

---

* I have kept Stephen Crane's misspellings throughout.

Linson, yet he was surprisingly fresh. "A wet towel cools the machinery," he said. He liked working at night. "I'm all alone in the world. It's great!"

The new story, called "The Pace of Youth," was a lighthearted tale of romantic love set in an Asbury Park–like seaside resort. In its witty depiction of the seemingly hopeless courtship of a carousel operator and a ticket taker who is the boss's daughter, it was the antithesis of *Maggie*, all sparkling light, filled with a tenderness and a *joie d'esprit* unlike anything Stephen had written before. As only Stephen Crane could have written *Maggie*, only he could have penned this story rich in his distinctive phrasing, imagery, and use of color, with the ironic narrative voice that was already a hallmark of his work. Here is Asbury Park: a "fairy scene of the night," where milling crowds, illuminated by artificial light, move to the seductive sound of the surf mingling with the music of the band playing at the pavilion. A girl in a red dress is seen from a distance on the beach, "crawling slowly like some kind of spider on the fabric of nature." Asbury Park's founder, Bradley, serves as the wealthy Stimson, the father of the beloved: a "fierce" comic character with "indomitable whiskers" and a fondness for his own signs. When the lovers manage to escape his watchful eye and elope, he is "defied by the universe" like one of the impotent little men of the Sullivan County tales. The pace of youth, represented literally by the couple's carriage flying into the future, has outstripped him. Even the rear window of the receding carriage looks back at the helpless father like a "derisive eye."

Here is Stephen's thwarted summer romance with Lily Munroe (the fictional girl is named Lizzie), but with the soaring happy ending that eluded them. Like the writer, who seems to society to be doing nothing and who has no financial security, the carousel operator spends his days standing on a narrow platform, underscoring the precariousness of his situation. He is "a sort of general squire in these lists of childhood," wrote Stephen. "He was very busy." Sick with love, he must satisfy himself by stealing glances at Lizzie, whose face is always seen, bridelike, behind the silvered netting of the cashier's box. It is money that stands between the lovers, the lack of it making the suitor unworthy in the father's eyes.

Writing to Lily in April, three months after seeing her again, apparently in New York, Stephen depicted himself as a young man flying strongly into the future. He wanted "Dearest L.B." to know that his months of hard work had paid off: he had written a book, and it had won him the admiration of Hamlin Garland and the powerful William Dean Howells.

Howells cared for the book "immensely." Its truth was "grim, not to say grimy," and "cultured ears" would find its profanity hard to accept, but Stephen had written "perhaps the best tough dialect which has yet found its way into print," and his artistry and "literary conscience" outweighed the book's weaknesses. He invited Stephen to tea. As Frederic Lawrence later told it, on the appointed day Stephen dressed in his best clothing amid high excitement at the Pendennis Club. His roommates cheered him as he set off for the great man's apartment at 40 West 59th Street.

Howells, a stocky man in his mid-fifties, with a big mustache and a kind face, was charmed by Stephen, who stayed late, talking about his work and "the semi-savage poor" he had studied for the novel. The older man worried that the book's profanity "would shock the public away." Stephen said he had felt some "stress" about having to include it. Howells was impressed with the young man's wisdom and kindness as he talked about the Bowery poor and about his perception that the street tough had to be tough because "everything was on him." Howells was nearly as taken with Stephen's person as with his intelligence. He was wonderful to look at — with a "strange, melancholy beauty," an "ironical smile," and "mystical, clouded eyes," Howells said later. Stephen was quiet upon returning to the Pendennis Club. Even to Lawrence, he said little about his important evening.

"They tell me I did a horrible thing, but, they say, 'its great,'" he wrote Lily. He told her that B. O. Flower, the editor of the *Arena*, who had published many of Garland's stories and articles, "has practically offered me the benefits of his publishing company for all that I may in future write." And "Albert Shaw of the 'Review of Reviews' wrote me congratulations this morning and to-morrow I dine with the editor of the 'Forum.'" He was now "almost a success," but he assured Lily that "applause" would not turn his head. His silence during the past months — all his hard work — had been for her. "I was trying to see if I was worthy to have you think of me. And I have waited to find out." He "thought if I could measure myself by the side of some of the great men I could find if I was of enough value to think of you, L.B." In closing he asked, did she care about the chorus of praise for his book? Had she forgotten? Forgotten *what*, he did not say.

On a snowy day in March, Stephen turned up at Linson's studio. Though he still wasn't making money, he was on a winning streak, writing more

prolifically than ever before. Along with "The Pace of Youth," as yet unpublished, and the beginning of a new slum novel, he had written an
amusing piece on bad erotic French novels called "Why Did the Young
Clerk Swear? Or, the Unsatisfactory French." It had been published in
the weekly humor magazine *Truth*.

While Linson painted, Stephen's eye was caught by some old Civil
War issues of the *Century* in an oak bookcase, and he began to read them.
Published between 1884 and 1887, the *Century*'s Civil War series was
largely devoted to famous battles and military leaders. Accompanied by
photographs, engravings, and maps of military campaigns, the articles
were rich in detail about the accouterments of war. Here were the blis-
tered feet and aching bones, the endless meals of hardtack and coffee, the
inspections and drills through mud and dust, details of military strategy
and tactics and the transmission of orders. Here also were the contents of
knapsacks and what soldiers ate in the dining barracks. One learned that
a soldier's canteen, bayonet, and tin cup collided on his body during a
march; that an airborne shell sounded like a steam locomotive; that officers were not allowed to trot their horses over bridges; that "in a real battle the officer gets in the rear of his men." There was a story about the
Union front rank that was more afraid of its own rear rank — whose
gunfire had singed their hair — than of the Rebs.

The writing, however, was lifeless and dry. It was war without the
music and color, without human feeling. And there were the standard
clichés about courage and heroism: "There were many deeds performed
in this action which were heroic"; "The tender hand of woman was there
to alleviate distress, and the picture of misery was qualified by the heroic
grit of those who suffered"; and so on. "Cold chills ran up and down my
back as I got out of bed after the sleepless night, and shaved, preparatory
to other desperate deeds of valor," ran a soldier's typical comment on his
feelings. Said another, "I had a fluctuation of desires; I was faint-hearted
and brave; I wanted to enlist, and yet — I felt like old Atlas, with the
world on his shoulders and the planetary system suspended around him."

Linson noticed that Stephen was squatting on the floor, Indian-style,
beside the bookcase, reading in silence. Finally he tossed a magazine
aside, and got to his feet. "I wonder that *some* of these fellows don't tell
how they *felt* in those scraps!" he said. "They spout eternally of what they
did, but they are emotionless as rocks!"

On subsequent visits to Linson's studio he kept returning to the
magazines as though pulled by invisible threads. While Linson painted,

Stephen rummaged through copies of the *Century*. Outside, the sounds of Broadway drifted in: horses' hooves, the clanging of the horse-drawn fire engine, megaphones calling to vehicles outside Daly's Theater near 29th Street, passersby walking, cabbies arguing, people laughing and talking. Stephen sprawled on the divan to read, leaving the discarded magazines on the floor. He seemed to be looking for something, Linson thought.

Soon the idea of writing a war novel overtook him. The subject had always been in him; he "had been unconsciously working the detail of the story out through most of his boyhood," he said later. He had soldiers in his ancestry, in his blood, and he himself "had been imagining war stories ever since he was out of knickerbockers." He had grown up in the post-war decade with still-youthful veterans living all around. Members of the famed Orange Blossoms regiment sat in the park across the street from the Drew Methodist Church in Port Jervis, and Stephen had drawn them out whenever he met them, he told Frederic Lawrence. He had absorbed the veterans' speech and their tales of life in army camps until they almost seemed like his own memories. By now, said Lawrence, Stephen "knew more of war as it appears to the private in the ranks than most of the historians did."

But, like the *Century* writers, the Civil War veterans Stephen met "had never told him just the things he wanted to know about. They would describe the position of the troops, and tell how this regiment marched up here while one marched down there; but as for their sensations in the fight they seemed to have forgotten them," he said later. They "were in no wise to be trusted."

He thought of writing a quick "potboiler" to sell to a newspaper, "something that would take the boarding school element — you know the kind," he would tell Louis Senger. But as he continued his Civil War reading, borrowing a book collection of the *Century* pieces from a neighbor, "I got interested in the thing in spite of myself, and I *had* to do it my way." A story and a character began to take shape. He resolved to write the best war story that was in him.

"He was immersed in dreams," said Linson of that spring of 1893. As Stephen pored over the magazines in Linson's studio, he said nothing about the novel forming in his mind and possibly now on paper. Instead he talked about escaping his own poverty. "If I had a new suit of clothes I'd feel my grip tighten on the future — it's ridiculous but it doesn't make me laugh," he told his friend. Remembering Stephen's dreamy state later, Linson sensed that the character in the war novel had stalked Stephen for months, "a shadowy accompaniment of his every move." One day Stephen stopped reading the *Century* articles: "I'm through with 'em now, CK," he said. "Your charming patience is appreciated!" And he left the magazines where he had tossed them.

Linson had the impression that Stephen wrote some version of the novel the same month he discovered the *Century* issues, in March of 1893. Stephen himself, who was careless about dates, would say only that he began writing the war tale in "the latter part of my twenty-first year . . . and completed it early in my twenty-second year." What is certain is that by July 1893 — thirty years to the month after the beginning of the great battle at Gettysburg — he started writing the novel in earnest. The Pendennis Club having disbanded for the summer, Stephen moved into Edmund's house in Lake View and wrote.

From the beginning, he wanted to show what it felt like to be in a war, to write "a psychological portrayal of fear." To this aim he left the battle unnamed — "it was essential that I should make my battle a type," he explained later — and conceived his story from the point of view of a young private. He was not interested in heaping laurels on bemedaled generals, and he knew enough about war to understand that privates did the killing. Borrowing his sister-in-law's maiden name, Fleming, for the youth, he wrote a working title on a piece of paper:

Private Fleming His various b

He started over on a clean page.

Private Fleming
His various battles

After their long gestation, the first words and paragraphs came to him with "every word in place, every comma, every period fixed," he later told Hamlin Garland, saying nothing about the research and concentration that had produced this miracle. It was as though he were taking dictation, writing "throughout with the unhesitating speed of one who did not have to contrive incident or think it through at all; it was simply the labor of writing," he told Linson.

The cold passed reluctantly from the earth and the retiring fogs revealed an army stretched out on the hill, resting. As

the landscape changed from brown to green the army awak-
ened and began to tremble with eagerness at the noise of rumors. It cast its eyes upon the roads which were growing
from long red th —

he deleted "red th" —

troughs of liquid mud to proper thoroughfares. A river, amber tinted in the shadow of its banks, purled at the army's
feet and at night when the stream had become of a sorrowful
blackness one could see, across, the red eye-like gleam of
hostile camp-fires set in the low brows of distant hills.

It was a marvelous opening paragraph. With the easy brilliance of
"the cold passed reluctantly from the earth," the perfectly placed word
"resting," the sentences moved, with flawless choreography, to the red
eyes of the campfires. Now he was off to Private Henry Fleming's deeply
personal and subjective experience of war. Stephen was well equipped for
battle; he had all the authentic details — the cracker boxes and tin dishes,
the hardtack and coffee, the canteen, haversack, and musket, the camp
rumors — to ground his story in reality. With his Sullivan County little
men and his experiments with color behind him, with the rhythms and
imagery of the Bible in him and a formidable innate gift with words, he
now summoned a mature artist's control to depict Henry Fleming's war.
A constantly changing landscape of hallucinatory images registered the
youth's "panic-fear": campfires appeared as red animal eyes, shells were
"strange war-flowers bursting into fierce bloom," an army looked like a
dragon, a crawling reptile, a serpent.
Filled with boyish dreams of the glory of war, Fleming leaves the
farm of his widowed mother to fight. But he quickly becomes disillu-
sioned by war's reality — the long delay before battle, the endless marching and drilling, the rumors going round the camp. He begins to worry
that when the battle finally does come, he will not be equal to it, that he'll
run. After making it through the first confusing skirmish, he begins to un-
ravel. He doesn't remember loading his gun. He breaks into a sweat, the
water running down his soiled face. He keeps wiping his eyes. He fires a
blank shot. Then he begins to lose himself. Feeling that he is "not a man
but a member" of an army, he is briefly paralyzed with fear. In the chaos
of smoke, fire, and noise, with men dropping "like bundles," Fleming be-

comes further disoriented, and when the regiment is attacked again, he is overwhelmed with terror, and runs.

The rest of the tale charts Henry's metamorphosis from fear to rage at the enemy, from guilt — at running away from his regiment and from a mortally wounded soldier who turns out to be Jim Conklin from his own regiment — to a kind of atonement, as he makes his way back to his regiment and fights like a savage. But the youth wins redemption at a heavy price. Stalked by his own cowardice, he fears that it will "stand before him all of his life." Even his head injury — from a rifle butt when he was on the run — is a bogus badge of courage, a reproach.

Working after midnight, when he was all alone in the world, Stephen followed Henry Fleming like a scout in the wilderness. Occasionally he lost the scent, faltered. "Fleming discovered the next morning," he began — and wrote nothing more on that page. On the second page he wrote:

> To his attentive audience he drew a loud and elaborate plan
> of a very successful

— he crossed out the word "successful" and wrote "brilliant" —

> campaign. When he had finished, the blue-clothed men
> scattered into small, arguing groups in the little rows of
> squat, brown huts.

Except for the comma after "squat," the sentence would appear in book form exactly as written in this draft. In some places, Stephen needed to revise more. A simple sentence in the novel's opening pages — "Smoke drifted lazily from barrel-chimneys" — was replaced by a picture of a dancing Negro teamster, an idea Stephen perhaps drew from a camping trip when he had seen a black man dancing in the woods.

> A negro teamster who had been dancing upon a cracker-box
> with the hilarious encouragement of two-score soldiers, was
> deserted. He sat mournfully down.

He restored his original sentence at the end:

> Smoke drifted lazily from a multitude of quaint chimneys.

The story of young Henry Fleming's trial by artillery fire in the Civil War was not radically new in subject matter; it echoed familiar themes and details of plot long available, though there is no telling whether Stephen had read any of the war stories of Zola, Frank Wilkeson, or Joseph Kirkland. These authors and others had written about war in brutally realistic narratives and tackled the subject of fear and cowardice in wartime. Some had written about war from the perspective of the private soldier — notably Wilkeson, in *Recollections of a Private Soldier in the Army of the Potomac,* and Warren Lee Goss, whose "Recollections of a Private" appeared in the *Century*. A book titled *Corporal Si Klegg and his "Pard,"* by Wilbur F. Hinman, chronicled the metamorphosis of a farm boy into a war veteran; marked with heavy dialect, it showed a young soldier wrestling with doubts about his courage, who later takes the flag from the hands of an injured standard bearer. These details also reappeared, yet were made new, in Stephen's novel.

One could pick up ideas anywhere. On Sunday, February 12, 1893, the month before Stephen started reading the old *Century*s, the *New York Times* published a Civil War story called "The Coward" above the initials "C.G.S." This piece of hackwork tells of a young Yankee soldier named Jamie Mayhew, whose first engagement comes at Vicksburg. Ridiculed as a "sissy," Jamie begs his sergeant to release him from fighting. "I will die if I have to go; I am a fearful coward!" he cries. The sergeant refuses, insisting that he is sick, not afraid, but Jamie manages to slip behind the front ranks anyway and flee, leaving many of his regiment to die. Like Henry Fleming, he ends up in a wood, where he feels safe from the action, but he worries about being shot for desertion. Captured by the enemy and forced to accompany them on their nocturnal raids, Jamie eventually redeems himself by warning the Union soldiers about a coming raid. He is wounded while making his way back to them, but he recovers and becomes a great hero, and eventually a minister, beloved by his congregation.

If Stephen borrowed ideas for his plot, he made them utterly his own. In style, treatment, and perspective, his war tale suggests no other, with the exception of Tolstoy's *Sebastopol*. Tolstoy is the only war writer he is known to have read, "the writer I admire most of all." *Sebastopol*, consisting of three nonfiction essays chronicling the defense of the Russian city during the Crimean War, seems to have most influenced Stephen's thinking or at least amplified it. The fledgling war writer found much to which he could respond in Tolstoy's book, which was available to Americans in an 1887 translation from the French by Frank D. Millet. Distinguished by graphic realism, an unremitting clinical view of wounded and dead men, and an unromantic depiction of war as a "house of pain," the essays Tolstoy wrote in his twenties claimed "truth" as their "hero" — something Stephen Crane might have said of his own story.

Tolstoy had showed how men *feel* in battle. His approach was impressionistic and ironic; he linked flowers with corpses, addressed man's vanity and self-delusion, and sympathized with the common man — all hallmarks of Crane's work. Having seen war firsthand, the Russian writer understood that in battle, men lose part of themselves. The young officer described in this passage from *Sebastopol* sounds, in the beginning, very much like Henry Fleming.

> The feeling of this desertion in the presence of danger, of death, as he believed, oppressed his heart with the glacial weight of a stone. Halting in the middle of the place, he looked all about him to see if he was observed, and taking his head in both hands, he murmured, with a voice broken by terror, "My God! am I really a despicable poltroon, a coward, I who have lately dreamed of dying for my country, for my Czar, and that with joy! Yes, I am an unfortunate and despicable being!" he cried, in profound despair, and quite undeceived about himself. Having finally overcome his emotion, he asked the sentinel to show him the house of the commander of the battery.

Tolstoy's war was grounded in reality. Stephen Crane's portrait of war, seen as an assault on the senses, was stunningly original. Not even the great Tolstoy had done this. Stephen imagined Henry Fleming's battle as a psychological and spiritual crisis. It is not the Confederate army on which Henry's fear focuses but nature, alternately friendly, hostile, and indifferent, which the youth sees through the distorting lens of his vanity and his ego. "The world was fully interested in other matters," Stephen wrote. A stream regards Henry with "white bubble eyes"; armies attack each other in "panther-fashion." Stephen drew on his religious upbringing and the violent rhetoric that had terrified him as a child to paint nature. Here, in "the cathedral light of the forest," the trees sang "a hymn of twilight," and the insects quieted in "a devotional pause." Lamblike eyes and "fierce-eyed hosts" peered from the forest. "War, the blood-swollen god" was fought in a "celestial battle," and "the chorus pealed over the still earth." "It seemed that there would shortly be an encounter of strange beaks and claws, as of eagles," Stephen wrote, harking back to the eagles of the Book of Revelations. Having returned to his regiment to fight, Henry "felt the daring spirit of a savage, religion-mad." He became a "war devil," he "had fought like a pagan who defends his religion."

Stephen mocked Henry's delusions with an ironic narrative, while letting what he later called the red devils in his own heart loose upon the page. In his celestial battle the youth saw demons, imps, and "swirling battle-phantoms." The fires of hell burned in the crimson rays of war, which made "weird and satanic effects." Soldiers in combat appeared as fiends with "black faces and glowing eyes." Henry heard the battle as a "furnace-roar." "The flames bit him," Stephen wrote, and the men of the regiment "stood as men tied to stakes." He used his natural feeling for color, his palette of reds, black, and yellow, to create some of his most conspicuous effects. Stephen told Frank Noxon that a passage in Goethe which "analysed the effect" of certain colors on "the human mind" influenced him. Red — the color of blood and fire — best expressed his feelings. Henry Fleming saw campfires as "red, peculiar blossoms." He experienced "the red sickness of battle." Influenced, perhaps unconsciously, by Kipling as well as Goethe, Stephen ended Chapter Nine with the sentence "the red sun was pasted in the sky like a wafer."*

In part, it is the insistence of the novel's religious imagery, which was both conscious and unwitting, that stamps it as the work of Stephen Crane. He could no more escape the religion that was in him than he could change his eye color or his bone structure. In creating the character of Fleming, he kept close to what he knew — to his honesty, as he would put it. He gave the youth his own eyes. He embraced his religious heritage while railing against it and controlling it with irony. Writing from within to show "war from within," he made the experience seem true.

Henry Fleming carried Stephen into the deepest part of himself. During a pivotal scene, Henry finds himself in a little sanctuary in the woods. Bathed in "a religious half-light," the sheltering bower welcomes him with a "religion of peace." "He conceived nature to be a woman with a deep aversion to tragedy," wrote Stephen. Then Henry parts the green doors of his sanctuary to be confronted by a corpse in a Union

---

* In *The Light That Failed* (1891), Rudyard Kipling described the shining sun as "a blood-red wafer, on the water."

army uniform, a "thing" with "liquid-looking eyes." Black ants trundle over the gray face, "venturing horribly near to the eyes." As he flees the green chapel, Henry imagines that the dead man will rise "and squawk after him in horrible menaces." The fascination with the corpse's face, with what happens to the body after death turns up in other scenes and images, in the upturned, "corpse-hued faces" of stricken soldiers, in the youth's first encounter with a dead soldier, at whom he longs to stare. The corpse is tawny-haired, like the author, and poor, the soles of his shoes "worn to the thinness of writing paper."

And so Stephen had arrived at himself. He would tell Linson that the tale was "the product of an utter discouragement, almost of despair." He thought it "a pity that art should be a child of pain, and yet I think it is." The pictures of dead soldiers reflected Stephen's sense of himself as puny and not long for this world — a self-image compounded and complicated by the early religious assault upon his senses, which was like a melody he could not get out of his head.

For Henry Fleming there was no easy heroism. Though the youth ultimately conformed to Victorian notions of duty and honor — a large part of what defined a man — his desertion in the field haunted him. He had no sustaining religious faith to comfort him, as other Civil War soldiers had, no Christian fatalism, no sense of true salvation. "He had been to touch the great death, and found that, after all, it was but the great death," Stephen wrote. "Scars faded as flowers." Much later, after he thought he had finished the novel, he added an ironic last line to show that Henry's dreams of eternal peace were the same old delusions. Nature would have the last word: "Over the river a golden ray of sun came through the hosts of leaden rain clouds." The last line of Tolstoy's "Sebastopol in December, 1854" also begins with an image of the sun shining through gray clouds above the ocean.* Perhaps more suggestively, in Helen Crane's tribute to Stephen's dead father, she had written in closing, "And so we laid his body away under the evergreens, amid the scenes of his childhood, as a flood of golden sunshine burst upon the scene."

Climbing the stairs to the garret of Edmund's house after the family had retired for the night, Stephen wrote "far into the night, if composition was going smoothly," said Edmund. Then he would sleep until noon and

---

* "Day closes; the sun, disappearing at the horizon, shines through the gray clouds which surround it, and lights up with purple rays the rippling sea."

perhaps take a cup of coffee while waiting for Mame, his sister-in-law, to prepare lunch. During the afternoon he taught football to the local boys, coaching them in tactics and organizing the first football games in Lake View. He played with his adoring nieces. While the girls assaulted him with paper clubs made from rolled-up newspapers, Uncle Stephen sat astride a chair like a general on his horse, dodging blows and holding his ground. At night in the garret, with memories of football still on him, he imagined bodies clashing in combat, running, rushing at each other. "As the story began to take shape," Stephen read it to Ed, saying that he wanted "only to know if [he] liked the story." He was not interested in his brother's literary opinion. "I liked the story," said Edmund.

Still pressed for money, Stephen decided to forgo the fun of camping with his friends. In late June he turned up at Linson's studio with two Bowery sketches, "An Ominous Baby" and "A Great Mistake." Linson was illustrating another of Stephen's little-man stories, an oddly insular and unpleasant work called "The Reluctant Voyagers," and Stephen wanted him to try his hand at illustrating the new tales as well.

These short works were minor bread-and-butter writing turned out for quick sale and would not add to his reputation. And yet they spoke poignantly of Stephen's sense of himself, of his deepening sense of displacement as a struggling writer and as someone who lacked a home. "The Reluctant Voyagers" carries two squabbling little men out to a sinister sea, where they fall prey to bad company and are ultimately made to look ridiculous in front of the society they thought they had escaped. The "Baby Stories," as Stephen called them, resurrect from *Maggie* a younger brother, Tommie, who dies in infancy early in the novel. In these tales, Stephen carried on the theme of the little man in the universe but the universe is now the city. It is society, rather than nature, that turns its back on the little man, here represented by a poor child. Each sketch depicts a tattered street urchin (blond and blue-eyed like Stephen) who steals something, only to be devoured for his actions — absorbed into the "swallowing cavern" of his poor neighborhood or caught by a fruit vendor, who is "undoubtedly a man who would eat babes that provoked him." It is the street urchin's outsiderness, his terrible longing when confronted with "the amassed joys of the world" which are denied him that comes through most vividly.

Shifting from war to the Bowery, Stephen carried Henry Fleming with him: babes wander "in a strange country," where ragged urchins with dirty faces suggestive of "scars and powder smoke" resemble "some wee battler in a war" — tattered, wounded soldiers. Then, returning to the war novel, he described the sweat running down the youth's soiled face, which resembled "that of a weeping urchin."

Though Stephen had asked only for his response to the war story, Edmund sometimes suggested a word change. Stevie "would consider the matter and then decide, oftener against than for the suggestion," said Edmund. "He had the confidence of genius."

Sometime between July and September, having written perhaps a third of the novel, Stephen stopped. Leaving Henry Fleming staggering against the pain of a rifle butt amid the chaos of scrambling men and horses hauling cannon and artillery, he began his final transcription of the novel, apparently starting again from the beginning.

◆

In the fall of 1893, he moved into a large studio apartment in the old Art Students' League building at 143–147 East 23rd Street in New York, with artists Nelson Greene, William W. Carroll, and R. G. Vosburgh, whom Stephen affectionately called "Indians." He was virtually penniless; lacking the money to buy a new pair of shoes, he turned up in New York wearing rubber boots. The war novel, still far from finished, was the most valuable thing he possessed. But the Indians "were glad to have him," said Vosburgh; "he added very little to the expense" and was good company.

The top floors of the building — the Art Students' League had already abandoned it for new lodgings on West 57th Street — were rented to artists, illustrators, writers, and musicians. Everyone was poor; the landlord, himself an artist, was understanding. Stephen and the Indians shared everything. Three men slept in the old double bed; the fourth man took the cot. They pooled their shoes and clothing. The first man up in the morning, or the one with a job interview, got the choicest selection from the community closet, and buttoned his coat "bravely over a stomach that had missed more than one meal," wrote Vosburgh. Stephen typically ate two meals a day, consisting of "a bun or two for breakfast and a supper of potato salad and sausages warmed over the little stove that heated the room, frequently eaten cold because there was no coal for the stove," said Vosburgh. They ate a lot of potato salad, bought at the Sixth Avenue Deli. When they had money, they treated themselves to a meal at a cheap restaurant, like the Hotel Griffin on West 9th Street, where one could get dinner with wine for fifty cents.

"Our life there was free, gay, hard working — and *decent*," said artist Frederick Gordon, who lived in one of the largest studios; the social atmosphere was "really congenial." Since no one had any money, the residents would gather in one of the studios to talk, smoke, and play cards for entertainment, the loser buying the beer. Stephen loved the old building, whose "staid puritanical" facade had "once contained about all that was real in the Bohemian quality of New York," he wrote. Frequently rebuilt over the years, it had three entrances and was a wondrous jumble of labyrinthine corridors and large studios that seemed to "rear their brown rafters over scenes of lonely quiet." On an old beam in the most remote studio, someone had written, in now faint chalk marks, a maxim attributed to Emerson: "Congratulate yourselves if you have done something strange and extravagant and broken the monotony of a decorous age." Stephen copied it down in his notebook.

From fall on into winter, he lived in the war novel. He worked nights, as he had in Lake View, from around midnight until four or five in the morning. Then he slept the better part of the day, said Vosburgh. The story was always with him. Reading a football report in the paper, Stephen would say, "That's bully! That's like war!" Underdressed and underfed, he stood for hours in a soaking rain watching the warships come into the harbor at Fort Wadsworth. He would return from one of his health-renewing excursions to Lake View, and in one swift stride briefly greet everyone in the studio, set down his small handbag, claim a sketching stool, pull out pen, paper, and ink bottle, and begin to write, as though resuming after only a brief interruption. David Ericson marveled at Stephen's concentration, his ability to hold the story in his head while his slowly moving pen trailed after it. Writing in ink on legal-sized paper, he seldom crossed through or interlined a word. "I have to make it easy for the boys who set the type; and I cant afford a type-writer," he told Linson. When he did change something, he rewrote the whole page, as if a clean script "cooled the machinery."

Sounding like Tolstoy, he told the Indians that "he did not expect to be great himself, but he hoped to get near the truth" in his writing. "Impressionism was his faith," said Vosburgh. "Impressionism, he said, was truth, and no man could be great who was not an impressionist, for greatness consisted in knowing truth." Sustained by his belief that the war novel would make him famous, he talked as if his coming fame were carved in oak next to Emerson's words. When he wasn't writing, he wrote the name that would be famous on paper, books, magazines, alongside poker scores on the heavy paper covering the card table — anything that was handy: Stephen Crane, Stephen Crane, Stephen Crane.

5

THE COMMANDING
POWER OF GENIUS

I t was a season of creativity and deprivation such as he had never
known. Outwardly cheerful, he did not tell his family how desperate
he was, and they seem not to have noticed. As far as Edmund was concerned, if his youngest brother was "poorly dressed and ill fed, it was simply because he stripped for the race. He held his career above his comfort, or any other personal consideration."

Sometimes he looked for work. On one particularly foul rainy day, he
returned to the old League building "utterly done up," remembered
Frederick Gordon. He'd been to see Edward Marshall, Sunday editor of
the *New York Press*. "He was thin — almost cadaverous," Marshall would
remember. Marshall felt that the demands of full-time reporting would
ruin Stephen as an imaginative writer, and according to Gordon he refused to take him on staff. But he said he would happily take any special
articles Stephen could come up with. Being "too proud" to tell Marshall
that he hadn't the nickel for carfare, Stephen walked all the way home in
his shabby shoes and no overcoat. By the time Gordon saw him he was
soaked through, "shivering and coughing" and "ripe for pneumonia."
Gordon put Stephen in the spare bed in his own large studio, where he
remained for a week.

A couple of pieces were published; an amusing parody of theatrical
melodramas called "Some Hints for Play-Makers" ran in *Truth* on November 4, 1893, and his first known fable, "How the Ocean Was Formed,"
appeared in *Puck* on February 7, 1894. Hamlin Garland recommended

Stephen to the magazine publisher Samuel Sidney McClure, telling him in a note to send "any work" he could Stephen's way "and for Mercy Sake! Dont keep him *standing* for an hour, as he did before, out in your pen for culprits."

Sometime that winter Stephen wrote an anguished letter to L.B., dwelling on her face, which he still loved and could not forget. Though he saw her occasionally in New York, he said it was not the same. The "fragrance of past joys" seemed as elusive as the smell of a hearty meal; and yet "it is beyond me to free myself from the thrall of my love for you; it comes always between me and what I would enjoy in life — always — like an ominous sentence — the words of the parrot on the death-ship: 'We are all damned.'" And yet he did not want to "escape" the memory of her, even if he could, for it was "the better part" of him. "I adore you," he wrote, "you are the shadow and the light of my life; — the whole of it." Unaccountably, he told Lily that he would be making "a very short trip" to Europe in a couple of weeks, and he begged her to write, to give some relief to his "infinitely lonely life." He could not help trying to impress her. "The *Arena Co* brings out a book of mine this winter," he wrote casually, evidently referring to his expectations of a deal to publish *Maggie*. "I wish you to get it, for it will show you how much I have changed." As in his previous letter, he told her of the critical praise for the book and of Howells's opinion that it was "quite extraordinary." He wanted her "to think well of the man you have made."

Poetry burst from him now, vivid images of black riders galloping out of the sea, riding "the ride of sin." Images of a bullying, blustering god, of forlorn wanderers in the desert. There was no labor before the birth; the poems came "in little rows, all made up, ready to be put down on paper," he told Hamlin Garland. Written in free verse, the "lines," as he called them, depicted figures in various states of sorrow and aloneness. A woman stands on an ocean shore, weeping for her dead lover, while "the King of the seas / Weeps too, old helpless man." A man who has "lived a life of fire" dies, realizing "that he had not lived"; another appears amid a "crimson clash of war." Almost without exception, the poems Stephen would gather under the title *The Black Riders* express a profound cynicism and terror of the world, reflecting both the intensity of the composition of the war novel and the Methodist preachings of his youth. God is variously depicted as cruel, indifferent, nonexistent; nature, as the malevolent force of the darkest Sullivan County tales.

The land of *The Black Riders* is soaked in sin, swathed in darkness, and populated with leaping devils, a seer, God, and angels. Snow and ice mingle with "burning sand," angels draw near a "fat church," puzzled by the "little black streams of people" coming and going. A man pursues the horizon. Mountains — so recurrent in the Sullivan County tales, *The Red Badge,* and other works — appear in several poems. The peaks of a mountain range assemble and march, singing as they go. Angry mountains ready themselves for battle. The winds whisper "Good-bye!" One man walks alone in a desert, another "on a burning road." Love walks alone, bloodied by the rocks and brambles that are "Heart's Pain."

Like Henry Fleming's hallucinatory view of war, some of the poems have a dreamlike quality. Certain fantastic images — the "clamor" of "a million tongues" talking at once, a blade of grass feeling ashamed before God in heaven on Judgment Day, the juxtaposition of corpses with toys — suggest the subconscious mind at work. Shades of red run through the lines as a leitmotiv, just as in the war novel; the lone figure who tries to make sense of the "intricate clamor of tongues" asks the frantic multitudes, "Why is this?" echoing Henry Fleming's query of the fleeing army before he is hit by a rifle butt. Through the strange landscape of the lines moves a figure who is solitary in a large, sometimes terrifying world that is as limitless as the ocean or as heaven and against which a person is no more than a blade of grass.

He had written the poems in "desperation," said Stephen. The lines were his confessional, his attempt to comprehend "the thoughts I have had about life in general." When God asks the blade of grass, "What did you do?" in life, it answers, "Oh, my lord, / Memory is bitter to me / For if I did good deeds / I know not of them" — words Stephen would apply to himself and his own accomplishments. He saw himself as small and ordinary, "very common uninteresting clay," "not the cream of mankind," "a small pale-yellow person with a weak air and no ability of pose." But if heaven existed — and his godlessness had not completely extinguished the possibility that it did — he liked to believe that it had room for all sorts of souls: a street girl, even a blade of grass with no ability of pose. At the honest answer of the blade of grass, God says, "Oh, best little blade of grass."

On a snowy day in mid-February 1894, he turned up at Linson's new studio near Sixth Avenue on West 22nd Street. Linson was working on a drawing when Stephen appeared with his gray rain ulster buttoned against the cold. Smiling mysteriously, he removed his derby, brushed the snow from it, then reached into his coat for some sheets of foolscap.

"What do you think I have been doing, CK?"

Linson waited, and Stephen placed his sheets on top of the drawing illuminated by gaslight. Linson had scarcely begun reading the lines when Stephen demanded to know what he thought of them. Linson told him that he hadn't had time to think; he was "seeing pictures." He wanted to know how Stephen had thought of them.

"They came, and I wrote them, that's all," he said, tracing his fore-head with a finger, as though trying to coax the memory from it. Linson told him he was "glad they're not Whitman," and Stephen laughed. All he cared about, he said, was that the poems brought pictures to Linson's mind. Later, when another visitor to the studio read a couple of pages and handed them back with the dismissive remark "I don't know much about poetry," Stephen abruptly left the room. Linson caught up with him at the street door.

"CK!" Stephen cried. "I know everyone can't like them, but I hate to give a man a chance to hit me in the back of the neck with an ax!"

On February 26, a blizzard enveloped the city in nearly a foot and a half of snow over a period of thirty hours. Fierce winds up to forty miles an hour tore through the streets. Drivers, muffled to the eyes, guided slipping horses uptown; traffic moved at a crawl. The wind lashed the faces of pedestrians, causing skin to burn "as from a thousand needle-prickings." They lowered their heads inside their coats, "stooping like a race of aged people," wrote Stephen, who was among them.

During a conversation about bread lines, Hamlin Garland had pro-posed that Stephen do a story on them. Stephen chose the day of the bliz-zard to stand outside in a snow-covered line of ragged men huddling together "like sheep" as they waited for a West Side charitable house to open. Wearing only a thin layer of clothing, he stayed in the punishing cold for some hours in conditions that would have tried a sturdier, better-fed reporter. He observed everything, from the sound of footsteps on the snow-covered cobbles to "the spongey brown mass that lay between the rails" of the streetcars, causing the horses to slip. He saw the wanderers huddling under the stairs below the elevated train and "the characteristic hopeless gait of professional strays." And then, that night, though suffering from exposure, he managed to get it all down on paper. "The Men in the Storm" was a carefully paced, effective mood piece that began and ended with the snow, a portrait of humanity as "important music, a melody of life" moving to the swirling storm's "pitiless beat."

The next day Linson discovered Stephen alone in the studio, lying in bed, looking "haggard and almost ill."

"Why didn't you put on two or three more undershirts, Steve?" he asked.

"How would I know how those poor devils felt if I was warm myself? Nit! Anyway, I didn't have the shirts, you mutt!" Stephen said, reaching under his pillow for the manuscript.

With "The Men in the Storm," Stephen began his tramp period, as Linson called it, his experiments in misery. He would disappear for days at a time, then eventually turn up, "looking as if he had lived in a grave." One day, he told Linson, he was sitting alongside a tramp in front of City Hall when an old friend passed by without recognizing him. Then the cops ordered him to move along. He was so altered that even CK failed to recognize him when he turned up at the studio.

On the recommendations of Garland and Howells, the newly formed Bacheller-Johnson Newspaper Syndicate gave Stephen an assignment to cover the Bowery's sordid flophouses. In early March, he and William Carroll dressed as tramps, put about thirty cents apiece in their pockets, and set off for the Bowery.

He was in his element, submitting to the game with a kind of relish. Here in the flophouse was life at its most raw: "strange and unspeakable odors . . . assailed him like malignant diseases with wings," he would write in "An Experiment in Misery." "They seemed to be from human bodies closely packed in dens; the exhalations from a hundred pairs of reeking lips; the fumes from a thousand bygone debauches; the expression of a thousand present miseries." Each time a door in this netherworld opened, "the unholy odors rushed out at him, like released fiends." He delighted in the saloon meals of watery soup "in which there were little floating suggestions of chicken," in the charitable house sign reading "Delectable Coffee 1¢"; in the little man who cried out in his sleep. Stephen took it upon himself to watch out for repeaters in his soup and bread lines, said Carroll. For three endless nights, while his companion lay awake in whatever joint they'd flopped in, Stephen slept soundly on the cold, filthy "5, 7 or 10¢ beds," untroubled by the bedbugs or anything else. Afterward, when he told his friends about these days, his storytelling

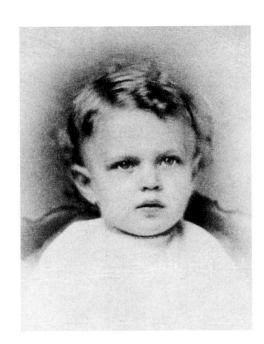

Stephen Crane, "our precious baby," about 1873. *Stephen Crane Collection, Department of Special Collections, Syracuse University Library*

Mary Helen Peck Crane, Stephen's mother, a "pleasant-faced little lady." *Crane Collection, Syracuse University*

Stephen's father, the Reverend Jonathan Townley Crane, was "without an evil habit." *Crane Collection, Syracuse University*

Agnes Elizabeth Crane, Stephen's sister, was his "good angel." *Crane Collection, Syracuse University*

Stephen, about 1879. "How you going to know about things at all less'n you *do* 'em?" *Crane Collection, Syracuse University*

Cadet Stephen Crane, Claverack College and Hudson River Institute, about 1889. He "had a perfectly henlike attitude toward the rank and file." *Crane Collection, Syracuse University*

BELOW: "Do you think *order arms* means to drop your gun?" Cadet Company B, Claverack College, about 1889. Crane is second from left. *Crane Collection, Syracuse University*

OPPOSITE: Arbutus Cottage, the Cranes' house in Asbury Park, where Frances E. Willard was a summer guest. *Crane Collection, Syracuse University*

The Syracuse University baseball team, 1891. Crane (front row, middle) stood up to the plate "like a professional." *Crane Collection, Syracuse University*

Lily Brandon Munroe, here with her husband, Hersey Munroe, was Stephen's "dearest" L.B., "the one of all." *Crane Collection, Syracuse University*

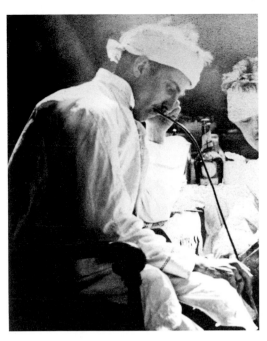

A wet towel "cools the machinery."
Stephen in New York, 1893.
Crane Collection, Syracuse University ·

BELOW: Stephen (left) and another man
asleep in the old Art Students League
building about 1893. Friends had piled
shoes and other objects near the bed
before taking the picture. *Clifton Waller
Barrett Library, Manuscripts Division, University
of Virginia Library*

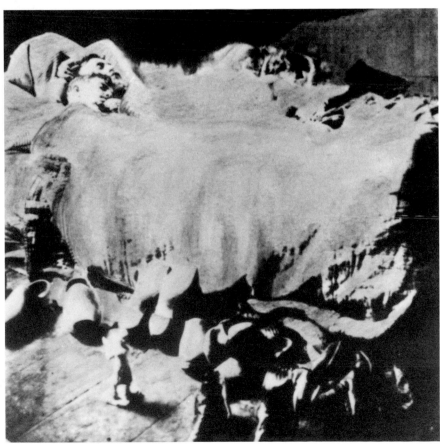

Stephen said Hamlin Garland (shown here in 1898) was "the first to over-whelm me with all manner of extraordinary language."

William Dean Howells in 1888. "How often I think of your kind and benevolent life," wrote Stephen.

"You'd think the book came straight from hell and they smelled the smoke." Stephen holds a banjo at the Pendennis Club party for *Maggie*, 1893. *Crane Collection, Syracuse University*

Stephen (right) with Lucius Button on the roof of Corwin Knapp Linson's studio at West 30th Street, New York, in 1893. *Crane Collection, Syracuse University*

BELOW: At Linson's studio Stephen began reading Civil War accounts in old issues of *The Century*. "He was immersed in dreams." *Crane Collection, Syracuse University*

Stephen's profile reminded the painter "of the young Napoleon — but not so hard, Steve." Oil painting of Crane at twenty-two by Corwin Knapp Linson.
Barrett Library, University of Virginia

was wonderfully vivid — it "made one see gas jets and dark interiors," said Carroll.

When their sojourn in hell ended, the tramps went to Linson's studio. It was another miserable day of driving rain and biting wind. The men in their soaking rags had no overcoats or umbrellas, and their toes were coming through their shoes. An artist friend of Linson's named Emile Stangé, who knew Stephen slightly, happened to stop by, and was shocked by his appearance. Years later he would remember the pools of water forming beneath the men's feet, and the picture of Stephen Crane standing there, his blond hair matted over his eyes, his thin chest shaking from spasms produced by a hollow cough. Stangé thought, "My lord! Has it come to this?" Stephen grinned and let CK explain the Bowery assignment. Stangé scolded Stephen for taking such risks with his health, but Stephen dismissed it.

Looking as poorly dressed and underfed as any Confederate army private, he became indifferent to his appearance. He turned up at William's house in Port Jervis in dirty clothes, which he slept in. He reeked of garlic and tobacco. His hair was windblown, his fingers tobacco-stained, remembered William's daughter Helen, who was five years old at the time. It was as though, in writing about Bowery life from behind the lines, he had become part of the wretched masses.

He seemed to revel in being lost. "He drank and smoked and like Robert Louis Stevenson he had a hankering after the women," said fellow reporter John Northern Hilliard. Chivalrous and idealistic about "true womanhood," he yet felt sexually free. There was golden-skinned Gertrude Selene (even the name was poetry); only eighteen, she was smartly dressed and intelligent and had "a marvelous figure," said Nelson Greene, who suspected that Stephen took her to bed. There were common street girls. "He took up with many a drab, and was not overly particular as to her age, race or color," said Hilliard. "Many a time I have heard him say he would have to go out and get a nigger wench 'to change his luck.' Time and time again he would bring a lady of the streets to his room." With prostitutes, Stephen got what "he was always looking for — the real, naked facts of life," said Hilliard. "And in seeking them, in living them, he was tolerant and absolutely unashamed."

"Don't forget me, dear, never, never, never," Stephen wrote L.B. in the spring of 1894. She was still "the only woman in life. I am doomed, I suppose, to a lonely existence of futile dreams. It has made me better. It has widened my comprehension of people and my sympathy with whatever they endure. And to it I owe whatever I have achieved and the hope of the future. In truth, this change in my life should prove of some value to me, for, ye gods, I have paid a price for it."

However unchanging his love for the beautiful, unattainable girl, a year had worked a big difference in him. Like the lost soldiers of the battle of the Wilderness, who had guided themselves with a compass, he had stayed his course, giving all to the war novel, to his art. And he had come through with his compass intact, his faith in his work unbroken. In writing Lily about his literary admirers and his prospects, he sounded more in command of himself, less urgent in his need to impress her, though he was still not above posturing. He claimed that he would have two books published that spring and would go to Europe afterward. He said he had renounced what he called "the clever school in literature," his "clever Rudyard Kipling style" — referring to the Sullivan County tales. He had struggled for two years to develop "a little creed of art which I thought was a good one," a creed he had learned was shared by Garland and Howells, he said, less than candidly. Though Stephen's art was highly subjective and poetic — impressionistic rather than realistic in the strictest sense — he felt that he, Garland, and Howells were fighting the same good fight. He felt that the winter he'd just spent "fixes me firmly," that the forces of the new realism were about to win.

In his lines he had written:

> I looked here
> I looked there
> No where could I see my love.
> And — this time —
> She was in my heart.
> Truly then I have no complaint
> For 'though she be fair and fairer
> She is none so fair as she
> In my heart.

His letter to Lily had a final sound: "Good-bye, beloved," he wrote.

He was feeling confident with good reason. He had "fifteen short stories in my head and out of it. They'll make a book," he wrote Hamlin Garland in April. Poems had been rushing out of him like a geyser — "five or six every day," he had told Garland in March, adding, "I wrote nine yesterday." This outpouring had come in spite of his having to write "in a box amid the clamor of the studio," where the lines were jeered and howled at by the Indians, who thought them hilarious. He gave Garland about thirty of the poems. The mentor was delighted with them and with the way they had sprung out of the "pale, reticent boy moving restlessly about the room." He simply could not reconcile the poems with the boy.

Garland recommended Stephen's poems to Howells, who thought them "too orphic" but referred Stephen to Henry Mills Alden, the editor of *Harper's Magazine*. When Alden turned the poems down, Howells wrote Stephen, "I wish you had given them more form, for these things so striking would have found a public ready made for them; as it is they will have to make one."

Then they would make one. What mattered to Stephen was that Howells and Garland were still firmly behind him — and Howells did not even believe in free verse. Stephen's faith in his work, together with his confidence in Howells's power in the literary world, would carry him. Along with the poems, he was writing an occasional Bowery study and, always, the war novel. At about the time he wrote his "dearest" — in early April 1894 — he finished a good working draft.

◆

Stephen began revising the novel with the clear eye of a writer who has the whole piece in hand. He saw, for instance, that to make his battle a type he needed to substitute common nouns for proper names, as he had done in the Sullivan County tales; he wrote "the youth" for Fleming, "the tall soldier" for Conklin, "his comrade" for "young Wilson." The revision did not always come easily. Above a sentence beginning "Conklin felt called," he wrote "a," then crossed it out and wrote "The first." Then he drew a line through that and wrote "The soldier." That wasn't right, either. He inserted "excited": "The excited tall soldier." Finally he settled on the plain phrase "The tall soldier."

At some point he changed eight or nine chapter endings and discarded an entire chapter — the twelfth — in which Fleming philosophizes about his place in the world and in relation to nature. Sometimes he cut too deep and had to restore material.

Even before Henry Fleming's adventures were generally known to the world, word about the talented Stephen Crane was getting out. Stephen had shown his lines to John Barry, editor of the *Forum*, who sent them to the avant garde publishing house of Copeland & Day. On April 14,

Barry read some of the poems at an event sponsored by the Uncut Leaves Society, honoring Frances Hodgson Burnett. The poet, he told the audience, had declined to read them himself, saying he'd "rather die than do it." Then Howells, in an interview published in both the *New York Press* and the *Philadelphia Press*, talked Stephen up as a young writer who "promises splendid things" and called *Maggie* "a remarkable book. There is so much realism of a certain kind in it that unfits it for general reading," yet the study of Lower East Side life told the truth, he said. Howells mentioned Stephen's name in the company of Mark Twain, Sarah Orne Jewett, George W. Cable, Mary E. Wilkins, and Hamlin Garland. The *New York Press* even ran excerpts from *Maggie* with the interview, along with a tentative appraisal of the book, which contained "the kind of truth that no American has ever had the courage (or is it bravado?) to put between book covers before."

Stephen was flush with ideas. He had sold five stories, including the unflinching "An Experiment in Misery" and its weak fictional sister "An Experiment in Luxury," which told of an uneventful evening spent at a millionaire's house, where the narrator felt out of place, "one of the outer barbarians." Both "Experiments" appeared in the *New York Press* that April. In May "An Ominous Baby" finally appeared in the *Arena*, with an editorial note that called attention to the sketch as a significant social study. The *New York Press* published a lighthearted piece about a railroad tramp, "Billy Atkins Went to Omaha."

Howells's public praise had been noticed, and others began to write about Crane, likening him to Tolstoy in his artistry and realism. Writing under the nom de plume "Holland," Elisha J. Edwards, a *New York Press* reporter who knew Stephen slightly, told a story about Stephen-the-starving-Bohemian, who was so near despair at the time *Maggie* was privately printed that he'd decided to quit writing. ("This is a fake," Stephen later wrote on a clipping for his scrapbook, "— not only a fake but a wretched, unartistic fake written by a very stupid man. But it was a great benefit.")

"They come in shools and say that I am a great writer," Stephen wrote Garland on April 18, 1894. He had been wanting to see Garland, but his toes were coming through his shoes. A few days later, however, he turned up at Garland's apartment. He brought an air of stale cigarette smoke with him, Garland noticed, and "a fat roll of manuscript sagging the side pocket of his shabby gray ulster." Garland asked whether it was poetry; Stephen "smiled sheepishly" and told him it was "a tale."

As Hamlin Garland would tell it more than thirty years later, he began reading the manuscript of the war novel while the hungry young author joyfully ate a steak that Garland's brother, Franklin, had cooked for lunch. Taken "captive" from Stephen's first stunning sentence, Garland read on, fully sensible of the value of what he was holding in his hands. "The finality which lay in every word, the epic breadth of vision, the splendor of the pictures presented — all indicated a most powerful and original imagination as well as a mature mastery of literary form," he wrote later. He hardly dared tell Stephen "how much I value this thing — at least not now," he said. Then he asked Stephen where the rest of the manuscript was.

"In hock," came the embarrassed reply. He had left it at a typist's and lacked the fifteen dollars needed to claim it.

Garland arranged for Stephen to go to the theater where Franklin, an actor with the Shores Acres Company, was performing. Franklin would give Stephen the fifteen dollars and a theater pass, and Stephen would retrieve the manuscript and bring it to Garland. Kindly telling Stephen not to trouble himself "about the borrowing, we all have to do that sometime," Garland said he was sure Stephen would be on his feet soon.

Stephen bought the rest of his manuscript back from the typist and returned with it to Garland's apartment. Garland was leaving for Chicago the next day, and he read the remainder of the war story hastily, pencil in hand. He corrected some of Stephen's spelling, grammatical errors (substituting "himself" for "he," for instance), and usage, occasionally crossing out a word and inserting another.* For the most part he queried Stephen's heavy use of dialect and, in the manner of a teacher correcting an errant student, sometimes impatiently drew a large cross through the offending passage. In his haste he overdid it, and added some new errors to the text. To the sentence:

> As he spoke his boyish face was voice was wreathed in a glee-
> ful smile

Garland interlined the word "and" after "face" and crossed out "was," so the sentence read:

---

* Fredson Bowers discusses Garland's corrections to *The Red Badge of Courage* in *The Works of Stephen Crane* 2: 193–96. A facsimile of the final draft of *The Red Badge* shows Crane's revisions.

As he spoke his boyish face and voice . . .

Stephen later caught the error and emended the sentence:

As he spoke his boyish face was wreathed . . .

After Garland left town, Stephen continued revising the manuscript. He went along with much of Garland's editing, which he showed no sign of resenting: "Don't forget to return to New York soon for all the struggling talent miss you," he wrote his literary father. He let one of Garland's interlinings stand and elsewhere darkened Garland's handwriting with his own pen. Trusting Garland's advice about the use of dialect, Stephen at first normalized the speech of the three key soldiers in the story — Wilson, Conklin, and Fleming — and lightened the dialect for Fleming's mother. Then he changed Fleming's dialogue, effectively setting him apart from the other soldiers. He worked on the manuscript with a sure sense of what he was after, cutting unnecessary words and improving the story's clarity, syntax, and style. He continued to tinker with the phrases denoting characters — "the loud soldier," "the tall soldier," and so on — playing with words until he came up with the right phrase: "the blatant soldier," for instance, finally became "the loud soldier." He deleted the word "young" in reference to Wilson, so that he would not be confused with "the youth," Henry Fleming.

He spent another month revising the story before submitting it for publication. At some point he crossed out his working title and, in a much larger, bolder hand, wrote

The Red Badge of Courage.
An Episode of the American Civil War
By Stephen Crane

Stephen never explained where the idea for the final title came from, though the words were in the novel. Envying the wounded soldiers, Henry Fleming "wished that he, too, had a wound, a red badge of courage." The image was perhaps originally suggested by Jacob Riis's *How the Other Half Lives*, in which Riis frequently used the word "badge" as a metaphor: "They are society's honest badge, these perennial lives of rags hung out to dry" and, most strikingly, "the white badge of mourning."

In the spring of 1894, with Garland's blessing, Stephen offered *The*

Red Badge of Courage to *McClure's Magazine*. Specializing in fine fiction and nonfiction, *McClure's* was quickly establishing itself as *the* magazine for Civil War literature, as the *Century* had been years before. Debuting in 1893 at the cheap price of fifteen cents an issue, when the magazine world's big three — the *Century, Harper's,* and *Scribner's*— cost twenty-five to thirty-five cents, *McClure's* was the baby of thirty-seven-year-old S. S. McClure, the Irish-born founder of the influential McClure's Syndicate and cofounder of the magazine. McClure was "the magazine man of the hour," as someone told Linson.

McClure delayed giving Stephen an answer on *The Red Badge* but threw him a bone in the meantime: an assignment writing about the Pennsylvania coal mines. Linson was to do the illustrations. McClure wanted to go to press with the story in August, but Stephen acted like a man with plenty of time. Linson found him sitting in a rocking chair on William's front porch in Port Jervis, "passing gibes" with Senger.

"S.S. wants you back in New York," Linson told him.

"The hell he does!" said Stephen. "What's up?" Linson said it was about the coal mine piece.

"You damned Indian!" he cried. "To scare a man like that!"

He felt fear in the mines. This place "in the sunless depths of the earth" was as sordid and unholy as anything he had seen in the Bowery. As in "An Experiment in Misery," he used images of hell to describe it: human figures appeared as "apparitions" and "spectres," their smiles "strangely satanic," their teeth "white as bleached bone." He felt the threat of a cave-in, the ominous roof, the "unmeasured, deadly tons above us." He had traveled helplessly down the elevator, plunging through "a swirling dark chaos," his mind struggling "to locate some coherent thing, some intelligible spot." The journey was endless; he seemed to be "tumbling among the stars. The only thing was to await revelation." And when the tumbling stopped, the darkness was still infinite and "inscrutable . . . a soundless place of tangible loneliness."

A swift flight up the elevator, and he was again in "the new world" that he had temporarily forgotten in the dark chamber below. As he began his ascent, impressions flickered by: "black faces and crimson and orange lights," the engineer working his lever from on high. Then the tunnel walls became "flecked with light," and the traveler returned to a green, pastoral world, an Eden juxtaposed with the sinister struggle being played out below.

An outstanding piece of literary reporting, "In the Depths of a Coal Mine" was written after two journeys into the mines at Dunmore. Stephen began putting his impressions on paper in the early morning hours after his first descent. One of his most moving passages concerned the plight of the mules who used up their lives "in the limitless night of the mines," deprived of sunlight and seasons and "the fragrant dream" of earth. Writing on lined legal paper by the morning light from the window of the Valley House hotel room he was sharing with Linson, he said, "CK, what did those mules' eyes look like down in those caverns?" It was six o'clock in the morning, and Linson was not yet awake.

"Like lenses?" he offered.

"Ye-eh, you hit it," Stephen told him. "Lenses it is." And he read the words out loud: "The mules were arranged in solemn rows. They turned their heads toward our lamps. The glare made their eyes shine wondrously like lenses."

"All right, all right," he said. (In the final piece, the last sentence was followed by: "They resembled enormous rats.")

He began with a striking personification of the coal-breaking machines: crouched upon the Pennsylvania landscape like giant, prehistoric creatures, the breakers eat and destroy everything around them. In its primitiveness and its looming, oversized scale, the image imparts a child's-eye view of the scene but is rendered with Crane's characteristic irony and his imagery of monsters and war. He was appalled by the misery he found underground, where all creatures "toil[ed] in this city of endless night." Armed with careful, measured, elegant prose, he found a way of controlling the personal effects of the experience through language.

The draft of the coal mine piece shows a quick and sure-footed reviser who did not struggle much with word choices. Stephen's interlined words are unerringly better than the originals — "structure" preferable to "buildings" in one sentence, "gaze" superior to "stare." He knew when he had been wordy, though his rewriting typically consisted of changing a single word rather than his syntax. He would rewrite only one sentence in the opening paragraph. "The smoke and dust from their nostrils had devastated the atmosphere" became "The smoke from their nostrils had ravaged the air of coolness and fragrance." In its religious imagery and its final, ironic contrast, reminiscent of the "golden ray of sun" coming "through the hosts of leaden rain clouds" at the end of *The Red Badge*, the piece was pure Crane. He completed the assignment in a week.

Afterward, dressed almost identically in trousers, dark vests, jackets, and derbys, Stephen and Linson stepped over the train tracks at the Dunmore mine. Stephen paused to flash a rare smile for the camera — perhaps in relief that he was back on the untarnished earth. They were staying at the house of the painter John Willard Raught. Like two boys returned from a great adventure, they had carried away souvenir miners' lamps — and promptly spilled oil on their host's carpet.

✦

While he waited for word from McClure on the war novel, he eased into summer, settling into Port Jervis like a rich man on holiday. The *New York Press* served up some minor pieces — a story called "Mr. Binks' Day Off" and a sketch, "Sailing Day Scenes," tales about getting away, leaving New York, strictly light fare. But the easy flow of summer, with its front porch rockers and jibes traded with friends, belied the excitement Stephen felt about the future. Certain that *The Red Badge* was going to bring him "fame and immortality," as Frederic Lawrence put it, he was also expecting the publication of his lines by Copeland & Day, though he'd received no formal offer from that publisher.

Camping deep in the woods of Pike County, Pennsylvania, on a remote site reached after a three-mile journey by country wagon, he came alive again. Along with CK, Lew Senger, and Frederic Lawrence, he was with a party of some twenty-five Lawrence relatives and friends celebrating Frederic's graduation from medical college. Supplies had to be brought in by local farmers and a milk train. For a whole month, from the last days of July until the end of August, he threw himself into the outdoor life. He went rowing, played baseball, and foraged the shores for firewood. He played cards, sang loudly and badly around the campfire, and perhaps even joined in the nightly barn dancing — all with the boyish enthusiasm of a twenty-one-year-old. He ate three meals a day and slept like an Indian on the ground, with his head inside the tent and his body outside, half in and half out of the world. The woods at Twin Lakes were filled with "the scent of a thousand fragrances," it seemed to Linson, the lake lighted with "a ghostly whiteness" which crept like a cat along the shore.

Plucking the strings of a guitar while he leaned against a tree, Stephen was the picture of health, his skin tanned a deep copper-brown. He "loved this life," said Lawrence. "Steve was happy there as a colt let loose in pasture." If he was anxious about his poetry and the war novel, he made light of it. "As Stephen Crane was traversing the little rope ladder that ascends the right hand side of the cloud-capped pinnacle of his thoughts, he fell and was grievously injured," he wrote in a mock newspaper called *The Pike County Puzzle* (so called because its news items and ads were filled with inside jokes about the campers and their activities at the site they called Camp Interlaken).

The four-page burlesque newspaper, on which Stephen collaborated with Senger and which was later printed at the *Port Jervis Union* newspaper office, was a clever, funny, uninhibited sendup of small country newspapers such as the *Union*, which still set type by hand and flourished in intense competition with other such papers. *The Pike County Puzzle* took aim at its rivals: "The Misleading Record," "The Weekly Hearth-Rug," "The Manayunk Cloud-burst," and the "Curry Ear-Trumpet." As Linson described it, "from captions to ads it looked like a conventional twelve-by-fifteen, four-page country paper — seen three feet away."

Filled with parodies of the local-interest stories carried in country papers, mixed with spoofs of international news, nonsense reports, letters to the editor, weather reports, and ads, the *Puzzle* formed a record of Stephen's month at Camp Interlaken, distorted and exaggerated for comic effect. In one item, a Mr. S. Energetic Brinson is reported to have used his lawn mower to trim his beard; "he now closely resembles Mr. Willie Astor of Condon." There was an article on a social event attended by the "fashionable crowd": "Miss L. C. Senger was attired in black crape man-o'war sails, with corinthian columns and light-houses wreathed across the front. Miss Ontario Bradfield's pearl gray sentry box overskirt was only matched by the Indian corn that grew exuberantly from her majolica ware hat."

Stephen did not spare himself.

> *To the Editor:* Can you direct me on the road to Rigg's?
>
> MAME PRONK.
>
> We are obliged to refer you to Stephen Crane. We hate to refer even our enemies to Stephen Crane, but he is a person who knows all about the road to Rigg's. He don't say he made the road himself, mind you, but even the original maker of it would throw down his hand and quit if he once confronted the knowledge of the road to Rigg's possessed by Stephen Crane.

To the Editor: What can I do with my voice?

STEPHEN CRANE.

In the spring, Stephen, you can plough with it, but after corn
ripens you will have to seek employment in the blue-stone
works. We have seen voices like yours used very effectively as
cider presses.

But the camping idyll was not entirely carefree. Stephen was disgusted
by the cuts made in his coal mine piece, which he thought showed editorial gutlessness. As written, "In the Depths of a Coal Mine," which was
first syndicated in various newspapers in late July and published in *Mc-
Clure's Magazine* in August, had contained a small discourse before the final
paragraph. In a somewhat rambling personal opinion better suited to an
editorial than to a literary reporting piece, Stephen had contrasted the
lives of the courageous miners with the "coal-brokers and other men who
make neat livings by fiddling with the market." Though he was usually
an astute editor of his own work, his impassioned feelings and social outrage had impaired his judgment in this case. And even now he was unable to see that the cuts had removed more fat than muscle. Linson
watched as Stephen read the piece in the newspaper, then flung it aside
with a grunt.

"The birds didn't want the truth after all," he said. "Why the hell did
they send me up there then? Do they want the public to think the coal
mines gilded ball-rooms with the miners eating ice-cream in boiled shirt
fronts?"

In late August, he wrote a high-handed note to Copeland & Day. "I
would like to hear from you concerning my poetry. I wish to have my out-
bring all under way by early fall and I have not heard from you in some
time. I am in the dark in regard to your intentions."

On August 28 his summer idyll ended, and he returned to Port Jervis
on the milk train. Almost immediately, he was plunged into battle with
Copeland & Day, who wanted to cut a number of his poems and asked
that Stephen supply new ones in their place. "We disagree on a multitude
of points," he wrote on September 9.

In the first place I should absolutely refuse to have my poems
printed without many of those which you just as absolutely
mark "No." It seems to me that you cut all the ethical sense

out of the book. All the anarchy, perhaps. It is the anarchy which I particularly insist upon. From the poems which you keep you could produce what might be termed a "nice little volume of verse by Stephen Crane" but for me there would be no satisfaction. The ones which refer to God, I believe you condemn altogether. I am obliged to have them in when my book is printed. There are some which I believe unworthy of print. These I herewith enclose. As for the others I cannot give them up — in the book.

"S. Crane is extravagantly young, and will outgrow his saucy little 'ethical meanings,'" wrote Louise Imogen Guiney, Copeland & Day's thirty-four-year-old reader and literary conscience, who had recommended the poems for publication. Poet and publisher briefly wrangled, then reached an agreement. The lines would be published under Stephen's suggested title, *The Black Riders and Other Lines*, with only a few omissions, as requested by the publisher and without any new poems written to take their place. Stephen found it "utterly impossible" to do more. He would receive a 10 percent royalty. Thanking Copeland & Day for their "tolerance of my literary prejudices," he turned his attention to *The Red Badge*, in the hands of the still silent McClure.

Since starting his magazine a year earlier, McClure had been overspending, and he now found himself in possession of a masterwork he could not afford to buy. While trying to stall Stephen with the coal mine assignment, he had kept him dangling on the novel, *piece,* evidently wanting to publish it and hoping to come up with the money to buy it. Stephen wrote Garland that McClure had been a "Beast" about the war novel, holding the manuscript for six months (actually five) without formally accepting it. Stephen was distracted and "near mad" from waiting. He sought the advice of Edward Marshall at the *New York Press*, who believed in him. Marshall suggested that Stephen offer the novel to Irving Bacheller of the Bacheller-Johnson Newspaper Syndicate, which was to begin publishing on October 29. Bacheller had never met Stephen Crane, but he'd heard about him from Marshall, "one of the most brilliant men on Park Row." Marshall's admiration was reason enough for Bacheller to meet Crane. Bacheller had formed the impression of a young writer who wasn't fully equipped to be a reporter — he wasn't "trained," he "lacked the 'iron-bound' nerve" — but he possessed a "great and unusual gift for vivid phrasing." The slender youth who stood in his office in mid-October with a handwritten manuscript immediately impressed the newspaperman with his "beautiful head and face," his blue-gray eyes and tanned skin. Stephen told Bacheller that he'd "be glad of" his "frank opinion" of the manuscript, whether he cared to use it or not.

Thirty years later Irving Bacheller remembered how he and his wife sat up most of the night reading the manuscript of *The Red Badge of Courage* aloud to each other, swept along by its vividness and power. The pages were slightly soiled from excessive handling, but the script was legible and handsome. Bacheller sent for Stephen the very next morning and offered to use 50,000 words in serialization.

"I had no place for a story of that length," wrote Bacheller, "but I decided to take the chance of putting it out in instalments far beyond the length of those permitted by my contracts. It was an experiment based on the hope that my judgment would swing my editors into line. They agreed with me."

His long months of waiting over, Stephen found himself suddenly caught in the whirl of impending publication. Asked for a typescript that could be cut up for newspaper serialization, he appealed to an old fraternity brother, John Henry Dick, for fifteen dollars, the cost of making a second typescript, since the first, which Stephen had given to McClure, was now outdated by revisions. "Beg, borrow or steal" the money, Stephen told him. Dick borrowed it from his employer at *Godey's Magazine* — Stephen never repaid him.

For more than a year, while working on *The Red Badge*, Stephen had published only the coal mine piece, "An Experiment in Misery," and two trifling newspaper articles. "He looked like one who had been fed for months on crackers and milk," wrote Elisha Edwards. But now everything seemed to be coming together. In the *New York Press* he found a receptive home for minor pieces on such topics as bohemian life in the League building (where he was again living) and ghosts on the New Jersey coast. He sold an interview with William Dean Howells to McClure, who syndicated it in a string of newspapers. He revised *The Black Riders* for Copeland & Day and was assured of their intention to publish the book in a form "more severely classic than any book ever yet issued in America." He also finished his second short Bowery novel, *A Woman Without Weapons*, which "leaves Maggie at the post," he told Garland. "It is my best thing."

"So much of my row with the world has to be silence and endurance that sometimes I wear the appearance of having forgotten my best friends, those to whom I am indebted for everything," he wrote Garland on November 15. "As a matter of fact, I have just crawled out of my fifty-third ditch into which I have been cast and I now feel that I can write you a letter that wont make you ill." But he told Garland about the war novel's imminent publication in the newspapers.

On the eve of *The Red Badge*'s appearance, Stephen wrote a sketch called "A Desertion," which shows a pretty girl guiltily returning home late to her Bowery apartment. While chattering to her father as he silently sits at a table, the girl suddenly realizes that he is dead. Like Henry Fleming on his first encounters with a corpse, she is both captivated and repelled by the dead body, wanting to "caress" it yet "loathing" it. Like Fleming, she fears that the thing might rise and pursue her. Stephen himself was a man pursued, a man with a "mystic shadow, bending near me," his hands heaped with corpses as he had written in his poetry.

While he was writing "A Desertion" (which went unpublished until 1900), two fictional pieces were published in the *New York Press*. "A Realistic Pen Picture," about a fire on a New York side street, appeared on November 25 under the headline "WHEN EVERY ONE IS PANIC STRICKEN." On December 2 "When Man Falls, a Crowd Gathers," depicted a crowd's fascination with a stricken man on the street. In each story a child is left alone — in a burning house or beside the body of a dead or ill parent. The scene of the house afire is rendered as an act of immolation, the last wisps of smoke suggesting "fragments of dark tissue." The "humming" flames and images of snakes turn the fire into an expression of "satanic wrath." In the second piece the crowd, more interested in gawking at the corpselike figure on the street than in helping him, closes in, holding lighted matches to the man's face — as the Port Jervis lynch mob had done to the Negro William had tried to save — while a young boy stands helplessly by. There is no fictional point to these sketches, no development of character or plot. They are simply exercises, all spectacle. "It thrilled the blood, this thunder," Stephen wrote.

Between the third and the ninth of December 1894, *The Red Badge of Courage* began appearing in some half-dozen newspapers in the United States: the *Philadelphia Press*, the *Kansas City Star*, the *Nebraska State Journal*, the *Minneapolis Tribune*, and finally the Sunday edition of the *New York Press*. (The *San Francisco Examiner* would run excerpts the following summer, between July 14 and July 21.) The serial was well placed, beginning

in the first half-dozen pages of the papers, with illustrations and decorated titles or an illustrated "T" leading off the great opening sentence,
"The cold passed reluctantly from the earth . . ."

Though the novel had been seriously cut for syndication — "pitilessly
compressed into seven columns" for the *New York Press*, said Curtis Brown,
the editor of the *Press*'s Sunday edition — it was causing a stir, "its quality
. . . immediately felt and recognized," said Irving Bacheller. The lead editorial in the *Philadelphia Press* of December 7 sounded the trumpets:

> If you have not been reading "The Red Badge of Courage,"
> by Stephen Crane, the story which has been running in
> "The Press" for three or four days, you have been missing
> one of the best war stories going. Stephen Crane is a new
> name now and unknown, but everybody will be talking
> about him if he goes on as he has begun.

This was followed by a tribute by "Holland," praising Stephen's
ability to intuitively understand the war fought before his birth, which he
had captured in "perhaps the most graphic and truthful" account that
had ever been published. "If Mr. Crane is careful, is true to his best im-
pulses, follows his intuitions and pays no heed to those who write this or
that about American fiction," he wrote, "he is quite likely to gain recognition before very long as the most powerful of American tellers of tales."

Curtis Brown happened to be in the *New York Press* office on December 9, the day *The Red Badge* appeared. He had just left the building when
he ran into Stephen at the corner of Beekman and Park. The day was
"bitter, wind-swept," remembered Curtis, but Stephen wore no overcoat.
It hardly mattered. He was all lit up, like a Christmas tree. Throwing his
arms around Brown, he said, "Oh, do you think it was good?"

"It's great," said Brown.

"God bless you," said Stephen. "And [he] hurried on to anywhere in
the sleet."

Talcott Williams, editor of the *Philadelphia Press*, begged Bacheller to
bring Stephen around to meet him. On December 15, twelve days after the novel's debut in Philadelphia, the young writer accompanied
Bacheller to Williams's office. "Word flew from cellar to roof that the
great Stephen Crane was in the office," remembered Bacheller. "Editors,
reporters, compositors, proof-readers crowded around him shaking his
hand. It was a revelation of the commanding power of genius."

II

THE
BATTLEFIELD

———◆———

6

YELLOW SKY

At the end of January 1895, Stephen boarded a train for what was to be "a very long and circuitous newspaper trip," as he put it. Irving Bacheller was sending him to various places in the West "for new color," he called it, with Mexico City to be the last stop.

By this time the West's shoot-'em-up frontier days were past; about the closest one could get to that era was Buffalo Bill Cody's Wild West Show. But with its wide-open spaces, its arid beauty, and its inherent sense of drama, the American West offered what historian Walter Prescott Webb called a "promise of something better." Travel was still mostly on horseback; a life of adventure could yet be found — in the cowboy, the plainsman, the peace officer.

For Stephen, a writer who was always pretending to be someone else, the lure of the West was powerful. It was preeminently a man's world; it stood for toughness, high-spiritedness, fierce independence, strong individuality, honesty, and courage, all qualities that Stephen prized. The cowboy, that uniquely American character, represented physical strength and gritty endurance, which Stephen was badly in need of. Out on the range for weeks at a time, cowboys lived a solitary life; the relationship between man and horse, and between man and nature, was central. Furthermore, they were cheerfully indifferent to middle-class mores, "wild in a well established tradition of Western wildness that involves drinking, fighting, fast and reckless riding . . . and of course, seducing." Stephen himself liked to gamble, ride, and whore. He was attracted to guns and admired the man who could stare down the barrel of a cocked revolver without losing his composure.

It was not simply the life of adventure that appealed to him; he could find plenty of trouble in the Bowery. It was, rather, adventure on a grand scale, played out on horseback on the limitless plains under an unending sky. Stephen relished the untamed outdoors, and he never looked better or felt healthier than when he was camping or riding. In the West he would enjoy an unencumbered, rambling life that came down to a horse, a saddle, a good pair of boots, and a gun. He could test his luck and ride off from ill health — or at least have the illusion of being strong. In this rough country far from home, he could tie a red kerchief around his neck, wear a gun belt so heavy that a woman would need both hands to pick it up, and experience what Hamlin Garland described in his own writings about the Great Plains as "a drama as thrilling, as full of heart and hope and battle, as any that ever surrounded any man."

But now, when Stephen took up his suitcase, it was filled with something more substantial than dreams: he had money in his pockets. He had two books going into production as he prepared to leave — or almost two. He had spent the last couple of months responding to Copeland & Day's queries about *The Black Riders*, looking at proofs, and wrangling over matters of type and design. "The classic form of the sample suits me. It is however paragraphed wrong," he had written. "There should be none. As to punctuation, any uniform method will suit me." He had tried to get a publication date out of them, and at least once had lost his temper: "There has been no necessity for you to wait impatiently to hear from me for I have answered each of the letters sent to me and, at any rate, you have had opportunities to inform me of it since the 31st Oct." He asked if they would send a publication announcement to his friends. Copeland & Day responded with a four-page prospectus, quoting Hamlin Garland's review of *Maggie* for the *Arena*, which called Stephen Crane a writer to be "reckoned with" and one "of almost unlimited resource," and reprinting one of Stephen's poems:

> "Truth," said a traveler,
> "Is a rock, a mighty fortress . . ."

Shortly before Christmas, Stephen had called on Ripley Hitchcock at D. Appleton, bringing along a couple of his newspaper stories. Impressed by these, Hitchcock asked Stephen if he had a book-length story. Stephen hesitated. He said that he had "one rather long story," just then appearing in severely shortened form in Bacheller's syndicate newspapers, and "some of the boys in the office seemed to like it." Hitchcock asked him to send the story immediately.

Stephen left New York for his western trip without having an answer from Hitchcock. From Cooke's European Hotel in St. Louis, en route to his first destination, Lincoln, Nebraska, he wrote Hitchcock, giving him his itinerary for the next month or so and the addresses where he could be reached. He sounded anxious and vulnerable. "Any news of the war story will be grateful to me," he wrote. "If you had not read the story, I would wish you to hear the Philadelphia Press staff speak of it. When I was there some days ago, I was amazed to hear the way in which they talked of it." He added that he would "be glad to hear from you at any time." Before moving on, he dispatched notes to Senger and Button, asking them to write him in Nebraska "in care of the State Journal." He would be there for ten days, he said; afterward he could be reached at the *New Orleans Times-Democrat* office. "Hello, Budge, I am en route to kill Indians," he chirped to Button. He already seemed to be missing his companions.

Stephen had been sent to Nebraska to cover the devastating drought that had begun the previous summer, when a fierce sun and hot south winds scorched great sections of the prairie, killing cattle and destroying crops and soil. Trees had been reduced to skeletons; once fertile farmland was now a useless desert. People were starving, and more than a dozen states had sent aid. By the time Stephen arrived, the disaster had already attracted veteran reporters such as Robert B. Pettie of the *Omaha World-Herald*, whose fifteen vivid articles on the Nebraska drought had been reprinted all over the country, and plucky Nelly Bly of the *New York World*. Just a few years older than Stephen, Bly (the pseudonym of Elizabeth Cochrane Seaman) was building a career as a daring investigative journalist. Bly specialized in sensational exposés; she had faked insanity to get herself committed to the women's prison on Blackwell's Island in New York, so that she could write firsthand about its scandalous conditions.

And yet Stephen's arrival on February 1 was treated in the local press as an event. The next day the *Nebraska State Journal* announced him as a reporter for "a large syndicate of newspapers of national reputation and influence. . . . Mr. Crane's papers have asked him to get the truth, whether his articles are sensational or not, and for that reason his investigation will doubtless be welcomed by the business of Nebraska." Apparently no one at the copy desk that day connected him to the Stephen Crane whose *Red Badge of Courage* had been serialized in the paper some two months earlier. The war story was not mentioned.

In the next six days he traveled some two hundred miles around Nebraska in fierce weather, interviewing Governor Holcomb and talking to farmers, who gave him his best quotations. After listening to one tale of hardship, he asked, "How did you get along?"

"Don't get along, stranger. Who the hell told you I did get along?"

His journey to the little prairie town of Eddyville, in north central Nebraska, coincided with a memorable twenty-four-hour storm. Making his way first, it seems, by train, he then proceeded by wagon for another forty-five miles in temperatures of eighteen below zero with lashing winds of sixty miles per hour. Branch-line trains were derailed; people were housebound. At least one family froze to death, and others were found frozen alongside their horses on the road. The wagon driver's face had turned a dark shade suggesting "a purple Indian from Brazil," Stephen wrote, while the team of brown horses, now covered with snow, struggled valiantly under the whip, wearing "an expression of unutterable patient weariness." At journey's end he retired to a room in Eddyville where the temperature was "precisely one and a half degrees below zero," apparently waiting out the storm.

Though he didn't exactly "get along," he produced a lengthy, fine piece titled "Nebraska's Bitter Fight for Life." While not radically different from what others had written, Stephen's piece was thorough, balanced, and poetic. Stirred by the devastation and suffering he saw in this once-fertile land under "an imperial blue sky"; moved by the pioneer spirit and the "steadfast and unyielding courage" of the Nebraska people, these "fearless folk, completely American," he felt the things he wrote about: the wind attacking the land like "wolves of ice" after the summer's terrible drought, when "the scream of a wind [was] hot as an oven's fury." Even among other memorable reports on the drought, Stephen Crane's stood out. "It was as if upon the massive altar of the earth, their homes and their families were being offered in sacrifice to the wrath of some blind and pitiless deity," he wrote after his own encounter with nature. As the drought begins, the hot winds come on quietly, sneakily at first, in little "panting" breaths like the wind from the tropics; the corn rustles with a "dry and crackling sound which went up from the prairies like cries"; the wind screams, the trees "gasp" as they die (as in the Sullivan County woods); "the corn [shivers] as from fever"; "the fingers of the storm clutch madly at" the people huddling inside their sod houses.

Upon arriving in Lincoln, Stephen had gone to the *State Journal* office to introduce himself. A young woman named Willa Cather was there when he "sauntered" in, as she put it, his face half hidden by his hat. Having done some of the copy editing on *The Red Badge* for the newspaper's publication of it in December, she recognized Stephen's name and stayed to observe him.

Writing under the pseudonym Henry Nicklemann five years later, Willa Cather, who was just two years Stephen's junior, would create something of a Dorian Gray portrait of him, a likeness of the man's soul that was part Crane, part Cather, as subjective as it was psychologically perceptive. Everything about him seemed dark to her. She remembered his blond hair as "black," his fair eyes as "dark," whiskers darkening his narrow face, the beginnings of a "thin dark moustache" visible above his upper lip. During the few days Cather observed Stephen around the *State Journal* office, his spirits were depressed, adding to the impression of darkness.

At the very beginning of the western trip he had so long anticipated, on the threshold of literary success, Crane seemed to Willa Cather "profoundly discouraged" — "tense, preoccupied," with the "self-centered air of a man who is brooding over some impending disaster," she wrote, noting that he carried a volume of Poe in his pocket. "Even his jokes were exceedingly drastic." He had already run out of money and had cabled Bacheller for more. "Only a very youthful enthusiasm and a large propensity for hero worship could have found anything impressive" in Crane, she stated. Obviously unhealthy, he said he was going West both to carry out this assignment for Bacheller and to "get rid of his cough." He told her he was poor, and his starved appearance — a "gaunt" face above a "narrow-chested" frame that was "thin to emaciation" — and shabby, ill-fitting clothes, confirmed it. Wearing "a slovenly apology for a tie" and shoes "badly run over at the heel," in need of a haircut and a shave, Crane looked worse than the most "disreputable" tramp printers who regularly turned up at the newspaper looking for work. And yet amid this ruin were his beautiful hands and eyes, the hands "delicately shaped," with "thin, nervous fingers." She would remember Stephen's eyes as "the finest I have ever seen, large and dark and full of lustre and changing lights, but with a profound melancholy always lurking deep in them. They were eyes that seemed to be burning themselves out."

Though still a student (she was a junior at Nebraska State University), Willa Cather was a rising star at the *Nebraska State Journal*. She already had her own column, which consisted mostly of theater reviews. Among actors she had made a name for herself as a critic of "biting frankness," and at the paper she had a "reputation for zest, intelligence and ferocity," according to one biographer. On campus she had further distinguished herself by wearing boyish suits and short hair, underscoring her serious, somewhat masculine, heavy featured face. Her lack of femininity and attractiveness may have put Stephen off, for he repeatedly frustrated her persistent attempts to draw him out.

He talked "in a wandering, absent-minded fashion, and his conversation was uniformly frivolous," she complained later. He seemed to shrink from serious conversation. But Cather was serious about writing, and she pursued him. Well read, admittedly "Maupassant-mad at the time," she "made a frantic effort to get an expression of opinion from him on 'Le Bonheur.' 'Oh, you're Moping, are you?' he remarked with a sarcastic grin, and went on reading a little volume of Poe." On another occasion she asked him

> whether stories were constructed by cabalistic formulae. At length he sighed wearily and shook his drooping shoulders, remarking: "Where did you get all that rot? Yarns aren't done by mathematics. You can't do it by rule any more than you can dance by rule. You have to have the itch of the thing in your fingers, and if you haven't, — well, you're damned lucky, and you'll live long and prosper, that's all." — And with that he yawned and went down the hall.

To Cather, Stephen seemed always on the verge of departing. Even when he was sitting, his long fingers would be restlessly tapping the copy paper. Though he gave an appearance of idleness, she sensed "that he was in the throes of work that told terribly on his nerves." He asked her how to spell a word when he was writing a letter, saying he didn't have "time to learn to spell." He didn't have time to dress properly, either: "It takes an awful slice out of a fellow's life," he said, looking at himself and smiling. But her persistence finally paid off. The night before Stephen left Nebraska, instead of moving toward the door when the conversation turned serious, he talked willingly, the words flooding from his heart in a bitter torrent.

It was eleven o'clock, and he was "deeply despondent" over money. He had expected the night mail to bring a check, and it hadn't. Cather came in fresh from the theater, wrote her notice, and then pulled up a chair near where Stephen was sitting on the ledge of the open window, overlooking the street. In his slow diction, he quoted some lines from *The Black Riders* and talked at length about the miseries of his trade and the agonies of composition. He never raised his voice.

> He gave me to understand that he led a double literary life; writing in the first place the matter that pleased himself and doing it very slowly; in the second place, any sort of stuff that would sell. And he remarked that his poor was just as bad as it could possibly be. He realized, he said, that his limitations were absolutely impassable. "What I can't do, I can't do at all, and I can't acquire it. I only hold one trump."
>
> He had no settled plans at all. He was going to Mexico wholly uncertain of being able to do any successful work there, and he seemed to feel very insecure about the financial end of his venture. The thing that most interested me was what he said about his slow method of composition. He declared that there was little money in story-writing at best, and practically none in it for him, because of the time it took him to work up his detail. Other men, he said, could sit down and write up an experience while the physical effect of it, so to speak, was still upon them, and yesterday's impressions made today's "copy." But when he came in from the streets to write up what he had seen there, his faculties were benumbed, and he sat twirling his pencil and hunting for words like a schoolboy.

They talked about *The Red Badge*. Stephen explained the relatively short period of its composition by his having unconsciously worked it out "through most of his boyhood." He told her about his soldier ancestors and the war stories he had imagined throughout his childhood. His imagination "was hidebound; it was there, but it pulled hard," he said. "After he got a notion for a story, months passed before he could get any sort of personal contact with it, or feel any potency to handle it. 'The detail of a thing has to filter through my blood, and then it comes out like a native product, but it takes forever.'" And he had earned only about ninety dollars for *The Red Badge* syndication, he told her. As their conversation ended and Cather got ready to go home, she tried to encourage him, saying "in ten years he would probably laugh at all his temporary discomfort. Again his body took on that strenuous tension and he clenched his hands, saying, 'I can't wait ten years, I haven't time.' "

Stephen seems not to have told Cather that he was waiting to hear from Appleton about the book publication of *The Red Badge*. The long wait was making him miserable. Finally, in early February, he received a letter of acceptance from Ripley Hitchcock. He later told his friend Willis Brooks Hawkins "that he would have burned the manuscript if it had come back again."

Appleton's offer was stingy. The author would receive no money up front; he would be paid a meager 10 percent royalty each year, but only after the publisher's own costs were recovered. There were no provisions for foreign rights. In his haste to get the novel published, Stephen agreed to the terms of the contract as stated in the letter, and wrote Hitchcock that he could correct the manuscript during his next stop, in New Orleans. Remarkably, someone at Appleton had expressed doubt about the novel's title; Stephen said that he would "have to reflect upon it." On June 17 he signed the contract for *The Red Badge of Courage*, as it was still called, the publisher apparently no longer thinking that Stephen should shorten the title.

Stephen left Nebraska with a set of impressions: a lone house on a vast prairie made invisible by enveloping "white clouds" of snow; the "soft blue" of the sky against a great expanse of white; the psychological isolation brought on by the weather, which forces everyone indoors. The best of what he gathered on the Nebraska prairie was not put into the reporting piece but saved for his fiction.

"He felt that he had the material for a thrilling story," reported the *State Journal* on February 14 in an announcement about Stephen's departure from Nebraska. But "when he returned to civilization and found that he could have met a meaner blizzard at about the same date if he had remained in New York, his disgust was copious enough to fill a furniture van."

From Nebraska his train took him to Hot Springs, Arkansas, a place colored in soft yellows and greens with pine-fragrant air and a stream Stephen described as precisely the color of lemon phosphate. Life in Hot Springs centered on its bathhouses. "A man becomes a creature of these conditions," Stephen wrote. "He is about to take a bath — he is taking a bath — he has taken a bath." His cough notwithstanding, he seems to have resisted the baths. From Hot Springs he went to the narrow, gaily lighted streets of New Orleans, where he attended the Grand Opera and stood in the swarming crowds on Canal Street during Mardi Gras. He soon left its vivid color for the "dull-hued" Texas prairie of "long low hills, like immense waves."

The seventeen reporting pieces Stephen wrote for Bacheller over the next three months suggest a writer hacking his way through the Texas brush country. After Nebraska, his assigned writing became curiously lifeless and uninspired, revealing little of what he was feeling. At each stop he dutifully recorded his impressions, dispatching pieces of local color like a tourist sending home picture postcards. He listened to small talk in saloons and collected pieces of local history like trinkets; he noted the changing landscape, the way people dressed, the prices of clothing and transportation, architecture — the outsides of things. Occasionally he even managed to scare up a good metaphor.

With so much to absorb, he seemed overwhelmed by the need to match his words to the speeding pace of the train. Without time for the new impressions to filter through his blood, he was creatively hobbled. He was soon so bored that he couldn't work up enough enthusiasm even to write Button about "the many strange things" he had seen.

Appleton had sent the *Red Badge* manuscript by express to him in New Orleans, and in revising it he had cut about two thousand words. He was still reflecting on the novel's title: "I am unable to see what to do with it unless the word 'Red' is cut out, perhaps. That would shorten it," he wrote Hitchcock on March 8.

His letters to friends reflected a variety of moods. He seemed happy as he left New Orleans, and he wrote a schoolboy's nonsense letter to Linson in a playful imitation of Louisiana Creole: "Table d'hotes sur le balconies just like spring. A la mode whiskers on the citizens en masse, merci, of the vintage de 1712"; "Ce matin I write un article sur le railways du South which were all made in hell." He answered a couple of letters from a journalist asking him for biographical information.

Writing to his Syracuse fraternity brother, Clarence Peaslee, and to John Hilliard, now literary editor of the *Rochester Post Express*, whom Stephen had known in New York, he essentially repeated himself, sounding like the weary veteran of many campaigns — especially of Henry Fleming's campaign, which he was not free of. He described his life as a "battle," a "war," that he had begun "with no talent, no equipment, but with an ardent admiration and desire." He noted that after recovering from college, he had "had to build up." Wanting most of all "to write plainly and unmistakeably, so that all men — and some women — might read and understand," he yet found literature a great labor. Dismissing his own success as "meagre," he added, "There is nothing to respect in art, save one's own opinion of it."

On March 5 he arrived in Galveston, a prosperous cotton-exporting city of some forty thousand residents. Welcomed in an item in the *Galveston Daily News*, which called Stephen Crane "one of the brightest and most entertaining special writers of the day," he checked into one of the city's best hotels and spent his first day drinking beer with the mayor and the newspaper's managing editor. He called the session "a distinctly homeric" struggle in which he'd managed to both toe the political line and hold his liquor. He found the natives friendly. They found him "quiet" and "unobtrusive," with an "impressive countenance." The prestigious Aziola Club, a businessmen's club, which required that its members be "gentlemen of good moral character," opened its doors to him. He admired the southern frankness he found in Galveston, the lack of suspicion toward a stranger. But this cosmopolitan island city seemed to hold little attraction for him. He watched the stevedores on the offshore cotton steamers and noted that people moved slowly in the summer heat, "with an extraordinary caution as if they expect to be shot as they approached each corner." (His piece on Galveston — a dull compendium of local history — was not published during his lifetime.)

Stephen was not looking for fine dining, sea bathing, or a new opera house but for the rugged West of legend. He wanted a one-horse town with a name like Tin Can or Yellow Sky, where a frequently kicked dog dozed in front of the saloon, and the town marshal fought it out in the dirt street with a drunken gunslinger. In his mind he had a picture of "the rough west [which] stood in naked immortality before the eyes of the gentle East." Though not naive about westerners — "Garland will wring every westerner by the hand and hail him as a frank honest man. I wont. No, sir" — he loved the "simple courtesy which leads Western men to donate the fighters plenty of room," "the straight out-and-out, sometimes hideous, often-braggart westerners" who seemed to him "the truer men. . . . They are serious, those fellows. When they are born they take one big gulp of wind and then they live."

"We in the east are overcome a good deal by a superficial culture which I think is the real barbarism," he wrote later. "Culture in it's true sense, I take it, is a comprehension of the man at one's shoulder. It has nothing to do with an adoration for effete jugs and old kettles." Writing about Galveston, Stephen complained that the easterner's "passion for differences" got in the way of understanding the westerner. "Travelers tumbling over each other in their haste to trumpet the radical differences between Eastern and Western life have created a generally wrong opinion," he wrote. People's fascination with differences "kept the sweeping march of the West from being chronicled in any particularly true manner."

On the train hurtling west over the Texas plains to San Antonio, it seemed that everyone he met — "business men, consumptive men, curious men and wealthy men" — envied his going to that city, which "seemed to symbolize for them the poetry of life in Texas."

In San Antonio, the oldest city in Texas, Stephen found some of the West that he was looking for. Here was the extreme southwestern outpost of the settled frontier, the land of the longhorn and wild horses; of Confederate war days and Mexican war raids and vigilante committees; of big cattle drives and pioneer settlers and cowpunchers and chili girls. As one historian put it, "Here the romance of life [was] thick enough to cut." Here was the lingering spirit of the Alamo.

Spanish-style buildings of white-washed adobe capped with red roofs were partly hidden in a lush tangle of bright green foliage; throughout was a scattering of church spires, and above it all, like a giant cupping hand, a sky of indigo blue. The prairie lay all around, "wrinkled into long low hills, like immense waves," wrote Stephen, "and upon them spreads a wilderness of the persistent mesquite, a bush that grows in defiance of everything." The Edwards Plateau to the northwest was visible as a bluish haze; to the southwest stretched the rolling, blossoming coastal plain. At sunset the sky flushed scarlet, like a Mexican serape; at night the moon lit the vast prairie.

But whatever poetry Stephen found in old San Tone was blurred by the rhythm of "the march of this terrible century." In a city ringing with church bells, the dominant chord in Stephen's ears was the relentless rumble of the trolleys, those "merciless animals. They gorge themselves with relics," he wrote in an echo of his words on the Scranton coal breakers. Though the romance of the place was not lost on him, the sight of people rushing off to make money overshadowed the pretty Mexican girls and the Mexican men with their ever-present cigarettes, wide-brimmed hats, and Americanized clothing. In Stephen's eyes, "the principal color of San Antonio" was the spirit of commerce.

In writing about the city, Stephen fell back on its glorious past. He bemoaned the disintegration of the two-hundred-year-old mission churches in the valley south of the city, victims of both nature and "relic hunters." And yet the march of progress had not extinguished the spirit of the Alamo. Never mind that "67,710 writers of the state of Texas have begun at the Alamo," he wrote. "The Alamo remains the greatest memorial to courage which civilization has allowed to stand." The building itself, a little limestone-walled fortress dwarfed by the city's taller modern buildings, had an "air of contemplative silence." To Stephen, the Alamo was "as eloquent as an old battle flag." It was poetry.

He found another kind of poetry in the local chili queens or chili girls. These Spanish waitresses who worked at the chili stands were celebrated for their dark beauty and their mastery of the arts of flirting and cigarette rolling (black tobacco wrapped in corn shucks). Memorable among them was Martha, a raven-haired beauty with dazzling white teeth, red lips, and a luscious figure. In his book *Glamorous Days*, Frank H. Bushick told of one night when he turned up in Martha's orbit with a young stranger. Martha wore a short, "flaming red" skirt that showed her bare ankles and a "bluish rebozo" that revealed her bare arms and neck and "full bosoms." She had a way of tossing her head back when she smiled, in the manner of Carmen, said Bushick, and when he greeted her on this night she fixed her "sparkling eyes" and red smile on his friend and said,

> "Who's your good lookin' compañero? He shure look good ter me."
>
> "Martha, you're looking prettier than ever tonight," said the compañero, as though they'd met before.
>
> "So sorry," she kids back, with a twinkling laugh and a shrug of the shoulder, "But I ain't got a nickel to geeve you. Does your mother know you're out?"
>
> "Yes," put in the man from up north, "Ive heard a lot about you and thats why I came around to see you."
>
> "Oh, my! You're a big kidder, too. Here, you must have a flower for that."

Martha was unfailingly good natured, but she was also up

to a few tricks. She knew that the man from up north was one of them reporters and she liked to see her name in the paper.

Plucking a rose from her corsage, she pinned it lightly on the coat of the *compañero*, who was Stephen Crane.

On March 12, as he was "about to venture into Mexico and sever . . . relations with the United States postal service," he wrote to Lucius Button — "merely an attempt to cajole a letter out of you," he admitted. He made much of a bore named Butler he'd met in New Orleans who happened to be from Akron, Ohio, Button's hometown. Sounding more irritable than playful, Stephen carried on about this "intolerable duffer," who had embarrassed him by pointing to people in the street and saying, " 'Look at that fellow!' People in New Orleans don't like that sort of thing, you know," Stephen wrote. Butler had invited him to visit in Akron on his way back to New York. "I modestly replied that while I appreciated his generosity and his courage, I had to die early in the spring and I feared that I would have to hurry home for the funeral but I had an open date in 1997 and would be happy to see him in hell upon that occasion."

It wasn't like him to get so rattled, to expend so many words on a harmless bore. What Stephen wasn't saying was that this duffer had made a disparaging remark about a girl he was interested in.

In January Button had given a tea at his New York apartment. There Stephen met young Nellie Crouse, who was visiting from Akron. Instantly smitten, he called on her once before leaving for the West and again found her "very attractive." He began to imagine that she was a kindred spirit. "To some sentence of mine you said, 'Yes, I know,' before I had quite finished. I dont remember what I had said but I have always remembered your saying 'Yes, I know.' I knew then that you had lived a long time." When he met the "awful chump" Butler in New Orleans and learned that he lived in Akron, he mentioned Nellie Crouse. It turned out that Butler knew her. To Stephen's appraisal of Miss Crouse as "very charming," Butler had agreed but added unaccountably, "rather queer girl, though."

Crossing the Rio Grande into Mexico on March 17, Stephen kept his eye on the view out the window and his ear on the conversation in the car. He was sitting in the train's smoking compartment with two American businessmen, an archeologist from Boston and a capitalist from Chicago, neither one of whom had any conversation. But he recorded their words anyway, in one of his rambling reporting pieces.

In Mexico he absorbed everything, from the street beggars to the pulque drinkers and later told CK that "there were certain traits that he sensed like a native." But he was acutely aware of what he could not do. After trying to write about the Mexican poor, he gave up, saying that as an artist he could "be sure of two things, form and color." He was unable to write with psychological perception about the people and the life in this foreign country. It seemed to him that "the most worthless literature of the world has been that which has been written by the men of one nation concerning the men of another." He could only observe, without judging, without translating.

He roamed the City of Mexico and wandered into the high plains. He took to this country, a land hard as the stone *metates* on which tortillas were made and as seductive as the fiery opals sold by street vendors. The women were "beautiful frequently . . . their black eyes as beautiful as gems," he wrote, though he missed the "sudden intelligence, comprehension, sympathy" he found in the eyes of American girls. He took in the street hustlers, the circus, the Circo Teatro Orrin, the dice and card games, the floating gardens beyond the Viga Canal, and whatever else caught his fancy. He loved the colors of Mexico — the red and purple clothing, the "vivid serapes," the yellow and white adobes, the "heavily blue" shadows under the mesquite, the brown women, the white dust, the great creamy-toned mountains, Popocatépetl and Iztaccíhuatl, which turned silver against the deep velvet blue of the night sky; "the long flare of crimson, purple, [and] orange" that was the western hills — "tremendous colors that, in the changes of the sunset, manoeuvered in the sky like armies." He had never seen anything in America to equal the dignity of the Paseo de la Reforma, the famous macadam drive in the City of Mexico approaching the Castle of Chapultepec. Here the Old World came alive; he was keenly aware of the buskin-clad feet that had walked the stones of the broad avenue "before the coming of carriages."

Mexico was a place where a man could lose himself if he had a mind to. He could disappear into the black streets at midnight or put on a derby and cutaway coat and melt into the evening swirl of well-dressed people. Carriages driven by coachmen in towering sombreros clattered along the *calle*, the air sweet smelling from the afternoon's rain. Or he could set out for the silent plains where "the world was declared to be a

desert and unpeopled," Stephen wrote. Across the flawless sky, a sheepherder could sometimes see dust rising, in "long, white streamers" from
another flock miles away. The only sounds to be heard were the breath of
horses and the jangling of spurs.

In April or May of 1895, wearing Mexican spurs "as large as pies," a
Smith and Wesson revolver, a sombrero, and a serape, Stephen hired a
fast little horse and a guide and rode out into the country on a true adventure that proved almost fatally thrilling. According to Corwin Knapp
Linson, the story Stephen told him later in an excited tumble of words
("for once his tongue found freedom," said Linson) was virtually the same
as that of his later short story "One Dash — Horses" ("one dash" means
"an all-or-nothing roll of the dice").

Stephen's "wild midnight" began somewhere out in the Mexican
desert. The hills to the west looked as though some giant hand had
carved them into peaks, then "painted [them] the most profound blue,"
Stephen wrote. "Above them, the sky was of that marvelous tone of
green — like still, sun-shot water — which people denounce in pictures."
He and his guide stopped at an adobe house for bed and board. While
they were sleeping, a torch-carrying band of drunken Mexicans arrived
at the house and burst into their room, threatening to kill Stephen if he
did not hand over his money, his fine gun, saddle, and spurs. The lead
bandit was fat and menacing, with jet black hair and eyes and a "little
snake-like moustache." Stephen froze. His knee joints turned "to bread."
He was unable to do more than sit up and stare at the fat bandit. This dis-
armed the bandit and bought Stephen some time. Then the guide (he is
called José in the story) woke, and the bandits roughed him up. Trying to
get a reaction out of Stephen, they threatened to kill the guide, but
Stephen maintained his outward calm, sitting up in bed and fixing them
with an impassive stare while fingering his revolver under the blanket.
Suddenly a guitar began playing. Some women arrived and called out to
the men, and they drifted off into another room.

Slowly Stephen roused himself and began to sneak away with his
guide. His big spurs made a crashing sound, like cymbals, he said later,
and he had to stop and remove them with trembling fingers. His horse
whinnied to him in greeting. When he reached the animal he fumbled
with the cinch, his hands still shaking.

He and his guide escaped, galloping over the "silent," misty blue
plains as dawn was breaking. Stephen's little horse was the superior animal, and he flew across the desert "with hoofs that were as light as blown

leaves." As Stephen rode he kept looking back over his shoulder. He began to hate José for being frightened too, and ordered him to ride fifty paces behind. When the guide objected, Stephen threatened to shoot him.

Finally he saw dust rising on the plain behind. "Crimson serapes in the distance resembled drops of blood on the great cloth of plain." The bandits got close enough for Stephen to hear a yell; a gun was fired. He began to imagine his capture, selfishly thinking only of himself, reflecting that after all, José was Mexican, and it was natural for *him* to die in this country. But he was a foreigner, a New Yorker. "He remembered all the tales of such races for life, and he thought them badly written."

Then luck stepped in to save him. Ahead of them the huge silvery sombreros of the Mexican *rurales* became visible against the lightening sky. These cavalry soldiers, who patrolled the plains, were crack shots. When Stephen and his guide reined up before them, the guide spilled out their story, identifying Stephen "as an American señor of vast wealth who was the friend of almost every governmental potentate within two hundred miles." Just then the *pistoleros* came galloping over the hill, some "fifty drunken horsemen" riding so hard they were unable to turn around, and ran smack into the cavalry. The rurales aimed their carbines, and an officer rode out to address the fat bandit. Threatening him, the officer finally gave the bandit's horse a great kick in the belly, and the whole pack of drunken rebels thundered away in a whirl of dust.

It would be months before Stephen was able to write about "my personal troubles in Mexico." "One Dash — Horses," which is only moderately successful as a short story, is a careful explication of a man's fear. The writing is painstakingly detailed, as though the composition were an exercise in steadying the writer's nerves, the plot perhaps taken too literally from life.

By May, Stephen had been in Mexico so long that his face had turned "the color of a brick side-walk. There was nothing American about me save a large Smith and Wesson revolver and I saw only Indians whom I suspected of loading their tomales with dog," he said. In this hardened and disconnected state, looking as scraggly as old mesquite, he was in a hotel in Puebla one day when he saw a young American woman who reminded him of Nellie Crouse. "I only saw her four times — one in the hotel corridor and three in the street. I had been so long in the mountains and was such an outcast, that the sight of this American girl in a new spring gown nearly caused me to drop dead," he wrote in a letter to

Nellie. "She of course never looked in my direction. I never met her. Nevertheless I gained one of those peculiar thrills which a man only acknowledges upon occasion. I ran to the railroad office. I cried: 'What is the shortest route to New York.' I left Mexico." On May 15 he checked out of the Hotel Iturbide and boarded a train. It was springtime, and the few remaining buffalo were making their way up north.

A few days later he was back in New York.

7

THE COMING MAN

He was back on familiar ground. He exchanged "the keening Rio Grande" for the dirty East River and boots with big silver spurs for shoes. He took up his old life and habits, wandering Manhattan's Lower East Side with his old *compañeros* and using Edmund's new house in the village of Hartwood, next to Port Jervis, as a home base.

He came home with a serape, "a deep tan, a very practical Spanish vocabulary," said Frederic Lawrence, a cache of colorful stories, a half-dozen luminous opals purchased from a street vendor who had no doubt taken him for more than the stones were worth, and empty pockets. He was "broke to the limit," said Nelson Greene. But he gave the opals away, letting his friends have their pick.

Strumming a guitar as he talked, he regaled his family with stories — about the night he was chased by bandits, about a religious procession he'd seen. "Magnificent! Magnificent!" he said.

He had been written about even in his absence. *The Black Riders* had scarcely been announced in *Publishers Weekly* when twenty-three-year-old Stephen Crane was being hailed in the *Bookman* as a young writer who was exciting "the highest hopes for his future career. The impression he makes on his literary coworkers is that he is a young man of almost un-limited resource." Citing *Maggie* as a "daring" book of "terrible direct-ness" and iconoclasm — the product of "rugged undisciplined strength in a youth of genius" — the article also noted the forthcoming publication of *The Red Badge of Courage*, and another novel under consideration by a publisher, currently titled *A Woman Without Weapons.*

Another piece in the *Bookman*, by Henry Thurston Peck, in response to an advance copy of *The Black Riders*, called Stephen "the Aubrey Beardsley of poetry." Noting the similar gimmickry in the poet's work — "the Beardsleyesque splash of black upon its staring white boards," the words "printed wholly in capitals," the unrhymed and unrhythmical lines, Peck wrote that "the general impression is of a writer who is bidding for renown wholly on the basis of his eccentricity." And yet Stephen Crane was "a true poet" whose lines had "a thought and a meaning." Peck even likened him to a young Walt Whitman — if Whitman had been "subjected to aesthetic influences" as a fledgling writer.

On May 11, 1895, *The Black Riders and Other Lines* arrived in the world, with an attention-getting cover and a respectable first printing of five hundred copies. A special edition of fifty copies was printed in green ink on gold-stamped white vellum, with a different binding. "I am particularly anxious to see the green ones," Stephen wrote the publisher. It was a small book, about six by four and a half inches; a child could pick it up without dropping it. On the cover, under the title, which was printed in large plain black capitals, a curling black orchid declared itself against a pale yellowish-gray background. The design, by a Copeland & Day artist, was an adaptation of a drawing by Frederick Gordon. It was surprisingly effective — strangely seductive and Oriental in its simplicity and color, and the more potent because the design was at odds with the title. The cover forced itself into one's line of vision. Along with the Copeland & Day imprint, the cover told the reader to expect something out of the ordinary.

It is the poems' flashes of strange imagery, their qualities of wisdom, irony, and skepticism that made *The Black Riders* notable. Though Stephen Crane was not the first to write in free verse — Emily Dickinson and Walt Whitman had paved the way — the form was not yet popular. And no one but Stephen Crane could have written

> I stood upon a high place,
> And saw, below, many devils
> Running, leaping,
> And carousing in sin.
> One looked up, grinning,
> And said, "Comrade! Brother!"

These were not the "lyrical outbursts" readers of poetry were used to. Stephen's themes of rebelliousness and the search for knowledge or truth were the familiar territory of the young writer; though he did not invent blasphemy, his portrayals of God as raging, wrathful, blustering, a "puffing braggart" to spit on, a figure lying "dead in Heaven" while angels sing hymns and drip blood from their wings could make a reader think that he had. What set *The Black Riders* apart from other late-nineteenth-century poetry was Stephen's daring and his "individual eyes," his "naturally primitive" quality, as later poets would put it. As in *Maggie* and *The Red Badge*, he had taken certain familiar themes and shaken them up, breathed new life into them with his original view of the world.

Describing *The Black Riders* as "small skeletons of poetry," an 1896 reviewer would say that "they often have enough freshness of conception to set the reader thinking. . . . One feels that a long journey has been taken since the Last Poems of Mr. Lowell were read."

Stephen had not needed screaming capitals and an attention-grabbing book design to enhance the more original poems.

> In the desert
> I saw a creature, naked, bestial,
> Who, squatting upon the ground,
> Held his heart in his hands,
> And ate of it.
> I said, "Is it good, friend?"
> "It is bitter — bitter," he answered;
> "But I like it
> "Because it is bitter,
> "And because it is my heart."
>
> •
>
> Many red devils ran from my heart
> And out upon the page.
> They were so tiny
> The pen could mash them.
> And many struggled in the ink.
> It was strange
> To write in this red muck
> Of things from my heart.

The Black Riders is a preeminently youthful effort. "There is nothing save opinion, / And opinion be damned," ended one. Many of the poems are parables rather than poetry. The work of an intelligent, precocious writer eager to set down his ideas "about life in general," they tend to be raw expressions of feeling and idea; they are not composed.

There are exceptions. The title poem shows a genuine attempt to create a poem through alliteration, repetition, and near-rhymes. It seems to have been worked all the way through.

> Black riders came from the sea.
> There was clang and clang of spear and shield,
> And clash and clash of hoof and heel,
> Wild shouts and the wave of hair
> In the rush upon the wind:
> Thus the ride of sin.

The poem numbered X is something more; here Stephen Crane became a poet.

> Should the wide world roll away,
> Leaving black terror
> Limitless night,
> Nor God, nor man, nor place to stand
> Would be to me essential
> If thou and thy white arms were there
> And the fall to doom a long way.

•

Upon Stephen's return to New York in May, he, Irving Bacheller, Edward Marshall, Richard Watson Gilder, Willis Brooks Hawkins, Post Wheeler, and others formed the Sign o' the Lanthorn Club (also called the Lantern Club) as a watering hole for journalists. They purchased a shanty on top of a house on William Street, near the Brooklyn Bridge, for fifty dollars and fixed the interior up with lanterns to make it look like a ship's cabin. They hired a cook, and lunch was served daily, with a banquet on Saturday nights. Eating at the Lantern Club on the day he was to turn in his expense account to Bacheller, "Stephen pulled out a big gun which he said was one of the considerable expense items" he'd had on his trip West, said Nelson Greene.

"Why, Steve, that's just like Doc Biggs' gun," Greene said without thinking.

As Greene remembered it later, Stephen simply replied that the gun "was one of his expenses" and said nothing more about it until the two of them had left the club and were waiting for the elevated train on Third Avenue. Then he turned on his friend.

"You damned fool. Why did you want to try to queer me like that," he said. "I borrowed the gun from Doc to pad out my expense account."

They talked about it briefly, and the storm blew over. "Everything became ok between us," said Greene.

Outwardly Stephen seemed unchanged — sociable, even garrulous. He fell into step with the same friends from before his trip and easily made new ones. Bunking with Greene for some weeks at his studio in the old League building, Stephen sat up late, talking with Greene and the new fellows in the building over beer and soft drinks and tobacco. As their conversation ranged over various weighty subjects — religion, politics, art, music, literature, and social issues — Stephen talked splendidly, said Greene, the result of his "straight" thinking and humanitarian feelings. Shining in conversation on virtually any subject he addressed, Stephen instinctively tuned himself down when he found himself in the company of inferior minds, said Greene. Many nights he could be found at "a dingy but quite clean tenement somewhere in the Thirtieth Streets west of Broadway," as Henry McBride remembered it, having dinner and throwing dice "for unpretentious stakes" with the Pike brothers and a group composed mostly of artists. The Pikes had been to France — Charley Pike had even posed for a series of Charles Dana Gibson illustrations on student life in Paris for the *Century*, which made him a standout among his friends — and they had found two French peasant women in the Bowery to cook for them and their friends nightly. The diners, who often included Stephen, ate country style at a table in the tenement kitchen, with the French women serving them from the stove.

He slept late in the mornings and got by largely on a diet of coffee and cigars. Greene's studio had a kitchenette, and he and Stephen "fussed up breakfast" there. Then, if he wasn't dining with the Pikes, he went to the Lantern Club for his "one square meal" of the day. He continued to retreat to Hartwood as needed, "to the temporary benefit of his health," said one club member. But Greene and some of the others were concerned enough about Stephen's dietary habits to say something to him. "We fellows thought Crane's constant smoking, too much coffee, lack of food and poor teeth — at 23 — would soon kill him off," said Greene. "We told him so and tried to make him go to a dentist. He had the worst teeth I ever saw on a human being — but he would do nothing about it."

In an age when dentistry was performed without anesthesia, and by itinerant practitioners who were not formally trained, Stephen may have reasoned that he was better off having rotting and perhaps abscessed teeth than subjecting himself to crude drills with steel burs or tooth extraction with a turnkey. The picture of a dentist's office, with its barbaric instruments and its spittoon, was more frightening than the reflection in the mirror.

During his first weeks back after his trip he tried to write, but the words escaped him. He told Greene "he had lost his producing power." But after a while "he got busy and turned out the first half of a Civil War short story, 'The Gray Sleeve.'"

While Stephen sat writing at a table in Greene's studio, Greene, who later became a cartoonist at *Puck*, picked up a pencil and sketched him sitting in a Windsor chair, writing with a steel pen on foolscap. An ink bottle, a cup of black coffee, and a coffeepot are carefully arrayed on the table around him, and a cigar protrudes from his mouth. His shoulders are hunched, his shirtsleeves are rolled to the elbows, and his bare arms are extended on the table in front of him, his whole body seeming to lean into the task at hand. What is striking about the portrait is the rawboned look of the subject. His upper body is reasonably slender, and his hands are long-fingered and gracefully formed, like a woman's. But his head is gaunt, severely carved, the lines of his chin, nose, and skull long, angular, and bony. His hair is back-combed and sparse. The man in the drawing looks uncannily like Stephen Crane as an old man, ravaged by illness.

Both "A Gray Sleeve" and "A Mystery of Heroism," a fine Civil War story that Stephen seems also to have written in the summer of 1895, had subtle overtones of his western trip and of his Mexican adventure in particular. "Gray Sleeve," an inferior piece of writing, turns on an unconvincing romantic attraction between a blond, deeply tanned infantry captain in the Union army and a young southern woman whose house the Yankees have broken into. The captain is a poor-looking suitor, acutely conscious of his dirty clothing and his bedraggled appearance.

"A Mystery of Heroism" suggests Stephen's paralyzing fear before the Mexican bandits. A thirsty soldier, taking the jeering challenge of some members of his company to get water in a field that is under heavy artillery fire, becomes an unlikely hero. At first he is numb to the risk he is taking, but when he finds himself in the thick of the firing, he becomes afraid. Like Henry Fleming, he finds that he has become a hero. But this soldier is wiser, learning something that Fleming doesn't: that one can feel fear and also be a hero. "This, then, was a hero," Stephen wrote. "After all, heroes are not much." In both stories danger is concealed — behind a maple grove, behind "a curtain of green woods," behind a house, behind a girl's dress, which hides a gun. Both carry the sense that violence can erupt unexpectedly. Horses are a steady presence in the narrative action — carrying riders, pounding the ground, kicking up dust, their hooves lifted to the sky when they fall in battle.

Stephen returned from his trip to write not directly of the West but of the Civil War; his own experiences were still too close.

Nelson Greene remembered that Stephen struggled through the writing of half of "A Gray Sleeve," then put his pen down. "He said he couldn't get anything out of himself." Stephen finished the story later, sometime after he moved out of Greene's studio.

He was "not in very good health," he told Copeland & Day. He had therefore left New York for Hartwood. Edmund's house overlooked the Mill Pond, where refuse timber from the lumber mill drifted.

Writing to Copeland & Day, he asked for news of *The Black Riders*; he had noticed that the book was "making some stir." Though he sounded as though he were planning to stay in the country a while, he seemed in no hurry for an answer. He gave the Lantern Club in New York City as his return address.

Throughout the summer of 1895, reviews of the little volume trickled in. Stephen took some hits — "so much trash," wrote his old newspaper, the *New York Tribune. Munsey's Magazine* disliked its free verse form. "Mr. Crane has thoughts. We are finding fault with him because they are not put into frank prose. Is this poetry?" The *Bookman* declared that they were "stamped with truth." Reviewing *The Black Riders* in June for the premier issue of the *Philistine*, Elbert Hubbard wrote that he didn't know why Stephen had titled the book so; "the riders might have easily been green or yellow or baby-blue for all the book tells about them, and I think the title 'The Pink Rooters' would have been better, but it doesn't matter."

A prosperous businessman, farmer, horseman, and former soap salesman turned novelist and journalist, Hubbard had recently become associated with the *Philistine*, the latest in a group of irreverent, satirical "little magazines" that offered an iconoclastic alternative to the big standards of the day, the *Century*, *Harper's*, and *McClure's*. Founded and edited by Harry Persons Taber, the *Philistine* was a product of Taber's artsy Roycroft Press in East Aurora, New York, which followed certain theories of art and design inspired by England's William Morris and his Kelmscott Press.

Eager to get Stephen for the *Philistine*, Hubbard wooed and flattered. He sent a complimentary issue of the magazine. Then the July issue ran a gleeful parody of Stephen's "I saw a man pursuing the horizon," titled "THE SPOTTED SPRINTER":

After the Manner of Mr. Steamin' Stork.

I saw a man making a fool of himself;
He was writing a poem,
Scratch, scratch, scratch, went his pen,
"Go 'way, Man," says I; "you can't do it."
He picked up a handful of red devils and
Threw them at my head.
"You infernal liar," he howled,
"I can write poetry with my toes!"
I was disquieted. I turned and
Ran like a Blue Streak for the Horizon,
Yelling Bloody Murder.
When I got there I
Bit a piece out of it
And lay down on my stomach and
Thought.
And breathed hard.

Hubbard trusted that Stephen would "not take to heart the little stunt on *The Black Riders*. We will take it all back in the next issue." He asked if Stephen would contribute "a bit of ms" to the fledgling magazine: "We will try awfully hard to help you," Hubbard cajoled. "You are the coming man I believe."

Apparently unperturbed by the parody, Stephen sent Hubbard two poems, "The chatter of a death-demon from a tree-top" and "Each small gleam was a voice." Hubbard accepted the poems, then asked Stephen if he wouldn't "present us these verses" — in the cause of promoting "liberty in Letters." The little magazine was not making any money, and other writers had been generous, he said. He offered bait in the form of a free full-page advertisement of *The Red Badge* in the magazine's September issue. Stephen agreed.

While asking Stephen to give them his work, Hubbard was not afraid to say that he had reservations about it. "I do not confess to an unqualified liking for your work," he wrote in July.

> When you hand me the book I am grown suddenly blind. It rather appeals to my nerves than to my reason — it gives me a thrill. Your work is of a kind so charged with electricity that it cannot be handled. It is all live wire. It eludes all ordinary criticism and it escapes before one can apply his Harvard Rhetorical Test. What is left? I'll tell you, we can stand off and hoot — if we have columns to fill we can fill them with plain hoot. Your lines show too much individuality to pass by and so we laugh and work the feeble joke.

Though he appeared to be a straight shooter, there was a bit of the con in Elbert Hubbard. Like the street vendors in Mexico who sold unsuspecting tourists gilded goods, Hubbard knew how to package his wares seductively and in a way that flattered the buyer's business savvy. He never ran the ad for *The Red Badge*.

Stephen read reviews of *The Black Rider* and pasted them into a scrapbook at Hartwood. He was alternately amused and wounded by them — chuckling, even laughing outright as he lay reading on his brother's couch, then refusing to read any more of them. Perhaps because of the bad press, however, he had second thoughts about having dedicated the book to Hamlin Garland without his permission. When he hadn't heard from Garland by mid-July, Stephen wrote him a note asking if he had seen *The Black Riders* and whether Garland minded the dedication.

Whether or not he was hurt by the critical reaction to his lines, he continued to be proud of the book, feeling that it was his best work. "To Curtis Brown — not at all reluctantly but with enthusiasm — From Stephen Crane," he inscribed one copy.

Over the summer he saw friends, shifting from New York to Hartwood and back again in his desultory way, and did what he had to do to make money. It was camping season. He preferred not to write in the summer, but he needed money. "I have considerable work that is not in the hands of publishers," he wrote invitingly to Copeland & Day, asking if they would be interested in his "favorites" — "eight little grotesque tales of the woods which I wrote when I was clever. The trouble is that they only sum 10000 words and I can make no more." Perhaps thinking of the critical howls over *The Black Riders*, he added that publication of his Sullivan County tales "would gain considerable lengthy abuse no doubt." Evidently Copeland & Day was interested, for he then wrote "My dear L.B.," asking her to send him the tales, for "there is no one in the world has any copies of them but you." But the tone of his note was casual. "Are you coming north this summer? Let me know, when you send the stories. I should like to see you again." He signed it, "Yours as ever   S.C."

He had high hopes for *A Woman Without Weapons*, which was under consideration with the publisher Edward Arnold. Like a new lover, this novel seemed more beautiful than its predecessors — "better than anything yet," he told Harvey Wickham when they ran into each other again.

Later retitled *George's Mother*, the slender new novel was essentially a companion piece to *Maggie*. Stephen had returned to the Bowery tenement where Maggie Johnson lived with her family to write a small, intimate tale about a mother and her dissolute son. Maggie Johnson even appears briefly as the neighbor whom George Kelcey adores from afar, but this is peripheral to the true love story, which is between mother and son. Here again was the Bowery crowd in all its bluster and swagger, the trite and idle saloon crowd, the grinding poverty and shame. Here was the deluded Crane hero, blinded to his actions by his ego. George falls into drunkenness as Maggie fell into prostitution. But the characters are better developed. In place of the stereotyped, brutal Mrs. Johnson is George's mother, Mrs. Kelcey. A former WCTU lecturer who wields pots and brooms "like weapons" and soldiers through her hard life "planning skirmishes, charges, campaigns" and attending prayer meetings, Mrs. Kelcey is Mary Helen Peck Crane turned vulgar and poor. George is Stephen taken to a far extreme — drinking and swearing with abandon, living in violation of his parents' teachings. Like Stephen, George both admires and resists his mother. To the son, "the correctness of her position was maddening," yet she is a figure of courage to him. In the end, she dies while he is getting ready to fight over stolen beer. If the novel suggests Stephen's own sense of guilt at letting his mother down, it is perhaps most autobiographical in the feeling of closeness between mother and son. Like Helen Crane, Mrs. Kelcey has lost five children before the birth of her last child. As the baby in the family born eight years after his youngest surviving sibling, Stephen perhaps felt much the way George did, seeing himself and his mother as figures alone and apart. Her last hopes had depended on him.

For months Bacheller had been releasing Stephen's journalistic pieces from the West in syndication, and throughout the summer this work turned up, like a group of tedious relatives, in scattered newspapers around the country. He had reduced his time in Mexico, which had changed and deepened him, to a series of dullish, wandering reports that ranged conscientiously over local scenery, customs, and items of interest to tourists but offered little more than glimmers of the heat and the local color. The material included three Mexico-inspired fables for which Bacheller got few takers; they ran in the *Nebraska State Journal* and the *New York Advertiser*. The fables — titled "The Victory of the Moon," "The Voice of the Mountain," and "How the Donkey Lifted the Hills" — all center on the theme of betrayal. Man betrays nature; a wife betrays her husband, the Strong Man of the Hills, whom she sees as dusty, ordinary, and uninteresting, for the old Moon.

On August 1 Stephen traveled "four deadly miles up the mountain" to the Twin Lakes campsite in Pike County. Two days later, seemingly as an afterthought, he wrote Ripley Hitchcock and asked him to send all proofs of *The Red Badge* to the local post office. In the next sentence he changed his mind. "As a matter of fact I don't care much to see page proof," he wrote. But he sent the note anyway.

Though he remained interested in seeing any publicity for the book and asked Hawkins to send him "anything in the way of notices," his mind seemed to dwell on *The Black Riders*, the book closest to his heart. On August 3, he requested that Copeland & Day send a copy of the book to Karl Knortz, who had translated Whittier and Longfellow into German. He was "anxious to see your frank opinion of it as expressed in the Leipsic publication," he wrote Knortz.

After a little more than a week "out of the world," Stephen was feeling renewed and eager for more company. He wrote Hawkins, asking him to come up. "I am cruising around the woods in corduroys and feeling great. I have lots of fun getting healthy. Feel great," he said again. "There are six girls in camp and it is with the greatest difficulty that I think coherently on any other subject."

✦

He rode through "the brown October woods" as swift as an eagle, one with his horse. Riding almost bareback, he gave the horse free rein, riding to beat all *pistoleros*. "Lord, I do love a crazy horse with just a little pig-skin between him and me," he wrote Hawkins. He loved the speed of the animal and the feel of the frosty fall air — the absence of clutter. "I missed my first partridge yesterday. Kehplunk. Bad ground, though. Too many white birches." Since arriving in Hartwood some days earlier, he hadn't "written a line yet. Dont intend to for some time."

Since its publication on September 27, *The Red Badge of Courage* (price one dollar) had taken off. The first notices had been overwhelmingly favorable; "they didn't skirmish around and say maybe — perhaps — if — after a time — it is possible — under certain circumstances — but," said Stephen. "No, they were cock-sure." Only a couple had taken shots at him. Still holding a grudge because of Stephen's parade piece, the *New York Tribune* wrote a "grind," as Stephen called it. The review called the novel "a chromatic nightmare" that was as "tedious as a funeral march" and "devoid of tragic power." The author was advised that "the exaggerated common-places of Tolstoi, the brutal coarseness of Zola, and the reduplicated profanities of Maeterlinck, are not commendable ideals for the student of literary art. Nor is decadent morbidity destined to win a commanding place in literature." But most reviewers found the tale powerful and authentic — seemingly a "most impressive and accurate record of actual personal experience," said the *Philadelphia Press*. Even those who didn't like the novel reacted to it strongly; this was clearly not a book to be dismissed.

Readers — who knew what fear was, whether or not they had fought in a war — believed Henry Fleming. They were moved by his battle with himself, by his struggle to measure up, and by his overwhelming shame, universal and timeless themes. They would never tire of the picture of a "fat soldier" trying to steal a horse from a dooryard when a plucky girl rushes out to stop him, to a chorus of cat calls from the regiment; or of the tattered soldier who falls in step with Henry after he flees the forest chapel and asks where he was hit; or of the awesome death of Jim Conklin; or of Henry and another soldier taking the flag from the dead color-sergeant.

The *Detroit Free Press* compared Stephen's style to Victor Hugo's, saying that *The Red Badge* "will give you so vivid a picture of the emotions and the horrors of the battlefield that you will pray your eyes may never look upon the reality." In an unsigned review in the *New York Press*, Edward Marshall defined the novel's reality as intensely personal. "At times the description is so vivid as to be almost suffocating," he wrote. "The reader is right down in the midst of it where patriotism is dissolved into its elements and where only a dozen men can be seen, firing blindly and grotesquely into the smoke. This is war from a new point of view, and it seems more real than when seen with an eye only for large moments and general effects." Other reviews, while favorable, observed that the writer was young; his prose needed discipline. The style needed toning, said the *New York Times*, which yet praised Stephen for creating "a picture which seems to be extraordinarily true, free from any suspicion of ideality, defying every accepted tradition of martial glory." It was, finally, a book that "commends itself to the reader."

The *Chicago Daily Inter-Ocean* was not won over. "Its author is evidently a theoretical soldier and never carried a knapsack or a gun, or heard the roar of battle." While acknowledging that "Mr. Crane tells some things well" and praising him for his "graphic" and "impressive" scenes of battlefield dead, the reviewer found him

> too profuse, profane, and prolix. He doesn't tell things as a soldier would, and he doesn't see things as a soldier did, and will make the real soldier tired to follow him. He has a small conception of the humor and comradeship and spirit of a regiment, or a great army, and leads the reader to believe a regiment of American soldiers is made up of a thousand dull automatons with a great amount of coarseness, if not brutality.

The Red Badge was born into a market hungry for fiction. Fiction dominated book sales in the United States, and the public wanted more. Though many of the top sellers were popular fare, such as Arthur Conan Doyle's detective stories, Richard Harding Davis's *Princess Aline* ("namby-pamby stuff," said the *Bookman*), and Anthony Hope's *Prisoner of Zenda*, a romantic comedy, serious literary fiction and nonfiction could outsell anything. Rudyard Kipling, then living in Vermont, was popular in both America and England. Emile Zola's romances were in demand. Expensive new editions of Honoré de Balzac were being published. Mark Twain and Henry James had been important influences for decades. The best-selling book in both America and England that year was George du Maurier's *Trilby*, based on the author's years as an art student in Paris. Hall Caine's novel *The Manxman* was also extremely successful, as was *So-*

cial Evolution, by Benjamin Kidd, and Max Norau's *Degeneration*, translated from the German, which argued that English romantic literature descended — and degenerated — from the German tradition.

Now *The Red Badge of Courage* seemed to be on everyone's mind. The book arrived on the literary scene "like a flash of lightning out of a clear winter sky; it was at once unprecedented and irresistible," remembered H. L. Mencken, who was about fifteen at the time. "Who was this astonishing young man? A drunken newspaper reporter in New York! One of Davis's heroes! The miracle lifted newspaper reporting to the level of a romantic craft, alongside counterfeiting and mining in the Klondike. More, it gave the whole movement of the nineties a sudden direction and powerful impulse forward."

As in America, the book produced a "sensation" in England. "Crane's work detonated . . . with the impact and force of a twelve-inch shell charged with a very high explosive," wrote Joseph Conrad. Soldiers, writers, and book lovers cheered this novel by "a man inspired, a seer with a gift for rendering the significant on the surface of things and with an incomparable insight into primitive emotions."

Four months after its publication, Stephen Crane's war tale would appear among the top six books on a scattering of bestseller lists throughout the country. Between February and July of 1896, *The Red Badge* claimed the number-one spot several times in New York, as well as in cities such as Cleveland and Denver. More briefly, it was a bestseller in England, last appearing on the lists for the March–April period.

Sales of this psychological novel may have been helped by American readers' strong interest in books on hypnotism and mental science and by the growing demand for books on "mental healing." Even the word "red" in the title, which Stephen had considered deleting to satisfy his publisher's desire for a shorter title, perhaps made the book more marketable. Two other top-selling books in America, and two in England, had "red" in the title.*

While the noise about *The Red Badge* went on, *The Black Riders* was causing its own stir. In August the poem "I saw a man pursuing the horizon" had been parodied in the *New York Recorder* ("I saw a meter measuring gas," it began); and Elbert Hubbard wrote to Stephen to say that

---

* In the United States, *The Red Republic* and *Red Men and White;* in England, *The Red True Story Book* by A. Lang and *The Red Cockade* by S. Weyman (this was also a bestseller in many parts of America).

"The chatter of a death-demon from a tree-top," published that month in the *Philistine*, had caused a lot of talk. In September the *New Orleans Picayune* attacked both Stephen and the *Philistine* for their pretensions in a parodic poem.

When *The Red Badge* was published, Stephen and Frederic Lawrence had gone to Wanamaker's and bought a copy of the red-orange book with black and beige lettering. Then they "tenderly carried it around the corner to the old Rathskellar, there to feast our eyes on its pages," wrote Lawrence. Stephen inscribed the book to his friend. He was suddenly flush with cash. At some point Appleton gave him "a few hundred dollars" and, said Willis Brooks Hawkins, he "came to me, joyously declaring that he had more money than his hand had ever clutched before. At once he began speculating on how he was going to spend it. 'First,' he said, 'I am going to have two pairs of trousers and, by gosh, a pair of suspenders for each.' What he really did buy first was a complete and expensive outfit for horseback riding — a Mexican saddle, elaborately decorated bridle, etc."

But just weeks after the reviews started coming in, Stephen's ambivalence toward the war novel began to show. While telling Hawkins to "clip anything you see in the papers and send it," he was already nervous about his big success and beginning to separate himself from it. "I have heard indirectly from Brentano's that the damned 'Red Badge' is having a very nice sale," he wrote Hawkins. As if to distance himself further, in mid-October he left New York and moved all his personal belongings to Edmund's house in Hartwood.

Before leaving New York he arranged a poker game in the loft on the top floor of 165 West 23rd Street, which he was sharing with Post Wheeler. Hawkins turned up with an acquaintance named Harry B. Smith, who assumed that the author of *The Red Badge of Courage* had either read Zola's *Le Débâcle* or was himself a soldier. The place had just enough furniture "for a small poker game," said Smith. Stephen had decorated the room with his Mexican saddle, Indian blankets, and a piece of pottery used as an ash catcher — "some kind of an Aztec damned thing," he drawled in explanation. Smith noted that Stephen was "just a kid," as Hawkins had said he was, "but thin, pallid, looking like a consumptive." When the poker game broke up at about three o'clock in the morning and the players were leaving, they noticed a girl asleep in Stephen's partitioned bed.

"Gosh!" said Crane. "I didn't hear her come in."

There were some facetious comments. "Is it Maggie?" asked one of the ribald, referring to Crane's story.

"Some of her," said Crane.

Stephen was now working on a new novel that had nothing to do with *pistoleros* or war. In a letter to Ripley Hitchcock on October 29, he managed a weak endorsement of the new work, titled *The Third Violet*. "The story is working out fine," he said; he had seven short, rough chapters already done (he neglected to say that he had begun the novel the year before). He wasn't sure he could produce more than 25,000 words altogether — perhaps 35,000, if Appleton wanted the novel. "Can you endure that length?" he asked Hitchcock, adding defensively: "— I mean, should you like the story otherwise, can you use a story that length?"

"I am not sure that it is any good," he wrote Hawkins. His opinion of the work seesawed; he couldn't decide whether the thing was "clever" or "nonsensical." The writing, though, was "easy . . . I can finish a chapter each day," he said. Three days after writing Hawkins that the novel was a third done, he reported in a letter to Elbert Hubbard that it was "over half finished." In any case, he had decreed that the work "must end in forty-five days."

"My Dear Mr. Crane," began the letter from the Committee for the Philistine Society dated November 5. "Recognizing your merit as a man and your genius as a poet, and wishing that the world should know you better, the Society of the Philistines tender you a dinner to take place at the Iroquois Hotel in Buffalo in about one month." Awaiting only Stephen's acceptance, said the letter, a date would be set and invitations would go out "to 200 of the best known writers, publishers and newspaper men of the United States and England." Stephen would, of course, be the guest of the Philistines, his transportation and accommodations provided for. The letter was signed by Elbert Hubbard, H. P. Taber, and three Buffalo newspapermen, William MacIntosh, managing editor of the *Buffalo News*, E. R. White, also of the *News*, and A. G. Blythe, of the *Buffalo Express*.

"What do you suppose made the Philistines do this dinner thing?" Stephen asked Hawkins. "Was it because I wrote for their magazine?"

There were bigger names the group could have chosen to honor. "You could have knocked me over with a gas-pipe when I got their bid," he wrote Hawkins, sending along a copy of the invitation he'd written out. To the banquet committee he wrote, "An acceptance, it seems to me, is a tacit admission of my worthiness in the circumstances." To Hawkins he panicked about his clothes. "My dress suit took to the woods long ago and my 1895 overcoat is not due until 1896. I have not owned a pair of patent leather shoes in three years," he wrote on November 8. "Write me at once and tell me how to get out of the thing. Of course I am dead sore but I think if you will invent for me a very decent form of refusal, I will still be happy up here with my woods."

Hawkins urged him to accept the invitation and promised to take care of his clothing problem. Stephen's relief was almost palpable. Though he blushed at himself for being "low enough to grab at your generosity," he was "delighted and charmed" by Hawkins's letter. As for the clothes, "my chest, bad luck to it, measures 35 inches — scant — and my leg is a 33 — worse luck. And foot — rot it — is a seven," he wrote. "There! It is over! I feel as if I have told you that I am a damned thief."

His misery at the idea of having to refuse the invitation now gone, he wrote his acceptance. He would go to the banquet and "have a dandy time, I know, . . . satisfied that it will do me an immense amount of good."

The banquet, to be held sometime in December, said Hubbard, was to be more than just a pleasant diversion: "You represent a 'cause' and we wish in a dignified, public (and at the same time) elegant manner, to recognize that cause." "I am getting frightened already," Stephen told Hawkins. "Imagine me representing a 'cause'." He repeatedly asked Hawkins to be there. He was counting on his presence.

Isolated in Hartwood, Stephen had been feeling the lack of camaraderie. At an exciting and pivotal moment in his career, when *The Red Badge* reviews were pouring in, and success finally seemed within his grasp, there was no one to share it with — "you know there is nobody here whom one can talk to about [the reviews] at all," he confided to Hawkins.

When he wasn't working on his new novel, he sometimes sailed out on the "blue crystal" lake in a little catboat. When she proceeded to windward, the boat tacked, leaning like a house shingle, he told Hawkins. The locals "are expecting my death shortly."

On November 19, he took the catboat out alone in a high wind —

"the stiffest breeze we've had in moons," he said later. And everything went wrong, as he wrote to Hawkins afterward.

> When I got near to the head of the lake, the boat was scud-
> ding before the wind in a manner to make your heart leap.
> Then we got to striking snags — hidden stumps, floating
> logs, sunken brush, more stumps, — you might have thought
> ex-Senator Holman of Indiana was there. Anything that
> could obstruct, promptly and gracefully obstructed. Up to
> the 5th stump I had not lost my philosophy but at the 22d I
> was swearing like cracked ice. And at the appearance of the
> 164th, I perched on the rail, a wild and gibbering maniac.

He could not remember ever being "so furiously and ferociously angry." He compared himself to Judge, Edmund's Belton setter. "When the girls run Judge out of the kitchen, his soul becomes so filled with hate of the world, that, outside, he pounces on the first dog he meets." The size of the dog didn't matter; collie or pup, "he whales them and they roar." The dog simply needed someone to take it out on. "This is the way I felt up at the pond," he told Hawkins. "But there was nobody there."

When Edmund read the first chapters of the new novel, "he finished them up without a halt," Stephen wrote Hawkins. Still, "he is an awful stuff in literature." Stephen wasn't sure he should trust his brother's judgment. "Understand, he thinks my style wouldn't be used by the devil to patch his trousers with. I think he — Teddie — discovered the fellow and the girl in the story and read on to find out if they married. He hung around for a time asking for more chapters but I sent him away."

Stephen worked on his novel as though he were outrunning an advancing army. On November 23 he was calculating that the end was "eight days" away. He asked Louis Senger to read the manuscript. "Up here, I miss some little public to impale," he said. Needing money, he was sending out what he could to editors who had asked him to contribute to their publications — a poem and a sketch to the *Chap-Book*, a tale to the *Bookman*— taking care to enclose stamps for returns. But he hadn't made "a cent, mainly because I want it so badly," he wrote Hawkins. *Leslie's Weekly* praised a story as "very stunning" but declined it because of another tale they were running. "Irving Bacheller had tried hard to accept a story of mine, but he said that he couldn't." Adding to his money worries was the knowledge that Hawkins was hard-pressed himself, apparently because he had either loaned Stephen money or was using money of his own to purchase Stephen's clothes for the banquet. "I begin to think you are disgusted with me," Stephen told him, but Hawkins reassured him: "I like this sorto' thing. Don't you let it bother you a bit. It isn't as if I were rich. Its one poor devil faking up a way for another poor devil to get his fingers into a pie."

Reviews of *The Red Badge* continued to stream in; there were more than forty by mid-November. Stephen had subscribed to a clipping service in Boston that billed only every three months. Though the favorable reviews still outweighed the negative ones — only "about six in the patch were roasts" — he was stung by some of the notices from his home territory. "New York, throughout, has treated me worse than any other city," he complained to Hawkins; the sole exception was the *Evening Post*. "Damn New York." He did not mention the unfavorable review William Dean Howells had written for *Harper's Weekly*. While acknowledging Stephen's ability to convey war's "sense of deaf and blind turmoil," Howells had disparaged his use of dialect, which he found unconvincing. In summary, he wrote that "on the psychological side the book is worth while as an earnest of the greater things that we may hope from a new talent working upon a high level, not quite as clearly as yet, but strenuously."

Whatever Stephen felt on reading Howells's review, he was too loyal and gentlemanly to disparage the man who had been "so generous with me," who had been "so much to me personally." He still regarded Howells as one of his literary fathers. As a reader, Howells had limitations. He had not seen the necessity for the profanity in *Maggie;* he had even disparaged Mark Twain's use of the word "hell" in *Huckleberry Finn*. Clearly, Howells was unable to appreciate — or even comprehend —*The Red Badge of Courage*. This was not realism. Howells's own realism was literal and constricted; it did not include impressionistic, psychological description, the poetic use of metaphor, the animistic and hallucinatory images of a mind under stress. This kind of writing was simply beyond him. He was "glad" that Stephen was getting his "glory young," yet he would "remain true to my first love, 'Maggie.' That is better than all the Black Riders and Red Badges," he would say. Stephen undoubtedly understood this. He had his own ideas about truth in writing, which was not the same as Howells's realism, "that misunderstood and abused word," Stephen called it. That was all right. What mattered was Howells's unwavering support.

The signs of his literary importance continued to appear. The *Union* proposed a piece on Stephen Crane as part of a series on eminent writers such as William Dean Howells, Hamlin Garland, Eugene Field, and Sarah Orne Jewett. To test the power of his name, Stephen had Walter Senger — Louis's brother — type one of Stephen's stories and send it to a magazine under Walker's name. When the story was rejected, Stephen sent it again under his own name. "It was instantly accepted," said Senger. And so he was a success. Yet he was broke. In October Appleton had sold the British rights of *The Red Badge* for thirty-five pounds without providing for an author's royalty.

The Philistine banquet was set for December 19. Invitations had been mailed to seven hundred "folks we hoped couldn't come," Hubbard said later — to seemingly every important literary man and woman the Philistine Committee could think of, including Irving Bacheller, Ambrose Bierce, Simon Brentano (of the New York bookstore), Stephen's publisher, Daniel Appleton, and his editor, Ripley Hitchcock. (Hitchcock was later "disgusted" to learn that his letter of regret had been printed in the souvenir menu with a crucial mistake — a remark referring to writers of genius as "prophets" was rendered as "puppets." "I was not in the least offended," Stephen assured him.)

Feeling "elated" by the acceptances ("none have yet confessed that they have never heard of me and wanted to know why in the devil you were going to dine me"), and indebted to Hubbard for all the trouble he was going to, Stephen was also embarrassed about the "hideously long list" of guests he had sent Hubbard to add to the Philistines' list. "I have been aroused at night by a dream of them all writing acceptances," he said.

He spent everything he had to get to Buffalo as cheaply as possible. He'd managed to scratch up a few items of good clothing (coat, vest, and trousers courtesy of Hawkins), buying "one full dress shirt and what goes with it. I have a damn fine hat," he wrote Hawkins shortly before leaving Hartwood. But he had "no overcoat save that little gauze one." He had borrowed Edmund's patent leather shoes "and I am sleeping with them under my pillow," he said. Hubbard had sent him train fare.

> "The time has come," the Walrus said,
> "To talk of many things;"

The lines from Chapter 4 of *Alice in Wonderland* were printed in capital letters across the top of the striking dinner menu produced by the Roycroft Press studio, in mocking tribute to *The Black Riders*. Below them, rocking horses mounted by black riders tumbled from the sky above a lone figure with outstretched arms running toward the sun at the earth's horizon line, an allusion to Stephen's "I saw a man pursuing the horizon."

The long table in the Colonial Parlor of the Genesee Hotel in Buffalo was banked with carnations and smilax. Henry Taber sat at the head in the role of chief host and toastmaster, the usually commanding Hubbard at the foot, looking "timid," thought a guest. Wearing his new and borrowed clothes, transformed into an "immaculate" figure for the evening, the guest of honor was seated at Taber's right. He had gathered his friends around him for support — Hawkins on the right, Frank Noxon, now a newspaperman and drama critic for the *Boston Record*, diagonally across from him. Thinking that Stephen would "feel freer" without them there, Nelson Greene and W. W. Carroll had declined the invitation.

Throughout the evening the wine and champagne flowed freely. After dinner Taber rose to deliver his speech in praise of Stephen Crane when he was interrupted. "Probably, the most unique —"

"Can 'unique' be compared?" someone asked. And the banquet in Stephen's honor turned into a roast. The air grew "tense" but was relieved by Robert Mitchell Floyd of Delaware, who jeered at the speakers "for their grouch," said a guest.

From where Frank Noxon sat, Stephen appeared to be "having the time of his life," but Hawkins saw that his friend was "in a blue funk." He would occasionally "nudge me and utter a nearly suppressed groan or half-whispered word of disapproval of what I knew he regarded as kindly-intentioned bosh; for he had repeatedly assured me that he had done nothing to warrant any part of this praise," said Hawkins.

Finally the table grew quiet. Hubbard introduced Stephen as "the strong voice now heard in America — the voice of Stephen Crane," and praised him "as man and genius." Stephen was called on to give "a few words." He reluctantly but graciously got to his feet.

Wetting his dry lips, he took a long moment before beginning to talk. The twenty-four-year-old author called himself "a working newspaper man who was trying to do what he could 'since he had recovered from college' with the machinery that had come into his hands — doing it sincerely, if clumsily, and simply setting forth in his own way his own impressions," William MacIntosh wrote in the next day's *Buffalo News*.

"I write what is in me, and it will be enough to follow with obedience the promptings of that inspiration, if it be worthy of so dignified a name," quoted another reporter. As for the squabbling that had preceded his speech, Stephen said that "the man who can't stand the gaff isn't a man at all; he's a hell of a bum sport" — and then he sat down. Here was a young man who didn't "take himself over seriously," wrote MacIntosh.

Outraged by what he called "the sight of a young ox led to the slaughter," Claude Bragdon, a prominent Rochester artist and illustrator, rose to leave. "I come here to do honor to Stephen Crane, not to ridicule him," he said. "I regret to take this step, but I can no longer remain in the room." Willis Hawkins rose and blocked him. He knew Stephen — he had "slept with him, eaten with him, starved with him, ridden with him, swum with him," and like everyone present he loved and admired him, he said. He assured Bragdon that Stephen Crane preferred the light-hearted tone of the evening to a solemn eulogy. Stephen nodded his head in agreement, the guests applauded, and Bragdon sat down. Just after midnight, the party "in honor and mockery of Mr. Stephen Crane," as one of the guests put it, broke up.

After the banquet, Stephen went home to East Aurora, New York, with Elbert Hubbard for a few days. Hubbard's twelve-year-old son would remember watching the "great personage" Stephen Crane coming down the plank walk to the house, Hubbard carrying his bag in a tending, parental way. At dinner that night, Stephen seemed to the boy "afraid and timid" and let his host do the talking. But East Aurora was trotting-horse country, and in this pretty setting smelling of horses and strap oil and straw Stephen was soon himself again. The two men rode in the relaxed, fearless style of men born to the saddle. Stephen, like a westerner, used long stirrups and loose rein, giving the horse her head; Hubbard held his reins high, elbows pointing out. Hubbard admired Stephen's "happy abandon" while sitting secure in the saddle. Stephen had his eye on one of Hubbard's mares, and he began haggling over a price as though he could afford her.

Back in Hartwood, having exchanged his evening finery for corduroys, he laughed when he heard that some guests invited to the banquet had regretted that they had not been able to be there to assist at the "Hanging of the Crane." Yet he continued to take the honor seriously. He sent Nellie Crouse William MacIntosh's newspaper article, copies of the Philistine Committee's letter of invitation, and his own reply. He "was very properly enraged at the word 'poet' which continually reminds me of long-hair and seems to me to be a most detestable form of insult," he told her.

Though others would feel that Hubbard had used Stephen to attract publicity for his magazine, the correspondence tells a different story. After the Philistine dinner and the visit to East Aurora, "Mr. Crane" became "Steve," or "Stevie," or "My Dear Poet;" "Mr. Hubbard" gave way to "Hub" or "Haitch." "I am always your friend," Stephen inscribed in a copy of *Maggie*. He made a point of reading Hubbard's 1894 novel *No Enemy (But Himself)*, and immediately wrote him a note of extravagant praise. For his part, Hubbard waved aside Stephen's offer in February to send him a check for the mare he wanted to buy — money he knew Stephen would have to "pinch . . . from various places" — and told him to bring the check when he came for the horse in the spring.

Stephen finished *The Third Violet*, an unsuccessful romance drawn from his courtship of Lily Munroe and his days among the artists at the old Art Students' League building. On December 27 he sent Hitchcock the manuscript, without enthusiasm and with apologies for sending the handwritten copy instead of a typescript. (Having had the novel typed locally with discouraging results, he'd decided that the handwritten copy was the more presentable. "Typewriting is too new an art for the woods," he explained to Hitchcock, adding that Hitchcock could charge the typing to his account, if necessary.) He was already feeling resentful of the comparisons to *The Red Badge* he knew were inevitable. "I hear that the damned book 'The Red Badge of Courage' is doing very well in England," he wrote Curtis Brown. And he confided that he did not expect Appleton to want the new novel. "It's pretty rotten work. I used myself up in the accursed 'Red Badge.'"

The noise about Stephen Crane was that he could write about war as few others could — as few writers ever had. Literate people and war veterans alike said that Crane was better than Zola, superior even to Tolstoy at depicting war as it really was. John Phillips of the McClure Syndicate offered him a contract to write a series on Civil War battlefields. Stephen was interested but wary. To begin with, he already had "a good many orders and requests," which were keeping him busy. And he was reluctant to take on additional work that would require him to give up his winter plans. For if he accepted the assignment, he wanted to do it properly. "One of the first things I would want to do, would be to visit the battlefield — which I was to describe — at the time of year when it was fought," he wrote Phillips. And then there was the problem of secondary research. "The preliminary reading and the subsequent reading, the investigations of all kinds, would take much time." (He didn't add that he was not interested in book research.) He would have to be scrupulous in the pieces that Phillips proposed.

> If I did not place the only original crown of pure gold on the heads of at least twelve generals they would arise and say: "This damned young fool was not there. I was however. And this is how it happened." I evaded them in the Red Badge because it was essential that I should make my battle a type and name no names.

He did not turn down the assignment. He thought he might take it on in the spring, when his workload was lighter, "and the anniversaries of the fights begin to occur." In the meantime, if Phillips would tell him which battle he wanted Stephen "to tackle" first, he would "try to do some reading on it," he said.

In Mexico the previous spring, the brightly colored serapes had reminded him of a Christmas cornucopia. Now it was Christmas in Hartwood, and his own serape draped the tea table in Edmund's house. This year, too, was ending with the prospect of a newspaper assignment that would send him traveling. "I am considering a start very shortly to some quarter of the world where mail is uncertain," he wrote Hitchcock. He envisioned "a far country where the women were said to go about displaying a 'very fetching' zone of nakedness by way of the waist-line," he told his friends. But he didn't have any money. He couldn't buy Hubbard's mare or even a new overcoat.

Writing to Curtis Brown, Hawkins, and Nellie Crouse on the last day of the year, he sounded dispirited. The Philistine banquet was behind him, *The Third Violet* was finished and mailed to the publisher, its fate uncertain. He told Curtis Brown he was "plodding along."

In December Stephen received an extremely gracious letter from his new English publisher, William Heinemann. "We think so highly of your work — of its actuality — virility & literary distinction that we have been very pleased to take special pains to place it before the British public," wrote Sidney Pawling, an editor and partner in the publishing house. Some one hundred copies of *The Red Badge* had been sent out to reviewers and "leading literary men" in England. Arthur Waugh noted in a London letter to the *Critic* "the great and deserved" success of *The Red Badge* in England, an infrequent occurrence for an American book, and "the more welcome" because Crane's novel had real literary value — it was "no vulgarly popular success." People all over England were reading *The Red Badge of Courage*, he said, and "the best-esteemed critics" admired it. Until now, "Mr. Stephen Crane" had "been practically unknown upon this side of the ocean. Now, however, everyone is asking about him."

8

RED HAIR

Hartwood, N.Y.
January 1st [1896]

Dear Mr Howells: Every little time I hear from some friend a kind thing you have said of me, an interest which you have shown in my work. I have been so long conscious of this, that I am grown uncomfortable in not being able to express to you my gratitude and so I seize the New Year's Day as an opportunity to thank you and tell you how often I think of your kind benevolent life.

Sincerely yours
Stephen Crane

By January 1896 the clamor about *The Red Badge* was beginning to overwhelm Stephen. At first gratified by the attention, he sent copies of one notice to his friends. (This in spite of telling Nellie Crouse that he "never encouraged friends to read my work — they sometimes advise one.") He was enjoying the effect of his success on his family. They were quite "swelled up," he wrote Hawkins. "Gee! I simply cant go around and see 'em near enough. It's great. I am no longer a black sheep but a star." Then the praise came thundering down on him. It had been easier to be the mark "for every humorist in the country," he said.

Facing another dinner in his honor, at the Author's Club, he was experiencing the same mixed feelings he'd had about the Philistine banquet. "In one sense, it portends an Ordeal but in the larger sense it overwhelms me in pride and arrogance to think that I have such friends," he wrote Hawkins. He needed a photograph of himself to send the *Bookman* for a February article; he wrote Senger for that. From Port Jervis on January 11 went a flurry of notes written that day:

> Dear L: If you dont send the photograph, I will do you.
> > Very truly yours
> > Stephen Crane

> Dear Louis: Have you sent it?
> > Sincerely yours
> > Stephen Crane

> Dear Louis Why dont you send it?
> > Faithfully yours
> > Stephen Crane

The next day he reluctantly left "the blessed quiet hills of Hartwood" for New York. "McClure is having one of his fits of desire to have me write for him and I am obliged to go see him," he wrote Nellie Crouse. Appleton had accepted *The Third Violet* for publication, and he needed to see Ripley Hitchcock about some revisions Hitchcock thought necessary. But he was "hanged if I stay in New York more than one day. Then I shall hie me back to Hartwood."

But he stayed away many days. Planning to do research on the series for McClure, he briefly left New York to visit some Civil War battlefields in northern Virginia, which just then "would be the very same color of things of the days the battle [of Fredericksburg] was fought." From Virginia he returned to New York, where he was feted and cheered. When he read the English reviews of *The Red Badge*, he felt proud but also "afraid, afraid that I would be satisfied with the little, little things that I have done," he later wrote Nellie Crouse. "For the first time I saw the majestic forces which are arrayed against man's success." He dined at the Lantern Club and was toasted by Irving Bacheller. He knew everyone there, "and to see all those old veterans arise and [look] solemnly at me, quite knocked the wind from me," he said. "When it came my turn to get up I could only call them damned fools and sit down again." The rest of his visit was so taken up with "silly engagements," he felt that he no longer owned "a minute" of his time. He was unable "to breathe in that accursed tumult," he told Hawkins. He could handle "being called a damned ass," he said to Hitchcock, "but this sudden new admiration of my friends has made a gibbering idiot of me. I shall stick to my hills."

He left town on January 26 so abruptly, even running out on Hawkins, that he afterward felt "utterly dejected," he wrote him. By way of apology, he sent his friend the original manuscript of *The Red Badge*, mailing it express. "You dont know how that damned city tore my heart out by the roots and flung it under the heels of it's noise," he wrote Hawkins. "On Friday it had me keyed to a point where I was no more than a wild beast and I had to make a dash."

Stephen could not elude the demand for more war stories. Between September 1895, when *The Red Badge* was published, and February 1896, he produced five new Civil War stories, four of them very fine. He told Ripley Hitchcock he thought they should "go ahead with The Third Violet. People may just as well discover now that the high dramatic key of The Red Badge cannot be sustained." *The Red Badge* had seemed "a pretty good thing when I did it," he wrote Nellie Crouse on January 13, but it no longer had any "attractions" for him. He needed to prove that he could do better work. He suggested that McClure send him "to the scene of the next great Street-car strike. I feel that I could do something then to dwarf the Red Badge, which I do not think is very great shakes."

The new tales — "Three Miraculous Soldiers," "The Veteran," "An Indiana Campaign," "An Episode of War," and "The Little Regiment" — again depicted military engagements without identifying them as particular battles, though "The Little Regiment" was based on the battle of Fredericksburg. The mentions of General Longstreet in "Three Miraculous Soldiers" and of Chancellorsville in "The Veteran" were anomalies in Crane's Civil War fiction. For Stephen, research-based writing — the "daily battle with a tangle of facts and emotions" — was especially arduous. A reader but not a scholar, he was handicapped by his paltry formal education. At first he found "The Little Regiment" with its research "awfully hard. I have invented the sum of my invention in regard to war and this story keeps me in internal despair," he wrote Hawkins. "However I am coming on it very comfortably after all." He even found a way to do it "that is not without a mild satisfaction," he wrote Nellie Crouse. When he finished the story in February, he felt that he had done his best work. He had also written "positively my last thing dealing with battle." To Nellie he wrote, "Hang all war stories."

The best of the new tales shimmered with the kind of authentic detail that persuaded readers of *The Red Badge* that Stephen Crane had served in the Civil War: the burning smell of gunfire on the cold night air; the noise of rumors going round the camps; the almost palpable presence of a giant, slumbering army; the rubber blanket on which a lieutenant lays out precisely measured coffee rations; the busy, impatient surgeon who is about to amputate a man's arm; the emotions of men in battle. Stephen found the poetry in war: "This aggregation of wheels, levers, motors, had a beautiful unity, as if it were a missile. The sound of it was a war-chorus that reached into the depths of man's emotion," he wrote in "An Episode of War." In "The Little Regiment" a wounded soldier rises from his dead comrades to return to his regiment: "When he arose, his clothing peeled from the frozen ground like wet paper."

Sometimes his powers failed him: "Three Miraculous Soldiers" was no more than popular magazine fare. And yet he was stretching himself, showing a deepening gift for characterization. His portraits of young boys, old men, and squabbling brothers were wonderfully true. In "An Indiana Campaign," a charming story about a veteran of the Indian War who is left to protect a sleepy town during the Civil War, he produced his best piece of comic writing to date. The impression in these tales is of a writer enjoying himself, letting go. "At the roadside a brigade was making coffee and buzzing with talk like a girls' boarding school," he wrote in "An Episode of War."

As if to underscore his decision to write no more about war, in "The Veteran" he kills off Henry Fleming. Now an old man, Fleming is a hero both to his young grandson, Jimmy, and to his town. He good-naturedly answers the same tired questions from civilians: "Could you see the whites of their eyes?" But one day Henry is asked if he was ever afraid "in them battles." The old man responds with startling honesty. He admits to running at Chancellorsville — a revelation that horrifies and humiliates young Jim. The story ends with Fleming dying in a barn fire while trying to rescue some colts.

> When the roof fell in, a great funnel of smoke swarmed toward the sky, as if the old man's mighty spirit, released from its body — a little bottle — had swelled like the genie of fable. The smoke was tinted rose-hue from the flames,

and perhaps the unutterable midnights of the universe will
have no power to daunt the color of this soul.

✦

Back among the Hartwood hills after his tumultuous visit to New York,
Stephen now applied himself to the task of winning Nellie Crouse in
Akron, writing her uncharacteristically long letters he called "chronicles."
Only his letters tell the story of the romance; Nellie's have not survived.
Written over a two-month period, from December 31, 1895, to March 1,
1896, they give the picture of a young man trying hard to impress a
woman who apparently showed some interest; he refers to "that lot of
things which you say you wish to know." She wrote back promptly at his
request and sent him her picture. The photograph "awed" him; "the light
of social experience in your eyes somewhat terrifies this poor outer pagan," he wrote. He was obvious, yet gentlemanly, about his interest in her.
Since meeting her a year earlier, he had regarded her as "a curiously potential attraction. I tell it to you frankly, assured that no harm could come
from any course so honest. I dont know what it is or why it is. I have never
analyzed it." Physically attracted to her, he persuaded himself that he saw
in her a "remarkably strong personality," a woman who was out of the ordinary. Every letter from her was impatiently anticipated, then endlessly
analyzed. In his second letter he asked her to "please keep in mind that
there is a young . . . corduroy-trousered, briar-wood [pipe] smoking young
man — in Hartwood, N.Y. who is eagerly awaiting a letter from you."

He could not account for the way he felt drawn to her after only one
meeting. How could "a practical and experienced person," he wrote, apparently straight-faced, "be so attracted by a vague, faint shadow — in
fact a young woman who crossed his vision just once and that a considerable time ago?" And yet her letters "reinforced" him. He was coming
to know her, and he knew that his "instinctive liking for you was not a
mistake."

He ventured closer. She was a kindred soul, he implied, perhaps the
only woman who had ever understood him. "No women — not even the
women who have cared for me — ever truly knew the best and worst of
me," he wrote on January 26. "There are three men in this world who
know me about as I am but no woman does." She had stirred something
in him, shaking loose a cornucopia of words about truth and simplicity
and courage and life's lonely struggle.

"I observe that you think it wretched to go through life unexplained. Not at all. You have no idea how it simplifies matters," he wrote, then attempted to explain himself. He was "quite honest and simple. On most occasions I contrive to keep myself that way but sometimes the social crisis catches me unawares." He had little use for society: "I have been told 84646 times that I am not the cream of mankind but you make a sort of an inference that I might myself think that I was of it, so I hasten to say that although I never line the walls or clutter the floors of ballrooms, my supreme detestation is dowdy women although they may be as intellectual as Mahomet."

Her photograph shows an intellectual-looking young woman who was far from dowdy. Above her pale skirt, which almost touches the ground, she is all dark velvet, wearing puffed sleeves, a high collar, and an elaborate velvet hat. Her left hand is concealed in a velvet muff; in the other hand she holds a small dog who stands on a low wall. Though dressed in the height of fashion, she appears anything but frivolous.

She was bored, weary of life; he was, too. "For my own part, I am minded to die in my thirty-fifth year," he wrote. "I think that is all I care to stand. I don't like to make wise remarks on the aspect of life but I will say that it doesn't strike me as particularly worth the trouble." Miss Crouse liked "the man of fashion"? So did he — "if he does it well. The trouble is . . . that the heavy social life demands one's entire devotions. Time after time, I have seen the social lion turn to a lamb and fail — fail at precisely the moment men should not fail." The important masculine virtues were knowing good poetry, music, and drama from bad; knowing "good claret and good poker-playing"; knowing "how to stand steady when they see cocked revolvers and death comes down and sits on the back of a chair and waits"; knowing how to "treat a woman tenderly not only when they feel amiable but when she most needs tender treatment." He presented himself as a gun-toting, horse-riding, courage-loving man who shied away from ballrooms and was reduced to inarticulateness in the presence of a charming young lady, and yet a literate thinking man, a man of taste and discernment. He was a man of both claret and cards, part saloon, part drawing-room. Like the corduroys he favored, he was both rugged and soft to the touch.

While affecting a casual attitude about his work, Stephen was careful to let Nellie know of upcoming publications, and he sent her the occasional story, though not his best work; the mediocre "A Gray Sleeve" was "not in any sense a good story and the intolerable pictures make it worse," he said. (He did not say it was a love story that suggested his attraction to her.) He sent "One Dash — Horses," which had a sensitive, romantic hero based on himself, he admitted. He gave her *The Black Riders*: "I might as well let you know the worst of me at once. Although *Maggie* perhaps is the worst — or the most unconventional — of me." He welcomed her opinion of his work — "I think your advice would have a charm to it that I do not find in some others" — and yet when she suggested in a letter that he could learn from the reviewers, he replied with a high-handed, self-assured diatribe that might have discouraged her.

> Oh, heavens! Apparently you have not studied the wiles of the learned reviewer very much or you never would have allowed yourself to write that sentence. There is only one person in the world who knows less than the average reader. He is the average reviewer. I would already have been a literary corpse, had I ever paid the slightest attention to the reviewers.

And he went on to tell her of the "enthusiastic" English reviews of *The Red Badge*.

There was a touch of desperation in Stephen's letters to Nellie; he tried too hard to win her, protesting his virtues too much, offering his opinions at excessive length. While encouraging the picture of himself as a successful young author on the rise, he skirted the financial part of success, which he could not give her. He scorned "the new-rich," he told her, the man who thought that having money was equal to being well-bred. He was contemptuous of men who wanted to be great in order "to be admired, to be stared at by the mob." When she suggested that she was intimidated by him, he tried to downplay his gifts. "I am afraid you laugh at me sometimes in your letters. . . . I am often marvelously a blockhead and incomparably an idiot. I reach depths of stupidity of which most people cannot dream. This is usually in the case of a social crisis. A social crisis simply leaves me witless and gibbering," he wrote, unintentionally creating an impression of a socially inept, clumsy man.

He became impatient to see her again. By his second letter, on January 6, he felt sufficiently encouraged to mention visiting her. He laid the groundwork by telling her he wanted to travel to Arizona to study the Apaches. Someone in Boston had asked him to write a play, and Stephen wanted to do something with Apaches in it. He would take the Erie Railroad. "This route leads through Akron, as I distinctly remember. Furthermore, — if I dont go to Arizona — I shall at any rate go to Buffalo and if you will please tell me that Akron is not far from Buffalo, I will make an afternoon — or possibly evening — call on you. Sure." He would "invade Akron," he wrote, then tried to make light of it. "You will feel embarrassed. I'll bet on it. Here is a young man who proclaims an admiration of you from afar. He comes to Akron. You dont care either way but then you feel a sort of a moral responsibility. Great Scott! What a situation!"

Two weeks later he sounded as though a visit to Akron were a certainty. He hoped that "when" he met her there, "it could be in riding weather. I could bring some toys and I dare say I could rent some kind of a steed in Akron. My pilgrimage to the west via the Erie will please me immensely if it achieve a ride, a tea and *An Evening Call*, in Akron. Considering, February weather, I can forego the ride." But he might go to Europe instead — that is, if she were going. Would she be coming East in the summer? "I hope so. I never work in the summer. It is one long lazy time to fool away." By February 11 Stephen had received a letter containing the news that she was sailing for Europe. "I wish you would tell me more about your European trip," he wrote back. "By the way, if you forbid me going over on the same boat, it must be because you think I am not clever."

Writing from a friend's apartment at 33 East 22nd Street on March 1, Stephen began his last letter to Nellie, which like the letter before it, contained no salutation. Perhaps feeling that he had passed the "Miss Crouse" stage with her but could not properly address her by her Christian name, he omitted her name altogether.

The young lady had put an end to his hopes. "Do you know, I have succeeded in making a new kind of an idiot of myself?" he began. His ever-growing success had put him on social display until he could no longer endure it. In Hartwood he had "sat before twelve fireplaces and drank 842 cups of tea," and finally escaped only to find things "worse" in New York; "mine own friends feel bitterly insulted if I do not see them twelve times a day — in short they are all prepared to find me grown vain. You know what I mean. That disgraceful Red Badge is doing so well that my importance has widened and everybody sits down and calmly waits to see me be a chump." He was "in despair. The storm-beaten little robin who has no place to lay his head, does not feel so badly as do I."

Dear me, how much am I getting to admire graveyards —
the calm unfretting unhopeing end of things — serene absence of passion — oblivious to sin — ignorant of the accursed golden hopes that flame at night and make a man run
his legs off and then in the daylight of experience turn out to
be ingenious traps for the imagination. If there is a joy of
living I cant find it. The future? The future is blue with
obligations — new trials — conflicts. It was a rare old wine
the gods brewed for mortals. Flagons of despair —

Prolonging his goodbye, Stephen didn't end the letter until two weeks
later, on March 18. He was writing from Washington, D.C., where Mc-
Clure had sent him to research a political novel. "Really, by this time I
should have recovered enough to be able to write you a sane letter, but I
cannot — my pen is dead. I am simply a man struggling with a life that is
no more than a mouthful of dust to him," he wrote.

When it was over, it hardly mattered to him that the epistolary romance had never turned into an actual love affair. His feelings were real.
He had committed words to paper — an act more real for a writer than
the life lived outside of writing. Nellie Crouse was essentially a fantasy. He
had put such a woman into *George's Mother* even before he met her: "An
indefinite woman was in all of Kelcey's dreams." And like his novel's
George, he was the "sublime king of a vague woman's heart." He had
risked his own heart for this woman; he had allowed himself to hope.

Though complimented by the attentions of the talented young writer,
Nellie Crouse could not love him. There is a hint of a reason in a comment Stephen made in a letter on January 12: "Why, in heaven's name,
do you think that beer is any more to me than a mere incident?" But she
saved his letters, and in later years she remained proud enough of their
association to exaggerate the relationship, telling her children that
Stephen Crane had once been "deeply in love with her."

Some weeks later — around April 1 — Stephen met Lily Brandon
Munroe by prearrangement at the old congressional library in Washington, D.C., and asked her to run away with him. The library was under
construction, and they were forced to talk through the noise. Stephen was
"miserable" and ill, Lily noticed. He told her that Bacheller wanted him
to go west again, and he planned to go to Mexico for his health. He
wanted her to divorce Hersey and go with him — to the West or to Europe if she preferred. He told her to bring her three-year-old son. But she

couldn't do it. If she had not been married or "if Crane had urged her," she would have gone with him, she said later, though Stephen "had less than nothing to offer her." He cried as he put her in the cab.

◆

"It was a woman!" Stephen had written Hawkins from Washington on March 15.

> Dont you see? Nothing could so interfere but a woman. How sorry I am that I treated you so badly and yet how absolute is the explanation — a woman. I shall want to know how angry you are. I am sure, of course that you have been very much offended but it is a woman, I tell you, and I want you to forgive me.

He had as usual left New York abruptly. Having "had enough tea," as he put it to Ripley Hitchcock, he went to "lazy Washington" with the intention of settling down to his political novel for McClure. (He intended to work on *Maggie* as well, which Appleton was to republish. He now hated the book.) He wanted "to know all the congressmen in the shop," he wrote Hitchcock. "I want to know Quay of Pennsylvania. I want to know those long-whiskered devils from the west." He had a sackful of good intentions.

In his apology to Hitchcock for leaving New York, Stephen called himself "eccentric." "I cannot help vanishing and disappearing and dissolving. It is my foremost trait," but he hoped Hitchcock would "forgive me and treat me as if you still could think me a pretty decent sort of chap."

He kept the identity of the woman to himself. From the Cosmos Club in Washington he sent out letters like flares. He swung from swaggering pleasure to despair, illuminating his high emotional state while revealing nothing. Viola Allen, a Claverack classmate, had requested a copy of *The Red Badge*, which he happily sent her. In his accompanying note, he assured her that he had not forgotten her nor any of the girls: "Anna Roberts! . . . Eva Lacy! . . . Jennie Pierce!" who had broken his heart. "Men usually refuse to recognize their schoolboy dreams. They blush. I dont. The emotion itself was probably higher, finer, than anything of my after-life, and so, often I like to think of it. I was such an ass, such a pure complete ass — it does me good to recollect it."

To an admirer, Stephen wrote: "My dear Miss Hill: I have been wondering if you are not making game of me."

> In the first place, I am such a small pale yellow person with a weak air and no ability of pose that your admiration, or whatever it may be — if admiration is too strong a term — causes me to feel that I am an imposter and am robbing you of something.

However, he must be honest with her.

> Ye Gods! I am clay — very common uninteresting clay. I am a good deal of a rascal, sometimes a bore, often dishonest. When I look at myself I know that only by dint of knowing nothing of me are you enabled to formulate me in your mind as something of a heroic figure. If you could once scan me you would be forever dumb.

Stephen was unable to cut through Washington's political types. "These men pose so hard that it would take a double-barreled shot-gun to disclose their inward feelings and I despair of knowing them," he wrote Ripley Hitchcock on March 30. After a month, he left the capital and returned home, abandoning the political novel.

He had "been a rampant wild ass of the desert with my feet never twice in the same place," he wrote Hubbard upon his return to New York. He was planning a trip to East Aurora in a couple of weeks and hoped to "chew the rag at great length" and reach an agreement on the purchase of "that noble horse." Then he was sick — too ill to leave the house when he had an appointment one morning. He begged Hitchcock to release him from correcting the proofs of the preface for the new edition of *Maggie*. "The proofs make me ill," he wrote on April 2. "Let somebody go over them — if you think best — and watch for bad grammatical form & bad spelling. I am too jaded with Maggie to be able to see it."

Fame dogged and encumbered him. He was parodied, pummeled, praised. As for the badge of "genius" pinned on him, he told *Demarest's*

Family Magazine, "genius is a very vague word; and as far as I am concerned I do not think it has been rightly used." To the *Book Buyer* he wrote: "I have never been in a battle, of course, and I believe that I got my sense of the rage of conflict on the football field. Whatever success I have had has been the result simply of imagination coupled with great application and concentration." His comings and leavings were noted in print, from the *New York Press* to the *Lotus.* His photograph was so often requested that in Washington he had tamed his hair, center-parted it, and sat for a formal studio portrait that showed off his wonderful large eyes and his mature, neatly trimmed mustache. He joined the Author's Club and was feted at the Lantern Club with a tribute by William Dean Howells. Someone wanted to set *The Black Riders* to music. Fledgling writers sought his advice. When Miss Belle Walker sent him a story, he wrote back, telling her: "Take the diamond out of that man's shirt immediately. Dont let him live another day with a diamond on his front. You declare him to be very swell and yet you allow him to wear a diamond as if he were a saloon proprietor or owned a prosperous livery stable." As for her story, he didn't think much of it, but "this need not discourage you for I can remember when I wrote just as badly as you do now." Many writers "far our superiors wrote just as badly," he added.

In the six months after his return from Washington, Stephen wrote three gun-filled yarns of Mexico — "A Man and Some Others," "The Wise Men," and "Five White Mice." His reporting pieces and stories appeared regularly in syndication for Bacheller and McClure. He was quite "beset" with requests for his work, he wrote Hitchcock. In both America and England, from small firms to major, from big magazines like the *Atlantic Monthly* to the little *Philistine* and the *Criterion* in St. Louis, invitations to contribute arrived by the battalion, it seemed.

Led by "avarice," Stephen made one bad blunder, giving "The Little Regiment" to a publisher whose manager was an old Claverack friend, thereby behaving discourteously to Appleton. This person had "conducted a campaign" for the story "as is seldom seen," he said in his defense, and he had given way. He was now at pains to reassure Hitchcock that he had no intention of playing one publisher against another. His "mind was most just and open," he said. "But, before God, when these people get their fingers in my hair, it is a wonder that I escape with all my clothes." Insisting that he didn't "care a snap for money until I put my hand in my pocket and find none there," he admitted that it would be easy to make a contract he would later regret. He wanted to remain loyal to Appleton, but he expected something in return. "I expect you to deal with me precisely as if I was going to write a *great* book ten years from now" — *The Red Badge* didn't count — "and might wreak a terrible vengeance on you by giving it to the other fellow. And so we understand each other," he wrote.

He submitted gracefully to requests for interviews, biographical information, and photographs. Herbert P. Williams, a reporter who interviewed Stephen for the July 18 issue of the *Illustrated American*, found a serious young writer who was willing to talk freely about his art.

> His method, he told me, is to get away by himself and think over things. "Then comes a longing for you don't know what; sorrow, too, and heart-hunger." He mixes it all up. Then he begins to write. The first chapter is immaterial; but, once written, it determines the rest of the book. He grinds it out, chapter by chapter, never knowing the end, but forcing himself to follow "that fearful logical conclusion"; writing what his knowledge of human nature tells him would be the inescapable outcome of those characters placed in those circumstances.

He had little faith in the reader's imagination:

> "Trust their imaginations? Why, they haven't got any! They are used to having everything detailed for them. Our imaginations are defunct for lack of use, like our noses. So whether I say a thing or suggest it, I try to put it in the most forcible way."

By the fall of 1896, Stephen had three novels in print: *The Red Badge, George's Mother,* and a greatly toned-down *Maggie.* Stephen had "plugged at the words which hurt," and the book was edited for the remaining profanity as well as for grammar and style. Reviewers swept down on each book with condemnation and praise. *George's Mother* was "sorry stuff," said the *Bookman.* "There is absolutely no reason why it should have been done at all. The whole thing is simply an incoherent fragment, told with no purpose and fraught with no interest." The *New York Times* disagreed. "Mr. Crane is giving ample proof that scenes of war are not the only ones he can describe with an artist's hand." *Maggie* was hailed as a triumph of truth, "written as pitilessly as *L'Assommoir*," said the *Book Buyer*. But Stephen's old employer, the *New York Tribune*, hit him hard. Crane had "no charm of style, no touch of humor, no hint of imagination." Reading *Maggie* was akin to "standing before a loafer to be sworn at and have one's face slapped twice a minute for half an hour."

There were endless reviews of *The Red Badge*. "It really seems a touch of that marvelous intuitive quality which for want of a better name we call genius," wrote Thomas Wentworth Higginson, who had commanded the First South Carolina Infantry (Colored) in the Civil War. But attacks on the novel were savage. Another veteran condemned it as "The Red Badge of Hysteria." The novel was "realism run mad, rioting in all that is revolting to man's best instincts, and utterly false to nature and to life," said the *Dial*. It was parodied in *Life* as "The Blue Blotch of Cowardice" — Stephen's Kiplingesque line at the end of Chapter 9, "The red sun was pasted in the sky like a wafer," turned into "Above, the sun hung like a custard pie in a burnt blanket" — and was dismissed as a cheap imitation of Ambrose Bierce. Bierce, who had himself fought in the Civil War, initially praised Stephen Crane's novel, telling a friend, "this young man ... has the power to feel. He knows nothing of war, yet he is drenched in blood. Most beginners who deal with this subject spatter themselves merely with ink." But when *The Red Badge* eclipsed his own work, Bierce turned on the author: *The Red Badge* was "the Crane freak." "There could be only two worse writers than Stephen Crane, namely two Stephen Cranes," he said.

"It was an effort born of pain — despair, almost," Stephen said of his book,

> and I believe that this made it a better piece of literature than it otherwise would have been. It seems a pity that art should be a child of pain, and yet I think it is. Of course we have fine writers who are prosperous and contented, but in my opinion their work would be greater if this were not so. It lacks the sting it would have if written under a great need.

•

Stephen regarded himself as "very very lazy, hating work, and only taking up a pen when circumstances drive me." He thought "a good saddle-horse is the one blessing of life." Riding was his "idea of happiness." With the one-hundred-dollar advance he'd requested from Hitchcock for *Maggie*, he was able to buy Hubbard's chestnut mare, which he'd been "crazy to get" since seeing him in December. One day the "noble horse" with the boyish name Peanuts arrived at Edmund's house with great fanfare in a boxcar from East Aurora. Stephen's nieces watched in excitement as their uncle rode him for the first time.

Now there were wild races on horseback, Stephen riding Peanuts, Edmund a trotting horse he had broken to saddle, on the bad roads leading into Hartwood. Galloping their mounts as fast as they could, the brothers gave no thought to the danger, said Edmund. They thundered into the village "striking the bridge over the Green brook once each, through the straight of the 'lane' and then taking reverse curves first right around the corner of the Tannery meadow and left around a stone wall corner."

Peanuts, it turned out, was a prankster who knew how to turn the latch on his stall. When he'd had his fill of the feedbags on the barn floor, he'd go back in — but without knowing how to shut the stall door behind him. Trotting on the road around Hartwood, he'd suddenly stop at an ordinary stick, gather all fours together, and jump it. It was this unpredictableness in the horse, whom Uncle Stephen called his Monkeyshines, that he loved, said Edith Crane.

◆

At two o'clock in the morning on September 16, Stephen left the Broadway Garden restaurant between 31st and 32nd streets in New York's Tenderloin district (so dubbed by a policeman in reference to its easy graft). He, two chorus girls, and another woman headed down Broadway. This area of the city, along Sixth Avenue from 14th Street to about 42nd Street, housed numerous legitimate businesses and entertainment — hotels, clubs, restaurants, bars, and theaters — but also a whole underworld of peepshows, opium joints, gambling dens, and prostitutes. Having agreed to write a series of newspaper articles on demimonde life for William Randolph Hearst, Stephen had been taking in its "garish" spirit. "Yes, the Tenderloin is more than a place. It is an emotion," he wrote.

As Stephen would tell it, one of the chorus girls was going to catch a cable car, and he escorted her to the corner of Broadway and 31st Street. Because of the hour, he kept the two other girls in sight as he put her on the Broadway car. He noticed two men walk toward them and quickly pass. The girls were "deep in conversation," as he wrote later in "Adventures of a Novelist."

Just as Stephen returned, a man appeared and grabbed the two women. Telling them that they were under arrest, the policeman in civilian clothes held them while they screamed and tried to slip free. Stephen told the officer that they had done nothing wrong. The officer threatened to arrest him. Then the chorus girl claimed to be Stephen's wife. Stephen backed her up — he felt he couldn't do otherwise — and the officer released her. He had the other girl, he snarled — a red-haired, well-heeled beauty named Dora Clark.

"Why arrest her, either?" Stephen asked.

"For soliciting those two men."

"But she didn't solicit those two men."

The officer asked if Stephen knew the woman; Stephen admitted that he didn't.

"She's a common prostitute."

Stephen considered this.

"Are you arresting her as a common prostitute?" he asked. He added that she'd been "perfectly respectable" during the time she'd spent with him and the chorus girls.

The policeman said that he was arresting her for soliciting. If Stephen and the chorus girl didn't "want to get pinched, too," they'd better stay out of it.

Stephen and the chorus girl accompanied the officer and Dora Clark to the Nineteenth Precinct on West 30th Street. As the officer, Charles Becker, took her away to be locked up, Dora called out that she wanted to appear before the magistrate. Stephen walked her friend, sobbing, out of the station house. Still crying, she told him that if he didn't go to court to speak up on Dora's behalf, he wasn't a man.

Stephen protested that he couldn't "afford to do that sort of thing." But when they parted, he stood on the street thinking. He felt "dishonored" for having left the precinct house without speaking up for Dora Clark; he'd been more concerned with "his bauble reputation" than with injustice. He returned to the Nineteenth Precinct.

Addressing the desk sergeant he had seen earlier, Stephen asked if there was anything he could do to make the girl "more comfortable for the night." Then he told the sergeant his version of the arrest.

The sergeant acknowledged that Becker might have been wrong, but he himself knew that the girl was a common prostitute. He had been behind that desk many years, and he "knew how these things go." Stephen had a good reputation. The sergeant advised him to stay out of it: "If you monkey with this case, you are pretty sure to come out with mud all over you." The two men debated a while, then Stephen went back to his apartment and set his alarm for Dora's appearance in court.

At eight-thirty the next morning, wearing a blue suit and a blue-and-white-striped shirt, he arrived at the imposing Jefferson Market Courthouse in Greenwich Village. Built just nineteen years earlier and modeled after Ludwig II's castle in Bavaria, the courthouse was a magnificent structure, with gables, pinnacles, and a clock tower soaring above the corner of West 10th Street and Sixth Avenue. Just three days earlier, Stephen had sat beside Magistrate Cornell to observe the court's workings for Hearst. Now he ran into a reporter he knew.

"Go home," said the reporter, after hearing Stephen's story; his presence there didn't look respectable. Stephen argued that it would be wrong to leave. It would be only "a temporary wrong," said the reporter, and again told him to leave.

Stephen waited inside the courthouse all morning. A *New York Journal* reporter who had been observing him without knowing who he was thought he looked nervous and pale. Finally Dora Clark was brought in and led to the bar, "sobbing violently." Stephen noticed that even after her night in jail she looked neat. Calling the young woman "an old offender," Patrolman Becker gave his testimony. Then the prisoner told how Becker and his colleagues had been harassing and arresting her for weeks, ever since a Patrolman Rosenberg had accosted her one night. In the dim light she had mistaken the dark-skinned man for a Negro and told him she wanted nothing to do with Negroes. The magistrate seemed about to rule against her when Stephen spoke up.

"Your Honor, I know this girl to be innocent," he said forcefully. "I am the man who was with her, and there is no truth in what the officer has charged!"

The magistrate asked Stephen to identify himself.

"I am Stephen Crane, the novelist," he said quietly. Feeling the condemning eyes of the court spectators now turned on him, Stephen told the judge how he had been in the Tenderloin "studying human nature" for some magazine stories on the night of the arrest.

As he talked, Dora Clark watched him, stunned. The judge released her.

Interviewed by a *New York Journal* reporter that evening, Stephen said,

"She was a woman and unjustly accused, and I did what was my duty as a man.

"I realized that if a man should stand tamely by, in such a case, our wives and sisters would be at the mercy of any ruffian who disgraces the uniform. The policeman flatly lied, and if the girl will have him prosecuted for perjury, I will gladly support her."

The reporter wanted to know whether Stephen had felt like Henry Fleming: had he been afraid to give his testimony?

Stephen smiled. "Yes," he said, he had felt like Fleming. He was "badly frightened," and he too would have run "could I have done so with honor."

Asked to describe Dora Clark, Stephen said, "Why, she was really handsome, you know, and she had hair — red hair — dark red."

Later, at the Nineteenth Precinct station house, the *Journal* reporter talked to two of Becker's fellow officers. They hoped Dora Clark would get herself arrested again that night, they said laughing. The reporter asked if it made any difference to them "that a man of world-wide reputation states that she committed no offense."

"Who is this Crane? An actor?"

"No. An author."

"Never heard of him before."

Patrolman Becker was "a good man," the officers said, a longtime member of the force. But they admitted that reporters had recently caught Becker making a similar false arrest.

The newspapers feasted on the story. On September 17 Stephen awoke to blaring headlines all over New York. The Stephen Crane story, as it had become, soon spread to Philadelphia, Boston, and beyond — the focus not on police corruption in New York but on Stephen's chivalry and courage. Crane "showed the 'Badge of Courage' in a New York police court," said the *New York Journal;* "He Wore No Red Badge of Courage, But Pluckily Saved a Girl from the Law," wrote another paper. He was "as Brave as His Hero," "a knight errant," — and so on.

After the first wave of publicity, however, the tone darkened. On September 18 the *Boston Herald* moralized that "Stephen Crane, novelist, had been distinguishing himself in the New York police courts in a manner that does credit to his heart, if not to his head." After summarizing the court proceedings, the writer added, "Here seems to be a novelette all ready made." The *Chicago Dispatch* agreed: "Stephen Crane is respectfully informed that association with women in scarlet is not necessarily a 'Red Badge of Courage.'"

On Sunday, September 20, the Hearst-owned *New York Journal* devoted considerable space to Stephen's account of the Dora Clark arrest. Manuscript drafts and fragments show that he struggled with the writing. Titled "Adventures of a Novelist," the piece was earnest but unimpressive, candid but unmoving. It was further compromised by the drawings and layout. A quarter of a page was devoted to a large, full-bodied sketch of lovely Dora Clark. There were drawings of Stephen and of Stephen and the girl facing the magistrate. While remaining steadily supportive of Stephen, the *Journal* had unintentionally bolstered the view that the case was about a beautiful, scandalous young woman rescued by a dashing, world-famous author.

On October 2, aided by two charitable organizations who provided her with legal funds, Dora Clark preferred charges against Patrolman Becker and Patrolman Conway. That same day the *Boston Traveler* attacked Stephen. "The chances are that the youthful literary prodigy was on a genuine 'lark,' and, when his companion was apprehended, invented the tale about searching for book material. That is the way it looks to a cold and unprejudiced world."

Two days later, early on a Sunday morning, Officer Becker, dressed again in civilian clothing, audaciously attacked Dora Clark in public. She was talking to a group of cabmen when Becker appeared. Enraged about the charges filed against him, he swore at her, kicked her, grabbed her by the throat, and finally knocked her to the ground, stopping only when bystanders came to her aid.

After agreeing to testify on Dora's behalf, Stephen decided to escape the heat for a few days, and went to Philadelphia to see Frederic Lawrence. The two sent a telegram to Police Commissioner Theodore Roosevelt, stating Stephen's intention to testify against Becker. Roosevelt was a new friend of Stephen's and he was confident that the commissioner "would see that he had a square deal."

The thirty-seven-year-old Roosevelt had been chairman of the Board of New York City Police Commissioners for a little more than a year. Called "the biggest man in New York," he was already rumored to be in line for the presidency. As thickset as Stephen was puny — "bull-necked, bull-chested," wrote a biographer, with short hair, a ruddy complexion, big teeth, and a booming voice, Roosevelt rushed at life with boundless, almost superhuman, energy. Described by a friend, *Evening Post* editor Joseph Bucklin, as a man of "inflexible honesty, absolute fearlessness, and devotion to good government which amounts to religion," Roosevelt had set about the herculean task of cleaning up the New York Police Department, world-famous for its corruption.

The year before the Dora Clark affair, the Lexow Committee, a special investigating force of the New York State Senate, had published a searing 10,576-page document detailing the department's practices of job peddling, bribery, and other illegal activities. The committee recommended "an indictment against the Police Department of New York City as a whole." Police corruption had invaded Tammany Hall, the Democratic party, and Wall Street; the police even rigged elections to keep the Democrats in office. A citizen could not oppose the department without fear of losing his job, or even his life. According to the Lexow Report, even "strong men" were afraid to testify against the police, which seemed "an invulnerable force." A reporter had been beaten with brass knuckles by a police captain. In his memoirs, Roosevelt would write: "From top to bottom, the New York police force was utterly demoralized by the gangrene. . . . Venality and blackmail went hand-in-hand with the basest forms of low ward politics. . . . The policeman, the ward politician, the liquor seller, and the criminal alternately preyed on one another and helped one another to prey on the general public."

Roosevelt had begun his campaign for police reform in 1895 with a series of celebrated "night patrols" of the Lower East Side. Accompanied by his trusted friend Jacob Riis, who was still New York's preeminent police reporter, or Richard Harding Davis of *Harper's Monthly* or Lincoln Steffens of the *Evening Post*, the pugnacious commissioner would wander the shadowy, gas-lit streets of the Tenderloin unrecognized. Policemen caught away from their posts were swiftly and "severely" dealt with. The commissioner himself appeared as complainant in at least one disciplinary hearing.

But for all Roosevelt's audacity, his actual power was limited. At about the time he took office, a bill altering the power structure of the police force was passed. The chief of police now had the right to act independently, and Police Chief Peter Conlin was blocking Roosevelt's efforts to reorganize the force. The board of police commissioners itself was fractured and corrupt. Though Roosevelt was the board spokesman, he was one of four commissioners and only the titular head. Commissioner Andrew D. Parker, in charge of the mighty Detective Bureau and an important underworld force, had been secretly working against Roosevelt with the support of Chief Conlin.

By 1896, both Roosevelt's enthusiasm for his job and his local popularity had deteriorated. Though nationally and internationally famous for his police reforms, he had antagonized nearly everyone in New York with his rigid enforcement of the Sunday blue laws, which forbade the sale of alcoholic beverages on Sunday. Finding his work "grimy," increasingly tired and depressed, Roosevelt was beginning to think that he had accomplished all that he could. Now concerned with getting "the Spaniards out of Cuba," he had his eye on a new job as secretary of the Navy.

Early that summer, apparently, S. S. McClure had introduced Roosevelt to Stephen. The publisher was considering having Stephen write a story on the New York police, and he brought the two men together "in the hope that some spark would ignite a flame." Roosevelt, it turned out, was an admirer of Crane's work, particularly *The Red Badge;* he apparently owned all of Stephen's books. He and Stephen and Jake Riis dined together on at least one occasion. Roosevelt invited Stephen to visit him at the Police Department, apparently to discuss matters relevant to Stephen's reporting assignments but to socialize as well. "I have much to discuss with you about 'Madge,'" he wrote on Police Department stationery, referring to *Maggie.* Hamlin Garland wanted to meet the commissioner, and Stephen tried to arrange a dinner at the Lantern Club, but Roosevelt couldn't make it.

It is not clear how much the two men liked each other personally. They had not yet got beyond "Mr. Roosevelt" and "Mr. Crane," but the tone of Roosevelt's letters was friendly. In August Stephen sent him an autographed copy of *George's Mother,* for which the commissioner thanked him in a letter. He wanted Stephen to autograph his copy of *The Red Badge* as well, "for much though I like your other books, I think I like that book the best." There was a sufficient rapport between them for Stephen to show Roosevelt the manuscript of "A Man and Some Others" before it was published. Roosevelt responded to the story, in which an American sheepherder is killed by Mexicans, with a suggestion: "Some day I want you to write another story of the frontiersman and the Mexican Greaser in which the frontiersman shall come out on top; it is more normal that way!" He and Stephen shared a love of books, of Tolstoy in particular, and of the West. Roosevelt, an Easterner, had been a pioneering cattleman in the wild Dakota Badlands in the 1880s, and like Stephen had been a sickly child who later thrived on the rugged, "superbly health-giving" open-air life of the West. Both men delighted in looking the part of the hard-riding cowboy, with the best gear, good guns, and the finest in tack and spurs.

In spite of their friendship, Stephen felt free to criticize the New York Police Department and, by implication, Commissioner Roosevelt, though he did so in a small-time newspaper, the *Port Jervis Evening Gazette*, and under the thin cover of his initials for a byline. While he was becoming acquainted with Roosevelt that summer, he was the paper's page-one metropolitan correspondent, which, in effect, required him to toss out bits of big-city news and freely offer his opinions. It was an easy assignment; he lazily reworked material published elsewhere into his columns.

Two of the three columns he wrote for the *Gazette* were critical of the New York police. On August 12, William Jennings Bryan opened his campaign as the Democratic candidate for president with a big rally in Madison Square Garden. As police commissioner, Roosevelt was responsible for protecting Bryan, but he was not at the Garden that night, and the event was spectacularly mismanaged by the police. Gatecrashers got in, ticket holders were kept out, and the press condemned the police. Writing to Stephen on August 18, Roosevelt tried to excuse the police on the ground that they were inexperienced at controlling large crowds. He added that "we have not had a single complaint of clubbing, or brutality from any man claiming to have suffered; the Managers of the meeting and the Manager of the Garden have both written us in the warmest terms." Nevertheless, Stephen's column for the August 20 edition of the *Gazette*, perhaps written before he received Roosevelt's letter, blasted the police for their "shameful performance." Referring to the previous police chief, Thomas F. Byrnes, whom Roosevelt had driven out of office in 1895, Stephen wrote that "such blundering . . . would not have been possible under the Byrnes regime."

It was a surprisingly impolitic remark. Though Byrnes had known how to get a job done, he had also elevated the practice of graft to remarkable heights. Presiding over a large force of precinct captains and inspectors who had bought their ranks, Byrnes had taken money from everyone, from the lowly Tenderloin greengrocer to the lords of Wall Street. He left office a very rich man. A streetwise reporter like Stephen Crane must have known something about the methods of the Byrnes regime. And given his intolerance of police brutality and vice, he would hardly have promoted thuggery over incompetence. Shooting from the hip in his August 27 column, he attacked Roosevelt more directly with a paragraph about the stringent enforcement of the blue laws, which had led to "systematic police persecution" of the city's "harmless and petty traders." And, just weeks before the Dora Clark arrest, he assailed a New York City policeman for wrongfully arresting a woman on Sixth Avenue. "This is a form of outrage that has become very frequent of late, and the disgrace and exemplary punishment of some of the official brutes would have a beneficial effect in serving as a warning to over zealous policemen," he wrote.

From the beginning, Roosevelt seems to have opposed Stephen's testifying at the October hearing on behalf of Dora Clark. After Stephen and Lawrence dispatched the telegram to the commissioner, Stephen rushed back to New York on the next train like Sir Galahad, said Lawrence, confident of Roosevelt's support. There is no record of a meeting between them, but Roosevelt told Hamlin Garland, "I tried to save Crane from press comment but as he insists on testifying, I can only let the law take its course." On October 10 *Harper's Weekly* reported that "Commissioner Roosevelt and other high authorities of the police force are skeptical of the accuracy of Mr. Stephen Crane's observation."

Whatever turned Roosevelt against Stephen, the change of heart was unalterable. Roosevelt stood by the police, persuaded that this writer he admired and seemed to like was dishonest and depraved. The explanation lies both in the rigid character of Theodore Roosevelt and in the underhanded activities of the New York police, who were busy digging up incriminating evidence on Stephen — raiding his apartment and talking to people in the Tenderloin who knew him. Stephen was an easy target. He was unmarried and free-living; he openly and unapologetically consorted with chorus girls and prostitutes in shady neighborhoods. Rumors of his amorous activities — specifically of his recently having lived with a woman in the Tenderloin — had probably reached Roosevelt's ears.

A happily married father, "in matters of morality," Roosevelt was "as prudish as a dowager," writes a biographer. Though he could appreciate Crane's "Madge" as a literary work, he was disgusted by men who visited prostitutes or kept mistresses. A man of "abnormal self-control," Roosevelt held himself to impossibly high standards. At the age of twenty-eight, already three years widowed, he had felt dishonorable, weak, and unfaithful to his dead wife's memory when he remarried. His "small hand" had "caressed only two women." For Roosevelt, who was little interested in the company of women anyway, marriage was the only acceptable way to have a sexual life.

As the October 15 police hearing approached, Stephen received some very public warnings about what would happen to him if he testified for Dora Clark. Ugly rumors circulated like odors through the Tenderloin. It was said that Stephen Crane had left town for Philadelphia "in order to avoid being subpoenaed in the case," that "he led a fast life among the women of the Tenderloin," that he even ran "an opium joint in his rooms." The word was that the police were trying to scare Crane away from testifying and that they had the evidence they needed to ruin him.

When the police raided his apartment, they found an opium layout. In May, McClure had published a piece by Crane on opium smoking in the Tenderloin, and it had been widely syndicated. Though far from sympathetic to the opium habit, "Opium's Varied Dreams" was evocative and precisely detailed, clearly suggesting that the writer had tried the drug. The substance left the first-time smoker feeling as though he'd "swallowed a live chimney-sweep," wrote Stephen, only to be immediately overtaken by an overwhelming thirst for "strong black coffee." Yet Stephen reacted to the police raid with surprising nonchalance. The opium layout in his room was "tacked to a plaque on the wall," he told the *Journal.* Anyone could see that it was a souvenir, something to add to his collection, like a piece of Mexican pottery. He wasn't worried. The *Journal* published Stephen's remarks in an October 11 article titled "Novelist Crane a Hard Man to Scare."

He was summoned to appear at police headquarters at three o'clock in the afternoon on October 15. Upon his arrival he was taken to a room where he apparently waited alone so that other witnesses would not influence his testimony.

Commissioner Frederick D. Grant, chairman of the New York Police Department's disciplinary committee, presided over the hearing. The middle-aged son of ex-president Ulysses S. Grant, Frederick Grant was a former soldier whom Roosevelt considered "easily misled." He had been described as liking "nothing so much as to sit and stare into space." Roosevelt seems to have had nothing to do with the proceeding, which was clearly not a matter of importance to him. He was spending much of his time giving speeches for the Republican presidential candidate, William McKinley.

At nine o'clock that evening, six hours after Stephen's arrival, the hearing against police officers Becker and Conway finally got under way. While Stephen waited in isolation, the police lawyer, also named Grant, did his best to demolish Dora Clark's credibility. Her real name, it

emerged, was Rubi Young, and she was a kept woman. A police roundup
had produced various Tenderloin people — cabmen, prostitutes, and the
like — to testify for the defense. Remarkably, they had all seen Dora Clark
soliciting at two o'clock in the morning on the night of September 16.
One of them, a prostitute known as "Big Chicago May," whose fingers
sparkled with diamond rings "as big as hickory nuts," claimed that Dora
Clark had tried to bribe her to give false testimony against Officer Becker.
Under questioning by Lawyer Newberger, counsel for Dora Clark, Big
Chicago May gave her occupation as "typewriter." She could neither
identify the kind of machine she used nor explain what the job entailed.

Finally, at one fifty-five in the morning, Stephen entered the courtroom. He was dressed in a suit, vest, and ascot, his tawny hair center-
parted. Lawyer Grant immediately accused him of listening at the door.
The courtroom was packed with reporters and spectators, and the police
had turned out *en masse*, which looked like intimidation. As Stephen gave
his testimony, an artist for the *Journal* sketched him in a variety of poses.
Sitting on a chair, he looked by turns animated and uncomfortable as he
was "subjected to a very severe cross-examination by the counsel for the
policeman," noted the *New York Times*. He crossed and uncrossed his legs.
He punctuated his testimony with outstretched arms or held his hands
gently in his lap. Curiously, some of the drawings made the slender writer
look stout.

He repeated the testimony he had given before the magistrate on
September 17. Lawyer Grant asked about his private life. Was it true that
Stephen had lived at a certain address on West Twenty-seventh Street?

"Yes, I lived in a flat house on West Twenty-seventh Street," he said
icily.

"With what woman did you live there?" asked Grant with a sneer.
Newberger told Stephen not to answer that. "It has absolutely nothing to
do with the case at hand," he said.

"I refuse to answer," said Stephen, sounding weary.

"On what ground?" asked Grant.

"Because it would tend to degrade me."

"Perhaps you think to answer this will tend to disgrace you. With
whom did you live at . . ." went the line of questioning.

On Newberger's advice, Stephen "refused to answer many of the
questions, and in his refusal he was supported by Commissioner Grant,"
reported the *Times*.

The reporters present saw the hearing as a trial of Stephen Crane's character. Though Commissioner Grant sustained many of Newberger's objections and had some questions struck from the record, he allowed the policemen's counsel to continue his insulting line of questioning. Stephen held his ground, giving answers the *Journal* described as "short, snappy, and to the point," his manner "cold as icicles." Lawyer Grant seemed particularly interested in the house Stephen had lived in on West 27th Street, and he implied that Stephen was living on money from Tenderloin women. Finally Stephen shielded his face with his hands "as if to prevent [the questions] from burning into his brain," wrote a reporter.

Commissioner Grant closed the case. Then the police captain, Chapman, "asked that one more witness be heard." The commissioner allowed it, and James O'Connor, janitor at the West 27th Street house where Stephen was alleged to have lived with a woman, testified that the novelist had lived there "for six weeks during the summer." Newberger objected to the testimony as inadmissible. Commissioner Grant excluded it, but it had been heard.

At two-thirty in the morning on October 16, the day after it began, "the longest trial ever held at police headquarters" ended. The court exonerated Charles Becker. On the steps outside on Mulberry Street a woman who had been a court spectator struck the janitor who had testified. A policeman grabbed her, then let her go.

Dawn arrived with sensational headlines: CRANE HAD A GAY NIGHT. RED BADGE MAN ON A POLICE RACK. The little newsboys in their caps and knickerbockers, the newsgirls in their somber, ankle-length dresses, had saleable copy. Every newspaper in the city carried the story. The *New York World* ran a large sketch of Stephen next to the headlines. The *New York Times* alone was restrained, reporting the news in a short, noncommittal article. The others took sides. The *Brooklyn Daily Eagle*, the *Press*, and the loyal *Journal* defended the author, decrying the assault on his reputation by the police department and warning that Crane's treatment in court might discourage other citizens from testifying against the police. (In faraway San Francisco, the *Wave* blasted the *Journal* as "positively the worst newspaper we can recall" and Stephen as "the veriest filth. We have yet to see even the 'Police Gazette' descend to such depths.") The *New York Tribune* reacted with vicious pleasure; several other newspapers turned against Stephen. Every journalist had an opinion; even "The Literary Den" page of the *Illustrated American* self-importantly weighed in — against Stephen.

The press accounts continued into November, when Dora Clark was arrested again, for fighting with another prostitute. "There was a man who did a brave deed and got blows for it," wrote the *Daily Tatler;* "some called him indiscreet; the rest kept silent. But this is a sadder part: The brave deed was lost like a street light in the morning. And this is the saddest part: That she whom he sought to save lost herself again."

Stephen's reputation was shattered. The *New York Tribune* cheered, saying the fad named "Stephen Crane" was over. Old friends like Frederic Lawrence and Corwin Knapp Linson stood by Stephen, Edward Marshall admired him for taking the fall "like a man," and a few literati supported him, but others turned on him or distanced themselves. His literary fathers were discomfited. Fifty-nine-year-old Howells was "greatly distrest by the incident until I put the matter before him in its true light," said an anonymous source. Garland sympathized with Stephen's loyalty but regarded his decision to testify as "stubborn" and "quixotic." Now thirty-six, Garland was writing historical romances in the hope of achieving greater popularity as a writer. He saw the Dora Clark affair as exposing Stephen's shady bohemian life "to the light" — his sentiments echoing a *New York Journal* headline: HIS BOHEMIAN LIFE IN NEW YORK LAID BARE FOR THE SAKE OF DORA CLARK. When the hearing was over, Garland advised Stephen to leave town. He didn't look well, Garland told him. He should go to his brother's house in Hartwood "and get back your tone," spend time writing a "big book."

Stephen shook his hand.

"I'll do it," he said.

A month later, on November 27, he left New York on a train bound for Jacksonville, Florida. He carried with him a chamois belt fitted with seven hundred dollars in Spanish gold, courtesy of the Bacheller-Johnson Syndicate, which was sending him to "the storm center of the world," Cuba, as a war correspondent. And he was traveling with a lady.

9

GOD SAVE

CRANE

The lady was Amy Leslie, the well-known drama critic of the *Chicago Daily News*. A year earlier she had sent her warm regrets to the Philistine Society dinner in Stephen's honor with the message: "My most gentle thoughts are tinged with envy of you who are so lucky as to meet Stephen Crane." Whether she had in fact already met Stephen or met him soon afterward is unknown, but in a New Year's Eve telegram to her that year he sounded friendly if not exactly intimate: "My dear Indian, did you really like the stuff?" And he wished her "a long, flaming '96." It is not known when they began their affair, but it seems certain that she was the woman Stephen had lived with at 121 West 27th Street in the summer of 1896.

They were sixteen years apart in age, she forty-one, he twenty-five that November. Judging by the photographic record, she was easily the most beautiful woman Stephen ever romanced. Small, blond, and plump, she had a striking face with well-drawn, theatrical features: large, deep-set, intelligent eyes, not unlike Stephen's, with a very direct gaze; high, well-rounded brows; and a wide, sensuous mouth. Her classically shaped long nose was also like Stephen's. One man would recall "a red, laughing mouth" and "the most beautifully white teeth I have ever seen." In her photographs Amy Leslie smiles softly. She is always elaborately dressed in clothes that look like costumes, with high, puffy sleeves and fancy trimmings of bows, beads, even ermine.

There was something both regal and festive about Amy. The writer

Ben Hecht said "she looks like a Mardi Gras." She led a glamorous life, attending theater openings and parties. Described as "brilliant" and "witty," with "a sharp tongue when she cared to use it," she was also vivacious, "always laughing, always good-natured." Hecht would compare her, even at an older age, to Sousa's " 'Spring Song' . . . bouncing, effervescent, indomitable, cyclonic, ululating, and incredible as her literary style. There is a high wind about Amy that blows your hat off. She is as hilarious as a feast day. Her conversation is as successful as a circus . . . And beside her nine women out of 10 still fade into tired school teachers."

Amy Leslie was called "the first important woman on a major American metropolitan newspaper." Known for her nurturing attitude toward actors, she had a reputation among theater people as a knowledgeable, sympathetic, generous reviewer. Though her reviews ranged from "rhapsodies of adulation" to cool dismissals of players and plays, she was known for her fairness. Having started out as an actress and singer, enjoying a modest success in such light operas as Edmond Audran's *La Mascotta*, at the Bijou Opera House in New York, and Gilbert and Sullivan's *H.M.S. Pinafore*, she brought great empathy to the role of critic. And she knew everyone in the theater, from Lillian Russell to Lillie Langtry.

Born Lillie West — she adopted "Amy Leslie" much later as a pen name — she had already led a full life before she met Stephen. Along with having a theatrical career, she had lived and studied in Paris and London. She had married the comedian Harry Brown around 1881 and had had a child, Frankie. But the marriage ended in 1889 (the date of their divorce is unclear), soon after four-year-old Frankie died of diphtheria. It was later said that Amy Leslie lost her only child, her marriage, and her singing voice, all at the same time. Retiring from the stage soon after Frankie's death, she began a new life as a theater critic. She may have been still legally married at the time she met Stephen. But though she lived in the male-dominated worlds of newspaper journalism and the theater, her name was seldom linked romantically to anyone else's. In the seven years between her son's death and the time when she is known to have been involved with Crane, Amy Leslie seems to have lived for her work.

While sharing a Tenderloin apartment with Stephen in the summer of 1896, she also maintained a permanent residence at the Grenada Hotel in Chicago. After the summer, she returned to Chicago, and the lovers presumably continued to meet when they could. With Stephen's work in New York and Amy's in Chicago, they may have planned to continue dividing their time between the two cities until a more desirable arrangement could be worked out.

Only Stephen's side of the correspondence with Amy — and evidently not all of it — exists. His letters reveal that Amy was in some kind of trouble — "what is now really a great trouble," Stephen wrote Hawkins. What is known is that on November 1, Stephen's twenty-fifth birthday, Amy gave him eight hundred dollars to put in a bank for her. They apparently met in Boston, where Stephen had covered a football game between Harvard and the Carlisle Indian School for the *New York Journal* the day before. After the weekend Stephen returned to New York, Amy to Chicago. On November 5 he deposited six hundred dollars in his own bank account.

As with almost everything else in the Crane-Leslie affair, the reason for this transaction is unknown. Clearly, from Stephen's letters, the affair was to continue after his return from Cuba — this was just a "temporary separation," he wrote her; "wait for me." In that case Amy would need a bank account in New York. Being casual about money, Stephen apparently decided to put her money into his own account rather than go to the trouble of opening a new account for her. Before leaving for Florida, he gave Hawkins five hundred dollars and arranged for him act as both his and Amy's banker, sending money to each as requested. Amy could draw on the account when she needed to.

Because Stephen expected to be catching a boat for Cuba soon after his arrival in Jacksonville, Amy was to travel with him only as far as Washington. From there Stephen would take another train south, and Amy would return to work in Chicago.

The moment of parting was hard. From what Stephen wrote later both to Amy and to Willis Hawkins, she was terribly upset — "I was positively frightened for the girl at the moment of parting and I am afraid and worried now," he wrote Hawkins on November 29, the day after his arrival in Jacksonville. In a note to Amy the same day, he said that "the few moments on your train at Washington were the most painful of my life and if I live a hundred years I know I can never forget them."

Amy seems to have been enraged by Stephen's high-handed arrangements with her money. Perhaps already in serious financial trouble, she was on the verge of moving out of the Grenada Hotel. Later she would refer to "two stormy interviews" with Stephen to get her money back — one perhaps occurring on the train to Washington.

•

Once he had arrived in Jacksonville, Stephen's head was filled with war, which he would be seeing for the first time. Mindful of the danger, he was concerned with making sure that his estate was in order and that both the people and the horse he loved were taken care of. Having lost or misplaced his will, he wrote his brother William a letter that he hoped would replace it. He appointed William his sole executor and allowed that one-third of his estate should go to him, with another third going to Edmund; George and Townley would each get one-sixth. His furniture at Hartwood would go to Ed, with mementos to other family members. Peanuts should remain with Ed's family and not be sold or should go to "somebody whom it is absolutely certain would not maltreat him." He wanted William Dean Howells, Hamlin Garland, and Ripley Hitchcock to serve as his literary executors, with Howells making decisions about "book publication of various collections of my stories which have appeared only in serial or magazine form." He concluded by sending "my love to you and Cornelia and all the babies" and defending his behavior in the Dora Clark case.

> If I should happen to be detained upon my journey, you must always remember that your brother in that case acted like a man of honor and a gentleman and you need not fear to hold your head up to anybody and defend his name. All that I said in my own article in the Journal is absolutely true, and for my part I see no reasons why, if I should live a thousand years, I should be ever ashamed or humiliated by my course in the matter.

Stephen's will made no provisions for Amy Leslie and did not mention the money he owed her, which would have been unseemly since they were not married and would have stirred up questions he didn't want his family asking.

Stephen's letters to Hawkins and to Amy suggest a consuming worry about her. Stephen asked his friend to "encourage" Amy "in every possible way" if he happened to see her, though "there is not one man in three thousand who can be a real counsellor and guide for a girl so pretty as Amy. . . ."

> Of course feminine nature is mighty peculiar and she might have that singular ability to get rid of mournful emotions

> which is possessed by a great many of her sex, but I was posi-
> tively frightened for the girl at the moment of parting and I
> am afraid and worried now. I feel that no one hardly could
> need a friendly word more than this poor child.

Amy's sister was married to a prosperous Chicago grain merchant. In Stephen's words she was "good hearted," but "weak, very weak," and could not be relied on to help Amy.

To Amy he wrote only a note, saying that he had "dictated a long letter" to her (the letter no longer exists), and "I could not very well tell you in it how much I loved you and how sorrowful I am now over our temporary separation." In the weeks to come, he continued to write Amy of his love and devotion. She was his girl, his "Blessed Girl," his "own girl," his "sweetheart," "beloved," "dearest." "Be brave, my sweet," he told her. He loved "you alone."

Yet for all his worries about Amy, he "was feeling very good," he wrote Hawkins. He had escaped the Dora Clark mess and had reached Jacksonville without being detained by the police, who still wanted to punish him for his testimony. He was about to witness war up close. In the meantime, while he awaited passage to Cuba, he was free to explore a new city at the very moment when it was "a hotbed of intrigue."

Jacksonville, named for General Andrew Jackson, was a popular winter resort. Tens of thousands of tourists from the United States and abroad flocked to "the southern Newport" and "the American Nice," as it was called. Easily accessible by both water and rail, this busy seaport in northeast Florida combined physical comforts with the allure of a tropical climate and exotic natural beauty. Though the city offered little entertainment outside the Park Opera House, and had no library of significance, no museums or art galleries, it was prosperous and picturesque, with paved roads and good hotels. Fine houses sat on wide streets shaded by live oaks. Lovely beaches of fine white sand led to the warm ocean.

Since the start of the year-old Cuban revolt against Spanish rule, Jacksonville had become the country's major filibustering port. Inflamed by the yellow journalism of Hearst's *New York Journal* and Joseph Pulitzer's *New York World*, American sympathies for the Cuban insurgents ran high. There was money to be made in smuggling arms to the Cuban rebels, though the appeal of this clandestine activity lay chiefly in its romance, which "catches the heart of the lad," wrote Stephen. "The same lad who longs to fight Indians and to be a pirate longs to embark secretly on one of these dangerous trips to the Cuban coast." The boyish love of adventure — "this delicious bit of outlawry in the evening of the nineteenth century," Stephen called it — brought important correspondents, artists, and political figures to Jacksonville. Sylvester Scovel of the *New York World*— who was celebrated for having marched across Cuba with Cuban general Antonio Maceo — was one of the journalists who joined Cuban leaders José Martí and José Alejandro Huau ("pronounced 'wow'") at Huau's cigar store at the corner of Main Street. The store served as a gathering place and recruitment center for volunteer fighters for the Cuban cause. Spies for the Spanish loyalists and self-important Pinkerton detectives conducting surveillance for Spain lurked about the city.

Out in the harbor, like a great glistening emblem of freedom, sat "the Cuban fleet" of filibustering ships — the *Three Friends*, the *Dauntless*, and the *Commodore*. It mattered nothing that they were mere tugs, "and small ones at that," noted Stephen; in fact, the *Commodore* was actually a fishing steamer. So revered was this little fleet, wrote Stephen, that just the sight of one of the tugs brought a grin to one's face. In Jacksonville the Cuban fleet was perhaps "better known than the battleships of the United States navy." The sound of the *Three Friends*' "long mournful whistle" late at night, the rumor of an impending expedition, was enough "to pick up a crew. Men jump at the chance," wrote Stephen.

He registered at Jacksonville's best hotel, the internationally known St. James, under the alias Samuel Carleton. A large brick and wooden building fronted by a wide promenade, with five hundred rooms, the elegant St. James was a mecca for the rich — hardly the best place for someone trying to be unrecognized. Stephen promptly found that getting passage on a boat was no easy trick, alias or not. Even the famous and well-connected Sylvester Scovel, who was using the alias "George H. Brown" and had the help of the local customs collector, was unable to get clearance to take a dispatch boat to Cuba because of neutrality and navigation laws. While other leg men waited out their time in brightly lit cafés and hotels, Stephen disappeared into the smoky back rooms of the seedy waterfront saloons. He sat quietly, said fellow *Journal* reporter Charles Michelson, drinking "innumerable bottles of beer," "listening to the talk of oilers, deck hands, sponge fishermen, wharf-rats and dock thieves, and all the rest of the human flotsam that is washed into a port that has the West Indies for a front yard," becoming "one of them."

Within a few days after Stephen's arrival, the *Daily Florida Citizen* reported that Samuel Carleton and two other men, who called themselves

George H. Brown and H. K. Sheridan, were "being closely watched by Spanish spies." Brown was reputed to be "an expert dynamiter" who would "do effective work for the Cuban cause." Samuel Carleton was identified as "an ex-Lieutenant in the army" who was "fully up to war tactics and maneuvers." Sheridan "will handle a melenite gun."

While waiting for a boat, Stephen visited the local brothels. Within days after his arrival in town he had met Lyda de Camp, madam of the well-known Lyda's, and Cora Taylor, proprietress of the finest bawdy house in Jacksonville, the Hotel de Dream. On December 4 he inscribed a book to Cora.

> Brevity is an element
> That enters importantly
> Into all pleasures of
> life and this is what
> makes pleasure sad
> and so there is no
> pleasure but only sadness
>   Stephen Crane

Another inscription, in Kipling's *The Seven Seas*, was addressed to "C.E.S." — Cora Ethel Stewart, which was Cora Taylor's legal name; the other, also to Cora, in a copy of *George's Mother*, was "to an unnamed sweetheart / Stephen Crane."

His letters to Amy became infrequent. In a short letter to his "own Sweetheart" on December 11, twelve days after his previous note, he implied that he had been too busy to write:

> every moment we have expected to get off and I have wished to save my last word for you. We have had a great deal of trouble to get a boat ready and I think within twenty-four hours we will be on our way to Cuba. It breaks my heart to think of the delays and to think that I might have had you with me here if I had only known. There is a great deal of work attached to the affair and I have hardly had time to breathe but always I think of you, night and day, my own love. Remember me sweetheart even in your dreams. From now on I will have time to write oftener and you may expect to hear now every day until starting from your poor forlorn

boy. I know you wont forget me. I know you love me and I
want you always to remember that I love you.

He signed it "Your lover."

As for writing every day, he kept his word for a few days. He wrote
again on the twelfth, appending a few lines on the following two days.
Judging by his letters, the "remarkable series of circumstances" that had
kept him in Jacksonville bothered him chiefly because he missed Amy.
He repeated the words about his broken heart and again emphasized his
extreme busyness — which had an element of danger, for he and the
other correspondents had been followed by Spanish spies. They seemed
"very harmless," he told her, and she needn't worry about him. Confined
to his hotel "in misery" while he waited for his ship (there was "a strict
rule about drinking and no one to play with," he wrote), he could "do
nothing but think of you. I love you, my sweetheart, my sweetheart." On
Monday he added that he was certain to leave the next day. "I love you,
mine own girl. Be good and wait for me. I love you."

Meanwhile Stephen had won the affection of one of Jacksonville's
most desirable scarlet women. At thirty-one, Cora Taylor prided herself
on looking younger. Like Amy Leslie, she was short, blond, and "generously built." Though not beautiful — "her features were a shade too
heavy for beauty," notes her biographer — she was very attractive. Her
stunning natural red-gold hair, worn in a simple coil, was complemented
by radiant, fresh coloring, and soft blue-gray eyes. In her carriage and
style of dress she "suggested affluence." And "there was about her an extraordinary vitality," which gave her great presence. Those who knew her
attested to her "class," her "great dignity and quiet charm." Her photographs, said another woman, did "not do her justice."

Born Cora Howorth in Boston to a good, "highly literate" family, she
had been raised "in an atmosphere in which art and its appreciation
formed an important part of daily life." Her father was a painter; her
paternal great-grandfather, George Howorth, a prominent Boston art
dealer and restorer. After the deaths of her parents, which left her a
wealthy young woman, she lived with an aunt in New York. And there
her life departed from the expected conventional route. At not yet twenty,
she lived out of wedlock with a man and worked as a hostess at a Tenderloin gambling house, the London Club. Two brief marriages followed.
The first, at twenty-one, was to a man in the dry goods business named
Vinton Murphy, who soon divorced her on the grounds of adultery. In

January of 1889 she married her lover, Captain Donald William Stewart, the son of a baronet, who had served with the 92nd Gordon Highlanders. Mrs. Stewart now took up a new life in London, where she and her husband resided at the elegant Grand Hotel in Charing Cross. Sometime around 1892 Cora left Stewart for a rich, Princeton-educated man, Ferris Thompson, who was named as corespondent in a divorce action that Stewart later dropped. Cora was apparently still Thompson's lover when she met Stephen Crane.

Like Amy Leslie, this sophisticated, worldly woman, who had shopped for clothes in Paris and traveled to Constantinople on the Orient Express, earned her own money. She was capable and strong, someone "who had never accepted defeat." She knew how to make her way in the world without a husband. She loved the theater, which she attended once or twice a week in Jacksonville. Her bookshelves showed an eclectic taste, with works by Shakespeare, Dickens, Ibsen, Matthew Arnold, Byron, Emerson, George Eliot, Benjamin Franklin, Kipling, Goethe, and others; travel writings by Isaac Taylor, Oscar Fay Adams's works on sexual equality, and at least one book by Stephen Crane.

Though she had been in Jacksonville just two years, Cora Taylor, as she now called herself, was a well-known figure about town. A curious mixture of scandal and propriety, she was never seen in public without her companion, Mrs. Mathilde Ruedy. When Cora stepped down from her handsome victoria at the post office, Mrs. Ruedy waited, holding a lace parasol. The victoria with its stately black horse, liveried coachman, and dusters on the seats (changed daily to match Cora's clothes) was as familiar a sight around town as its ample blond mistress. On the street men looked at Cora; the ladies snubbed her.

Called "Ma" or "Miss Cora" by a favored few guests, Cora ran her "sporting house" as an elegant establishment. It was a decided cut above brothels like Lyda de Camp's on Ward Street. The Hotel de Dream, named for its previous owner, Ethel Dreme, stood on the corner of Ashley and Hawk streets in the La Villa district, "at a safe remove" from the other brothels. Set up as a furnished boarding house that served good meals and operated as a nightclub in the evenings, the hotel sold beer and champagne but no hard liquor. Miss Cora disapproved of drunkenness. Gentlemen guests of the hotel made their own arrangements with the girls who worked for Cora; the girls did not live there. Early in the evening men and women would socialize downstairs or play at the roulette

Stephen in the spring of 1895. "I am simply a man struggling with a life that is no more than a mouthful of dust to him." *Barrett Library, University of Virginia*

The first page of the final manuscript of *The Red Badge of Courage*. "You've got to feel the things you write if you want to make an impact on the world." *Barrett Library, University of Virginia*

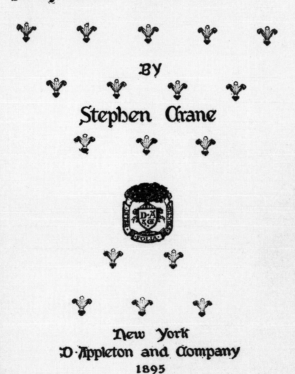

The title page of *The Red Badge*, "a revelation of the commanding power of genius." *Barrett Library, University of Virginia*

How could he "be so attracted by a vague, faint shadow?" Nellie Crouse of Akron, Ohio, winter 1896. *Crane Collection, Syracuse University*

"I did what was my duty as a man." Illustration accompanying "Adventures of a Novelist," Crane's account of Dora Clark's arrest, *New York Journal*, September 20, 1896.

"Why, she was really handsome, you know, and she had hair — red hair — dark red." Newspaper illustrations for reports of the Dora Clark affair.

Amy Leslie as a young woman. "There is not one man in three thousand who can be a real counsellor and guide for a girl so pretty as Amy." *Harvard Theatre Collection, The Houghton Library*

Amy Leslie, then drama critic for the *Chicago Daily News,* in 1895. *The Chicago Sun-Times © 1996*

Amy Leslie in later years. *The Chicago Sun-Times © 1996*

THE ST. JAMES,
JACKSONVILLE, - - FLA.
J. R. CAMPBELL, Prop'r.

Sunday –

My Blessed Girl: I have dictated a long letter to you today but as it was dictated to a stenographer I could not very well tell you in it how much I loved you and how sorrowful I am now over our temporary separation. The few moments on your train at Washington were the most painful of my life and if I live a hundred years I know I can never forget them. I want you to be always sure that I love you. We start tomorrow night probably but if you have

Stephen wrote this love letter to Amy from Jacksonville, where he awaited passage to Cuba, late in 1896. *Dartmouth College Library*

THE ST. JAMES,
JACKSONVILLE, - - FLA.
J. R. CAMPBELL, Prop'r.

written today I will get it before the boat sails. Be good, my darling, my sweet. Dont forget your old hubber. I think of you at all times and love you alone.

Your lover.

P.S.: We are at the St James and my name is Samuel Carleton. I must hurry this to get it off on the northern mail. Be brave, my sweet.

"A good saddle-horse is the one blessing in life." Stephen in Jacksonville, December 1896. *Crane Collection, Syracuse University*

Stephen's "unnamed sweetheart," Cora Taylor, about 1889. *Crane Collection, Syracuse University*

wheel while their charming hostess — who was the main attraction — graciously moved among them in the parlor. A man called the Professor played the piano. One of the guests might buy Miss Cora a drink, but the correspondents from out of town lacked the nerve to suggest anything more. "Fact is, she was a cut above us in several ways, notably poise and surety of command of herself and others," said Ernest McCready. Miss Cora represented class; "if she had any false notes I was then all too un-skilled in recognizing authentic 'class' or lack of it, to detect any." Later in the evening, couples left the hotel or withdrew to the upstairs bedrooms. Miss Cora and Mrs. Ruedy retired to Cora's private apartment, to which only a favored few guests were ever invited.

Stephen came to the Hotel de Dream as Samuel Carleton in the company of Ralph Paine and Ernest McCready. At the end of an elegant dinner party, one of the guests revealed Samuel Carleton's true identity. "The news pierced the lady's very liver," said McCready. It happened that Cora was reading one of Stephen's books. And he was *the* writer of the moment, "whose mud-bespattered name signified to Cora the bright-est star of genius." By all accounts, the attraction on Cora's part, at least, was overwhelming. She fell instantly in love.

He had his picture taken on horseback and on December 12 wrote Amy that he was sending it to her. The picture had been Scovel's idea. He and Stephen and some of the others had put on correspondents' garb — matching pants and shirt, English riding boots, and a cap that empha-sized Stephen's boyish looks — and posed for the camera on livery stable horses. He looked fine in the saddle.

He was still in town on the fifteenth, the day he'd "seemed sure" to leave. He was there two days later. He had arranged to ship out on the *Commodore*, but the acting secretary of the treasury was unwilling to grant the boat clearance to carry arms to Cuba. Stephen apparently filled much of the time with Cora Taylor; there are no more known let-ters to Amy Leslie written that month. Then, on December 24, departure seemed imminent. Stephen telegraphed Hawkins for fifty dollars and asked for news of Amy. "Leave soon telegraph frankly amys mental con-dition." He was "troubled over Amy," he said in closing.

Finally, on the last day of the year, the *Commodore* received clearance to carry arms to the Cuban port of Cienfuegas, about fifteen hundred miles from Jacksonville. That afternoon the cargo was loaded. Stephen watched as black stevedores lifted "box after box of ammunition and bundle after bundle of rifles." The *Florida Times Union* reported that there were "203,000 cartridges, 1,000 pounds of giant powder, 40 bundles of rifles, 2 electric batteries, 300 machetes," and other supplies worth more than four thousand dollars. "It might have been the feeding time of some legendary creature of the sea," Stephen wrote later. And yet it was only "a test cargo" to test the law, reported the *New York Herald;* the load was actually "very small." There was no attempt at secrecy; Spanish spies were invited to observe the operation. "She loaded up as placidly as if she were going to carry oranges to New York, instead of Remingtons to Cuba," wrote Stephen.

When it came time to leave at eight o'clock on New Year's Eve, good-byes were exchanged on deck "in two languages." Stephen felt a tug "of melancholy." He thought of those he was leaving "in the remote North." Against protest by the Spanish vice-consul, who knew that the shipment of war supplies was intended for the insurgents, the *Commodore* pulled away to the cheers of the Cubans on shore. She blew her whistle three times. To Stephen it sounded like a wail. Then he remembered that he was a gun-runner now, and his mood improved. "When a man gets the ant of desire-to-see-what-it's-like stirring in his heart, he will wallow out to sea in a pail," he would write. "The thing surpasses a man's love for his sweetheart."

As the 123-foot, 178-ton coal-burning tug carrying twenty-eight or twenty-nine men headed toward the ocean by way of the narrow St. Johns River, she was enveloped in fog. The lower end of the river was dark and tropical, its shores layered with great vines, Spanish moss, cypresses, and live oaks. Farther down was the open passage to the sea. Just two miles out of Jacksonville, while still on the St. Johns, the *Commodore* hit a mud bar in the fog and ran aground. "In this ignominious position we were compelled to stay until daybreak," wrote Stephen. In the morning the captain of the cutter *Boutwell* attached a line to the steamer and pulled her out of the mud. It was New Year's Day, 1897, and as the tug set out again the southern sun "fell full upon the river," wrote Stephen, bathing it in gold as in a painting by Winslow Homer. Spectators on shore and people on passing ships cheered as she left. Then the steamer was beached again. This time she reversed her engines and managed to free herself just as the *Boutwell* approached.

"Are you fellows going to sea to-day?" called the *Boutwell* captain.

Captain Murphy answered yes.

"Well, gentlemen, I hope you have a pleasant cruise," said the captain, raising his hat. No one thought to examine the steamer's hull.

At sea the *Commodore* promptly headed into the eye of a southeast squall. The tug, heavy with cargo, pitched and bucked like a rodeo bronco, said Stephen. Water "swarmed over her bow." Many of the Cubans fell sick and lay down on the deck or took to their bunks. Stephen and Captain Murphy "were about the only ones" on board who weren't seasick. As the steamer plunged south over the rough sea, Stephen kept the captain company in the pilothouse, "smoking and telling yarns." He had shipped out as a twenty-dollar-a-month seaman, and he was determined to act the part. The ship's cook was impressed: Crane "never quailed when he came on deck and saw the foaming and raging billows," he said.

At first Stephen was too excited to sleep. Then, when he tried to sleep, he was distracted by a valise on deck that threatened "with every lurch of the ship" to hit him. The cook thought they wouldn't get out of this alive. And yet he sensed that if they did, he and Stephen Crane would see each other again — "down at Coney Island, perhaps." Even the old seaman at the wheel thought he'd quit filibustering after this trip.

Stephen settled into a corner of the pilothouse and was almost asleep when the chief engineer came running up the stairs. There was a problem in the boiler room, he told the captain. By the time Captain Murphy got there, several inches of water had covered the floor. The pumps were down. The engine room looked like a scene "taken from the middle kitchen of hades," wrote Stephen. In this "insufferably warm" place, "faintly" burning lights cast "mystic and gruesome shadows" while "soapish sea water" washed over the steaming, roaring, clattering machinery. "It was a devil of a ways down below." He joined a human chain of Cubans led by the ship's oiler, Billy Higgins, who filled buckets and passed them down the line.

Nothing worked. Captain Murphy ordered the men to use their buckets to pile wood, oil, and alcohol into the room in the hope that with a larger fire the tug could work up enough steam to get them to Mosquito Inlet, some sixteen miles due west and one hundred miles down the coast from Jacksonville. But the water put out the fires. Stephen overheard talk about sending up a rocket. He climbed to the slippery deckhouse to help Higgins and "two colored stokers" wrest a lifeboat from its place. He cheerfully removed his new shoes and "tossed them overboard," saying with a laugh, "Well, Captain, I guess I won't need them if we have to swim."

Even with four men working to free the lifeboat, it seemed to weigh "as much as a Broadway cable car." They "could have pushed a little brick school-house along a corduroy road as easily." Higgins raged at Stephen and the two black stokers. Finally the lifeboat started to move, and they eased it into the water.

Some of the men panicked. A coal heaver entered the hold with a package of dynamite, telling the captain that "they might as well let that off at once." Murphy took it from him gently, then shouted, "Lie there, you cowardly dog! Obey orders, and we'll all get off."

A young sailor ran up the rigging and tried to stand on his head. Another kneeled before the captain, praying to be thrown overboard. A Negro stoker was so swaddled in life preservers that "he looked like a feather-bed," wrote Stephen. Murphy cursed him. A Cuban panicked and tried to get into one of the lifeboats ahead of time. Stephen knocked him down onto the leeway, stunning him.

As Stephen worked, he smoked a cigarette. When he wasn't working, he stood on the bridge, looking through glasses for a glimmer of the Mosquito Inlet lighthouse. The ship rocked from side to side so violently, "her yards almost touching the waves," that it seemed to the steward that Stephen "would be swept off." Then the *Commodore*'s whistle sounded. "This cry on the sea at night" sang of "despair and death," wrote Stephen. There was something different in its melody — "as if its throat was already choked by the water." Amid the wind and the spraying water, it seemed "a song of man's end."

Three lifeboats were lowered into the ocean, and men tumbled into them. When the third boat hit the water, the captain told the men remaining on board that anyone who wanted to go should go now. Seven men climbed in. Stephen stayed on deck with Captain Murphy, Higgins, the oiler, and the steward, C. B. Montgomery. All that remained was a ten-foot dinghy — much smaller than the lifeboats. The captain told Stephen to get in first. He was dropped in, then handed a five-gallon water jug. The other three got in next, the captain, whose left arm was in a sling, going last. Though the dark waves around the sinking tug threatened to swamp the dinghy, the captain said, "Boys, we will stay right near the ship till she goes down." They gladly obeyed.

At ten o'clock in the morning of January 2, a Saturday, after six hours of rowing, one of the *Commodore*'s lifeboats reached shore two miles north of Mosquito Inlet. Two hours later a second boat came in. An empty boat washed up at Port Orange. Sixteen Cuban men had survived the sinking, sixteen miles off the coast of Florida; the fate of the rest was unknown.

When news of the disaster reached Jacksonville, Cora Taylor asked Morton, the room clerk at the St. James, to find out what he could. Writing at nine o'clock that night, apparently from Mosquito Inlet, where he had traveled, he reported that Stephen was not among the "eleven men" who had turned up in town. One man claimed to have seen Stephen get into the third boat, which was then swamped, wrote Morton. There were "conflicting stories as to the empty boat being washed ashore. Some say it has been washed ashore at Port Orange — others say not. The Operator at New Smyrna tells me that he has it pretty straight that it came in, bottom up. God save Crane if he is still alive!"

✦

It took her a long time to die. The men in the dinghy joked that maybe she wouldn't sink at all. The waves around the sinking tug were "monstrous," wrote Stephen — "as high as I have ever seen them hereabouts," said Captain Murphy. "They rolled in on us, threatening to dash us against the sinking tug, and we expected every moment to be overthrown. It was pitch dark, and you could not see your hands before your face." Each time the dinghy rose on a swell, the four men crammed close together saw "the swaying lights of the dying Commodore." In the "biting" wind, as the waves washed over the men and chilled them, they kept bailing out the dinghy; this kept their blood circulating, kept them warm. At dawn the sinking ship's outline gradually came into focus in the gray morning light.

The accounts of what happened next differ in small details. In his short story "The Open Boat," Stephen would remember that the men in the dinghy had rowed only yards away from the sinking tug when a cry rang out. The third lifeboat, carrying the first mate, had returned to the ship, apparently to retrieve something he had forgotten. Then the lifeboat was staved, apparently by the monstrous waves around the ship, and the men climbed onto the *Commodore*'s stern and flew a distress flag.

Keeping the dinghy some twenty yards distant, the captain told the stranded men to make rafts. They did as instructed, then begged the captain to take them in tow. He agreed, and the men in the dinghy set about making a towline. Then Murphy directed the men to jump. Two jumped and got hold of rafts; then the first mate dove to his death — knowingly, it looked to Stephen. He was not wearing a lifebelt, and in the turn of his head and hands Stephen thought he discerned "rage, rage, rage unspeakable . . . in his heart." Tom Smith, the man whom Stephen had earlier overheard saying he was going to quit filibustering, was the next to jump and grab on to a raft. Three men remained on board the sinking *Commodore*.

As the men in the dinghy constructed the towline, the wind and the water worked against them, and the dinghy took in a lot of water. Suddenly a black stoker on one raft threw the men a line to tow him; they tried to, but "there was an enormous sea running," and the dinghy was in constant danger of overturning. Stephen was at one oar, facing the rafts and the stoker; the cook controlled the line. All at once the stoker started "pulling on the line hand over hand," pulling the dinghy toward him and getting ready to spring into it. The water was breaking over the towline; there seemed only one thing to do: "The cook let go of the line," wrote Stephen. The stoker drowned.

Afterward the men in the dinghy attempted to get a line from the chief engineer, but the rafts separated and shattered in the water. Water swamped the dinghy. While Stephen and the others bailed out, the *Commodore* sank, just fifty yards from the dinghy, the sea swallowing the remaining men on board. They went down without so much as a "murmur." The men in the dinghy exchanged words "that were still not words, something far beyond words," wrote Stephen.

The dinghy remained by the rafts for another twenty minutes. Finally, with the high seas and the mighty wind threatening to overturn the small craft, the men gave in to the wind and allowed the dinghy to be carried off.

The oiler steered with one oar, Stephen with the other. The steward, Montgomery (called "the cook" in "The Open Boat"), squatted at the bottom of the boat, his eyes fixed on "the six inches of gunwale which separated him from the ocean." The injured captain lay dazed and depressed, unable to shake the last terrible picture of the seven who drowned — the look of their "seven turned faces" — and the sight of the *Commodore* as she went down. He directed his crew in a voice that was "beyond oration or tears."

In this new existence bordered on all sides by water, Stephen rowed, keeping his eyes level with the sea. The waves were the color of slate and capped with "foaming white," and they were "barbarously abrupt and tall," he wrote. In this wall of water he found "a terrible grace." He rowed.

They told the time of day by the color of the water. When it was "emerald-green, streaked with amber lights, and the foam was like tumbling snow," it was "broad day." The point of their compass was the great cone-shaped lighthouse at Mosquito Inlet. Topped with a high-powered hydraulic lamp designed by George Gordon Meade, commander of the Union army at Gettysburg, its light could be seen eighteen nautical miles away. As the men in the dinghy rowed toward it through the "towering" sea, pausing occasionally to bail out the boat, the light was the size of a pinhead.

Always they were in danger of overturning. So precarious was their position that when a bird tried to land on them, the captain shooed it away with his good arm — carefully, lest he capsize the boat. When they needed to change places, they did so with the care of high-wire performers, for "it is easier to steal eggs from under a hen than it was to change seats in the dinghy," wrote Stephen.

That first day, their state of mind was serene; in spite of the biting cold, they were warmed by their camaraderie, "by the subtle brotherhood of men," and no captain had a more obedient or willing crew. "The correspondent," wrote Stephen, "who had been taught to be cynical of men, knew even at the time [that] this was the best experience of his life." He sensed that the others knew it too, though none of them said so.

As they rowed toward the lighthouse, it turned from a pinhead to "a little gray shadow." Even when the men slept, they did not really sleep, and the rowing became a "diabolical punishment . . . a horror to the muscles and a crime against the back." Eventually they got close enough to shore to make out a house, and the red brick lighthouse suddenly "reared high." It was late afternoon on January 2 when they approached land. There were no signs of life on shore. The dinghy was about a quarter of a mile out, and the men dared not bring her in any farther because the surf was so rough. They flew a distress flag; the captain fired his pistol. No rescue came. The men's optimism turned to rage. They began swearing. "If I am going to be drowned," Stephen thought, "— if I am going to be drowned — if I am going to be drowned — Why, in the name of the seven mad gods who rule the sea, was I allowed to come this far and contemplate sand and trees?" A squall was coming up from the southeast, and the sea was becoming more perilous. The captain directed his crew to take the dinghy farther out, where the waters were calmer. They would try again the next morning.

At one point that afternoon they seemed on the brink of rescue. A man appeared on shore and began frantically waving his coat to them. Then others joined him on the beach, and the man went on waving his coat. The men in the dinghy could not interpret the signal: was the man warning them of something, telling them that help was on its way, or simply having sport with them? They waited, but no help came, and the emerald water turned a sinister black.

"A night on the sea in an open boat is a long night," wrote Stephen. They rowed all night, keeping their eyes on the light to the north. Stephen and the oiler took turns, each man rowing until his strength gave out, then waking the other and carefully changing places in the open boat. Rowing kept them warm; the moment they stopped, their teeth began to chatter. While Stephen rowed, Montgomery and the oiler huddled together.

The night was so dark and the tall waves so black and silent that "often one was almost upon the boat before the oarsman was aware." During one of his turns at the oars, Stephen heard "a long swishing astern of the boat." Then he saw "a gleaming trail of phosphorescence, like blue flame," a shape that "might have been made by a monstrous knife." The shark was almost close enough to touch with an oar, and as there was no one awake to talk to, Stephen "swore softly into the sea." He rowed on as the shark's fin sliced the water around the boat. Fatigue knocked the fear out of a man being circled by a shark. Stephen thought that "if he had been a picnicker" sighting the creature from shore he would have felt more fear than he felt now.

As he rowed, a verse he had learned in childhood floated into his head:

> A soldier of the legion lay dying in Algiers,
> There was lack of woman's nursing, there was dearth of
>   woman's tears;
> But a comrade stood beside him, and he took that
>   comrade's hand,
> And he said: "I never more shall see my own, my native land."

In the morning they saw land again, cottages and a windmill on the dunes, but no people. After some thirty hours of rowing, they had little strength left, and they decided to take the dinghy in as far as they could, then swim when the boat swamped. The inshore rollers were high. Beyond tiredness, Stephen merely thought it would be a shame if he drowned. A soldier of the legion lay dying in Algiers . . .

As they brought the dinghy in, the waves thrashed them.

"Look out, boys!" called the captain. There were only two life preservers. The captain directed Stephen and Montgomery to put them on, "they being the least able to help themselves," though the captain's own arm was broken. The sound of the surf grew louder, and the men became "nervous." Big rollers hit them, and hit them again; on the third one they went over.

The captain called out to Stephen to make sure that his lifebelt was adjusted and "up on his body."

"All right, captain, I'll do as you command," Stephen called back "cheerfully."

The water was ice cold. Stephen experienced a jumble of sensations: the noise of the water, the image of his comrades swimming toward shore, the oiler strong and fast and ahead of the rest of them. He saw "the cook's great white and corked back," the captain "hanging with his one good hand to the keel of the overturned dinghy," the water jar he himself had carried into the dinghy bobbing "gayly over the seas." The waves carried the dinghy and its belongings, and the swimmers had to watch out for flying oars and the boat and other objects.

At first Stephen found the swimming fairly easy; then he entered a current. The captain, seeing that he was in trouble, called him to the overturned dinghy. But as Stephen made his way there, a wave picked him up, hurled him over the dinghy and "far beyond it," to waist-high water. He was so weak and the undertow was so strong that his legs buckled. He became aware of a man running toward him down the beach, peeling off his clothes. Once in the water the man dragged Montgomery out. He was about to assist the captain when Murphy directed him to Stephen instead.

"Thanks, old man," said Stephen. Then he noticed the oiler lying face down in the water.

When he felt land beneath his feet, his strength left him. Then the beach came alive with running figures carrying blankets, hot coffee, clothes, flasks. Stephen saw a "dripping shape . . . carried slowly up the beach."

The way to sleep lay up a little embankment on the Halifax River in Daytona Beach. A pretty Victorian clapboard house was Stephen's sanctuary that Sunday night; his comrades were put up at the Surfcrest cottage on the dunes. The residents did everything they could for the men, fed them, gave them medical treatment.

Before resting, Stephen sent off some telegrams, including one to Cora Taylor, who immediately telegraphed back:

> Telegram received. Thank God your safe have been almost
> crazy.
>
> C.T.

In a second telegram, she told Stephen to come to Jacksonville by special train that day, as regular trains did not run on Sunday, and "never mind overcharges." Exhausted, suffering from exposure, and broke — he'd had to throw his gold-filled money belt into the sea — Stephen decided to stay where he was. The next morning Cora took a train to Daytona to bring him home.

Fred Niver, who worked the telegraph in the railroad office at Daytona Beach, observed Stephen and Cora in the train station's waiting room the next day, after Cora arrived on the noon train. They sat in a corner, all wrapped up in each other, "hugging and kissing like lovebirds until time for the afternoon northbound train. That's the last I saw of them."

A crowd of some two hundred Cubans was at the Jacksonville train station to greet Stephen and some of the other *Commodore* survivors. And when a tattered Stephen Crane walked into the St. James Hotel later that evening, wearing the same sailing clothes he'd shipped out in four days earlier, now "shrunk to half [their] former size," he found a female admirer waiting for him. Miss Lillian Barrett, a guest of the hotel, had been shadowing him for some time in hopes of getting his autograph for her album. Stephen caught sight of the nine-year-old girl and waved to her.

"Where's that album?" he called out.

Lillian eagerly retrieved the book from the clerk's desk and gave it to Stephen. He wrote:

> Stephen Crane, Able Seaman; S S Commodore, January 4,
> 1897.

Telegrams fluttered in like confetti. "Congratulations on plucky and successful fight for life," wrote Edward Marshall, now a foreign correspondent for the *New York Journal*. The message told Stephen not to wire but to "write fully from Jax. will wire money today." Hawkins sent money as well as an official message of "praise and congratulation — praise for your manly bearing in the presence of danger, and congratulation for your deliverance from that danger," from the Sign o' the Lanthorn.

The disaster was widely reported, making the front page of many newspapers outside of Jacksonville, including the *New York Times* and the *Atlanta Journal*. Some reports announced that Stephen Crane had drowned. There were persistent rumors that the *Commodore* had been sabotaged — a charge reported as a fact in the *New York Times*. Battered and worn from his ordeal, his broken left arm in a sling, Captain Murphy told the Cubans in Jacksonville that the sabotage story "is a damned lie," and attributed the sinking to a mechanical problem in the pumps. Able Seaman Stephen Crane agreed. On January 6, in response to a query, he telegraphed the *Atlanta Journal* that "the ship was probably not scuttled." "The *Commodore* was a fine boat," he told the *New York World*. "She carried her load like a cork and breasted the waves like a duck, and she was buoyant and did not seem to strain at all. It is rather queer, to say the least, that such a leak occurred."

But the rumors of treachery persisted. The need to affix blame and generate good newspaper copy produced more ugly allegations. The captain was blamed for ignoring the advice of river men who were said to have warned him that the old wooden tug could not support the heavy cargo she was carrying. Everyone had an opinion. Paul F. Rojo, the Cuban commandant of the *Commodore*, told the *Florida Times-Union* that he thought the ship's engineer had been drunk and neglecting his duties. The steward, Montgomery, refuted that accusation. He spoke of a mysterious Spaniard who had visited him on board just before the *Commodore* left port and had begged him not to go: "You risk your own life," said the stranger. When the *Commodore* ran aground in the St. Johns River, Montgomery had had what he called a "premonition." He told the *Florida Times-Union* that he now suspected that the tug's steering gear had been tampered with.

Stephen emerged from "the best experience of his life" with his reputation enhanced, if not restored after his battering in the Dora Clark affair. Both of his surviving comrades from the dinghy praised him publicly. "Crane is a man every inch of him, and he acted throughout with true grit," said Captain Murphy. The *Chicago Tribune* called him "plucky." The *New York World* ran an article under the heading "Crane Knocks Down a

Coward." One New York newspaper offered him "$1,000 for 1,000 words" about the event. He turned it down, honoring his commitment to Bacheller instead.

"I am unable to write a thing yet but will later," he wired Bacheller on January 4, then wrote "Stephen Crane's Own Story," a thousand-word account of the wreck, focusing on the *Commodore*'s short voyage up to the sinking. It was syndicated on January 7 under a different title. Though a creditable piece of writing, it was not the best that was in him. He had not written of his real ordeal at sea, which began not with the sinking of the *Commodore* but with his descent into the ten-foot dinghy. Though he "would prefer to tell the story at once, because from it would shine the splendid manhood of Captain Edward Murphy and of William Higgins, the oiler," he was not yet up to it.

The affair with Cora Taylor, which had begun for Stephen as a brief pleasure with an unnamed sweetheart, had turned to love, or something approximating love. With his sea adventure still fresh, Stephen wrote into one of Cora's books a paraphrase of one of his better poems.*

> to C.E.S.
> Love comes like the tall
> swift shadow of a ship at
> night. There is for a mom-
> ent, the music of the water's
> turmoil, a bell, perhaps, a
> man's shout, a row of gleam-
> ing yellow lights. Then the
> slow sinking of this mystic
> shape. Then silence and a
> bitter silence — the silence
> of the sea at night.
> Stephen Crane

---

* The original had been published in the *Bookman* in 1896:
  I explain the silvered passing of a ship at night / The sweep of each sad lost wave / The dwindling boom of the steel thing's striving / The little cry of a man to a man / A shadow falling across the greyer night / And the sinking of the small star. / Then the waste, the far waste of waters / And the soft lashing of black waves / For long and in loneliness. / Remember, thou, oh ship of love / Thou leavest a far waste of waters / And the soft lashing of black waves / For long and in loneliness.

He was her writer now, her literary lover; he wrote to her in poetry, on the flyleaves of books. There are no surviving letters from Stephen to Cora, but the scanty evidence shows that he wrote to her with a certain reserve — to C.E.S. from Stephen Crane — and in metaphor rather than directly, passionately, as he wrote to Amy Leslie. Cora was the woman who was there, ready to do anything for him, and for the moment, at least, he was content to be with her.

A Jacksonville doctor who met Stephen at the Hotel de Dream during this time was struck by Cora's quiet happiness as she hovered over Stephen, "filling up the glasses and just patting him every once in a while, right like a mother whose boy had come home with a Sunday school prize." The doctor, who had been with one of Cora's girls earlier in the evening and was about to leave, was invited to join Cora and the celebrity writer in her private apartment, where the two were dining on "quail on toast, and some watercress salad, and two or three bottles of champagne. . . . It was on the house, Cora said." Cora had sent a messenger down to the doctor's room at midnight to ask him to "help entertain a friend" — a gesture that seems odd at a time when lovers would presumably want their privacy. The doctor sat down, and the conversation stretched into the next day, breaking up "after seven in the morning. You could see she was simply crazy about him." As for Stephen, he was morose and looked "rather slouchy" — his dirty shirt appeared to have been worn for a week. "If he ever said anything pleasant about anybody, it was not while I was around," said the doctor.

Though he needed rest, he wanted action. More than "woman's nursing," he needed time alone in a room to write the story of his ordeal. He began to talk of leaving town. "I will stay in Jacksonville until another expedition starts for Cuba," he told the *Atlanta Journal* on January 7. Yet five days later, he was en route to New York. "I am feeling stronger, and after a short rest I shall make new plans for my visit to Cuba," he told the *Port Jervis Union*. He applied for a passport to Cuba, Mexico, and the West Indies.

10

THEY SAY

SMOLENSKI WEPT

He looked like a man from a grave," said Louis Senger. "He jerked and thrashed in his sleep, and sometimes cried out in anguish." And yet he wrote with the control of an athlete at the top of his form, both physically and psychologically. Stephen apparently began writing "The Open Boat" in Jacksonville, leaving for New York when it became clear that he could not work there, even by hiding out in a bar — such was the reach of Cora's loving arms. He finished the story about a month later in New York.

From its sublime first sentence — "None of them knew the color of the sky" — to its lyrical last lines, "The Open Boat" is the work of a writer at the height of his powers. Written in a measured prose that catches something of the sea's rhythm, Crane's 9,000-word story, generally regarded as his masterpiece, is a straightforward yet complex rendering of his experience in the dinghy. Charting both the narrator's inner life and the action at sea, the two levels of consciousness move out through the narrative like twin rings of water. There are no false steps. "It is the writing of somebody who cannot go wrong . . . who is authentic," said the English novelist and editor Ford Madox Hueffer (who later changed his name to Ford Madox Ford).

"Shipwrecks are apropos of nothing," Stephen wrote. He had written about shipwrecks before, in his as yet unpublished tale "The Reluctant Voyagers" and in another unpublished piece, "The Wreck of the 'New Era.'" In "The Reluctant Voyagers," his little men, seemingly yanked from the Sullivan County woods, take to the sea as bumbling, helpless babes and are rocked to sleep by the lullaby sound of the "lapping waves" on the small craft. (Stephen used the same image to greater effect in "The Open Boat," where the correspondent's sleeping comrades in their ragged clothes look like "babes of the sea.") Written in 1891–92, "The Wreck of the 'New Era'" told of an 1854 shipwreck off the coast of New Jersey, in which the spectators on shore were forced to watch helplessly as many people on board drowned — an uncanny harbinger of Stephen's real-life drama in the dinghy.

In writing "The Open Boat," Stephen felt compelled to speak not only for himself but for his comrades in the dinghy, to whom he dedicated the manuscript. He appended a subtitle, "A tale intended to be after the fact. Being the experience of four men from the steamer Commodore," and later read the story to Captain Murphy before it was published. It was important that he get it right. He knew, of course, that truth in fiction had nothing to do with a slavish adherence to facts; he had rendered a psychological truth in *The Red Badge* by making his battle a type. But as his work matured and he continued to develop his own theories of realism, he reached higher, marrying the reporter to the artist, moving further outside himself.

The point of view in "The Open Boat" is free of Henry Fleming's self-centeredness. Although Crane's is the controlling vision through which the reader feels what the men in the dinghy feel, he keeps himself down, becoming part of the ensemble of captain, cook, oiler, and correspondent. (Only the drowned oiler, Billy Higgins, is ever referred to by name.) The story is at once personal and universal, the orphans in the dinghy seen as mere specks on the vast sea, part of the larger cosmic picture. Stephen Crane's sea story, "the most poignant religious story in American literature," became a tale about life and death and man's place in the world. In the end, the babes of the sea move from anonymous figures whose own self-absorption prevents them from knowing the color of the sky to enlightened beings who can interpret their experience.

"When it came night, the white waves paced to and fro in the moonlight, and the wind brought the sound of the great sea's voice to the men on shore, and they felt that they could then be interpreters," Stephen wrote in closing.

That he could write the story so soon after the event, reaching new literary heights while still grappling with personal aftershock, is remarkable. He didn't believe in inspiration; he believed "that an enthusiasm of concentration in hard work is what a writer must depend on to bring him to the end he has in view." And yet concentration alone was not enough. It had taken him months to write his merely fair story about the frightening chase by *pistoleros* in Mexico. His one piece about the Dora Clark fiasco was unexceptional. And yet such is the mystery of artistic creation that in only a month's time he had produced a masterpiece.

During Stephen's short time in New York that winter, he moved about the city apparently without fear of the police, who had not forgotten his betrayal in the Dora Clark affair. He was aware of the rumors still circulating about him, and he complained to Linson about the "mountain of lies." But he was not about to play the role of criminal by hiding.

On January 19 he attended the annual French ball given by the Cercle Français de l'Harmonie in Madison Square Garden. His presence there was no secret. Asked by a Boston reporter how the ball impressed him, Stephen said: "There is the reflection of the light upon the white shirt bosoms of the men. . . . That is about all I can see." Police Captain Chapman, Charles Becker's superior in the Dora Clark affair, was also there. A story got around later that as Stephen was leaving with friends, the police tried to arrest him for drunkenness.

As midnight approached one cold night in January or February, Stephen stood contemplating the pavement under the Sixth Avenue elevated, near 33rd Street and Broadway. He wore a long, rust-colored overcoat, the collar turned up against the chill wind, and a black felt hat pulled low over his eyes. Before he could escape, a reporter named William Dunlevy called out to him, "Oh, Crane! Here's a man who can't sleep until he meets you."

The man was Robert H. Davis, a *Journal* reporter with whom Stephen had recently broken an appointment. Stephen had contracted to go to Greece as a correspondent covering the impending war with Turkey — a backup plan in case he couldn't get to Cuba — and he was supposed to see Davis about the arrangements.

He offered Davis a limp handshake. Plainly uninterested in conversation, he said something about going up Broadway toward Herald Square "in search of kindred spirits," but Davis managed to keep him talking.

Davis had been wanting to meet the famous "Stevey Crane," as Dunlevy called him, for he was the talk of Park Row and Grub Street. One newspaper hack had told the newly hired Davis that Crane was an epileptic and a drug addict. Davis longed to talk to Crane about *The Red Badge*, and he wanted to pass along a compliment from Ambrose Bierce. He brought up Greece, something "about covering a war in the country for which Lord Byron was prepared to shed his blood."

"No man should be called upon to report a war in a country that he loves," said Stephen, adding that since "Greece means nothing to me" — and neither did Turkey — he'd "do a better job than Lord Byron could have done." He imagined it would be cold there after Florida.

"By the way, this is a hell of a town," Stephen told Davis. "I never come here without feeling the necessity for taking immediate steps to go elsewhere."

"Hardly the place for a minister's son," said Davis.

"Well, for that matter, is there any place exactly suited to a minister's son?" said Stephen.

"We are not understood."

"You, too?"

This discovery changed Stephen from unfriendly to talkative, though he was reluctant to discuss himself. As he spoke, a cigarette dangled from his mouth, punctuating his words "like a baton," said Davis.

"This is the point of view," Stephen told him. "The bartender's boy falls from the Waldorf roof. The minister's son falls from a park bench. They both hit the earth with the same velocity, mutilated beyond recognition."

Davis had just offered to buy Stephen a drink at the Imperial Bar when a young woman approached them. Tossing his cigarette into the street, Stephen removed his hat, pressed one hand to his heart, and bowed. Under the shadowy arc lights on Broadway, his face became as beautiful as a painting. Warmed by the sight of the girl, his sallow skin took on a coral tone, said Davis. His long tawny hair fell into a soft lock on his white forehead, and his mouth was graced with an "elusive smile." Until that moment Davis had wondered at the descriptions he'd heard of Crane's famous eyes, which didn't seem remarkable to him. Suffused now with "an almost indescribable luminous beauty, . . . they were large, the iris seemingly out of proportion to the pupil, blue in general tone, brilliant, flashing."

"A stranger here?" said Stephen, speaking to the girl "with the utmost delicacy," said Davis.

She hesitated a moment.

"Well, suppose I am a stranger. Can you show me anything?"

"Yes, I can show you the way out, but if you prefer to remain —" Stephen bowed again.

The girl buttoned her coat button at the throat, and Davis noticed that "the light seemed to go out of Stephen Crane's eyes as though some one had turned down a lamp from within."

"You shouldn't hang out here, kid," she said in a rough voice. "You look cold. You can't stand it. This fat guy can."

And she walked off in the direction of Delmonico's.

"This is a long cañon," Stephen told Davis. "I wonder if there *is* a way out. Come, now you can have your picon and ginger ale. I'll *not* have the same."

Sitting at the bar later with their feet propped against the brass railing, Davis told Stephen what Ambrose Bierce had said about *The Red Badge* — that this writer who knew nothing of war had the power to feel, was drenched in blood. Seemingly unaffected by the compliment, Stephen slid his untouched whiskey glass back and forth along a wet spot on the walnut bar and chain-smoked.

Noticing a tub of rubber plants in a corner of the restaurant, he said, "If we were in Cuba now, there would be five murderers with drawn machetes behind those Brooklyn palms. Two of them would be candidates for office."

He continued to slide his glass on the bar. Had Davis read Bierce's "Occurrence at Owl Creek Bridge"? he asked.

Davis said he had.

"Nothing better exists," said Stephen. "That story contains everything. Move your foot over."

He wanted to know about Bierce's personality. Davis told him what he knew about Bierce and said he didn't think he would "be appreciated until long after he is dead."

"Has he plenty of enemies?"

"More than he needs," said Davis.

"Good. Then he will become an immortal," said Stephen. He stood up and gave Davis a warm handshake.

"Good night!" he said. "I hope to see you when I get back from Greece."

His whiskey sat on the bar, untouched. The next day Davis told a reporter about meeting Stephen Crane. When he added that Stephen had never touched his drink at the Imperial Bar, the reporter responded with a "raucous guffaw." The story got around the *Journal* office, causing "a fit of laughter" after each telling. Davis decided to keep quiet about Stephen's chivalrous behavior toward the street girl.

Having finished "The Open Boat," on February 10 he was back in Jacksonville, eager for another crack at Cuba. "He is confident of making the shores of that island before the war is ended," reported the *Florida Times-Union*. William Hearst's yacht, the *Buccaneer*, had arrived in port, and it was said that Crane and Charles Michelson would use her as a dispatch boat — a claim denied by the man in charge of the yacht, Theodore Hilborn.

By March 11 Stephen had lost hope of getting to Cuba. The navy's revenue cutters were enforcing neutrality laws by forming blockades along the Florida coast, and after more than "a month among the swamps wading miserably to and fro in an attempt to avoid our derned U.S. navy," as Stephen put it in a letter to William, he gave up. He returned to New York, bound for Greece.

Stephen may have seen Amy Leslie during these months in and out of New York, for she was precisely informed of his earnings. Badly in need of money, she had been hounding Hawkins. In two messages in January and February, she referred to checks coming in to Stephen from Bacheller — "one from the syndicate and the other from the herald."

Linson found his friend quite transformed from the old days. He was no longer the ragged bohemian with holes in his shoes; he was groomed and brushed — "a rather dandified Steve," said Linson. He wore a suit that fit, and had a real mustache instead of a shading. When he took his usual place on the couch, he sat rather than sprawled. Linson had been to Greece, and Stephen plied him with questions.

"Willie Hearst is sending me for the war," he said. "What I'll do among those Dagoes I don't know. What are they like, CK? How did you chin their lingo?"

He seemed worried that the war might be over before he got there. Though Linson was seeing him for the first time since the *Commodore* sinking, Stephen's only reference to the event was casual. To Linson's description of a Greek drink called *retsinato*, Stephen said, "No thanks! Not for this Indian! Nearly cashed in down in Florida."

Over dinner that night in a restaurant on 23rd Street at Fourth Avenue, Stephen showed his usual reserve when talking about women. But he said he'd met a girl in Jacksonville whom he planned to marry. She was older, she had "suffered from unfortunate circumstances." Linson didn't ask for details. They "could sail on the same steamer and be married in England," said Stephen, "but there were tongues. The weasels would draw blood anyway." Still, "he hated to leave her alone, but his job was to go on to Greece and come back when the stew was over."

"What would you do, CK?"

"If you love her, marry her," said Linson.

Curiously, Stephen never mentioned the girl's name.

Whether because he hated to leave Cora alone or because she was determined not to be left, they decided that she would follow him abroad. (She apparently left Jacksonville without paying her bills. On March 22 a warrant for nonpayment of debt was issued, and the Hotel de Dream furniture was seized by the sheriff.) Stephen spent five or six days in New York saying his goodbyes, putting an extra six or seven hundred dollars in his pocket by promising McClure "first option on the serial publication of his next stories," and writing another piece about the *Commodore* called "Flanagan and His Short Filibustering Adventure."

While he was in New York, on March 19, Willis Hawkins made another payment to Amy Leslie in the amount of $12.95, which left him $4.00 out of pocket. The entire $500 Stephen had given him in November was now gone in payments to both Amy and Stephen — a fact Stephen seems to have been unaware of. Stephen was flush. In addition to the loan from McClure, he was to get $300 for "The Open Boat," which his agent, Paul Revere Reynolds, had sold to *Scribner's*. He had other expectations as well. Heinemann had published *The Little Regiment* in its Pioneer Series on February 6. *The Third Violet* would be published in May, and he expected to finish "Flanagan" before he left the country.

Though Stephen had planned to make a flying trip to Port Jervis to say goodbye to his brothers and "chin" for a couple of hours, "Flanagan" was turning out to be a long story and his time was "most tragically short." Edmund hurried to New York to see him. Stephen gave him a copy of *An Army Wife*, by Charles King, as a farewell gift, "E.B. Crane from Stephen March 19, 1897 on his departure for bretn."

The next day, Saturday, March 20, he sailed for Liverpool on the Cunard liner *Etruria*.

✦

London welcomed him like an old friend. He met his English publisher, William Heinemann, and Heinemann's partner, Sidney Pawling, who had written to him so graciously about *The Red Badge* after its English publication. Richard Harding Davis, who was himself about to depart for Greece as correspondent for the *Times* of London, threw a formal luncheon for Stephen at the Savoy to introduce him to some of the local literary establishment: Anthony Hope, Justin H. McCarthy, Sir James Barrie, and Harold Frederic, who had praised *The Red Badge* in a glowing review in the *New York Times* a year earlier. The luncheon was interrupted by the arrival of a lance sergeant on horseback, who carried a large envelope marked "On Her Majesty's Service." The guests assumed that Turkey had declared war on Greece, and their host called away to the front. But the envelope revealed only a letter of regret from Sir Evelyn Wood, who had been detained at the War Office and was unable to attend the luncheon. Davis gave Stephen the letter as a souvenir.

During his whirlwind three-day visit to London, Stephen charmed the British press with his unassuming personality and his "extreme and refreshing modesty, being conspicuously free of the tendency to self-advertisement which is so often characteristic of the Novelist's Progress," as Arthur Waugh wrote in the *Critic*. Stephen joked to reporters that "he was off to Crete because, having written so much about war, he thought it high time he should see a little fighting." Even his rival Davis was impressed. Though Davis had been in Jacksonville when Stephen was there, the two men had not met. "He is very modest sturdy and shy," Davis wrote his mother. "Quiet unlike I imagined." In a letter to Nellie Crouse, Stephen had once called Davis a "stuffed parrot," someone with "the intelligence of the average saw-log"; whether he liked Davis better in person is unknown. But the meeting was friendly enough that the two men agreed to sit together on the train to Paris.

The Davis-Crane relationship was ambivalent at best. Long before they met, they had been compared in print as writers — a fact that in itself might discourage a friendship. In his Lower East Side days Stephen had taken heart when Hamlin Garland, in the *Arena*, rated him the better writer; R. G. Vosburgh remembered that Stephen often quoted Garland's words, which had helped sustain him. Linked in an 1896 article in *Leslie's Weekly* as belonging to one of the "new groups of writers, or schools . . . who . . . are inaugurating a new and brighter period in our literary history," the two had a number of things in common. Davis had attended

Lehigh College in Pennsylvania, a nearby rival of Lafayette; like Stephen, he did not graduate. Both men were athletic. Both had lived and worked in New York as newspapermen, and their journalism had informed their fiction. Both had mothers who were writers.* But as a biographer of Davis notes, they were "fundamentally different."

Each had something the other lacked and was sensitive about lacking. Davis was the image of the dashing war correspondent: handsome in a rather bland way, with a trim nose and smallish eyes, and immaculately groomed, poised. "Read by multitudes of nubile maidens with accelerated heart beats and retarded breaths," said Claude Bragdon, Davis was the kind of man who got the nice girl, the Nellie Crouse. "The social crisis" never seemed to catch *him* unaware.

From Davis's perspective, Stephen had both genius and greatness as a writer. Though Davis had made his name as a war writer, he was generous enough to salute the seven-years-younger Crane as the superior talent, a gesture that would seem rare among writers of any caliber. After the book publication of *The Red Badge*, Davis had told his brother that "Stephen Crane seems to have written the last word as far as battles or fighting is concerned." The luncheon for Stephen in London was apparently given in a spirit of goodwill and genuine camaraderie. And yet, to the conventional Davis, as to Theodore Roosevelt, there was something distasteful about Stephen personally, a disturbing lack of inhibition, which later brought out some of Davis's less attractive qualities.

Whether by prearrangement or coincidence, on April 1 the two men met at the station of the London train to Paris. On the platform Davis caught sight of the golden-haired Cora, whom he later described in a letter as "a bi-roxide blonde who seemed to be attending to [Crane's] luggage for him and whom I did not meet." Davis and Stephen settled in on the train together while Cora and Mrs. Ruedy, her companion from Jacksonville, removed to a separate compartment. But Stephen was embarrassed. Of his correspondent-hero in the novel *Active Service* he later wrote that he "was understood by all to declare that his prehensile attributes had not led him to cart a notorious woman about the world with him."

In the rush of the next few days, he and Cora passed from one new sight to another, gliding from London to Paris and on to Marseilles, where he

* Davis's mother was the novelist Rebecca Harding Davis.

boarded the French steamer *Guadiana*. He was filled with the coming war, with seeing what he had so long imagined. He'd have gone out to sea in a pail.

The four-day voyage to Greece was uneventful until the passengers were informed that the ship had changed course. Instead of going to Piraeus, the port of Athens, they were heading to Suda Bay on Crete's northern coast to deliver mailbags to the European fleet — the Concert of Powers, as it was called. The long struggle for the island of Crete having erupted in violence and bloodshed between the Turks and the Greeks, Great Britain, France, Russia, Italy, Germany, and Austria had come in and formed an international protectorate.

In his first dispatch Stephen described "the top-gear of warships, stacks of tan, of white, of black, and fighting masts and the blaze of signal flags." The sight was "very unlike the pictures in the illustrated papers which appear always to have been sketched from balloons." And yet, personifying war in his characteristic way, he saw the warships as "great steel animals"; the torpedo boats reminded him of "a shadow on the water," like the shark circling his dinghy two months earlier.

From the Grand Hotel d'Angleterre in Athens on April 10, he paused to write a breathless letter to William announcing that he would soon be leaving for the "frontier." About to see war at long last — the elephant, as Civil War soldiers had called it — the romantic boy who had wanted a military career rose to the surface, pushing aside the great war writer, the savvy ironist. He was told that his literary reputation had preceded him. Though Stephen had no military qualifications, he somehow had the idea that his fame would land him at the forefront of the action. "I expect to get a position on the staff of the Crown Prince [Constantine]," he wrote Will. "Won't that be great? I am so happy over it I can hardly breathe. I shall try — I shall try like blazes to get a decoration out of the thing but that depends on good fortune and is between you and I and God." He had observed even the famous Greek sights with indifference: "Athens is not much ruins, you know. It is mostly adobe creations like Mexico although the Acropolis sticks up in the air precisely like it does in the pictures," he wrote William. The Parthenon was not the Alamo. What really interested him was "the exhibition of foreign war-ships." And he returned to the position on the crown prince's staff. It seemed "a sure thing," he wrote. "It really isn't so much for a foreigner of standing to get on the staff but then it sounds fine and it really is fine too in a way. I am so happy tonight I can hardly remain silent and write. I hope and pray that you are all well and that I see you all again. Love to everyone."

Stephen was with the cheering crowd in the Place de la Constitution in Athens on April 17, when Turkey declared war on Greece. He was moved by the sound of the cheering, which was "deep-throated and meaningful" — it "stirs the heart," he wrote. He was touched by "these people of the mountains," by the crowds in every public place "aiming to go and fight the Turks."

The next day Stephen headed off to Epirus in the northwest, pausing first to send one hundred dollars to Amy Leslie — at the wrong address, it would turn out, for Amy had moved. In Epirus he saw only skirmishing, so he left for Thessaly, where he had heard there was more action. In Florence, Richard Harding Davis heard that a correspondent named William Peel had been wounded in the fighting in Thessaly. "Thank God it wasn't Stephen Crane," he wrote in a letter.

Cora apparently remained behind in Athens. She had decided to become the Greek war's first woman war correspondent. Writing under the pseudonym "Imogene Carter" for the *New York Journal*, a job Stephen had gotten her, she filed her first dispatch on April 26 — an appealing, if light, piece about war seen through a woman's eyes. Imogene Carter had also been among the jubilant crowd at the Place de la Constitution the day war was declared. She had seen the Greek volunteers return after the heavy fighting in Thessaly, and she shared Stephen Crane's interest in the wounded — "the clumsily bandaged, unwashed and wan," the upturned faces with their "rolling eyes," she wrote, sounding like Stephen.

In *Active Service*, the novel Stephen would write about the Greek war, the correspondent hero, Rufus Coleman, finds himself tempted by a beautiful actress named Nora Black while he is in love with a respectable girl named Marjory. This "duality" in his mind thrills him; it is "a great fine game to play." And it does not interfere with his most compelling interest, the war in Greece. In the midst of his conflicting desires for two women, he finds "it easy to fasten his mind on the prospective war." The echoes in the names Cora/Nora and Marjory/Amy and the striking beauty of regal Nora Black — an actress, as Amy Leslie had been, with flashing eyes and a gorgeous smile — recall the two women in Stephen's life, yet neither of the fictional characters exactly represents Cora Taylor or Amy Leslie. Nora Black is the dark lady of the tale, who tries to come between Marjory and Coleman. A spirited yet conventional girl, Marjory is really the ideal woman Stephen had not won — part Lily Brandon Munroe, part Nellie Crouse — the dream he had always found elusive. Apparently loving both Amy and Cora, yet feeling flanked by whichever woman he was with — Cora in Greece, Amy in New York — he did not choose but simply let things take their course.

"I enclose a pony [twenty-five dollars] for Amy," Stephen wrote Hawkins from Athens on April 27. "Give her my love. Tell her there is lots more coming. Just off again to see fight. I love Amy." He expressed irritation with a mutual friend, Leonard Fairman, who had occasionally served as a go-between in the Hawkins-Leslie transactions and was evidently becoming a problem. "Tell Fairman go to hell," Stephen wrote in a postscript. He seemed unaware that he was inconveniencing Hawkins, causing him to spend money out of his own pocket. As it turned out, Hawkins was through with serving as Stephen's banker; when the money for Amy arrived, he sent it back.

The Greeks had been hit hard in Thessaly, and in Athens the news of Greek losses caused rioting among the citizenry. On April 27 Stephen met up with Richard Davis and John Bass, who headed the *New York Journal* staff, at the Place de la Constitution, where an angry crowd had gathered. Davis later wrote his mother that Stephen was "not a day ahead of me as we start from here together. . . . He has not seen as much as I have for several reasons but then when a man can describe battles as well as he can without seeing them why should he care."

Three days later Davis, Crane, and Bass were among a group of correspondents leaving Athens by steamer for the scene of combat in Thessaly. Davis was dismayed to find the "bi-roxide blonde" still with Stephen. She turned out to be "a Lady Stuart who has run away from her husband to follow Crane," he wrote his family. "She is a commonplace dull woman old enough to have been his mother and with dyed yellow hair. He seems a genius with no responsibilities of any sort to anyone." Davis and Bass were happy to get "shut of them at Velestinos after having had to travel with them for four days."

If Cora felt slighted by Davis, she did not find it worthy of a diary entry. In an excited style filled with dashes, she set down a vivid impressionistic record of her journey to the front. On the second day the steamer stopped at Chalkis, where they "got left" and had to be taken by dispatch boat to catch up with the steamer. At Stylis, they went ashore by sailboat.* Carriages took them on to Lamia, arriving at midnight. "Bunked on Floor wierd Hotel — Cafe — Soldiers," Cora wrote. The next morning they drove to Domoko. Whole villages were fleeing the advancing

---

* I have used Crane's spellings of Greek place names throughout.

Turks, and the Americans found themselves part of a mass of goat flocks and shepherds, volunteer soldiers wearing cartridge belts and carrying guns on their shoulders, refugees moving household goods topped with children — a "torrent" of "man tumbling over beast, beast over man," wrote Stephen in the story "Death and the Child." The Americans "stopped to lunch by [a] spring," Cora noted in her diary, then pressed on, reaching the "grim old tumbled down" town of Domoko at five in the afternoon. Two hours later they were on the road again, moving with the stream of humanity and animals to Pharsala, where they were stopped by sentries. They parted company with Davis and Bass, who headed to Velestino. Stephen and some of the other correspondents went to the seaport town of Volo; Cora set off in search of a bed for the night. Volo was "surrounded by mountains," she wrote. "War ships. Greek fleet — one English — one French — lumpy looking mountains with patches brown, red-Brown, yellow different greens black rocks and shadows — House, shops closed."

An article called "Imogene Carter's Adventure in Pharsala," a collaborative effort by Stephen and Cora, detailed Cora's night spent on a billiard table in a filthy coffeehouse. Her "maid," as Cora called Mrs. Ruedy, had broken down in tears at the poor supper of black bread and cheese, and the plucky woman correspondent had sent her away — *where* is unclear — though this left Cora in the risky position of being "the only woman in Pharsala or within many miles of it." While Cora slept intermittently on the billiard table, a Greek patrolled the place with a rifle. Throughout the night soldiers knocked on the door for a drink, and at daylight the woman correspondent finally emerged from her blanket on the billiard table, put on her hat, and joined the group of soldiers who now filled the room.

The next day Cora traveled to Greek headquarters in Pharsala in hopes of getting an interview with Crown Prince Constantine. She carried a letter from the American minister, Eban Alexander, but the crown prince had ordered a retreat from Pharsala and was too busy to meet with her. After waiting some time, she rejoined Stephen in Volo.

While he waited to see full-fledged war, Stephen continued turning out copy. Writing as Imogene Carter, he described a dragoman telling the female correspondent the name of a high-ranking Greek officer: to Carter "the name sounded only like a term in chemistry to me and I have never been able to do better with it." Writing in a dispatch as Stephen

Crane on May 1, he sounded irritable; the hoped-for job on the crown prince's staff had not materialized. The 131 correspondents, including himself, who were posted in Athens, Constantinople, and on the frontier were getting in the way of the armies, he wrote. Particularly offensive were the English correspondents, with their know-it-all attitude about war. Understanding war is not possible, he believed; "if there is a man who knows aught of that mystic thing, he is a man with no tongue." There was a type of American correspondent Stephen loathed too. He imagined such a reporter's journal entry: "I am the only correspondent up to the present time who has been able to penetrate to the fastnesses of Larissa. During the terrible journey across the desert that surrounds this city I was three times prostrated by the heat and had five horses die under me. My dragoman, Murphy, had his ears frost-bitten." The war correspondence coming out of Greece had been "terrifying in its assininity," he wrote. Correspondents wrote "absurd" interviews and expected to be decorated for it.

Just as the Turks were assaulting the Greeks at Velestino in a major offensive, Stephen came down with dysentery. As the first day of heavy fighting raged on without him, he remained in Volo with Cora, whose diary, amid a hail of dashes, noted, "mouse ill — 8 P.M."

The next day, May 5, he was back on his feet, and he and Cora set off for the fighting. They arrived at the front at noon on the second day. Davis and John Bass had been there from the beginning and had seen the whole battle from the Greek trenches. Davis was disgusted by Stephen's late arrival, blaming the bi-roxide blonde (Stephen told him he'd had a toothache). "Crane came up for fifteen minutes and wrote a 1300 word story on that," Davis wrote his family. "He was never near the front but dont say I said so. He would have come but he had a toothache which kept him in bed. It was hard luck but on the other hand if he had not had that woman with him he would have been with us and not at Volo and could have seen the show toothache or no toothache." And later, less charitably: "There was nothing to be said about what Crane did except that he ought to be ashamed of himself."

Here at last was war. The Turks' assault on General Constantine Smolenski's Greek forces at Velestino was Stephen's "first big battle," as he acknowledged in his *Journal* report. He also admitted that other reporters saw more than he did — "I was rather laid up." Until now he had seen only "skirmishes and small fights." "The roll of musketry was tremendous," he would write.

> From a distance it was like tearing a cloth; nearer it sounded like rain on a tin roof and close up it was just a long crash after crash. It was a beautiful sound — beautiful as I had never dreamed. It was more impressive than the roar of Niagara and finer than thunder or avalanche — because it had the wonder of human tragedy in it. It was the most beautiful sound of my experience, barring no symphony. The crash of it was ideal. This is one point of view. Another might be taken from the men who died there.

The sound of war was also, he said, like "an empty beer-bottle" hurled at you "with marvellous speed" — not so unlike the sounds of howling urchins wielding gravel and oaths in a tenement alley.

John Bass — "a Harvard graduate, and a most charming and attractive youth," said Davis — was curious to see how the great war novelist would behave "in a real battle." He followed Stephen "up the steep hill to where the Greek battery, enveloped in smoke, was dropping shells among the black lines of Turkish infantry in the plain below." When they reached the top, Bass sought cover in a trench. Stephen stayed out in the open. To all outward appearances, he might have been in an amphitheater watching a ball game. He found an ammunition box, sat down "amid a shower of shells and casually lighted a cigarette," said Bass. As he watched the show, his pale, thin face registered no surprise.

"It is a great thing to survey the army of the enemy," Stephen wrote. "Just where and how it takes hold upon the heart is difficult of description." One felt a "terrible" power in the "long dark lines" of the army. "It could reach and pull down the clouds, this thing. It could let two seas meet, this thing." He was impressed with the Greek army's perseverance: "They fought with the patience of salaried bookkeepers — never tired, never complaining." Looking at war the way a painter regards a "great canvas," he was caught by the beautiful swordsmanship, by the accurate aim of the Greek artillery. He watched a battery officer send a man to the rear for his field glasses. The soldier misunderstood the order, returning with a bottle of wine instead, and though the officer bawled him out, Stephen noticed that the soldier "never let go of that bottle of wine." From his artillery box Stephen reflected that "from a distance it was like a game. No blood, no expressions of horror were to be seen; there were simply the movements of a tiny doll tragedy." He had imagined war this way. "The tiny riders were beating the tiny horses," he had written in *The Red Badge*. And yet some aspects he had not imagined, things one could not get from books, such as the slow pace of the fighting. "The swiftness in the chronology of battles is not correct in most books," he reflected. "Evidently one has time to get shaved or lunch or take a bath often in battles whose descriptions read like whirlwinds." In *Active Service* Rufus Coleman realizes that until seeing war he has been only a student. "The universities had not taught him to understand this attitude" of the soldiers who stood up and talked casually in the trenches when they were not under fire.

John Bass watched Stephen watch the artillerymen swiftly load and fire the cannon.

"Crane, what impresses you most in this affair?" he asked. Stephen reached for another cigarette. He used his hat to push his long hair out of his eyes, said Bass. Then he spoke quietly. "Between the two great armies battling against each other the interesting thing is the mental attitude of the men," he said. "The Greeks I can see and understand, but the Turks seem unreal. They are shadows on the plain — vague figures in black, indications of a mysterious force."

Night fell, and the battle continued. Though the "stout, bull-necked" General Smolenski directed the Greeks from a mile or two away, the men felt comforted and secure knowing that the commander they respected was there. "By the red flashes" of artillery fire that lit the darkness, Stephen could make out the shapes of the wounded as they were carried off to Volo. Though the Greeks had fought successfully and hard, they were finally ordered to retreat. "They say Smolenski wept," Stephen wrote in his dispatch. The correspondent remained at his post until "the last mountain gun was loaded on the mules," said Bass. And then, on the way down the hill they encountered "a fat waddling puppy" the size of "a cake of soap." Stephen picked it up "and immediately christened it Velestino, the Journal dog."

Cora was also at the battle of Velestino, watching the fight with the second battery of mountain howitzers; she too was "among the last to leave the field." "Shells screamed about me as I went toward the station," she wrote in a dispatch, "and I had one narrow squeak. The soldiers were amazed at the presence of a woman during the fighting." As they left the area Stephen's horse took what appeared to be a shell fragment in his back; Stephen escaped unharmed. With the pup Velestino in hand, he and Cora managed to get on the train to Volo. The Turks shelled the train, but it arrived at its destination intact.

By May 10 the Turks had reached the hilltops around Volo. With the advance guard of the enemy pressing down on them, Stephen and Cora fled the city by ship to Chalkis. Every ship, tug, sailboat, and fishing vessel in the harbor was filled with women and children; only the English Red Cross ship sat empty. Stephen raged against "the English Red Cross idiot" who was neglecting the starving refugees. "It is a case for the opening of skies, but no skies open," he wrote in a piece syndicated by Hearst under the title "The Blue Badge of Cowardice." He blamed the ship's chief surgeon — "a particularly splendid ass ... He had some rules — God knows what they were — and he was the kind of fool to whom a rule is a holy thing. ... I promise myself the pleasure of writing about him later on."

He left Volo with pictures of war branded on his mind. He had seen a lieutenant shot through the neck while standing in a trench to roll a cigarette. He'd watched as the lieutenant's servant rushed to him, kneeling and weeping over the body, oblivious to the danger. Soldiers had had to drag the man to safety by his legs. After the Greek defeat at Velestino, Stephen had sat next to "a man covered with bloody bandages," who had talked to him the whole time "in wild Greek." He had seen plenty to make him angry. The German officers were "hired assassins," he wrote; everywhere there were wailing babies and silently suffering peasant women. The most vulnerable people were left hungry and homeless. "Nobody pays for these things in war," he wrote.

During the second week of May, Stephen and Cora returned to Athens for some rest. There, with John Bass, they sat for formal photographs at the studio of C. Boehringer. Continuing to maintain a certain discretion, the couple posed separately, and Stephen sat for a portrait with Bass. He wore correspondent's khakis or riding breeches, buttoned below the knee, tall riding boots, a "tunic well marked with buttoned pockets," as he later wrote, and a broad-brimmed hat. He held the ever-present cigarette pinched between his right forefinger and his thumb. "He looked well," Frederic Lawrence thought when he saw the picture. "The eyes might be a bit more sunken, the cheek bones more prominent, but the main change was in the heavy mustache that was to distinguish him henceforth. Of ill health there was no suggestion." Cora, looking robust and plump, wore a tunic over her long skirt, crisscrossed with straps holding a canteen and a leather bag. A small hat was perched on her head.

Sylvester Scovel of the *New York World* was also in Athens. In a letter to his wife, Frances, he wrote that "Stephen Crane is here with Mrs. Stewart. I was afraid that she would ruin him, but really her influence has, so far, been the reverse. He has done such good work since that his publishers and others are increasing their offers for future work." Scovel was impressed that Cora had gone to the front, where she had been under heavy artillery fire and had remained until the battle was over. She "was the last noncombatant to leave the place after the battle," he wrote.

> But poor woman, how will it end. She urges him along, but even if he wished to, he cant marry her, as her husband Sir Donald Stewart, son of the British Commander in Chief of India will not divorce her.
>
> Stephen was very glad to see me and, I to see him. He is true steel. They took my boat off my hands, and went to the front day before yesterday.
>
> I dont know when I shall see them again. If you were here it would be embarrassing if they were here too. Lady Stewart is received by some of the most prominent people and even the Queen may receive her. How's that for the Greeks who are said to be the only moral people in this part of Europe?

On May 17 Cora and Stephen were off again, heading north to Domoko on a dispatch boat leased by the *New York World*, which Scovel had lent them. But Prince Constantine had given orders to abandon the town and had already left himself. Stephen hung around the Greek army's Thermopylae division of 15,000 soldiers, who were always the last to retreat and the first to advance. From the top of the old Acropolis, he peered through his field glass at the advancing Turks. "There are the elements of a first-class scrap right here in the range of my field glass," he wrote. After witnessing Greek retreat after retreat, he was anxious "to write a dispatch telling of a full-blown Greek victory for a change."

From Bay St. Marina Stephen and Cora took the dispatch boat to the lovely, lemon-scented town of Stylidia, where he helped the Greek army evacuate civilians to Chalkis. That same day, in Chalkis, he and Cora boarded the *St. Marina*, an ambulance ship packed with "eight hundred bullet-torn men," some wounded at Domoko, some dead, "jammed together in an insufferably hot hole, the light in which is so faint that we cannot distinguish the living from the dead." The "suffering freight" arrived at Piraeus to a chorus of cheers in support of the war.

An armistice was signed between Greece and Turkey on May 20, ending the thirty-day war.

In writing about war after witnessing it for the first time, Stephen Crane the war correspondent was virtually indistinguishable from Stephen Crane the war novelist. His sympathies were with the wounded and the private soldier. While other correspondents interviewed the top-ranking men — the king, the crown prince, General Smolenski — he sought out the private soldier. Writing his dispatches as letters, he gave them an accessibility and an immediacy. "I send this from Volo and before you print it the Turks will be here," he wrote from the battle of Velestino. He often sounded more like a novelist then a reporter: "In front of the doors of a house that was being used as a field hospital, many stretchers were crowded awaiting their turns, as carriages in front of a New York theater around eight o'clock crowd and await their turns." Listening to a speaker at the Place de la Constitution, he was distracted by the man's bobbing white hat, and his dispatch became "The Man in the White Hat." He could no more confine himself to straight reporting than he had been able to conform to a school curriculum. It was not that he disliked reporting, it was the cut-and-dried nature of it that put him off. He noted that the windows of the king's palace were "heavily curtained as if it had closed its eyes purposely to this scene in the square below it."

While learning to be a war correspondent and enjoying it, the dispatches show, he was also storing material for his fiction. "A Fragment of Velestino" was in part a rehearsal for the fine short story he would write about the Greek war, "Death and the Child." "The sky was of a fair and quiet blue," he wrote in the dispatch. "In the radiantly bright atmosphere of the morning the distances among the hills were puzzling in the extreme. The Westerner could reflect that after all his eye was accustomed to using a tree as a standard of measure, but here there were no trees."

There was a majesty in the wounded that Stephen found "inexpressible" — like war itself, which was "a mystic thing." It was the wounded who "defined" war, who "explained the meaning of all that racket." Their upturned faces were worse than a corpse's, "because [their] eyes looked here, there, everywhere in slow sweeps." The color of war was

THEY SAY SMOLENSKI WEPT

red: from "the terrible red of [a] man's face, which was of the quality of flame as it appears in old pictures" to the blood-red poppies, war blossoms "miraculously preserved from the countless feet," in "the crimson outburst of shell after shell," in the kilted, red-capped Efzones, the best infantry troops in the Greek army, in the Turkish flag, a "tiny blood-red banner," in the red fez.

The *Commodore* disaster and the trauma in the dinghy colored Stephen's introduction to war, shaping the way he saw it. In the babbling, choking voices of the fleeing Greek refugees, he heard the sound of drowning men. Witnessing the firing of a shell, he was revisited by the hellish glow of the tug's engine room, "the blare of furnace fires." In "Death and the Child," the correspondent, Peza, feels like "a corpse walking on the bottom of the sea." The shells passing overhead remind him of "the first sight of the sea during a storm," and "he [seems] to feel against his face the wind that races over the tops of cold and tumultuous billows." The figures he sees from a distance in combat are "fantastic smokey shapes which resembled the curious figures in foam which one sees in the slant of a rough sea: The plain, indeed, was etched in white circles and whirligigs like the slope of a colossal wave." The sight of men falling and dying reminds him of "the captain . . . washed off the bridge at sea during a storm."

Stephen was acutely aware of what had brought him to Greece: twenty-seven hours in an open boat, police harassment, damnable lies, the mutilation of his name, his own need for heroism, for a decoration, for adventure. "They went on and on," he would write in *Active Service*, referring to Coleman.

> Visions of his past were sweeping through Coleman's mind precisely as they are said to sweep through the mind of a drowning person. But he had no regret for any bad deeds; he regretted merely distant hours of peace and protection. He was no longer a hero going to rescue his love. He was a slave making a gasping attempt to escape from the most incredible tyranny of circumstance. He half vowed to himself that if the God whom he had in no wise heeded, would permit him to crawl out of his slavery he would never again venture a yard toward a danger any greater than may be incurred from the police of a most proper metropolis. If his juvenile

and uplifting thoughts of other days had reproached him he would simply have repeated and repeated: "Adventure be damned."

At the end of "Death and the Child," the exhausted correspondent struggles to a hilltop gasping for breath "in the manner of a fish." There stands a child abandoned by his parents when they fled the war. "Are you a man?" he asks the correspondent. And in the aftermath of his ordeal, Peza, who is bloody, dirty, ragged — so war-torn that he resembles "a creature" — faces "the sovereign child" with the humility of a little blade of grass confronting God in the kingdom of Heaven. And he understands that he is just a man, nothing more; "the definition of his misery could be written on a wee grass-blade."

11

LIVING TALLY

In early June, the famous young American author was sighted in the Strand in London. Boyish and slender, with a thick blond mustache, Stephen was fresh with youth and triumph and possibility. Reviews of *The Third Violet* were out, his dispatches from the brief war in Greece were appearing in both English and American newspapers, and his brilliant story "The Open Boat" was in the June issue of *Scribner's*. The literary world speculated about what Crane would do next. "He will probably 'conclude,' as you say, that nothing pays him like fiction," wrote Arthur Waugh in the *Critic*. "The unanimity of the reviewers, indeed, must sometimes suggest to him that he merits the envy of the gods."

Stephen could have pointed out that though the English reviewers were generally kinder, American reviewers were panning *The Third Violet*. The novel's subject was "trivial," the dialogue "inane," wrote the *San Francisco Argonaut*. The *Literary Digest* could not find "a word to be said in favor of *The Third Violet*, whose reason, even for its name, does not appear till we reach the last page." The *Critic* found it "inconceivable that even for an experiment in inanity a writer should be willing to follow up a book like 'The Red Badge' with such a vacuous trifle as 'The Third Violet.'" Stephen wrote an apologetic inscription in a copy of the novel:

> . . . This book
> is even worse than any
> of the others

His war letters had been parodied in the *Lewiston* (Maine) *Journal:*

> I have seen a battle.
> I find it very like what I wrote up before.
> I congratulate myself that I ever saw a battle.
> I am pleased with the sound of war.
> I think it is beautiful.
> I thought it would be.
> I am sure of my nose for battle.
> I did not see any war correspondents while I was watching
>   the battle except I.

He wasn't making any money to speak of. Though *The Red Badge* had gone through fourteen printings in America and six in England, his contract with Appleton ensured that the book would have to sell a lot of copies before Stephen saw any money from his paltry American royalty of 10 percent. He still had nothing from the English sales.* And yet he was a success, and "in England, nothing succeeds like success," Arthur Waugh said of him.

After the armistice Stephen and Cora had spent some two weeks on holiday in Paris. There, apparently, they hatched a plan. If Cora could not get a divorce, they would simply call themselves Mr. and Mrs. Stephen Crane and live in England. Since Cora's husband was British and her father-in-law a baronet, establishing themselves in England would seem to carry some risk. But English society was far more tolerant of such unions than America was. In fact, unmarried cohabitation — known as "irregular marriage" or "living tally," in the common vernacular — seems to have been popular in nineteenth-century England. Though Cora would have no claim to any of Stephen's money or property if he should die first or abandon her, there was otherwise little legal risk in the arrangement. Even if Captain Stewart decided to prosecute her for bigamy, the courts would be likely to impose a lenient sentence. And Stephen's family and friends, including Amy Leslie, were less likely to learn the truth if "the Cranes," as they would now be known, lived abroad. Clearly uncomfortable with his pretend marriage and with a

---

* Some of Appleton's publishing records were later sold at auction, so one has to rely largely on summary lists of printings Appleton made many years later. These lists do not mention the size of the printings.

choice that had forced him into exile, Stephen did not explain the arrangement to his family or friends. When he wrote home, he gave his publisher, William Heinemann, as his return address.

They arrived in England with Mathilde Ruedy; two young Greek men they had brought out of the war zone with them, Adoni Ptolemy and his twin brother; and the war puppy, Velestino, whom Stephen had already immortalized in a piece called "The Dogs of War," published in the *Journal* on May 30. They found temporary lodgings in the village of Limpsfield, Surrey, twenty miles south of London. After several days in rented rooms, they moved into a large brick villa in Limpsfield Chart, Oxted, on the Surrey-Kent border. The house was called Ravensbrook, after the ravens that had supposedly settled at the nearby brook during the Roman occupation of Britain.

The Limpsfield-Oxted area, home to members of the socialist Fabian Society, founded in 1883 by George Bernard Shaw and other middle-class intellectuals, was something of a magnet for writers. The English poet, critic, and biographer Edmund Gosse and the elderly Pre-Raphaelite poet Algernon Charles Swinburne lived there. The Scottish novelist Robert Barr lived at nearby Hillhead, in Woldingham. Harold Frederic, an American novelist as well as the London bureau chief of the *New York Times*, lived within walking distance of Stephen, at Homefield, Kenley, with his young common-law partner, Kate Lyon, and their three children. Frederic, whose novel *The Damnation of Theron Ware* had been published to great acclaim the year before, was an early champion of *The Red Badge*. He had predicted that Crane's book would live "as one of the deathless books which must be read by everybody who desires to be, or seem, a connoisseur of modern fiction."

Edward Garnett lived on the High Chart, near Limpsfield. A writer, publisher's reader, and perceptive critic who shared Harold Frederic's admiration for Crane's work, Garnett considered him a "unique" talent and "of the young school of American writers . . . the genius." He would soon praise *George's Mother* as "a masterpiece" in its *"method."* Garnett's wife, Constance, was a superb English translator of Russian novels. There were so many Russian visitors coming and going at their house, the Cearne, that Garnett dubbed the house and its stone cottage Dostoevsky Corner. Gracie's Cottage next door was then occupied by Ford Madox Hueffer and his pregnant young wife, Elsie. The fair, bearded Hueffer, half German and the grandson of the great Pre-Raphaelite painter Ford Madox Brown, dressed in smock and gaiters; Elsie, tall and slender, a dark, rather exotic-looking contrast to her husband, wore "richly colored garments of the William Morris style and wore earrings and a great amber necklace," said the Garnetts' son, David.

Garnett, Hueffer, and Stephen were much of an age, and after an awkward start, when Stephen, who spoke in a western drawl and peppered his colorful talk with Bowery slang, mistook the modern Gracie's Cottage for an ancient ruin, exclaiming, "That's a bully ol' battlement!" they all became friendly. Hueffer, who later told many embellished and inaccurate stories of Stephen Crane, would remember him stepping into this English scene "in breeches, leggings, and shirt-sleeves, with a huge Colt strapped to his belt." He was received by "all the intensely highbrow Fabians of Limpsfield," said Hueffer. The group also included Edward Pease, the society's "dourly kind" secretary, as another writer described him, and his "jolly, commanding" wife Margery, who often hosted Fabian Society meetings at their house. Stephen sent one of the Ptolemy brothers, whom he called "a butler in shirt sleeves," to work at the Peases'. But he found that he missed the way the Greek man shaved him, and he often walked over to the Peases' before breakfast to be shaved. The elder Pease disapproved of the American Crane's "defection from middle class standards."

Ravensbrook was large, damp, and expensive, a collection of empty rooms awaiting furniture. It now housed five people needing to be fed. While Cora set about transforming their "primitive establishment" into a home — buying old oak furniture, filling up the conservatory with "beautiful flowers" — Stephen went to work at a gallop. He wrote prolifically for both the English and the American market, shifting with ease from saleable hackwork to literary fiction, writing to make money. In June he wrote to Edmund asking him to locate his unpublished western stories "The Wise Men" and "The Five White Mice" among his possessions in Hartwood and send them to England.

In this quintessentially English setting of timber-framed brick houses, shops made of local sandstone and tile, and low rubble walls sprouting lichens, tiny ferns, and mosses, Stephen's mind turned west toward home. As though the distance from his native ground had made him thirsty for the sights of home, he wrote about America as he had never done before, in some of his finest stories. He returned in his imagination to the distinctly American scenes that had formed him: Main Street, with its barbershop and post office, its gas-lighted shop windows and leisurely evening strollers under the electric arc lamps, a band playing in the park.

The American Southwest, the Texas scrub. Reticent, gun-toting characters with weathered faces, hands brick red from the sun. The great Rio Grande, winding like a woman's hair ribbon through the vast dry spaces beneath the endless sky.

In late June he began work on *The Monster*, a novella set in a New York State town he called Whilomville, based on Port Jervis. He also wrote up his impressions of London for the newspapers. Throughout the summer he lived in two worlds. Taking in the "new phenomena" of London — the Thames, the Houses of Parliament, the porters and cabmen — he listened to the late-night sounds of the city, which seemed silent compared to the ceaseless roar of New York. Riding over the narrow, gas-lit, cobbled streets in a hansom cab, he found himself on an imaginary train in Whilomville, where little Jimmie Trescott was "engine Number 36, and he was making the run between Syracuse and Rochester. He was fourteen minutes behind time . . ."

A powerful, shattering story of disfigurement and social ostracism, *The Monster* tells of a Negro hostler named Henry Johnson, who acts with selfless courage to save the life of his employer's young son, Jimmie Trescott, in a house fire and is burned nearly to death. Expected to die, Johnson is hailed as a hero by the citizens of Whilomville and eulogized in the local paper. But the hero does not die. Through the tireless efforts of Dr. Trescott, Johnson lives — as a freak, a monster "with no face" — and is shunned by Whilomville's revolted citizens, who turn out to be the real monster of the tale. Blamed for saving Johnson's life, Dr. Trescott loses his patients, and his wife is snubbed by the local ladies. The story ends with Dr. Trescott bleakly counting his wife's unused teacups on her "at home" day.

A near-perfect tale, it is beautifully crafted, with a strong sense of place and vivid characterizations, flawed only by certain stereotypes — notably the town's black residents, who live in "Watermelon Alley." In scene after marvelous scene, with a shifting point of view, Crane ponders the tragedy through the good folk of Whilomville. We hear the talk at Reifsnyder's barbershop as faces are being shaved; the bloodthirsty gossip of Carrie Dungen and the acid-tongued spinster Martha Goodwin. Childless old Judge Hagenthorpe rubs the ivory head of his cane as he debates with Dr. Trescott the morality of saving Henry's life for *this* — an exchange brilliantly played out against the single unwinking eye of Henry Johnson, peering God-like from his cocoon of bandages.

Even the smallest details of the novella are written with passion and cunning. In a comic tour de force, Stephen lets the monster loose on the town. Faceless and half-witted, Henry turns up at Bella Farragut's house in Watermelon Alley to court her as in days of old — sending fat Mrs. Farragut flying out of her armchair and over a high board fence. He makes a surprise appearance at the window of little Theresa Page's house, where a children's party is in progress, a wickedly funny bogeyman scene. Arguably Stephen's best performance to that point, the novella works on the reader as a kind of controlled howl, searing in both its subject matter and its evocative language. The prose is at times flashy, filled with intricate punning and extended metaphors, at times understated and taut. Nothing is wasted, everything tells.

The spectacular fire in which Henry Johnson is defaced is written as a stunning seduction scene with biblical overtones. Carrying Jimmie Trescott in his arms as he gropes through the burning house, Henry remembers the private stairway leading to the little apartment the doctor uses as a laboratory, which has its own outside door, and he makes his way there, only to be trapped. Exploding chemicals have transformed the room into a kind of hellish Eden, "like a garden in the region where might be burning flowers." In the midst of this fire garden Henry encounters "a delicate, trembling shape like a fairy lady. With a quiet smile she blocked his path and doomed him and Jimmie. Johnson shrieked, and then ducked in the manner of his race in fights. He aimed to pass under the left guard of the sapphire lady. But she was swifter than eagles, and her talons caught in him as he plunged past her." Henry is knocked down and falls on his back at the base of the doctor's desk. Chemicals in glass jars are shattering on the desk, and one of them contains a red liquid, "a ruby-red snake like thing," which oozes across the desk and down the side and consumes Henry's face. This too is carried out as a seductive dance.

> It coiled and hesitated, and then began to swim a langorous way down the mahogany slant. At the angle it waved its sizzling molten head to and fro over the closed eyes of the man beneath it. Then, in a moment, with mystic impulse, it moved again, and the red snake flowed directly down into Johnson's upturned face.
>
> Afterward the trail of this creature seemed to reek, and amid flames and low explosions drops like red-hot jewels pattered softly down it at leisurely intervals.

Though not literally autobiographical, the novella drew on people and places Stephen knew. The patriarchal, courageous Dr. Trescott suggests both the Reverend Jonathan Townley Crane and William Crane, who later told one of his daughters that "the characterization flattered him." In a letter to Will, Stephen later acknowledged that Port Jervis entered his head "while I was writing [*The Monster*], but I particularly dont wish [the townspeople] to think so because people get very sensitive and I would not scold away freely if I thought the eye of the glorious public was upon me."

Perhaps because the violence done to Henry Johnson is so savage, his injuries something the mind resists imagining, people close to Stephen later sought to explain the fictional character by identifying a real-life model. Cora would claim that "Henry Johnson was a real man" in that he was based on a black man Stephen had seen who had been "burned horribly about the face." William Crane identified a Port Jervis ash hauler named Levi Hume as Henry Johnson. William's daughter, Edna, would remember that the children of her generation "often met [Hume] with his cart as we drove around town with our pony. He was an object of horror to us, for it could truthfully be said of him, 'He had no face.'" Certainly Stephen could have found a real-life model anywhere, for there were plenty of disfigured Civil War veterans around during his boyhood. There was even a hostler named Henry Johnson in Port Jervis — German, not black — who died of typhus in 1894. And that same summer the *Port Jervis Union* ran a story of a horrific crime that took place in Buffalo, when a woman threw a pint of corrosive acid into the face of another woman.

Into the disfigurement scene in Trescott's laboratory went both real and imagined pieces from life. The 1892 lynching of the black man William had tried to save, when the lynchers held lighted matches against the victim's face. The descent with Linson into the "impenetrable night" of the Pennsylvania coal mine, where a little flame not unlike a fairy lady had appeared and seemed to dance before Stephen. The nights spent with William Carroll in the Bowery flophouses, where the light was dim and vile odors had rushed out "like released fiends." The *Commodore*'s "insufferably warm" engine room, with its faintly burning lights and its "mystic and gruesome shadows," a place right out of hell's "middle kitchen." The lifeless shape of Billy Higgins is in the seemingly dead body of Henry Johnson carried from Dr. Trescott's laboratory and laid on the grass. More recently, in Greece, Stephen had been saturated with sights of wounded men; in his mind he held a fresh set of images of bleeding, "bullet-torn men" — some of them shot in the face, some dead. And he had been entombed with eight hundred injured soldiers on the *St. Marina.*

As far back as *Maggie*, he had been imagining fire scenes, pictures of disfigured faces, of the dead. In that book, as smoke from an oil lamp pervades the air, "the wine from an overturned glass dripped softly down upon the blotches of a man's neck." He had conceived the resurrection of a seemingly dead man, "a thing," as Henry Johnson is called, in "The Little Regiment." The fictional fire in Stephen's 1895 newspaper piece contained many of the same images and details he used to greater effect in *The Monster.*

Whatever pieces of real life found their way into the work are of secondary importance. What comprises the *real life* of the story is the feeling with which it was written, its passion and psychological truth. *The Monster* was Crane's response to the forces that had shaped him: small-town life, with its narrow-minded conventionality; the oppressive religiosity of his upbringing, with its terrifying images of the lake of fire, its punishing themes of eternal damnation and retribution. Seen by some scholars as a Christ story, the tale is rich in religious imagery and biblical allusion. The "solemn and terrible voice" of the Methodist church bells sets the tone in Whilomville. From the opening scene, in which Dr. Trescott is observed shaving his lawn "as if it were a priest's chin," to the moment when the horribly disfigured Henry Johnson steps into the Negro shanty to which he has been exiled and is finally seen in "the full revelation of the light," the tale is lit with religious references. The fiery fairy lady who attacks Henry Johnson comes at him "swifter than eagles," a phrase that appears three times in the King James version of the Old Testament.

The Monster also sprang from Stephen Crane's perception of himself as unattractive, a view complicated by his fragile health, which hinted to him that death and disfigurement lay close at hand. Henry Johnson was Stephen himself, carried to a hideous extreme. Into the black man Stephen poured his deepest feelings about his differentness and the forces that sought to destroy him. He had posed and strutted before Nellie Crouse, and where had it got him? Like Henry Johnson before the fire, dressed as a swell in lavender trousers to go courting, Stephen himself had preened and been savaged by society. Like Stephen, the rising literary star and rescuer of a prostitute, Henry rises to local prominence as Dr. Trescott's hostler and risks his life in an unselfish and courageous act, only to be assailed by flames that are "alive with envy, hatred and malice." The novella's unnerving fire scene — a complex mingling of religious, racial, and sexual images — has at its center a fairy lady who dooms the man and seals his fate.

Until now, his poetry had best expressed his ideas "about life in general." Not since *The Black Riders* had he written with such soul-wrenching agony. He was proud of *The Monster*, which he finished writing in about two months.

That September Stephen wrote a marvelous western story, "The Bride Comes to Yellow Sky." Riding through the streets of London that summer, he had noticed a young man dressed in evening clothes and a top hat and was reminded of a story he'd heard about an ex-sheriff from Tin Can, Nevada, who'd brought home a new top hat from Chicago. Then Spike Foster got hold of the new hat and went on a bender at the Red Light Saloon. Staggering into the square, he let out a yowl in imitation of a mountain lion and was dragged off by his friends. The sheriff's top hat, left behind, was used for target practice. Though slight, the story had comic potential. Stephen told it in his "London Impressions" column, which began appearing in the English *Saturday Review* on July 31. But he had not finished with it. As he rode through the streets of London, he saw a "newly-married pair" whirling east across the Texas plains in a "great Pullman."

Here was Texas again, perfectly evoked with a few strokes of the pen: "vast flats of green grass, dull-hued spaces of mesquite and cactus, little groups of frame houses, woods of light and tender trees." "To the left, down a long purple slope, was a little ribbon of mist where moved the keening Rio Grande." Stephen Crane "of the false East," a Jerseyman, he called himself, caught the spirit of the American West like a native.

Written when Stephen had been living openly in England with Cora for several months, presenting himself there as married but continuing to conceal the relationship from his family and friends at home, "The Bride" was a lighthearted expression of Stephen's personal dilemma. In this tender, exuberant sendup of the western gunslinger story, Jack Potter, sheriff of the town called Yellow Sky, has gone to San Antonio to marry "a girl he believed he loved." He has taken his bride "without consulting Yellow Sky for any part of the transaction, and now, as the Pullman nears home and he approaches the hour of reckoning, he feels himself "sweeping over a horizon, a precipice." A "traitor to the feelings of Yellow Sky" who has "gone headlong over all the social hedges," Potter begins to comprehend the consequences of his act. Waiting for him is the drunken Scratchy Wilson, who's been busy shooting up the Weary Gentleman Saloon.

Mingling parody with a vivid sense of place, "The Bride" is Stephen's comic masterpiece and his truest love story. Jack Potter and his bride are a grownup version of the eloping young couple in "The Pace of Youth." "The bride was not pretty, nor was she very young" — and yet there is a certain innocence about this mature couple, who do not know each other well or comprehend the danger, in the form of a drunken gunslinger, that waits around the corner of Potter's adobe house. The surprise of the story is its sweetness. Like Jack Potter, Stephen Crane had grown up and taken his bride.

He posed with Cora for a picture at Ravensbrook. With his fair hair looking freshly washed, his mustache drooping, Stephen appeared many years younger than the round-faced, matronly-looking Cora. Most striking about the photograph is the apparent lack of connection between them. Cora is off in the background next to Mrs. Ruedy, separated from Stephen by a tangle of plants and a table in the conservatory. Leaning comfortably against the small table, she is turned toward him. He sits cross-legged and unsmiling, looking as sealed off as uncut pages. He gazes at nothing in particular.

"London Impressions" was followed by a series of trivial, unsigned "European Letters" sent to the *New York Press* under the name Imogene Carter — light fare ranging over female topics such as the local fashions, the luggage of the King of Siam, the garden at Buckingham Palace, and the danger of petroleum hair wash. With a large household to support and furnish, Stephen needed money as never before.

That summer Stephen received word that Edmund's two-and-a-half-year-old son, little Bill, had died. In August the puppy Velestino died of distemper. Just two hours later — "because you are the only one who will understand" — Stephen wrote Sylvester Scovel a grief-stricken note. The puppy had "died in Cora's bedroom with all the pillows under him which our poverty could supply. For eleven days we fought death for him, thinking nothing of anything but his life. He made a fine manly fight, with only little grateful laps of his tongue on Cora's hands, for he knew that she was trying to help him." They buried him in the collar Scovel had given him. Stephen asked Scovel to send any pictures he had of the dog.

But of the death of Edmund's son he didn't "know what to say." To his brother he wrote, "I cant say the conventional thing and yet there are so few phrases which I could use to express to you how I feel about the death of brave bold little Bill. Good old Bill and the way he used to smoke my pipes! Give my love to Mame and the kids."

In August, Stephen and Cora were en route to a birthday luncheon for Harold Frederic at Kenley when their carriage horse ran away with them. The driver was unable to control the animal, and the trap overturned. Cora claimed in a letter to Scovel that they were almost killed. (Stephen downplayed the accident, writing Edmund that he was "rather badly shaken up.") They arrived at Kenley "covered with dust and blood," said Cora. They spent the next weeks recuperating under the care of Harold and Kate, first at Kenley, then in the little fishing village of Ahakista, in Dunmanus Bay, Ireland, where Frederic had the loan of a house. During their "delightful three weeks in the wilds," as Cora put it, Stephen got around well enough to write some careful, if unmemorable, observations of the local life. "The only result finally of the accident will be a small scar on the side of my nose," he wrote Edmund. Where it served him — in letters to William, who was in a position to send him money, and Amy Leslie, to whom he still owed money — he was not above working on the recipient's sympathy.

Neither Amy nor Stephen knew that Hawkins had returned Stephen's last checks to Amy, mailed from Greece. Stephen had never received them. While still in Ireland, on September 12, Stephen wrote a careful letter in response to one he'd received from an obviously angry Amy. Addressed to "My dear Amy," the letter sounded caring and concerned. She'd been hearing rumors — apparently about Cora. "You know better than to believe those lies about me," Stephen wrote in a smaller hand than he had used before. "You know full well what kind of a man I am. As soon as I get home I shall want to know who told you them." Writing on hotel stationery decorated with a drawing of a dreamy lake surrounded by sharply peaked mountains — the view from the hotel where he was staying in Glengariff — he said he was "sorry to have you write to me in the way that you did because I will always be willing to do anything in the world for you to help you and see that you do not suffer. I never intended to treat you badly and if I did appear to do so, it was more by fate or chance." Stephen was clearly anxious to avoid inflaming her further, but the romance was over. He had been "doing very decently in London" until the carriage accident, he wrote, which had prevented him from sending her more money. As soon as she let him know that she had got the hundred dollars from Hawkins, he would "rake up more." For now — well, he himself had had to borrow money to get to Ireland. "Keep up heart, Amy. Trust me and it will all turn out right. . . . Dont think too badly of me, dear. Wait, have patience and I will see you through straight. Dont believe anything you hear of me and dont doubt my faith and my honesty." He signed it "Yours as ever C."

His callousness toward Amy notwithstanding, he had in truth left no pocket unchecked in his quest for money. A few days before writing to her, Stephen had written another letter to Edmund asking him to send "any odd bits of writing you find at H.," even the inferior sea tale "The Reluctant Voyagers." Back at Ravensbrook in the fall, he continued his hackwork. He wrote a short piece on the Afridi people of northern India in the *New York Press*. His "Irish Notes," written for the *Westminster Gazette* and the English *Saturday Review*, began appearing in England in October and were reprinted at home in the *Journal*.

Stephen began what he described as "a big novel" based on his Greek war experiences, *Active Service*. And he found enough artistry in reserve to write "Death and the Child," which is laced with troubling images of snakes and dead, upturned faces, images that run like certain glittering threads through so much of his work, from *The Red Badge* to *The Monster*, as well as in his most banal work. Again he links death with seduction. The bullets make a "silken, sliding, tender noise," calling the soldiers to their deaths. "Peza could feel himself blanch; he was being drawn and drawn by these dead men slowly, firmly down as to some mystic chamber under the earth where they could walk, dreadful figures, swollen and blood-marked. He was bidden; they had commanded him; he was going, going, going."

That October, in an effort to sell his work more quickly, Stephen agreed to give his American literary agent, Paul Revere Reynolds, 10 percent of everything he sold; he would henceforth "refer everything" he wrote to Reynolds, "giving you the clear field which is your right. You will have the whole management as in the theatrical business." Stephen had met Reynolds earlier that year in New York, at a party given by Irving Bacheller. He had decided that working with an agent was the best way to free himself from "the ardent grasp of the S. S. McClure Co.," to whom, by his own calculations, he still owed five hundred dollars and who "seem to calculate on controlling my entire out-put." The *Journal* claimed he was in debt to them — "I say I am not," he wrote Reynolds. Nevertheless, he had sent them a piece from his "Irish Notes" but had heard nothing from them.

Stephen was full of ideas for making money. He thought that he and Reynolds could "do large things" in the newspaper business. "The *Herald* pays me $100 per article of between 3000 and 4000 words. The *World* has never paid me over $50 and expenses but could be brought to $75 or $100, I think. Now that of course is a big graft to pay as long as I am here in Europe." And he had "another scheme" in mind: Reynolds should pay a visit to Curtis Brown, still the Sunday editor of the *New York Press*, and tell him "*in the strictest* confidence" that the author of the pieces he had occasionally run under the name Imogene Carter

> is also named Stephen Crane and that I did 'em in about twenty minutes on each Sunday, just dictating to a friend. Of course they are rotten bad. But by your explanation he will understand something of the manner of the articles I mean to write only of course they will be done better. Ask him if he wants them, signed and much better in style, and how much he will give. Then if he says all right you might turn up a little syndicate for every Sunday. You can figure out that I should get about £10 per week out of it. Then — you do the business — I do the writing — I take 65 per cent and you take 35. The typewriting expenses in New York we share alike. You do a lot of correspondence, that's all — and keep your eyes peeled for new combinations.

His letters now took on a hard, pay-up-or-else tone. Bolstered by the admiration of local writers and by Cora, who thought that every word from Stephen's pen was golden, he believed he should be paid for those words. He had his own notions about what his stories should fetch. "My terms for a story of between five and ten thousand words is $500. This does not include English rights," he had written a prospective editor or publisher in September, greatly inflating his usual payment, which was about five cents a word or less. He felt that "the American rights alone of 'The Monster,'" which was 21,000 words, should "easily" pay back his debt to McClure, even after Reynolds's commission — or that at least the novella would "pay them a decent amount of" what he owed. He judged the American rights of "The Bride," which was 4,500 words, "to be worth $175."

In attaching price tags to the new fiction, Stephen was taking into account the quality of the work, which he knew to be first-rate. He had shown "The Bride" to some of his English friends, all of whom "say it is my very best thing," he wrote William. "'The Bride Comes to Yellow Sky' is a daisy and don't let them talk funny about it," he instructed Reynolds. In September McClure had both the short story and the novella in their possession.

In October, though it had been only a month, Stephen wrote an irritable letter to John Phillips of the McClure syndicate. "What on earth have you done with *The Monster*?" Apparently sensing that the novella's subject matter might be offputting, he added, "for heaven's sake give the story a chance." As for "The Bride," he would tolerate no doubts about it.

> I hope you liked The Bride Comes to Yellow Sky but I could
> see a slight resemblance to some of your other mistakes if
> you didn't. I have delivered to you over 25000 words against
> my debt but I dont see myself any better off than if I had
> asked you to wait until I got damned good and ready to pay.
> I have worried poor little Robert [McClure] for money until
> he wails and screams like a mandrake when I mention it.
> Now please tell me where I am at. What has happened? Did
> I write a story called *The Monster*? Did I deliver it to you?
> And what happened after that?

McClure held on to *The Monster* until mid-December, when they finally rejected it. The novella was published in *Harper's Magazine* the following year.

"We are happy — very happy," Cora wrote to Scovel on October 17. "Stephen is working very hard on a new book *[Active Service]* which will be his best I think." She and Stephen wanted Scovel and his wife to come "for a long visit."

In his letters to Amy, Edmund, and William, Stephen suggested that England was a pied à terre; he would "stay over here and lay for another war," but then he'd go home and settle in Hartwood or Port Jervis. Since July — virtually since touching ground in England — he'd been angling for a foreign correspondent's assignment. Having failed to get one to South Africa, he set his sight on the Sudan. There was trouble brewing between the Anglo-Egyptian army and the Maltese forces, and Stephen felt certain that the English forces would be going to Khartoum. The Bachellers had asked him to go to the Klondike, where the gold rush had begun at Bonanza Creek the year before, and he was considering that assignment as well.

In an unusually long letter to William he struggled to present himself as a mature, responsible man while admitting that he needed his brother's financial help. He did not admit to spending more than he earned, furnishing a large house, supporting other adults, or entertaining his friends. Depicting himself as a hard-working, world-traveling author, he attributed his money problems to "dreadfully hard luck." He had been victimized by publishers who had not paid up, people in America who wanted to bring him down. In three months he had "earned close to 2000 dollars," but been paid "only £20.17s 3d — about 120 dollars," he wrote. "In consequence I have had to borrow and feel very miserable indeed. I am not sure that I am not in trouble over it. McClures, with security of over 1000 dollars against my liability of four hundred, refuse to advance me any money. And yet they think they are going to be my American publishers."

Admired in England, he thought himself attacked at home. "There seem so many of them in America who want to kill, bury and forget me purely out of unkindness and envy and — my unworthiness, if you choose," he wrote. He worried about the effect on his family, and asked William "to promise never to pay attention to it, even in your thought. It is too immaterial and foolish. Your little brother is neither braggart or a silent egotist but he knows that he is going on steadily to make his simple little place and he cant be stopped, he cant even be retarded. He is coming."

He stopped short of asking William for money. "I am just thinking how easy it would be in my present financial extremity to cable you for a hundred dollars but then by the time this reaches you I will probably be all right again," he wrote. "I believe the sum I usually borrowed was fifteen dollars, wasnt it? Fifteen dollars — fifteen dollars — fifteen dollars. I can remember an interminable row of fifteen dollar requests." But he suggested that Helen sell his stamp collection and share the profits with him. He acknowledged that "I have managed my success like a fool and a child but then it is difficult to succeed gracefully at 23. However I am learning every day. I am slowly becoming a man."

"Are you a man?" the orphaned child asks the correspondent at the end of "Death and the Child."

III

THE
MANOR

◆

12

WARM AND ENDLESS

FRIENDSHIP

I n the midst of his unrest, Stephen escaped to London to have lunch with Sidney Pawling and Joseph Conrad. The introduction to Conrad was at Stephen's request; he admired the Polish writer, who was also published by Heinemann. Conrad later said he was flattered when Pawling told him Stephen Crane wanted to meet him. He had read *The Red Badge* with admiration and become "even more interested in the personality of the writer," he said. He sensed that Stephen would understand his own work. Writing to Edward Garnett just before the luncheon, Conrad said, "I *do* admire him. I shan't have to pretend."

That afternoon — October 15, 1897 — the two writers shook hands over the tablecloth at a London restaurant "with intense gravity and a direct stare at each other," wrote Conrad, "after the manner of two children told to make friends." Conrad had come knowing nothing about Stephen personally, except that he "was quite a young man." Stephen had "very steady, penetrating blue eyes, the eyes of a man who not only sees visions but can brood over them to some purpose," Conrad wrote years later. "His manner was very quiet, his personality at first sight interesting."

On the surface, Conrad would seem to have nothing in common with Crane. The Polish-born writer — his given name was Jósef Teodor Konrad Korzeniowski — was nearly forty, "a very old forty," writes a biographer, "with a twenty-year career at sea behind him." A highly literate man who had come late to writing, he had lived in very different worlds from Stephen's. Short, dark, and intense, with thinning hair and a close-cut black beard that reached a point at his chin like an exclamation, Conrad was so foreign as to seem exotic — a polished European to Stephen's shaggy American. Writer friends would recall his broad seaman's shoulders and nervously gesturing arms and hands. Coupled with an exaggerated politeness, the gesturing arms seemed Oriental. His narrow, almond-shaped dark eyes could look "very troubled" as well as "brilliant." Like Stephen's eyes, they could be penetrating, narrowing as he listened or talked, then softening and becoming warm.

H. G. Wells later pointed out that Conrad had learned English from books "long before he spoke it and had formed wrong sound impressions of many familiar words." Because he also spoke with a heavy French accent and tended to lapse into French when speaking about "cultural or political matters," his speech took some getting used to. Both Wells and Henry James had thought Conrad "the strangest of creatures" upon first meeting him. But talking to Stephen Crane also required some adjustment. As Conrad said later, Stephen "talked slowly with an intonation which on some people, mainly Americans, had, I believe a jarring effect," adding, "but not on me." From the moment they shook hands across the table, there was a connection between them. "Whatever he said had a personal note, and he expressed himself with a graphic simplicity which was extremely engaging," Conrad said of Stephen. "We were friends from the first."

We have only Conrad's account of the meeting. Stephen talked that afternoon with "intense earnestness," showing his desire to be understood. Speaking in his "deliberate manner" about his Greek war experiences, he sounded casual, his voice "careless." Then he would raise his deep-set eyes — which were blue-gray, like the sea — and Conrad would see "that secret quality" which instantly revealed Stephen Crane's soul. Writing about that day decades later, Conrad thought that it "had a character of enchantment about it."

The luncheon stretched on until four in the afternoon, when Pawling, a "friendly and debonair" man, who had also been absorbed by Stephen's tales, noticed the time and left the writers to continue their talk alone. And so they set off into the streets of London like "two tramps without home, occupation, or care for the next night's shelter" — the young blond American and the dark, bearded European forming an amiable study in contrasts. A concert of powers. They walked without a destination, simply to be talking together. As they passed the Green Park and Kensington Gardens, Stephen told Conrad about the American Southwest and Mexico, conjuring up visions of mesquite and "the plum-colored infinities of the great Texas plains" in his distinctive drawl. Conrad had never been to these places, but as they passed a clump of "grimy brick houses" he saw Mexico, in all its serape colors. At Oxford Street came the majestic Painted Desert. He was so absorbed by Stephen's vivid word pictures that he did not see London that day. He failed even to see the oncoming traffic until Stephen jerked him away. "You will get run over," he said quietly.

That first day they talked about their work only briefly. Conrad said something about Stephen's having "seen no war before he went to Greece," and Stephen said, "No. But the 'Red Badge' is all right." Conrad said he had never doubted it. Wanting to show Stephen that he had read the novel, he shyly offered, "I like your General." Stephen "knew at once what I was alluding to but said not a word," recalled Conrad. They continued their walk in silence, "elbow to elbow," and after they passed Hyde Park Corner, Stephen spoke: "I like your young man — I can just see him." "Nothing could have been more characteristic of the depth of our three-hour-old intimacy than that each of us should have selected for praise the merest by-the-way vignette of a minor character," wrote Conrad.

Later they stopped for tea at a dreary shop, where they were allowed to linger while they talked, said Conrad. Like Stephen, Conrad had been psychologically orphaned even before his parents died. Conrad's father was a religious mystic who had left him with a sense of the universe as meaningless and absurd. The dark-bearded writer had spent much of his life in exile and privation, without a home to return to. Married only a short time, he needed an anchor — and yet like Stephen he remained intrigued with the world of adventure, the idea of life as a battle fought amid nature's indifference, the personal price of courage. Though Stephen had not seen much of the world, Conrad discerned that he had an "imaginative grasp of facts, events, and picturesque men." He was young, to be sure. But in Stephen's face, in his marvelous eyes, Conrad saw a life that "had been anything but a stroll through a rose garden."

Over tea the two writers agreed that "though the world had grown old and weary, yet the scheme of creation remained as obscure as ever, and . . . there was still much that was interesting to expect from Gods and men." They left the tea shop, and Conrad sent off a telegram to his wife in Essex, telling her he "would not be home that night." Stephen seems not to have told Conrad about Cora; Conrad had the impression, he said years later, that Stephen was staying in London that night. "He seemed to have no care in the world." They continued their undirected tramping, forgetting dinner. At Piccadilly Circus the subject turned to Balzac. It was now ten o'clock, but Stephen pressed his literate new friend to tell him everything he knew about Balzac and "La Comédie Humaine." Finally Conrad insisted that they stop for dinner. All through the meal — through the clatter of crockery and rushing waiters — Stephen urged him on about Balzac. It was eleven o'clock when they shook hands at the Pavilion.

"Did not we have a good pow-wow in London?" Stephen wrote his new friend the following month. On November 16, having exchanged books and compliments, feeling an even deeper understanding with Stephen, Conrad answered, "The world looks different to me now, since our long pow wow. It was good. The memory of it is good." Stephen had eagerly read the proofs of Conrad's *The Nigger of the Narcissus*, and he hastened to tell "My dear Conrad" that

> the book is simply great. The simple treatment of the death
> of Waite is too good, too terrible. I wanted to forget it at
> once. It caught me very hard. I felt ill over that red thread
> lining from the corner of the man's mouth to his chin. It was
> frightful with the weight of a real and present death. By such
> small means does the real writer suddenly flash out in the sky
> above those who are always doing rather well.

He had written notes to Irving Bacheller and others in America who might help Conrad sell the novel's American rights.

"I must write to you before I write a single word for a living to-day," Conrad replied. "I was anxious to know what you would think of the end. If I've hit you with the death of Jimmy I don't care if I don't hit another man." He had some doubts about the novel's ending, but "when I feel depressed about it I say to myself 'Crane likes the damned thing' — and am greatly consoled." And yet he couldn't help wondering

> — (human nature is a vile thing) . . . whether you meant half
> of what you said! You must forgive me. The mistrust is not of
> you — it is of myself; the drop of poison in the cup of life. I am
> no more vile than my neighbours but this disbelief in oneself is
> like a taint that spreads on everything one comes in contact

with; on men — on things — on the very air one breathes.
That's why one sometimes wishes to be a stone breaker.
There's no doubt about breaking a stone. But there's doubt,
fear — a black horror, in every page one writes. You at any
rate will understand and therefore I write to you as though we
had been born together before the beginning of things.

Stephen had invited him to lunch at Ravensbrook, but Conrad's wife
was "not presentable just now." Her advancing pregnancy forbade travel.
Conrad therefore urged Stephen to "show your condescension by coming
to us first."

Twelve days later, Stephen went alone to the drafty little house Conrad called a "damned jerry-built rabbit hutch" at Stanford-le-Hope, Essex. Conrad's wife, Jessie, would later say that her husband had somewhat prepared her "for someone at once unusual and with a charm
peculiarly his own." She too was taken with Crane. She "appreciated him
intuitively almost as soon as I did myself," said Conrad. Stephen's behavior toward the very pregnant Mrs. Conrad "was slightly nervous and not
a little shy," she said. Though she was just twenty-four — two years
younger than Stephen — and a small woman, Jessie Conrad felt maternal toward the "very slight and delicate" writer — "the first American
author I had met," she said. He seemed "little more than a boy." And she
"was greatly amused by his queer drawl" and the tales he told of his new
dogs. He leaned on his r's and said "dawg" for dog, like a Texas cowboy.
Years later, that evening would come back to her in a picture of Stephen
perched on his chair while the three of them took their coffee, talking
"gravely on the merits of his three dogs, Sponge, Flannel and Ruby."

Jessie Conrad immediately perceived that her husband and Stephen
"were on the easy terms of complete understanding," which endeared
Stephen to her. Conrad was in a bad way, dealing with rejections, waiting
for the book publication of *The Nigger of the Narcissus*, which had been serialized in the *New Review*, committing himself neither to serious reading
nor to writing. He was not looking forward to the birth of their child,
which he hadn't wanted.* The visit of a literary comrade and empathetic
friend was just what he needed, thought Jessie. She wisely left the writers

---

* In a letter to Stephen, Conrad had urged him to visit before "the circus begins here
and . . . the house is full of doctors and nurses" — when "there will be no peace for
the poor literary man."

alone to smoke and talk late into the night. Stephen went off early the next morning before Jessie arose, leaving Conrad with copies of "A Man and Some Others" and "The Open Boat."

Worried about his mounting debts and feeling depressed — even "hopeless," in Conrad's view — Stephen returned to Ravensbrook through a storm. The day after he left Stanford-le-Hope, a high tide smashed the seawall, wiped out the railway line, and flooded the marshes, wrote Conrad: "Great excitement." As though picking up a musical beat, Stephen began to compose another western tale, "The Blue Hotel," this one set in a violent storm like the "hideous and unnatural snow storm" of his 1895 reporting trip to Nebraska, a time when he'd also been at a low psychological ebb.

About "A Man and Some Others," Conrad wrote on December 1, "Garnett is right."

> I can't spin a long yarn about it but I admire it without re-serve. It is an amazing bit of biography. I am envious of you — horribly. Confound you — you fill the blamed land-scape — you — by all the devils — fill the seascape. The boat thing is immensely interesting. I don't use the word in its common sense. It is fundamentally interesting to me. Your temperament makes old things new and new things amazing. I want to swear at you, to bless you — perhaps to shoot you — but I prefer to be your friend.
>
> You are an everlasting surprise to one. You shock — and the next moment you give the perfect artistic satisfaction. Your method is fascinating. You are a complete impression-ist. The illusions of life come out of your hand without a flaw. It is not life — which nobody wants — it is art — art for which everyone — the abject and the great hanker — mostly without knowing it.

Writing more ambivalently to Edward Garnett several days later, Conrad tempered his praise of Stephen's work. He thought the stories "excellent" but oddly limited. While praising Stephen for his "very indi-vidual" eye, his artistic expression, and his "concise" thought, which is "connected, never very deep yet often startling," he reduced Stephen's achievement to a surface trick: "He is the only impressionist and only an impressionist." In effect, Stephen Crane should be "immensely popular" with readers: he had "strength . . . rapidity of action . . . that amazing faculty of vision"; he had "outline, he has colour, he has movement, with that he ought to go very far." And yet Conrad sensed that he wouldn't. He

> could not explain why he disappoints me — why my enthu-
> siasm withers as soon as I close the book. While one reads, of
> course, he is not to be questioned. He is the master of his
> reader to the very last line — then — apparently for no rea-
> son at all — he seems to let go his hold. It is as if he had
> gripped you with greased fingers. His grip is strong but while
> you feel the pressure on your flesh you slip out from his
> hand — much to your own surprise. That is my stupid im-
> pression and I give it to you in confidence.

Given the passionate enthusiasm of his letter to Stephen, Conrad's remarks to Garnett sound oddly disparaging and unkind. Even his comment about Stephen as a person seems to downplay his regard for the man he felt he had been born with "before the beginning of things": "He is strangely hopeless about himself. I like him." While feeling a genuine and fast-deepening kinship with Stephen — who was the first of his English acquaintances to call him "Joseph"; everyone else called him "Conrad" — and greatly admiring his talent, Conrad was experiencing the dark side of a close friendship between writers talented enough to be a threat to each other. Though truly wishing Stephen well, he hardly wanted to be outstripped by the younger writer — who had, in his early success, already eclipsed *him*. "It must be remembered that as an author he was my senior," Conrad said without bitterness later on — "as I used to remind him now and then with affected humility."

Conrad was still developing as a stylist in English, and just then critics were calling him a Crane imitator: "Mr. Joseph Conrad has chosen Mr. Stephen Crane for his example, and has determined to do for the sea and the sailor what his predecessor had done for war and warriors," wrote W. L. Courtney in the *Daily Telegraph* of December 8. Though rating Conrad's style as "a good deal better than Mr. Crane's," the reviewer dismissed *Narcissus* as a Crane progeny. "It has the same jerky and spasmodic quality," the same "spirit of faithful and minute description — even to the verge of the wearisome," he wrote. Conrad wrote a defensive reply to the reviewer the next day, "[disclaiming] all allegiance to realism, to naturalism," but without mentioning Stephen's name. To Stephen he would write more humbly. "Do you think I tried to imitate you? No Sir! I may be a little fool but I know better than to try to imitate the inimitable." He had never read such a "mean-spirited" review.

As Conrad "[struggled] along feeling pretty sick of it all," Stephen kept up his frantic pace. While working on his Greek war novel and "The Blue Hotel," he revised his western gambling tale, "The Five White Mice." He oversaw the proofs of the English edition of a story collection built around "The Open Boat" and tried to scrape up a pound or a shilling wherever he could. He sent a copy of *The Black Riders* to a book reviewer, Henry Dauvray, hoping to induce him to translate the poetry into French. He wrote an admiring piece on Harold Frederic, which he thought would be right for *Cosmopolitan* magazine. "Stephen is fat, for him, and works hard," Cora wrote Sylvester Scovel on December 18. "He is so content and good quite the old married man. . . . We go a little into society though seldom into London."

In his letters Stephen sounded like a man with a noose around his neck. "I send you the child story of the Greek business," he wrote Paul Revere Reynolds in December, sounding too rushed even to remember the title ("Death and the Child"). "McClure has a call on it. He should give $300 for it — at least. The English rights are sold." He had asked McClure for a two-hundred-dollar advance on the book rights of his new novel even before he started it. "I wouldn't have done it if I was not broke," he told Reynolds. "For heaven's sake raise me all the money you can and *cable* it, *cable* it sure between Xmas and New Year's. Sell 'The Monster!' Don't forget that — cable me some money this month."

"We are so pleased that there is a chance of your coming with your wife to England next summer," Cora wrote serenely in the letter to Scovel. "We have ever so many more chairs and tables than when you were here." And she invited them to make Ravensbrook their "headquarters."

As the year ended, Stephen's money crisis worsened. McClure continued to sit on *The Monster*, neither accepting nor rejecting it. "It might make me come a cropper if I dont get that money directly," Stephen wrote Reynolds on December 20. Reynolds had managed to "pinch" thirty-nine pounds from somewhere, but though the money "came in very handily," Stephen was still "awfully hard up." From across the sea he tossed figures at his agent, trying to dress up the balance sheet as best he could. He had written 1,200 words of the new novel, which he projected would be "at least 75000 words," and he expected it to be popular — "we should make a big serial amount and a round sum in advance." He calculated the unfinished "Blue Hotel" at 1,000 words. He would get the new story to Reynolds "in about two weeks." His understanding of copyright law and international rights was weak. Reynolds needed to remind Stephen that *he* had exclusive agency rights to "Death and the Child"; Stephen could not simply send it where he wanted to.

Then things got even worse. Amy Leslie decided to sue Stephen for the $550 he still owed her. After receiving Stephen's letter from Ireland in September, she had repeatedly tried to meet with Willis Hawkins to get the $100 "Steve" had sent her, which she "badly" needed, she told Hawkins. Writing that fall and winter in a hand that became progressively shakier, she first approached him politely. Receiving no answer, she wrote again from Cincinnati, where she was apparently reviewing a play. Again she got no reply, but her New York lawyer, George B. Mabon, managed to meet with Hawkins, who agreed to talk with Amy upon her return to New York. Then Hawkins failed to keep an appointment at Mabon's office. Amy went to the office herself several times; Hawkins was always out. Finally she left him another note on his business stationery. Apparently untroubled by the threat of a lawsuit, Hawkins wrote Mabon on December 28 that he had paid out all the money he'd been given by "a friend" in just the "prescribed [manner]" he had been asked to pay it, and had receipts for each payment. "When that sum was paid out, my connection with the matter ceased." He admitted having returned the last sum of money "from the same friend" and held a receipt for that, too. "I presume you will agree with me that I do not have to receive and disburse money for friends if I do not wish to." Before Stephen got wind of the matter and could write William, his royalties from Appleton had been attached.

✦

The Chicago newspapers carried the story on the front page: AMY LESLIE VS. STEPHEN CRANE, read the headline in the *Chicago Tribune;* CRANE SUED BY AMY LESLIE, said the *Chicago Times-Herald.* With the exception of the *Daily News,* Amy's employer, five Chicago papers briefly reported the warrant of attachment suit filed in New York Supreme Court on January 3, 1898. The suit against Stephen Crane's property in the amount of $550 for "breach of contract, express or implied, other than a contract to marry," was reported in matter-of-fact small items in the *New York Times* and the *New York Daily Tribune*. According to the *Chicago Tribune*, Amy Leslie said that "by force of two stormy interviews with the novelist" — when, she did not say — "she had managed to get $250.00" of the $800 she had given Stephen to deposit in the bank, "but then Crane went abroad and is now in London." She had learned that the novelist "owns some property in the city, both real and personal, and she prays for an attachment against it." The *Chicago Chronicle* noted that Stephen Crane "became best known in September, 1896, when he showed the 'Badge of Courage' in a police court" in the Dora Clark affair. "He is popular among New York literary folk," the paper added. None of the press accounts offered an explanation for Amy Leslie's giving Stephen Crane $800 to deposit in the bank or suggested a personal relationship between the two.

"Literary circles are greatly disturbed by the breach of peace between Miss Amy Leslie of Chicago and Stephen Crane of New York, and there is occasion for fear that the clash may lead to the formal abrogation of the literary treaty between the two cities," intoned the *Chicago Evening Post* on January 6. While acknowledging that Stephen's action seemed "at the worst, a violation of honorable business principles," the paper took Amy's side and warned that Crane, who seemed to be hiding out in London, should not feel safe even with an ocean between him and the woman wronged. "If we know Miss Leslie and the staunch Chicago heart that thumps in recollection of her wrongs, Stephen is in imminent danger wherever he may be." He had invited Miss Leslie's wrath and "the scorn and contumely of the best literary thought of the country." If he had a red badge of courage, he would "have plenty of opportunity to exhibit it."

Four thousand miles away, surrounded by souvenirs and sentimental objects in his English study — books, a picture of Cora in correspondent's garb in Greece, inscribed to "me old pal Stevie," a Mexican blanket and pottery, a carved wooden figure, his spurs — Stephen continued to work. "The Bride Comes to Yellow Sky" was coming out in *McClure's* in February, and he was anxious to get the original illustrations, even if he had to buy them. He also wanted the illustrations for "The Little Regiment." He wrote a note to John Phillips, asking him to handle the matter. "That's a good boy," he said.

During January he sent Reynolds a small sketch and a political piece he thought suitable for newspaper publication. He dispatched some poetry to Elbert Hubbard for the *Philistine*, wrote a table of contents for the English edition of "The Open Boat," worked on "The Blue Hotel" and presumably on his novel. He wrote the occasional business and personal letter. "Crane wrote me . . . a penitent letter for not replying to mine at Xmas," Conrad wrote Edward Garnett on January 15. "He says he finds it easier to write *about* me, but *where* he says not."

He felt "heavy with troubles" and "chased to the wall" by his English expenses. His letters to Reynolds showed the strain. "Don't kick so conspicuously about the over-charge on the damned manuscript," he wrote after billing Reynolds for half the cost of having them typed in London. "If I was a business man, I would not need a business man to conduct my affairs for me. I will try to do better but if I shouldn't, don't harangue me. The point is of minor importance." He had had to travel to London to pressure S. S. McClure's brother, Robert, to release *The Monster*. Robert agreed and said he'd inform the New York office and Reynolds to that effect. Though Stephen had already accepted an offer from *Harper's*, which would pay $450 for serial rights to the novella and a $250 advance for book publication of *The Monster and Other Stories*, he remained bitter about "that scotch ass" McClure, who had "handicapped" the thing by holding on to it for so long. "In all the months I have been in England I have never recieved a cent from America which has not been borrowed. Just read that over twice!" Stephen wrote Reynolds. "The consequences of this have lately been that I have been obligated to make arrangements here with the English agents of American houses but in all cases your commission will be protected." And he pushed ahead. "I expect to mail you a story of 10000 words on Saturday," he wrote on January 31. "I am going to write about a thousand or twelve hundred more dollars in short stuff and work only on my big book. In the meantime every hundred dollars is a boon!"

On February 1 Stephen was served with a summons to answer Amy Leslie's claim. William handled the matter from New York. On February 5 he wrote to George Mabon, asking "what it will take in cash to settle" the claim. Mabon, who was anticipating a spring court date, answered that an offer "must approximate the full amount of the claim to receive attention." William replied that he would consult with Stephen — and here the written trail ends. The suit was settled out of court for an unknown sum.

The lawsuit told heavily on Cora's nerves. Harold Frederic had again invited the Cranes to share the Dunmanus Bay house in Ireland — apparently for the whole spring — with Kate and the children. Cora responded with a letter that sent Frederic reeling. In a return letter he said that he had been unaware of how much the Cranes' life had changed since the previous autumn, when they "were still in the chrysalis stage so to speak of house-keeping and you were both relatively fresh from the hap-hazard, bohemian life of the campaign in Thessaly." Acknowledging that "since last Autumn Ravensbrook has defined for itself a system and a routine of its own — quite distinct, as is natural, from the system of Homefield — and that an effort to put these two side by side under one roof would naturally come to grief," he graciously invited the Cranes, along with Mrs. Ruedy and Adoni, to be their guests for three weeks during the spring.

By the first week of February Stephen had finished "The Blue Hotel" — another "daisy," he called it in a letter to Reynolds. Though he had originally expected the writing to take only a month, the tale kept growing, in number of words and in complexity. In the end it took him longer to write this 10,000-word short story, which he called a "novelette," than it had taken him to write *The Monster*. It was one of his finest short stories, and he knew it. He hoped Reynolds could get at least five hundred dollars for it. But he sent it without strings, so that Reynolds could sell it to *Harper's* for *The Monster* story collection.

In "The Blue Hotel," a man's vanity and distorted perception of events collide with the mysterious forces of nature and fate to bring about his destruction during a blizzard in a western outpost town.

> The Palace Hotel at Fort Romper was painted a light blue, a shade that is on the legs of a kind of heron, causing the bird to declare its position against any background. The Palace Hotel, then, was always screaming and howling in a way that made the dazzling winter landscape of Nebraska seem only a gray swampish hush. It stood alone on the prairie, and when the snow was falling the town two hundred yards away was not visible.

Thus began "The Blue Hotel."

Working with the themes and literary devices he had made unmistakably his own, Crane brings three unnamed travelers — a "quick-eyed Swede," a "tall bronzed cowboy," and a "little silent man from the East" — to the memorably blue Palace Hotel. There, as the snow obliterates the world outside and seems to seep into the human action, helping to direct its course, the travelers join a card game. The strange Swede, his head muddled by stories he'd heard of the gunfighting American West, sees the local men through the deformed lens of his imagination and succumbs to paranoia. Convinced that the men mean to kill him, he suddenly accuses the owner's son, Johnnie Scully, of cheating. The men fight it out. The Swede beats the young man, but soon afterward, while celebrating his victory at the saloon, he aggressively insists that a gambler drink with him, and is knifed to death. In a witty ironic-comic touch, the dead Swede's eyes fix themselves upon the "dreadful legend" of the cash register, which reads, "This registers the amount of your purchase."

It was one of Stephen Crane's darkest tales. "No other Crane fiction — except, perhaps, 'The Monster' — expresses such a violence of disgust with man and his condition," Ralph Ellison would write. "The Blue Hotel" is "The Bride" gone bad; the Swede is Scratchy Wilson turned deadly serious. Stephen used his own condition — his depression and hopelessness, his feelings of anger and persecution, his strong sense of fighting a battle alone in exile — to dazzling effect. In the "turmoiling sea of snow" that entombs the Palace Hotel, in the quarreling gloom of the men playing cards, in the "formidably menaced" Swede, Stephen expressed an overpowering feeling of entrapment and doom. The blizzard itself becomes a virtual character in the story, remaining with the reader long after the details of the plot have faded from memory.

The story ends with the revelation that Johnnie Scully *has* been cheating at cards. Sounding Stephen's own often repeated refrain about manly behavior, the easterner reflects that none of the men present stood up and got involved when they should have. "Every sin is the result of a collaboration," he says — reflecting Stephen's role in the Dora Clark affair, his entanglement with Amy Leslie, and perhaps even his fake marriage to Cora. In the Palace Hotel, where the "humming" cooking stove is a recurring image, the women stay out of sight, emerging only to descend, like birds of prey, upon a man badly beaten in a fight. Then they spirit him away to the kitchen, where the stove is. The easterner tells the cowboy, "Usually there are from a dozen to forty women really involved in every murder."

In February Stephen confided to his agent that settling in England had run him some $2,000 into debt. Even with the payment from *Harper's* for *The Monster*, he was $1,200 in the hole, which he could have easily climbed out of "if it were not for that black-mail at Appletons." The attachment of his royalties had knocked him silly, he said. Things were so bad that "a ten pound note even fills me with awe." But he would "beat it." He would "bombard" Reynolds "with stuff." If Reynolds sold "The Blue Hotel" to *Harper's*, he was to instantly cable the money to Stephen. "Get me through this [month] and I am prepared to smile," he wrote.

Smiling, faintly, for a hired photographer (sent for "regardless of expense," said Joseph Conrad), Stephen posed for a group photograph in front of the door to Ravensbrook to commemorate the Conrads' first visit to their home, five weeks after the birth of their son, Borys. "Though the likenesses are not bad it is a very awful thing," Conrad said later. "Nobody looks like him or herself in it."

Having been warmly invited by Cora, who had sent them "a beautiful box of flowers" two days after the baby's birth, the Conrads arrived for a ten-day visit in mid-February. They brought the baby and Jessie's sister, Dolly. The new mother was tired and suffering from stomach trouble she attributed to nursing the baby. Conrad was still depressed and unable to work, finding the whole baby business "a ghastly nuisance"; he had sat apart from his wife, baby, and sister-in-law on the train to Ravensbrook. Yet it was a successful visit all around, and it deepened the writers' friendship. Conrad arrived bringing paper and good intentions, determined to "have a real good time." Stephen was brimming with ideas for a collaborative play that would make them both money. Though doubtful about such a proposition, Conrad was willing to consider it. "I believe you can do anything," he told Stephen.

The writers sat together in the memento-filled study while Stephen worked amid constant interruptions by the three dogs, which always had entrée to his study. To Conrad they seemed to number thirty: "they pervaded, populated and filled the whole house," he wrote later. "A scratching would be heard at the door. Crane would drop his pen with alacrity to throw it open — and the dogs would enter sedately in single file, taking a lot of time about it, too." After a settling-down commotion — "grunts, sniffs, yawns, heavy flops, followed by as much perhaps as three whole minutes of silence" — there would be another scratching at the study door. "Then, never before, Crane would raise his head, go meekly to the door — and the procession would file out at the slowest possible pace," said Conrad. Oblivious to the comedy in the situation, Stephen played his role with "absurd gravity," until an afternoon when the procedure had been repeated five or six times, and Conrad "could not help bursting into a loud interminable laugh and then the dear fellow asked me in all innocence what was the matter. I managed to conceal my nervous irritation from him and he never learned the secret of that laugh in which there was the beginning of hysteria."

On all sides there was courtesy and an effort to please. The Cranes brought in friends to help entertain the Conrads and admire the baby — Garnett, Frederic, and Hueffer, who had children of their own, Jack Stokes, Frederic's literary assistant, and Robert Barr. Conrad addressed Cora respectfully as "Mrs. Crane"; Cora was delighted with Conrad's French accent and manners and the tales of his "wonderful adventures" in the South Sea Islands. Jessie Conrad enjoyed herself "immensely," she said later. She was amused by Adoni's efforts at the role of butler and by his clumsy attempts to speak English: "Mr. Conrad, Mr. Stokes he come, he want you, Mr. Crane." At table the Greek moved a comfortable chair next to Jessie's as a bed for the baby. When Jessie gave the baby a bath, Adoni crept into the room to watch. Jessie was deeply touched by "the royal preparations for the small person's arrival" and by Cora and Stephen's interest in the child. Having been "impatiently expected," the baby was fussed over by each. "Stephen declared he had some distinct claim to our precious baby," said Jessie. "Cora too was very much taken up with the child, but in a different way." Neither Stephen nor Cora seems to have been disturbed by the baby's nightly crying, and the women apparently lived under the same roof for ten days without female tension or rivalry. In the group photograph outside Ravensbrook, Cora wears a cap that matches Stephen's and holds baby Borys; Mrs. Ruedy wears the same cap, and she and Stephen each hold one of the black dogs Conrad described as belonging "to some order of outlandish poodles." Conrad, admittedly suffering "from a severe case of extinction" amid all the fuss over the infant, stands stiffly in the doorway behind the others.

"I miss you horribly," Conrad wrote Stephen upon returning to Stanford-le-Hope. "In fact Ravensbrook and its inhabitants have left an indelible memory. Some day — perhaps next year — we must take a house together — say in Brittany for 3 months or so. It would work smoothly — I am sure."

✦

On the evening of February 15, 1898, several days before the Conrads arrived at Ravensbrook, the U.S. battleship *Maine* exploded in Havana Harbor under suspicious circumstances, killing some 262 people. With Pulitzer's *World* and Hearst's *Journal* leading the American charge, the yellow press was quick to cry Spanish sabotage. But President McKinley moved cautiously, waiting for the report of the Court of Inquiry before taking action. As the president waited and American political tensions mounted, a war with Spain began to seem inevitable. In early March McKinley requested and got $50 million from the House Appropriations Committee to prepare for war. Plans to construct new battleships, destroyers, and torpedo boats were under way; an auxiliary fleet was to be purchased from abroad.

As the coming war beckoned, Stephen again talked to Conrad about collaborating on a play. While insisting that he had "no dramatic gift" and would only be a "hindrance" to his friend, Conrad was flattered by the suggestion. He was also in need of money. Following a dinner at the Savage Club in London one evening, the two writers drifted off alone and talked about the play until "the last train," remembered Conrad. That night anything seemed possible: even a melodramatic play bordering on the ludicrous was sure to make money. As they talked, they drafted the play, "interrupting each other eagerly," adding to each other's ideas. It would be called *The Predecessor*, said Stephen, and would involve a man who impersonates a dead man "in the hope of winning a girl's heart." It would be set on a ranch in the Rocky Mountains. In one scene the man and the girl would stand alongside "their dead ponies after a furious ride (a truly Crane touch)," to which Conrad objected. "A boundless plain in the light of a sunset could be got into a back-cloth, I admitted; but I doubted whether we could induce the management of any London theatre to deposit two stuffed horses on its stage," he said.

Finally, on March 28, the long-awaited report on the *Maine* was made public. Though Spain was not accused outright of sabotage, the explosion was attributed to an external device and the U.S. Navy absolved of all blame. That same day Cora wrote a letter to Sylvester Scovel.

> Dear Harry: Stephen is coming on the ship that carries this letter to America, as correspondent in the U.S. Spain row. I suppose you will see him as doubtless Key West will be the headquarters for newspaper men. We have thought it best for me to remain in England. I am writing to you to ask you and your good wife — if ye be in the same town, to look after him a little. He is rather seedy and I am anxious about

him, for he does not care to look out for himself. Adoni goes
with him but you know what the Greek servant is. And if he
should be ill I beg you to wire me.

Joseph Conrad later recalled "the cloudy afternoon" in April he and
Stephen had spent "rushing all over London" to get him an assignment
and the money needed to leave for the impending war in Cuba. "The
problem was to find £60 that day, before the sun set, before dinner, before the 'six forty' train to Oxted, at once, that instant — lest peace
should be declared and the opportunity of seeing a war be missed."
Stephen's request for an assignment was turned down at several places.
One man wanted forty-eight hours to consider the proposition, but
Stephen didn't have time to wait. Conrad finally suggested *Blackwood's
Magazine*. The publisher guaranteed Stephen the money he would need
to leave the country. Long afterward Conrad was haunted by the picture
of Stephen's "white-faced excitement," a look that had frightened him.
"Nothing could have held him back," he wrote. "He was ready to swim
the ocean."

On April 7, with war still undeclared, *Blackwood's Magazine* issued
Stephen a sixty-pound advance for articles "from the seat of war in the
event of a war breaking out" between the United States and Spain. It was
to be paid in two installments — forty pounds at the outset for Stephen to
take with him and another twenty to Cora on April 16. With perhaps
some additional money from the *Harper's* advance on *The Monster*, but
nothing from "The Blue Hotel," which had been rejected by the *Century*,
Scribner's, and the *Atlantic*, Stephen left Oxted. Cora and the rest of the
household — including Adoni, apparently, whom Stephen could not afford to take — remained at Ravensbrook to fend off local creditors. He
and Cora had talked about looking for cheaper lodgings in another part
of England and had planned to visit an ancient manor house in East Sussex that Edward Garnett had told them about. But there was no time for
that now. Stephen shipped out from Liverpool aboard the *Germanic* on
April 13. When the ship stopped at Queenstown, Ireland, on the fourteenth just before heading across the Atlantic Ocean, Stephen sent a
telegram to the person for whom he felt a "warm and endless friendship,"
Joseph Conrad.

13

THE BEST MOMENT

OF ANYBODY'S LIFE

On April 21, 1898, shortly before midnight, the *Germanic* crossed into New York Harbor. Just hours later, United States warships painted lead gray for battle left Key West for Havana. Congress had passed resolutions recognizing Cuba's independence and disclaiming any American intention to establish sovereignty there. A war resolution was imminent. At sea off the Cuban ports the Atlantic Squadron, under the command of white-bearded Rear Admiral William T. Sampson, formed a blockade and waited for the Spanish fleet to arrive.

Stephen rushed around New York collecting money and a passport. In addition to *Blackwood's*, he was to report the war for the *New York World*, for which he was reportedly paid $3,000. On April 24 he left for Key West, planning to stop in Washington to see Lily Munroe's sister, Dot. Then he received word "that there was to be a big fight off Havana and I was to go there instantly. I flew," he wrote Dot later from somewhere "off Havana." "Will you forgive me? I have not changed in the least and you may be sure that the S. Crane you knew so well long ago would not seem thoughtless if he could help it."

On April 25 the United States declared war, and the following day Stephen found Key West swarming with reporters — some two hundred and fifty, he calculated. Every American newspaper had sent from five to twenty-five field reporters to cover the war, along with their regular correspondents. Edward Marshall was there representing the *New York Journal*, Ernest McCready the *New York Herald*, Sylvester Scovel the *World*. The

Philadelphia Press reporter Ralph Paine later noted that though most of these newsmen were "first-class," they were not war correspondents per se: "This dignity belonged to Richard Harding Davis," representing both the *New York Herald* and the *London Times*, to the English correspondents, and to Stephen Crane. The uninitiated, like Paine, "never tired of listening to their yarns." While the army massed in Tampa, the reporters who gathered at the navy's port in Key West passed their time like well-fed gentlemen at a summer hotel. "This was the rocking-chair period of the war," said Davis. Dressed in immaculate, freshly creased flannel trousers and straw hats, the correspondents spent hours "idling on a hotel verandah and paying court to a smartly dressed summer girl," wrote Frank Norris, the reporter from *McClure's*. They gambled at a nearby resort dubbed the Eagle Bird. Ralph Paine would remember that Stephen was often at the roulette wheel there, gambling alone and offering a "tired smile" as he drawled out the words

> Oh, five white mice of chance
> Shirts of wool and corduroy pants,
> Gold and wine, women and sin,
> All for you if you let me come in —
> Into the house of chance.

He was soon running out of money.

As the American warships waited for Admiral Pascual Cervera y Topete's Spanish fleet to enter their two-hundred-mile net along Cuba's northern coast, the dispatch tugs and yachts hired by the newspapers fanned out behind them like a school of fish. Occasionally some small eruption occurred, providing copy for the quick reporter. He then "ran to Key West, blow high, blow low, to reach the cable office," as Paine said. The well-connected Richard Harding Davis was aboard Admiral Sampson's flagship, the *New York*, on April 27 when it shelled the earthworks at Matanzas and exchanged fire with some Spanish soldiers. No one was injured, but Davis exulted at witnessing the little spectacle up close. Only one press boat had been anywhere near the action; even the celebrated Stephen Crane had "missed the bombardment," Davis wrote his family. It was the first day of Velestino all over again. "I have made I think my position here very strong and the admiral is very much my friend as are also his staff," Davis wrote his family. "Crane on the other hand took the place of Paine who was exceedingly popular with every one and it has made it hard for Crane to get into things."

But Stephen had his connections too. Through his friendship with Sylvester Scovel, who was also acquainted with Admiral Sampson, Stephen was on board the *New York* for its two-day inspection of the Bay of Mariel, thirty-five miles west of Havana, on April 29 and 30. During this idle period of the war, he interviewed people, kept his ears open, and made the most of small things, turning out occasional copy with the unmistakable Crane touch. "The boatswain of the *New York* has a voice like the watery snuffle of a swimming horse," he wrote in "Sampson Inspects Harbor at Mariel." Writing about the toll that inaction was taking on the Key West fleet, he described the torpedo boats spinning "like tops . . . in the mad waters of the Florida Strait."

He himself was not spinning so much as unraveling. He looked like a dirty bed sheet. He skipped baths and shaves. On board the dispatch tug *The Three Friends,* he wore rank pajamas or "duck trousers grimed and fouled with all manner of pitch and grease and oil," said Frank Norris. His untucked white shirt was unbuttoned at the neck and rolled to the elbows, emphasizing his deeply tanned neck, face, and hands. His mustache was shaggy, his hair "hung in ragged fringes over his eyes." He looked so bedraggled and weatherbeaten that one of the photographs taken of him on the tug was later misidentified as having been taken after his rescue from the sunken *Commodore.*

Stephen found a correspondent's work "drudgery," said Norris. He was an artist; he needed time to form his sentences. He used his suitcase as a lap desk for writing his dispatches, pausing to take swallows of beer out of a bottle held on the floor between his bare feet. Sometimes he failed. "The sun is over the yardarm," he'd say, and "the corkscrew is mightier than the pen." He was hardly the picture of a war correspondent, let alone "a great genius," wrote the disgusted Norris. "You want to see the war correspondent in all his glory, leaping from the dispatch boat before she is even made fast to the dock, dashing ashore in all the panoply of pith helmet, norfolk jacket and field glasses." But even Norris conceded that Stephen Crane and Sylvester Scovel, whom he later disguised in print as The Young Personage and The Press, "approached more nearly to the ideal type of war correspondent than any I had yet seen." Both "were tanned to the color of well worn saddles" and had "the little calloused spot" on the bridge of their noses "that comes with the long use of field glasses."

At leisure to write his own stuff and deal with literary business, Stephen wrote a long Whilomville tale to fill out *The Monster* volume for *Harper's*. A lackluster, drawn-out yarn about a boy who runs away from home (tellingly populated by women), "His New Mittens" reflected Stephen's preoccupation with the word count. He wrote Reynolds that he thought the story was worth "about £40"; he also thought Harper's should "cough up that other $125," the remainder of the book advance. Already he needed money. *Collier's* had offered $300 for "The Blue Hotel" on the condition that it be cut to 7,500 or 8,000 words. He agreed to those terms but said that he could not cut the story himself. "Let Collier's do the cutting," he wrote Reynolds on May 8.

As the American blockade dragged into the second half of May and the Spanish fleet played cat and mouse with the navy, Stephen found adventure where he could. One night when *The Three Friends* was returning to Key West, a gunboat mistook the tug for a Spanish ship and rammed it, showering the correspondents with soot. Stephen turned the incident into a dispatch called "Narrow Escape of the Three Friends." Another time he went with Paine and some other correspondents on an expedition to Haiti. As Paine told it, *The Three Friends* steamed across a sea so rough that some of the men could not even hold a pad on their laps and were forced to lie prone on the floor to write. Then they landed on a dark beach at Le Môle St. Nicholas. With its thatched-roof houses, stone ruins, and steady drum beat, the place seemed like the Congo. On the beach the correspondents were surrounded by natives carrying ancient rifles with rusty bayonets, who followed them as they tried to find the dispatch office. They were continually stopped by sentries calling out "Qui vive!" and they got nowhere. The Haitians did not understand the Americans' bad French; the Americans — Paine, representing the *Philadelphia Press*, Ernest W. Mc-Cready of the *New York Herald*, and Harry Brown, whom Paine called the "dean of the 'Herald' war staff" — could not interpret the natives' "corrupt French patois." Stephen alone enjoyed himself. "As usual," said Paine, "he refused to take the responsibilities of daily journalism seriously. He had been known to shorten the life of a managing editor."

Appealed to for advice, Stephen grinned. "Me? If I caught myself hatching a plot like this, I wouldn't write another line until I had sobered up," he said. "Steady boys, the night is still young, and I have a hunch that there'll be lots more of it. This opening is good."

Even when a Haitian poked Harry Brown with a bayonet as he reached into his pocket for a bribe, Stephen remained unruffled.

"Stick around, Harry," he said. "Age has dulled your feeling for romance. We can beat this game yet."

Eventually, Bill, the young deck hand of *The Three Friends*, saved the day by answering the "Qui vive!" with "I-AM-THE-BOSS!" — which apparently sounded like something equally authoritative in the Haitians' French.

"Bill, you are a wonder," said Stephen. "But darn you, you are too impossible for fiction. I shall have to get good and drunk to do you justice. And you told them you were the boss and got away with it?"

Bill led the way, and the correspondents followed him through the lines, echoing his "I-AM-THE-BOSS! Salute, you black sons-of-guns!" as they encountered the sentries. Some of the sentries even saluted the Americans.

"I wonder if we could blast the secret out of a French dictionary," Stephen mused. "Probably not. We shall never know. It is just one of those things."

The next night, having heard from Bill about a lovely girl he'd met on the island — "an awful pretty girl, and there was mighty little tar baby about her" — Stephen "went native," said McCready. He was barefoot, "clothed only by exceedingly soiled blue-striped pajamas, an equally soiled brown beard of a week's well-fertilized herbage — and his circumbient Breath. This last was protection enough for all ordinary purposes. Indeed, it would have sufficed in the still undiscovered stratosphere," said McCready. But Stephen accomplished his mission anyway. He apparently failed in his other great plan for the evening — to steal rum from two drunken men who had hidden it in a barque in the shark-infested harbor.

On May 28 the navy finally caught up with the Spanish fleet. Commodore Winfield Scott Schley found the enemy in Santiago Harbor. In the coming days his flying squadron, reinforced by Admiral Sampson with the *New York* and the *Oregon*, blocked their exit route. On the twenty-ninth, Stephen was on the dispatch boat *Somers N. Smith* with six other correspondents, including Scovel and *Collier's Weekly* photographer Jimmy Hare, looking for Cervera's fleet about 160 miles north of Jamaica. Suddenly they were chased by what they thought was a Spanish warship. Though the pursuer turned out to be an American auxiliary cruiser, the *St. Paul*, Stephen used the experience in a dispatch. He wrote it like a tale, heavy with dialogue. The *World* promptly published it.

•

While Stephen played war games, exchanged yarns with his fellow correspondents, and joined in the evening singing — making "a good second" to Scovel's "very good tenor," noted one newsman — Cora planned for his return to England. He had been writing and sending her money — regularly, it seems. (Stephen's letters to Cora have not survived.) Presumably to keep the liaison private, he sent the money to Paul Revere Reynolds, who mailed it to John Scott-Stokes in London, who then passed it on to Cora. Having temporarily escaped the Oxted creditors by spending several weeks with the Frederics in Ahakista after Stephen's departure, Cora was now forced to fend them off alone while she planned an escape. In consultation with Stephen, she negotiated to rent Brede Place, the manor house in East Sussex that Garnett had suggested. With Stephen's approval, she even hired an architect to look at the old house and determine what it would cost to make it livable. Cora proposed to the owners that along with an annual rent of £40 — an astonishingly low figure, even given the house's dilapidated condition — the Cranes would make improvements by building "a small conservatory" and fixing up the stable. This would actually equal "over £120 a year rent," as she figured it, including improvements. She was anxious to get started. She wanted to be "already in camp" when Stephen returned from Cuba.

With no end to the blockade in sight, Admiral Sampson turned his attention to the establishment of a protected American base in Cuba. The blockading ships had been forced to travel eight hundred miles to Key West for coaling and small ship repairs. Now a perfect site for a base was found at Guantanamo Bay, on Cuba's southeastern tip. On June 6, Commander B. H. McCalla and a hundred Marines on the *Marblehead* and the *Yankee* easily seized the lower bay. This opened the way for the First Marine Battalion landing of some 647 men, who arrived on the U.S.S. *Panther* on June 10. The American flag was raised, and the camp christened Camp McCalla.

Stephen witnessed the landing from *The Three Friends* with Paine and McCready. The water around the bay looked to him like "blue steel." To the east a village was burning, transforming the palm trees into shivering "gory feathers." That night, when the other correspondents steamed off in the tug to Port Antonio, Jamaica, to cable their dispatches, Stephen, untroubled by the need to do the same, went ashore with the Marines.

They had an abundant supply of cigarettes and good whiskey, noted Paine, and "a hawser could not have dragged [Crane] away from the show." His plan was "to gather impressions and write them as the spirit moved," said Paine.

The Marines made camp and dug a few trenches. The bay had been taken so easily that some of the men were bathing naked when they suddenly found themselves under fire. It came from the chaparral, where the enemy couldn't be seen, and the Marines returned fire blindly. There was no time to scramble into their clothes. They burst from the water and grabbed their cartridge belts and rifles. Signalmen flashed messages to the *Marblehead* out in the bay, and she shelled in the direction of the enemy. But nothing stopped the assault — the Marines were up against "practicos, or guides, who knew every shrub and tree on the ground," wrote Stephen. Hour after hour the firing continued.

Stephen spent that night with the four Marine signalmen in the trenches, which faced the water. The signalmen had to use lanterns and, standing up to hold one lantern still while moving the other in the wigwagging code, they became illuminated targets. The Escuadra de Guantanamo, said to be "the most formidable corps in the Spanish army of occupation," was hidden just a few hundred yards away. Every time a signalman stood up, Stephen's heart leaped into his mouth, for he knew that "all Spain [would] shoot at him." From his place in the trench he automatically rolled away, in case a man was hit and fell on him.

He greatly admired the courage of the Marines and the bravery of the signalmen, who did their job with seeming disregard for their own personal safety. He watched their faces, bathed in yellow lantern light. They betrayed nothing save the attitude of "a man intent upon his business." Though he would write honestly of his own fear in battle, Stephen himself seemed to be a model of composure. Even Richard Harding Davis would say that

> in his devotion to duty, and also in his readiness at the exciting moments of life, Crane is quite as much of a soldier as the man whose courage he described. . . . It never occurs to Crane that to sit at the man's feet as he did close enough to watch his lips move and to be able to make mental notes for a later tribute to the marine's scorn of fear, was equally deserving of praise.

Another observer wrote that it would be a long time before he forgot Stephen Crane's "calmness . . . on the night of the 11th of June on top of that red gravel hill."

Before the battle was over, Stephen would hear a man die. He did not then realize that the man he heard "dying hard" was Assistant Surgeon John Blair Gibbs, whom he himself had gone out to look for before heavy fire forced him to drop to the ground. "For the moment I was no longer a cynic," wrote Stephen. "I was a child who, in a fit of ignorance, had jumped into the vat of war." The enemy got so close that the Marines used revolvers to return their fire. Four Marines were killed, one wounded. A story got around that two of the dead men, who were killed at close range, were stripped and "horribly mutilated" — a detail Stephen reported as fact in a dispatch on June 12. The detail was not printed. It turned out that the bodies looked mutilated because of the devastating Mauser bullets used by Spanish snipers, which caused a "frightful tearing effect," wrote Stephen.

In his superb war tale "Marines Signaling Under Fire at Guantanamo," Stephen would write of "this prolonged tragedy of the night":

> The noise; the impenetrable darkness; the knowledge from the sound of the bullets that the enemy was on three sides of the camp; the infrequent bloody stumbling and death of some man with whom, perhaps, one had messed two hours previous; the weariness of the body, and the more terrible weariness of the mind, at the endlessness of the thing, made it wonderful that at least some of the men did not come out of it with their nerves hopelessly in shreds.

Stephen himself was so charged up after one of these nights that even when daylight came he couldn't sleep. "It always took me . . . some hours to get my nerves combed down," he wrote. "But then it was great joy to lie in the trench with the four signalmen, and understand thoroughly that night was fully over at last, and that, although the future might have in store other bad nights, that one could never escape from the prison-house which we call the past."

The nights were long. "The day broke by inches, with an obvious and maddening reluctance," wrote Stephen. Then the island flushed violet in the tropical sun. At daybreak on June 14, the fourth day, Stephen reluctantly rose from a restless night on the ground in chilly air to walk six miles along the coast to Cuzco with Captain George Elliott, a detachment of 160 Marines from Companies C and D, and fifty Cubans. Their mission was "to drive the enemy from the well and destroy it." The night before, Elliott had invited Stephen to go along as his aide. Stephen eagerly accepted the invitation, then became so frightened at the prospect of the next day's battle, he said later, that he could not sleep. He was bitterly cold, "bitterly afraid." He began to hope that he'd get sick and be unable to go. But though he was inadequately dressed and his sore feet were already poulticed in wet clay, he was healthy, and he went as planned.

Both in his dispatch and in a story about the fighting at Cuzco, Stephen portrayed himself as an alternately passive, fearful, and attentive observer who had tagged along because he wanted the others to think well of him. He walked on the lee side of the steep ridges to avoid the fire. He was so afraid of falling that he was tempted to grab on to the cactus growing in thick clumps on the ridge. When Captain Elliott moved into dangerous territory, Stephen dropped farther behind. But he responded quickly to the captain's requests, earning Elliott's respect with his willingness to serve, and he spoke in a cheerful tone that was in truth "a black lie," Stephen admitted. With his "heart in his boots," he carried messages to company commanders, who unlike himself did not seem afraid. He thought of running but didn't.

In spite of his shaky condition, made worse by the exhausting march up the hills along the coastline in blazing heat, he was captivated by the battle fought at close range, by the soldiers' faces, "the color of beetroot." A man who had been shot looked simply "weary, weary, weary." He watched the signalers, again in awe. As Sergeant John H. Quick signaled to the *Dolphin* using a handkerchief tied to a long stick — boldly silhouetted on the bare ridge, his back a perfect target for Spanish fire — Stephen and the others instinctively moved away. But Quick kept to his work, his face "as grave and serene as that of a man writing in his own library." He showed no fear. "It seemed absurd to hope that he would not be hit; I only hoped that he would be hit just a little, little, in the arm, the shoulder, or the leg," wrote Stephen. Quick was later awarded the Congressional Medal of Honor. Stephen himself was officially cited for his "material aid during the action" at Cuzco.

His fellow correspondents finally caught up with him. *The Three Friends* had returned from Port Antonio while the battle at Cuzco was still going. The cruisers were firing shells right over the soldiers' heads, and the Marines were scrambling up the ravines, said Ernest McCready. The Marines had fought without letup for some thirty hours, too busy even to bury their dead. Ralph Paine came across the dead soldiers, laid out in a row between the tents and covered with blankets. Then Paine went off to join the action; McCready went in search of Stephen.

He found him sitting alone on a rock, contemplating the battle. Though Stephen was not in the line of fire, he was close enough so that smoke blew over him. But he seemed oblivious to any danger. Only a year earlier he had posed in proper war correspondent's attire on a fake rock in a photographer's studio in Athens. Now, tired and dirty and looking much older than he had then, he was still stimulated by the drama before him and by "the prospect that presently it would be a whole lot worse," said McCready.

McCready had a difficult time getting Stephen to leave the rock. He had not slept in two days, and he was irritable and rude. Looking at McCready "with visible dislike," he demanded a cigarette.

"You think, for God's sake, that I'm going away now on your damned boat, and leave all this?" he said, gesturing toward the battle.

McCready got angry. He told Stephen "to forget the scenery & the 'effects'" and remember the obligations of a newspaper man. But he knew full well that Stephen could not have cared less about "mere news gathering."

Stephen explained that he'd been with the Marines through it all, had shared their food, and "he'd be damned if he'd stir from his rock. As for me, I could do what I damned well liked — I was simply distracting his attention." McCready finally got him to leave by bribing him with cigarettes (Stephen took them all) and with the promise of ale and scotch on the boat.

"Oh, be damned to it!" Stephen said.

As they headed back through the bush, Stephen complained about McCready's fast pace.

"What the hell's the rush?" he said, pointing out that this fighting was nothing compared to that of the night before.

"There was no fear in him so far as battle, murder or sudden death was concerned — in the observation of any who saw him in places where the average man feels a chill wind momentarily, or is afraid he's about to get the wind up," said McCready.

Back aboard *The Three Friends* and under the restoring influence of

food, drink, and tobacco, Stephen revived enough to tell his fellow correspondents the stories he would later write. Long afterward Ralph Paine
could see him — "sprawled on deck, rolling cigarettes and talking in a
slow, unemotional manner," his tired eyes brightening as he told of the
brave signalmen. His storytelling was so electric, his vivid words like "colors to be laid on a canvas with a vigorous and daring brush," said Paine,
that the men temporarily forgot the real battle still going on on land.

Bribed with more cigarettes and ale, Stephen finally agreed to dictate his dispatch to McCready. "It was a ridiculous scene," remembered
Paine. "McCready, the conscientious reporter, waiting with pencil and
paper — Crane, the artist, deliberating over this phrase or that, finicky
about a word, insisting upon frequent changes and erasures, and growing
more and more suspicious."

"Read it aloud, Mac, as far as it goes," Stephen told him. "I believe
you are murdering my stuff."

McCready replied that he'd deleted "a few adjectives." This was
news; he needed "the straight story of the fight."

Suddenly one of the cruisers fired a thundering shot from the bay,
and Stephen left to join the Marines. McCready had to write Stephen's
dispatch himself from the notes he had taken.

On June 17 Stephen joined forces with Sylvester Scovel and Alexander Kenealy, also of the *World*, to establish a news headquarters near Santiago. From the dispatch boat *Triton*, Stephen and Scovel plunged into the
water on two Jamaican horses. Once ashore, they found a third horse for
Kenealy and some insurgents to guide them into the Cuban hills. The
trails were so steep that the men had to lie flat on their ponies. They then
decided to pinpoint the location of the Spanish fleet in Santiago Harbor.
In the hills that first day they found Colonel Cebreco's insurgent camp,
where half-naked, "ragged" soldiers slouched about. They wore full cartridge belts and carried 1873 Springfield rifles, wrote Stephen. They were
downtrodden and hungry but as hardy as the island's tall guinea grass,
and they were ready to help the American correspondents. Scovel and
his men asked for a guide to take them over the mountains; Cebreco
gave them five. As they climbed the first ridge — high above the sea, with
green peaks and lush woods filled with bird song — Stephen thought "it
was the kind of country in which commercial physicians love to establish
sanitariums."

Before dawn the next day, June 18, they reached another insurgent camp. With fifteen guides now leading the way, the correspondents left their horses behind for an arduous nine-mile trek on foot. As they ascended a 2,000-foot mountain, they passed within rifle range of Spanish campfires. When they reached the top, the correspondents dropped to the ground. Then the Cubans drew their machetes and parted the foliage before them like a curtain, exposing the whole of Cervera's fleet.

Later, Stephen and Scovel carried this information directly to Admiral Sampson on board the *New York*.

It was June 22. As part of a tripartite plan devised by Admiral Sampson, Brigadier General William R. Shafter, commander of the Fifth Corps, and General Calixto García Iñiguez of the *insurrectos*, American troops landed at the village of Daiquirí, eighteen miles east of Santiago. Thus began the first phase of the Santiago campaign. All day long, under a blue sky, Stephen watched the landing of 6,000 men and uncounted horses commanded by Major General Joseph "Fighting Joe" Wheeler. The sea was rough, and two of the men from the Tenth Cavalry and several horses were drowned when their boat overturned as they approached shore. "It is horrible to think of them clasped in the arms of their heavy accoutrements," wrote Stephen, perhaps remembering the money belt he had had to discard in the dinghy. In this otherwise largely uneventful landing, he was also moved by the sight of "the ragged Cuban infantry," who let out a great cheer at the Americans' arrival. In the end, though, this momentous, long-awaited day somehow failed to seem grand.

On June 23, American troops entered the little fishing village of Siboney, seven miles west of Daiquirí. First came General Henry Ware Lawton's Second Division, then Brigadier Shafter by sea, landing troops and supplies, and Wheeler, leading the Cavalry Division, which consisted of the Regulars and the First Volunteer Cavalry. Popularly known as the Rough Riders, Teddie's Terrors, and Wood's Weary Walkers, the First Volunteer Cavalry was commanded by Colonel Leonard Wood and Lieutenant Colonel Theodore Roosevelt, who had resigned his post as assistant secretary of the navy in order to fight. On June 24, the army moved from Siboney toward Las Guásimas, the mountain pass where the Spanish were waiting.

The Rough Riders were just disappearing over the hill that morning when Stephen arrived in Siboney by dispatch boat in the company of Ernest McCready, Edward Marshall of the *New York Journal*, and Burr

McIntosh, a photographer for *Leslie's Weekly*. Hearing that the Rough Riders "had gone out with the avowed intention of finding the Spaniards and mixing it up with them," the press set off after them.

The cavalry advanced on foot. Colonel Wood and 500 Rough Riders made up the left flank on the westerly side of the mountain, called the "ridge trail"; General S. B. M. Young, some 470 Regulars, and the First and Tenth Negro Cavalry formed the right flank up the "valley road," the Camino Real. The way to Las Guásimas was a hard, steep trail of "dense Cuban thickets" infested with land crabs and with mosquitoes carrying yellow fever. The woods were so dry that Stephen feared they would ignite under the scorching early morning sun. The climb exhausted even the most "wiry" and "stalwart" soldiers; "there were frequent halts." The Rough Riders discarded blankets, blouses, tents, and even precious coffee along the way. Stephen and his colleagues passed these odd leavings as they struggled to catch up. Once they reached the Rough Riders, Ed Marshall joined Roosevelt and Richard Harding Davis at the front of the line, where any fighting would be. Both Marshall and Davis had been Roosevelt favorites since his police commissioner days, when they'd given him good press. Stephen, still a pariah with Roosevelt because of the Dora Clark affair, declined to go with them. Amazing Marshall "with his apparent indolence," he remained in the extreme rear.

The Rough Riders marched through the woods "making more noise than a train going through a tunnel," wrote Stephen. They had yet to fight, and some of the correspondents were better versed than they in the ways of the Cubans and the Spanish. As Teddie's Terrors advanced, laughing and talking, Stephen became more afraid than he had ever been before. He alone seemed to recognize that "the beautiful coo of the Cuban wood-dove" was actually the deadly "Spanish guerilla wood-dove which had presaged the death of gallant marines." The sergeant had just given the order to stop talking, adding that there was a Spanish outpost ahead, when they were pounded with heavy sniper fire from three directions. The woods rang with the unmistakable drawn-out sound of high-speed Mauser bullets. "These Mauser projectiles sounded as if one string of a most delicate musical instrument had been touched by the wind into a long, faint note, or that overhead some one had swiftly swung a long, thin-lashed whip," wrote Stephen. The Spanish used smokeless powder, and in the dense jungle the Americans couldn't see where the fire was coming from. It seemed as if the regiment was firing on itself.

Now the Rough Riders became soldiers, advancing upon the enemy with a boldness that "by any soldierly standard, was magnificent," wrote Stephen. Their sheer audacity — moving across open ground under heavy fire, falling as they went — soon scared the Spanish into a retreat. Sixteen American soldiers were killed, eight of them Rough Riders. Thirty-four men were wounded. In two hours, which seemed like a half-hour to Stephen, the skirmish was over. Davis came upon Stephen "smoking a pipe" and appearing "badly rattled as he thought we were surrounded." The rumors began. "Everybody was wounded. Everybody was dead." A soldier told Stephen, "There's a correspondent up there shot all to hell." And he led him to Ed Marshall, hit close to the spine.

When the firing was over, Marshall regained consciousness to find Stephen and Davis standing over him. Stephen greeted him.

"Hello, Marshall! In hard luck old man?"

"Yes, I'm done for."

"Nonsense! You're all right, old boy. What can I do for you?" Marshall asked Stephen to file his dispatches — after he filed his own — and to find some of his *Journal* colleagues to assist him. Deciding that Marshall was "doomed," Stephen found some soldiers to carry him to the surgeon. The regiment had no stretchers, so the wounded man had to be carried on a tentcloth. Stephen was unable to get a horse or a mule for the trip back to Siboney, so he walked the three miles of rough jungle trail in the suffocating heat. At Siboney he cabled Marshall's dispatch, somehow located a stretcher, and arranged for some men to carry Marshall back to the coast on it. He eventually found Acton Davies and George Coffin on one of the *Journal*'s dispatch boats and filled them in on Marshall. Stephen "was probably as tired then as a man could be and still walk," said Marshall. "But he trudged back from the coast to the field hospital where I was lying, and saw to it that I was properly conveyed to the coast." Marshall survived, but he lost a leg and was paralyzed from the waist down.

Later Stephen reported the ambush of Lieutenant Colonel Roosevelt's Rough Riders in a matter-of-fact dispatch, saying that the attack occurred when the First Volunteer Cavalry struck Spanish lines while they were "noisily" talking. The Rough Riders' heavy losses were "due to the remarkably wrong idea of how the Spaniards bushwhack." He credited the cavalry for their "superb" bearing, which "could not be finer" in the face of an unseen enemy. In the end, wrote Stephen, "it was simply a gallant blunder" that caused the losses at Las Guásimas.

Stephen's dispatches did not help his cause with Roosevelt, who seemed to have Stephen in mind when he complained, long afterward, that "the first reports sent back to the coast were of a most alarming character, describing, with minute inaccuracy, how we had run into an ambush." Furthermore, now that he himself had experienced war firsthand, Roosevelt could say, "I did not see any sign among the fighting men, whether wounded or unwounded, of the very complicated emotions assigned to their kind by some of the realistic modern novelists who have written about battles" — though he was willing to concede that "there was doubtless . . . a good deal of panic and confusion in the rear where the wounded, the stragglers, a few of the packers, and two or three newspaper correspondents were." Richard Harding Davis, loyal to Roosevelt, maintained that the Rough Riders had simply "[blundered] into an ambuscade." But historians and eyewitnesses like Edward Marshall concurred with Crane, down to the detail of the Spanish wood-dove call, which heralded the firing.

Whatever Stephen's feelings about Roosevelt, he admired the Rough Riders, and he ungrudgingly gave them their due in print. But he was most concerned with reporting honestly, and, as always, his strongest sympathies lay with the unheralded soldier — on this occasion, General S. B. M. Young's brigade, the First Regular Cavalry. While all five correspondents present at Las Guásimas had tailed the brown-clad Rough Riders like schoolboys following a pretty girl, the Regulars, in blue, fought without an audience. Stephen wrote that it was not until after the skirmish ended that the press even knew the Regulars were engaged on the right flank. They all took the Regulars for granted, he explained, knowing that they would fight gallantly, knowing that they never failed. "Our confidence in them has come to be a habit. But, good heavens! it must be about time to change all that and heed them somewhat. Even if we have to make some of the volunteers wait a little."

Military conditions had been hard in Cuba, Stephen had reported. Even before the action began, the navy had run out of eggs, onions, and ice, and things were worse after the Las Guásimas battle. Fresh supplies were not getting to the men, and even the elite Rough Riders were out of sugar, meat, and tobacco. A good breakfast might consist of hardtack and tomatoes cooked in bacon grease. Hardtack — the saltless, often wormy biscuit and the soldier's staple — did not go down well in the tropical Cuban climate. Like the hungry insurgents, the Rough Riders had taken to frying mangoes. Some of the soldiers learned from the Cubans how to roll dried leaves, roots, and manure for a smoke. The correspondents were even worse off, having run out of food immediately upon landing in Cuba. Though they carried credentials from the secretary of war instructing "all commanding officers to furnish forage and rations" at the "cost price," said Edward Marshall, they had to beg the soldiers for food. Marshall later said that he "ate only one meal while I was in Cuba." For nearly a week after arriving the hungry men were forced to sit around in sweltering 100-degree heat, waiting for the next battle. They waited in a blood-soaked place with red-spattered leaves and rotting corpses picked at by vultures, land crabs, and, most offensive of all, scavenging Cubans, who helped themselves to the dead soldiers' equipment, clothing, and supplies, infuriating the American soldiers. Many men became ill.

About a week after the Las Guásimas skirmish, Stephen gave photographer Jimmy Hare a tour of the battlefield. Hare had come to the war late, and he particularly wanted to know the famous author of *The Red Badge of Courage*. He'd heard that Scovel "usually found it very difficult to get Crane's copy," and now he could see why. Using one cigarette to light the next, Stephen told Hare that he had signed with the *World* for the military pass so he could gather material for a war novel. Hare thought Stephen "a charming fellow, fond of a drink and not too fond of work" — though he could be infuriating.

That evening they met again in the correspondents' camp. Suddenly Scovel rushed in "with news so important that even Crane looked up to listen," said Hare. There was to be a battle the next morning. In a twin objective, General Lawton would attack the village of El Caney and capture the fort there, while the other divisions, including the Rough Riders, assaulted San Juan Hill, four miles to the south. From San Juan Hill Santiago was clearly visible. After Lawton captured the fort at El Caney, severing Santiago's northern supply route, he would join forces with the rest of the command and move toward the San Juan Heights. The Fifth Corps was to begin moving into position that night. Scovel assigned Stephen to Lawton's advance, which is where the real action was to be — at least until after the fall of El Caney. Since Hare was on his own, Stephen agreed to partner with him as far as El Pozo, a hill four miles south of El Caney, which offered a good vantage point for both battles. Lawton's men would pass through El Pozo, then head north and camp about a mile farther up the trail; the other troops would position themselves around the hill. Hare wanted to get going right away so as to be ready with his camera when the action started. But Stephen, seemingly nervous, "fingered his whiskey glass," said Hare, and claimed that there was no reason to start for the battle now; four in the morning was soon enough. They should rest in the interim. "It'll be the soldiers who do the fighting. All we have to do is report afterward what they did."

The others agreed with Stephen and headed for their hammocks. But Stephen, unable to sleep, poured another drink. He'd "sit up awhile with a sick friend," he said.

He was sleeping like the dead when Jimmy Hare tried to rouse him in the dark — no amount of shaking or profanity stirred him beyond mumbled excuses. Finally Hare set off for El Pozo alone, raging against Stephen. He would "cover the blarsted war alone!" he said. He had just left the correspondents' shack when Stephen appeared at his side, apologizing profusely. He offered to show Jimmy the Las Guásimas battlefield — forgetting that they'd seen it together not twenty-four hours earlier. They tramped along the dark, muddy ground for some time without talking, then Hare finally relented. "Nobody could stay angry with Stephen Crane for very long," he said later.

At El Pozo they parted company, and Stephen headed north, where Lawton's force was bivouacked.

He moved like an observation balloon through the events of the following day, July 1. He was there from the time the first gun was fired on the pink, cloudless morning, which turned suffocatingly hot. "They're off!" he heard someone say. He watched the long "artillery duel" between Captain George S. Grimes's battery and the Spanish, which began an hour after Lawton's attack on El Caney. The Spanish battery had the advantage of smokeless powder, but Grimes's men hurled their shrapnel directly into the Spanish trenches, opening the way to Kettle Hill and San Juan Hill. With Burr McIntosh, Henry J. Whigham of the *Chicago Tribune*, and the artist and illustrator Frederic Remington, Stephen watched the disastrous flight of Colonel Joseph E. Maxwell's Signal Corps balloon over the Camino Real. "Huge, fat, yellow, quivering," it invited a hail of sniper fire and tipped off the location of the Americans' advance column. "Suddenly the conflict became a human thing," wrote Stephen. He became preoccupied with finding his toothbrush. The sight of thousands of Regulars marching past with their toothbrushes stuck in their hatbands put him to shame, he said.

Nothing much was supposed to happen at San Juan Hill until Lawton got there. But the planned easy conquest of El Caney turned into an

all-day battle with the heavily fortified village. Stephen and the other correspondents were watching the action when the unexpected happened
right under their noses. Tired of waiting for orders and impatient with
Lawton's long delay, the other divisions, led by the newly promoted
Colonel Theodore Roosevelt and the Rough Riders, bypassed the Regulars to take Kettle Hill. Roosevelt's order was to support the Regulars in
an assault on the hills, but he thundered up on his little horse, Texas, waving his hat and challenging stricken soldiers to follow him, his blue kerchief flapping like a flag in a hailstorm of Mauser bullets. Then the
Rough Riders assisted the Regulars, members of the First and Tenth
Cavalry, and other regiments in their attack on nearby San Juan Hill,
driving the Spanish from their fortifications. "It was impatience suddenly
exalted to one of the sublime passions," wrote Stephen in a long dispatch.
"It will never be forgotten as long as America has a military history."

All Stephen had been able to see from El Pozo was "a thin line of
black figures moving across a field." The "gentle green hills of San Juan"
reminded him of home, "the sloping orchards of Orange County." Suddenly the Rough Riders "disappeared in the forest. Then somebody
yelled: 'By God, there go our boys up the hill!'" He continued:

> There is many a good American who would give an arm to
> get the thrill of patriotic insanity that coursed through us
> when we heard that yell.
>
> Yes, they were going up the hill, up the hill. It was the best
> moment of anybody's life. An officer said to me afterward:
> "If we had been in that position and the Spaniards had
> come at us, we would have piled them up so high the last
> man couldn't have climbed over." But up went the regiments
> with no music save that ceaseless, fierce crashing of rifles.
>
> The foreign attachés were shocked. "It is very gallant, but
> very foolish," said one sternly.
>
> "Why, they can't take it, you know. Never in the world,"
> cried another, much agitated. "It is slaughter, absolute
> slaughter."
>
> The little Japanese shrugged his shoulders. He was one
> who said nothing.

Then came the grim aftermath, the long, sad procession of the
wounded, which Stephen saw all too vividly. Some soldiers held on to a

friend or used a rifle for a crutch. Others walked unaided. Some stopped, "to answer the universal hail 'How is it going?' . . . Their slit trousers exposed red bandages. A few were shot horribly in the face and were led, bleeding and blind, by their mates." Stephen saw "horribly mangled" Cubans being carried to the rear of the battery. And all the while the shooting from the Spanish lines continued. Green-garbed guerrillas hid in the trees and fired on anyone in their range — even the wounded, even an ambulance driver. Stephen marveled at "that profound patience" of the wounded men.

After Roosevelt's charge Stephen set off with McIntosh and Whigham in the direction of the firing. The battle was going full force, and when they reached the bottom of San Juan Hill they found Scovel hastily writing his dispatch under a tree while a man with a horse waited. Scovel warned them not to go up there — sharpshooters were picking off everyone who passed. They saw a man whose left jaw had been blown away, witnessed a man being shot down, saw another right after he was hit through the knee. Heard his terrible scream, saw the blood gushing. The scream was unusual, noted Stephen; soldiers typically "went over like men of wet felt, quietly, calmly." The firing got so close to the correspondents that McIntosh finally persuaded them to head back to El Pozo. It seemed that McIntosh had yellow fever. Within minutes after leaving him near El Pozo, Stephen and Whigham returned to the firing.

Jimmy Hare came across Stephen riding a "pinto pony and wearing, of all incredible garments, a gleaming white raincoat." He headed up toward the crest of San Juan Hill like "a shining target." Though it was about 100 degrees and the battle was still going, Stephen seemed as "cool and unconcerned as if he had been at a garden party," said Hare. "Only the horse was showing any trace of nervousness." Stephen invited Hare to come with him. Though the photographer had just come from San Juan Hill, he went along anyway, walking behind the pinto when Stephen would not dismount. "If they aim at me, so much the better," Stephen said. "No Spaniard ever hits the thing he aims at." When Hare positioned himself behind the pony, Stephen said he was sorry the pony wasn't larger. He was in high spirits. The Spanish fire was "uproarious, and the air simply whistled," he wrote. Noting Hare's white-faced nervousness, Stephen later confessed that he was "delighted" by the quivering figure at his shoulder.

Hare said, "Say, this is pretty hot, ain't it?"

"Yes Jimmie, you can take it from me that this is patent, double extra what-for," said the war veteran solemnly.

Stephen selected a trail away from the slippery grass so that his horse would have an easier climb. Suddenly they found themselves at the place later dubbed the Bloody Ford. This was San Juan Creek, at the bottom of San Juan Hill, where the Rough Riders had been deployed and the signal balloon had been shot down.

Already muddy from rain, the creek had turned red from the blood of injured and dying men. Under a spray of bullets, the regimental surgeon of the Third Cavalry, George J. Newgarden, was doing what he could for the wounded men. In this gruesome dressing station, framed by mosquito bogs, the men lay on top of each other. At first Stephen and Hare were too shocked to move. They saw before them "a hundred broken men, the human wreckage brought from a few square yards of the battlefield. . . . Many a doctor fell across the body of the man he was helping," as Hare's biographer wrote.

Stephen got off the pinto and started talking to the wounded men. Then one of them caught his eye. Lying in the red mud in the midst of this "miserable huddle" was Reuben McNab, a tall, freckled boy Stephen had known at Claverack. He was now a corporal with the Seventy-first New York Volunteers, "with a hole through his lung. Also several holes through his clothing." And the sight of this boy, "identified intimately in my thought with the sunny irresponsible days at Claverack, when all the earth was a green field and all the sky was a rainless blue" —

> the apparition of Reuben McNab, the schoolmate lying there in the mud with a hole through his lung, awed me into stutterings, set me trembling with a sense of terrible intimacy with this war which heretofore I could have believed was a dream — almost. Twenty shot men rolled their eyes and looked at me. Only one man paid no heed. He was dying, he had no time. The bullets hummed low over them all. Death, having already struck, still insisted upon raising a venomous crest. "If you're goin' by the hospital, step in and see me," said Reuben McNab. That was all.

Stephen gave the pinto to his old schoolmate for the trip back to Siboney.

Later that bloody day, under heavy firing, Stephen appeared on the ridges overlooking Santiago, still wearing the long white rubber raincoat. The Americans' hold on the ground was precarious. They were tired, and the Spanish were still heavily entrenched. At about three that afternoon, Leonard Wood, now a brigadier general, was directing the Rough Riders as they helped hold the line under intense fire. Suddenly, said Richard Harding Davis, Stephen strolled "to the crest and stood there as sharply outlined as a semaphore, observing the enemy's lines, and instantly bringing upon himself and us the fire of many Mausers." He smoked a pipe as he watched the action, as calm as though he were watching a matinee performance at a New York theater, said Davis. Everyone else was in the trenches. Wood, who was himself called "the Ice-Box" for his coolness in battle, ordered Stephen to get down. "You're drawing the fire on these men," he said. Stephen seemed not to hear him — or was determined not to hear. He moved away. Davis understood Stephen well enough to know that he hated "anything that savored of a pose" and, not wanting "to see him killed," he called out to him, "You're not impressing anyone by doing that, Crane."

This "instantly" brought Stephen to the ground, and he "crawled over to where we lay."

"I knew that would fetch you," Davis told him.

Stephen grinned. "Oh, was that it?"

But he had been only temporarily shamed. Like a man under a spell, he stood up again to get a closer look at the smoke and flames. Davis jumped up and forced him to the ground. In that instant a bullet tore Davis's hat off, and another nicked "the leather case of his field glasses."

News of Stephen's exploits got around. Depending upon the observer, Stephen Crane was either the bravest man one had ever seen under fire or the most reckless.

Other men had acted recklessly in war. Before his great ride up Kettle Hill, Theodore Roosevelt had remained on his horse under a massed assault that had other Rough Riders crawling on the ground. Rough Rider Captain "Bucky" O'Neill had walked back and forth smoking a cigarette while under the same "killing hailstorm" of Mauser fire, claiming that there wasn't a Spanish bullet that could kill him. Roosevelt, who was seen as setting a courageous example for his men, soon got off his horse. But O'Neill kept walking and was promptly shot through the mouth and killed.

Civil War literature offered tales of men who bravely exposed themselves to fire by standing tall. Hadn't General "Stonewall" Jackson earned his nickname by standing as upright at Manassas as a stone wall? Stephen might have remembered an incident in *Sebastopol* in which Tolstoy describes his officer as sitting on a cannon "rolling a cigarette with such coolness" and talking "with such natural calmness, that you recover your own *sang-froid*, in spite of the balls which are whistling here in greater numbers."

Perhaps borrowing from such real-life models in order not to show fear, Stephen maintained a state of calm exaltation under fire to recover his own sang-froid. He felt fear all right. Yes, sir, he knew what it was to have his heart in his mouth. To feel like "a mere corpse. My limbs were of dough and my spinal cord burned within me as if it were a red-hot wire," he would write. But his fear of showing fear outweighed his fear of injury or death. Stephen Crane was a product of his time; duty and honor were inseparable from his notion of masculinity. He was no skulker. He might have reasoned that if he died while standing upright in a war, he would at least die with honor.

But following the battle for San Juan Hill, a new element crept into his risk-taking; he seemed to be challenging the bullets to hit him. Bragdon Smith of the *New York Journal* saw Stephen standing under a tree whose leaves had been sheared by bullets, "calmly rolling a cigarette" in the midst of Mauser fire that struck down several men standing nearby. Unperturbed, Stephen "finished rolling his cigarette and smoked it without moving away from the spot where the bullets had suddenly become so thick," said Smith.

A week later, on July 8, suffering from a high fever and wearing the clothes he had worn for the last three weeks, Stephen was put on a transport ship, the *City of Washington*, at Siboney and sent to the United States for medical treatment. He had become aware of the fever on July 6. From San Juan Hill on a sunny afternoon, he was observing an exchange of prisoners. There had been a long wait, and he had begun to feel "a langorous indifference to everything in the world," he wrote. Then he became confused about where he was and what was happening: "I didn't know whether London Bridge was falling down or whether there was a war with Spain." He had an unreasonable craving for pickles. But perhaps he had actually become sick days earlier. The picture of him fingering a whiskey glass with trembling hands on the eve of the San Juan Hill triumph and appearing the next day in a long rubber raincoat under a tropical sun — seeming cool and acting in outrageous ways — suggests that he had.

Once on board the transport, Stephen was told by a regular army doctor that he had yellow fever. Ordered to isolate himself from the other sick and wounded men on board, he spent the next five days lying limply on a little rug on deck, his head resting against the flagstaff.

During his last days in Cuba he'd slept out in the open with Scovel, McIntosh, and Davis. Davis had had an attack of sciatica. After the firing on San Juan Hill subsided, Stephen and Jimmy Hare took Davis back to camp at Sevilla. Afterward Stephen slept "on a pile of saddles and provender, with a blanket over him," then on the hard floor of a covered ruin. Now, as he lay on the deck of the *City of Washington* surrounded by men who were far worse off— "poor bandaged chaps looking sadly down at the waves" — he carried pictures in his mind of those last days in Cuba. The barricaded red-tile-roofed houses of San Juan. Dog-tents shining white on the slope of San Juan Hill. The church in the plaza at El Caney, which had been turned into a makeshift hospital for the captured Spanish wounded. "Framed . . . in the black archway was the altar-table with the figure of a man upon it. He was naked save for a breech-cloth, and so close, so clear was the ecclesiastic suggestion, that one's mind leaped to a fantasy that this thin pale figure had just been torn down from a cross." Stephen could still hear the "chattering refugees" streaming out of Santiago to El Caney. And he could see the faces of Lawton's men as they moved into position on San Juan Hill on July 2. "There wasn't a high heroic face among them. They were all men intent on business." The expression on those faces was beyond words. It was something sacred.

> One cannot speak of it — the spectacle of the common man serenely doing his work, his appointed work. It is the one thing in the universe which makes one fling expression to the winds and be satisfied to simply feel. Thus they moved at San Juan — the soldiers of the United States Regular Army. One pays them the tribute of the toast of silence.

At ten o'clock in the morning on July 13, the *City of Washington* pulled into Hampton Roads opposite Old Point Comfort, Virginia. It bore a cargo of some two hundred wounded men, most of them from the Seventy-first New York Infantry. The ship flew a yellow flag — "the grim ensign of the plague," said Stephen. A launch carrying an anxious-looking woman approached and circled. Watching it, Stephen was reminded of "the fourth element of war": the loved ones left behind, the wives and families. He became absorbed by the sight of the watchful face of the little woman on the launch as she scanned the faces of the wounded for her husband; "my heart sank with the fear that she was not going to find him." Then one of the men of the Twenty-fourth Infantry recognized the woman as the wife of his colonel. The colonel called out, "Alice!" and the woman saw him and buried her face in her hands. In that moment, Stephen and the other men on the transport saw "the other part" of war. "And in a vision we all saw our own harbor-lights," he wrote. "That is to say those of us who had harbor-lights."

Afterward he settled onto the verandah of the Chamberlain Hotel at Old Point Comfort to watch the procession of his wounded shipmates. Many of them couldn't walk and so were carried on stretchers to the Fort Monroe Hospital. Having been correctly diagnosed with malaria, Stephen had sufficiently recovered to be able to stay at the hotel. He had even managed to write his long dispatch of the San Juan battle. From his place on the verandah, wearing the filthy rags he'd worn for some four weeks, he was surrounded by girls in their summer dresses, "like a bank of flowers." As he watched his wounded shipmates pass, he felt as though he were seeing them for the first time. "I had never known that they looked like that," he would write in "War Memories." "Such a gang of dirty, ragged, emaciated, half-starved, bandaged cripples I had never seen." The bank of flowers wept. The wounded soldiers "hung their heads like so many jail-birds."

He spent the next weeks resting, regaling sympathetic women with the tale of his wretched voyage from Cuba, and enjoying the attention. He had endured devastating chills and shaking, a hot stage lasting perhaps eight hours, then a wet stage, or fever. Finally he had begun sweating; he felt drained. Now he felt better. When someone at the hotel approached him with a copy of *Pictures of War*, a new collection of some of his previously published Civil War tales, he inscribed it with his old sense of humor:

> Know you that when you
> possess this book, you
> are free of others' envy.
> Stephen Crane

•

He traded his war rags for a new suit costing a modest twenty-four dollars, which the *New York World* refused to pay for. For reasons that remain unclear, the *World* was unhappy with its star correspondent. Though Stephen had filed more than twenty dispatches in the three months he'd been covering the war, Don C. Seitz, the *World*'s business manager, whose memories were distorted by personal dislike of Stephen, would later claim that the *World* received nothing from him until July 1, when they got a "dull" dispatch based on his "leisurely stroll with a scouting party of Marines, which resulted in the death of two recruits and of Dr. Gibbs, the army surgeon." Seitz thought that the *World* had not gotten its money's worth out of Crane.

To a certain extent, Stephen had brought this situation on himself. Lawless and dirty, he looked like a degenerate and did not answer to any authority; the other correspondents never saw him take notes. Even Henry N. Cary, who managed the *World*'s field staff in Cuba, would describe Stephen as "a drunken, irresponsible and amusing little cuss" who kept him "busy trying to get a little work out of him."

The real trouble seems to have been an unsigned dispatch the *World* received in the middle of July, when Stephen was recovering from malaria in Virginia. Datelined Port Antonio (Jamaica), July 15, the dispatch implied that the officers of the Seventy-first New York Volunteer Regiment had acted with cowardice in the aftermath of the San Juan Hill charge. The *World* published the piece on the front page of its July 16 issue and immediately suffered the fallout. Though it was actually written by Sylvester Scovel and was accurate, Seitz claimed that Stephen Crane was the author. In an editorial, the *New York Journal* blasted its rival for the unpatriotic accusation against the Seventy-first Regiment. At first the *World* stuck by its story. But public opinion was against the paper, and Joseph Pulitzer quickly tried to redeem the *World*'s reputation with a proposal to raise money for a monument to the fallen heroes of the Seventy-first. The *World* ran articles in support of the regiment's eagerness to fight. But Hearst only increased his attack, and the duel in ink continued.

In the midst of this uproar, Stephen's deeply felt piece in support of the unheralded regular soldier, "Regulars Get No Glory," appeared in the *World* as well as in the *Philadelphia Press* and the *Boston Globe*. Then Stephen himself turned up at the *World*'s New York office and was promptly fired.

According to Seitz, Stephen had asked the paper's financial manager, John Norris, for another advance. As Norris "gleefully" told Seitz, he responded with "Don't you think you have had enough of Mr. Pulitzer's money without earning it?"

"Oh, very well, if that is the way you look at it, by-by," said Stephen.

He signed with Hearst's *New York Journal.* He would return to Cuba in August and report the Puerto Rican campaign. But first he had to take care of his health. That same week he traveled to Saranac Lake in the Adirondacks to see the prominent tuberculosis specialist Dr. Edward Livingston Trudeau.

14

THE ASHES

OF LOVE

D ear Madam," Dr. Trudeau would write Cora from the sanatorium at Saranac on September 16,

> Your husband had a slight evidence of activity in the trouble
> in his lungs when he came back here this summer but it was
> not serious and he had improved steadily I understand since
> he came. I have only examined him once but he looked
> very well and told me he was much better than last time I
> saw him.

It was the dreaded nineteenth-century disease, and it was nearly always a death sentence. The word itself — consumption — was enough to strike terror into the hearts of its victims. Over the course of the nineteenth century, tuberculosis would claim the lives of some seven million people worldwide; fifty million were openly sick. Two of Stephen's stomping grounds — New York and London — were "the worst affected cities," writes a historian. There was no medicine to treat it, no remedy except rest, a change of climate, and a healthy diet, sometimes at a sanatorium. And it was a chronic illness. Even those who recovered and resumed their lives were "never fully cured," writes an expert. "In the tiny calcified scars that show up on the chest x-rays, like little tombstones, the relentless germ lives on."

Stephen Crane suffered from pulmonary tuberculosis, the most common form of the disease, which typically appears in childhood. While Dr. Trudeau's letter told little about the course of Stephen's treatment, it revealed much about the length of his illness. The word "activity" suggests that an x-ray showed scarring from an earlier bout with the disease, notes an expert. "If it was a question of recent disease, he would describe it differently, eg evidence of active tb or evidence of primary disease etc."

If examined closely, the record suggests that Stephen in fact had had tuberculosis since childhood and that he knew it, had always known it. The sickly child who was a worry to his parents and frequently absent from school was, from the beginning, extremely thin, his build of the type called "phthisoid" in the medical literature — a characteristic of tuberculosis. From earliest childhood Stephen's health had improved when he was removed to the country, where he could breathe fresher air. The restorative horseback rides, his attraction to the West — where he went for his health, he told Willa Cather and Lily Munroe — further suggest that Stephen had long been conversant with the recommendations that consumptives benefited both from riding and from living in the West.

Though he is not known to have contracted the disease from anyone in his parents' household, the most likely means of transmission is repeated exposure to someone with the disease living under the same roof. The minute, airborne bacterium is inhaled when an infected person coughs or even exhales, though it can also be contracted from infected cow's milk and from chicken. The great majority of people who come into contact with the bacterium do not become sick; the healthy body resists it. But when a person with a weak immune system encounters it — usually by living with an infected person over a long period of time — the bacillus gets into the lungs and grows until it becomes "a cheesy boil."

The letters and diaries of Jonathan and Mary Helen Crane offer certain details about family illnesses that sound like tuberculosis. Jonathan's sister Agnes died in the Crane home in 1867 after "bleeding at the lungs." And though this occurred four years before Stephen's birth, some of the Crane children later showed symptoms characteristic of the disease. George looked "emaciated" and suffered from a bad cough. Nellie left home at seventeen or eighteen to recover from an unnamed illness that caused Helen to worry that her daughter's life would be marked by "disease and suffering." Most provocatively, in December of 1874, when Stephen was three, Jonathan wrote his father-in-law, "Will . . . seems well & has had [no] more bleeding at the lungs, or signs of it, no cough, or irritation of the throat or lungs." William is known to have been ill at least since the previous summer. Even when he returned to college sometime during the winter of 1874–75, his health was dubious.

It would be a matter of time before Stephen's disease spread into his body's airways to form new boils or tuberlike clusters, from which the name "tuberculosis" derives. The nineteenth-century term "consumption" best captures the progression of the disease, which consumes the organs in its path. Eventually the bacteria shut down the lungs, making it hard to breathe. In the acute stage, the blood vessels are attacked, causing the victim to cough up blood. Death from tuberculosis is suffocation; the victim drowns in his own blood.

As Stephen told Willa Cather in 1895, he couldn't wait ten years for his success; "I haven't time." He was convinced he would die young, he told Lily B. earlier. If he had had chronic tuberculosis since childhood, or had healed tuberculosis then and realized it, he certainly knew that the disease would eventually get him. He was concerned enough to consult Dr. Trudeau — again — during the summer of 1898.

Given Stephen's personality, his feverish approach to his work, and his penchant for risk-taking, one wonders whether he lived and worked on the ragged edge because he knew he hadn't much time. His health improved from time to time, yet he was "still wedded to an enemy," as another consumptive said of himself. He was powerless to stop his fate, so why not experience life as fully as possible? Why not stand even closer to the precipice in order to better feel the things he was writing about? Better death by a bullet than by a bacterium.

Dr. Trudeau was America's preeminent expert on tuberculosis and the founder of the country's first sanatorium for the disease, the Cottage Sanatorium at Saranac Lake. He himself had battled pulmonary tuberculosis since he was a young man and had lost his daughter to the disease five years earlier. Though in his letter to Cora he described Stephen as looking "very well," one wonders whether Stephen had asked the doctor to sound optimistic. The *Journal* reporter Charles Michelson saw Stephen only days later and found him "shambling, with hair too long, usually lacking a shave, dressed like any of the deck hands, hollow-cheeked, sallow, destitute of small talk, critical if not fastidious, marked with ill health — the very antithesis of the conquering male." Seeing him stripped for a seawater shower aboard a tug bound for Puerto Rico, Michelson noted that Stephen's twenty-six-year-old body was already "the wreck of an athlete's frame — once square shoulders crowded forward by the concavity of a collapsed chest; great hollows where the once smooth pitching muscles had wasted; legs like pipestems — he looked like a frayed white ribbon, seen through the veil of green as the seas washed over him."

The siege of Santiago had brought a more feared destroyer than bullets: malaria and dysentery, with cases of yellow fever suspected as well. As many as five thousand men were ill at one time. Sickness had seriously thinned the lines of blue and brown on San Juan Heights.

After that battle the Spanish surrendered, and Cuba was liberated from the yoke of Spanish imperialism. Then came "the deadly monotony of waiting," wrote one soldier. With the truce remaining to be worked out and Cuba not yet returned to the Cubans, the Americans devised a campaign to conquer other Spanish territories, including Puerto Rico. They took Ponce, Puerto Rico's second largest city, without significant resistance.

Sent to cover the Puerto Rican campaign for Hearst, in late July Stephen sailed against a strong headwind from Pensacola Naval Base to Puerto Rico on a *Journal*-chartered tug with Michelson and some others. The passage was rough, and many of the men were seasick, but Stephen Crane, this frayed ribbon of a man, seemed to have an iron constitution. He told Michelson that he'd never been seasick, not even in the dinghy. Then he told him the open-boat story — "phrase for phrase, for entire paragraphs" as it was written, Michelson later discovered — while the tug moved through the Gulf Stream.

Apparently feeling better for the enforced rest away from the war zone and in company with people he felt at ease with, Stephen proved a rare companion during the three-day journey. Talkative and slangy and full of the devil, but cool as the North Atlantic if need be, he was "as merry and considerate a shipmate as anybody could ask" for, said Michelson. He told his mates about the great manor house he had taken in England, Brede Place. The others took to calling it Mango Chutney and imagined Stephen as "a liverish British squire, with an East Indian background," said Michelson.

Stephen greeted potential trouble with an unruffled attitude and considerable wit. The day an American cruiser approached the tug in the blockade zone, where she didn't belong, and "swept" off again at their "cheery" greeting, he quipped: "Like a fat dowager duchess who has been asked by a scrubwoman where she bought her hat." He called another would-be adventure an "onion," a term he had invented early in the war when an unfamiliar craft approached his ship in the blockade zone, only to call out, "Can you let us have some onions?" Thereafter, adventures that missed fire were "onions." While his mates were seasick, Stephen "drew attention to the convulsive jerk of their shoulders as they bent miserably over the low rail, mentioning that men died with just such a spasm," wrote Michelson. "It was not lack of sympathy, or callousness. . . . It was simply that motion-picture mind of his registering impressions. It was an instinct, stronger than pity, or love, or fear." Roused to adventure when they reached the coast of Puerto Rico, he was found "baiting the captain to run in close" to a Spanish destroyer inshore. When the captain was asked why he had responded to Crane's baiting, he said, "You don't think I'm going to let this damned frayed tholepin think he's got more guts than me, do you?" And Stephen became Lord Tholepin of Mango Chutney. The ribbing amused him even more than it did his mates, said Michelson.

"Viva!" The sound of Mauser bullets that had characterized the war in Cuba was now replaced with a cheer. Seeing the Americans as benefactors rather than invaders, the Puertorriqueños were overwhelmingly eager to surrender. They even held a parade in honor of General Nelson Miles, commander of the United States armed forces and the army's highest ranking officer.

Upon arrival in mosquito-infested Ponce on August 1, Stephen promptly disappeared. Michelson and the others knew where to find him — "in a back-street cantena, with the wastrels of Ponce — drunkards, drabs, and tin-horn gamblers. They did not know a word of his language nor he a word of theirs," wrote Michelson. Neither did it matter that Stephen was an invader and the locals were the conquered. "He was accepted into the easy brotherhood of the thriftless without question." With the local riffraff, Stephen was in his element. But to the military brass at Ponce "he seemed a social bankrupt," said Michelson. "Possibly the explanation is that he wanted to hear about the reactions of these men under their adventures, while they wanted to hear a literary lion roar, and, the ground being respectively distasteful, their minds never met."

Stephen created his own adventures. He slipped into Juana Díaz, some nine miles from Ponce, ahead of the advance posts, and handled the town's surrender himself. Richard Harding Davis and Charles Michelson would tell two different versions of the story. In Davis's, Stephen rode into town ahead of the other correspondents who had passed the advance posts. Wearing a slouch hat and a khaki suit with leggings and smoking a cigarette, he accepted the keys of the cartel, then divided the town's men into two groups: "good fellows" and "suspects" — an entirely arbitrary process.

"Anyone whose appearance Crane did not approve of, anyone whose necktie did not suit his fancy, was listed as a 'suspect,'" said Davis. Stephen permitted the "good fellows" to serve as his bodyguards and hosts; the "suspects" were "ordered to their homes." The surrender of Juana Díaz was followed by a celebratory night in the plaza. At dawn the next morning, Stephen was sitting over his coffee in front of the town's only café, surrounded by bodyguards, when the American regiment of eight hundred finally arrived. The colonel was fully sensible of the great honor of having the author of *The Red Badge of Courage* there to write about his conquest of the town. Greeting Stephen happily from his horse, the colonel said he was glad to see him. Had Stephen been marching with the colonel's men?

Stephen shook his head.

"'I am sorry,' said the Colonel. 'I should like you to have seen us take this town.'"

"'This town!' said Stephen in polite embarrassment. 'I am really very sorry, Colonel, but I took this town myself before breakfast yesterday morning.'"

In Michelson's version of the story, Stephen rode into Juana Díaz ahead of the advance line to get breakfast for himself and the other correspondents before the military arrived. Pretending to have been sent ahead to order breakfast for "the American governor of Puerto Rico," he then introduced Mumford, a correspondent "in immaculate whites" who looked the part. When the brigadier general and his staff appeared, Stephen lied about what had happened, saying that the locals had heard the correspondents call Mumford "governor," apparently because he looked like a governor, and had served them breakfast.

On August 12, President McKinley signed a peace protocol proclaiming an armistice. When it was time for the correspondents to sail home, they re-sold their horses to the horse dealer and gathered at the *embarcadero* four miles below Ponce. Everyone was there except Stephen. As Michelson would tell it, he set off to look for Crane. About halfway to Ponce he encountered the horse dealer and noticed that the string was complete except for Stephen's horse, "a hammer-headed, spur-scarred, hairy-hoofed white beast hardly bigger than a goat," said Michelson, "with all the bad habits that could be grafted on original sin by ignorance and bad treatment." A kicker and a biter, the horse had had to be hobbled apart from the other horses. Stephen called him "El Dog," and they "got along like sweethearts," said Michelson. He asked the dealer where the animal was. The man shrugged his shoulders and indicated a nearby thicket. There Michelson found Stephen saying goodbye to the pony. One of his arms was draped over the horse's neck, and his cheeks were tear-stained. El Dog turned an unfriendly white eye to the intruder. Afterward, as the two correspondents walked back to the *embarcadero*, where the steamer was waiting, Stephen offered no explanations.

The war was not over for Stephen; something was left unfinished. The war in his mind he had not yet put on paper, for his dispatches had caught very little of this. In Key West, he dutifully cabled Cora, telling her of his whereabouts. But instead of continuing on to England, in the third week of August he returned to Cuba, slipping into Spanish-occupied Havana like a spy, without a passport and "without permission from anybody," he later admitted. It was a risky act. The Spanish evacuation of Havana was to take place gradually. American troops would not move in until fall, taking charge on January 1, 1899. In the meantime there were American peace officers in the city and some two hundred Spanish troops in and around Havana. Though the tension was primarily between the Spanish soldiers and the Cuban revolutionaries who entered the city against orders, the attitude toward Americans was constantly changing, Stephen said later. As he checked into Havana's Grand Hotel Pasaje, nine other correspondents were imprisoned on a harbor steamer.

Thus began a period of self-imposed exile. It started openly enough, with Stephen living at a very public hotel among other correspondents. He wrote a few unengaging dispatches. The others didn't see him at the Spanish censor's office. He spent part of his days drinking beer at the American Bar next door to his hotel. The correspondents gathered there from ten in the morning until ten at night — "or until a riot broke out," said Walter Parker, a correspondent for the *New Orleans Times-Democrat*. "Crane was usually the last to show up in the morning." He was unhurried and extremely reserved, a calm, companionable, listening presence who "rarely discussed himself," said Parker. But he listened keenly to the talk of any man who had had extraordinary experiences. He was often broke, and men would "pass a gold centen to him to enable him to pay his American bar bill." Stephen repaid them with "his Cuban revolutionary affiliations," wrote Parker — principally a well-connected, hot-tempered Cuban he had saved from drowning during the *Commodore* sinking. The Cuban greeted Stephen as though he were royalty, dropping to his knees to kiss Stephen's hand or the hem of his coat. Through this Cuban, Stephen and the other correspondents were able to slip by the Spanish authorities on their nocturnal adventures into forbidden territory. They crawled through tunnels, sneaked into Canaña fortress, where some four thousand Spanish soldiers who had mutinied were being held prisoner; inspected the city's Spanish defenses, and set off to "find and interview the Cuban patriot army."

One night Stephen's Cuban friend took them to a *danza*, where money was being raised illegally for the Cuban cause. Stephen was sitting with his friend and the friend's "really beautiful girl," as Parker described her. A drunken correspondent sitting in the row in front of them kept tilting his chair against the girl's chair until she complained. All at once the Cuban was on his feet with a knife flashing in his hand. Stephen jumped up, caught the knife, and cut his own hand. The Cuban fell to his knees, kissing the hem of Stephen's coat. Stephen wrapped his bleeding right hand in his handkerchief, thrust it into his pocket, and left. When he didn't show up at the bar the next morning, Parker and some of the other correspondents went to his hotel. The door was locked. They eventually climbed over the half-wall partition and found Stephen in a bad way from the hand wound. They got a doctor to treat it, but it was "many days" before the hand began to heal, said Parker. Even then Stephen tended to favor it, holding it in his pocket. "He was not the same after the incident, was more reticent and less regular in his habit of joining us every morning," said Walter Parker.

"He is a juggler who is perfectly sure that he will catch the knife by the handle every time," wrote a *Life* reviewer in praise of *The Monster*. In August *Harper's Magazine* published the novella with wonderful illustrations by Peter Newell. "The reader can't escape the suspicion that perhaps Mr. Crane is not juggling with real knives — and if he did catch the wrong end it would not hurt him."

And then came another day when Stephen failed to turn up at the bar. After several days had passed, the correspondents went to his hotel room. They "found that he had had a personal shock," wrote Parker. "The affair was wholly personal and the details are nobody's business," Parker explained. And then he provided some of the details. Stephen, he said, had "found a girl, living in Havana, whom he had previously known elsewhere in the world. On her mantel there was a photograph of a handsome Cuban. After some discussion with the girl, Crane left the house . . . and lived the life of a complete recluse. He desired to see no one and had no liking for companionship."

Stephen's encounter with this woman seems to have coincided with the *Journal*'s decision to sever his expense account — presumably because he was not sending newsworthy dispatches. He left the expensive Hotel Pasaje without paying his bill and moved in with an Irish-born New Yorker named Mary Horan, who took in penniless Cuban lodgers. The correspondents learned that Stephen was writing something called "The Ashes of Love." He would not show them the work.

In hiding, he wrote a series of ten self-indulgent poems, titled them "Intrigue," and sent them off to Reynolds to complete the volume of poetry that would be called *War Is Kind*. Of historical rather than literary interest, the "Intrigue" poems were a raw expression of Crane's feelings. They give a picture of a writer whose emotions have overwhelmed his literary judgment and toughness.

> Thou art my love
> And thou are the ashes of other men's love

he wrote in the first and longest poem. Filled with fresh pain — his heart "still beat[s] for thee, beloved" — the poems tell of a love affair that has ended, leaving the poet raving with bitterness and feelings of betrayal. The sound of this woman's laughter "[defines] the measure of my pain; / I knew that I was alone, / Alone with love, / Poor shivering love . . ." While offering few clues to the woman's identity, the poems suggest that she is young — "Bell-voiced, happy," "chattering girlishly to other girls," "careless with the stout heart of unscarred womanhood" — though Stephen had called even the middle-aged Amy Leslie his "girl." Clearly, the love affair had been sexual and passionate. The poet remembers happier days, when he had "heard your quick breaths / And seen your arms writhe toward me." He has "seen thy face aflame / For love of me, / Thy fair arms go mad, / Thy lips tremble and mutter and rave."

Most telling, and more important, perhaps, than the woman's identity, which remains unknown, the poems show that even after Cora, Stephen continued to court a certain kind of woman, a respectable Lily or Nellie. Notwithstanding his sobering adult experiences with war, illness, money, serious literary work, and women, he was a boy in love. With this elusive woman of the "Intrigue" poems he was never quite himself; he "was impelled to be a grand knight, / And swagger and snap my fingers, / And explain my mind fully." He needed to prove himself worthy of her:

> God give me medals
> God give me loud honors
> That I may strut before you, sweetheart
> And be worthy of —
> — The love I bear you

In needing her, Stephen showed the worst side of himself, the appalling insecurity and adolescent jealousy that set him swaggering instead of walking, trying to impress a girl's father with his French. While the "lost sweetheart" of the "Intrigue" poems is carefree, a woman for whom "life . . . was all light melody," his is a dark personality. He copes with "the drip of the blood / From my heart." He is tormented by "the shadow of another lover" behind her, this "shade" forever coming "between me and my peace." His doubts have undone him sexually and psychologically. "My love grew like a genie / For my further undoing" — and ultimately cost him the woman. "He had your picture in his room / A scurvy traitor picture." Vacillating between love and hate, wishing her and the other man grief, wondering if she ever thinks of him now, whether she remembers when she loved *him*, he ends the last poem in the series on a note of reconciliation:

> Thou lovest not me now,
> But thou didst love me,
> and in loving me once
> Thou gavest me an eternal privilege,
> For I can think of thee.

The following month, October, he felt sufficiently recovered to write a lighthearted newspaper piece on Cuba's courtship rituals. Apparently thinking of his encounter with a lost love in Havana, he wrote:

> Time moves at its allotted speed slowly over the years; nothing changes, routine is routine. And in the end, what? Who

knows? Perhaps our fine young man sights a woman who rightly or wrongly blots out in four minutes the memory of the girl he has arduously courted for three years. Then, again, perhaps not.

It was hardly worth discussing: "Men seek the women they love, and find them, and women wait for the men they love, and the men come." And in the end these agonies "count[ed] for nothing against the tides of human life, which are in Cuba or Omaha controlled by the same moon."

He wrote to no one, it seems — not to Cora, his family, or anyone else — except for Paul Revere Reynolds. Once in a while one of the correspondents would drop in on him "to learn how he was making out," but his days of companionable drinking at the bar had ended. It was as if he had vanished.

"Have you heard anything from Stephen Crane or his Wife — how he has come out of the American & Spanish War," William Blackwood wrote Joseph Conrad. He had never received any articles from Stephen.

A rumor got around that Stephen had been "done away with" by locals hostile to the press. On September 10 a gossip column in the *Florida Times-Union* reported that Stephen had entered Havana ten days earlier, posing as a tobacco buyer. The Spanish police were said to have been shadowing him for several days before he disappeared; now "fears for his safety are entertained by his friends," said the paper. Someone sent the item to Cora, who responded with a flurry of urgent requests for help. She wrote to John Hay, the United States secretary of state and former ambassador to England, Secretary of War Russell A. Alger, and Reynolds. She urged Hay, who was a friend of Stephen's, to "ask the President to instruct the American commission to demand Mr. Crane from the Havana police," and she begged Reynolds to use his influence with William Randolph Hearst, as the *Journal* people in London were "behaving very shabily." Hearst "has no right to allow a man like Stephen Crane to be missing for over three weeks without using means to find him," she added. She was "almost distracted with grief and anxiety" and in "*great* need of money." She had not heard from Stephen since August 16, and in the meantime she had been served with two summonses. She was still living at Ravensbrook and feared eviction.

The Hearst press reported that Stephen Crane was hiding in a Havana rooming house. Cora, deciding to travel to Cuba to fetch him back to England, appealed to Robert Barr to help her raise the money. Barr was disgusted with Stephen — "I should hate to put down in black and white what I think of Stephen Crane," he wrote Cora. He now thought that the initial report that Stephen had been imprisoned in Havana was "a put-up job" and that Stephen had no intention of returning — an opinion shared by Harold Frederic and apparently by James Creelman, the *Journal*'s London representative, who had been sending Cora's letters to Stephen and was sure he had received at least some of them. Barr was deeply sympathetic to Cora's plight. "If, in these circumstances, you think it worth while to go after such a man, then there is nothing to do but consider the ways and means," he wrote. Though Barr himself was too far in debt to lend her travel money, he wrote to the German Lloyd and American shipping lines, requesting that they give Cora passage with deferred payment. He explained that Cora's husband had been imprisoned by the Spanish in Havana and that he would pay for his wife's passage after his release. Barr also suggested that Cora try to get an advance from William Heinemann on the understanding that Stephen would give him future work.

People spotted him on the streets of Havana. He was seen sitting in a café listening to stragglers until they ran out of talk. At the end of the day he would retreat to his room to turn out his six hundred words. He wrote in his painstaking way, without aid of a dictionary or reference books of any kind, which slowed his pace even more. "He did nothing with regularity," said Otto Carmichael, a correspondent for the *Minneapolis Times* who met Stephen in a café at about this time and soon became his friend. He lived on light drinks and coffee, in the Cuban way, but did not take much alcohol. "This was somewhat remarkable at a time and place of excessive drinking." His health was "wretched."

While he remained lost to the world, Stephen sent out dispatches and war tales like messages in bottles. They bobbed up regularly in the *Journal*. "Now this is It!" he wrote Reynolds on September 27. Having apparently written through his personal crisis in the "Intrigue" poems, he had produced a superb Cuban war tale. Titled "The Price of the Harness" — referring to "the price the men paid for wearing the military harness, Uncle Sam's military harness," explained Stephen — the piece revisited the battles of El Caney and San Juan Hill from the perspective of the private soldier, personified by the fictive Private Nolan, a name he also used in other pieces. Where the "Intrigue" poems had lacked poetry, poetry was everywhere present in the new war tale: in "the grace of a man whose rifle has become absolutely a part of himself," in the sound of infantry fire, "that continual drumming which, after all, sounds like rain on a roof," in "the wire-string note of the enemy's bullets" and the "bitter ballad" of wounded men, "the visible messengers of bloodshed, death." Subtle and lyrical, filled, but not choked, with familiar Crane imagery, the prose was crisp, streamlined, and fresh. "Here were scattered tiny white shelter-tents, and in the darkness they were luminous like the rearing stones in a graveyard," he wrote. "The Price of the Harness" was the best sustained piece of its kind he had written to date and a superior war tale by any-one's standards. "If you dont touch big money for it I wonder!" Stephen wrote Reynolds. He instructed his agent to cable him when it was sold and to send the English copy to Blackwood, to whom he still owed sixty pounds.

That story was soon followed by "a *peach*," another Cuban war tale ti-tled "The Clan of No-Name," which dealt with an assault upon a block-house. It was framed by the slender story of a man who wins a girl he loves by default when the man she loves — the man in the photograph she has — dies in battle. The girl is named Margharita (the name faintly echoed the Marjory of Stephen's as yet unfinished novel *Active Service*), and the man who wins her is Smith, a suitor approved by her mother, a lover tormented by "dream-rivals." Of Smith — a name as undistinguished as Stephen felt his own to be — he wrote, "It was part of his love to be-lieve in the absolute treachery of his adored one. So whenever he heard the whirl of her skirts in the hall he felt that he had again leased happiness from a dark fate." Stephen loved the story "devotedly." He instructed Reynolds to "sell it to anybody if the price is grand enough. Otherwise remember that *Blackwood's* have a call on me." Though usually a good judge of his own work — he reserved his greatest enthusiasm for "The Bride Comes to Yellow Sky," "The Blue Hotel," and *The Monster* — Stephen was curiously overpraising about this latest war tale, his judgment clouded, perhaps, by the love story, into which he put some of the feelings he'd poured into the "Intrigue" poems. "I *love* this story," he said again in a postscript to Reynolds. Perhaps he wasn't so sure about it.

When he wrote about love, Stephen's youth was evident. The stories failed because he took romantic love seriously. As Frederic Lawrence said of him, "despite all experience he was persistently and unalterably ro-mantic in his conception of women — many of whom, it need scarcely be added, did not deserve it. This brought him close to catastrophe." The Margharita seen walking in a moonlit garden while bathed in the "shivering gleam" of the electric light never springs to life or moves us like the beauty seen through "the silvered netting" of the cashier's box in "The Pace of Youth." The writer himself believes the clichés, is dazzled by the shivering gleam. He cannot penetrate the surface to turn Margharita into a flesh-and-blood woman; she remains mysterious and inaccessible. In both "The Pace" and "The Bride" — written, it seems, when Stephen was *not* in the throes of romantic love — he had been able to look at it objectively, and he soared.

Visiting the Conrads in their new house at Ivy Wells in October, Cora succumbed to jealousy and insecurity. The visit "was marred by her very real anxiety as to [Stephen's] possible whereabouts, and a fierce jealousy as to his possible fancy for someone he might meet," wrote Jessie Conrad. "In vain I assured her of my complete conviction that Stephen was deeply attached to her" and that his first thought as soon as he was able to get a letter through would be of her."

If Stephen was worried about anyone on the home front, it was not apparent to Otto Carmichael, who was sent by Major General J. F. Wade, chairman of the American Evacuation Commission in Cuba, to tell Stephen that he was holding a London cablegram for him. Carmichael delivered the message and Stephen thanked him, then forgot about it. The next day a second cablegram arrived, asking whether Stephen had received the first. Carmichael again conveyed the message.

"Say, didn't you tell me something about a cablegram yesterday?" Stephen said.

Carmichael told him he had and explained the second cable.

"Yes, I see," Stephen said. "Using the government to find me. Anyway, I'm much obliged."

Later Stephen dismissed the cable, saying it probably came from "some tradesman" to whom he owed money. He went on ignoring the cablegrams until the secretary of war himself began making inquiries into his whereabouts. Finally shamed, Stephen called on General Wade and expressed "regret at having caused so much trouble," as Wade wrote the adjutant general. "I do not know his business or why he has not corresponded with his family." The correspondents in Havana who were questioned about Stephen's whereabouts maintained that he "had not been out of the city."

On October 18, Cora finally received a letter from the British consul at Havana, assuring her of Stephen's physical safety. Stephen was neither ill nor imprisoned by the police, but he was "in some sort of difficulty," Cora wrote in a letter to Reynolds. Aware now that she had no real influence with Stephen, she urged Reynolds to write "and tell him of the important work there is to be done here. Ever so many people have written for stories etc."

Stephen resumed his business in Havana, cranking out war tales and newspaper pieces. He wrote about the mood in Havana, the crowded city sidewalks, the poverty, the price of things, seemingly covering any topic that had anything to do with Cuba. He recycled stories from his war tales, and in his war tales he used bits from his reporting work, writing too much, producing reams of forgettable copy. He took on some serious issues, such as the reckless behavior of certain American regiments sent to occupy Santiago. He was, as always, desperate for money — "Hit him hard," he told Reynolds when he sent "Marines Signaling Under Fire at Guantanamo" for McClure; "Hit him beastly hard." And he fired off one impatient letter after another, instructing Reynolds to respond to queries instantly and send money for work he had mailed from Havana just days earlier. "I have got to have at least fifteen hundred dollars this month, sooner the better. For Christ's sake get me some money quick here by cable," he wrote on October 20. "When in *Christ's* name do I get any money," he wrote the next day. A week later: "If I dont receive a rather fat sum from you before the last of the month, I am *ruined.*" He said he was determined to stay in Havana and clear his debts to the *Journal* and the Hotel Pasaje. He wanted Reynolds to ask the *Journal* to double his pay; without an expense account, he said, he could not "afford to write for twenty dollars a column."

In England, left alone to battle increasingly angry creditors, Cora was virtually penniless. When she could, she would gather up the dogs and, with Mrs. Ruedy, take refuge with friends.

When her own finances were most dire, she took in the three young children of Harold Frederic and Kate Lyon. In August, Frederic had had a stroke, which left him paralyzed on one side. Afterward he grew steadily worse and developed rheumatic fever. Attended at Homefield by Kate, a Christian Scientist, and another practitioner named Althie Mills, Frederic refused medical treatment and died of heart failure on October 19.

Two days later, there was a coroner's inquest in Kenley, and a scandal erupted. Along with the matter of medical neglect during Frederic's fatal illness, there was the matter of his illegitimate family, now forced into

public light. The *New York Times* tried to protect their former London bureau chief by reporting that he had died in London, his official residence,
with his legal wife and children. But the *Times* savagely attacked the
Christian Science practitioner Althie Mills as "a miserable creature" who
had been after "the sick man's gold" and deserved a prison sentence.
On November 5, both Kate Lyon and Althie Mills were indicted for
manslaughter. When the trial began the next day, Cora staunchly accompanied Kate to court.

Kate's crisis underscored the tenuousness of Cora's own unlawful
marriage, which had never been at greater risk, with Stephen apparently
having deserted her. She had no legal rights. Even if she chose to take
Stephen to court, she could expect nothing from a legal system that
would view her as an unchaste woman. While rallying around Kate and
the children, offering the children sanctuary, cosponsoring a fund for
their support, and writing letters of appeal to everyone she could think of,
even poor writers like Conrad and Robert Barr, Cora did all she could to
bring Stephen home.

Though Stephen must have been aware of both the Frederic-Lyon
scandal and Cora's poverty, his letters to Reynolds — the only letters he
wrote during this period that are known to have survived — talked solely
of his work and his own troubles. He had "completed about 15000 words
of Cuban stories" for a war book he was targeting for spring. "I am working like a dog," he told Reynolds, and he finished his letter with the usual
lament. "When — oh, when, — am I to have some money? If you could
only witness my poverty!"

Cora appealed to Joseph Conrad for help in getting Stephen back to
England. Conrad assured her that he'd do what he could, but he cautioned her that his chances of success were *"most* remote." He chose his
words carefully, hiding any thoughts he had about Stephen's true situation in Havana. "What kind of trouble is Stephen in? You make me very
uneasy. Are you *sure* you can bring him back. I do not doubt your influence mind! but not knowing the circumstances I do not know how far it
would be feasible. In Stephen's coming back to England is *salvation* there
is no doubt about that."

Conrad himself had no money to send Cora — "I've only £8 in the
bank and am in debt to publishers so heavily that I can't go to them for
more. Or else I would do it, believe me," he wrote. But he approached
David Meldrum, head of Blackwood's London office, asking that the
publisher lend Stephen £50, with Stephen's work, Cora's furniture, and

Conrad's work as security. Should Cora and Stephen be unable to repay the loan, Conrad was prepared "to furnish them copy to the amount advanced."

"I only wish I had something to pawn or sell," he wrote Cora later. Blackwood himself was still angry with Stephen for reneging on the promised Spanish-American War copy ("a short letter from Stephen saying he could not send anything would have made all the difference," said Conrad). Conrad therefore advised Cora to work through Meldrum, who admired Stephen's work and was the more friendly of the two men.

But Meldrum proved a prudent businessman. While appealing to his friends in London's publishing industry on Stephen's behalf, he advised Blackwood against advancing the Cranes more money — even after Blackwood received Stephen's superb "The Price of the Harness" and accepted it for publication in *Blackwood's Magazine*. Neither Cora's furniture nor the promise of future work from Stephen Crane was adequate security for such a loan. Such a promise was in fact "legally, absolutely worthless," wrote Meldrum. And he had doubts about Stephen's character. "I fancy he is more foolish than you know. I can find no justification for the man, though I can make many excuses for one with such a strange and all-on-the-edge temperament as his," he wrote Blackwood.

Like a pauper's wife reduced to foraging in the larder for the last crumbs of bread, Cora unearthed some old stories and sketches from Stephen's papers at Ravensbrook and approached the London literary agent James B. Pinker about them. Pinker, who represented Henry James and Joseph Conrad, was doubtful about the wisdom of sending publishers such youthful literary efforts, but Cora prevailed by bringing Stephen himself in on the dealings.

The lure of money finally smoked Stephen out of hiding and opened the door to direct communication with Cora. Whatever her feelings about Stephen's abandonment — and she was too intelligent, too sophisticated a woman to see it any other way — she desperately wanted him back. This woman, who could publicly stand alongside another woman accused of manslaughter and who could write with magnificent outrage to a matron who had indignantly refused to contribute to the fund for Harold Frederic's illegitimate children, was not too proud to use every means available to get back her man.

Cora's letters and diaries, and the reminiscences of those who knew her, suggest a complaisance in her relations with Stephen that amounted to worship. Once she was in direct communication with him again, she let him know there would be no tears or recriminations, no demand for explanations. All she desired was his return. Cora was a formidable opponent in her dealings with others, sharp-tongued when provoked. To the indignant matron she had written, "To me, the supreme egotism of women who never having been tempted, and so knowing nothing of the temptation of another's soul, set themselves upon their pedestals of self-conceit and conscious virtue, judging their unfortunate sisters guilty alike, is the hardest thing in life." But she would surrender everything for Stephen, her Mouse. She and Stephen apparently corresponded as though they were merely discussing the household accounts, picking up where they'd left off the week before.

Pinker was soon negotiating a contract for an unwritten novel. At the same time, Cora continued to raise money by approaching publishers on her own. After she asked publisher Grant Richards for seventy-five pounds and Pinker asked him for a hundred, the London agent patiently advised her, "I think it would be better if you did not mention terms if you communicate with any publisher, for fear we should not name the same," he wrote on December 9. And he took the precaution of reminding her that she would need formal power of attorney to act for Stephen.

As the end of the year approached, Cora intensified her efforts to get Stephen home. Conrad wrote to Stephen through Reynolds. John Scott-Stokes got him a fifty-pound advance from Heinemann, then cabled that the money for his return would be sent through General Wade. ("Mrs. Crane got the cash and has sent it off to Havana to bring Stephen back," Conrad wrote Meldrum. "I know you will like to hear that she got over that trouble.") Urging Reynolds to "advise Mr. Crane to return to England," Cora emphasized Stephen's "great vogue here," the "favorable notices" he always received in England — unlike America, she implied. His continued great work depended upon his return to England, she said, adding, "A man must have pure wholesome air if he wishes to succeed in art." Furthermore, "he has a great future and a wonderful home awaiting him." ("My letters are one long inky howl," she confided to her manuscript book.) The wonderful home, Stephen knew, was the romantic and private Brede Place, with its great acreage and stable. By now Cora had not only committed Stephen to renting Brede, she had arranged for two of Kate's children to go there ahead of her with their governess while Kate, recently acquitted with Althie Mills in Frederic's death, got on her feet again.

Stephen was finally worn down. He had even been reduced to ca-

bling William for money, and he was perhaps further shamed into returning by the fifty pounds that came to him through General Wade rather
than directly. He left Havana, left the nightly fights between the Cubans
and the Spanish at the Café Inglaterra and his "dalliance with two
morena damozels," as one observer put it. On Christmas Eve he sailed
for New York on the *City of Washington*.

Several friends who saw him in New York — including Hamlin Garland, who met Stephen in the McClure office in late December — were
struck by the change in his appearance. Garland noted in his diary that
"the wonderful boy" he had championed looked "dingy" and "soaked
with nicotine," though he was "mentally alert and as full of odd turns of
thought as ever. He strikes me now as he did in early days as unwholesome physically — not a man of long life. He is now unusually careless in
his dress." To William Dean Howells, Stephen seemed restless, a result of
his "malarial fever."

"The horror of the last few months is at an end," Cora wrote Moreton Frewen, the owner of Brede Place. By the end of the month she was
able to report that "Mr. Crane is in New York settling up some business
affairs, but sails next Saturday week." And with her long wait nearly at an
end and bright vistas before her, she sent "over three hundred very choice
roses" to Brede Place. They might have been a flourish of trumpets.

15

———

LORD THOLEPIN OF

MANGO CHUTNEY

I t took a month of legal wrangling and frantic appeals to literary agents to get the Cranes out of Oxted. From the time Stephen stepped onto English soil on January 11, 1899, he was bombarded with summonses. They owed the grocer, the butcher, and the dairy. They owed a year's rent on Ravensbrook and a staggering £98.9s for the balance on a piano bought for Cora nearly two years earlier. Cora proposed to Pinker that she write up her experiences as a war correspondent in Greece — an idea that appealed to the editor of *Wide World*, though he would not advance her a shilling without seeing some copy. Stephen pressured William, asking now for a loan of $500 to save him from bankruptcy. Sounding like a man who had simply fallen on hard times, he complained that his Appleton royalties had amounted to a mere *"thirty-five dollars"* for the year. By now William had heard that Stephen had a wife, and Stephen used the occasion to sound a note of genteel poverty. "Yes, it is true I am married to an English lady [Cora was technically English by her marriage to Captain Donald Stewart] and through her connections we have this beautiful old manor but we are beastly short on ready money owing to my long illness." He feebly excused himself for failing to stop to see William and the family on his way through New York; he "was near to going smash" in England, he said, and had therefore been obliged to get back the moment he could raise the money to leave Havana. "So I have run by you in the dark again," he wrote, calling himself "the wayward brother."

———

But William did not send the money, and Stephen no sooner arrived in Oxted than he was "all fuzzy with money troubles," contending with yet another writ from "a leading creditor," he wrote Reynolds. A day of meeting with the head of Stokes's London office left Stephen so depleted he failed to keep an appointment afterward with Pinker. "I am unwell," he later explained.

Perhaps because he lacked the energy, he remained in Oxted nearly a week before finally making the excursion by carriage to Brede Place. Having seen the house with his own eyes and tramped over its lovely park with Cora, he became "mad over the place."

Brede Place sat on a hillside a half-mile from the public road, at the end of a winding Sussex lane framed by high hedges and ancient oaks. The house presided over a hundred-acre private park. A treasured piece of English architecture described by one historian as "lyric," Brede Place was considered one of England's finest examples "of the small country houses of the time of Henry VII." Dating to the fourteenth century, with Tudor and Elizabethan additions, it was laid out in the shape of an *E* in homage to Elizabeth, constructed of small Tudor bricks and local sandstone that had long since turned gray from the ravages of weather and neglect. It had pointed roofs, an abundance of chimneys, and narrow, diamond-paned windows that would seem to admit little light. There was neither electricity nor indoor plumbing. Sixteenth-century privies perched on the slope behind the house; "primitive earth closets" inside provided its "only sanitation." Except for occasional use as a game-keeper's refuge, the house had been unoccupied for a century. Beyond its massive arched wooden door and large stone entryway, the primitive interior was fitted with fine oak paneling, a great central fireplace that smoked and "would have roasted an ox," said Moreton Frewen's daughter, Clare Sheridan, and a small private chapel.

Adding to the aura of romance was a resident ghost. Legend had it that Brede's medieval owner, Sir Goddard Oxenbridge, haunted the house. Though the scanty historical record depicted the man as a harmless, devoutly religious knight, the Sir Goddard of local lore was a giant-sized ogre who ate little children. The neighborhood children had reportedly revenged themselves by sawing Sir Goddard in half at the little bridge over the stream at the bottom of Brede's hill, thereafter known as the Groaning Bridge. At night the house issued strange rattling noises probably caused by wind blowing through the monkholes and the falconry. Doors fastened by old wooden latches slipped open. One guest would describe hearing an array of sounds — "babies crying," the distant "trundling" of a coach-and-four, "the horses' hoofbeats pounding louder and louder over my head." From their nests in the ivy outside the windows came the *hoo-hoo-hoo* of white owls. Brede Place was irresistible.

Something about the manor revived Stephen, gave him fresh hope. "Stephen said that a solemn feeling of work came to him there so I am delighted," Cora wrote Edward Garnett.

The nominal rent of forty pounds annually would be no obstacle. Furthermore, the Cranes would rent the house from the kindest of landlords, who had himself lived a life of adventure and understood what it was to be hard pressed. Moreton Frewen was the forty-five-year-old son of an English squire, a colorful, charming, amusing man who was "absurdly fond" of Americans and a friend to writers. He had been an early champion of Kipling. After squandering his inheritance when young, Frewen had engaged in a series of moneymaking ventures that left him worse off. He purchased vast, unsecured range lands in Wyoming, where he fought off Sioux Indian raids at his log cabin; he invented something called a Gold Crusher, became an ardent bimetalist, and wrote a book called *The Economic Crisis*, which earned him the nickname "Mortal Ruin." Nothing about Stephen Crane's life could have shocked him. He himself had engaged in foreign intrigue in India and romantic intrigue in England, where he'd once shared a mistress — the actress Lillie Langtry — with the Prince of Wales. Frewen had known Buffalo Bill in his hunting-scout days, was a friend of prominent Americans, including Senator Cabot Lodge and Theodore Roosevelt, and brother-in-law to the widowed Lady Randolph Churchill. His wife, Clara, was one of the three beautiful American Jerome girls. Though Brede Place had been in the Frewen family for hundreds of years, Moreton and Clara had never lived there. Frewen had only recently purchased the house from a brother, then promptly mortgaged it. While renting it to Stephen Crane for a pittance, the Frewens themselves were teetering on the edge of bankruptcy and living largely on the charity of friends.

"I must raise heaven and earth between now and the middle of February," Stephen wrote Reynolds after seeing Brede Place. "I must have every pennie you can wrest from the enemy." Chief among the enemy was *Harper's*. Having disagreed with Stephen about the word count for *The Monster* story collection and about the suitability of some of the stories he had submitted, they had given him only half of the agreed-upon advance. They refused to give him more. "I think that collection of re-spectable old women has treated us rather badly," Stephen wrote Reyn-olds. He decided he could no longer afford to write for America's big three — *Harper's*, *Scribner's*, and the *Century*. He would concentrate on pub-lishing in the English magazines instead.

Through Pinker he contracted with the English publisher Methuen to write an unspecified 70,000-word novel. It was due just six months later, on August 1, and Stephen would receive a one hundred–pound ad-vance. He sent both Pinker and Reynolds inferior small work for quick cash — two Whilomville tales, "Lynx-Hunting" and "The Angel-Child"; a dull Spanish-American War tale called "God Rest Ye, Merry Gentle-men," which revisited war correspondents' experiences at Daiquirí, Si-boney, and Las Guásimas, and other light fare that showed his creative exhaustion. While trying to sound optimistic about these small efforts — "We all think that this is the best story that I have done for many a moon," he told Reynolds about the unworthy "Angel-Child" — he knew they didn't amount to much. "We like it a little," he wrote Pinker upon sending him the same story for English publication. "The next story will be a better one."

There was always the next story, the next big break. Considering the good reviews he got in England and the vastly more economical life that he and Cora envisioned for themselves at Brede, he calculated that he "could live for half what I've been usually spending," repay all his debts by year's end, and still make £1,500 that year. "For God sake jump the game with all four feet," he instructed Reynolds. For his part, he would "borrow money from pretty near everybody in the world." He would charm the loan out of William with descriptions of enchanting Brede, emphasizing the high cost of living there. He would even ask his new agent, Pinker, to stand as guarantor of his debts.

In the end, Stephen's English friends freed him from his entangle-ments at Oxted. Moreton Frewen dispatched his own solicitor, Alfred D. Plant, to mediate between Stephen and his creditors. Plant worked out an arrangement whereby Pinker would send him small sums of Crane's small earnings, which the lawyer would then parcel out to the creditors before Stephen received any. Though Plant managed to stave off further legal action, the battle was already lost. Stephen continued to borrow. At Stokes's suggestion, he agreed to what he himself downplayed as "a little temporary mortgage" on all his Appleton books — *The Red Badge*, *Maggie*, *The Little Regiment*, and *The Third Violet* — in exchange for a loan from them. Finally he asked Pinker to serve as guarantor for his debt to the Ravensbrook landlord by simply agreeing that the rent "will be paid, time not specified." Stephen had met with the landlord's solicitors, Morrison and Nightingale, and had come away with the wrong understanding that Pinker's guarantee was all it would take to enable him to move to Brede. Though Stephen had seemed slightly uncomfortable about asking Pinker such a favor — "of course I dont want to let you in for any strange game," he told him — he asked anyway, making light of the risk to Pinker. "Really your position would be simply that of a buffer-state," he wrote. He saw it as the only way to move to Brede "and get a fair chance at myself."

Having asked, he considered himself at liberty to go, and he and Cora and the dogs at last left Ravensbrook and joined their ready-made family at Brede, whose "very atmosphere makes our heads lighter," he wrote Clara Frewen.

Months later he lay stretched out on the grass at Brede, smoking and laughing as he watched eighteen-month-old Borys Conrad struggle to walk by himself. His pleasure in the baby was obvious and deep and un-like his pleasure in anything else. Joseph Conrad would remember that the only time he ever heard Stephen laugh outright was "in connection with the child" — "the boy," Stephen called him. Stephen's absorption in Borys puzzled Conrad and made him jealous. He would look out a win-dow at Brede and see the two of them being "very still; staring at each other with a solemn understanding," speaking a wordless language that left *him* on the outside. And Stephen "seemed to be everlastingly taking the boy's part," said Conrad. He could not, for instance, understand why Conrad would not get the baby a dog: "Hang it all, a boy ought to have a dog." And another time: "Joseph, I will teach your boy to ride." The two men were sitting inside at Brede Place during the dog discussion. Conrad was trying to work. Beyond the narrow diamond-paned windows sat Borys, well supported by pillows, on a blanket. His red stocking cap had slipped over one eye. "Behold the boy . . ." said Conrad, and Stephen laughed. "He dropped his preaching on the dog theme while I went on with my work," wrote Conrad.

The Conrads arrived for a fortnight's visit in June, as May's "blaze of azaleas" was giving way to wisteria and scarlet hawthorn. The solemnly beautiful house commanded the hill like an old warrior, its once-golden fa-cade telling a tale of suffering and neglect. It seemed a fitting metaphor for its new young master, variously dubbed "Baron Brede" and "the Duke" by Robert Barr and Cora. Both Jessie and Joseph Conrad were startled by the change in Stephen's appearance; husband and wife "looked apprehensively at each other." As Jessie saw it, the hard experiences in the Spanish-American War had operated on a fragile constitution.

Stephen had driven himself hard during his first months at Brede, "doing more work now than I have at any other period of my life," he'd written Reynolds. In May he'd finished *Active Service*, writing "at a clipping gait of some ten thousand words per week," he said. He had stories coming out in both England and America, some in syndication. *The Monster and Other Stories* was in production, and *War Is Kind*, his second collection of poems, was published in America in May. (It was not published in England.)

War Is Kind, which included the self-indulgent "Intrigue" poems Stephen had written in Cuba, was not likely to add to his literary reputation. Nature, seen from the shifting perspectives of different observers, was a largely godforsaken landscape colored in black, gray, blood-red, and blue; a sinister, primitive world of "whispering snakes," "blood and torn grass," bloody horses, mountains, bleak deserts and lonely black water. The sounds were "the screams of cut trees," and "the chatter of a death-demon from a tree-top." But nature also sang "good ballads of God": on a "blue night" a "chorus of colors came over the water, / Little songs of carmine, violet, green, gold." A man asks a workman to weave a dream of "sunlight, / Breezes and flowers" for his love, a "cloth of meadows." God is punishing, indifferent, nonexistent. God is love, nature's beauty, present. Man sins, journeys, searches, ultimately fruitlessly, and yet the question persists: does God exist? The answer is ambiguous.

Although on the whole *War Is Kind* lacked the freshness of *The Black Riders*, Stephen had taken a few steps forward as a poet and had produced some of his best verse. "A slant of sun on dull brown walls, / A forgotten sky of bashful blue," began one. "I have heard the sunset song of the birches, / A white melody in the silence," began another. "Each small gleam was a voice — / A lantern voice —" he had written, using color to impressive effect. But his characteristic imagery and themes were, overall, less striking and successful. The verse was too raw; little was composed.

Reviewers pounced on the small gray-blue volume with the absurd art nouveau illustrations by Will Bradley, finding the book ridiculous, adolescent, unmemorable, evidence of a man who "was profoundly weary," "losing his grasp." Rupert Hughes panned it in the *Criterion*; Willa Cather in the *Pittsburgh Leader*. She wrote:

> Mr. Crane is insulting the public or insulting himself, or he has developed a case of atavism and is chattering the primeval nonsense of the ages. His *Black Riders*, even as it was, was a casket of polished masterpieces when compared with *War Is Kind*. And it is not kind at all, Mr. Crane, when it provokes such verses as these — it is all Sherman said it was.

Stephen's best stories — "The Bride Comes to Yellow Sky," "The Blue Hotel," "The Open Boat," and *The Monster*— had earned him only about 2.7 cents a word, and the inferior Whilomville tales 5¼ cents a word, at a time when Kipling was earning up to 23 cents a word.* None of his books after *The Red Badge* had sold well; *Maggie, The Little Regiment*, (a story collection), *The Third Violet, The Open Boat and Other Stories*, and *Pictures of War* had had only one printing each in England.

His debts had chased him to the walls of the ancient manor. A creditor from Cuba had even turned up at Reynold's office in America with a draft for $305.88. In his more frayed moments, Stephen confessed to William, he thought, "I can't quite do it." And yet he persisted, buying a typewriter to speed production, talking in the same confident way about the money he would earn, forever a dreamer. He told Reynolds he thought he could get a few thousand dollars in serial rights for the 79,000-word *Active Service;* he lied to William, telling him that "the American serial rights are worth about $3,000" and that he would get the money in May.

He had spent months courting his brother for a five-hundred-dollar loan, trying hard to present himself as a mature man who was eager to reestablish ties with his family and be helpful to them. He was, he said, living a modest, work-centered existence that would imminently pay off, now with a devoted wife who "feels the same interest in the stories that I feel myself." In fact, he hoped to bring Cora to visit the family in America as soon as they got out of debt. Finally he succeeded in getting a mere hundred dollars from William, but with strings: William's troublesome eldest daughter, Helen, would spend the spring with Stephen and Cora.

In *War Is Kind* he had written:

* James B. Stronks, "Stephen Crane's English Years: The Legend Corrected."

The successful man has thrust himself
Through the water of the years,
Reeking wet with mistakes,
Bloody mistakes,
Slimed with victories over the lesser
A figure thankful on the shore of money.

If Stephen looked as gray and in need of repair as the English manor he now called home, his guests felt amply rewarded by the time spent under his roof. A visit to Brede Place was a lark. Mark Barr, a distant cousin of Robert's, asked Stephen why the stone entrance hall was sunken. H. G. Wells, visiting from nearby Sandgate, knew the answer: "in the old days," he explained, such floors "were strewn thick with rushes" — and Stephen immediately proposed an excursion into the meadow and brook to collect rushes. They ran into Joseph Conrad, who helped gather the green bundles and carry them back to the house.

The house was still largely "uninhabitable," said Conrad. Stephen cheerfully described the outside as "ulterior splendor. The inside is mainly chops and potatoes." Cora had done her best to furnish some half dozen of its many rooms with the lovely oak pieces she'd found in Oxted and with some four-poster beds lately used as chicken coops, which she'd had rubbed down. Even so, the cavernous rooms seemed only half-filled. Cora had taken the old ballroom as her boudoir. Her four-poster sat on a dais, with furniture huddled around it. Jessie Conrad remembered kissing Cora good night one evening and watching her retire to the little candle-lighted island on the dais, which looked like a "doll's" room. In a far corner of the chamber, a small passageway opened into the room where Conrad and Stephen sat deep in conversation. From a distance it seemed to Jessie that their heads hung suspended in air.

Guests stayed "in the unhaunted wing of the manor house," said Mark Barr, where beeswax candles provided the only light. "Bats flew about my ceiling and walls until the candle was put out and they settled down to share the room with me," said another guest, A. E. W. Mason. As Mark Barr told it, on one occasion, when both he and H. G. Wells were visiting, Stephen asked if he'd like "to sleep in the haunted room." Barr said yes, then grew suspicious when he saw Stephen and Wells whispering and grinning in the hall. Once settled into his bedchamber for the night, Barr armed himself with a pail of water, then unintentionally fell asleep. He awoke in the night to the sound of creaking stairs. The door was wide open. Barr got up, flung the pail of water out into the stairs, crying, "I've got you two ghosts!" — but there was no response. Another time Stephen asked Barr, who was a scientist, if he could treat some firewood with chemicals so that when Henry James visited he would take the colored flames for ship's timbers — the joke worked.

The house was brimming with people. The Cranes' "simpler" life now included Kate Lyon's two youngest children, four-year-old Barry, and Heloise, age six. They and their nurse, Mrs. Lily Burke, were staying with Stephen and Cora until Kate got on her feet again. A retinue of servants, some of whom Moreton Frewen had insisted remain with the house, kept things running. White-bearded Mack was both coachman and gardener. There was a drunken cook, Vernall, and her husband, Chatters, who carried in the well water and did the outdoor work; an old butler named Richard Heather; a coachman and his wife who lived over the stables; and a serving man. Various "slatternly" women and girls supplemented the regular staff, said Jessie Conrad. Fearing the ghost, the day help insisted on returning to the village at sunset.

The Frederic children ran about in bare feet, wearing old-fashioned garments of "some coarse bronze plush," said Jessie Conrad. The dogs — more numerous than ever — ruled the roost as they had at Ravensbrook and tore through the village and neighboring property. Stephen refused to pay for the damage they did. Even when a local shepherd threatened to sue for the destruction to his lambs and sheep, Stephen disregarded it "in a somewhat lofty manner," said Jessie Conrad. One day the Conrads and Cranes were returning from an excursion when the horses "shied violently" at the drive. Everyone in the trap "gasped and held our noses." Before them, level with the horses' heads, the carcasses of four or five sheep swung from the trees. "Stephen's face turned deathly pale with anger while he muttered curses under his breath," said Jessie Conrad. She once saw the elderly butler, "his face set in the most benevolent expression . . . escort the dogs to the head of the stone steps then solemnly kick each one down the steep flight."

Dinner at Brede was played out like a theatrical farce. "The chances of dinner — at eight — were often very small, especially when there were many people expected," said Jessie.

> The cook would appear and announce in the most truculent
> tone that she was even at that moment departing. Cora
> Crane, at her wits' end for the moment, would wring her

hands and appeal to Stephen. He in turn would give her one glance and solemnly ring the bell. Like clockwork the old butler appeared and handed a bottle of brandy to the thirsty woman, who retired with no further comment to her kitchen, and an hour or so later a perfect dinner would be served, complete in every detail. One night the old butler, who had primed himself a trifle early, knocked over the lamp and set the table alight.

The Cranes were "delightful hosts," said Mark Barr. Stephen was a good listener and a good talker, funny, fun-loving, and kind, utterly lacking in vanity or pretension. He could take a joke, even it if wore thin. Conrad, who greatly admired "The Open Boat," loved to tease Stephen about his famous description of the waves as "barbarously abrupt": the carriage ride that morning had been barbarously abrupt, he would say; or he would beg Stephen not to be so barbarously abrupt. Stephen always smiled. He liked to sing and strum a guitar of an evening. He loved games. "You are the greatest of the boys," Conrad told him. As for Cora, her hospitality was "more than charming." She set a generous table. Guests were never made to feel the Cranes' financial pinch, which kept old Heather washing and drying the flat silver between courses. Cora eagerly went along with whatever Stephen wanted. His happiness, well-being, and work were of paramount importance to her — something that endeared her to his friends, whether they actually liked her or not.

Living for Stephen, wholly concerned with their life together, Cora seems to have been absorbed into him. The woman who had cut such a distinctive figure in Jacksonville now appeared as a fuzzy postscript to Stephen Crane. Even her handwriting had become so like Stephen's that it was virtually impossible to tell his script from hers. Only the coronets on her brushes, toilet silver, and trunks stored in the attic, ending with the initial *S*, bespoke another identity.

Stephen, the record shows, did not write or talk about his feelings for Cora, yet friends described him as devoted and protective of her. In later reminiscences of some of his friends, Cora was conspicuously absent. One gets the sense that though she was not the woman Stephen's friends would have chosen for him and did not add much to the pleasure of being with him, neither did she detract from it. The Cranes' English acquaintances generally accepted her as Stephen's wife (in fact some of them, like A. E. W. Mason, did not know the truth) and appreciated her devotion to him and her kindness to them. But he was clearly the drawing card. Mason rated her as "below" Stephen "mentally: he aimed at more" — a view that seems to have been shared by Stephen's other friends. Like Conrad — whose true feelings about Cora are unknown — Henry James, living at nearby Lamb House, in Rye, treated her cordially and respectfully as "Mrs. Crane," though he regarded her fastidiously as a woman with a "past." Robert Louis Stevenson's widow, who did not know Cora, described her as "nine or ten years older than Mr. Crane and 'all the tongues are wagging.'" The more liberal-minded H. G. Wells, who had lived out of wedlock with the woman who became his wife and who spent a lot of time at Brede, appraised her as "an energetic lady" who gave "her ailing young husband a good time." Mrs. Mark Barr, "herself a great lady," staunchly defended Cora. Mark Barr is said to have considered Cora educated.

People tended to focus on Cora's physical size and her clothes, as if there weren't much else of interest about her. (Mark Barr also described her as "an ample 'negro mammy' sort of person.") Even Jessie Conrad, whose memoirs of the Cranes were overwhelmingly affectionate and discreet, essentially dismissed Cora as "of a somewhat monumental figure," a woman who "affected a statuesque style of dress." Hueffer called her "large, fair and placid." Though Cora dressed well enough when the occasion required, such as a trip into London, at Brede she put away her corset and wore loose-fitting "medieval" costumes, as Hueffer described them, consisting of tunics and skirts that she made herself and Greek sandals. "I haven't any more clothes than a rabbit," she said. She sometimes allowed her heavy golden hair to stream loose down her back when company was in the house.

To Jessie Conrad, who had more opportunities to observe the Cranes now that they lived just a short ride from the Conrads' current house, Pent Farm, in Stanhope, it seemed that Cora's "strange fancy for inviting people in such shoals to visit the house" made life excessively hard for the anxious writer laboring in a little upstairs room. And she blamed Cora for the slatternliness of the female servants, whose presence caused "much unfavorable gossip" in the village. Jessie was sure this must have pained the "highly strung and sensitive" Stephen. Clare Sheridan described the "vivid impression" Cora had made "on my childish mind. She was what my father called 'a terror' — the worst type of bossing American woman. . . . She overpowered & overshadowed and overlaid Crane and everyone else in her vicinity! How Crane could stand her —

THE MANOR

these are the things I heard my parents say to one another. It didn't matter of course that they never paid the rent."

Jessie Conrad's perception that Cora cluttered Stephen's life with
people virtually against his will was inaccurate and unfair. They had each
approached Brede with the intention of reforming. They would live quietly and frugally until they got out of debt, they vowed. Cora was sincere
when she told Edward Garnett before they moved, "I hope that the perfect quiet of Brede Place and the freedom from a lot of dear good people,
who take [Stephen's] mind from his work, will let him show the world a
book that will live."

But the plan had soon gone awry. Both Stephen and Cora began issuing invitations. Someone they knew was coming to London; it would be
fun to have him out to luncheon, show her the house. Someone —
Pinker, Alfred Plant, the Frewens — had been so good to them, they
could hardly do less than invite them for a casual visit. A photograph
taken of Stephen that summer shows him descending the front steps at
Brede, his right hand extended in eternal greeting. And of course they
wanted to see their friends. Cora understood that given the intensity of
Stephen's daily labors alone, he needed replenishment from the world
outside. It was helpful to have Conrad or Garnett visit; time spent with
empathetic, supportive friends was a necessary pleasure in a writer's life.
Even so, she sometimes protested that they had just had a houseful of
company, that perhaps Stephen ought to rest. Uninvited guests — whom
Stephen also attracted, in spite of Brede's inconvenient distance from
London — were another matter. He called them "lice."

On Cora's part, the relentless socializing seems to have been largely
an effort to please Stephen. She sensed that she needed to bring in others
in order to hold onto her dear one. From the beginning, their union had
included other people: Mrs. Ruedy, the Ptolemy brothers, correspondents, friends. At moments when a man and woman would seemingly
want to be alone — after Stephen's rescue from the *Commodore*, following
his eight-month absence in the Spanish-American War — Cora asked
people to join them, thinking this would divert Stephen. While he was
still en route to England in early January she invited Edward Garnett to
accompany them on their upcoming day trip to Brede Place. (Garnett apparently declined.) They had scarcely arrived at Brede when she began
inquiring into American adoption laws, writing Harold Frederic's executor, Judge Alton B. Parker of the New York State Court of Appeals, of

their desire to adopt little Barry Frederic.* The desire to please Stephen was mixed up with her need to anchor him with obligations — to children, to a house. But the impression that others had of Cora as the sole engineer of the Cranes' people-choked life was enhanced by her looks and personality. She was the more overtly social of the two, a managing, self-confident woman. People thought she must dominate the retiring and frail Stephen, who was more inclined to listen than talk, who was apt to slip away from people, from life.

Though both Stephen and Cora knew that the Brede idyll could not last — the Frewens might reclaim the house when the year's lease was up — they quickly wedded themselves to the place. Stephen hung his Mexican blanket in the stone entrance hall. They inscribed their books "Crane / Brede Place" or "Mrs. Stephen Crane / Brede Place." They had calling cards printed. Even before moving in, they had begun using their new embossed stationery. "We love Brede with a wildness which I think is a little pathetic," Stephen wrote Clara Frewen. "During these late heavy storms the whole house has sung like a harp and all the spouts have been wailing to us. It is rather valkyric."

Day after day, Stephen closed the narrow wooden door of his study and wrote. He worked in the modest room overlooking the front door of the house — "the porch room," he and Cora called it. It had a small fireplace with a plain slate mantel and oak wainscoting bordered at the top with carved grinning faces. The room itself was sparsely furnished, with a long writing table and a sleeping couch. He had hung a few pictures on the walls. His writing table faced the windows, which looked west over the rolling green park dotted with sheep. The village church spire was visible in the distance.

During his two-week visit in June, Conrad would accompany Stephen to the porch room while he worked. Settling himself at the opposite end of the long table, with his back to Stephen, he took up his book and read for two hours, until Stephen announced, "I won't do any more now, Joseph." Conrad was amused by one feature of Stephen's daily ritual: as he started to work, he poured himself a little ale from a small jug brought into the room at about ten; then he scarcely touched it. When he put down his pen, having filled three long sheets of paper with his careful

* Kate Lyon's role in this is unknown.

handwriting ("with no more than half a dozen erasures — mostly single words — in the whole lot," noted Conrad), he would drink the flat ale "as if moved by some obscure sense of duty." Then the two friends would stroll around the front of the house until lunch was ready.

✦

It was August 29, 1899. "Feeling vile," Stephen said in an irritable-sounding letter to Henry Sanford "Arnold" Bennett, a Canadian friend. He had just had tea at Henry James's, which didn't help matters. "My God how does he stand those bores who pester him," he wrote. "Mrs. Humphrey Ward was there. What an old cow! She has no more mind than a president. Nice to us, though." The crack about Mrs. Ward followed a nastier comment about Oscar Wilde, who was sick with syphilis.

> About Wilde and his troubles a mere stranger and runaway dog like me can't be supposed to care. I met him once. We stood and looked at each other and he bleated like a sheep. With those bad manners that are so awfully much mine I laughed in his face. He tried to borrow money from Dick Davis when he was being tried after insulting Davis all across London. Something pretty poor in him. And I owe my brothers too much money to bother about helping with sub- scriptions for a mildewed chump like Wilde. Blood, etc. If Harris and the rest of Wilde's friends really want to help him they ought to send him express to Weir Mitchell or some specialist in his kind of malady. Perhaps it is because I lived on borrowed money and ate in lunch-wagons when I was trying to be someone that these magnified sinners in good duds bore me so. That isn't what Conrad would call a senti- ment of generosity but it is mine.

His arrows were not reserved for strangers like Mrs. Ward and Wilde. Henry James, who was only a casual friend, had provoked Stephen by not defending Harold Frederic's name against the scandalmongers. "He professed to be er, er, er much attached to H. and now he has shut up like a clam," Crane wrote in a letter to William, mocking the Master's halting syntax. Everything Stephen said — even in defense of or out of concern

Stephen Crane, war correspondent, posing on a fake rock for a studio photograph in Athens, 1897. *Barrett Library, University of Virginia*

Cora in Athens, 1897. She was "among the last to leave the field." *Crane Collection, Syracuse University*

Stephen and Cora in the conservatory at Ravensbrook, the first house they rented in England, about 1897. *Barrett Library, University of Virginia*

"I expect to mail you a story of 10000 words on Saturday." Stephen at work in the study at Ravensbrook. *Barrett Library, University of Virginia*

"'IF YOU AIN'T AFRAID, GO DO IT THEN'"

Illustration by Peter Newell for "The Monster," *Harper's New Monthly Magazine*, August 1898.

Joseph Conrad (1895), for whom Stephen felt "a warm and endless friendship."

The Conrads' first visit to Ravensbrook, February 1898. Left to right: Jessie Conrad's sister Dolly, Stephen (holding a dog), Joseph Conrad, Jessie, Mrs. Ruedy, and Cora, holding the infant Borys. "Though the likenesses are not bad it is a very awful thing." *Crane Collection, Syracuse University*

Marshall.
Crane.   Morrison.
Bengough.   Exton.
                    Greene.

Breakfasting with Captain Greene, Daiquiri, June 23d.

Stephen (second from left) with other correspondents and Rough Riders at breakfast on Daiquiri Beach, Cuba, June 23, 1898. *Photo by Burr McIntosh*

"The very antithesis of the conquering male." Crane aboard *The Three Friends* en route to Cuba, 1898. *Barrett Library, University of Virginia*

Crane aboard *The Three Friends*.

"We love Brede Place with a wildness which I think is a little pathetic." Brede Place as it looked when Stephen and Cora lived there.

Brede Place in 1989. Stephen's porch room is above the front door, at left. *Photo by Bob Ward*

Stephen descending the front steps at Brede, his right hand extended in eternal greeting, August 1899. *Barrett Library, University of Virginia*

"Feeling vile." Stephen in August 1899. *Crane Collection, Syracuse University*

Stephen put in "hours of terrific work" in the porch room at Brede Place, September 1899. *Barrett Library, University of Virginia*

"Lord Tholepin of Mango Chutney." A cartoonist's depiction of Stephen at Brede Place.
Barrett Library, University of Virginia

"I haven't any more clothes than a rabbit."
Cora in medieval dress at Brede, 1899.
Barrett Library, University of Virginia

Stephen's life "had been anything but a stroll through a rose garden." This photograph, taken in 1899, appeared in the book *Napthali*, by C. L. Hind.

Riding was always Stephen's "idea of happiness." This photo was taken late in 1899. *Barrett Library, University of Virginia*

"When you come to the hedge — that we must all go over — it isn't bad." The Villa Eberhardt in Badenweiler, Germany, where Stephen spent his last days (his room was on the second floor, at right). *Photo by Linda Davis, 1989*

The last photograph taken of Stephen, Brede Place, 1900, with his favorite dog, Sponge, a dog with "soul." *Barrett Library, University of Virginia*

for someone — had a razor's edge. "You are wrong about Hueffer," he wrote Bennett. "I admit he is patronizing. He patronized his family. He patronizes Conrad. He will end up by patronizing God who will have to get used to it and they will be friends." And, more baldly, to another correspondent: "Please have the kindness to keep your mouth shut about my health in front of Mrs. Crane hereafter. She can do nothing for me and I am too old to be nursed. It is all up with me but I will not have her scared. For some funny woman's reason, she likes me. Mind this."

On the surface he acted the part of a twenty-seven-year-old man with a long life before him. He divided his time between work, family life, and pleasure. He assumed responsibility for his niece, Helen, who had arrived in June when Mrs. Ruedy left — albeit with financial help from William. He often rode over to Pent Farm to visit Conrad. Sometimes he talked "freely, and at others he would sit for an hour without speaking," said Conrad. He took rides in the park on one of the manor's two large bays; the horses were called Hengist and Horsa "because they were true 'Kentishmen!'" he told Mark Barr, a cigarette in his mouth. He galloped over the wet Sussex lanes in darkness, as heedless of danger as he had been in Hartwood, when he and Edmund had taken their horses around reverse curves at breakneck speed. The romantic Hueffer, who once found Stephen lying in the road under the leg of a fallen horse, saw him as "a frail eagle astride a gaunt elephant."

Feeling indebted to the Frewens for Brede Place, where he and Cora had been living rent-free without complaint from their landlords, Stephen agreed to provide Lady Randolph Churchill with a long war story for her new *Anglo-Saxon Review*, but he neglected to negotiate a price. He was to write an unspecified novel for Methuen and was under contract to Stokes for its American publication. He thought he would write about the Revolutionary War. To Pinker he tried to sound optimistic. "If you can stick to your end, all will go finely and I will bombard you so hard with ms that you will think you are living in Paris during the siege," he wrote. In July he had broken with Paul Revere Reynolds and given Pinker full control over his literary affairs.

As his health deteriorated, Stephen's writing tended to fall into one of three categories: Whilomville stories, war tales, and "tales of western American life similar to 'Twelve O'Clock,'" he wrote Pinker. In the Whilomville tales he resurrected Jimmie Trescott, Henry Johnson, and Alex Williams from *The Monster*, the fire victims magically appearing without scars. He had no time to create new characters. Stories were now to be paid for by his agent upon receipt — before they were sold. "A rattling good war story" of 5,330 words required an immediate £40 from Pinker; "a whacking good Whilomville story" necessitated £150, an amount Stephen had to have "within the next ten days," and which he would earn by writing more Whilomville stories — "for they are sure and quick money," he wrote Pinker. As he saw it, he had already earned £40 of the £150 with the rattling good war tale.

His life told on his face. At twenty-eight he had deep parentheses around his mouth and shadows under his large eyes. And yet his face mirrored "every emotion," wrote a reporter. The superb, shining gray-blue eyes, which Hueffer likened to "great orbs," a horse's eyes, drew you in, lassoed you. His gaze was "intensely concentrated," said Edward Garnett. But he was as skinny as rope. Even dressed in summer white flannels with a jacket and tie, he seemed to be swimming in his clothes.

He was obviously ill on the occasion of writer Edwin Pugh's first visit to Brede Place. Nevertheless, said Pugh, "Stevie" had invited him to come and stay as long as he liked. He met Pugh at the Rye station with horse and trap. Bending his tawny head and his "pale Mephistophelian face" to scrutinize his guest, Stephen said, "This looks like Edwin Pugh." He talked little on the long ride home but hummed steadily:

> I'll be there, I'll be there!!
> When the Hully Gee is calling I'll be there —
> Sure as you're born!

His bad health notwithstanding, Stephen played a mean game of handball, firing balls at Pugh like bullets from every possible angle in Brede's little "damp garden." Pugh found him a thoroughly engaging host. His sense of humor was "profound: so profound that usually he practised it merely to amuse himself"; his wit was "like liquid silver." He spoke lovingly of people he liked, praised others' books extravagantly. In the middle of a stream of compliments, he'd interrupt himself: "O hell! what's the use of words, anyway, when you want to say something?" He told stories about the Greek war in an exaggerated western drawl. Along with his swaggering, the drawl was Stephen's way of playing — acting out his work, experimenting with new guises. There was nothing phony about him, no artifice. He was simply young and creative. He liked costumes. As Pugh remembered it, Stephen told stories like this:

Say, when I planted these hoofs of mine on Greek soil I felt
like the hull of Greek literature, like one gone over to the
goldarned majority. I'd a great idea of Greece. One catches
these fleas at Syracuse, N'Yark. So I said to the chocolate-
box general of the Greek army: 'Can I go into the fighting
line?' And he says to me like a Denver Method: 'Not in those
trousers, sonny.' So I got back at him with 'How near may I
get to the fighting line, then?' And he said in his eloquent
way, 'Not less than two miles.'

Stephen stopped to fill his glass. Drained it. He resumed, "solemnly":
"That commanding officer was right for sure. I never was within two
miles of the fighting line. But I was mostly two miles nearer the Turks
than the Greek army was. Bekase they ran like rabbits."

By the end of August Cora was worried enough about Stephen's health
to ask Pinker for twenty pounds so that her husband might take "a few
days holiday" when he accompanied Helen to the Rosemont-Dézaley
school in Lausanne in September. Cora did not mention that she was going along with them as far as Paris or that they would be taking nineteen-
year-old Edith Ritchie. Edith was Kate Lyon's niece and Mark Barr's sister-in-law. In Paris she and Cora saw the sights and window-shopped.
George Lynch, a handsome war correspondent the Cranes called "the
wild Irishman," joined them. And when Stephen returned to Paris from
Lausanne, they all met friends for a round of "lunches, dinners, theaters,
cafés-chantants, and [more] sightseeing," said Edith. Cora and Stephen
mailed penny candy home to the dogs.

That request to Pinker was coupled with another for thirty-five
pounds to pay a wine dealer who was threatening legal action if Stephen's
bill was not paid immediately and yet another for forty pounds for a
4,000-word Whilomville story Pinker would get by Monday. "The wine
man must be satisfied and Mr. Crane must have a change or I fear he will
break down and we can't have that," Cora wrote Pinker.

By early September he was already breaking down, feeling "like
hell." "The clock work is jiggling badly," he wrote the undersecretary
of war, George Wyndham. Calling his ailment "fistula or vistula," he
wanted to know what Wyndham knew about Germany's Black Forest "as
a health resort." "The truth is that Cuba libra just about liberated me
from this base blue world," he said. But with others he continued to

downplay his illness. After his short holiday in Lausanne and Paris, Stephen wrote Moreton Frewen that he was "still seedy" following "a slight attack of Cuban fever." Though malaria is chronic, and Stephen was almost certainly truthful about the attack, the vague terminology was a deliberate counterfeit, used both to protect Cora (and spare himself her hovering) and to maintain his privacy. No one needed to know that he also had tuberculosis. The revelation would hardly inspire confidence in his publishers and creditors.

One night he dreamed that he was an actor performing on a stage before an audience. Playing a prisoner, he wore manacles on his wrists and ankles. During the play a fire broke out in the theater. Everyone — audience and fellow cast members — ran for the doors, forgetting him.

He told Cora and Edith Ritchie about the dream, wondering whether it would make a good story. He had the women tie his hands and ankles so that he could see how one moved in such circumstances. Edith would remember him struggling with his tethers all one morning, "trying, over a given distance, to hop or roll or work along like an inchworm, all in deadly seriousness." Stephen's dream became a 1,500-word short story called "Manacled." It was one of two good stories he managed to produce during this period. Crisply written, with echoes of *The Monster*'s humming, invitingly colored flames, it ended with the hobbled hero about to perish.

As the year wound down, Stephen seemed torn between his love of home and his need to escape. He made plans for an elaborate, old-fashioned Christmas party, complete with a ball and a play, while simultaneously trying to wrangle a correspondent's assignment to cover the Boer War in the Transvaal. He wanted to leave "early in the new year." He applied for a visa. He became increasingly suspicious of his publishers, whom he suspected of withholding payments. *Harper's*, he was sure, was "under the influence of the McClures" and would thus not pay more for his stories. He lost things, he forgot story titles. With so many words flying off his pen, he was confused about whether he had given the same story two titles, and sent it to two different publications or whether there were actually two stories. It was perhaps during this time that he began a story called "The Squire's Madness" — an unsuccessful tale about a writer living in a manor in Sussex and apparently losing his mind.

He was losing his publishers' respect, angering Stokes by continually asking for advances. He even succeeded in trying the patience of the saintly Pinker. Plagued with demands from both Cora and Stephen, who now asked him to deposit unearned money directly into Cora's account at

Lloyd's Bank in Oxted, Pinker finally snapped. "I confess that you are becoming most alarming," he wrote Stephen. "You telegraphed on Friday for
£20; Mrs. Crane, on Monday, makes it £50; today comes your letter making it £150, and I very much fear that your agent must be a millionaire if he
is to satisfy your necessities a week hence, at this rate." He had advanced
the Cranes £230 that he had not collected in sales. "I mention this to impress you less with an obligation to me than to yourself. There is a risk of
spoiling the market if we have to dump too many short stories on it at
once" — a comment to which Cora took great exception. "This is a fatal
thing to say to a writing man. Particularly to Stephen Crane," she wrote
back. Pinker could sell a thousand of his stories if he had them, she said; the
Whilomville stories were as good as cash. She and Stephen appreciated
what Pinker had done for them, but why did he not insist that publishers
"pay cash for Mr. Cranes stories?" "They have always had to pay cash before this." She and her husband would need "every possible pennie" Pinker
could send them in the next fortnight, and if Pinker did not deposit £40 in
Cora's bank account that very day (October 26), the Cranes would be issued a writ on an unpaid bill. And she told Pinker to write "all right" upon
receipt of her letter, "if you have sent £40 to my account at Oxted so that I
may be sure that this troublesome cheque is paid."

On November 4 Stephen sent Pinker "a double extra special good
thing" — a 1,500-word war tale that filled him with fresh hope. "It is so
good — for me," he wrote, "that I would almost sacrifice it to the best
magazine in England rather than see it appear in the best paying magazine." Nevertheless, he had calculated the word count in pencil on the
back of each page. Certain of the story's theatrical possibilities, he sent a
copy to the actor Sir Johnson Forbes-Robertson, "in an attempt" he told
Pinker, "to make him see that in a thirty minute sketch on the stage he
could so curdle the blood of the British public that it would be the sensation of the year, of the time." He continued, "I suppose many men stir
you with tumultuous sentiments concerning work which they have completed but — anyhow you take a copy of this story home with you and
read it, and let me know your opinion." He especially needed his agent's
praise on this one. "This is something which you do not always do," he
advised him. And he needed to hear promptly of sales, even the smallest
ones. Such news gladdened his heart, he said.

Written in lean, taut prose, "The Upturned Face," at first titled "Burial," depicts the burial of a soldier in the Spanish-American War. The

short short story derives its tension from the exposed face of the corpse, which unnerves the soldiers who are assigned to bury it. Using favorite words and imagery with chilling restraint — the face of the corpse is "chalk-blue"; a voice is reduced to a "babble" — Stephen achieved a powerful psychological portrait of what he called "the singing of the nerves." It was the best thing he had written in about a year, since his finest Spanish-American War tales, and perhaps as good as anything he had ever done. Composed amid so much hackwork and in a state of crumbling health, the tale was something of a miracle — a lone rose blooming in a garden of weeds.

He had first sketched the idea in a brief scene in "The Price of the Harness." But even before the war he'd discussed it with Conrad, who referred to it as "the 'Dead Man' story." In the two years leading up to its writing, Stephen had been drenched in sights of wounded and dead men — "fearsome sights that will shake you to the roots of your being," as Tolstoy wrote in *Sebastopol*. He had seen friends like Reuben McNab and Edward Marshall lying shot up and near death on the battlefield. "Well, of course . . . a man we've messed with all these years . . . impossible . . . you can't, you know, leave your intimate friends rotting on the field. . . . Go on, for God's sake, and shovel, *you*," he wrote in "The Upturned Face." But like *The Monster*, "The Upturned Face" was rooted deeply in Stephen himself. Though the story was fed by his experiences in the Greek and Cuban wars, it was also the product of Stephen's long awareness of his own illness — heightened just now, when the clockwork was jiggling badly — and his long preoccupation with death.

Just as Henry Fleming, on first encountering a corpse, circles the body and stares at it again and again, Stephen, in his fiction and war reporting, circled corpses, pondering the Question. Looking at the faces of wounded and dead soldiers in Greece and Cuba, he had considered "the terrible red of [a] man's face, which was of the quality of flame as it appears in old pictures." He had noted the "weary, weary, weary" expression of an injured man, the lack of nobility in a dead man's face. "There was expressed in this thing none of the higher thrills to incite, for instance, a company of romantic poets," he wrote at Velestino. He had observed the glances that reflected a "strange wonder and wistful questioning of the future." In a sense, "The Upturned Face" was Stephen's own burial tale, his shroud. It was all up with him; the undiscovered country beckoned. At the end of the story the reader is left with the image of the dead soldier's face and the bald sound of dirt falling on it — "plop."

16

THE RED ROOM

He decided to color everything in the porch room — walls, ceiling, and carpet — a "bright scarlet," said Mark Barr. Barr, a chemist, tried to dissuade Stephen with " 'scientific' reasons, determined by Charcot," but to no avail. Stephen had no interest in science, and he turned a deaf ear whenever Barr and H. G. Wells discussed it. His writing room would be red.

During Stephen's "hours of terrific work" in the red room (perhaps a metaphorical red, for it is uncertain whether Stephen went through with his proposed color scheme), Cora spared him "all interruption and annoyance," said Edith Ritchie. Either Edith or Cora would mix his drinks — one teaspoon of whiskey, the rest soda — which he nursed throughout his long sessions with the pen. He found he could not write on a typewriter after all. He lit one cigarette after another. Like the whiskey, the cigarettes served largely as a touchstone, something to steady him. He'd take one drag, then let the cigarette burn out while he wrote or talked. Then he'd relight it or toss it away. Edith, who spent five months with the Cranes, did not think Stephen smoked even six cigarettes a day.

When work was going well, he'd say, "This is good, by God it's good!" After work, if he felt well enough, he would gallop over the park on one of the bays. Perhaps once a week, Henry James bicycled the seven miles over from Rye. The Cranes and Edith went to Lamb House to tea. Edith later recalled an occasion when Stephen was winning an argument with James. James suddenly erupted: "'How old are you?' 'Twenty-seven,' said Stephen. 'Humph,' said Mr. James, 'prattling babe!'"

Stephen relished merriment and play, the noise of young people, and "delightfully foolish games like 'Animal Grab'" or Blind Man's Bluff, said Edith, which were played "in the beautiful panelled hall," which echoed with the sounds of "Stephen roaring like a lion, Cora twittering like a canary, Mr. Wells barking like a dog." When Henry James called, Edith was asked to sing. After a while, Cora would say, "Now, let's have a concert," and Edith would gather up the five puppies and resume singing and playing the piano while the puppies howled. The Cranes and Henry James would grow weak with laughter. When the house was full of company, everyone took turns telling stories around the great fireplace. As Stephen became excited, "the studied Americanisms" began to disappear from his deep voice, said Hueffer, and he would talk "a rather classical 'English.'" Sometimes, after Edith had gone to bed, Cora would knock on her bedroom door. "Stephen wants some music," she would say. "Slip into your dressing gown and bring your comb." First they would all raid the pantry — H. G. Wells and his wife, Joseph Conrad, A. E. W. Mason, perhaps — then sing through the tissue paper covering their combs while Stephen conducted with the toasting fork.

To Edith Ritchie, "Mummy Crane" and "Mr. Crane" seemed deeply in love, a couple in "perfect sympathy and understanding." Stephen "adored" Cora, Edith said. She had no inkling that they were not legally married.

Cora had suggested that Stephen "write a popular novel for money something that everyone will read" — a potboiler, she might have said. Stephen got angry. "I will write for one man," he said, "banging his fist on the table & that man shall be myself etc etc," Cora wrote in her notebook. He had written "The Upturned Face" for himself. He might have said the same of all his best work. Now, in November of 1899, the 80,000-word *Active Service*, which he'd described as "full of love and war," was published — and gave the lie to Stephen's claim that he wrote only to please himself. The story of a correspondent and newspaper editor named Rufus Coleman, who wins the girl he had earlier lost, Marjory Wainwright, after rescuing her and her family in the Greek war, the novel was as banal as Stephen's best work was original. While trying to convince himself of his seriousness of purpose, Stephen had in fact written it for money. This big book was strictly popular fare, and the worse for taking itself seriously. Here was Stephen Crane as Richard Harding Davis. Here was "the impact of a dollar upon the heart," as he had written in a poem.

In trying to write a novel that was part adventure story, part love story, Stephen was at odds with himself. As he'd once told Willa Cather, what he couldn't do, he couldn't do at all. Written around the first-rate short fiction that followed his natural bent, including "Death and the Child," Stephen's one superior story of the Greco-Turkish conflict, *Active Service* got the creative leavings. Though Stephen was inscribing profound experiences — his first exposure to war, his love affairs with Cora and Amy Leslie, and his sense of inferiority and unworthiness as a suitor of nice girls — the result was curiously shallow. Little of his inner life got into the text. He was perhaps too close to it all — still living it, almost — to have a novelist's necessary detachment. But one also senses that he lacked the impulse to write about the women in his life straight. As for writing about war — it was not to be used as a backdrop for romance.

Both the actress, Nora Black, and the professor's daughter, Marjory, are essentially female types of the sort found in ladies' magazines and bad plays. They have none of the feeling of the plain Texas bride or the amusement-park angel; Stephen's imagination had not pulled that hard. Devoid of irony, singular prose, and literary value, *Active Service* was ultimately a portrait of Stephen's life as he wished it could be. Rufus Coleman shares Stephen's disreputable aura (he is "rather — er — prematurely experienced"), works for a sleazy newspaper, and is suspected of drinking too much and carrying on with Nora Black. He suffers, as Stephen did, from the rumors about him — which is the whole point of this novel. Albeit unintentionally, through Coleman, Stephen rewrote his own history. Coleman resists the actress, gets the girl, and even wins over her parents. Furthermore, he is rich, reputed to earn $15,000 a year — more than three times what Marjory's professor father earns.

While working on the novel in February of 1899, Stephen had written a letter out of the blue to his old Syracuse professor, the Reverend Charles J. Little. Long ago, he said, the professor had heard some false information about him and had "told me to beware — that I was going very wrong indeed." Sounding the same note he had written in letters to William, Amy Leslie, Nellie Crouse, and others — sounding like Rufus Coleman, who tells Marjory Wainwright that he knows somebody has been telling her stories about him — he wrote, "I was worse than I should have been but I always had a singular faculty of having it said that

I was engaged in crimes which are not of my accomplishments. Indeed, this singular faculty has followed me out of college into real life." He wanted the professor to know that his kind interest in him had made a difference in his life — that it had in fact helped him form a "creed of conduct." He downplayed his career: "It is a little thing to talk about but I have written several little books. . . . It is indeed such a little thing"; he possessed "some silly talent." With *Active Service* Stephen had, in effect, returned to campus and proved his professors wrong about him.

He had tried to sound optimistic about the novel — "I am confident that it will be the most successful book that I have ever published," he wrote Pinker as he was finishing it. But he knew that it was rotten work. "I fear that in later years people who wish the house well will be saying that Stephen Crane did *not* write 'Active Service' in the room over the porch at Brede Place," he admitted to Moreton Frewen. He worried that the novel would "undermine whatever reputation for excellence I may have achieved up to this time," he told Clara Frewen. "May heaven forgive it for being so bad."

The early critical reaction was mixed. Praised in England for its "admirably sketched and sustained" characterizations, its "ingenious and entertaining" plot, its vivid descriptive writing and "invincible" American optimism, the novel was panned in the United States. The *New York Times* wondered "whether the author of 'Active Service' himself really sees anything remarkable in his news-papery hero." The *San Francisco Argonaut* found it "tiresome," the characters unreal "vulgarians masquerading in the guise of their betters." *Book News* told Stephen to stick to the battlefield. In the *Pittsburgh Leader*, Willa Cather wrote:

> Every page is like the next morning taste of a champagne supper, and is heavy with the smell of stale cigarettes. There is no fresh air in the book and no sunlight, only the "blinding light shed by the electric globes." . . . It is a grave matter for a man in good health and with a bank account to have written a book so coarse and dull and charmless as *Active Service*. Compared with this "War was kind" indeed.

✦

Miserable weather kept many of the local people away from the Cranes' grand Christmas party. A driving rainstorm, complete with thunder and lightning, was followed by a big snowfall. One who braved the icy roads, Charles Lewis Hind, editor of the *Academy*, remembered the halting trip up the hill to Brede village in the special omnibus Cora had hired from a London carriage maker to carry guests from the Rye railway station. "Again and again we had to alight and push, and each time we returned to our seats on top." But the cheeriness of the manor soon offset the cold outside. A fire burned in the cavernous central fireplace; lighted candles flickered against the richly paneled walls of the long hall, which Cora and Edith Ritchie had festooned with ropes of holly and greenery.

The festivities got under way on Christmas, with a traditional Christmas dinner in the old kitchen, below the puddings and hams hanging from the ceiling. The party consisted only of Mark Barr and his wife, Edith Ritchie and her parents, and A. E. W. Mason. Cora had put Stephen's favorite foods on the lavish menu: roast turkey stuffed with chestnuts, giblet gravy, cranberry sauce, a variety of vegetables, and an assortment of nuts and pies, all washed down with plenty of liquor — champagne, claret, and Green Mint. More houseguests began trickling in the next day, with some fifty people in attendance by the twenty-eighth. H. G. Wells and his wife, Jane, brought their own blankets and bedding as requested and captured one of the few private bedrooms available, a room overlooking the main gateway, which had a portcullis and an owl's nest. Mason also had a private room. He was warned to open its two massive doors with great caution, for one led directly into the chapel, where the Cranes stored apples; with no electric lights, a misstep in the dark would send him plunging some thirty feet down to the ground floor. Most of the other houseguests were put up in rooms dubbed the girls' and boys' dormitories, fitted with cots rented from a local hospital. "Husbands and wives were torn apart," said Wells. To reach the makeshift sanitary equipment indoors, the men had to walk through the girls' dormitory. "Consequently the wintry countryside next morning was dotted with wandering melancholy, preoccupied, men guests," wrote Wells. But the manor's primitiveness was no hindrance to the revelers' enjoyment. It "meant nothing to us, for we were all of us young," said Mason.

Most of the literary notables who'd been invited were absent. Conrad was unable to come; Robert Barr was not up to it. "I loathe a crowd," he explained in a letter to Cora. Henry James kept his distance. When Mason passed Lamb House in his dog cart, he found James standing apprehensively at the garden gate. James warned him about the actresses who were likely to be at the Cranes' party. "Some of those poor wantons have a certain haggard grace," James told him gravely.

"Surely there has never been such a house party," remembered Charles Lewis Hind. It began with the play, called *The Ghost* after Sir Goddard Oxenbridge. On the evening of December 28, after a brief rehearsal at the manor, the troupe gave a performance for the village children at the Brede schoolhouse. Then everyone trudged back through heavy snow for the real performance. Though the show was free of charge, the Cranes had had a program printed, and even tickets. Starring Mason as the Ghost, with assorted other guests making up the rest of the cast, the play depicted the Ghost of Brede appearing in disguise before a group of tourists a half a century in the future, in the year 1950.

The text consisted of "some awful rubbish" Stephen had written himself, with minor contributions from literary friends "to make the thing historic," he explained to H. B. Marriott-Watson. Stephen had spent months soliciting contributions from local writers, asking for even "a mere word — any word," such as " 'it,' 'they,' 'you,' " — anything at all to "identify themselves with this crime." Conrad submitted "This is a jolly cold world"; Edwin Pugh donated the memorable line "He died of an indignity caught while chasing his hat by the Strand." In this way the play, such as it was, had come about courtesy of what Stephen called a "distinguished rabble": Henry James, Robert Barr, George Gissing, Rider Haggard, Joseph Conrad, H. B. Marriott-Watson, H. G. Wells, Edwin Pugh, A. E. W. Mason, and Stephen Crane. Stephen lifted the music from Gilbert and Sullivan and borrowed the characters from works by the play's contributors: Dr. Moreau wandered in from Wells's *Island of Doctor Moreau*, Tony Drum was seized from Edwin Pugh's *Tony Drum, Cockney Boy*. Miranda was apparently taken from Mason's *Miranda of the Balcony* and Marriott-Watson's *Heart of Miranda*; Crane's own Rufus Coleman appeared on leave from *Active Service*; and so on. It was an "awful" play, said Hind, which greatly amused its participants.

Over the course of three days the Cranes' houseguests acted in the play or served as audience and "revelled until two or three every night," said Wells. They descended the stairs at midday for a breakfast of bacon and eggs, American sweet potatoes, and beer. Wells led a game of broomsticks on the slippery hall floor; Stephen contributed an American touch by trying to teach some of the men poker. When they failed to apply themselves seriously to the game, he was humorless. "In any decent saloon in America, you'd be shot for talking like that at poker," said the Kid from the Weary Gentleman Saloon. The kid was "profoundly weary," Wells realized in retrospect. At the time, in the midst of the "marvellous Christmas Party," Stephen seemed merely "sulky and reserved." Charles Lewis Hind saw him as a spectator rather than a participant at his own party, a quiet figure watching the merriment from a corner of the great hall fireplace — "not unamused, but very silent. He seemed rather bewildered by what had happened to him." Though Cora was attentive to the smallest detail — she and Edith wrote out cards daily, pairing dinner partners, which they left on the bed of each guest — she seemed an oddly "aloof" hostess. She did not appear until luncheon. "To tell the truth, she rather slopped about the house," said Mason. "We were, during that Christmas, chiefly a stag party and she certainly made no efforts by her dress, etc. to attract anyone." In Mason's eyes, "Crane seemed devoted to her and yet not in very close touch with her."

On the last evening, December 29, there was a ball. True to Henry James's prediction, dangerous girls turned up, though it is uncertain whether any were actresses. Hind would recall being "presented to bevies of beautiful American girls in beauteous frocks." Even Stephen danced that night. While the little orchestra brought in from London played tunes ranging from barn dances to waltzes, with titles like "Run Away Girl" and "The Belle of New York," the dancers moved through the long hall in the flattering light of dozens of candles fitted into huge iron sconces, which Cora had had custom-made by the village blacksmith. The sconces had not been provided with grease guards, however, and the dancers' backs developed a telltale sign — "a patch of composite candlewax, like flash on the coat of a Welsh Fusilier," said Wells.

In the night, after the guests had retired, Cora came to the Wellses' room. Stephen had suffered a lung hemorrhage, which he'd tried to hide from her. "He 'didn't want anyone to bother,'" Cora told Wells. She asked Wells to fetch a doctor. He climbed onto one of the manor's bicycles. "My last clear memory of that fantastic Brede House party is riding out of the cold skirts of a wintry night into a drizzling dawn along a wet road," he said later.

Cora asked Stephen whether he had enjoyed the party. Yes, he had, he told her, "every bit of it."

After the hemorrhage, he worked from bed. He plugged away at a new novel he referred to as an Irish romance. He inscribed copies of his books for strangers and friends ("A long 20th Century to you and yours," he wrote Margery Pease in a copy of *The Monster and Other Stories*) and promptly answered letters in his firm hand. News of *The Ghost* had gotten into the local papers, stirring up interest and creating more work for him. By some accounts the Christmas play written by Stephen Crane and a galaxy of important authors had real merit. Those who hadn't seen it called it "amusing," "original," "the most amazing play ever produced," and "a remarkable piece of literary patchwork," which had "lately been allowed to waste its sweetness on the Sussex air." Sir Beerbohm Tree wanted to know if *The Ghost* could follow *A Midsummer Night's Dream* at Her Majesty's Theatre. (A. E. W. Mason assured him that it could not.)

When the Frewens' son, Hugh, asked for a copy of the play, Stephen wrote a gracious letter on January 1, 1900, describing himself as "desolated by your request because I fear it is the result of a misunderstanding." The play "was a mere idle string of rubbish made to entertain the villagers and with music frankly stolen from very venerable comic operas such as 'The Mikado' and 'Pinafore.' The whole business was really beneath contempt to serious people and it would be inconsiderate, even unkind, of me to send it you. The names of the authors was more of a joke than anything." Less kindly, Cora said in a letter to Clara Frewen that they had had to write down for their intended audience. "You see we knew that to reach the back of the Sussex villagers heads it would have to be very simple." She invited the Frewens for a visit the following week.

Life at Brede Place proceeded in its characteristic way. The issuing of social invitations was exceeded only by pleas to Pinker for money. In a chatty letter to Clara Frewen, Cora said she was looking forward to the "very jolly" time they would have planning a maze and laying out the shrubbery. To Pinker on January 2 she casually mentioned that Stephen was "ill again" but working from bed. Aware of their indebtedness to the English agent, she was careful to include an expression of gratitude in the first urgent request for money in the new year: "I don't know what Mr. Crane would do without your kind help through these long days of trying to get straight," she wrote, and then asked that he immediately deposit twenty pounds in her account at Brown & Shipleys.

Three days later, Stephen's own hasty note to Pinker showed the strain of his illness:

> My Dear Pinker: I must have the money. I cant get on with-
> out it. If you cant send £50 by the next mail, I will have to

find a man who can. I know this is abrupt and unfair but self-preservation forces my game with you precisely as it did with Reynolds.

Yours faithfully,

S. Crane

A startled Pinker, who had sent a check for twenty pounds on the same day Stephen wrote his threatening note, responded with a telegram asking whether Stephen was breaking their agreement. The Cranes were baffled. "Mr. Crane intended no threat and will keep all engagements made with you," wrote Cora. "He does not understand what your telegram means and it has quite upset his days work." She insisted that Stephen always honored his agreements, and she urged Pinker to deposit another thirty pounds in her bank account. Pinker remained steadfast, supplying them with what money he could. "I am sure it is not necessary for me to tell you that you and Mr. Crane may always count on all the help I can give, but as you know, the demands on my help have been greater in extent and persistency than was ever contemplated," he wrote in conclusion.

In early February a county magistrate and bibliophile named Thomas Parkin gave a luncheon in Stephen's honor at Fairseat, his estate in Hastings. One of the guests, a Miss Bothem-Edwards, was shocked by Stephen's appearance. "Already months ago . . . it was easy to see that Stephen Crane's years, if not months, were numbered," she wrote later. Now, at the luncheon, the contrast between his looks and those of the other guests was "painful. . . . Poor Stephen Crane had that white, worn-out, restless look betokening complete nervous exhaustion. He took no tea and did not join in general conversation, but moved about uneasily as if in search of something he could not find."

He was then grinding out chapter after chapter of a new novel, a swashbuckling tale about an Irish blade named the O'Ruddy, written as a satiric romance. Stokes had agreed to take the Irish romance in place of the now abandoned Revolutionary War novel and Methuen would take it as the unspecified novel Stephen had contracted to write for them. At the same time Stephen was keeping his eye on the Boer War. In January, scarcely a week after his hemorrhage, the *New York Journal* published a thoughtful piece by him protesting the censorship of correspondents in the Transvaal. More of his thoughts on the war appeared in the *Journal* in February, and he even queried the paper about a correspondent's assignment, telling them that his health had improved. But "the good thing in his life had slipped by him," said H. G. Wells. And Stephen knew it.

In print he had never been more visible. Along with *Active Service* and *The Monster and Other Stories*, his short fiction and nonfiction were appearing on both sides of the Atlantic. The strange little-man tale he'd written in 1893, "The Reluctant Voyagers," was syndicated in American newspapers; a deadly dry series called "Great Battles of the World," for which Stephen was paid $1,000, was appearing under his name in *Lippincott's Magazine*.* *Harper's Magazine* published another Whilomville tale, "The Knife"; *Ainslee's Magazine* ran "The Upturned Face."

Reviewers weighed in with both praise and indictments of his writing. In the *Criterion*, Rupert Hughes reaffirmed his long-standing faith in Crane's "genius," in spite of the writer's "grammatical carelessness," which at times amounted to "absolute illiteracy." The flaws in his work notwithstanding, "Mr. Crane seems to me to be the most definite and individual of all our book-writers, and I credit him with having written some of the best pages America has contributed to literature." One reviewer rejected *The Monster* as "grim" and "unpleasant." Julian Hawthorne, in *Book News*, said it was "an outrage on art and humanity. Something is fundamentally out of gear in a mind that can reconcile itself to such a performance." As for the novella's comic touches, Stephen had thrown them away by writing about "the tiny trivialities of a New York country town." In February Stephen was cited in an article in the *Literary Digest* as a writer "of the new school" who carried his literary descriptions to extremes in order "to be vivid and striking." And the point was illustrated with a passage from *The Red Badge*, the book Stephen could not escape.

By the end of March Stephen had finished twenty-four chapters of the romance. He had continued to write more about the Boer War for the *Journal* and had put what appears to be the merest of finishing touches — the occasional use of favorite words like "oath" and "swarmed" — to Kate Lyon's hastily assembled "Great Battles" tales, which meant "sure quick money." He had arranged to write "little Cora" stories for *Harper's Bazaar*. These Whilomville tales, borrowing from stories Cora had told Stephen about her own childhood, would pay "$50 per thousand words for the American serial rights." But there was never enough money. A request in March that Pinker deposit £15 "to my wife's credit at Brown

* Kate Lyon was researching and actually drafting these histories, presumably without remuneration; they were virtually unrecognizable as Crane's work.

Shipleys" was followed four days later with a reminder that Stephen would need "a good sum" — in fact £100. Pinker was to wire his response "rather ambiguously because my post-master is my grocer," wrote Stephen. Alfred Plant had to "have ten pounds to pay some Oxted man"; and "£22 before Wednesday or a bailiff will be here and also deposit £20 to my wife's a/c at Brown Shipley." Though Methuen had paid Stephen a £70 advance for the romance (Cora had asked for another advance, which was refused), he worked on it reluctantly. He worried that he had made a mistake by "abandoning my lucrative short story game for this long thing which doesn't pay (much) until the end." Still, he expected the novel "to pull me out much more than even," he told Pinker.

Conrad would remember "a flying visit" Stephen made to Pent Farm when both writers were overwhelmed with worry. He turned up looking "harassed," stretched out on the couch, and fell into one of his silences. Conrad pulled up a chair. He was reminded of Stephen's great opening line in "The Open Boat." The men in the dinghy, absorbed by their endless rowing and ever watchful of the danger of overturning, could not see anything above water level. Suddenly Conrad spoke: "None of them knew the colour of the sky."

Stephen sat bolt upright. The words seemed familiar, but he looked as though he couldn't place them.

"Don't you know that quotation?" Conrad asked him.

Suddenly he did. "The startled expression passed off his face. 'Oh, yes,' he said quietly, and lay down again."

On March 31, Cora left Brede Place to meet Helen Crane in Paris. After less than a year at the school, and against her parents' better judgment, Helen was leaving Lausanne. In a letter enclosed with chapters 24 and 25 of the Irish romance, Stephen asked Pinker to send Cora twenty pounds at the Hotel St. Petersburg so that the two women would not be stranded there.

Two hours after Cora departed for Paris, Stephen began hemorrhaging. Without his knowledge, the cook, Vernall, sent Cora a telegram. Cora flew into action. She wired to William Crane, Moreton Frewen, Lafayette Hoyt de Friese, an American friend living in London, and the American Embassy in London before returning to Brede with Helen. The embassy's secretary, Henry White, sent a nurse and a prominent physician, Dr. J. T. Maclagen, to Brede at Cora's expense.

She and Helen took the night boat across the English Channel and arrived home to find Stephen in alarming condition. After the first hemorrhage, he suffered a series of hemorrhages over about nine days. She engaged two nurses. She wrote Dr. Maclagen a check for fifty pounds, then wrote a note to *Lippincott's Magazine* asking for an advance on the next battle article to cover it. "I don't think they will hesitate as it was a matter of saving Stephen Crane's life," she wrote Pinker. She did not sleep for three days, except to nap.

On April 11, Stephen was moved to the downstairs hall. From here he could more easily be taken outside into the sunshine on warm days once his health improved. "He seems to get weaker every day and my anxiety is very great," Cora wrote Clara Frewen. "There has been no return of hemorrhage but he suffers so horribly from the abscess, which is too deep-seated to open from the outside while he is in such a weak state."

Cora took over all of Stephen's literary correspondence, and wrote to Pinker and anyone else who might advance or lend money — even those who clearly could not, notably Conrad. In an anguished letter, Conrad wrote that his future was "already pawned" to his publishers. Kate Lyon professed herself willing to do whatever she could to get the writing "in a shape that won't positively disgrace Stephen." Though he had not been representing Crane lately, Paul Revere Reynolds had sold a piece on the Boer War for one hundred dollars — fifty dollars more than Stephen had asked him to get — and said he was willing to advance Stephen money on stories before they were sold, as Pinker did. But his medical bills piled up. Cora was soon writing Reynolds for money but without offering any stories. William insisted that he had no money to send, his bank account was "very much depleted," but he suggested that Stephen and Cora come to America and stay with his family during Stephen's convalescence. He complained about getting the news of his brother's health from the London dispatches in the morning papers. "We find this unsatisfactory," he wrote.

In her letters Cora shifted from optimism to frank expressions of worry, writing lucidly to one person and unclearly to another. Having begun a letter to Clara Frewen with a candid account of Stephen's health, she veered off into a newsy ramble about some outdoor improvements to be made at Brede — even illustrating the letter with sketches of the manor and hill and of an old battle-ax found on the property. Kate Lyon was alarmed. "My dearest girl," she wrote in early April, "*what* is the matter with Stephen? I could not tell from your letter." In her letters to Pinker, Cora was careful to sound optimistic: Dr. Maclagen "was so encouraging that I am glad." But a note from the doctor suggests that he was in fact trying to keep Cora's spirits up, probably at Stephen's request, while not encouraging her to think that he could recover. Stephen seemed improved and was even taking "his nourishment well," Cora wrote to Pinker — on the same day she told Clara Frewen that Stephen seemed weaker by the day. She reassured the agent that Stephen's contractual obligations would be fulfilled — "I have notes of end of novel so it could be finished & no one will lose — if that thought should occur," she wrote in April. Pinker was upset about Cora's high-handed extravagance, but she insisted that the large expenditures for a specialist and nurses and medicines were necessary. "Now, Mr. Pinker," she wrote on April 11:

> It was a matter of life & death to have the Specialist down. I
> could not leave any stone unturned. You might not have gone
> to office on Saturday or Friday. I had to write to Lippincott at
> the same time I wrote you. One cannot stand upon ceremony
> at such a moment, and indeed I was almost distracted. Pray
> forgive my seeming lack of courtesy to yourself.

By mid-April, she was reporting to both Pinker and H. G. Wells that the doctors were hopeful — provided that Stephen could get through ten days without another hemorrhage. "He is much better & very cheerful," she wrote Wells on the fifteenth. He was even reading his mail "for the first time." She told Pinker that the doctor said Stephen could work in about three weeks' time, though he would first need to recover somewhere on the sea for a few weeks. She considered Bournemouth, then St. Helena, and finally Badenweiler, Germany, in the Black Forest, recommended by one of the specialists, Dr. Mitchell Bruce. The plans for Stephen's recuperation became steadily more elaborate and expensive.

When Stephen seemed strong enough, the servants carried his bed outside to a sheltered spot under a corner of the house, where he could take the sun and fresh air considered essential to recovery from tuberculosis. A. E. W. Mason was a frequent visitor now. Stephen asked him to read the Irish romance and consider finishing it, "since he would not be alive to do so." Stephen was not looking forward to the trip to Badenweiler, though Mason noticed that he pretended to for Cora's sake. Mason understood that the doctor considered Stephen's recovery virtually hopeless. At least one of the doctors blamed the primitiveness of Brede Place, with its lack of indoor plumbing and its poor ventilation, for some of the damage to Stephen's health. There was some truth in this, but Brede was not the cause of his illness.

Before leaving for the Black Forest, Stephen drew up a new will with Alfred Plant to replace the one he had written in a letter to William from Jacksonville only three and a half years earlier. With his nurse, Charlotte E. Gardner, witnessing, Stephen named Cora his sole beneficiary until her death or remarriage, in which event half of Stephen's income would be held in trust for his namesake, Edmund's infant son Stephen, and the other half divided equally between Edmund and William. Cora was to receive all of his personal belongings. The careful wording — Cora was called "my dear wife Cora Howarth Crane" rather than simply "my wife" — was an effort to protect Cora's legal rights in the event that someone came forward with proof that they were not married. William and Plant were to be coexecutors and trustees, with Plant investing any remaining monies after Stephen's debts were paid.

"Stephen is not up to letter writing so I am answering your very cheerful letter to him," Cora wrote Wells on April 25. Stephen still had the "dreadful abscess" in either his bowels or his rectum, she wrote uncertainly, which was causing him terrible suffering and an "alarming" loss of strength. He again had "Cuban fever." Dr. Bruce, who had recommended the Nordrach treatment in Badenweiler, examined Stephen's lungs and pronounced the right lung "unaffected" — an astounding diagnosis that Cora readily believed. Dr. Maclagen, who apparently had not examined Stephen recently, advised Cora in a letter to keep her husband home, at least "for the next 2 months."

Until virtually the hour of their departure for the Black Forest, Cora sent out appeals for money. She considered renting out Brede. She kept up the pressure on Pinker: the English climate was "simply death to lung Trouble," but Stephen "has a chance to get well & live for years if we can get him out of England." She even cabled John Hay at the War Department in Washington for a few hundred dollars to save Stephen's life. Moreton Frewen and Lady Randolph Churchill started a fund for Stephen's Badenweiler trip. Frewen wrote to John Hay, Joseph Pulitzer, and J. P. Morgan. Andrew Carnegie donated fifty pounds. William Crane insisted that he could not help, but encouraged Cora and Stephen to come to Port Jervis or go to New Mexico. "My wife would love to nurse him back to health," William added. He would try to locate his copy of *A Consumptive's Struggle for Life* to send Stephen, and he recommended Dr. Howe's breathing tube, which had helped him. "Stephen can tell you that I have blown on Dr. Howe's tube over twenty years, and I am sure that it has done me great good," he wrote Cora.

Just before they left Brede, Cora told Conrad the truth and asked him to come to Dover to see Stephen off. The night before, Jessie had had a dream about Stephen. It had been months since he had written, and neither she nor Conrad had heard that his health had worsened. And yet in her dream Stephen was being spirited away "to some seaport town a long distance from Brede Place" by invalid carriage, stopping somewhere en route to change the horses that had been driven so gently along the road. The dream had been so vivid, she said later, that she woke Conrad to tell him about it. Then came Cora's letter.

"I have Conrad very much on my mind now," Stephen dictated to Cora in a letter to Henry Sanford Bennett. Stephen said that he had been thinking about how the Civil List might help his friend. He understood that the List did not exclude English residents who were born outside the country from receiving financial assistance. "Garnett does not think it likely that his writing will ever be popular outside the ring of men who write." Conrad "is poor and a gentleman and proud. His wife is not strong and they have a kid. If Garnett should ask you to help pull wires for a place on the Civil List for Conrad please do me the last favor of talking about it to that relative of yours who has something to say about these things. I am sure you will."

Stephen left Brede Place on the morning of May 15, when the park was in bloom. Cora's roses mingled now with the park's primroses and azaleas. ("I am sure when the time comes that you go into residence we will always be remembered by our rose garden," Cora had written the Frewens less than eighteen months earlier.) Stephen left England with an entourage, as he had entered it less than two years earlier, consisting now of nurses Annie Taylor and Charlotte Gardner, the Cranes' manservant, Richard Heather, Helen Crane, Dr. Ernest B. Skinner, a local doctor, Cora, and his favorite dog, Sponge, a dog with "soul," said Edith Ritchie. In Stephen's most recent photograph, taken at Brede, Sponge had sat alongside him on a bench in the sunlight against the gray house. Stephen, dressed in jacket and tie, patterned flat hat, and English riding boots, smiled down at the black dog.

In agony from the terrible abscess in his bowels, which required "constant care," said Cora, Stephen was carried on an air mattress atop a stretcher in a carriage to Rye, where the party changed horses and took a special invalid carriage on to Dover. They settled into the Lord Warden Hotel overlooking the sea, where Stephen would rest for an indefinite period before continuing across the Channel. He had brought along the unfinished manuscript of the romance and dictated to Cora when he was able.

The new passport application he had shakily signed in Dover suggests that a physical transformation had occurred during these long years of wandering. Instead of measuring five feet eight inches, he was inaccurately described as five feet ten inches tall and twenty-nine years old — as if his odyssey had lengthened, as well as aged him. His complexion, on his various passports, had likewise gradually changed from "clear" to "medium" to "dark," and his eyes from "grey" to "grey blue" to "Lt. blue." The full mouth adorned with a drooping tawny mustache was now "ordinary."

Friends came to Dover to see the shadow in the bed. Wells found Stephen "lying still and comfortably wrapped about before an open window" overlooking the blue sea. "He was thin and gaunt and wasted, too weak for more than a remembered jest and a greeting and good wishes." Henry James, whose agitation about the dying man was "painful to witness," said Ford Madox Hueffer, was unable to come. Hoyt de Friese was "broken-hearted. . . . Seldom in my life have I found such affection for *anyone* . . . and now to lose him in his very youth! I can't realize or believe it." Robert Barr, who had thought since Stephen's hemorrhage at the Christmas party that it was "all over with the boy, he might last two years," brought along a promising young novelist named Stewart Edward White, whom he thought could finish Stephen's novel. Mason had declined to do it, so Stephen had asked Barr, who was reluctant. Barr and White put up at the Lord Warden but were forbidden by the doctor to see Stephen until the next day. They passed the evening reading Stephen's manuscript, written "in Crane's beautiful handwriting," remembered Barr.

"There was a thin thread of hope that he might recover, but to me he looked like a man already dead," Barr wrote soon after seeing Stephen. As he spoke, in a voice scarcely above a whisper, the best of him emerged; there was "all the accustomed humour in his sayings," said Barr. Stephen told Barr that he looked unnatural without a cigarette in his hand "and urged me to light one so that he could have a sniff of it, and condemned his physician." Then he told Barr to light his pipe "so that he might caress the bowl of it."

Having been instructed by both Cora and the doctor "to agree to anything Stephen asked," Barr unhappily consented to finish the novel, adding that Stephen "could not have made a worse choice." In his whispering voice Stephen said "he was well acquainted with my self-conceit, and did not credit in the least my assumption of incapacity." He accused Barr of being afraid of the critics. If Barr split "the last sentence he had written," said Stephen, he might jump in from there. "They'll all think you began with a new chapter, so you can defy them to point out the junction." Stephen wasn't sure how the novel should end, except that it should be at Brede Place, which he had written into the story.

In Cora's presence, Stephen played along with Barr's talk of visiting him in Germany that summer. They would take "some convalescent rambles together" in the Schwarzwald, said Barr. "I'll look forward to that," said the dim voice. Then Stephen smiled and winked. Finally he told Cora, "Don't you understand that men want to be alone together sometimes?"

After Cora left the room, Stephen spoke freely. "Robert, when you come to the hedge — that we must all go over — it isn't bad," he said. "You feel sleepy — and — you don't care. Just a little dreamy curiosity — which world you're really in — that's all."

When the Conrads arrived in Dover, Jessie and little Borys stayed with Cora while Conrad went alone to see Stephen, his "old Pard." "One glance at that wasted face" told him the story. The trip to the Black Forest "was the most forlorn of all hopes," Conrad said later. Nevertheless he "put on jolly manners" during the twenty minutes they spent together. Stephen looked out the window at the blue Channel. "How beautiful life is," he said. His last words to Conrad, "breathed out" in what remained of his voice, were, "I am tired. Give my love to your wife and child." Conrad left him, then paused at the door to look back. Stephen had "turned his head on the pillow" so that he was facing the sea, where "the sails of a cutter yacht glided slowly across the frame, like a dim ghostly shadow against a grey sky." Conrad and Jessie spent some time trying to comfort Cora and said their last goodbye. Afterward Conrad poured out his heart to his wife. Stephen's appearance had deeply affected him: "It is the end, Jess. He knows it is all useless. He goes only to please Cora, and he would rather have died at home!"

On May 24 the entourage crossed the English Channel to Calais, then took a salon carriage to Basel, Switzerland, where they rested for a few days at the expensive Hotel Trois Rois. Even at Dover, Cora had been skipping meals to ensure that their money would get them to Badenweiler. It was all turning out to be more costly than she'd been told. She was hard hit by the six francs a day at the Hotel Trois Rois and the extra charges due to Stephen's illness. From Basel the little party traveled the final thirty kilometers to Badenweiler. The carriage moved past beautiful scenery that Stephen could only have glimpsed: mountainsides rising from fields that would be blanketed in giant sunflowers later in the summer. On and on went the carriage, carrying its passengers about 1,400 feet up the Blauen Mountain into the southern Black Forest, the Markegrafferland. Then they ascended winding hills into Badenweiler, a fairy-tale village nestled in the forest with a wonderful view of the Alps. The air smelled of flowers. The town was situated in what is known as the Dreilandereck, where Switzerland, France and Germany meet, a European counterpart to Port Jervis, set at the corner of New York, Pennsylvania, and New Jersey.

They took rooms at the Villa Eberhardt, Hans Luisenstrasse 44, at the bottom of a steep hill. Stephen's stretcher had to be carefully angled and supported up a series of steps for the final ascent into the house. All around, the dark, pine-covered hills rolled like waves, with the same bluish cast as the hills around Port Jervis.

It was May 28. Stephen had journeyed 600 miles from East Sussex, and 3,850 miles from where he had started in America, his strength leaving him, it is fair to say, with every jostle and bump of the carriage.

Even after the carriage stopped, the movement in his head was unending. He relived his life; he continued his novel. Words marched like troops through his mind. "Upon our arrival at the little wayside inn, I left the devoted Doctor Chord and my long sword. Paddy, Jem and I then proceeded to find Strammers —" he dictated in a whisper to Cora. The hero of his novel, the O'Ruddy, had entered a green garden, a "little special rose garden." Lady Mary was weeping there. Horses galloped, people ran. Cora took down the words on folded sheets of Lord Warden stationery.

When she was not attending to Stephen or serving as his amanuensis, Cora wrote letters, including an appeal to Pinker for money, and jotted words down in a notebook. There were things she wanted to remember, and perhaps write, about Stephen — scraps of his talk, things he'd told her about his childhood and life, her own perceptions. "A worshiper of everything beautiful in life, he could see rosy lights under the most sordid clouds and had the moral courage to write his true impressions." She quoted him: "The true artist is the man who leaves pictures of his own time as they appear to him."

From England, Moreton Frewen sent a welcome twenty-five pounds. Cora responded with a long letter on June 3. "I've only sad news to write you," she began. "There seems little hope of cure."

Stephen was now under the care of Dr. Albert Frankel, who at thirty-six was head of the Hilaherin sanatorium in Badenweiler. He was an eminently qualified physician, well trained in the study of both tuberculosis and heart disease and active in the Heidelberg Institute of Pharmacology. Like Dr. Trudeau, Frankel had contracted tuberculosis himself as a young man, and he brought a special empathy and understanding to the treatment of consumption patients. But something about this particular young patient affected him deeply: his "hard suffering," the "singular personality" that shone through it. Dr. Frankel told Cora that Stephen had "the most wonderful eyes he ever saw: 'They read the world' he said."

Stephen's case sufficiently alarmed Frankel that he requested a consultation with Professor Brueiler of Freiburg, to whom Dr. Mitchell Bruce had written before advising Cora to take Stephen to Badenweiler. Frankel could not understand "why the lung trouble was not discovered when Mr. Crane was examined in Dec.," Cora wrote Moreton Frewen.

Nothing brought down Stephen's fever. The nurses changed his sheets as often as three times a day, Cora wrote Frewen, adding that the fever was "not due alone to the lung but is the remains of the yellow fever and the Cuban fever" — proof, perhaps, that she was still not seeing that Stephen had tuberculosis. She must attribute his symptoms to something else, such as the war, which lent blamelessness and self-sacrifice to the tragedy. "My husbands brain is never at rest," she wrote Frewen. "He lives over everything and talks aloud constantly. It is too awful to hear him try to change places in the 'open boat!!' " She was going mad listening to him, she said. The nurses finally gave her something to help her sleep.

"Visions of his past were sweeping through Coleman's mind precisely as they are said to sweep through the mind of a drowning person," Stephen had written in *Active Service*. In his delirium he played with the rector's children. When he bobbed again to the surface of consciousness, he worried so much about money that Cora lied to him, saying she had three hundred pounds in cash. In the new novel, the O'Ruddy finally got some missing papers he was after: "If I lose them I will lose my life at the same time," he cried. Stephen continued to dictate the words. "I myself do not care for the collection of papers, but I like riding in the open air on a good horse." Stephen's idea of happiness.

In the evening of June 3, Cora wrote again to Moreton Frewen — a distracted note about an army canteen she'd invented. A technical engineer had been testing it, and Cora hoped Frewen would invest. "Stephen is not quite clear in his mind tonight," she added in closing.

That day Stephen dictated more of the romance, now called *The O'Ruddy*. It was becoming less coherent. "Look under it & you'll find him," Cora wrote, then added a question mark in parentheses. The narrative was filled with action — people scampered, rode horses. A horse went lame. Men on horses galloped through a Sussex rain while wind swept the tops of the hedges. Then the men rode more carefully, through the darkening English landscape toward their destination.

Stephen had almost reached his own destination. On June 4 he told Cora, "I leave her gentle, seeking to do good, firm, resolute, impregnable." He said he wished to be buried with his parents, at the Evergreen Cemetery in Elizabeth, New Jersey. Cora cabled William, telling him that Stephen was near death.

He had come to the hedge. The doctor gave him a shot of morphine to ease the way, and Cora saw it go to his heart, saw his muscles contract. The doctor then tried to revive the heart with a camphor injection, but he was gone. Stephen Crane died at three in the morning on June 5, 1900 — "the same sinister hour which carried away our friend Frederic nineteen months before," wrote Robert Barr. He was twenty-eight years old, the age his beloved sister Agnes had been when she died so many years earlier.

"It was only the last year that he overcame his bashfulness about hearing the sound of his own voice," Cora wrote in her notebook. "Beautiful hands & glad his hair was cut during illness so he would not be a bald old man."

Joseph Conrad, who kept a picture of Stephen on his desk, liked to remember his friend as he was in life — young and on a day when he was feeling well. On the Conrads' first visit to Brede Place, he had ridden out on one of the large bays to meet them — Joseph, Jessie, and Borys riding in the open trap while he trotted alongside. Never looking better than when he was on horseback, said Conrad, and proud of his seat in the saddle, Stephen was happy that day. As he kept pace with the trap, Conrad said, "If you give the boy your seat I will be perfectly satisfied." And Stephen smiled all the way to the door.

EPILOGUE

INTERPRETERS

He would have smiled at the picture. There he was laid out in a stable behind the undertaker's shop in London. Horses occupied a few of the stalls; his coffin stood in another. The silence was punctuated by their snuffling. The religious symbolism of the stable would not have been lost on him. He might have thought, too, of Henry Johnson, bowed and faceless, his head swathed in a heavy crepe veil. A broken figure sitting on a box behind Dr. Trescott's stable, to be tormented by little boys. Stephen's own box had been fitted with a little glass pane for viewing the corpse — the upturned face.

Curtis Brown was in London when Stephen's body returned from Badenweiler. Having received a card telling him that he could see the body on a certain day at 82 Baker Street — "just opposite to where Sherlock Holmes was supposed to have lived," wrote Brown — he went to pay his last respects. He presented the card to a woman in the undertaker's small shop, and she said, "Outside, under the archway." He passed through the stable yard cluttered with carts to get to Stephen's coffin in the stall. The coffin was supported by trestles, and the face Curtis Brown saw through the glass told a tale of great suffering. The body was alone in the stable; no other visitors came. Brown lingered a while, "thinking over our talks together; and then went slowly away, with a heavy heart."

Stephen was buried in the Crane family plot in Elizabeth, following a Methodist funeral at the Central Metropolitan Temple on Seventh Avenue in New York, where President Grant had worshiped after his retirement from office. Frederic Lawrence and Stephen's old landlady from 1064 Avenue A were there; Willis Brooks Hawkins and Ripley Hitchcock were two of the pallbearers. All of Stephen's brothers came except Townley. His sister Nellie Murray-Hamilton arrived carrying a bouquet of blue pansies, Stephen's favorite flower. Cora was swathed "in heavy mourning." On this hot day, June 28, the small church was only a third to half full — the newspaper accounts varied. To the young Wallace Stevens, covering the service for the *New York Tribune*, it was a depressing affair. The mourners looked down at the heel, the prayers were "perfunctory, the choir worse than perfunctory with the exception of its hymn 'Nearer My God to Thee,'" and the address was "absurd." Afterward, no one in the street seemed to pay any attention to the hearse and small entourage of carriages clattering over the hot cobbles. Stevens "realized much that I had doubtingly suspected before — There are few hero-worshippers," he told his diary. "Therefore, few heroes," he added later.

In four years Stephen had published five novels, two volumes of poetry, three big story collections, two books of war stories, and countless works of short fiction and reporting. And yet in three years he had earned just over $1,200 for his entire American output, at a time when the country's per capita income was $1,200 annually.* He had received £20 from the English sales of *The Red Badge of Courage* — apparently from the goodness of Heinemann's heart, since Crane's contract had not been amended to include an author's provision for foreign rights.

Stephen Crane quickly became the stuff of legend. The rumors that had started even before his death now grew more fabulous. The *New York Evening Sun* suggested that Stephen wrote *The Red Badge* in three days. (In time the figure would be ten days.) Stephen himself was "the outcast child of an eminent family in New York, an Australian sailor, a German actor and an ex-convict," in one account. A favorite story told how Crane had been drafted by a professional baseball team — a tale that perhaps originated in a comment Stephen himself made in a *Leslie's Weekly* interview: "They used to say at Syracuse that I was cut out to be a professional baseball player." At Syracuse an inscription appeared in the cupola where Stephen had presided over the smoking outlaws: "sunset 1891 May / Steph Crane." Many years later a Delta Upsilon brother named

---

* Joseph Katz, "The Estate of Stephen Crane," *Studies in American Fiction* 10 (2): 135–50 (Autumn 1982).

Frederick D. Hopkins said that he had seen another brother, Lewis Edward Collings, cut the legend into the wall himself sometime around 1907, as a practical joke. But the story stuck: the inscription was genuine.

Though most of the stories about Stephen Crane tended toward the romantic, uglier rumors about his drug use and alcoholism also persisted, fueled in part by the New York police vendetta against him in the wake of the Dora Clark affair — a crusade that lasted long after Stephen's death. The stories were fueled, too, by jealousy (Hamlin Garland said in print that he feared Stephen had taken opium) and by Stephen's unwholesome appearance, which may have been mistaken for the seedy thinness and sallowness of a morphine addict or drunk. Nearly a century after his death, his name is still disfigured.

Most ridiculous was the frequently leveled charge that Crane had not fulfilled his early promise. Even Joseph Conrad would say that Stephen's death was a greater loss to his friends than it was to literature: if he had lived, there would have been no "further possible revelation." (Conrad was "horribly" upset by Stephen's death, which delayed his own work, he admitted. And he remained so devoted to Stephen's memory that he wrote about him for publication, even without payment.) H. G. Wells said that "even before his death, Crane's right to be counted in the hierarchy of those who have made a permanent addition to the growing fabric of English letters was not only assured, but conceded." Edward Garnett believed that Stephen Crane's genius would receive only "grudging, inadequate recognition" — a result of the mediocrity of American literary taste, he added.

The Red Badge of Courage — that accursed, damnable book, in Stephen's view, which had pegged him as a war writer just as he was bursting from the starting gate and eclipsed everything he did afterward — would be popularly regarded as his only masterpiece, though several of his stories are worthy of that medal. Few writers could match any one of Crane's great short works — "The Blue Hotel," "The Bride Comes to Yellow Sky," "The Open Boat," "The Upturned Face," *The Monster* — even in the course of a long career. The best of his war tales — "The Price of the Harness," "Marines Signaling Under Fire at Guantanamo" — are masterful. Had Stephen Crane lived, wrote A. J. Liebling in a 1961 *New Yorker* piece, he "might have been the great correspondent that the First World War failed to produce." "I do not think that American criticism has yet done justice to the unsurpassable beauty of Crane's best writing," said H. G. Wells. "And when I write those words, *magnificent, unsurpassable*, I mean them fully. He was, beyond dispute, the best writer of our generation, and his untimely death was an irreparable loss to our literature." Willa Cather, who never blinked when appraising Crane's work, praised him for "dealing altogether with the surfaces of things, but in a manner all his own. He died young, but he had done something real. One can read him today."

In 1901, the year after Stephen's death, both Lily Brandon Munroe and Amy Leslie remarried. Not long after her last tearful meeting with Stephen in Washington, D.C., Lily had divorced her first husband. She became Mrs. George F. Smillie and settled into a happily married long life in Norristown, Pennsylvania. Still a beautiful woman at the age of almost eighty, she remembered Stephen Crane as "the most sincere and natural person she had ever known." True to Stephen's prediction, every time she saw the ocean, she thought of him.

At the age of forty-five, Amy Leslie married seventeen-year-old Frank Buck, a bellboy at the Virginia hotel, where she had long lived. The Chicago newspapers, who printed Buck's age as twenty-something, amused themselves with the story of the prominent drama critic and the bellboy, "the boy bridegroom." Almost fourteen years later, Buck filed for divorce, "charging cruelty," according to the *Chicago Daily News*. And yet the couple remained lifelong loyal friends. In his 1941 memoir, Buck, now famous as the Bring 'Em Back Alive man, called Amy Leslie "the finest woman I ever knew."

Of Stephen Crane, Amy Leslie would say nothing. Her silence — and her anger when asked about him — perhaps spoke more eloquently than anything she might have said. When a former *Daily News* colleague, Vincent Starrett, who was writing a monograph on Crane, ran into her on the street and asked whether she would let him read any of his letters she might have saved, she snapped, "Certainly not!" and swept off. Ashton Stevens, who took over Starrett's Crane research, recklessly inquired about the letters while in a private dining room with the drama critic "and was threatened with a wine bottle," said Starrett.

Theodore Roosevelt turned so completely against Crane that even years after the writer's death, when Roosevelt was president, he talked about Crane with hot disgust. Jimmy Hare, the news photographer who had known Stephen in Cuba, was on a train with Roosevelt when one of the president's secretaries, George B. Cortelyou, handed the president a copy of Crane's collection of Cuban war tales, *Wounds in the Rain*. A Hare biographer related what happened next.

"You knew this fellow Crane rather well, didn't you, Jimmy?" said Roosevelt.

"Yes, sir, very well indeed," said Hare.

Roosevelt clicked his teeth.

"I remember him distinctly myself. When I was police commissioner of New York I once got him out of serious trouble."

Jimmy Hare recalled the story but misplaced it as something connected to Crane's research for *Maggie*.

"Nonsense!" thundered the president. "He wasn't gathering any data! He was a man of bad character and he was simply consorting with loose women."

Red-faced with anger, Hare rose to his feet. "That is absolutely not so! Nothing could be farther from the truth," he told the president.

"Roosevelt stared, and Cortelyou gasped," wrote Hare's biographer. Then Hare recovered himself and resumed speaking, now calmly.

"I'm sorry," he told the president. But his voice was curt. "You see, I happen to know the story behind that incident. My friend, Crane, was merely taking the part of an unfortunate young woman who was being hounded by the police; that was the whole reason for his getting into a scrape with the law."

Roosevelt continued to stare at the photographer. Then his eyes softened.

"All right, Jimmy," said the president. "Have it your own way."

Eventually some justice emerged from the Dora Clark affair, though it came too late for Stephen to know about it. In 1915, Patrolman Charles Becker was convicted of "complicity in the murder of his gambling partner, Herman Rosenthal" and became the first New York police officer to die in the electric chair.

A few months after paying his last respects to Stephen in the London stable, Curtis Brown and his wife received an invitation from Mrs. Stephen Crane to an "at home." The Browns went to Cora's small, furnished house in Kensington, where they met the woman calling herself Stephen's widow — "a generously built blonde with curiously unresponsive pale blue eyes," remembered Brown.

In the midst of her grief — "all the infernal tangle and misery of my life," she called it — Cora remained wedded to Stephen, treasuring her memories of their brief time together, cherishing his every written word. She wrote on the clean side of his draft pages — even on an early version of "The Blue Hotel" — linking her words to his. She wrote letters to his friends on black-bordered stationery embellished with the monogram *CC*. And she continued to harass poor Pinker about money. (Robert Barr would finish *The O'Ruddy*, Stephen's worst novel, in 1903.) She soon alientated the English agent for good. Eventually, relations between Cora and William Crane grew chilly over his tight control of Stephen's estate. Meaning well, Cora sent Edmund mementos of Stephen, including his blood-stained spats. "Papa's heart was broken," wrote Edmund's daughter, Edith. "Maybe the stains were not what he thought, but we were all distressed."

For a time Cora entertained thoughts of becoming a writer. She finished a few of Stephen's lesser stories and wrote a few of her own, without much success. She wanted to write a small biography of Stephen but was unequal to the task. Following his funeral and a visit with his family, she returned to London, intending to settle there. But less than two years later she was back in the United States. Eventually she lost touch with Stephen's family.

In 1901 a great fire gutted nearly two square miles of the old city of Jacksonville, including the Hotel de Dream. The following year, during a building boom, Cora returned to the city and managed to borrow the money to build a two-story, fourteen-bedroom brick bawdy house with an annex and stable, which she named the Court. Business flourished. In June 1905, Captain Donald Stewart died, and Cora married twenty-five-year-old Hammond McNeil, a good-looking, trigger-happy alcoholic who listed his occupation as railroad conductor. "Cora Crane, widow," was forty-one. Soon after the marriage, McNeil murdered a local man, young Harry Parker, in a jealous rage. McNeil's father stepped in, sending Cora and her maid off to England for a long holiday to put them out of reach at his son's murder trial. McNeil was acquitted, and in 1909 he rewarded Cora with a divorce.

In 1910 Cora suffered a slight stroke. Then, on September 4 of that year, she noticed a car stuck in the sand in front of her oceanfront house at Pablo Beach, south of Jacksonville, and went out to offer assistance. After helping to push the car out, she returned to the house and collapsed. She died later that day. She was buried in Jacksonville's Evergreen Cemetery under the name "Cora Crane."

•

Cora's love for Stephen Crane — which endured in spite of his attempt to abandon her in Cuba and in spite of the poverty and debt she inherited upon his death — spoke to the magic of the man. He was one of those rare beings of great personal charm and charisma who was equally attractive to both men and women. When describing Stephen Crane, men could sound as passionate as if they were writing about a woman. He was "a god — an Apollo with starry eyes," said Ford Madox Hueffer (now Ford). "I have never had this feeling about any other man. . . . Crane had a way of dropping lightly down the stairs that I have always envied." Of someone he met on a trip to Germany, Ford wrote his wife, "but as for Levin I'm sure you'd have fallen in love with him. He's in face *exactly* like Stephen Crane." "What a brutal, needless extinction — what an unmitigated unredeemed catastrophe!" Henry James wrote Cora. "I think of him with such a sense of possibilities and powers!"

Syracuse kept Crane's baseball. The house where he died in Baden-weiler became something of a tourist attraction; long after his death, said Alexander Woollcott, people in the beer garden would direct tourists to the room where Crane died. A visitor to Badenweiler today finds the lovely town in the Black Forest still proud of its fleeting association with the American writer.

People fell in love with Stephen. A slight acquaintance named E. R. Woodruff would sum up that personal quality that made him so memorable and affecting:

> Stephen Crane was so quiet and retiring when any opportunity was offered to make himself conspicuous, particularly in connection with his writing. . . . The charm of the man was so subtle it is hard to define but it was very real. I have seen him sit quietly a whole evening, watching and listening to the talk of the group with no other indication of his interest than a quick nod or a smile. I didn't know him well but as I think of him I remember him as always standing by watching and measuring people and such. Even in the thick of things he seemed a man apart, a slight boyish figure with a mop of light hair and shining eyes which saw everything. A most alive person, so alive that the news of his death seemed a mistake.

NOTES

_____

SELECTED

BIBLIOGRAPHY

_____

INDEX

NOTES

The following abbreviations are used in the notes.

Correspondence   Stanley Wertheim and Paul Sorrentino, eds., *The Correspondence of Stephen Crane*, 2 vols. (New York: Columbia University Press, 1988)

JTC   Jonathan Townley Crane

Log   Stanley Wertheim and Paul Sorrentino, eds., *The Crane Log: A Documentary Life of Stephen Crane, 1871–1900* (New York: G. K. Hall, 1994)

MHPC   Mary Helen Peck Crane

SC   Stephen Crane

SCrN   *Stephen Crane Newsletter,* edited by Joseph Katz (Columbus: Ohio State University Press, 1966–1970)

Work   Wilson Follett, ed., *The Work of Stephen Crane*, 12 vols. (New York: Alfred A. Knopf, 1925–1927)

Works   Fredson Bowers, ed., *The Works of Stephen Crane*, 10 vols. (Charlottesville: University Press of Virginia, 1969–1976)

All of the letters from Stephen Crane's parents are in the Clifton Waller Barrett Collection at the Alderman Library, University of Virginia. Along with the University of Virginia, the libraries at Syracuse University and Columbia University house the major Crane collections. Melvin H. Schoberlin's unpublished biography, "Flagon of Despair," is at Syracuse, as is the other material by Schoberlin cited in these notes. Other documents pertaining to Crane's life and work are at Dartmouth College, the University of Connecticut at Storrs, Yale University, the University of Minnesota, and other libraries listed in the *Correspondence*.

All of the letters I've quoted to and from Stephen Crane are in the *Correspondence*. Many of the reviews and other documents mentioned appear in full or in part in the *Log*. But I have cited the *Log* primarily for items that are not easy to find elsewhere. In writing about Crane's work, I have relied on the ten-volume *Works*, edited by Fredson Bowers. I have used only the introductions to the twelve-volume *Work*, edited by Wilson Follett.

I. HOW DO YOU SPELL "O"?

Edmund B. Crane's "Notes" on his brother Stephen is with the Thomas Beer Papers at Yale. Much of it is excerpted in the *Log*.

page

3   *loud summons . . . a grotesque:* Lyndon Upson Pratt, "The Formal Education of Stephen Crane," *American Literature* 10 (1939): 460–71.

ghastly white: Michael Robertson, *Stephen Crane at Lafayette* (Easton, Pa.: Friends of Skillman Library, 1990), p 7.

extremely nervous: ibid. p. 7.

4   *he was suddenly:* SC, "A Mystery of Heroism," *Works* 6: 54.

fimming . . . We boys: Edmund B. Crane, "Notes on the Life of Stephen Crane by His Brother, Edmund B. Crane."

the final . . . clung to his sister's: Melvin H. Schoberlin, "Flagon of Despair: Stephen Crane," unpublished manuscript, p. 8.

5   *Upon my mother's . . . numerous: Correspondence,:* p. 166.

could have wrapped: Helen R. Crane, "My Uncle, Stephen Crane," *American Mercury* 31 (January 1934): 25.

without an evil: MHPC in Thomas A. Gullason, ed., *Stephen Crane's Career: Perspectives and Evaluations* (New York: New York University Press, 1972), p. 33.

eloquent: Leslie's Weekly, 28 May 1896.

a pleasant: Port Jervis Daily Union, Feb. 16, 1880, quoted in Joseph Katz, "Stephen Crane's Concept of Death," *Kentucky Review*, 4, no. 2 (Winter 1983): 52.

a book of: Edna Crane Sidbury, "My Uncle, Stephen Crane, as I Knew Him," *Literary Digest International Book Review* 4 (1926): 248.

The baby is: JTC to George Peck, 11 November 1854.

6   *Here it is:* Sidbury, "My Uncle," p. 248.

almost forgot: JTC journal, 12 September 1859, in Gullason, *Career,* p. 13.

repulsive . . . deformities: JTC diary, in Stanley Wertheim, "Another Diary of the Reverend Jonathan Townley Crane," *Resources for American Literary Study* 19 (1993): 40.

dressed in dark: Post Wheeler to Melvin H. Schoberlin, 25 December 1947.

I find that . . . Pray for me: MHPC to parents, 14 March 1848?

7   *I had hoped:* JTC to George Peck, 9 August 1849?

my better half: JTC to Peck, 3 October 1849?

getting weary: MHPC to parents, 20 November 1864.

I have plenty: MHPC to parents, 2 November 1857?

Sunday Evening: JTC to George Peck, February (no year recorded).

8   *full of joy:* JTC journal, 10 April 1865, in Gullason, *Career,* p. 12.

8   *The whole place:* JTC journal, 15 April 1865, in Gullason, *Career,* p. 12.
     a day of: ibid., 16 April 1865.
     I hope Sherman: MHPC to parents, 20 November 1864.
     failing: MHPC to father, 13 August 1855? (year unclear).
     Mr. C: MHPC to parents, 19 November 1865.

9   *visions:* MHPC to parents, 20 November 1864.
     taking care: MHPC to mother, 16 February 1862.
     I guess: MHPC to parents, 2 November 1869.
     the enemy: JTC journal, 2 April 1867, in Gullason, *Career,* p. 18.
     our colony: JTC journal, 15 October 1866, in Gullason, *Career,* p. 17.
     my beloved . . . bleeding at the lungs: JTC journal, 15 January 1867, in Gullason,
          Career, p. 18.
     fits: MHPC to mother, 8 March (year unknown).
     to strengthen: MHPC to mother, 1 July 1865.
     debilitated: MHPC to mother, 9 February 1864.
     difficulties . . . destined to a life: MHPC to parents, April 1867.
     Well, God: JTC journal, 14 October 1866, in Gullason, *Career,* p. 17.

10   *from our:* JTC journal, 18 October 1866, in Gullason, *Career,* p. 17.
     to the better: JTC journal, 6 August 1867, in Gullason, *Career,* p. 19.
     our precious: MHPC to father, 16 April 1872.
     uncommonly strong: JTC to George Peck, 16 April 1872.
     much improved: JTC journal, 5 July 1872, in Gullason, *Career,* p. 20.
     fat and: JTC to George Peck, 16 September 1873.
     so sick: JTC journal, 20 October 1873, in Gullason, *Career,* p. 21.
     I suppose: JTC to George Peck, 16 September 1873.

11   *bright and . . . he loved:* Edmund B. Crane, "Notes."
     be able to: Jesse T. Peck, D.D., *The True Woman; Or, Life and Happiness at Home and
          Abroad* (New York: Carlton & Porter, 1857), p. 152.
     poisonous reptile: quoted in Christopher Benfey, *The Double Life of Stephen Crane*
          (New York: Knopf, 1992), p. 31.
     That brethren: MHPC, "Rev. Jonathan T. Crane, D.D." in Gullason, *Career,*
          p. 34.

12   *promised at least:* JTC diary, 26 March 1878, in Wertheim, "Another Diary,"
          p. 43.
     on the false: Port Jervis Evening Gazette, 25 May 1878.
     The day coach . . . How was I: Post Wheeler and Hallie E. Rives, *Dome of Many-
          Coloured Glass* (Garden City, N.Y.: Doubleday, 1955), pp. 21–22.

13   *the great difficulties:* Port Jervis Evening Gazette, 11 June 1878.

14   *Did nothing:* JTC journal, 11 August 1866, in Gullason, *Career,* p. 16.
     weird marks . . . Ma, how do you: Edmund B. Crane, "Notes."
     novel reading: Peck, *True Woman,* p. 154.
     trashy literature: Port Jervis Evening Gazette, 11 January 1879.
     a true picture: JTC journal, 21 May 1866, in Gullason, *Career,* p. 16.

15   *I'd Rather Have:* SC, "I'd Rather Have —," *Works* 10: 73.
     Stevie is not . . . Stevie is well: Log, p. 21.

15   *to an unusually:* Port Jervis Evening Gazette, 16 February 1880.

16   *the audience was:* Port Jervis Daily Union, in Katz, "Stephen Crane's Concept of Death," p. 53.

      as a flood: MHPC, "Rev. Jonathan T. Crane, D.D.," in Gullason, *Career,* p. 5.

      Oh. my Father . . . oyster-like: diary of Agnes Elizabeth Crane, 11 November 1880, in Paul Sorrentino, "Newly Discovered Writings of Mary Helen Peck Crane and Agnes Elizabeth Crane," *Courier* 21 (1986): 127–29.

17   *extraordinary settlement:* American Baedeker, 1893.

      Ocean Grave: Ames Williams to Melvin H. Schoberlin, undated.

      the Summer Mecca: quoted in Victor A. Elconin, "Stephen Crane at Asbury Park," *American Literature* 20 (November 1948): 275.

      temptation . . . graduates: New York Daily Tribune, 1 August 1889, p. 4.

18   *Mother has hope . . . spirit of fun:* Carl F. Price, "Stephen Crane, A Genius Born in a Methodist Parsonage," *Christian Advocate* 98 (n.d.): 866–67.

      magnetic: anonymous, in *Log,* p. 31.

      she was Stephen: Price, "Stephen Crane," pp. 866–67.

      range the neighborhood: anonymous, in *Log,* pp. 31–32.

      the growing taste: MHPC, "Change of Base," in Gullason, *Career,* p. 36.

      bird-like: anonymous, in *Log,* p. 31.

      her intelligence: Asbury Park Journal, 8 December 1883.

      planned her work . . . Stephen solemnly: Helen Crane, "In New Jersey," *Newark Star-Eagle,* 8 July 1926.

19   *many rare graces:* Asbury Park Journal, 28 June 1884.

      delicate: Edmund B. Crane, "Notes."

      and could outwalk . . . he would box: Post Wheeler interview and memorandum, 3 November 1947, Stephen Crane Collection, Syracuse University Library.

20   *85 or above:* Catalogue of the Public Schools of Asbury Park and Ocean Grove (1883–84), in Thomas A. Gullason, "Stephen Crane's Sister: New Biographical Facts," *American Literature* 49 (1977): 236.

      grimy, smoky: SC, "Uncle Jake and the Bell Handle," *Works* 8: 3–7.

2. GREAT BUGS AT ONONDAGA

21   *a temporary aberration:* Asbury Park Shore Press, March 1886.

      mental troubles . . . feeble: Asbury Park Shore Journal, 13 March 1896.

22   *Master Stephen:* Asbury Park Tribune, 29 June 1887.

      with a cloud . . . a very loud: quoted in Schoberlin, "Flagon," pp. 22–23.

      As the Professor . . . Stephen's most marked: Wilbur F. Crane, in *Log,* p. 39.

23   *$160.00 per year . . . we would do:* SCrN 2, no. 4 (Summer 1968): 2.

      the happiest: Correspondence, p. 12.

      simply pie: Harvey Wickham, "Stephen Crane at College," *American Mercury* 7 (March 1926): 292.

      morning prayers . . . very backward: Claverack College and Hudson River Institute catalogue, 1 August 1888.

      high reputation . . . as [if] in a terrestrial: Wickham, "Stephen Crane," pp. 291–92.

24   *to win recognition:* Schoberlin, "Flagon," p. 9.

24 *We . . . don't:* SCrN 2, no. 4 (Summer 1968): 3.
    far in advance . . . Plutarch's lives: A. Lincoln Travis to Mansfield J. French, circa
      20 March 1930.
    perfectly hen-like . . . drop your gun: Wickham, "Stephen Crane," p. 294.

25 *the stripes: Asbury Park Daily Press,* 19 June 1888.
    the bathing suit: New York Tribune, 3 August 1888.
    paid him for: Willis Fletcher Johnson, "The Launching of Stephen Crane," *Lit-
      erary Digest International Book Review* 4 (1926): 288.
    love feast . . . Four Christian: SC, "Mr. Yatman's Conversions," *Works* 8: 532.
    the pleasant-faced: Asbury Park Daily Press, 30 August 1889.
    the veritable: Arthur Oliver, "Jersey Memories — Stephen Crane," *Proceedings of
      the New Jersey Historical Society* 16 (1931): 456.

26 *yellow and:* Post Wheeler to Melvin H. Schoberlin, 25 December 1947.
    You all know: Asbury Park Daily Press, 2 July 1888.
    seething summer city: SC, "Asbury Park as Seen by Stephen Crane," *Works* 8: 654.
    the livery: SCrN 2, no. 4 (Summer 1968): 4.
    It was his . . . self-deprecation: Wickham, "Stephen Crane," p. 293.
    extremely irregular: Schoberlin, "Flagon," p. 9.

27 *slightly sheepish . . . enjoyed a certain:* Wickham, "Stephen Crane," pp. 294, 291,
      296, 294, 293, 295, 296.
    madly, in the: Correspondence, p. 212.
    a damn nice . . . My God: Wickham, "Stephen Crane," p. 296.
    learned many . . . He had: Schoberlin, "Flagon," p. 17.

28 *Only women:* Wickham, "Stephen Crane," p. 293.
    more or less . . . intimacy with other: Schoberlin, "Flagon," p. 17.
    the long looked for . . . The village dominie: SC, "Baseball," *Works* 8: 567–78.

29 *he was fed up:* Schoberlin, "Flagon," p. 35.
    longing for some: Correspondence, p. 34.
    bronzed and sturdy: SC, "Avon Seaside Assembly," *Works* 8: 501.
    all over six feet: SC, "Avon's School by the Sea," *Works* 8: 505.

30 *a very drab:* Earl G. Swem, in David E. E. Sloane, "Stephen Crane at Lafa-
      yette," *Resources for American Literary Study* 2 (1972): 103.
    raise[d] more hell: Correspondence, p. 35.
    the entire sophomore: Robertson, *Crane at Lafayette,* p. 6.
    I send you: Correspondence, p. 35.

31 *gazing at the clear:* Pratt, "Formal Education," p. 467.
    mark my words . . . left a big: Correspondence, p. 35.
    the third lowest: Robertson, *Crane at Lafayette,* p. 8.
    his family affairs: Ernest G. Smith, "Comments and Queries," *Lafayette Alumnus*
      2 (February 1932): 6.
    dropped from the rolls: Robertson, *Crane at Lafayette,* p. 8.
    Funny fowls: J. E. Anderson to Max J. Herzberg, 21 October 1921, Newark
      Public Library.
    delight: Edmund B. Crane, "Notes."

32 *dandy . . . I expect to see: Correspondence,* p. 36.
    more to play: Correspondence, p. 232.

32   *a Crimson sweater:* Clarence Loomis Peaslee, "Stephen Crane's College Days," *Monthly Illustrator* 13 (August 1896): 27.

      His skin: Mansfield J. French, "Stephen Crane, Ball Player," *Syracuse University Alumni News* 15 (January 1934): 3.

      soon became a feature: "A Varsity Boy," *Syracuse Standard,* in Paul Sorrentino, "New Evidence on Stephen Crane at Syracuse," *Resources for American Literary Study* 15 (Autumn 1985): 181.

      like a professional: Peaslee, "Crane's College Days," p. 27.

      unable to line . . . give a hop: French, "Stephen Crane," pp. 3–4.

33   *to bound back:* Peaslee, "Crane's College Days," p. 27.

      biting sarcasms: French, "Stephen Crane," p. 3.

      the best player: Peaslee, "Crane's College Days," p. 27.

      a fierce contempt: Frederic M. Lawrence, *The Real Stephen Crane,* ed. Joseph Katz (Newark, N.J.: Newark Public Library, 1980), p. 2.

      When I ought . . . the cut-and-dried: Correspondence, p. 99.

      Lounging about . . . a bulldog pipe: Lawrence, *Real Stephen,* pp. 2–3.

34   *daringly clad:* William McMahon, in Sorrentino, "New Evidence," p. 182.

      would not be bossed: George F. Chandler, "I Knew Stephen Crane at Syracuse," *Courier* 3 (March 1963): 13.

      a freshie: Price, "Stephen Crane," p. 867.

      Tut, tut: Elbert Hubbard, "As to Stephen Crane," *Lotos* 9 (1896): 676.

35   *unimpressive:* Peaslee, "Crane's College Days," p. 28.

      talked about how hard: Chandler, "I Knew Stephen Crane," p. 13.

      a haunting solicitude . . . Most men: Frank Noxon, "The Real Stephen Crane," *Step-Ladder* 14 (January 1928): 4–6.

      always cool: Peaslee, "Crane's College Days," p. 28.

      He has sung: SC, "The King's Favor," *Works* 8: 570.

      complimentary: Noxon, "Real Stephen Crane," p. 4.

36   *southeast of Brighton . . . had perhaps:* SC, "Great Bugs at Onondaga," *Works* 3: 578–80.

37   *invaders:* SC, "Greed Rampant," *Works* 8: 8.

      College life is a waste: Chandler, "I Knew Stephen Crane," p. 13.

3. THE GIRL WHO BLOSSOMED IN A MUD PUDDLE

Ames Williams's interview with Mrs. George F. Smillie (Lily Brandon Munroe) is at Syracuse, as are the other letters pertaining to L. B. The lynching incident was reported in the *New York Tribune,* 4 June 1892, and the *Port Jervis Evening Gazette,* 8 June 1892.

38   *bunches of scrub oaks:* SC, "Hunting Wild Hogs," *Works* 8: 201.

      scarred: SC, "Sullivan County Bears," *Works* 8: 201–2.

      tangled forests . . . This country may: SC, "Hunting Wild Hogs," pp. 201–2.

      His bones were not: Price, "Stephen Crane," p. 867.

      the old gnarled: SC, "The Last of the Mohicans," *Works* 8: 199.

      wonderful yarn-spinners . . . siren voice: SC, "Hunting Wild Hogs," p. 207.

39   *Great train-loads . . . wriggling, howling:* SC, "Arriving at Ocean Grove," *Works* 8: 221.

  virtuous bushwhacker: SC, "The Way in Sullivan County," *Works* 8: 221.

  has made a careful: SC, "Biology at Avon-By-The-Sea," *Works* 8: 546.

  bright-hued: SC, "Arriving," p. 546.

  liars: SC, "The Way," p. 220.

  devotional exercises . . . a bunch: SC, "On the Banks of the Shark River," *Works* 8: 548.

40   *big bundle . . . was in some respects:* Johnson, "Launching of Stephen Crane," 288–90.

  reality as the author: Hamlin Garland, "Ibsen as Dramatist," *Arena* 2 (June 1890): 72.

  by all odds . . . the novelist be true: SC, "Howells Discussed at Avon-By-The-Sea," *Works* 8: 508.

41   *laconic:* Hamlin Garland, "Stephen Crane as I Knew Him," *Yale Review* 75, no. 1 (Autumn 1985): 1.

  a nonsmoking teetotaler . . . hoarded every: Jean Holloway, *Hamlin Garland: A Biography* (Austin: University of Texas, 1960), pp. 71–73.

  wonderful boy: quoted in *American Literary Realism* 6 (Summer 1973): 249.

  Hamlin Garland was: Correspondence, p. 55.

  loved this life: Lawrence, *Real Stephen,* p. 4.

42   *Shortly after dusk: Log,* p. 66.

  its nightly glitter: Thomas Beer, *Stephen Crane: A Study in American Letters* (New York: Knopf, 1923), p. 79.

  one of the great: quoted in Van Wyck Brooks, *John Sloan: A Painter's Life* (New York: E. P. Dutton), p. 55.

  was open and plain: R. G. Vosburgh, "The Darkest Hour in the Life of Stephen Crane," *Criterion,* n.s. 1 (February 1901): 26–27.

43   *congestion of the brain: Asbury Park Shore Press,* 7 November 1890, p. 1.

  confined to her bed: Asbury Park Journal, 28 November 1891, p. 5.

  Suddenly it struck: SC, "The Octopush," *Works* 8: 232.

  listening pines: SC, "The Mesmeric Mountain," *Works* 8: 268.

  unseen live things: SC, "The Cry of a Huckleberry Pudding," *Works* 8: 256.

  black water: SC, "Octopush," p. 233.

  in a wilderness . . . congenial and alive: SC, "A Ghoul's Accountant," *Works* 8: 240.

44   *cave-damp:* SC, "Octopush," p. 233.

  mummy-like: SC, "Ghoul's Accountant," p. 241.

  an infinitely sallow: SC, "Four Men in a Cave," *Works* 8: 227.

  wild cry: SC, "The Black Dog," *Works* 8: 246.

  Troops of blue: SC, "Octopush," p. 231.

  The sun sank: SC, "Mesmeric Mountain," p. 270.

  The sun slid: SC, "Octopush," p. 232.

  with the world: Correspondence, p. 187.

45   *so seldom cleaned:* Beer, *Stephen Crane,* p. 79.

  a cigarette dangling: Ames Williams interview with Mrs. George F. Smillie (Lily Brandon Munroe), 1 January 1948.

45   *a small boy . . . Hot spiced rum:* SC, "The Broken-Down Van," *Works* 8: 275–80.
    a bird: Correspondence, p. 44.

46   *very beautiful . . . exquisitely feminine:* Mrs. Frederick B. Smillie to Miss Mary Benjamin, 15 February 1963.
    if he ever found: Edith Crane to Thomas Beer, 30 December 1933.

47   *very fond of violets . . . not a handsome:* Williams interview.
    extremely brilliant: Frederick B. Smillie to Melvin H. Schoberlin, 23 March 1949.
    very idealistic . . . whenever she saw: Williams interview.
    dearest, the one: Correspondence, p. 57.
    were very much . . . many letters: Williams interview.

48   *the sombre-hued gentlemen:* SC, "Meetings Begun at Ocean Grove," *Works* 8: 508.
    a bit of interesting: SC, "On the Boardwalk," *Works* 8: 518.
    a young man: SC, "The Seaside Hotel Hop," *Works* 8: 528.
    was not highly . . . Treat your notions: Oliver, "Jersey Memories," p. 454.

49   *the cool, shaded Auditorium:* SC, "Meetings Begun," p. 508.
    fierce and passionate . . . Do not appear: SC, "Boardwalk," pp. 515–19.
    bronzed, slope-shouldered . . . summer gowns: SC, "Parades and Entertainments," *Works* 8: 521–22.
    Well, Stevie: Oliver, "Jersey Memories," p. 428.
    The bona fide: SC, "Parades," p. 522.

50   *raised hob:* William K. Devereux, in "Take Orders from Harvey? No, Says Billy Devereux," *Newark Star-Eagle,* 8 November 1921.
    un-American . . . the Holy Bible: New York Tribune, 24 August 1892.
    who claim . . . reviled like a pickpocket: Asbury Park Daily Press, 22 August 1892, reprinted in Gullason, *Career,* p. 38.
    a bit of random: New York Tribune, 23 August 1892.

51   *susceptible [to] garbling:* Johnson, "Launching of Stephen Crane," p. 290.
    The article . . . a hankering: Asbury Park Daily Press, 25 August 1892.
    just a bit: Oliver, "Jersey Memories," p. 459.
    a much agitated . . . showing him the item: Johnson, "Launching of Stephen Crane," p. 290.
    glum as a king . . . No! You've got: Oliver, "Jersey Memories," pp. 454–63.

52   *a special article trade: Correspondence,* p. 45.
    Didn't live nowhere . . . some smoking: Jacob A. Riis, *How the Other Half Lives* (New York: Dover Publications, 1971), pp. 2, 50, 202.

53   *in search of the local:* Lawrence, *Real Stephen,* p. 7.
    boss reporter: Edith Patterson Meyer, *Not Charity but Justice: The Story of Jacob A. Riis* (New York: Vanguard Press, 1974), p. 60.

54   *of womanhood:* Riis, *The Other Half,* p. 122.
    blossomed in a mud puddle . . . for the honor: SC, *Maggie: A Girl of the Streets, Works* 1: 24, 7.

55   *No other wrote:* Corwin Knapp Linson, *My Stephen Crane,* ed. Edwin H. Cady (Syracuse: Syracuse University Press, 1958), p. 20.
    Did you ever: Lawrence, *Real Stephen,* p. 6.
    From a window . . . gave up loads: SC, *Maggie,* pp. 7, 25, 13, 65, 11.

56   *You can't find . . . A story must:* Linson, *My Stephen,* p. 18.

56   *to show that environment . . . one makes room:* Correspondence, p. 52.
       it would be difficult . . . stark brutality: Johnson, "Launching of Stephen Crane,"
           p. 289.
       bitter: Garland, "Crane as I Knew Him," p. 3.
       great: Hamlin Garland in *SCrN* 3, no. 2 (Winter 1968): 1.

57   *haggard purse:* Linson, *My Stephen*, p. 13.

4. THE NOISE OF RUMORS

58   *rumpled . . . gray-blue intensity:* Linson, *My Stephen*, p. 2.
       That boy has . . . Neither Mr. Podsnap: Johnson, "Launching of Stephen Crane,"
           p. 289.

59   *The reader of this book:* Hamlin Garland, "Roadside Meetings of a Literary No-
           mad," Part 4, *Bookman* 70 (January 1930): 524.
       so that passengers: Noxon, "Real Stephen Crane," p. 5.
       sensation: Correspondence, p. 232.
       to gentlemen . . . I wrote across: Linson, *My Stephen*, pp. 21–27.

60   *genius for phrases:* Garland, *Roadside Meetings*, p. 524.
       a kind of horror . . . try something else: Correspondence, pp. 49–51.
       genuine interest: Linson, *My Stephen*, p. 33.
       having received no reply: Correspondence, p. 51.
       heartbreaking note: William Dean Howells to Cora Crane, in "Saturday Review
           of Books and Arts," *New York Times*, 8 September 1900, p. 597.
       working in the right: Correspondence, p. 52.
       turban-like . . . A wet towel: Linson, *My Stephen*, pp. 28–29.

61   *fairy scene . . . He was very busy:* SC, "The Pace of Youth," *Works* 5: 3–12.
       Dearest L.B.: Correspondence, p. 55.

62   *immensely:* Howells to Cora Crane, "Saturday Review," p. 597.
       grim, not grimy . . . literary conscience: William Dean Howells, "Life and Letters,"
           Harper's Weekly 39 (8 June 1895): p. 533.
       the semi-savage . . . strange, melancholy: Howells to Cora Crane, "Saturday Re-
           view," p. 597.
       They tell me . . . thought if I could measure: Correspondence, p. 55.

63   *in a real battle:* Warren Lee Goss, "Recollections of a Private, III," *Century* 29
           (March 1885): 767–77.
       There were many . . . The tender hand: Warren Lee Goss, "Recollections of a Pri-
           vate, IV," *Century* 31 (January 1886): 467–74.
       Cold chills ran . . . I had a fluctuation: Warren Lee Goss, "Recollections of a Pri-
           vate, I," *Century* 29 (November 1884): 107–13.
       I wonder that: Linson, *My Stephen*, p. 37.

64   *had been unconsciously . . . had been imagining:* SC, in Willa Cather, *The World and
           the Parish: Willa Cather's Articles and Reviews, 1893–1902*, ed. William M.
           Curtin. (Lincoln: University of Nebraska Press, 1970), 2: 776.
       knew more of war: Lawrence, *Real Stephen*, p. 13.
       had never told: Chicago Sunday Inter-Ocean, 15 March 1896.
       were in no wise: SC, *The Red Badge of Courage*, *Works* 2: 9.

64   *potboiler . . . I got interested:* Louis C. Senger to Hamlin Garland, 9 October
        1900.

        He was immersed . . . Your charming patience: Linson, *My Stephen*, pp. 36–38.

65   *the latter part:* Correspondence, p. 167.

        a psychological portrayal: ibid., p. 322.

        it was essential: ibid., p. 161.

        every word in place: Garland, "Crane as I Knew Him," p. 9.

        throughout with the unhesitating: Linson, *My Stephen*, p. 44.

        The cold passed . . . stand before him: SC, *Red Badge*, p. 3.

67   *Fleming discovered . . . Smoke drifted lazily:* Early Draft of Manuscript of *Red Badge*,
        Works 2: 143–80 passim.

68   *sissy . . . I will die:* C.G.S., "The Coward," *New York Times*, 12 February 1893, p. 18.

        the writer I admire: Correspondence, p. 232.

69   *house of pain . . . The feeling:* Leo Tolstoi, *Sebastopol*, translated from the French by
        Frank D. Millet (New York: Harper & Brothers, 1887), pp. 26, 122, 174–75.

        The world was fully . . . stood as men: SC, *Red Badge*, pp. 3–135 passim.

70   *analysed the effect:* Noxon, "Real Stephen Crane," p. 6.

        red, peculiar blossoms . . . the red sun: Red Badge, pp. 17, 70, 58.

        war from within: Ripley Hitchcock quoting Crane, introduction to, *Works* 2: l.

        a religious half-light . . . worn to the thinness: SC, *Red Badge*, pp. 3–135 passim.

71   *the product of . . . a pity that:* Linson, *My Stephen*, p. 44.

        He had been to touch . . . Over the river: SC, *Red Badge*, pp. 3–135 passim.

        Day closes: Tolstoi, *Sebastopol*, p. 43.

        far into the night . . . I liked: Edmund B. Crane, "Notes."

72   *swallowing cavern:* SC, "An Ominous Baby," *Works* 8: 50.

        undoubtedly a man: SC, "A Great Mistake," *Works* 8: 50–52.

        in a strange country . . . some wee battler: SC, "Ominous Baby," pp. 47–49.

73   *that of a weeping:* SC, *Red Badge*, p. 34.

        would consider: Edmund B. Crane, "Notes."

        were glad . . . a bun or two: Vosburgh, "Darkest Hour," p. 338.

74   *Our life there:* Frederic C. Gordon to Thomas Beer, 25 May 1923.

        staid puritanical . . . Congratulate yourselves: SC, "The Art Students' League Build-
        ing," *Works* 8: 313–15.

        That's bully: Vosburgh, "Darkest Hour," pp. 338–39.

        I have to make it: Linson, *My Stephen*, p. 33.

5. THE COMMANDING POWER OF GENIUS

76   *poorly dressed:* Edmund B. Crane, "Notes."

        utterly done up: Gordon to Beer, 25 May 1923.

        He was thin: Edward Marshall, "Stories of Stephen Crane," *San Francisco Call*;
        reprinted in *Literary Life* 24 (December 1900): 71.

        too proud . . . ripe for pneumonia: Gordon to Beer, 25 May 1923.

77   *any work:* Log, pp. 95–96.

        fragrance of past . . . to think well: Correspondence, pp. 57–58.

        The ride of sin: SC, *The Black Riders and Other Lines*, *Works* 10: 3.

77   *in little rows:* Hamlin Garland, "Stephen Crane: A Soldier of Fortune," *Saturday Evening Post* 173 (28 July 1900): 16–17.

the King of . . . why is this?: SC, *Black Riders,* pp. 22, 39, 9, 11, 9.

78   *desperation:* Wickham, "Stephen Crane, p. 297.

the thoughts I have had: Correspondence, pp. 232–33.

What did you: SC, *Black Riders,* p. 11.

very common . . . a small pale-yellow: Correspondence, p. 209.

Oh, best: SC, *Black Riders,* p. 11.

79   *What do you think . . . I know everyone:* Linson, *My Stephen,* pp. 49–51.

as from a thousand . . . pitiless beat: SC, "The Men in the Storm," *Works* 8: 315–22.

80   *haggard and almost . . . How would I:* Linson, *My Stephen,* p. 58.

looking as if: Corwin Knapp Linson, "Little Stories of 'Steve' Crane," *Saturday Evening Post* 175 (11 April 1903): 19–20.

strange and unspeakable . . . in which there: SC, "An Experiment in Misery," *Works* 8: 283–93.

5, 7 or 10¢: William H. Carroll, untitled reminiscence, with covering letter to Thomas Beer, 20 March 1924.

81   *My lord:* Linson, *My Stephen,* p. 59.

He drank and smoked: John Northern Hilliard to Thomas Beer, 1 February 1922.

true womanhood: Corwin Knapp Linson to Thomas Beer, 30 April 1923.

a marvelous figure: Nelson Greene to Melvin H. Schoberlin, 21 July 1947.

He took up: Hilliard to Beer, 1 February 1922.

Don't forget me . . . fixes me firmly: Correspondence, pp. 57–58.

82   *I looked here:* SC, *Black Riders,* p. 6.

fifteen short stories: Correspondence, p. 65.

five or six . . . pale, reticent boy: Garland, "Stephen Crane: A Soldier," p. 6.

83   *too orphic: Correspondence,* p. 75.

I wish you: ibid., p. 62.

the youth . . . The tall soldier: SC, *Red Badge* and Early Draft of Manuscript, pp. 193–96.

84   *rather die: New York Tribune,* 16 April 1894.

promises splendid things: Edward Marshall interview with William Dean Howells, "Greatest Living American Writer," *New York Press,* 15 April 1894.

the kind of truth: New York Press, 15 April 1894.

one of the outer: SC, "An Experiment in Luxury," *Works* 8: 293–301.

This is a fake: Log, p. 103.

They come in shools: Correspondence, p. 65.

a fat roll . . . In hock: Garland, *Roadside Meetings,* p. 197.

85   *about the borrowing: Correspondence,* p. 66.

86   *Don't forget to return: Correspondence,* pp. 68–69.

They are society's . . . the white badge: Riis, *The Other Half,* pp. 41, 126.

87   *the magazine man . . . you damned:* Linson, *My Stephen,* pp. 64–66.

in the sunless . . . the fragrant dream: SC, "In the Depths of a Coal Mine," *Works* 8: 590–600.

88   *CK, what did:* Linson, *My Stephen,* p. 68.

toil[ed] in this city: SC, "In the Depths," p. 597.

88   structure ... *The smoke and dust:* first draft of "In the Depths of a Coal Mine,"
       Works 8: 600.
       the smoke from: SC, "In the Depths," p. 590.
89   *fame and immortality:* Lawrence, *Real Stephen,* p. 12.
       the scent of a thousand: Linson, *My Stephen,* p. 75.
       loved this life: Lawrence, *Real Stephen,* p. 4.
90   *As Stephen Crane ... To the Editor:* SC, "Pike County Puzzle," *Works* 8: 608–35.
91   *coal-brokers:* first draft of "In the Depths," p. 606.
       The birds didn't: Linson, *My Stephen,* p. 70.
       I would like: Correspondence, p. 72.
       We disagree: Correspondence, pp. 73–74.
92   *S. Crane is:* Louise Imogen Guiney to Fred Holland Day, in Stephen Maxfield
       Parrish, *Currents of the Nineties in Boston and London: Fred Holland Day, Louise
       Imogen Guiney, and Their Circle* (New York: Garland, 1987), pp. 269–70, in
       James B. Colvert, "Fred Holland Day, Louise Imogen Guiney, and the Text
       of Stephen Crane's *The Black Riders,*" unpublished paper.
       utterly impossible: Correspondence, p. 74.
       tolerance of: ibid., p. 75.
       Beast: ibid., p. 79.
       one of the most brilliant: Irving Bacheller, *From Stores of Memory* (New York: Farrar
       & Rinehart, 1933), p. 110.
       trained ... I had no place: Irving Bacheller, *Coming Up the Road: Memories of a North
       Country Boyhood* (Indianapolis: Bobbs-Merrill, 1928), pp. 276–77.
93   *Beg, borrow: Correspondence,* p. 80.
       He looked like: Marston LaFrance, "A Few Facts about Stephen Crane and
       'Holland,'" *American Literature* 37 (1965): 198.
       more severely classic: Correspondence, p. 77.
       leaves Maggie ... As a matter: ibid., p. 79.
94   *caress:* SC, "A Desertion," *Works* 8: 80.
       mystic shadow: SC, *Black Riders,* p. 6.
       fragments of ... It thrilled: SC, "The Fire," *Works* 8: 338–44.
95   *pitilessly compressed:* Curtis Brown, *Contacts* (New York: Harper & Brothers,
       1935) p. 261.
       its quality: Bacheller, *Coming Up,* p. 78.
       If you have not ... If Mr. Crane: LaFrance, "A Few Facts," pp. 195–202.
       bitter, wind-swept ... God bless you: Curtis Brown, *Contacts,* p. 261.
       Word flew: Bacheller, *Coming Up,* pp. 278–79.

6. YELLOW SKY

99   *a very long: Correspondence,* p. 93.
       for new color: Bacheller, *From Stores of Memory,* p. 111.
       a promise: Walter Prescott Webb, *The Great Plains* (New York: Grossett & Dun-
       lap, 1931), p. 510.
       wild in a well established: Larry McMurtry, *In a Narrow Grave: Essays on Texas*
       (New York: Touchstone Books, Simon & Schuster, 1989), pp. 24–25.

100   *a drama:* Hamlin Garland in Webb, *Great Plains,* p. 453.

      The classic form . . . There has been: Correspondence, p. 81.

      reckoned with: ibid., p. 87.

      Truth: Works 10: 17.

101   *one rather long:* Ripley Hitchcock, preface to *The Red Badge of Courage* (New York: Appleton, 1900), pp. v–vi.

      Any news . . . in care of: Correspondence, p. 95.

      Hello, Budge: ibid., p. 96.

      a large syndicate: article reprinted in Bernice Slote, "Stephen Crane in Nebraska," *Prairie Schooner* 43 (1969): 193.

102   *How did you . . . the fingers of the storm:* SC, "Nebraska's Bitter Fight for Life," *Works* 8: 409–20.

103   *sauntered . . . the finest I have:* Cather, *World and the Parish,* 2: 772–74.

104   *biting frankness . . . reputation for zest:* Hermione Lee, *Willa Cather: Double Lives* (New York: Pantheon, 1989), p. 40.

      in a wandering . . . in ten years: Cather in *World and the Parish,* pp. 773–77.

106   *that he would have:* SCrN 3 (Spring 1967): 4.

      have to reflect: Correspondence, p. 97.

      white clouds: SC, "Nebraska's Bitter Fight," p. 420.

      He felt that . . . when he returned: Nebraska State Journal, 14 February 1985, p. 4, quoted in Slote, "Stephen Crane," p. 195.

      A man becomes: SC, "Seen at Hot Springs," *Works* 8: 422.

107   *dull-hued:* SC, "The Bride Comes to Yellow Sky," *Works* 5: 109.

      long low hills: SC, "Stephen Crane in Texas," *Works* 8: 473.

      the many strange: Correspondence, p. 101.

      I am unable: ibid., p. 100.

      Table d'hotes: ibid., p. 99.

108   *battle . . . There is nothing:* ibid., pp. 97–99.

      one of the brightest: "Personal," *Galveston Daily News,* 7 March 1895, p. 3, reprinted in introduction, *Stephen Crane in the West and Mexico,* ed. Joseph Katz (Kent, Ohio: Kent State University Press, 1970), p. xviii.

      a distinctly homeric: reprinted in *Log,* p. 128.

      gentlemen of good: Edward Simmen, "Stephen Crane and the Aziola Club of Galveston: A New Crane Letter," *Journal of Modern Literature* 7 (February 1979): 171.

      with an extraordinary: SC, "Galveston, Texas, in 1895," *Works* 8: 477.

      the rough west: SC, "Moonlight on the Snow," *Works* 5: 185.

      Garland will: Correspondence, p. 136.

      simple courtesy: SC, "London Impressions," *Works* 8: 687.

      The straight: Correspondence, p. 136.

      We in the east: ibid., p. 136.

109   *passion for differences . . . kept the sweeping:* SC, "Galveston, Texas," pp. 474–75.

      business men . . . seemed to symbolize: SC, "Crane in Texas," p. 468.

      Here the romance . . . mesquite wilderness: Frank A. Bushick, *Glamorous Days* (San Antonio: Naylor, 1934), p. 9.

      wrinkled into long . . . as eloquent: SC, "Crane in Texas," pp. 468–73.

110   *flaming red . . . who's your good:* Bushick, *Glamorous Days*, pp. 98–100.
111   *about to venture . . . I modestly replied:* Correspondence, pp. 100–101.
        very attractive . . . rather queer: ibid., pp. 181–82.
112   *there were certain:* Linson, *My Stephen*, p. 87.
        be sure of two . . . the most worthless: SC, "The Mexican Lower Classes," *Works* 8:
            436.
        beautiful frequently: SC, "The City of Mexico," *Works* 8: 430.
        vivid serapes: SC, "The Viga Canal," p 8: 433.
        heavily blue: SC, "A Man and Some Others," *Works* 5: 62.
        the long flare: SC, "The Viga," p. 434.
        before the coming: SC, "The Wise Men," *Works* 5: 36.
        the world was declared . . . as large as pies: SC, "A Man," pp. 52–58.
113   *for once:* Linson, *My Stephen*, p. 87.
        painted [them] . . . fifty drunken: SC, "One Dash — Horses," *Works* 5: 13, 16, 15,
            22, 24.
114   *my personal troubles:* Correspondence, p. 162.
        the color of a brick . . . She of course: Correspondence, p. 162.

7. THE COMING MAN

The Louis Zara papers — research for his 1961 novel, *Dark Rider,* based on the life of
Stephen Crane — are at Ohio State University.

116   *The keening Rio Grande:* SC, "The Bride Comes to Yellow Sky," p 5:111.
        Magnificent: Recollection of Edith Crane to Louis Zara.
        a deep tan: Lawrence, *Real Stephen*, p. 12.
        broke to the limit: Nelson Greene, "I Knew Stephen Crane," in Stanley Wert-
            heim, ed., "Stephen Crane Remembered," *Studies in American Fiction* 4 Spring
            1976), p. 52.
117   *the highest . . . rugged undisciplined:* article quoted in *Log*, p. 131.
        the Aubrey Beardsley: Log, p. 131.
        I am particularly: Correspondence, p. 111.
        I stood: SC, *Black Riders*, p. 7.
118   *lyrical outbursts: New York Times Book Review*, 14 September 1930, p. 2.
        puffing braggart . . . dead in Heaven: SC, *Black Riders*, pp. 3, 41.
        individual eyes: New York Times Book Review, 14 September 1930, p. 2.
        naturally primitive: John Berryman, *Stephen Crane: A Critical Biography* (New York:
            Farrar, Straus & Giroux, 1950), p. 275.
        small skeletons: Anonymous, "Six Books of Verse," *Atlantic Monthly* 77 (February
            1896): 271.
        In the desert . . . There is nothing: SC, *Black Riders*, pp. 4, 13, 19, 43, 34, 25, 27, 28.
119   *about life:* Correspondence, pp. 232–33.
        Black Riders . . . Should the wide world: SC, *Black Riders*, pp. 3, 7.
        Stephen pulled out . . . Everything became ok: Greene, "I Knew Stephen," pp.
            50–53.

120 *a dingy but quite . . . for unpretentious:* Henry McBride, "Stephen Crane's Artist Friends," *Art News* 49 (October 1950): 46.

fussed up breakfast . . . one square meal: Greene, "I Knew Stephen," pp. 51–52.

to the temporary: J.L.H. (identity unknown), quoted in Edith F. Crane to Thomas Beer, 30 December 1933.

We fellows . . . he got busy: Greene, "I Knew Stephen," p. 52.

122 *This, then was . . . a curtain of green:* SC, "A Mystery of Heroism," *Works* 6: 49–53.

He said he couldn't: Greene, "I Knew Stephen," p. 52.

not in very good . . . making some stir: Correspondence, p. 104.

so much trash: New York Tribune, 9 June 1895.

Mr. Crane has thoughts: Munsey's Magazine, July 1895, quoted in *Log,* p. 135.

stamped with truth: Bookman 2, no. 6 (February 1896).

the riders might: Philistine, June 1895, quoted in *Log,* p. 135.

123 THE SPOTTED: reprinted in *Log,* pp. 136–37.

not take to heart: Correspondence, p. 109.

present us these: ibid., p. 114.

124 *I do not confess:* ibid., p. 115.

To Curtis: Brown, *Contacts,* p. 261.

I have considerable work: Correspondence, p. 111.

125 *My dear L.B.:* ibid., p. 112.

better than anything: Wickham, "Stephen Crane," p. 297.

like weapons . . . the correctness: SC, *George's Mother, Works* 1: 119, 120, 134.

126 *four deadly miles: Correspondence,* p. 118.

As a matter: ibid., p. 116.

anything in the way: ibid., p. 118.

anxious to see: ibid., p. 117.

out of the world . . . There are six: ibid., p. 118.

127 *the brown October . . . Don't intend:* ibid., pp. 127, 128.

they didn't skirmish . . . grind: ibid., p. 144.

a chromatic nightmare . . . most impressive: New York Tribune, Philadelphia Press, 13 October 1895.

will give you: Detroit Free Press, 7 October 1895.

128 *At times:* Edward Marshall, unsigned review, *New York Press,* 13 October 1895, reprinted in *Log,* p. 143.

a picture which seems: New York Times, 19 October 1895.

Its author is: Chicago Daily Inter-Ocean, 19 October 1895.

namby-pamby stuff: The Bookman, vol. 1: February 1895–July 1895 (New York: Dodd, Mead, 1895), pp. 190–91.

129 *like a flash:* H. L. Mencken, introduction to *Work* (Follett, ed.), vol. 5.

sensation: Joseph Conrad, *Last Essays* (Garden City, N.Y.: Doubleday, 1926), p. 119.

I saw a meter: reprinted in *Log,* p. 139.

130 *tenderly carried it:* Lawrence, *Real Stephen,* p. 13.

a few hundred: Willis Brooks Hawkins, "All in a Lifetime," *SCrN* 3 (Spring 1967): 4–5.

130   *clip anything . . . I have heard:* Correspondence, p. 127.

    for a small poker . . . "Gosh!" said Crane: Harry B. Smith, *First Nights and First Editions* (Boston: Little, Brown, 1931), pp. 177–78.

131   *The story is . . . Can you endure:* Correspondence, p. 128.

    I am not sure . . . clever: ibid., p. 140.

    easy . . . I can: ibid., p. 136.

    over half . . . must end: ibid., p. 138.

    My dear Mr. Crane: ibid., pp. 134–35.

    What do you . . . an acceptance: ibid., p. 140.

132   *My dress suit:* ibid., p. 135.

    low enough . . . have a dandy: ibid., pp. 139–40.

    you represent a 'cause': ibid., p. 135.

    blue crystal: ibid., p. 140.

    I am getting frightened . . . you know: ibid., pp. 143–44.

    are expecting my death: ibid., p. 136.

133   *The stiffest breeze . . . But there was:* ibid., p. 145.

    He finished them: ibid., p. 144.

    eight days . . . Irving Bacheller: ibid., p. 148.

134   *I begin to think:* ibid., p. 149.

    I like this: ibid., p. 156.

    about six . . . Damn New York: ibid., p. 144.

    sense of deaf: William Dean Howells, *Harper's Weekly,* 26 October 1895, quoted in *Log,* p. 146.

    so generous: Correspondence, p. 254.

    glad . . . that misunderstood: ibid., p. 188.

135   *It was instantly:* Louis Senger, quoted in Linson, *My Stephen,* p. 90.

    folks we hoped: Elbert Hubbard in *SCrN* 4 (Summer 1970): 11.

    disgusted: Correspondence, p. 158.

    I was not: ibid., p. 159.

    elated . . . I have been aroused: ibid., p. 152.

    one full dress: ibid., p. 154.

136   *I saw a man:* SC, *Black Riders,* p. 14.

    timid: Noxon, "Real Stephen Crane," p. 8.

    immaculate: Willis Brooks Hawkins, in *SCrN* 3, no. 1 (Fall 1968): 6–7.

    feel freer: Greene, "I Knew Stephen," p. 53.

    Probably the most . . . having the time: Noxon, "Real Stephen Crane," p. 8.

    in a blue funk: Hawkins, in *SCrN* 3, no. 1: 6–7.

    the strong voice . . . a few words: Bookman 2 (9 February 1896): 469.

    a working newspaper: William MacIntosh, *Buffalo Evening News,* 20 December 1895, reprinted in Kenneth Dirlam and Ernest F. Simmons, *Sinners, This Is East Aurora* (New York: Vantage, 1964), p. 27.

137   *I write what:* Bookman 2: 468.

    take himself: MacIntosh, *Buffalo Evening News,* in Dirlam and Simmons, p. 27.

    the sight of: Claude Bragdon, "The Purple Cow Period," *Bookman* 69 (July 1929): 478.

    slept with him: quoted in Noxon, "Real Stephen Crane," p. 8.

137   *in honor:* David Gray, in *SCrN* 4, no. 4 (Summer 1970): 5.

   great personage: Elbert Hubbard II, 1 December 1927, reprinted in Paul Sorrentino, "The Philistine Society's Banquet for Stephen Crane," *American Literary Realism* 15, no. 2 (Autumn 1982): 234.

   happy abandon: Hubbard, "As to Stephen Crane," p. 677.

   was very properly: Correspondence, p. 162.

138   *I am always:* ibid., p. 158.

   pinch . . . from various: ibid., p. 204.

   Typewriting is too new: ibid., p. 160.

   I hear that: ibid., p. 161.

   a good many orders . . . try to do: ibid., pp. 160–61.

139   *I am considering:* ibid., p. 159.

   a far country: Wickham, "Stephen Crane," p. 297.

   plodding along: Correspondence, p. 161.

   We think so highly: ibid., p. 151.

140   *The great and deserved:* Arthur Waugh, "London Letter," *Critic,* 28 December 1895, quoted in *Log,* p. 157.

8. RED HAIR

Stephen Crane's letters to Amy Leslie and hers to Willis Brooks Hawkins are at the Dartmouth College Library. For my understanding of Theodore Roosevelt — in particular, his childhood and his character — I am completely indebted to two marvelous biographies: *Mornings on Horseback,* by David McCullough, and *The Rise of Theodore Roosevelt,* by Edmund Morris. Morris's book, along with Olov W. Fryckstedt's superbly researched piece "Stephen Crane in the Tenderloin," told me almost everything I needed to know about the workings of the New York Police Department in the late nineteenth century, the power structure of the Board of Police Commissioners, and the Dora Clark affair. For my knowledge of Amy Leslie, I am indebted to my husband, Chuck Yanikoski, who did some impressive detective work and proved an indefatigable and imaginative researcher. Virtually all I know about Cora Taylor Crane comes from *Cora Crane: A Biography of Mrs. Stephen Crane,* by Lillian Gilkes, and from the work of Elizabeth Friedmann.

141   *Dear Mr. Howells: Correspondence,* p. 165.

   never encouraged friends: ibid., p. 171.

   swelled up: ibid., p. 175.

   for every humorist: ibid., p. 195.

   In one sense: ibid., p. 175.

142   *Dear L:* ibid., p. 179.

   the blessed quiet . . . back to Hartwood: ibid., p. 181.

   would be the very: ibid., p. 177.

   afraid, afraid: ibid., p. 187.

   and to see: ibid., p. 185.

   silly engagements: ibid., p. 184.

143   *to breathe:* ibid., p. 189.

143   *being called:* ibid., p. 191.

   utterly dejected . . . On Friday: ibid., p. 189.

   go ahead with: ibid., p. 191.

   a pretty good: ibid., p. 181.

   to the scene: ibid., p. 193.

   daily battle: ibid., p. 198.

   awfully hard: ibid., p. 175.

   that is not without: ibid., p. 198.

144   *positively my last thing:* ibid., p. 205.

   Hang all war stories: ibid., p. 198.

   This aggregation: SC, "An Episode of War," *Works* 6: 91.

   When he arose: SC, "The Little Regiment," *Works* 6: 20.

   At the roadside: SC, "An Episode of War," p. 91.

   Could you see . . . When the roof: SC, "The Veteran," pp. 82–86.

145   *that lot: Correspondence,* p. 172.

   awed . . . the light: ibid., pp. 197–98.

   a curiously . . . remarkably strong: ibid., p. 182.

   please keep in mind: ibid., p. 172.

   a practical . . . instinctive liking: Correspondence, p. 184.

   No women: ibid., p. 185.

146   *I observe . . . I have been told:* ibid., p. 171.

   For my own: ibid., p. 180.

   the man of fashion: ibid., p. 200.

   good claret . . . treat a woman: ibid., p. 201.

147   *not in any sense:* ibid., p. 171.

   I might as well: ibid., p. 198.

   I think your: ibid., p. 171.

   Oh, heavens . . . enthusiastic: ibid., pp. 180–81.

   the new-rich: ibid., p. 202.

   to be admired: ibid., p. 203.

   I am afraid: ibid., pp. 184–85.

148   *This route leads:* ibid., p. 172.

   invade Akron: ibid., p. 182.

   when . . . it could be: ibid., p. 185.

   I hope so: ibid., p. 198.

   I wish you: ibid., p. 203.

   Do you know . . . Really, by this: ibid., pp. 207–8.

149   *An indefinite woman . . . sublime king:* SC, *George's Mother,* p. 137.

   Why, in heaven's: Correspondence, p. 181.

   deeply in love: Edith Lundgren (Nellie Crouse's daughter) to Melvin H. Schoberlin, 24 June 1948.

   miserable . . . had less than: Ames Williams interview with Mrs. George Smillie (Lily Brandon Munroe), 30 January 1948. (And see Frederick B. Smillie to Lillian Gilkes, 7 March 1955, Crane Collection, Syracuse University.)

150   *It was a woman!: Correspondence,* pp. 212–13.

   had enough tea . . . forgive me: ibid., p. 213.

150   *Anna Roberts:* ibid., p. 212.

151   *My dear Miss:* ibid., pp. 208–9.

    These men pose: ibid., p. 218.

    been a rampant . . . that noble horse: ibid., p. 229.

    The proofs make: ibid., p. 224.

152   *genius is:* ibid., p. 230.

    I have never: ibid., p. 228.

    Take the diamond: ibid., p. 217.

    beset . . . I expect: ibid., p. 235.

153   *His method:* Herbert P. Williams interview, "Mr. Crane as a Literary Artist," *Illustrated American*, 18 July 1896.

    plugged at: Correspondence, p. 200.

    sorry stuff: Henry Thurston Peck, *Bookman* (July 1896), quoted in *Log*, p. 189.

    Mr. Crane: New York Times, 21 June 1896.

154   *written as pitilessly: Book Buyer*, July 1896, in *Log*, p. 189.

    no charm: New York Tribune, 31 May 1896.

    It really seems: Thomas Wentworth Higginson, *Philistine*, July, 1896, in *Log*, p. 186.

    realism run mad: J. L. Onderdonk, quoted in *Log*, p. 183.

    Above, the sun: Paul M. Paine, *Life*, 23 April 1896.

    This young man . . . There could be: Ambrose Bierce, *New York Press*, 25 July 1896, quoted in *Log*, p. 197.

    It was an effort: Correspondence, p. 232.

    very very lazy: ibid., p. 205.

    a good saddle-horse: ibid., p. 205.

155   *crazy to get:* ibid., p. 197.

    noble horse: ibid., p. 229.

    striking the bridge: Edmund B. Crane, "Notes."

    garish . . . Yes, the Tenderloin: SC, "The Tenderloin as It Really Is," *Works* 8: 114, 392.

156   *deep in conversation . . . a temporary wrong:* SC, "Adventures of a Novelist," *Works* 8: 656–61.

157   *sobbing violently . . . studying human nature: New York Journal,* 17 September 1896.

158   *She was a woman . . . a good man: New York Journal,* 17 September 1896.

    showed the 'Badge . . . Stephen Crane is: quoted in Olov W. Fryckstedt, "Stephen Crane in the Tenderloin," *Studia Neophilologica* 34 (1962): 135–63.

159   *The chances are:* editorial, *Boston Traveler*, 2 October 1896, p. 4.

    would see that: Lawrence, *Real Stephen*, p. 17.

    the biggest man: quoted in Edmund Morris, *The Rise of Theodore Roosevelt* (New York: Ballantine Books, 1979), p. 504.

    bull-necked: ibid., p. 524.

160   *an indictment . . . an invulnerable:* Fryckstedt, "Stephen Crane," p. 144.

    From top to bottom: Roosevelt, quoted in Morris, *Rise of Theodore Roosevelt*, pp. 485–86.

161   *grimy:* ibid., p. 539.

    the Spaniards: Morris, ibid., p. 526.

161   *in the hope:* Peter Lyon, *Success Story: The Life and Times of S. S. McClure* (New York: Scribner's, 1963), p. 140.

   I have much: Correspondence, p. 241.

   for much though . . . Some day: ibid., p. 249.

   superbly health-giving: David McCullough, *Mornings on Horseback* (New York: Simon & Schuster, 1982), p. 340.

162   *we have not: Correspondence,* p. 249.

   shameful performance: SC, "Poor Police Arrangements at the Bryan Meeting," *Port Jervis Evening Gazette,* 20 August 1896, reprinted in Joseph Katz, "Stephen Crane: Metropolitan Correspondent," *Kentucky Review* 4, no. 3 (Spring 1893): 44.

163   *systematic police . . . This is a form:* SC, "What an Observant Correspondent Sees Worth Noting," *Port Jervis Evening Gazette,* 20 August 1896, reprinted in Katz, "Metropolitan Correspondent," p. 44.

   I tried to save: quoted in Garland, "Roadside Meetings," p. 528.

   in matters of: Morris, *Rise of Theodore Roosevelt,* p. 25.

   abnormal self-control: ibid., p. 512.

   small hand: ibid., p. 25.

164   *in order to avoid . . . an opium joint: New York Journal,* 11 October 1896.

   swallowed alive . . . tacked to a plaque: SC, "Opium's Varied Dreams," *Works* 8: 666–67.

   easily misled: Henry F. Pringle, *Theodore Roosevelt* (New York: Harcourt, Brace & World), p. 95.

   nothing so much: Morris, *Rise of Theodore Roosevelt,* p. 490.

165   *as big as hickory . . . typewriter:* Fryckstedt, "Stephen Crane," pp. 135–63.

   subjected to . . . refused to answer: New York Times, 17 October 1896.

166   *short, snappy: New York Journal,* 17 October 1896.

   as if to prevent: quoted in Fryckstedt, "Stephen Crane," p. 156.

   asked that one: ibid., p. 157.

   the longest trial: New York Journal, 15 October 1896, in *Log,* p. 212.

   positively the worst: San Francisco Wave, 7 November 1896.

167   *There was a man: Daily Tatler,* 21 November 1896, reprinted in *SCrN* 4, no. 4 (Summer 1970): 7.

   like a man: Marshall, "Stories of Stephen Crane," pp. 71–72.

   greatly distrest: Howells, quoted in Berryman, *Stephen Crane,* p. 146.

   stubborn . . . big book: Garland, "Roadside Meetings," p. 528.

   The storm center: Bacheller, *Coming Up,* p. 292.

9. GOD SAVE CRANE

168   *My most gentle:* copy in Stephen Crane Collection, Newark Library.

   My dear Indian: quoted in Amy Leslie, "Books and Their Builders," *Chicago Daily News,* 22 July 1896.

   a red, laughing: Frank Buck, *All in a Lifetime* (New York: Robert M. McBride, 1941), p. 52.

169   *she looks like:* Ben Hecht, quoted in obituary of Amy Leslie, *Chicago Daily News,*
         5 July 1939.
         brilliant . . . witty: Charles Yanikoski telephone interview with James W. West,
         11 December 1992.
         a sharp tongue: Vincent Starrett, *Born in a Bookshop: Chapters from the Chicago Re-*
         nascence (Norman: University of Oklahoma Press, 1965), p. 92.
         always laughing: Buck, *All in a Lifetime,* p. 52.
         'Spring Song': Hecht, *Chicago Daily News,* 5 July 1939.
         the first important: Rita M. Plotnicki, quoted in Charles S. Yanikoski, "Amy
         Leslie Reconsidered," unpublished paper.
         rhapsodies of adulation: Ben Hecht, "Wistfully Yours," *Theatre Arts* 35 (July 1951):
         12–13.
170   *what is now:* Correspondence, p. 267.
         temporary separation: ibid., p. 268.
         wait for me: ibid., p. 271.
         I was positively: ibid., p. 267.
         The few moments: ibid., p. 268.
         two stormy interviews: "Amy Leslie vs. Stephen Crane," *Chicago Tribune,* 4 January
         1898, p. 1.
171   *somebody whom . . . If I should:* Correspondence, pp. 265–66.
         encourage . . . weak, very weak: ibid., p. 267.
172   *dictated a long:* ibid., p. 268.
         Blessed girl . . . Be brave: ibid., pp. 269, 270, 271.
         you alone: ibid, p. 269.
         a hotbed: Bill Walter, "On the Waterfront: The Treasure of 'The Open Boat,'"
         Florida's Coastal Magazine, June 1989, p. 3.
         the southern Newport: Helen A. Cooper, *Winslow Homer Watercolors* (New Haven:
         Yale University Press, 1986), p. 152.
         catches the heart . . . this delicious: SC, "The Filibustering Industry," *Works* 9:
         94–99.
173   *pronounced 'wow':* William Randel, "Stephen Crane's Jacksonville," *South At-*
         lantic Quarterly 62 (Spring 1963): 268–69.
         and small ones . . . to pick up: SC, "Filibustering Industry," pp. 94–99.
         innumerable bottles . . . one of them: Charles Michelson, quoted in introduction to
         Work (Follett, ed.), vol. 8.
174   *being closely watched . . . will handle:* Daily Florida Citizen, 2 December 1896.
         Brevity is an element: Correspondence, p. 269.
         to an unnamed: ibid., p. 270.
         own Sweetheart . . . I love you: ibid, pp. 270–71.
175   *generously built:* Brown, *Contacts,* p. 265.
         her features . . . there was about her: Lillian Gilkes, *Cora Crane: A Biography of Mrs.*
         Stephen Crane (Bloomington: Indiana University Press, 1960), pp. 21, 324.
         class: Ernest McCready, quoted ibid., p. 27.
         great dignity: Edith R. Jones, "Stephen Crane at Brede," *Atlantic Monthly* 194
         (July 1954): 60.
         not do her justice: Edith Crane to Melvin H. Schoberlin, undated.

175   highly literate . . . in an atmosphere: Gilkes, *Cora Crane*, pp. 30, 33.
176   who had never: ibid., p. 282.
        at a safe remove: ibid., p. 24.
177   Fact is . . . The news pierced: Ernest McCready, quoted ibid., pp. 27–29.
        whose mud-bespattered: ibid., p. 29.
        seemed sure: Correspondence, p. 271.
        Leave soon: ibid., p. 272.
178   box after box: SC, "Stephen Crane's Own Story," *Works* 9: 85.
        203,000 cartridges: Florida Times-Union, 1 January 1897, p. 6.
        It might have: SC, "Own Story," p. 85.
        a test cargo: New York Herald, 3 January 1897.
        She loaded up . . . of melancholy: SC, "Own Story," p. 85.
        When a man: SC, "Flanagan and His Short Filibustering Adventure," *Works* 5: 95.
        In this ignominious . . . swarmed over: SC, "Own Story," pp. 6, 87.
179   were about the only . . . never quailed: Murphy, quoted in R. W. Stallman, "Journal-
           ist Crane in That Dinghy," *Bulletin of the New York Public Library* 72 (April
           1968): 265.
        with every lurch . . . two colored stokers: SC, "Own Story," p. 88.
180   tossed them: Murphy, in Stallman, "Journalist Crane," p. 265.
        as much as . . . they might as well: SC, "Own Story," p. 90.
        Lie there: New York World, 4 January 1897.
        he looked like: SC, "Own Story," p. 91.
        her yards almost: Steward Montgomery, in Stallman, "Journalist Crane," p. 266.
        This cry on the sea . . . Boys, we will stay: SC, "Own Story," p. 91.
181   eleven men . . . conflicting stories: Correspondence, p. 273.
        monstrous: SC, "Own Story," p. 92.
        as high as: Murphy, quoted in New York World, 5 January 1897.
        the swaying lights: SC, "Own Story," p. 92.
        biting: New York Herald, 5 January 1897.
182   rage, rage . . . The cook let go: SC, "Own Story," p. 93.
        murmur: New York Herald, 5 January 1897.
        that were still: SC, "Own Story," p. 94.
        the six inches . . . A soldier of the legion: SC, "The Open Boat," *Works* 5: 68–92
           passim.
185   Look out . . . All right, captain: New York World, 5 January 1897.
        the cook's great . . . a dripping shape: SC, "Open Boat," pp. 90, 91, 92.
186   Telegram received: Correspondence, p. 274.
        never mind: ibid., p. 276.
        hugging and kissing: Charles LaPoint, "The Day That Stephen Crane Was Ship-
           wrecked," *Daytona Beach Sunday News-Journal*, 22 April 1962.
        shrunk to half: Richmond Barrett, "Correspondence," *American Mercury* 32 (June
           1934): xx–xxii.
        Stephen Crane, Able: Correspondence, p. 276.
        Congratulations on plucky: ibid., p. 275.
187   praise and congratulation: ibid., p. 279.
        is a damned lie: Florida Times-Union, 5 January 1897, p. 1.

187   *the ship was probably:* Correspondence, p. 277.

       she carried her load: New York World, 5 January 1897.

       You risk your own . . . premonition: Florida Times-Union, 5 January 1897.

       The best experience: SC, "Open Boat," p. 73.

       Crane is: New York World, 5 January 1897.

188   *$1,000 for:* according to an unidentified Asbury Park newspaper, reprinted in
       Log, p. 239.

       I am unable: Correspondence, p. 277.

       would prefer to tell: SC, "Own Story," p. 94.

       to C.E.S.: Correspondence, pp. 279–80.

       I explain: SC, Works, 10: 48.

189   *filling up . . . If he ever said:* quoted in Branch Cabell and A. J. Hanna, *The St.
       Johns: A Parade of Diversities* (New York: Farrar & Rinehart, 1943), p. 281.

       woman's nursing: SC, "Open Boat," p. 85.

       I will stay: Atlantic Journal, 6 January 1897.

       I am feeling: Port Jervis Union, 15 January 1897, quoted in *Log,* p. 240.

10. THEY SAY SMOLENSKI WEPT

190   *He looked like:* quoted in *Correspondence,* p. 263.

       None of them knew: SC, "Open Boat," p. 68.

       It is the writing: Ford Madox Ford, *Portraits from Life* (Boston: Houghton Mifflin,
       1937), p. 37.

       Shipwrecks are apropos: SC, quoted in introduction to *Works* 5.

191   *lapping waves:* SC, "The Reluctant Voyagers," *Works* 8: 18.

       babes of the sea: SC, "Open Boat," p. 83.

       the most poignant: James B. Colvert, introduction to *Works* 10.

       When it came: SC, "Open Boat," p. 92.

       that an enthusiasm: SC, in *Book Buyer* 13, no. 3 (April 1896); 140.

192   *mountain of lies:* Corwin Knapp Linson to Thomas Beer, 30 April 1923.

       There is the reflection: Boston Evening Record, 21 January 1897, p. 4.

       Oh, Crane! . . . raucous guffaw: Robert H. Davis, introduction to *Work* (Follett,
       ed.), vol 2.

195   *He is confident: Florida Times-Union,* 10 February 1897, p. 8.

       a month among: Correspondence, p. 281.

       one from the syndicate: Amy Leslie to Willis Brooks Hawkins, 6 February 1897.

       a rather dandified . . . No thanks! Linson, *My Stephen,* pp. 99–101.

196   *suffered from unfortunate . . . What would you:* Corwin Knapp Linson to Thomas
       Beer, 30 April 1923.

       If you love: Linson, quoted in Schoberlin to Edith Crane, 27 July 1948.

       first option: J. C. Levenson, introduction to *Works* 5.

       chin . . . most tragically: Correspondence, pp. 281–82.

197   *extreme and refreshing . . . he was off:* Arthur Waugh, "London Letter," *Critic,* 17
       April 1897.

       He is very modest: Richard Harding Davis, quoted in Scott C. Osborn, "The

'Rivalry-Chivalry' of Richard Harding Davis and Stephen Crane," *American Literature* 28 (March 1956): 53.

197   *stuffed parrot: Correspondence*, p. 186.

new groups: Leslie's Weekly, 1 June 1896, p. 381.

198   *fundamentally different:* Arthur Lubow, *The Reporter Who Would Be King: A Biography of Richard Harding Davis* (New York: Scribner's, 1992), p. 145.

Read by multitudes: Claude Bragdon, *Merely Players* (New York: Knopf, 1929), p. 70.

The social crisis: Correspondence, p. 185.

Stephen Crane seems . . . a bi-roxide blonde: quoted in Osborn, " 'Rivalry-Chivalry' " p. 53.

was understood by all: SC, *Active Service, Works* 3: 230.

199   *the top-gear . . . shadow:* SC, "An Impression of the 'Concert,'" *Works* 9: 5–12.

frontier . . . It really isn't: Correspondence, p. 285.

200   *deep-throated:* SC, "The Spirit of the Greek People," *Works* 9: 13.

these people: SC, "Stephen Crane Says Greeks Can't Be Cured," *Works* 9: 14–15.

Thank God: quoted in Osborn, " 'Rivalry-Chivalry,'" p. 53.

the clumsily bandaged: Imogene Carter, "War Seen Through a Woman's Eyes," *Works* 9: 267.

duality . . . it easy to fasten: SC, *Active Service*, p. 157.

201   *I enclose: Correspondence*, p. 287.

Tell Fairman: ibid., p. 287.

not a day: quoted in Osborn, " 'Rivalry-Chivalry,' " p. 54.

got left . . . Bunked: Cora Crane, "Manuscript Notes," *Works* 9: 273.

202   *torrent:* SC, "Death and the Child," *Works* 5: 121.

stopped to lunch . . . War ships: Cora Crane, "Manuscript Notes," pp. 272–73.

maid . . . the name sounded: Imogene Carter, "Imogene Carter's Adventure in Pharsala," *Works* 9: 269–70.

203   *if there is a man . . . absurd:* SC, "Greek War Correspondents," *Works* 9: 16–18.

mouse ill: Cora Crane, "Manuscript Notes," p. 273.

Crane came up: quoted in Osborn, " 'Rivalry-Chivalry,' " p. 54.

first big battle . . . with marvellous speed: SC, "Stephen Crane at Velestino," *Works* 9: 35.

204   *a Harvard graduate:* quoted in Charles Belmont Davis, ed., "Campaigning in Cuba," in *Adventures and Letters of Richard Harding Davis* (New York: Scribner's, 1917), p. 207.

in a real battle . . . amid a shower: John Bass, "How Novelist Crane Acts on the Battlefield," *New York Journal*, 23 May 1897.

It is a great . . . They fought: SC, "A Fragment of Velestino," *Works* 9: 34, 25.

great canvas: SC, *Active Service*, p. 136.

never let go: SC, "Crane at Velestino," p. 26.

205   *The tiny riders:* SC, *Red Badge*, p. 38.

The swiftness: SC, "Crane at Velestino," p. 25.

The universities: SC, *Active Service*, p. 126.

Crane, what impresses: Bass, "How Novelist Crane."

stout, bull-necked: Richard Harding Davis, *A Year from a Correspondent's Note-Book* (New York: Harper & Brothers, 1898), p. 239.

205   *By the red flashes . . . They say Smolenski:* SC, "Crane at Velestino," pp. 20, 22.

      The last mountain . . . a fat waddling: Bass, "How Novelist Crane," reprinted in *Log*, p. 254.

      a cake of soap: SC, "The Dogs of War," *Works* 9: 50.

      among the last: Sylvester Scovel to his wife, Frances, 19 May 1897, quoted in *Log*, p. 260.

      Shells screamed: Imogene Carter, "Imogene Carter's Pen Picture of the Fighting at Velestino," *Works* 9: 272.

206   *The English Red Cross:* SC, "The Blue Badge of Cowardice," *Works* 9: 47.

      a man covered . . . hired assassins: SC, "Crane at Velestino," pp. 27, 21.

      Nobody pays for: SC, "Blue Badge," p. 47.

      tunic well marked: SC, *Active Service*, p. 163.

      He looked well: Lawrence, *Real Stephen*, p. 19.

207   *Stephen Crane is:* Scovel to his wife, Frances, 19 May 1897, quoted in *Log*, pp. 260–61.

      There are the elements . . . suffering freight: SC, "Stephen Crane Tells of War's Horrors," *Works* 9: 53–54.

208   *I send this:* SC, "Crane at Velestino," p. 23.

      In front of: SC, "My Talk with 'Soldiers Six,' " *Works* 9: 63.

      heavily curtained: SC, "The Man in the White Hat," *Works* 9: 69.

      The sky was: SC, "Fragment," p. 27.

      inexpressible: SC, ibid., p. 29.

      a mystic thing: SC, "Greek War Correspondents," p. 17.

      defined . . . explained the meaning: SC, "Fragment," p. 29.

      because [their] eyes: SC, "My Talk," p. 64.

      The terrible red . . . the crimson outburst: SC, "Fragment," p. 29.

209   *tiny blood-red:* SC, "Impression of the 'Concert," p. 6.

      the blare of . . . fantastic smoky shapes: SC, "Death and the Child," pp. 127, 129, 133, 140.

      when the captain: SC, "Fragment," p. 41.

      They went on: SC, *Active Service*, pp. 191–92.

210   *in the manner of a fish . . . the definition:* SC, "Death and the Child," p. 141.

11. LIVING TALLY

211   *He will probably:* Arthur Waugh, "London Letter," *Critic*, 26 June 1897.

      trivial: San Francisco *Argonaut*, 14 June 1897.

      a word: *Literary Digest*, 19 June 1897, quoted in *Log*, p. 267.

      inconceivable: *Critic*, 26 January 1897.

      This book is: *Correspondence*, p. 292.

212   *I have seen:* *Lewiston Journal*, 18 May 1897.

      in England, nothing: Waugh, "London Letter," in *Log*, p. 266.

      irregular marriage: Stephen Parker, *Informal Marriage, Cohabitation and the Law, 1750–1989* (New York: St. Martin's Press, 1990), p. 14.

      living tally: Ginger S. Frost, *Promises Broken: Courtship, Class and Gender in Victorian England* (Charlottesville: University Press of Virginia, 1995).

213   *as one of the deathless:* Harold Frederic, "Stephen Crane's Triumph," *New York Times,* 26 January 1896.

unique . . . masterpiece: Edward Garnett, "Mr. Stephen Crane: An Appreciation," *Academy* 55 (1898): 483–84.

214   *richly colored:* David Garnett, *The Golden Echo,* quoted in Arthur Mizener, *The Saddest Story: A Biography of Ford Madox Ford* (New York: World, 1971), p. 37.

That's a bully . . . in breeches: Ford Madox Ford, *Thus to Revisit* (London: Chapman and Hall, 1921), p. 106.

all the intensely: Ford, *Portraits from Life,* p. 28.

dourly kind . . . jolly, commanding: Miranda Seymour, *A Ring of Conspirators: Henry James and His Literary Circle, 1895–1915* (Boston: Houghton Mifflin, 1989).

a butler . . . defection: Michael Pease to Melvin H. Schoberlin, 27 November 1948.

primitive establishment: Correspondence, pp. 299–300.

215   *engine Number 36 . . . It coiled:* SC, *The Monster, Works* 7: 9, 24.

217   *The characterization:* Edna Crane Sidbury, quoted in Linson, *My Stephen,* p. 78.

while I was: Correspondence, p. 446.

Henry Johnson was: Cora Crane, quoted in *Academy,* 2 March 1901.

often met [Hume]: Sidbury, in Linson, *My Stephen,* p. 78.

impenetrable: SC, "In the Depths," p. 594.

like released fiends: SC, "Experiment in Misery," p. 287.

insufferably warm . . . middle kitchen: SC, "Own Story," p. 89.

218   *bullet-torn:* SC, "War's Horrors," p. 53.

the wine from: SC, *Maggie,* p. 74.

a thing: SC, "Little Regiment," p. 19.

as if it were . . . alive with envy: SC, *Monster,* pp. 19, 9, 34, 24.

219   *about life in general:* Correspondence, pp. 232–33.

newly-married . . . To the left: SC, "The Bride Comes to Yellow Sky," *Works* 5: 108, 111.

of the false East: Correspondence, p. 242.

a girl he believed . . . The bride was not: SC, "Bride," p. 111.

220   *because you are:* Correspondence, p. 295.

know what to say: ibid., p. 294.

221   *rather badly shaken:* ibid., p. 296.

covered with dust . . . delightful three weeks: ibid., p. 300.

The only result finally: ibid., p. 296.

My dear Amy . . . Yours as ever: ibid., pp. 297–98.

222   *any odd bits:* ibid., p. 296.

a big novel: ibid., p. 301.

silken, sliding: SC, "Death and the Child," p. 139.

refer everything . . . in the strictest: Correspondence, p. 305.

223   *My terms for:* ibid., p. 299.

the American rights: ibid., p. 305.

224   *say it is my very best:* ibid., p. 301.

What on earth: ibid., pp. 307–8.

We are happy . . . for a long visit: ibid., p. 300.

stay over here: ibid., p. 296.

225   *dreadfully hard luck . . . I have managed:* ibid., pp. 301–2.

12. WARM AND ENDLESS FRIENDSHIP

229 *even more interested:* Joseph Conrad, "Stephen Crane: A Note Without Dates," *Bookman* 50, no. 6 (February 1920): 529.

I do admire: Joseph Conrad to Edward Garnett, 14 October 1897, in *Letters from Joseph Conrad, 1895–1924,* ed. Edward Garnett (Indianapolis: Bobbs-Merrill, 1928), p. 115.

with intense gravity . . . His manner: Joseph Conrad, introduction to Beer, *Stephen Crane,* p. 6.

a very old: Frederick R. Karl, *Joseph Conrad: The Three Lives* (New York: Farrar, Straus & Giroux, 1979), p. 14.

230 *very troubled:* H. G. Wells, *Experiment in Autobiography* (Philadelphia: J. B. Lippincott, 1967), p. 525.

brilliant: Edward Garnett, quoted in Karl, *Joseph Conrad,* p. 336.

long before he spoke . . . the strangest: Wells, *Experiment,* p. 525.

talked slowly . . . We were friends: Conrad, "Stephen Crane: A Note," p. 529.

intense earnestness . . . Nothing could have: Conrad, introduction to Beer, *Stephen Crane,* pp. 6, 14, 11, 15, 11, 12.

231 *imaginative grasp of:* Conrad, "Stephen Crane: A Note," p. 529.

had been anything . . . though the world: Conrad, introduction to Beer, *Stephen Crane,* pp. 6, 7, 16.

would not be home: Conrad, quoted in "Joseph Conrad, Stylist, Is No Stylist at All, He Avows," *Newark Evening News,* 8 May 1923.

232 *He seemed to have:* Conrad, introduction to Beer, *Stephen Crane,* p. 16.

Did not we: Correspondence, p. 310.

The world looks: ibid., p. 312.

My dear Conrad: ibid., p. 310.

I must write . . . show your condescension: ibid., pp. 312–13.

233 *damned jerry-built:* quoted in Karl, *Joseph Conrad,* p. 381.

for someone: Jessie Conrad, "Recollections of Stephen Crane," *Bookman* 63, no. 2 (April 1926): 134.

appreciated him: Conrad, introduction to Beer, *Stephen Crane.*

was slightly . . . very slight: Jessie Conrad, "Recollections," p. 134.

the first American: Jessie Conrad, *Joseph Conrad and His Circle* (New York: E. P. Dutton, 1935), p. 56.

gravely on the merits . . . were on the easy: Jessie Conrad, "Recollections," p. 134.

the circus begins: Correspondence, p. 313.

234 *hopeless:* Joseph Conrad to Edward Garnett, 5 December 1897, reprinted in *Log,* p. 281.

Great excitement: Correspondence, p. 315.

hideous and unnatural: SC, "Nebraska's Bitter Fight," p. 410.

Garnett is right: Correspondence, p. 315.

excellent . . . He is strangely: Conrad to Garnett, *Log,* p. 281.

235 *It must be remembered:* Conrad, introduction to Beer, *Stephen Crane,* p. 5.

Mr. Joseph Conrad: W. L. Courtney, *Daily Telegraph,* 8 December 1897, quoted in *Log,* p. 282.

235   *[disclaiming] all:* Conrad, quoted in *Log*, p. 282.

236   *Do you think . . . [struggled] along:* Correspondence, p. 319.
        Stephen is fat: ibid., p. 316.
        I send you . . . For heaven's sake: ibid., pp. 320–21.
        We are so pleased: ibid., p. 316.
        It might make me: ibid., p. 318.
        at least 75000 . . . in about two: ibid., pp. 317–18.

237   *Steve:* Amy Leslie to Willis Brooks Hawkins, 22 September 1897.
        a friend . . . I presume: Willis Brooks Hawkins to George B. Mabon, 28 December 1898, reprinted in *Log*, p. 284.
        Amy Leslie vs.: Chicago Tribune, 4 January 1898, p. 1.
        Crane sued: Chicago Times-Herald, 5 January 1898, p. 1.
        breach of contract: quoted in *Log*, p. 285.

238   *by force of . . . owns some property: Chicago Tribune,* 4 January 1898.
        became best known: Chicago Chronicle, 5 January 1898.
        Literary circles . . . have plenty: Chicago Evening Post, 6 January 1898, p. 4.
        That's a good boy: Correspondence, p. 329.

239   *heavy with troubles:* ibid., p. 331.
        chased to the wall: ibid., p. 327.
        a scheme: ibid., p. 332.
        Crane wrote me: Joseph Conrad to Edward Garnett, 15 January 1898, reprinted in *Log*, p. 286.
        Don't kick . . . The consequences: Correspondence, p. 327.
        I expect to mail: ibid., p. 332.
        what it will take: William Crane to George B. Mabon, 5 February 1898, reprinted in *Log*, p. 286.
        must approximate the full: George B. Mabon to I. Seisfield, 15 February 1898, reprinted in *Log*, p. 290.

240   *were still in the chrysalis: Correspondence,* p. 339.
        The Palace Hotel . . . This registers: SC, "The Blue Hotel," *Works* 5: 142, 143, 169.

241   *No other Crane fiction:* Ralph Ellison, "Stephen Crane and the Mainstream of American Fiction," in *Shadow and Act* (New York: Random House, 1964), p. 75.
        turmoiling sea . . . Usually there are: SC, "Blue Hotel," pp. 4, 170.

242   *if it were not . . . Get me through: Correspondence,* pp. 336–37.
        regardless of expense . . . Nobody looks: Conrad, introduction to Beer, *Stephen Crane,* p. 18.
        a beautiful box: Jessie Conrad, "Recollections," p. 134.
        a ghastly nuisance: Correspondence, p. 328.
        have a real good time . . . I believe: ibid., p. 341.
        they pervaded . . . could not help: Conrad, introduction to Beer, *Stephen Crane,* p. 18.

243   *wonderful adventures:* Cora Crane, quoted in *Correspondence,* p. 342.
        immensely: Jessie Conrad, *Conrad and His Circle,* p. 58.
        Mr. Conrad . . . Cora too: Jessie Conrad, "Recollections," p. 134.
        to some order . . . from a severe case: Conrad, introduction to Beer, *Stephen Crane,* p. 18.
        I miss you: Correspondence, p. 335.

244   *no dramatic gift:* Correspondence, p. 325–26.

   the last train . . . A boundless plain: Conrad, introduction to Beer, pp. 29, 30.

   Dear Harry: ibid., pp. 356–57.

245   *the cloudy afternoon . . . He was ready:* Conrad, introduction to Beer, *Stephen Crane,*
   pp. 31, 32, 33.

   from the seat of war: J. C. Levenson, introduction to *Works* 5, quoted in *Log,*
   p. 296.

   warm and endless: Correspondence, p. 347.

13. THE BEST MOMENT OF ANYBODY'S LIFE

246   *that there was to be:* Correspondence 2: 360.

247   *first-class . . . never tired:* Ralph D. Paine, *Roads of Adventure* (Boston: Houghton
   Mifflin, 1922), pp. 92–93.

   This was the rocking-chair: Richard Harding Davis, *The Cuban and Puerto Rican
   Campaigns* (New York: Scribner's, 1898), p. 50.

   idling on a hotel: Franklin Walker, ed., *The Letters of Frank Norris* (San Francisco:
   Book Club of California, 1956), p. 17.

   tired smile . . . ran to Key West: Paine, *Roads,* p. 193.

   missed the bombardment . . . Crane on the other: Charles Belmont Davis, ed., *Adventures and Letters of Richard Harding Davis* (New York: Scribner's, 1917),
   pp. 234–35.

248   *The boatswain:* SC, "Sampson Inspects Harbor at Mariel," *Works* 9: 106.

   like tops: SC, "Stephen Crane's Pen Picture of C. H. Thrall," *Works* 9: 108.

   duck trousers . . . hung in ragged: Norris, in Walker, ed., *Letters,* pp. 16, 17.

   drudgery . . . the corkscrew: Paine, *Roads,* p. 222.

   a great genius . . . that comes with: Norris, in Walker, ed., *Letters,* pp. 17, 10, 14.

249   *about £40:* Correspondence, p. 360.

   Let Collier's: ibid., p. 359.

   Qui vive! . . . an awful pretty: Paine, *Roads,* pp. 224–28.

250   *went native . . . clothed only:* E. W. McCready to B. J. R. Stolper, 31 January 1934.

251   *a good second:* SCrN 4, no. 2 (Winter 1969): 2.

   a small conservatory: Cora Crane to Clara Frewen, 4 June 1898, reprinted in *Log,*
   pp. 307–8.

   already in camp: Correspondence, p. 363.

   blue steel . . . gory feathers: SC, "War Memories," *Works* 6: 226.

252   *a hawser could not . . . to gather:* Paine, *Roads,* p. 24.

   practicos . . . a man intent: SC, "Marines Signaling Under Fire at Guantanamo,"
   Works 6: 194–200.

   in his devotion: Richard Harding Davis, "Our War Correspondents in Cuba
   and Puerto Rico," *Harper's New Monthly Magazine* 98 (May 1899): 941.

253   *calmness:* Correspondence, p. 478.

   dying hard . . . I was a child: SC, "War Memories," p. 226.

   horribly mutilated: SC, "In the First Land Fight Four of Our Men Are Killed,"
   Works 9: 129.

   frightful tearing effect: SC, "Only Mutilated by Bullets," *Works* 9: 131.

253   *this prolonged . . . But then it was:* SC, "Marines Signaling," pp. 196–97.
      The day broke: SC, "War Memories," p. 227.
254   *to drive the enemy:* SC, "The Red Badge of Courage Was His Wig-Wag Flag,"
      Works 9: 134.
      bitterly afraid . . . the color of beetroot: SC, "War Memories," pp. 228, 232, 233.
      weary, weary: SC, "Wig-Wag Flag," p. 139.
      It seemed absurd: SC, "Marines Signaling," p. 199.
      material aid: Report of the Secretary of the Navy for the Year 1898 (Washington, D.C.,
      1898), 1: 845, quoted in *Correspondence,* p. 364.
255   *the prospect . . . There was no fear:* E. W. McCready to B. J. R. Stolper, 22 January
      1934.
256   *sprawled on deck . . . the straight story:* Paine, *Roads,* pp. 244–46.
      ragged . . . it was the kind: SC, "Hunger Has Made Cubans Fatalists," *Works* 9:
      149.
257   *It is horrible . . . the ragged Cuban:* SC, "Crane Tells the Story of the Disembark-
      ment," *Works* 9: 132–33.
258   *had gone out . . . dense Cuban thickets:* SC, "Stephen Crane at the Front for the
      World," *Works* 9: 142.
      wiry . . . stalwart: Kenneth F. Harris, "Cavalrymen at Guasimas," in *The
      Chicago Record's War Stories* (Chicago: Chicago Record, 1898), p. 66.
      with his apparent: Marshall, "Stories of Stephen Crane," pp. 71–72.
      making more noise . . . Spanish guerilla: SC, "Crane at the Front," pp. 143–45.
      These Mauser: SC, "Wig-Wag Flag," p. 137.
259   *by any soldierly:* SC, "Crane at the Front," p. 144.
      smoking a pipe: quoted in Osborn, " 'Rivalry-Chivalry,' " p. 55.
      Everybody was wounded . . . doomed: "Crane at the Front," pp. 144–45.
      was probably as tired: Marshall, "Stories of Stephen Crane," pp. 71–72.
      noisily . . . it was simply: SC, "Roosevelt's Rough Riders' Loss Due to a Gallant
      Blunder," *Works* 9: 146.
260   *the first reports . . . there was doubtless:* Theodore Roosevelt, quoted in Frank Frei-
      del, *The Splendid Little War* (New York: Bramhill House, 1958), p. 112.
      [blundered] into: Richard Harding Davis, quoted in Freidel, *Splendid Little War,*
      p. 108.
      Our confidence: SC, "Hunger Has Made," p. 148.
261   *all commanding officers:* Edward Marshall, quoted in Charles H. Brown, *The Cor-
      respondents' War: Journalists in the Spanish-American War* (New York: Scribner's,
      1967), p. 308.
      ate only one meal: Edward Marshall, *The Story of the Rough Riders* (New York:
      Dillingham, 1899), p. 76.
      usually found it . . . fingered his whiskey: Cecil Carnes, *Jimmy Hare, News Photogra-
      pher: Half a Century with a Camera* (New York: Macmillan, 1940), pp. 60–63.
262   *It'll be the soldiers . . . Nobody could stay:* Carnes, *Jimmy Hare,* p. 63.
      They're off! . . . that profound patience: SC, "Stephen Crane's Vivid Story of the
      Battle of San Juan," *Works* 9: 156, 157, 158, 160.
264   *went over like men:* SC, "War Memories," p. 248.
      pinto pony . . . No Spaniard: Carnes, *Jimmy Hare,* pp. 70–71.

264   *uproarious and . . . Yes Jimmie:* SC, "War Memories," p. 246.

265   *a hundred broken:* Carnes, *Jimmy Hare,* p. 70.

     miserable huddle . . . the apparition: SC, "War Memories," pp. 247–48.

266   *to the crest . . . Oh, was that:* Richard Harding Davis, *Notes of a War Correspondent* (New York: Scribner's, 1910), reprinted in *Log,* p. 325.

     the leather case: Fairfax Downey, *Richard Harding Davis and His Day* (New York: Scribner's, 1933), p. 161.

     killing hailstorm: Morris, *Rise of Theodore Roosevelt,* p. 653.

267   *rolling a cigarette:* Tolstoi, *Sebastopol,* p. 36.

     a mere corpse: SC, "War Memories," *Works* 6: 237.

     calmly rolling: Landon Smith, quoted in Arthur Brisbane, "Some Men Who Have Reported This War," *Cosmopolitan,* September 1898, p. 537.

     A langorous indifference . . . I didn't know: SC, "War Memories," p. 259.

268   *on a pile:* Burr McIntosh, *The Little I Saw of Cuba* (London: F. Tennyson Neely, 1899), reprinted in *Log,* p. 326.

     poor bandaged chaps . . . hung their heads: SC, "War Memories," pp. 261, 254.

269   *know you:* Correspondence, p. 367.

270   *dull:* Don C. Seitz, "Stephen Crane: War Correspondent," *Bookman* 76 (February 1933): 138.

     a drunken: Henry N. Cary to Vincent Starrett, 30 March 1922, quoted in *Log,* p. 321.

     gleefully . . . Oh, very well: Seitz, "Stephen Crane," pp. 139–40.

14. THE ASHES OF LOVE

272   *Dear Madam:* Correspondence, p. 370.

     the worst affected . . . In the tiny: Frank Ryan, M.D., *The Forgotten Plague: How the Battle Against Tuberculosis Was Won — and Lost* (Boston: Little, Brown, 1993), pp. 8, 155, 156.

273   *If it was:* Frank Ryan to Linda H. Davis, 16 February 1994.

     a cheesy boil: Ryan, *Forgotten Plague,* p. 16.

     bleeding at the lungs: JTC journal, 12 January 1867, in Gullason, *Career,* p. 18.

     emaciated: JTC to George Peck, 15 August 1851.

     disease and suffering: MHPC to Mr. and Mrs. George Peck, 6 June 1867.

     Will . . . seems: JTC to George Peck, 16 December 1874.

274   *still wedded:* Sheila M. Rothman, *Living in the Shadow of Death: Tuberculosis and the Social Experience of Illness in American History* (Baltimore: Johns Hopkins University Press, 1995), p. 173.

     shambling . . . the wreck: Charles Michelson, introduction to *Work* (Follett ed.), vol. 12.

275   *the deadly monotony:* Chief Yeoman James Taft Hatfield, quoted in Freidel, *Splendid Little War,* p. 261.

     phrase for phrase . . . Possibly the explanation: Michelson, introduction to *Work* (Follet, ed.), vol. 12.

277   *good fellows . . . "This town!":* Richard Harding Davis, "How Stephen Crane Took Juana Dias," in George Lynch and Frederick Palmer, eds., *In Many*

Wars by Many War Correspondents (Tokyo: Tokyo Printing Company, 1904), reprinted in *Log*, pp. 334–35.

277   *the American governor . . . got along like:* Michelson, introduction to *Work*, vol. 12.

278   *without permission:* SC, "Stephen Crane Fears No Blanco," *Works* 9: 188.

      or until a riot . . . He was not the same: memorandum by Walter Parker re: Stephen Crane, March 1940, New York Public Library.

279   *He is a juggler:* Robert Bridges, *Life*, 1 September 1898, reprinted in *Log*, pp. 338–39.

      found that he had had . . . found a girl: Parker memorandum.

280   *Thou art . . . Thou lovest:* SC, "Intrigue," *Works* 10: 62–69.

281   *Time moves . . . count[ed] for nothing:* SC, "How They Court in Cuba," *Works* 10: 205.

282   *to learn how:* Walter Parker to H. L. Mencken, 2 March 1940.

      Have you heard: William Blackwood to Joseph Conrad, 30 August 1898, in Joseph Conrad, *Letters to William Blackwood and Davis S. Meldrum*, ed. William Blackburn (Durham, N.C.: Duke University Press, 1958).

      done away with: Helen R. Crane, "My Uncle, Stephen Crane," *American Mercury* 31 (January 1934): 28–29.

      fears for his safety: Florida Times-Union, 10 September 1898.

      ask the President: Correspondence, p. 371.

      behaving very shabily . . . has no right: ibid., p. 371–72.

      almost distracted: ibid., p. 371

283   *I should hate . . . If, in these circumstances: Correspondence*, p. 374.

      He did nothing . . . wretched: Otto Carmichael, "Stephen Crane in Havana," *Prairie Schooner* 43 (1969): 203.

      Now this is It!: Correspondence, p. 373.

      the price the men paid: ibid., p. 387.

      the grace . . . Here were scattered: SC, "The Price of the Harness," *Works* 6: 100, 101, 102, 98.

284   *If you dont: Correspondence*, p. 373.

      a peach: ibid., p. 379.

      dream-rivals . . . It was part: SC, "The Clan of No-Name," *Works* 6: 134.

      devotedly . . . I love this story: Correspondence, p. 379.

      despite all experience: Lawrence, *Real Stephen*, p. 16.

      shivering gleam: SC, "Clan," p. 119.

285   *was marred:* Jessie Conrad, "Recollections," p. 134.

      Say, didn't . . . Yes, I see: unsigned article by Otto Carmichael, *Omaha Daily Bee*, 17 June 1900, reprinted in *Log*, pp. 343–44.

      regret at having . . . had not been out: National Archives, reprinted in *Log*, p. 347.

286   *in some sort of difficulty: Correspondence*, pp. 379–80.

      Hit him hard . . . I have got: ibid., p. 380.

      When in Christ's: ibid., p. 381.

      If I dont: ibid., p. 383.

      afford to write: ibid., p. 381.

287   *a miserable creature: New York Times*, 28 October 1898.

      completed about 15000 . . . When — oh, when: Correspondence, p. 385.

287   *most remote . . . What kind:* ibid., pp. 383–84.
       I've only £8 . . . I only wish: ibid., p. 386.

288   *legally, absolutely:* Meldrum to Blackwood, 30 November 1898, in Conrad, *Letters to William Blackwood,* reprinted in *Log,* p. 353.

289   *To me, the supreme: Correspondence,* p. 403.
       I think it would: ibid., p. 399.
       Mrs. Crane got: Conrad to Meldrum, 21 December 1898, reprinted in *Log,* p. 357.
       advise Mr. Crane . . . A man must: Correspondence, p. 388.
       My letters: quoted in *Log,* p. 353.

290   *dalliance with two:* Edwin Emerson, *Pepys's Ghost* (Boston: Richard G. Badger, 1900), reprinted in *Log,* p. 357.
       the wonderful boy: Hamlin Garland diary entry, 28 December 1898, reprinted in *Log,* p. 359.
       malarial fever: Edwin H. Cady, *The Realist at War: The Mature Years, 1885–1920, of William Dean Howells* (Syracuse: Syracuse University Press, 1958), p. 213.
       The horror . . . over three hundred: Correspondence, p. 405.

15. LORD THOLEPIN OF MANGO CHUTNEY

291   *thirty-five dollars . . . So I have run: Correspondence,* p. 416.
292   *all fuzzy . . . a leading:* ibid., p. 418.
       I am unwell: Correspondence, p. 428.
       mad over the place: ibid., p. 420.
       lyric: Edmund Austen, *Brede: The Story of a Sussex Parish* (Rye, England: Adams & Son, 1946), p. 29.
       of the small: Augustus J. C. Hare, *Sussex* (London: George Allen, 1896), p. 47.
       primitive earth closets: Allen Andrews, *The Splendid Pauper* (New York: J. B. Lippincott, 1968), p. 195.
       would have roasted: Clare Sheridan, *My Crowded Sanctuary* (London: Methuen, 1946), p. 13.

293   *babies crying:* Edith R. Jones, "Crane at Brede," p. 59.
       Stephen said: Correspondence, p. 420.
       absurdly fond: Andrews, *Splendid Pauper,* p. 53.
       I must raise heaven: Correspondence, p. 418.

294   *I think that collection:* ibid., p. 422.
       We all think: ibid., p. 424.
       We like it: ibid., p. 425.
       The next story: ibid., p. 428.
       could live for half . . . borrow money: ibid., p. 419.
       a little temporary mortgage: ibid., p. 428.

295   *will be paid . . . Really your position: Correspondence,* p. 433.
       very atmosphere: ibid., p. 440.
       in connection with . . . He dropped: Conrad, introduction to Beer, *Stephen Crane,* pp. 20, 21.
       blaze of azaleas: Sheridan, *Crowded Sanctuary,* p. 11.

296   *looked apprehensively:* Jessie Conrad, "Recollections," p. 135.

296   *doing more work:* Correspondence, p. 463.
        at a clipping gait: ibid., p. 455.
        whispering snakes . . . Each small gleam: SC, *War Is Kind, Works* 10: 46–69.
        was profoundly weary: Amy Lowell, introduction to *Work* (Follett, ed.), vol. 6.

297   *Mr. Crane is:* Willa Cather, quoted in *Log,* p. 385.
        I can't quite: ibid., p. 446.
        the American serial . . . feels the same: ibid., p. 456.

298   *The successful man:* SC, *War Is Kind,* p. 54.
        in the old days: quoted in Mark Barr, "The Haunted House of Brede," in
          Wertheim, "Stephen Crane Remembered," p. 57.
        uninhabitable: Conrad, introduction to Beer, *Stephen Crane,* p. 25.
        ulterior splendor: Correspondence, p. 447.
        doll's: Jessie Conrad, "Recollections," p. 135.
        in the unhaunted: Mark Barr, "Haunted House," p. 57.
        Bats flew: A. E. W. Mason to Vincent Starrett, 4 October 1945.
        to sleep in . . . I've got you: Mark Barr, "Haunted House," p. 58.

299   *slatternly:* Jessie Conrad, "Recollections," p. 135.
        some coarse bronze: Jessie Conrad, *Conrad and His Circle,* p. 72.
        in a somewhat lofty . . . his face set: Jessie Conrad, "Recollections," p. 136.
        The chances of dinner: Jessie Conrad, *Conrad and His Circle,* p. 73.

300   *delightful hosts:* Mark Barr, "Haunted House," p. 57.
        You are the greatest: Correspondence, p. 516.
        more than charming: ibid., p. 335.

301   *below:* A. E. W. Mason to Melvin H. Schoberlin, 21 January 1948.
        past: Leon Edel, *Henry James, the Master: 1901–1916* (New York: J. B. Lippincott,
          1972), p. 62.
        nine or ten years: quoted in Gilkes, *Cora Crane,* p. 124.
        an energetic lady: Wells, *Experiment,* p. 522.
        herself a great: A. J. Liebling, "The Dollars Damned Him," *New Yorker,* 5 August
          1961, p. 59.
        an ample: Barr, quoted in Donald Pizer, ed., *Hamlin Garland's Diaries* (San
          Marino, Calif.: Huntington Library, 1968), p. 121.
        of a somewhat monumental: Jessie Conrad, *Conrad and His Circle,* p. 72.
        large, fair and placid: Ford Madox Ford, *Return to Yesterday* (New York: Horace
          Liveright, 1932), p. 62.
        medieval: Ford, *Portraits from Life,* p. 36.
        I haven't any: Cora Crane, quoted in Edith R. Jones, "Crane at Brede," p. 60.
        strange fancy . . . highly strung: Jessie Conrad, "Recollections," p. 136.
        vivid impression: Clare Sheridan to Ames Williams, 7 June 1945.

302   *I hope that:* Correspondence, p. 413.
        lice: ibid., p. 407.

303   *We love Brede:* ibid., p. 440.
        During these late: ibid., p. 465.
        I won't do . . . as if moved: Conrad, introduction to Beer, *Stephen Crane.*

304   *Feeling vile:* Correspondence, p. 507.
        He professed: ibid., p. 496.

305   *You are wrong:* ibid., p. 497.

       Please have the kindness: ibid., p. 504.

       freely, and at others: quoted in "Joseph Conrad, Stylist."

       because they were true: Mark Barr, "Haunted House," p. 57.

       a frail eagle: Ford, *Portraits from Life,* p. 30.

       If you can stick: Correspondence, p. 498.

306   *A rattling good:* ibid., p. 490.

       a whacking good . . . for they are: ibid., p. 494.

       every emotion: New York World, 10 June 1900, reprinted in *Log,* p. 447.

       great orbs: Ford Madox Ford, "Stevie & Co.," *New York Herald Tribune,* 2 January 1927, p. 4.

       intensely concentrated: Edward Garnett, *Friday Nights: Literary Criticisms and Appreciations* (London: Jonathan Cape, 1922), p. 203.

       pale Mephistophelian face . . . That commanding: Edwin Pugh, "Stephen Crane," *Bookman* 67 (December 1924): 162–64.

307   *a few days holiday:* Correspondence, p. 508.

       the wild Irishman . . . lunches, dinners: Edith R. Jones, "Crane at Brede," pp. 57, 60.

       The wine man: Correspondence, p. 508.

       like hell . . . The truth is: ibid., p. 515.

308   *still seedy:* ibid., p. 524.

       trying, over a given: Edith R. Jones, "Crane at Brede," p. 58.

       under the influence: ibid., p. 520.

309   *I confess:* ibid., pp. 539–40.

       This is a fatal . . . if you have sent: ibid., pp. 541–42.

       a double extra . . . This is something: ibid., pp. 543–44.

310   *chalk-blue . . . the singing:* SC, "The Upturned Face," *Works* 6: 297, 298.

       the 'Dead Man': Correspondence, p. 417.

       fearsome sights: Leo Tolstoy, *The Sebastopol Sketches,* translated by David McDuff (New York: Penguin Books, 1986), p. 48.

       Well, of course: SC, "Upturned Face," p. 300.

       the terrible red: SC, "Fragment," p. 29.

       weary: SC, "Wig-Wag Flag," p. 139.

       There was expressed . . . strange wonder: SC, "Fragment," pp. 39, 34.

16. THE RED ROOM

311   *bright scarlet:* Mark Barr, "Haunted House," p. 57.

       hours of terrific work: Edith Ritchie Jones to Thomas Beer, 6 February 1923.

       This is good: Cora Crane's Notebook, in Wertheim, "Stephen Crane Remembered," p. 60.

312   *How old . . . Now, let's have:* Edith R. Jones, "Crane at Brede," pp. 57–59.

       The studied Americanisms: Ford, *Thus to Revisit,* p. 109.

       Stephen wants . . . adored: Edith R. Jones, "Crane at Brede," p. 58.

       write a popular: Cora Crane's Notebook, in Wertheim, "Stephen Crane Remembered," p. 60.

       full of love: Correspondence, p. 447.

313   *the impact of a dollar:* SC, *War Is Kind*, p. 57.

rather — er — prematurely: SC, *Active Service*, p. 218.

told me to beware . . . some silly talent: Correspondence, pp. 429–30.

314   *I am confident:* ibid., p. 457.

I fear that: ibid., p. 454.

undermine whatever: ibid., p. 481.

admirably sketched: Athenaeum, 11 November 1899.

ingenious and entertaining: Spectator, 11 November 1899.

invincible: London Morning Post, 14 December 1899.

whether the author: New York Times, 18 November 1899.

tiresome: San Francisco Argonaut, 20 November 1899.

Every page: Willa Cather, *Pittsburgh Leader*, 11 November 1899, quoted in *Log*, p. 406.

315   *Again and:* Charles Lewis Hind, quoted in *Bulletin of the New York Public Library* 56 (December 1952): 592.

Husbands and wives . . . Consequently: Wells, *Experiment*, p. 523.

meant nothing: A. E. W. Mason to Vincent Starrett, 4 October 1945.

I loathe a crowd: Correspondence, p. 534.

316   *Some of those:* A. E. W. Mason to Melvin H. Schoberlin, 21 January 1948.

Surely there has never: C. Lewis Hind, *Authors and I* (New York: John Lane, 1921), reprinted in *Log*, p. 412.

some awful rubbish . . . distinguished rabble: Correspondence, pp. 548–49.

awful: C. Lewis Hind, *Naphtali* (New York: Dodd, Mead, 1926), p. 121.

revelled until two . . . sulky and reserved: Wells, *Experiment*, pp. 522–24.

317   *not unamused:* Hind, *Authors*, in *Log*, p. 412.

aloof . . . Crane seemed devoted: A. E. W. Mason to Melvin H. Schoberlin, 21 January 1948.

presented to bevies: Hind, quoted in *Log*, p. 412.

a patch of composite . . . my last clear: Wells, *Experiment*, pp. 523–24.

every bit of it: quoted in Edith R. Jones, "Crane at Brede," p. 61.

A long 20th Century: Correspondence, p. 574.

318   *amusing . . . a remarkable:* Sussex Express; Surrey Standard & Kent Mail, 5 January 1900; *Daily Chronicle*, 13 January 1900; *Manchester Guardian*, 13 January 1900; all quoted in *Correspondence*, pp. 569, 570.

desolated by your request: Correspondence, p. 569.

You see we knew: ibid., p. 570.

very jolly: ibid., p. 571.

ill again . . . I don't know: ibid., p. 572.

My Dear Pinker: ibid., p. 575.

319   *Mr. Crane intended:* ibid., pp. 577–78.

I am sure: ibid., p. 579.

Already months ago: quoted in *Log*, p. 424.

320   *the good thing:* Wells, *Experiment*, p. 524.

genius . . . Mr. Crane seems: Rupert Hughes ["Chelifer"], *Criterion*, 6 January 1900, reprinted in *Log*, p. 420.

grim: Critic, February 1900, quoted in *Log*, p. 423.

320   *an outrage . . . the tiny trivialities:* Julian Hawthorne, *Book News,* February 1900, quoted in *Log,* p. 422.

of the new school: "The New Art of Description in Fiction," *Literary Digest,* 10 February 1900, quoted in *Log,* pp. 424–25.

sure quick money: Correspondence, p. 605.

$50 per thousand: ibid., p. 603.

to my wife's credit . . . rather ambiguously: ibid., p. 605.

321   *have ten pounds . . . £22 before:* ibid., p. 607.

abandoning my lucrative: ibid., p. 607.

a flying visit . . . The startled expression: Conrad, introduction to Beer, *Stephen Crane,* p. 14.

322   *I don't think: Correspondence,* p. 615.

He seems to get weaker: ibid., p. 620.

already pawned: ibid., p. 643.

in a shape: ibid., p. 617.

very much depleted: ibid., p. 616.

My dearest girl: ibid., p. 617.

was so encouraging: ibid., p. 615.

323   *his nourishment:* ibid., p. 621.

I have notes: ibid., p. 618.

Now, Mr. Pinker: ibid., pp. 621–22.

He is much better: ibid., p. 624.

since he would not: A. E. W. Mason to Melvin H. Schoberlin, 21 January 1948.

324   *my dear wife:* Stephen Crane's will, 21 April 1900, reprinted in *Log,* p. 433.

Stephen is not up . . . for the next: Correspondence, p. 632.

simply death: ibid., p. 638.

has a chance: ibid., p. 642.

My wife would love: ibid., p. 644.

325   *Stephen can tell you:* ibid., p. 628.

to some seaport: Jessie Conrad, "Recollections," pp. 136–37.

I have Conrad: Correspondence, p. 651.

I am sure: ibid., p. 405.

soul: Edith Ritchie Jones to Thomas Beer, 6 February 1923.

constant care: Correspondence, p. 646.

326   *clear . . . ordinary:* SCrN 3, no. 2 (Winter 1968): 4; SCrN 3, no. 4 (Summer 1969): 6–7; SCrN 4, no. 1 (Fall 1969): 4–5.

lying still: H. G. Wells, "Stephen Crane from an English Standpoint," *North American Review* 171 (August 1900): 233.

painful to witness: Ford, "Stevie & Co.," p. 4.

broken-hearted: Gilkes, *Cora Crane,* pp. 251–52.

all over: ibid., p. 229.

in Crane's beautiful: Robert Barr, quoted in *Log,* p. 440.

There was a thin: Robert Barr to Vincent Starrett, 8 June 1900; reprinted in Vincent Starrett, "Stephen Crane: An Estimate," *Sewanee Review* 28 (July 1920): 11.

and urged me . . . I'll look forward: Robert Barr, quoted in *Log,* p. 440.

327   *Don't you understand:* Cora Crane's Notebook, in Wertheim, "Stephen Crane Remembered," p. 60.

        Robert, when you come: Barr, quoted in Starrett, "Stephen Crane," pp. 411–12.

        One glance: Conrad, "Stephen Crane: A Note," pp. 530–31.

        put on jolly manners: Conrad to John Galsworthy, 26 May 1900, quoted in *Log*, p. 438.

        How beautiful life is: "Joseph Conrad, Stylist."

        breathed out . . . the sails: Conrad, "Stephen Crane: A Note," p. 530.

        It is the end: Jessie Conrad, "Recollections," p. 137.

328   *Upon our arrival . . . little special:* Crane's dictated notes, *Works* 4: 360.

        A worshiper: Cora Crane's Notebook, in Wertheim, "Stephen Crane Remembered," p. 59.

329   *I've only sad news:* Correspondence, p. 655.

        hard suffering: Gustav Faber, *Badenweiler: Ein Stück Italien auf deutschem Grund* (Freiburg: Verlag Karl Schillinger, n.d.), p. 213.

        the most wonderful: Cora Crane's Notebook, in Wertheim, "Stephen Crane Remembered," p. 60.

        why the lung . . . He lives over: Correspondence, pp. 655–56.

        Visions of his past: SC, *Active Service*, pp. 191–92.

        If I lose: Crane's dictated notes, p. 360.

330   *Stephen is not quite clear:* Correspondence, p. 657.

        Look under it: Crane's dictated notes, p. 361.

        I leave her gentle: Cora Crane's Notebook, in Wertheim, "Stephen Crane Remembered," p. 59.

        the same sinister: Barr, quoted in Starrett, "Stephen Crane," p. 412.

        It was only: Cora Crane's Notebook, in Wertheim, "Stephen Crane Remembered," pp. 60–62.

        If you give the boy: Conrad, introduction to Beer, *Stephen Crane*.

EPILOGUE: INTERPRETERS

The story about the allegedly fake Crane inscription in the cupola st Syracuse appeared in "A Friend's Memory of Boyish Prank Reveals Crane 'Inscription' Hoax," *Syracuse Post-Standard*, 23 October 1955. Alexander Woollcott's comment is paraphrased from his book *Enchanted Isles* (New York: G. P. Putnam's Sons, 1924), p. 135.

331   *just opposite . . . thinking over:* Brown, *Contacts*, p. 265.

332   *in heavy mourning:* Edith Crane to Melvin H. Schoberlin, 8 December 1948.

        perfunctory . . . Therefore, few heroes: Wallace Stevens, 18 June 1900, in Holly Stevens, ed., *Letters of Wallace Stevens* (New York: Knopf, 1966), p. 41.

        the outcast child: "Playlot to Rise at Birthplace of Stephen Crane," *New York Herald Tribune*, 1 January 1940, p. 2.

        They used to say: Correspondence, pp. 231–32.

333   *further possible:* Joseph Conrad, "Stephen Crane: A Note," p. 530.

        horribly: The Collected Letters of Joseph Conrad, ed. Frederick R. Karl and Laurence Davies (Cambridge: Cambridge University Press, 1983) 2: 292.

333   *even before:* Wells, "Stephen Crane from an English Standpoint," p. 241.

grudging, inadequate: Edward Garnett, quoted in George Monteiro, "Stephen Crane: A New Appreciation by Edward Garnett," *American Literature* 50, no. 3 (November 1978): 456.

might have been: Liebling, "Dollars Damned Him," p. 71.

I do not think: Wells, quoted in Peter Molyneaux, "Had Stephen Crane Returned," *Texas Monthly* 3, no. 4 (April 1929): 505.

334   *dealing altogether:* Willa Cather, *Not Under Forty* (New York: Knopf, 1968), p. 91.

the most sincere: Ames Williams interview with Mrs. George F. Smillie (Lily Brandon Munroe).

the boy bridegroom: Chicago Daily Inter-Ocean, 17 July 1901, p. 3.

the finest woman: Buck, *All in a Lifetime,* p. 258.

Certainly not!: Starrett, *Born in a Bookshop,* p. 93.

335   *You knew this . . . All right, Jimmy:* Carnes, *Jimmy Hare,* pp. 128–29.

complicity in the murder: Wertheim and Sorrentino, in *Correspondence,* p. 223.

a generously built blonde: Brown, *Contacts,* p. 265.

all the infernal: Cora Crane to Poultney Bigelow, 19 November 1900, reprinted in Stanley Wertheim, "Cora Crane's Thwarted Romance," *Columbia Library Columns* 36, no. 1 (November 1986): 35.

336   *Papa's heart:* Edith F. Crane to Alice Beer, 6 July 1948, Schoberlin Collection.

337   *a god:* Ford, *Portraits from Life,* p. 23.

but as for Levin: quoted in Mizener, *Saddest Story,* p. 95.

What a brutal: Correspondence, p. 659.

Stephen Crane was: E. R. Woodruff to Max Herzberg, undated, Newark Library.

SELECTED

BIBLIOGRAPHY

Aikman, Duncan, ed. *The Taming of the Frontier — by Ten Authors.* New York: Minton, Batch & Co. 1925.

Alger, R. A. *The Spanish-American War.* New York: Harper & Brothers, 1901.

Altman, Lawrence K. "Stymied by Resurgence of TB, Doctors Reconsider a Decades-Old Vaccine." *New York Times,* 15 October 1992.

Anderson, Harold MacDonald. "The American Newspaper. Part I: The War Correspondent." *Bookman* 19 (March 1904): 24–41.

Anderson, Margaret P. "A Note on 'John Twelve' in Stephen Crane's *The Monster,*" *American Notes and Queries* 15 (October 1976): 23–24.

Anderson, Sherwood. Introduction to *Midnight Sketches.* Vol. 11 of *The Work of Stephen Crane.* Edited by Wilson Follett. New York: Knopf, 1925.

Andrews, Allen. *The Splendid Pauper.* New York: J. B. Lippincott, 1968.

Anonymous. "Novels of American Life." *Edinburgh Review* 187 (April 1898): 386–414.

———. "Six Books of Verse." *Atlantic Monthly* 77 (February 1896): 267–72.

Austen, Edmund. *Brede: The Story of a Sussex Parish.* Rye, England: Adams & Son, 1946.

Bacheller, Irving. *Coming Up the Road: Memories of a North Country Boyhood.* Indianapolis: Bobbs-Merrill, 1928.

———. *From Stores of Memory.* New York: Farrar & Rinehart, 1933.

Barr, Robert. "Stephen Crane: An Estimate." *Sewanee Review* 28 (July 1920): 422.

Barrett, Richmond. "Correspondence." *American Mercury* 32 (June 1934): xx–xxii.

Barry, John D. "A Note on Stephen Crane." *Bookman* 13 (April 1901): 148.

Beer, Thomas. Introduction to *The O'Ruddy.* Vol. 7 of *The Work of Stephen Crane.* Edited by Wilson Follett. New York: Knopf, 1926.

———. "Mrs. Stephen Crane." *American Mercury* 31 (March 1934): 289–95.

———. *Stephen Crane: A Study in American Letters.* New York: Alfred A. Knopf, 1923.

Belleville, Bill. "*Commodore* Wreck Prototype of 'Open Boat.'" *Oceans* 20 (May–June 1987): 58–59.

Benfey, Christopher. *The Double Life of Stephen Crane.* New York: Alfred A. Knopf, 1992.

Bennett, Alma Jean. "Traces of Resistance: Displacement, Contradiction, and Appropriation in the Criticism of Amy Leslie, 1895–1915." Ph.D. diss., Kent State University, 1993.

Berryman, John. *Stephen Crane: A Critical Biography.* New York: Farrar, Straus & Giroux, 1950.

Binder, Henry. "Donald Pizer, Ripley Hitchcock, and *The Red Badge of Courage.*" *Studies in the Novel*, 11, no. 2 (Summer 1979): 216–23.

Blow, Michael. *A Ship to Remember: The Maine and the Spanish-American War.* New York: William Morrow, 1992.

Bowers, Fredson, ed. *The Works of Stephen Crane.* 10 vols. Charlottesville: University Press of Virginia, 1969–1976.

Boyd, Thomas. "Semper Fidelis." *Bookman* 60 (December 1924): 409–12.

Bragdon, Claude. *Merely Players.* New York: Knopf, 1929.

———. "The Purple Cow Period." *Bookman* 69 (July 1929): 465–78.

Brazelton, Ethel M. Colson. *Writing and Editing for Women.* New York: Funk & Wagnalls, 1927.

Brooks, Van Wyck. *Howells: His Life and World.* New York: E. P. Dutton, 1959.

———. *John Sloan: A Painter's Life.* New York: E. P. Dutton, 1955.

———. *Sketches in Criticism.* New York: E. P. Dutton, 1933.

Brown, Charles H. *The Correspondents' War: Journalists in the Spanish-American War.* New York: Scribner's, 1967.

Brown, Curtis. *Contacts.* New York: Harper & Brothers, 1935.

Bruccoli, Matthew, and Joseph Katz. "Scholarship and Mere Artifacts: The British and Empire Publications of Stephen Crane." *Studies in Bibliography* 22 (1969): 277–87.

Buck, Frank. *All in a Lifetime.* New York: Robert M. McBride, 1941.

Bullard, F. Lauriston. *Famous War Correspondents.* Boston: Little, Brown, 1914.

Bushick, Frank. *Glamorous Days.* San Antonio: Naylor, 1934.

C.G.S. "The Coward." *New York Times*, 12 February 1893.

Cabell, Branch, and A. J. Hanna. *The St. Johns: A Parade of Diversities.* New York: Farrar & Rinehart, 1943.

Cady, Edwin H. Introduction to *Tales, Sketches, and Reports.* Vol. 8 of *The Works of Stephen Crane.* Edited by Fredson Bowers. Charlottesville: University Press of Virginia, 1973.

———. *The Realist at War: The Mature Years, 1885–1920, of William Dean Howells.* Syracuse: Syracuse University Press, 1958.

Caldwell, Mark. "Resurrection of a Killer." *Discover*, December 1992.

Carmichael, Otto. "Stephen Crane in Havana." *Prairie Schooner* 43 (Summer 1969): 200–204.

Carnes, Cecil. *Jimmy Hare, News Photographer: Half a Century with a Camera.* New York: Macmillan, 1940.

Cartwright, Gary. *Galveston: A History of the Island.* New York: Macmillan, 1991.

Cather, Willa. Introduction to *Wounds in the Rain.* Vol. 9 of *The Work of Stephen Crane.* Edited by Wilson Follett. New York: Alfred A. Knopf, 1926.

———. *Not Under Forty.* New York: Knopf, 1968.

———. *The World and the Parish: Willa Cather's Articles and Reviews, 1893–1902.* Edited by William M. Curtin. 2 vols. Lincoln: University of Nebraska Press, 1970.

——— [Henry Nickleman]. "When I Knew Stephen Crane." Reprinted in *Prairie Schooner* 23 (1949): 231–36.

Cazemajou, Jean. *Stephen Crane (1871–1900): Écrivain journaliste. Études anglaises* 35. Paris: Librairie Didier, 1969.

Champney, Freeman. *Art and Glory: The Story of Elbert Hubbard.* New York: Crown, 1968.

Chandler, George F. "I Knew Stephen Crane at Syracuse." *Courier* 3 (March 1963): 12–13.

Church, Joseph. "The Black Man's Part in Crane's *Monster.*" *American Imago* 45 (Winter 1988): 375–78.

Claverack Township: The History and Heritage. Town of Claverack Historical Society, 1883.

Claverack: Old and New. Claverack, N.Y.: F. H. Webb, n.d.

Clendenning, John. "Rescue in Berryman's *Crane.*" In *Recovering Berryman: Essays on a Poet.* Edited by Richard J. Kelly and Alan K. Lathrop. Ann Arbor: University of Michigan Press, 1993.

———. "Thomas Beer's *Stephen Crane:* The Eye of His Imagination." *Prose Studies* 14 (May 1991): 68–80.

Colvert, James B. "Crane, Hitchcock, and the Binder Edition of *The Red Badge of Courage.*" In *Critical Essays on Stephen Crane's The Red Badge of Courage.* Edited by Donald Pizer. Boston: G. K. Hall, 1990.

———. "Fred Holland Day, Louise Imogen Guiney, and the Text of Stephen Crane's *The Black Riders.*" Unpublished paper.

———. Introduction to *Bowery Tales.* Vol. 1 of *The Works of Stephen Crane.* Edited by Fredson Bowers. Charlottesville: University Press of Virginia, 1969.

———. Introduction to *Great Short Works of Stephen Crane.* New York: Perennial Library, 1968.

———. Introduction to *Poems and Literary Remains.* Vol. 10 of *The Works of Stephen Crane.* Edited by Fredson Bowers. Charlottesville: University Press of Virginia, 1975.

———. Introduction to *Reports of War.* Vol. 9 of *The Works of Stephen Crane.* Edited by Fredson Bowers. Charlottesville: University Press of Virginia, 1971.

———. Introduction to *Tales of War.* Vol. 6 of *The Works of Stephen Crane.* Edited by Fredson Bowers. Charlottesville: University Press of Virginia, 1970.

———. "The Origins of Stephen Crane's Literary Creed." In *A Mirror for Modern Scholars.* Edited by L. A. Beaurline. New York, 1966.

———. "*The Red Badge of Courage* and a Review of Zola's *La Debacle.*" *Modern Language Notes* 71 (February 1956): 98–100.

———. *Stephen Crane.* New York: Harcourt Brace Jovanovich, 1984.

———. "Stephen Crane's Literary Origins and Tolstoy's *Sebastopol.*" *Comparative Literature Studies* Vol. 15, no. 1 (March 1978): 66–82.

———. "Stephen Crane's Magic Mountain." In *Stephen Crane: A Collection of Critical Essays.* Edited by Maurice Bassan. Englewood Cliffs, N.J.: Prentice Hall, 1967.

———. "Structure and Theme in Stephen Crane's Fiction." *Modern Fiction Studies* 5 (Autumn 1959): 199–208.

———. "Unreal War in *The Red Badge of Courage.*" Unpublished paper.

Conrad, Borys. *My Father: Joseph Conrad.* London: Calder & Boyars, 1970.

Conrad, Jessie. *Joseph Conrad and His Circle.* New York: E. P. Dutton, 1935.

———. "Recollections of Stephen Crane." *Bookman* 63 (April 1926): 134–37.

Conrad, Joseph, *The Collected Letters of Joseph Conrad. 2 vols.* Edited by Frederick R. Karl and Laurence Davies. Cambridge: Cambridge University Press, 1983.

———. Introduction to *Stephen Crane: A Study in American Letters*, by Thomas Beer. New York: Alfred A. Knopf, 1923.

———. *Last Essays.* Garden City, N.Y. Doubleday, 1926.

———. *Letters from Joseph Conrad 1895–1924.* Edited by Edward Garnett. Indianapolis: Bobbs-Merrill, 1928.

———. *Letters to William Blackwood and David S. Meldrum.* Edited by William Blackburn. Durham, N.C.: Duke University Press, 1958.

———. "Stephen Crane: A Note Without Dates." *Bookman* 50 (February 1920): 529–31.

Conway, John D. "The Stephen Crane–Amy Leslie Affair: A Reconsideration." *Journal of Modern Literature* 7, no. 1 (February 1979): 3–13.

Cooper, Helen A. *Winslow Homer Watercolors.* New Haven: Yale University Press, 1986.

Crane, Edmund B. "Notes on the Life of Stephen Crane by His Brother, Edmund B. Crane." Unpublished manuscript, University of Connecticut.

Crane, Ellery Bicknell. *Genealogy of the Crane Family.* Vol. 2. Worcester, Mass.: Press of Charles Hamilton, 1900.

Crane, Helen. "In New Jersey." *Newark Star-Eagle*, 8 July 1926.

Crane, Helen R. "My Uncle, Stephen Crane." *American Mercury* 31 (January 1934): 24–29.

Crane, Jonathan Townley. *Holiness, the Birthright of All God's Children.* New York: Nelson & Phillips, 1874.

Crane, Robert. "Family Matters: Stephen Crane's Brother, Wilbur." Paper given to Stephen Crane Society, annual meeting of the American Literature Association, San Diego, Calif., 29 May 1992.

Crane, Stephen. "The Monster." *Harper's New Monthly Magazine* 97 (August 1898): 343–76.

Crane, Stephen. *The Red Badge of Courage.* New York: D. Appleton, 1895; reprint, Norton, 1962.

Damon, S. Foster. *Amy Lowell: A Chronicle.* Boston: Houghton Mifflin, 1935.

Davis, Charles Belmont, ed. *Adventures and Letters of Richard Harding Davis.* New York: Charles Scribner's Sons, 1917.

Davis, Richard Harding. *The Cuban and Puerto Rican Campaigns.* New York: Charles Scribner's Sons, 1898.

———. "A Derelict." *Scribner's Magazine* 30, no. 2 (August 1901): 130–52.

———. "How Stephen Crane Took Juana Dias." In *In Many Wars by Many War Correspondents.* Edited by George Lynch and Frederick Palmer. La Crosse, Wisc.: Sumac Press, 1976.

———. *Notes of a War Correspondent.* New York: Charles Scribner's Sons, 1911.

————. "Our War Correspondents in Cuba and Puerto Rico." *Harper's New Monthly Magazine* 98 (May 1899): 938–48.

————. *A Year from a Correspondent's Notebook.* New York: Harper & Brothers, 1898.

Davis, Roberts H. Introduction to *Tales of Two Wars.* Vol. 2 of *The Work of Stephen Crane.* Edited by Wilson Follett. New York: Alfred A. Knopf, 1925.

Davis, T. Frederick. *History of Jacksonville and Vicinity.* Jacksonville, Fla.: San Marco Bookstore, 1925.

De Forest, John William. *A Volunteer's Adventures: A Union Captain's Record of the Civil War.* New Haven: Yale University Press, 1946.

Dell, Floyd. "Stephen Crane and the Genius Myth." *Nation* 119: 637–38.

Dirlam, H. Kenneth, and Ernest E. Simmons. *Sinners, This Is East Aurora.* New York: Vantage Press, 1964.

Downey, Fairfax. *Richard Harding Davis and His Day.* New York: Charles Scribner's Sons, 1933.

Eby, Cecil D., Jr. "The Source of Crane's Metaphor, 'Red Badge of Courage.'" *American Literature* 32 (May 1960): 204–7.

Edel, Leon. *Henry James: A Life.* New York: Harper & Row, 1985.

————. *Henry James, the Master: 1901–1916.* Philadelphia: J. B. Lippincott, 1972.

Edmiston, Susan, and Linda D. Cirino. *Literary New York.* Boston: Houghton Mifflin, 1976.

Elconin, Victor A. "Stephen Crane at Asbury Park." *American Literature* 20 (November 1948): 275–89.

Ellison, Ralph. "Stephen Crane and the Mainstream of American Fiction." In *Shadow and Act.* New York: Random House, 1964.

Emerson, Edwin, Jr., *Pepys's Ghost.* Boston: Richard G. Badger, 1900.

Ezzell, Carol. "Captain of the Men of Death." *Science News* 143 (6 February 1993): 90–92.

Faber, Gustav. *Badenweiler: Ein Stück Italien auf deutschem Grund.* Freiburg: Verlag Karl Schillinger, n.d.

Feldman, Abraham. "Queries." *American Notes and Queries* 8: 185–86.

Fine, David M. "Abraham Cahan, Stephen Crane and the Romantic Tenement Tale of the Nineties." *American Studies* 14 (Spring 1973): 95–107.

Follett, Wilson. "The Second Twenty-Eight Years." *Bookman* 68 (January 1929): 532–37.

————, ed. *The Work of Stephen Crane.* 12 vols. New York: Alfred A. Knopf, 1925–1927.

Ford, Ford Madox. *Joseph Conrad: A Personal Remembrance.* New York: Octagon Books, 1964.

————. *The March of Literature.* London: George Allen and Unwin, 1939.

————. *Portraits from Life.* Boston: Houghton Mifflin, 1937.

————. *Return to Yesterday.* New York: Horace Liveright, 1932.

————. "Stevie & Co." *New York Herald Tribune,* 2 January 1927.

————. *Thus to Revisit.* London: Chapman & Hall, 1921.

Foster, Malcolm. "The Black Crepe Veil: The Significance of Stephen Crane's *The Monster.*" *International Fiction Review* 3 (July 1976): 87–91.

Frederic, Harold. "London on the War." *New York Times Magazine,* 1 October 1898.

Freidel, Frank. *The Splendid Little War.* New York: Bramhall House, 1958.

French, Mansfield J. "Stephen Crane, Ball Player." *Syracuse University Alumni News* 15 (January 1934): 3–4.

Frewen, Hugh Moreton. *Imogene: An Odyssey.* Sydney, New South Wales: Australian Publishing, 1944.

Fried, Michael. *Realism, Writing, Disfiguration: On Thomas Eakins and Stephen Crane.* Chicago: University of Chicago Press, 1987.

Friedmann, Elizabeth. "Cora Before Crane: The Prologue." Paper delivered at Stephen Crane Conference, Virginia Polytechnic Institute and State University, Blacksburg, Va., 29 September 1989.

———. "Cora's Travel Notes, 'Dan Emmonds,' and Stephen Crane's Route to the Greek War: A Puzzle Solved." *Studies in Short Fiction* 27 (Spring 1990): 264–65.

Frost, Ginger S. *Promises Broken: Courtship, Class and Gender in Victorian England.* Charlottesville: University Press of Virginia, 1995.

Fryckstedt, Olov W. "Stephen Crane in the Tenderloin." *Studia Neophilologica* 34 (1962): 135–63.

Galen, Nina. "Stephen Crane as a Source for Conrad's *Jim*." *Nineteenth-Century Fiction* 38 (June 1983): 78–96.

Garland, Hamlin. "Ibsen as Dramatist." *Arena* 2 (June 1890): 72.

———. *My Friendly Contemporaries: A Literary Log.* New York: Macmillan, 1932.

———. "Roadside Meetings of a Literary Nomad." Part 4. *Bookman* 70 (January 1930): 514–28.

———. "Stephen Crane as I Knew Him." *Yale Review* 75, no. 1 (Autumn 1985): 1–12.

———. "Stephen Crane: A Soldier of Fortune." *Saturday Evening Post* 173 (28 July 1900): 16–17.

Garner, Stanton. "Stephen Crane's 'The Predecessor': Unwritten Play, Unwritten Novel." *American Literary Realism 1870–1910* 13, no. 1 (Spring 1980): 97–100.

Garnett, Edward. *Friday Nights: Literary Criticisms and Appreciations.* London: Jonathan Cape, 1922.

———. "Mr. Stephen Crane. An Appreciation." *Academy* 55 (17 December 1898): 483–84.

———. "Some Remarks on American and English Fiction." *Atlantic Monthly* 114 (December 1914): 747–56.

Geismar, Maxwell. *Rebels and Ancestors: The American Novel, 1890–1915.* Boston: Houghton Mifflin, 1953.

Gilkes, Lillian. *Cora Crane: A Biography of Mrs. Stephen Crane.* Bloomington: Indiana University Press, 1960.

———. "The London Newsletters of Stephen and Cora Crane: A Collaboration." *Studies in American Fiction* 4 (Autumn 1976): 172–201.

———. "A New Stephen Crane Item." *Studies in American Fiction* 5 (Autumn 1977): 255–57.

———. "Stephen and Cora Crane: Some Corrections, and a 'Millionaire' Named Sharefe." *American Literature* 41 (May 1969): 270–71.

———. "Stephen Crane and the Biographical Fallacy: The Cora Influence." *Modern Fiction Studies* 16 (Winter 1970–71): 441–61.

Goss, Warren Lee. "Recollections of a Private, I." *Century* 29 (1 November 1884): 107–13.

———. "Recollections of a Private, II." *Century* 29 (2 December 1884): 279–84.

———. "Recollections of a Private, III." *Century* 29 (5 March 1885): 767–77.

———. "Recollections of a Private, VI." *Century* 31 (3 January 1886): 467–74.

Gregory, Horace. "Stephen Crane's Poems." *New Republic* 63 (25 June 1930): 159–60.

Gullason, Thomas A. "A Cache of Short Stories by Stephen Crane's Family," *Studies in Short Fiction* 23, no. 1 (Winter 1986): 71–106.

———. "The Cranes at Pennington Seminary." *American Literature* 39 (January 1968): 530–41.

———. "The Fiction of the Reverend Jonathan Townley Crane, D.D." *American Literature* 43 (May 1971): 263–73.

———. "The First Known Review of Stephen Crane's 1893 *Maggie*." *English Language Notes* 5 (1968): 300–2.

———. "The Last Will and Testament of Mrs. Mary Helen Peck Crane." *American Literature* 40 (1968): 232–34.

———. "New Light on the Crane–Howells Relationship." *New England Quarterly* 30 (September 1957): 389–92.

———. "The Sources of Stephen Crane's *Maggie*." *Philological Quarterly* 38 (October 1959): 497–502.

———. "Stephen Crane at Claverack College: A New Reading." *Courier* 27, no. 2 (Fall 1992): 33–45.

———. "Stephen Crane's Sister: New Biographical Facts." *American Literature*, 49 (May 1977): 234–38.

———. "The Symbolic Unity of 'The Monster.'" *Modern Language Notes* 75 (December 1960): 663–68.

———, ed. *Stephen Crane's Career: Perspectives and Evaluations*. New York: New York University Press, 1972.

Hafley, James. "'The Monster' and the Art of Stephen Crane," *Accent* 19 (Summer 1959): 159–65.

Hageman, E. R. "The Death of Stephen Crane." *Proceedings of the New Jersey Historical Society* 77 (July 1959): 173–84.

———. "Stephen Crane Faces the Storms of *Life*, 1896–1901." *Journal of Popular Culture* 2 (Winter 1968): 347–60.

Hallam, George. *Riverside Remembered*. Jacksonville, Fla: Drummond Press, 1976.

Hare, Augustus J. C. *Sussex*. London: George Allen, 1896.

Harriman, Karl Edwin. "The Last Days of Stephen Crane." *New Hope* 2 (October 1934) 7–9, 19–21.

———. "A Romantic Idealist — Mr. Stephen Crane." *Literary Review* 4 (April 1900): 85–87.

Harris, Kenneth F. "Cavalrymen at Guasimas." In *The Chicago Record's War Stories*. Chicago: Chicago Record, 1898.

Hart, James D. *The Oxford Companion to American Literature*. 5th ed. New York: Oxford University Press, 1983.

Hecht, Ben. "Wistfully Yours." *Theatre Arts* 35 (July 1951): 12–13.

Heilbrun, Carolyn G. *The Garnett Family*. New York: Macmillan, 1961.

Herford, Kenneth. "Young Blood — Stephen Crane." *Saturday Evening Post* 172 (18 November 1899): 413.

Hind, C. Lewis. *Authors and I.* New York: John Lane, 1921.

———. *Naphtali:* New York: Dodd, Mead, 1926.

Hitchcock, Ripley. Preface to *The Red Badge of Courage.* New York: Appleton, 1900.

Hoffman, Daniel G. "Crane's Decoration Day Article and *The Red Badge of Courage.*" *Nineteenth-Century Fiction* 14 (June 1959): 78–80.

———. *The Poetry of Stephen Crane.* New York: Columbia University Press, 1956.

———. "Stephen Crane's First Story." *Bulletin of the New York Public Library* 64 (May 1960): 273–78.

Holloway, Jean. *Hamlin Garland: A Biography.* Austin: University of Texas, 1960.

Hopkins, Ernest Jerome, ed. *The Complete Short Stories of Ambrose Bierce.* New York: Doubleday, 1970.

Hough, Robert L. "Crane and Goethe: A Forgotten Relationship." *Nineteenth-Century Fiction* 17 (September 1962): 135–48.

Howells, William Dean. "Frank Norris." *North American Review* 175: 769–78.

———. Letter to Cora Crane in "Saturday Review of Books and Arts," *New York Times,* 8 September 1900.

———. "Life and Letters." *Harper's Weekly* 39 (8 June 1895): 532–33.

———. "Life and Letters." *Harper's Weekly* 40 (25 January 1896): 79.

———. *Literature and Life.* New York: Harper & Brothers, 1902.

Hubbard, Elbert. "As to Stephen Crane." *Lotos* 9 (1896): 674–78.

Hughes, Rupert. "The Genius of Stephen Crane." *Criterion* 22 (6 January 1900): 24.

Huneker, James Gibbons. *Steeplejack.* 2 vols. New York: Scribner's, 1922.

Ireland Guide. Irish Tourist Board and the Irish Tourist Association, 1951.

Jean-Aubrey, G. *Joseph Conrad: Life and Letters.* Vol. 1. New York: Doubleday, Page, 1927.

Johnson, Clarence O. "Stephen Crane and Zola's *Germinal.*" *American Notes and Queries* 16 (November 1977): 40–43.

Johnson, Willis Fletcher. "The Launching of Stephen Crane." *Literary Digest International Book Review* 4 (April 1926): 288–90.

Jones, Claude. "Stephen Crane at Syracuse." *American Literature* 7 (March 1935): 82–84.

Jones, Edith R. "Stephen Crane at Brede." *Atlantic Monthly* 194 (July 1954): 57–61.

"Joseph Conrad, Stylist, Is No Stylist at All, He Avows." *Newark Evening News,* 8 May 1923.

Judd, Alan. *Ford Madox Ford.* Cambridge, Mass.: Harvard University Press, 1991.

Kahn, Sy. "Stephen Crane and the Giant Voice in the Night: An Explication of 'The Monster.'" In *Essays in Modern American Literature.* Deland, Fla.: Stetson University Press, 1963.

Karl, Frederick R. *Joseph Conrad: The Three Lives.* New York: Farrar, Straus & Giroux, 1979.

Katz, Joseph. "The Estate of Stephen Crane." *Studies in American Fiction* 10 (Autumn 1982): 135–50.

———. "The Maggie Nobody Knows." *Modern Fiction Studies* 12 (Summer 1966): 200–212.

———. "Solving Stephen Crane's Pike County Puzzle." *American Literature* 55 (May 1985): 171–82.

————. "Some Light on the Stephen Crane–Amy Leslie Affair." *Mad River Review* 1 (Winter 1964–65): 43–62.

————. "Stephen Crane: Metropolitan Correspondent." *Kentucky Review* 4, no. 3 (Spring 1983): 39–51.

————. "Stephen Crane's Concept of Death." *Kentucky Review* 4, no. 2 (Winter 1983): 52–53.

————. "Whitman, Crane and the Odious Comparison." *Notes and Queries* 14 (February 1967): 66–67.

————, ed. *Stephen Crane in the West and Mexico.* Kent, Ohio: Kent State University Press, 1970.

————, ed. *Stephen Crane Newsletter.* Columbus: Ohio State University Press, 1966–1970.

Kazin, Alfred. *On Native Grounds.* New York: Harcourt, Brace & World, 1942.

Kearny, Thomas. *General Philip Kearny: Battle Soldier of Five Wars.* New York: G. P. Putnam's Sons, 1937.

Keet, Alfred Ernest. *Stephen Crane: In Memoriam.* New York: "Privately printed for fifty appreciative friends," 1930(?).

Keller, Alan. *The Spanish-American War: A Compact History.* New York: Hawthorn Books, 1961.

Kibler, James E., Jr., "The Library of Stephen and Cora Crane." *Proof* 1 (1971): 199–246.

Kitchen, J. M. W., M.D. *Consumption: Its Causes, Prevention, and Cure.* New York: G. P. Putnam's Sons, 1885.

Knapp, Daniel. "Son of Thunder: Stephen Crane and the Fourth Evangelist." *Nineteenth-Century Fiction* 24 (December 1969): 253–91.

Kolata, Gina. "First Documented Case of TB Passed on Airliner Is Reported by the U.S." *New York Times,* 3 March 1995.

Kwiat, Joseph J. "The Newspaper Experience: Crane, Norris, and Dreiser." *Nineteenth-Century Fiction* 8 (September 1953): 99–117.

Kyles, Gillian G. M. "Stephen Crane and 'Corporal O'Connor's Story.' " In *Studies in Bibliography,* vol. 27. Edited by Fredson Bowers. Charlottesville: The University Press of Virginia, 1974.

LaFrance, Marston. "A Few Facts about Stephen Crane and 'Holland.' " *American Literature* 37 (1965): 195–202.

LaPoint, Charles. "The Day That Stephen Crane Was Shipwrecked." *Daytona Beach Sunday News-Journal,* 22 April 1962.

LaRocca, Charles, J. *The Red Badge of Courage: Stephen Crane's Novel of the Civil War: An Historically Annotated Edition.* Fleischmanns, N.Y.: Purple Mountain Press, 1995.

Lawrence, Frederic M. *The Real Stephen Crane.* Edited by Joseph Katz. Newark, N.J.: Newark Public Library, 1980.

Lee, Hermione. *Willa Cather: Double Lives.* New York: Pantheon, 1989.

Leslie, Amy. "Books and Builders." *Chicago Daily News,* 22 July 1896.

————. *Some Players.* Chicago: Herbert S. Stone, 1899.

Leslie, Anita. *Mr. Frewen of England.* London: Hutchinson, 1966.

Leslie, Shane. *Studies in Sublime Failure.* London: Ernst Benn, 1932.

Levenson, J. C. Introduction to *The O'Ruddy*. Vol. 4 of *The Works of Stephen Crane*. Edited by Fredson Bowers. Charlottesville: University Press of Virginia, 1971.

———. Introduction to *The Red Badge of Courage*. Vol. 2 of *The Works of Stephen Crane*. Edited by Fredson Bowers. Charlottesville: University Press of Virginia, 1975.

———. Introduction to *Tales of Adventure*. Vol. 5 of *The Works of Stephen Crane*. Edited by Fredson Bowers. Charlottesville: University Press of Virginia, 1971.

———. Introduction to *Tales of Whilomville*. Vol. 7 of *The Works of Stephen Crane*. Edited by Fredson Bowers. Charlottesville: University Press of Virginia, 1969.

———. Introduction to *The Third Violet and Active Service*. Vol. 3 of *The Works of Stephen Crane*. Edited by Fredson Bowers. Charlottesville: University Press of Virginia, 1976.

Lewis, Edith. *Willa Cather Living: A Personal Record*. New York: Farrar, Straus & Giroux, 1976.

Liebling, A. J. "The Dollars Damned Him." *New Yorker*, 5 August 1961 pp. 48–72.

Linder, Lyle. "Applications from Social Science to Literary Biography: The Family World of Stephen Crane." *American Literary Realism* 7 (Summer 1974): 280–82.

Linson, Corwin K. *My Stephen Crane*. Edited by Edwin H. Cady. Syracuse: Syracuse University Press, 1958.

Linson, Corwin Knapp. "Little Stories of 'Steve' Crane." *Saturday Evening Post* 175 (11 April 1903): 19–20.

"Literary Folk — Their Ways and Their Work." *Saturday Evening Post* 173 (28 July 1900): 19.

Littledale, Clara S. "Newark Discovers a Little Brick Shrine." *New York Herald Tribune*, 15 November 1925.

Lowell, Amy. Introduction to *The Black Riders and Other Lines*. Vol. 6. *The Work of Stephen Crane*. Edited by Wilson Follett. New York: Alfred A. Knopf, 1925.

Lubow, Arthur. *The Reporter Who Would Be King: A Biography of Richard Harding Davis*. New York: Scribner's, 1992.

Lynn, Kenneth S. *William Dean Howells: An American Life*. New York: Harcourt, Brace, Jovanovich, 1970.

Lyon, Peter. *Success Story: The Life and Times of S. S. McClure*. New York: Scribner's, 1963.

MacShane, Frank. *The Life and Work of Ford Madox Ford*. New York: Horizon Press, 1966.

Mangum, A. Bryant. "Crane's Red Badge and Zola's." *American Literary Realism* 9 (Summer 1976): 279–80.

———. "The Latter Days of Henry Fleming." *American Notes and Queries* 13 (May 1975): 136–38.

Marshall, Edward. "The Santiago Campaign: Some Episodes." *Scribner's Magazine* 24 (September 1898): 273–76.

———. "Stories of Stephen Crane." *San Francisco Call;* reprinted in *Literary Life* 24 (December 1900): 71–72.

———. *The Story of the Rough Riders*. New York: Dillingham, 1899.

———. "A Wounded Correspondent's Recollections of Guasimas." *Scribner's Magazine* 24 (September 1898): 273–76.

Martin, Ralph G. *Jennie: The Life of Lady Randolph Churchill*. Vol. 2: *The Dramatic Years, 1895–1921*. Englewood Cliffs, N.J.: Prentice Hall, 1969.

Martin, Thomas E. "Stephen Crane: Athlete and Author." *Argot* 3 (March 1935): 1–2.

Maurice, Arthur Bartlett. "Old Bookman Days" *Bookman* 66 (September 1927): 20–26.

Mayfield, John S. "S.C. at S.U." *Courier* 8 (Spring 1968): 8.

———. "Stephen Crane's Bugs." *Courier* 3 (September 1963): 22–31.

Maynard, Reid. "Red as a Leitmotiv in *The Red Badge of Courage*." *Arizona Quarterly* 30 (Summer 1974): 135–41.

McBride, Henry. "Stephen Crane's Artist Friends." *Art News* 49 (October 1950): 46.

McCullough, David. *Mornings on Horseback*. New York: Simon & Schuster, 1982.

McDougall, Walt. *This Is the Life!* New York: Alfred A. Knopf, 1926.

McIntosh, Burr. *The Little I Saw of Cuba*. London: F. Tennyson Neely, 1899.

McMurtry, Larry. *In a Narrow Grave: Essays on Texas*. New York: Simon & Schuster, 1989.

———. *Lonesome Dove*. New York: Pocket Books, 1986.

McPherson, James M. *For Cause and Comrades: Why Men Fought in the Civil War*. New York: Oxford University Press, 1997.

Mencken, H. L. "Various Bad Novels." *Smart Set* 40 (July 1913): 153–60.

———. Introduction to *Major Conflicts*. Vol. 10 of *The Work of Stephen Crane*. Edited by Wilson Follett. New York: Alfred A. Knopf, 1926.

———, ed. *A Mencken Chrestomathy*. New York: Alfred A. Knopf, 1949.

Meyer, Edith Patterson. *Not Charity But Justice: The Story of Jacob A. Riis*. New York: Vanguard Press, 1974.

Michelson, Charles. Introduction to *The Open Boat*. Vol. 12 of *The Work of Stephen Crane*. Edited by Wilson Follett. New York: Alfred A. Knopf, 1926.

Milne, Gordon. *Stephen Crane at Brede: An Anglo-American Literary Circle of the 1890's*. Lanham, Md.: University Press of America, 1980.

Mitchell, Lee Clark. "Face, Race and Disfiguration in Stephen Crane's *The Monster*." *Critical Inquiry* 17 (Autumn 1990): 174–92.

Mizener, Arthur. *The Saddest Story: A Biography of Ford Madox Ford*. New York: World, 1971.

Modlin, Charles E., and John R. Byers, Jr. "Stephen Crane's 'The Monster' as Christian Allegory." *Markham Review* 3 (May 1973): 110–13.

Molyneaux, Peter. "Had Stephen Crane Returned." *Texas Monthly* 3 (April 1929): 503–7.

Monteiro, George. "For the Record: Amy Leslie on Stephen Crane's *Maggie*." *Journal of Modern Literature* 9, no. 1 (1981–82): 147–48.

———. "Stephen Crane: A New Appreciation by Edward Garnett." *American Literature* 50, no. 3 (November 1978): 465–71.

Moorman, Lewis J., M.D. *Tuberculosis and Genius*. Chicago: University of Chicago Press, 1940.

Morace, Robert A. "Games, Play and Entertainments in Stephen Crane's 'The Monster.'" *Studies in American Fiction* 9 (Spring 1981): 65–81.

Morison, Elting E., ed. *The Letters of Theodore Roosevelt*. Vol. 1. Cambridge, Mass.: Harvard University Press, 1951.

Morris, Edmund. *The Rise of Theodore Roosevelt*. New York: Ballantine Books, 1979.

Moscow, Henry. *The Street Book*. New York: Hagstrom, 1978.

Noxon, Frank. "The Real Stephen Crane." *Step-Ladder* 14 (January 1928): 4–9.

O'Connor, Richard. *Hell's Kitchen*. Philadelphia: J. B. Lippincott, n.d.

O'Donnell, Thomas F. "De Forest, Van Petten, and Stephen Crane." *American Literature* 27 (January 1956): 578–80.

———. "John B. Van Petten: Stephen Crane's History Teacher." *American Literature* 27 (May 1955): 196–202.

Okada, Ryoichi. "Another Source of Crane's Metaphor, 'The Red Badge of Courage.'" *American Notes and Queries* 14 (January 1976): 73–74.

Oliver, Arthur. "Jersey Memories — Stephen Crane." *Proceedings of the New Jersey Historical Society* 16 (October 1931): 454–63.

Osborn, Neal J. "Crane's *The Monster* and *The Blue Hotel*." *Explicator* 23 (October 1964): item 10.

Osborn, Scott C. "Notes and Queries: Stephen Crane and Cora Taylor: Some Corrections." *American Literature* 26 (November 1954): 416–18.

———. "The 'Rivalry-Chivalry' of Richard Harding Davis and Stephen Crane." *American Literature* 28 (March 1956): 50–61.

———. "Stephen Crane's Imagery: 'Pasted Like a Wafer.'" *American Literature* 23 (November 1951): 362.

Otis, Edward O., M.D. *The Treatment of Advanced (Hopeless) Cases of Phthisis*. Boston: Damrell & Upham, 1895.

Paine, Ralph D. *Roads of Adventure*. Boston: Houghton Mifflin, 1922.

Parker, Hershel. "The Dates of Stephen Crane's Letters to Amy Leslie." *Papers of the Bibliographical Society of America*. 75, no. 1 (1981): 82–86.

———. *Flawed Texts and Verbal Icons: Literary Authority in American Fiction*. Evanston, Ill.: Northwestern University Press, 1984.

Parker, Stephen. *Informal Marriage, Cohabitation and the Law, 1750–1989*. New York: St. Martin's Press, 1990.

Parrish, Stephen Maxfield. *Currents of the Nineties in Boston and London: Fred Holland Day, Louise Imogen Guiney, and Their Circle*. New York: Garland, 1987.

Peaslee, Clarence Loomis. "Stephen Crane's College Days." *Monthly Illustrator* 3 (August 1896): 27–30.

Peck, Jesse T., D.D. *The True Woman; Or, Life and Happiness at Home and Abroad*. New York: Carlton & Porter, 1857.

Petry, Alice Hall. "Stephen Crane's Elephant Man." *Journal of Modern Literature* 10 (June 1983): 346–52.

Pizer, Donald. "The Garland-Crane Relationship." *Huntington Library Quarterly* 24 (November 1960): 75–82.

———. "'The Red Badge of Courage Nobody Knows': A Brief Rejoinder." *Studies in the Novel* 11 (Spring 1979): 77–81.

———, ed. *Hamlin Garland's Diaries*. San Marino, Calif.: Huntington Library, 1968.

Pratt, Lyndon Upson. "An Addition to the Canon of Stephen Crane." *Research Studies of the State College of Washington* 7 (1939): 55–58.

———. "The Formal Education of Stephen Crane." *American Literature* 10 (January 1939): 460–71.

———. "A Possible Source of *The Red Badge of Courage*." *American Literature* 11 (March 1939): 1–10.

Price, Carl F. "Stephen Crane: A Genius Born in a Methodist Parsonage." *Christian Advocate* 98 (n.d.): 866–67.

Pringle, Henry F. *Theodore Roosevelt.* New York: Harcourt, Brace & World, 1956.

Pugh, Edwin. "Stephen Crane." *Bookman* 67 (December 1924): 162–64.

Quigley, Michael. "The Writer and the Madam." *Times-Union and Journal* (5 December 1982): 11–12.

Ralph, Julian. "A Recent Journey Through the West." *Harper's Weekly* 39 (9 November 1895): 1064.

Randel, William. "The Cook in 'The Open Boat.'" *American Literature* 34 (November 1962): 405–11.

———. "From Slate to Emerald Green: More Light on Crane's Jacksonville Visit." *Nineteenth-Century Fiction* 19 (March 1965): 357–68.

———. "Stephen Crane's Jacksonville." *South Atlantic Quarterly* 62 (Spring 1963): 268–74.

Raymond, Dora Neill. "San Antonio: The Unsainted Anthony." In *The Taming of the Frontier — by Ten Authors.* New York: Minton, Batch, 1925.

Raymond, Thomas L. *Stephen Crane.* Newark, N.J.: Carteret Book Club, 1923.

Riis, Jacob A. *How the Other Half Lives.* New York: Dover Publications, 1971.

Robertson, Michael. *Stephen Crane at Lafayette.* Easton, Pa.: Friends of Skillman Library, 1990.

Rosenthal, Elisabeth. "Doctors and Patients Are Pushed to Their Limits by Grim New TB." *New York Times,* 12 October 1992.

———. "TB, Easily Transmitted, Adds a Peril to Medicine." *New York Times,* 13 October 1992.

Rothman, Sheila M. *Living in the Shadow of Death: Tuberculosis and the Social Experience of Illness in American History.* Baltimore: Johns Hopkins University Press, 1995.

Rubens, Horatio S. *Liberty: The Story of Cuba.* New York: Brewer, Warren & Putnam, 1932.

Ryan, Frank, M.D. *The Forgotten Plague: How the Battle Against Tuberculosis Was Won — and Lost.* Boston: Little, Brown, 1993.

San Antonio: The Flavor of Its Past, 1845–1898. San Antonio: Trinity University Press, 1975.

Schoberlin, Melvin H. "Flagon of Despair: Stephen Crane." Unpublished manuscript, n.d.

Seitz, Don C. *Joseph Pulitzer: His Life and Letters.* New York: Simon & Schuster, 1924.

———. "Stephen Crane: War Correspondent." *Bookman* 76 (February 1933): 137–40.

Seymour, Miranda. *A Ring of Conspirators: Henry James and His Literary Circle, 1895–1915.* Boston: Houghton Mifflin, 1989.

Shay, Felix. *Elbert Hubbard of East Aurora.* New York: William H. Wise, 1926.

Sheridan, Clare. *My Crowded Sanctuary.* London: Methuen, 1946.

———. *Naked Truth.* New York: Harper, 1928.

Sidbury, Edna Crane. "My Uncle, Stephen Crane, as I Knew Him." *Literary Digest International Book Review* 4 (March 1926): 248–50.

Simmen, Edward. "Stephen Crane and the Aziola Club of Galveston: A New Crane Letter." *Journal of Modern Literature* 7 (February 1979): 169–72.

Sloane, David E. E. "Stephen Crane at Lafayette." *Resources for American Literary Study* 2 (Spring 1972): 102–5.

Slote, Bernice. "San Antonio: A Newly Discovered Stephen Crane Article." *Prairie Schooner* 43 (Summer 1969): 176–83.

———. "Stephen Crane in Nebraska." *Prairie Schooner* 4 (Summer 1969): 192–99.

Smiley, Nixon. *Yesterday's Florida*. Miami, Fla.: E. A. Seeman, 1974.

Smith, Ernest G. "Comments and Queries." *Lafayette Alumnus* 2 (February 1932): 6.

Solomon, Eric. "Another Analogue for 'The Red Badge of Courage.'" *Nineteenth-Century Fiction* 13 (June 1958): 63–67.

"Some Men Who Have Reported This War." *Cosmopolitan* 25 (September 1898): 556–57.

Sorrentino, Paul. "New Evidence of Stephen Crane at Syracuse." *Resources for American Literary Study* 15 (Autumn 1985): 179–85.

———. "Newly Discovered Writings of Mary Helen Peck Crane and Agnes Elizabeth Crane." *Courier* 21 (1986): 103–134.

———. "The Philistine Society's Banquet for Stephen Crane." *American Literary Realism* 15 no. 2. (Autumn 1982): 232–38.

The Spanish American War: The Events of the War Described by Eye Witnesses. Chicago: Herbert S. Stone, 1899.

Specter, Michael. "Neglected for Years, TB Is Back with Strains That Are Deadlier." *New York Times*, 11 October 1992.

———. "TB Carriers See Clash of Liberty and Health," *New York Times*, 14 October 1992.

Spofford, William K. "Crane's *The Monster*." *Explicator* 36 (Winter 1978): 5–7.

Stallman, R. W. "Journalist Crane in That Dinghy." *Bulletin of the New York Public Library* 72 (April 1968): 260–77.

———. *Stephen Crane: A Biography*. New York: George Braziller, 1968.

———. *Stephen Crane: A Critical Bibliography*. Ames: Iowa State University Press, 1972.

———. "Stephen Crane's 'Apache Crossing.'" *Prairie Schooner* 43 (Summer 1969): 184–86.

———, and E. R. Hagemann, eds. *The New York City Sketches of Stephen Crane and Related Pieces*. New York: New York University Press, 1966.

Starrett, Vincent. *Born in a Bookshop: Chapters from the Chicago Renascence*. Norman: University of Oklahoma Press, 1965.

———. "Stephen Crane: An Estimate." *Sewanee Review* 28 (July 1920): 405–13.

Stevens, Holly, ed. *Letters of Wallace Stevens*. New York: Knopf, 1966.

Stone, Edward. "Crane and Zola." *English Language Notes* 1 (September 1963): 46–47.

Stronks, James B. "Garland's Private View of Crane in 1898 (with a Postscript)." *American Literary Realism* 6, no. 3 (Summer 1973): 249–50.

———. "Stephen Crane's English Years: The Legend Corrected." *Papers of the Bibliographic Society of America* 57 (1963): 340–49.

Taylor, Robert. *Saranac: America's Magic Mountain*. Boston: Hougton Mifflin, 1986.

Taylor, Thomas W. *The Beacon of Mosquito Inlet: A History of the Ponce de Leon Inlet Lighthouse*. Allandale, Fla.: Thomas W. Taylor, 1993.

Tenenbaum, Ruth Betsy. "The Artful Monstrosity of Crane's *Monster*." *Studies in Short Fiction* 14 (Fall 1977): 403–5.

Tennant, Roger. *Joseph Conrad*. New York: Atheneum, 1981.

Tolstoi, Leo. *Sebastopol*. Translated from the French by Frank D. Millet. New York: Harper & Brothers, 1887.

Tolstoy, Leo. *The Sebastopol Sketches*. Translated by David McDuff, New York: Penguin Books, 1986.

Ubell, Earl. "Can We Stop Tuberculosis Again?" *Parade*, 9 October 1994.

Vosburgh, R. G. "The Darkest Hour in the Life of Stephen Crane." *Criterion*, n.s. 1 (February 1901): 26–27.

Walker, Franklin, ed. *The Letters of Frank Norris*. San Francisco: Book Club of California, 1956.

Walter, Bill. "On the Waterfront: The Treasure of 'The Open Boat.'" *Florida's Coastal Magazine*, June 1989.

Warner, Michael D. "Value, Agency and Stephen Crane's 'The Monster.'" *Nineteenth-Century Fiction* 40 (June 1985): 76–93.

Weatherford, Richard M., ed. *Stephen Crane: The Critical Heritage*. London: Routledge & Kegan Paul, 1973.

Webb, Walter Prescott. *The Great Frontier*. Lincoln: University of Nebraska Press, 1951.

———. *The Great Plains*. New York: Grosset & Dunlap, 1931.

Webster, H. T. "Wilbur F. Hinman's Corporal Si Klegg and Stephen Crane's *The Red Badge of Courage*." *American Literature* 11 (November 1939): 285–93.

Wells, H. G. *Experiment in Autobiography*. Philadelphia: J. B. Lippincott, 1967.

———. "Stephen Crane from an English Standpoint." *North American Review* 171 (August 1900): 233–42.

Wells, Lester G. "The Iron Monster, the Crackling Insects of Onondaga Country, and Stephen Crane." *Courier* 3 (March 1963): 1–7.

Werstein, Irving. *Turning Point for America: The Story of the Spanish-American War*. New York: Julian Messner, 1964.

Wertheim, Stanley. "Another Diary of the Reverend Jonathan Townley Crane." *Resources for American Literary Study* 19 (1993): 35–49.

———. "Cora Crane's Thwarted Romance." *Columbia Library Columns* 36 (November 1986): 26–37.

———. "Garland and Crane: The Education of an Impressionist." *North Dakota Quarterly* 35 (Winter 1967): 23–28.

———. "*The Red Badge of Courage* and Personal Narratives of the Civil War." *American Literary Realism* 6 (Winter 1973): 61–65.

———. "Stephen Crane and the Wrath of Jehova." *Literary Review* 7 (Summer 1964): 499–508.

———. "Stephen Crane in the Shadow of the Parthenon." *Columbia Library Columns* 32 (May 1983): 2–13.

———. "Stephen Crane Remembered." *Studies in American Fiction* 4 (Spring 1976): 45–64.

———. "Stephen Crane's 'Battalion Notes.'" *Resources for American Literary Study* 6 (Spring 1976): 79–80.

Wertheim, Stanley, and Paul Sorrentino. *The Correspondence of Stephen Crane.* 2 vols. New York: Columbia University Press, 1988.

————. *The Crane Log: A Documentary Life of Stephen Crane 1871–1900.* New York: G. K. Hall, 1994.

————. "Thomas Beer: The Clay Feet of Stephen Crane Biography." *American Literary Realism* 22 (Spring 1990): 2–16.

Wheeler, Post, and Hallie E. Rives. *Dome of Many-Coloured Glass.* Garden City, N.Y.: Doubleday, 1955.

Wickham, Harvey. "Stephen Crane at College." *American Mercury* 7 (March 1926): 291–97.

Wilford, John Noble. "Tuberculosis Found to Be Old Disease in New Wold." *New York Times*, 15 March 1994.

Williams, Ames W. "Stephen Crane: War Correspondent." *New Colophon* 1 (April 1948): 113–23.

Williams, Herbert P. "Mr. Crane as a Literary Artist." *Illustrated American* 20 (18 July 1896): 126.

Wilson, Harold S. *McClure's Magazine and the Muckrakers.* Princeton: Princeton University Press, 1970.

Wilson, Joseph E. *The Cuban Crisis as Reflected in the New York Press (1895–1898).* New York: Columbia University Press, 1934.

Winter, Kevin O. *Florida: The Land of Enchantment.* Boston: Page, 1918.

Wolford, Chester L. *The Anger of Stephen Crane: Fiction and the Epic Tradition.* Lincoln: University of Nebraska Press, 1983.

Woodress, James. *Willa Cather: Her Life and Art.* New York: Pegasus, 1970.

Woollcott, Alexander. *Enchanted Isles.* New York: G. P. Putnam's Sons, 1924.

Yanikoski, Charles S. "Amy Leslie Reconsidered." Unpublished paper, 1996.

Ziff, Larzer. *The American 1890s: Life and Times of a Lost Generation.* New York: Viking Press, 1966.

INDEX

Active Service, 198, 222, 284, 296, 316, 320, 329
   evaluation of, 312–14
   excerpt from, 209–10
   plot and characters, 200, 313 14
"Adventures of a Novelist," 159
Aesthetics (Véron), 40
Ainslee's Magazine, 320
Alamo, 109–10
Alden, Henry Mills, 83
Alexander, Eban, 22
Alger, Russell A., 282
Allen, Viola, 150
American Day parade, 49–51
American Press Association (APA), 52
"Angel Child, The," 294
Anglo-Saxon Review, 305
Appleton, Daniel, 100, 130, 131, 135, 152–53, 212, 212n, 294
   British rights for *Red Badge*, 135
   payment for *Red Badge*, 106
   republishes *Maggie*, 150
   SC's royalties, 237, 242, 291
   and *Third Violet*, 138, 142
Arbutus Cottage, 17, 19, 25, 59
Arena, 40, 54, 77, 84, 100, 197
Army Wife, An (King), 196
Arnold, Edward, 125

Art Students' League building, New York, 73–74, 93, 120, 138
Asbury Park Daily Press, 25, 50
Asbury Park Journal, 43
Asbury Park/Ocean Grove, New Jersey, 11, 17, 19, 21, 25
   as setting for story, 61
Asbury Park Tribune, 22
"Asbury's New Move," 22, 22n, 28
"Ashes of Love, The," 280
Associated Press (AP), 50
Athens, 199, 200–201, 206
Atlanta Journal, 187, 189
Atlantic Monthly, 152, 245
Author's Club, 141–42, 152
Avon-by-the-Sea, 29, 40, 53

"Baby Stories," 72
Bacheller, Irving, 119, 133–34, 135, 142, 222, 225, 232
   first meeting with SC, 92–93
   on quality of *Red Badge*, 95
   sends SC to American West and Mexico, 99
   sends SC to cover war in Cuba, 188
Bacheller-Johnson Newspaper Syndicate, 80, 167
   serialization of *Red Badge*, 92–93, 101

Bacheller-Johnson Newspaper Syndicate (*cont.*)
  syndication of SC's reports and stories, 126, 152
Badenweiler, Germany, 324–30, 337
  Cranes' trip to, 327–28
Balzac, Honoré de, 128, 232
Barr, Mark, 298–301, 305, 307, 311, 315
Barr, Robert, 213, 243, 296, 298, 315, 316, 336
  Cora's letters of appeal, 282, 287
  disgusted with SC's hiding in Havana, 282–83
  finishing Irish romance, 327
  on SC "already dead," 326
  and SC's death, 330
Barrett, Lillian, 186
Barrie, Sir James, 197
Barry, John D., 59–60, 83–84
Baseball, 26–28, 30, 32–34, 41, 48, 337
Bass, John, 201, 203–4, 206
  on SC's courage in Greece, 204–5
Beardsley, Aubrey, 117
Becker, Patrolman Charles, 156–59, 164, 166, 192
  death in electric chair, 335
Beer, Thomas, 42, 45
Bennett, Henry Sanford "Arnold," 304, 305, 325
Bierce, Ambrose, 135, 154, 194
"Billy Atkins Went to Omaha," 84
Black Forest, 323–24, 327–28, 337
Black Riders and Other Lines, The, 92, 117, 134, 147, 219, 236
  excerpts, discussion, criticism, 77–78, 116–19, 122, 125, 136
  parodies of, 123, 129
  publication, 100, 117
  revisions, 93
  to be set to music, 152
  War Is Kind compared to, 296
Blackwell's Island prison, 101
Blackwood, William, 282
Blackwood's magazine, 284, 287–88
  sends SC to Cuba, 245
"Blue Blotch of Cowardice, The" (parody), 154
"Blue Hotel, The," 236, 237, 238, 249, 336

payment for, 297
plot, evaluation of, 240–41, 284, 333
rejections, 245
Bly, Nellie, 101
Blythe, A. G., 131
Boer War, 308, 319, 320, 322
Book Buyer, 152, 154
Book News, 314, 320
Bookman, 116–17, 128, 133, 142
  on *George's Mother,* 153
  on SC's poems, 122
Borland, Armistead "Tommie," 24, 45
  on Crane at Claverack, 26–28
Boston Globe, 270
Boston Herald, 158
Bothem-Edwards, Miss, 319
Bowers, Fredson, 85n
Bowery, 42, 45. *See also George's Mother; Maggie*
  dialect and profanity, 55, 56, 60
  flophouses story, 80–81
  SC's sketches of life in, 54–55, 72, 87, 94
Bradley, James, 49, 60
Bradley, Will, 296
Bragdon, Claude, 137, 198
Brede Place, 251, 275, 290, 292–93, 294, 324
  Christmas house party (1899), 315–18
  Conrad on first visit, 330
  Cranes living at, 296–325
  ghosts and, 292–93, 298–99
  lifestyle described, 298–300, 302, 311–12
  and SC's poor health, 323–24
  written into Irish romance, 327
Brentano, Simon, 135
"Bride Comes to Yellow Sky, The," 241
  evaluation of, 284–85, 333
  payment for, 223, 297
  plot and characters, 219–20
  published in *McClure's,* 238
Brooklyn Daily Eagle, 166
Brown, Curtis, 95, 124, 138, 223, 335
  SC letter to, 139
  visit to SC's coffin, 331
Brown, Ford Madox, 213
Brown, Harry, 169, 249–50
Bruce, Dr. Mitchell, 323, 324, 329
Brueiler, Professor, 329

Bryan, William Jennings, 162
Bryant, William Cullen, 24
Buck, Frank, 334
Bucklin, Joseph, 160
Buffalo News, 131, 136
"Burial." *See* "Upturned Face, The"
Burke, Lily, 299
Burnett, Frances Hodgson, 84
Bushick, Frank H., 110
Button, Lucius, 52, 101, 107, 111
Byrnes, Thomas F., 162

Cable, George W., 84
Caine, Hall, 128
Camp, Lyda de, 174, 176
Carleton, Samuel (alias), 173–74
Carmichael, Otto, 283, 285–86
Carnegie, Andrew, 324
Carr, Louis, 38, 41, 43
Carroll, William W., 73, 80, 136, 217
Carter, Imogene. *See also* Taylor, Cora: in
    Greece at front
  Cora's dispatches as, 200, 202
  SC writing as, 202, 220, 223
Cary, Henry N., 270
Cather, Willa, 273, 274, 313
  review of *Active Service,* 314
  review of *War Is Kind,* 297
  on SC's appearance and behavior in
    Nebraska, 103–6
  on SC's writing, 334
Cebreco, Colonel, 256
Century magazine, 59, 68, 120, 245, 294
  Civil War series, 63–65, 87
Cervera y Topete, Admiral Pascual, 247,
    250
Chancellorsville, battle of, 143, 144
Chandler, George, 37
Chap-Book, 133
Chapman, Police Captain, 192
Chicago Chronicle, 238
Chicago Daily Inter-Ocean, 128
Chicago Daily News, 168, 237, 334
Chicago Dispatch, 158–59
Chicago Evening Post, 238
Chicago Times-Herald, 237
Chicago Tribune, 188, 237–38, 262
Chili girls, 110–11

Christian Science, 286–87
Churchill, Lady Randolph, 305, 324
City of Washington (transport ship), 267–68,
    290
Civil War. *See also Red Badge of Courage, The*
  SC's battlefield series, 138–39, 142
  SC's stories of, 121–22, 143–44
"Clan of No-Name, The," 284–85
Clark, Dora, affair of, 155, 241, 258, 333,
    335
  arrest, 156–59
  newspaper coverage, 158–59, 166–67
  and Roosevelt, 159, 163
  SC's testimony in court, 163–67, 172
Claverack College, 22–25, 26–28, 265
Coal mine report, 87–89
Coffin, George, 259
Coleman, Rufus (character in *Active
    Service*), 312–13, 316
Collier's Weekly, 249, 250
Collings, Lewis Edward, 333
Commodore (ship), 173, 217. *See also* "Open
    Boat, The"
  carrying arms to Cuba, 177–78
  Cuban sailor saved by SC, 278–79
  sinking of, 179–85, 209
Conlin, Police Chief Peter, 160–61
Conrad, Borys, 242, 243, 295, 327, 330
Conrad, Jessie, 285, 327, 330
  and baby at Cranes' house, 243
  on Cora's appearance, and servants, 301
  on life at Brede Place, 298–99
  and SC, 233, 325
  on SC on return from Cuba, 296
Conrad, Joseph, 245, 282, 288, 298, 310,
    315–16
  background and appearance, 230, 231
  and birth of child, 233, 233n
  critical comparison with SC, 235–36
  efforts to get money to SC, 287–89
  feelings about Cora, 301
  first meeting with SC, 229–32
  friendship with Cranes, 233–34, 242–43,
    295, 300, 312
  and Hueffer, 305
  last goodbye to SC, 325, 327
  on *Red Badge,* 129
  SC attempts to place on Civil List, 325

Conrad, Joseph (*cont.*)
  and SC's dogs, 233, 242–43
  on SC's happiness on horseback, 330
  on SC's work habits, 300, 303–4
  SC worried and "harassed," 321–22
  on SC's writing, 234–35, 333
Constantine, Crown Prince, 199, 202, 207
Consumption. *See* Tuberculosis
Consumptive's Struggle for Life, A (no author), 324
Conway, Patrolman, 159, 164
Cooper, James Fenimore, 14
Copeland & Day, 84, 89, 91, 93, 100, 117, 122, 126
  SC's arguments with, 91–92
  and Sullivan County sketches, 125
Corporal Si Klegg and His "Pard" (Hinman), 68
Cortelyou, George B., 334–35
Cosmopolitan, 57, 236
Cottage Sanatorium, Saranac Lake, 271, 274
"Coward, The " (C.G.S.), 68
Crane, Agnes (aunt), 9
Crane, Agnes (sister), 5, 14, 29, 38
  character and personality, 16–18
  illness and death, 19, 273, 330
Crane, Anna (sister-in-law), 42–43
Crane, Cora. *See* Taylor, Cora
Crane, Edith (niece), 46, 155, 336
Crane, Edmund "Ed" (brother), 16, 31, 42, 45, 53, 139, 214, 336
  death of son, 220–21
  Hartwood house as SC's home base, 65, 116, 122, 130, 139, 142
  horseback racing with SC, 155, 305
  in New York before SC's trip to Greece, 196
  and *Red Badge*, 71, 72
  and SC's childhood, 4, 11, 14
  on SC's "confidence of genius," 73
  SC's letters to, 214, 222, 224
  and SC's poverty, 76
  SC's wills, 171, 324
Crane, Edna (niece), 217
Crane, Fannie (sister-in-law), 17, 19
Crane, George (brother), 19, 171, 273

Crane, Helen (niece), 81, 225, 305, 307, 321, 325
Crane, Luther (brother), 16, 19, 21–22
Crane, Mary Helen Peck (mother), 125
  appearance and character, 6–7
  children, 7–9
  death, 43
  family illnesses, 9–10, 19, 273–74
  after husband's death, 16–18
  and local press corps, 22, 25
  and temperance movement, 4, 11–12, 22
  tribute to husband, 71
  writings, 14, 29
Crane, Nellie (sister), 273, 332
Crane, Reverend Jonathan Townley (father), 21
  background and career, 6–9, 11–12
  character and personality, 4–6
  and children, 5–10
  death, 15–16
  Dr. Trescott character based on, 217
  against Holiness Movement, 11–12
  rhetoric and writings, 13–14
CRANE, STEPHEN
  baseball and, 26–28, 30, 32–34, 41, 48, 337
  birth, 10
  character: grit and determination, 4, 19–20, 187; self-assurance, 34, 35; solicitude for others, 35, 74; truthfulness, 22
  childhood, 4, 10–15: illnesses, 10, 15, 273
  courage, 4, 19–20, 205–6, 252–53, 255–56, 264, 266–67
  drinking and smoking, 29, 31, 58, 81, 120, 194, 205, 255, 256, 261, 262, 267, 311
  education: Asbury Park public schools, 17–20; paltriness of formal, 143; Pennington Seminary, 21–22; Claverack College, 22–25, 26–28; Lafayette College, 2–3, 29–31, 33–34; Syracuse University, 31–37
  family: illnesses and deaths, 9–10, 19, 21–22, 42–43, 273–74; reaction to *Red Badge* success, 141
  father's death, 16
  horseback riding, 99–100, 127, 130, 137, 154–55, 162, 305, 311, 329, 330

mother, 6–12, 17, 21, 25, 29

mother's death, 43

news reports by, 25, 29, 39–41, 46, 48–50, 53

payments, for work, 106, 212, 223, 270–71, 293–94, 297, 308, 332

physical appearance, 41, 58, 62, 76, 79–81, 89, 93, 189, 195; blond mustache, 206, 211, 220; Cather's description, 103–4; in Cuba, 248, 290, 296; at end of life, 306, 319, 326; eyes, 58, 103, 229, 230, 337; in Puerto Rico, 274–75

quoted: on Ford Madox Hueffer, 305; on Hamlin Garland, 41; on Henry James, 304; on his parents, 5; on Oscar Wilde, 305; on Richard Harding Davis, 197

royalties, 92, 106, 135, 212, 237, 242, 291

speech mannerisms, 230, 312

view of self, 78

wills, 171, 324

and women, 27–28, 81–83, 110–11, 126, 130–31, 139, 193, 194–95; personal charm, 337; romantic conception of, 284; sense of unworthiness, 313

work habits, 53–54, 60–61, 71–72, 300, 303–4; carelessness with manuscripts, 41

CHRONOLOGY OF ADULT LIFE:

1891

camping, 38–39, 41–42

in Lake View with Ed, 42, 45, 71–72

meeting with Garland, 40–41

stories and articles, 35–36

Sullivan County tales, 38–39, 43–44

trips into New York City, 42, 45

writing for *New York Tribune*, 33–34, 39–41, 46, 48–51

1892

American Day Parade piece, 49–51

finances, 45

Lily Munroe romance, 46–48

in New York City, 52–64, 71–81

poverty, 53, 72, 76

1893

Bowery stories, 72, 79–81, 84

and Lily Munroe, 61–62, 77, 81–82

in New York City, 73–75, 79–81

war novel, 63–73, 83–87

writing poetry, 77–78, 82–83, 91

1894

camping, and burlesque newspaper, 89–91

stories and newspaper pieces, 79–89, 93–94

1895

finances, 104, 105–6, 133, 135

Greene's sketch of, 121

at Hartwood, 122, 130, 142

health, 120–21, 122

and Lily Munroe, 125

looking for publishers, 124–25

Mexican vs. American girls, 112, 114–15

New York lifestyle, 116, 119–21

Philistine Society dinner, 131–32, 135–37

sailing, 133

Western/Mexican trip, 99–115

1896

advice to new writers, 152

Amy Leslie affair, 168–70

Civil War and Mexican stories, 121–22, 143–44, 152

Dora Clark affair, 155–59, 163–67, 172

formal studio portrait, 152

and Nellie Crouse, 145–49

novels in print, 153

opium den story, 164

requests for work, 152

on reviewers, 147

and Roosevelt, 161–62

and success, 141–43, 151–52

1897

Amy Leslie's lawsuit, 237–40, 242

Commodore disaster and rescue, 178–186

finances, 196, 212

in Greece as war correspondent, 203–10

in Jacksonville, 172–75, 177–78, 189, 195

in London, with Conrad, 229–32

to London with Cora, 198–99

loving both Amy and Cora, 200–201

in Paris with Cora, 212

poem paraphrased for Cora, 188

Crane, Stephen, *1897* (*cont.*)
  at Ravensbrook: carriage accident,
    221; fame, 211; finances, 222, 223, 225,
    234, 239, 241–42; hoping for war
    correspondent job, 224–25; household
    and friends, 213–14; writing *Active
    Service*, 222; writing play with Conrad,
    244
1898
  finances, 249
  fired by *New York World*, 270
  in Havana, 278–89; and Cuban friend,
    278–79; finances, 278, 280; health,
    283; knife wound, 279; return to
    England, 290–92; writing about love,
    280–82, 284–85
  pulmonary tuberculosis, 271–72
  as war correspondent in Cuba, 246–67:
    bravery in battle, 252–55, 266–67;
    Haiti expedition, 249–50; in Key
    West, 246–49; Las Guásimas ambush
    of Rough Riders, 257–60; to U.S. for
    medical treatment, 267–68
  as war correspondent in Puerto Rico,
    275–76; farewell to "El Dog," 277–78
1899
  awareness of death, 310
  Brede Place, Crane's love for, 292–93,
    303
  Christmas house party, 314–18
  Cora accepted as wife, 300–301
  and dogs, 295, 299, 312, 325
  finances, 291–95, 308–9
  friends and lifestyle, 295–96, 298–304,
    311–12, 318
  health worsens, 305–7, 317–18, 319
  hemorrhaging, 317, 321, 323
  horseback riding, 305, 311
  and Irish romance, 317, 319, 320, 323
  "manacled" dream, 308
  in Paris, 307
  Ravensbrook, departure from, 291,
    294–95
  stories and tales, 305–6
  work habits, 303–4, 311
1900
  awareness of death, 327
  Badenweiler sanatorium, 325–30
  burial, 331–32
  death, 330; legends and rumors after,
    332–33
  finances, and Pinker, 318–22
  and Irish romance, 328
  work in print, and reviews, 320
  POETRY (*see also Black Riders, The;* God, in
    SC's poetry; "Intrigue"; *War Is Kind*)
  ". . . chatter of a death-demon from a
    tree-top," 130
  first poem, 15
  "God give me medals . . . ," 281
  "I explain the silvered passing of a ship
    at night . . . ," 188
  "I looked here . . . ," 82
  "I saw a man pursuing the horizon"
    parody, 129
  imagery, 77–78
  "Oh, best little blade of grass," 78
  "Thou art my love . . . ," 280, 281
  "Thou lovest not me . . . ," 281
  " 'Truth,' said a traveler . . . ," 100
  WRITINGS (*see also* titles of newspaper
    articles, novels, stories)
  betrayal theme, 126
  on Cuban courtship rituals, 281
  early work, 20
  earnings per word, 297
  faith in, 82–83
  irony in, 39–40
  major themes of, 24
  method, 153
  meticulousness, 54
  minor newspaper pieces, 93
  mountain imagery, 78, 112
  and research, 143
  Sullivan County tales, 38–39, 43–44
  and terror, 4
  total work published and total income,
    332
  tragedy and irony in *Maggie*, 56
  "vivid phrasing," 92
  war tales, 294, 305, 310, 333, 335
  word count and price tags, 223
Crane, Townley (brother), 17, 22, 40, 52,
    171, 332
  character and career, 14, 25–26
  death of second wife, 42–43

defense of SC's JOUAM story, 50
SC writing news reports for, 25, 29
Crane, Wilbur (brother), 16, 19, 22
Crane, William (brother), 17, 22, 29, 59,
  81, 171, 195, 221
  Amy Leslie's lawsuit, 237, 239
  as character in *Monster*, 217
  daughter sent to England, 297, 305
  letters to, 199, 304, 313
  lynch mob in Port Jervis, 46, 94, 217
  SC's appeals for money, 289–90, 291,
    294
  SC's death, 330
  SC's estate, 336
  SC's last illness, 321, 324
  SC letter to, 225
Creelman, James, 293
Crete, 199. *See also* Greco-Turkish War
Criterion, 152, 297, 320
Critic, 140, 197, 211
Crouse, Nellie, 111, 114, 198, 218, 280
  SC's epistolary romance with, 137–38,
    139, 141–49, 197, 313
"Cry of a Huckleberry Pudding, The," 57
Cuba, 167, 170, 172–73, 195. *See also*
  Cubans; Havana; Spanish-American
  War
  SC waiting to go to, 167, 170, 172–73
  SC's war stories, 283–84, 335
Cubans
  insurgents in Santiago, 256–57, 260–61
  in Jacksonville, 172–73, 186
  and sinking of *Commodore*, 178–81
  SC's friend in Havana, 278–79

Daily Florida Citizen, 173–74
Daily Tatler, 167
Daiquir', Cuba, 257, 294
Damnation of Theron Ware, The (Frederic),
  213
Dauvray, Henry, 236
Davies, Acton, 259
Davis, Rebecca Harding, 198n
Davis, Richard Harding, 128, 160, 200,
  268, 313
  on Cora, 198, 201
  with Rough Riders, 258–59
  Savoy luncheon for SC, 197

on SC in line of fire, 266
on SC's behavior at Velestino, 203
on SC's bravery in battle, 252
on SC's taking of Juana Diaz, 277
war correspondent in Cuba, 247–48
war correspondent in Greece, 201
Davis, Robert H., 192–94
"Death and the Child," 208, 225, 313
  ending, 210, 225
  images, excerpts, 222
  selling of, 236–37
Delta Upsilon Fraternity, 3, 30, 32, 34, 37,
  332–33
Demarest's Family Magazine, 151–52
"Desertion, A," 94
Detroit Free Press, 127
Devereux, William K., 50
Dial, 154
Dick, John Henry, 93
Dickinson, Emily, 117
Dogs, 10, 133, 233, 299, 307, 312, 325. *See*
  also Velestino
  access to SC's study, 242–43
  SC's favorite, 325
"Dogs of War, The," 213
Doyle, Arthur Conan, 128
du Maurier, George, 128
Dunlevy, William, 192
Dysentery, 275

Eddyville, Nebraska, 102
Edwards, Elisha J., 84, 93, 95
El Caney, battle of, 261–63, 268, 283
"El Dog" (horse), 277–78
Elliott, Captain George, 254
Ellison, Ralph, 241
El Pozo Hill, 261–64
Emerson, Ralph Waldo, 74, 75
England. *See also* Brede Place; London;
  Ravensbrook
  Cora and SC settle in, 212–14
  Red Badge success in, 129, 129n, 138,
    140
  SC's success in, 289
  and unmarried cohabitation, 212
English, Phoebe "Pete," 31
"Episode of War, An" 143–44
Ericson, David, 46, 74

"Estate of Stephen Crane, The" (Katz), 332n
"European Letters" (Imogene Carter), 220
Evening Post, 134, 160
Evil That Men Do, The (Fawcett), 54
"Experiment in Luxury, An," 84
"Experiment in Misery, An," 80–81, 84, 87, 93

Fabian Society, 213, 214
Fables, 76, 126
Fairman, Leonard, 201
Fawcett, Edgar, 54
Field, Eugene, 135
"Five White Mice, The," 152, 214, 236
Flack, Reverend Arthur H., 23–24, 26
"Flanagan and His Short Filibustering Adventure," 196
Fleming, Henry (character in *Red Badge*), 83, 94, 107, 158, 191
   and Bowery stories, 72–73
   changes in dialogue, 86
   creation of, 66–69
   heroism of, 122
   psychological and spiritual crisis, 69–70
   readers' identification with, 127
   in "Veteran," 144
   view of war, 78
Florida Times-Union, 178, 187, 195, 282
Flower, B. O., 62
Floyd, Robert Mitchell, 136
Forbes-Robertson, Sir Johnson, 309
Ford, Ford Madox. *See* Hueffer, Ford Madox
Forum, 59–60, 62, 83
"Four Men in a Cave," 44
"Fragment of Velestino, A," 208
France, 199, 387
Frankel, Dr. Albert, 329
Frank Leslie's Illustrated Newspaper, 19, 29
Frederic, Barry, 303
Frederic, Harold, 197, 236, 243, 251, 283, 330
   Cora's care for children of, 286–89, 302–3
   and Cranes' carriage accident, 221

   death of, 286–87, 289
   invitation to Cranes, 239–40
   Red Badge as "deathless book," 213
   SC's defense of, 304
Free verse, 83, 117
French, Mansfield, 32
Frewen, Clara, 293, 295, 303, 314, 318, 322, 323
Frewen, Hugh, 318
Frewen, Moreton, 290, 292–93, 299, 308, 314
financial help to Cranes, 324, 329
   SC's last illness, 321, 329–30

Galveston Daily News, 108
Garcia Iñiguez, General Calixto, 257
Gardner, Charlotte E., 324, 325
Garland, Hamlin, 59, 61, 65, 77, 82, 84, 100, 108, 135, 161, 163
   advises SC to leave New York, 167
   background and character, 41
   Black Riders dedicated to, 124
   compares Crane with Davis, 197
   editing of *Red Badge*, 85–86, 85n
   as literary executor, 71
   on *Maggie*, 56
   and "new realism," 40–41
   on SC's appearance, 290
   on SC's "genius for phrases," 60
   SC's gratitude to, 93–94
   as SC's mentor, 79, 80, 83
   on SC as opium addict, 333
Garnett, Constance, 213
Garnett, David, 214
Garnett, Edward, 213, 234–35, 239, 243, 293, 325
   visits Cranes, 243, 302
   on SC's work, 333
George's Mother, 63, 149, 161
   first title, 117, 125
   plot, 125–26
   reviews, 153–54, 213
Germany, 199, 387
Ghost, The (Christmas play), 316, 318
"Ghoul's Accountant, A," 43–44
Gibbs, John Blair, 253
Gilbert and Sullivan, 169, 316
Gilder, Richard Watson, 56, 119

Gissing, George, 316

Glamorous Days (Bushick), 110–11

God, in SC's poetry, 77–78, 92, 117–18, 209–10, 296

"God Rest Ye, Merry Gentlemen," 294

Goethe, Johann Wolfgang von, 70

Goodwin, Clarence N., 32

Gordon, Frederick, 74, 76, 117

Goss, Warren Lee, 68

Gosse, Edmund, 213

Gracie's Cottage, 213, 214

Grant, Commissioner Frederick D., 164, 166

Grant, Lawyer, 165–66

"Gray Sleeve, A," 121–22, 146–47

"Great Battles of the World," 320, 320n

Great Britain, 199

"Great Bugs at Onondaga," 36

"Great Mistake, A," 72

Greco-Turkish war, 194, 195, 199, 217–18, 231

  and "Death and the Child," 210, 313

  faces of wounded and dead soldiers, 208–9, 310

  German officers in, 206

  SC and Cora as war correspondents, 199–208, 291

  SC's war tales, 306–7

Greece, SC as war correspondent in, 192, 194–95, 196, 199, 200–210

"Greed Rampant" (play), 36–37, 39

Greene, Nelson, 73, 81, 136

  on SC in 1895, 119–22

  on SC's poverty, 116

Grimes, Captain George S., 262

Guantanamo Bay, 251, 252

Guiney, Louise Imogen, 92

Haggard, Rider, 316

Haiti expedition, 249–50

Hare, Jimmy, 250, 261, 264, 268

  defends SC to Roosevelt, 334–35

Harper's Bazaar, 320

Harper's Magazine, 83, 87, 160, 240, 245, 279, 320

  payment refused, 293–94

  payments from, 308

  publishing *Monster*, 224, 239, 249

Harper's Weekly, 40, 163

Hartwood, New York, Edmund's home in, 116, 120, 224

  arrival of SC's horse, 155

  Christmas at, 139

  as SC's home base, 65, 122, 130, 142

Hartwood Park Association, 41–42

Hathaway, Odell, 29, 30, 32

Havana, 246

  and love poems by SC, 280–81

  newspaper pieces and stories about, 278–86, 290

  SC's exile in, 278–89

  SC's war tales, 283–86, 335

Hawkins, Willis Brooks, 119, 126, 127, 130–31, 332

  letters to, 139, 143–44, 150, 170, 171

  money sent to Jacksonville, 177, 187

  payments to Amy Leslie, 195, 196, 201, 221–22, 237

  and Philistine dinner, 131–32, 134–35, 136, 137

  on SC's pride in *Red Badge*, 141

Hawthorne, Julian, 320

Hay, John, 282, 324

Hearst, William Randolph, 195, 244, 270, 282

Hearst newspapers, SC as war correspondent for, 275

Heather, Richard (butler), 299–300, 325

Hecht, Ben, 169

Heinemann, William, 139, 196, 197, 213, 283, 289

Higgins, Billy (ship's oiler), 179–80, 184–85, 191, 217

Higginson, Thomas Wentworth, 154

Hilborn, Theodore, 195

Hilliard, John Northern, 81, 107

Hind, Charles Lewis, 315–16, 316–17

Hinman, Wilbur C., 68

"His New Mittens," 249

Hitchcock, Ripley, 58–59, 100–101, 106, 126, 135, 138, 332

  letters to, 150–52

  as literary executor, 171

  and *Third Violet*, 142, 143

Holiness, the Birthright of All God's Children (Jonathan Crane), 4, 11

"Holland," 84, 95

Hope, Anthony, 128, 197

Hopkins, Frederick D., 333

Horan, Mary, 280

Horses. *See also* Crane, Stephen: horseback riding; Spanish-American War in Crane's writings, 122, 320, 330

   Peanuts, 155, 171

Hotel de Dream, 174, 176–77, 196, 336

Hotel Pasaje, Havana, 278, 286

Hotel Trois Rois, Basel, 327–28

Hot Springs, Arkansas, 106

"How the Donkey Lifted the Hills," 126

"How the Ocean Was Formed," 76

How the Other Half Lives (Riis), 52–53, 86

Howells, William Dean, 40–41, 60, 77, 82, 93, 135, 167, 290

   attempts to help SC, 80

   and *Maggie*, 61–62

   and *Red Badge*, 134

   SC's gratitude, 141

   as SC's literary executor, 171

   SC's poems "too orphic," 83

   SC's work praised, 84, 152

Howorth, George, 175

Hoyt de Friese, Lafayette, 321, 326

Huau, José Alejandro, 173

Hubbard, Elbert, 130–32, 137, 151, 238

   parody of SC's poem, 122–23

   Philistine dinner, 131–32

   publishes SC's poems, 123–24, 129–30

   SC's friendship with, 137–38

Hudson River Institute, 22, 23

Hueffer, Elsie, 213–14

Hueffer, Ford Madox, 190, 243

   on Cora's style of dress, 301

   in Limpsfield, 213–14

   on SC's appearance, 337

   on SC at Ravenswood, 214

   SC on, 305

   on SC's speaking "English," 312

   on Wells at SC's death, 326

Hughes, Rupert, 297, 320

Hugo, Victor, 127

Hume, Levi, 217

"Hunting Wild Hogs," 40

Illustrated American, 166

"Imogene Carter's Adventure in Pharsala" (Crane/Taylor), 202

"Indiana Campaign, An," 143–44

"Indians" (SC's New York roommates), 73, 83

"In the Depths of a Coal Mine," 87–89, 91

"Intrigue," 280, 281, 284, 293, 296. *See also War Is Kind*

"Irish Notes," 222

Irish romance, 317, 319, 323, 327, 330. *See also O'Ruddy, The*

Jackson, General Andrew, 172

Jacksonville, 175–76, 195, 197, 336

   "Cuban fleet" in, 173

   spies in, 173, 178

James, Henry, 128, 230, 288, 299

   and Christmas party, 315, 316, 317

   on Cora, 301

   friendship with Cranes, 311–12

   SC on, 304

   on SC's death, 337

   SC's last days, 326

Jefferson Market Courthouse, 157

Jewett, Sarah Orne, 84, 135

Jews, 36–37, 39

Johnson, Henry (character in *Monster*), 215–18, 305–6, 331

Johnson, Willis Fletcher, 25, 33

   impressed by SC's work, 40, 51

   and JOUAM parade story, 50

   on *Maggie*, 56, 58–59

JOUAM (Junior Order of United American Mechanics), 49–51, 56

Juana Diaz, Puerto Rico, 276–77

Kansas City Star, 94

Katz, Joseph, 332n

Kelmscott Press, 123

Kenealy, Alexander, 256

Kettle Hill, battle of, 262, 263, 266

Key West, 246–47, 251

Kidd, Benjamin, 129

King, Charles, 196

"King's Favor, The," 35

Kipling, Rudyard, 70, 70n, 82, 128, 174

amount earned per word, 297
Kirkland, Joseph, 68
"Knife, The," 320
Knortz, Karl, 126

Lafayette College, 3–4, 29–31, 30, 33–34
Lake View, New Jersey, 42, 45, 72
Lantern Club, 119, 120, 142, 152, 161
Las Guásimas, battle of, 257–59, 294
"Last of the Mohicans, The," 40
Lawrence, Frederic, 52, 53, 55, 59, 62, 64,
    130, 159, 163, 167, 332
  camping with SC, 38, 41, 89
  on SC's appearance in Athens
    photograph, 206
  on SC's conception of women, 284
  on SC at Lafayette, 33–34
  on SC's meticulous writing, 54
  on SC's return from Mexico, 116
Lawton, General Henry Ware, 257,
    261–63, 267
Le Débâcle (Zola), 130
Leslie, Amy, 195, 212, 241, 313
  Hawkins as agent for payments to, 195,
    196, 201, 221–22, 237
  lawsuit, 237–38
  letters to, 172, 174–75, 177, 221–22, 224,
    313
  and SC, 167–70
  after SC's death, 334
  SC's debt to, 171
Leslie's Weekly, 133, 197, 258, 332
Lewiston (Maine) Journal, 212
Lexow Committee, 160
Liebling, A. J., 333
Life magazine, 154, 279
Light That Failed, The (Kipling), 70n
Limpsfield-Oxted area. See Oxted,
    England
Linson, Corwin Knapp (CK), 167, 192, 196
  camping with SC, 89
  and coal mine report, 87–89, 217
  first meeting with SC, 58
  illustrations for stories, 72
  SC's Creole letter to, 107
  SC's Mexican adventure, 113–14
  on SC as "rather dandified," 195–96
  on SC's "tramp period," 80

SC's visits to studio, 62–65, 78–79, 81
Lippincott's Magazine, 320, 322
Literary Digest, 211, 320
Little, Reverend Charles J., 33, 313–14
"Little Cora" stories, 320
"Little Regiment, The," 143–44, 152, 218,
    238
Little Regiment, The, 196, 294, 297
London
  SC's casket in stable, 331
  SC's first visit, 197–98
  SC's meeting with Conrad, 229–32
  tuberculosis and, 272
"London Impressions," 219, 220
Longstreet, General James, 143
"Lord Tholepin of Mango Chutney,"
    275, 276
Lotus, 152
Lynch, George, 307
"Lynx-Hunting," 294
Lyon, Kate, 213, 239, 289, 307, 322
  children of, with Cora, 299, 303n
  Frederic's death and manslaughter
    indictment, 286–87
  research for "Great Battles," 320, 320n

Mabon, George B., 237
McBride, Henry, 120
McCalla, Commander B. H., 251
McCarthy, Justin H. Jr., 197
McClure, Robert, 239
McClure, Samuel Sidney, 77, 161
  stalls on Red Badge, 92
  SC's debt to, 222
  and SC's need for money, 286
McClure's Magazine, 87, 93, 247, 308. See
    also McClure's Syndicate
  coal mine piece, 91
  Red Badge submitted to, 87
  and SC's work, 236
McClure's Syndicate, 87, 138, 149
  seeks SC's work, 142
  stalls on Monster, 224, 236, 239
  syndication of SC's reports and stories,
    152, 196
McCready, Ernest, 177, 246, 249–50, 251,
    257
  on SC in battle, 255–6

McIntosh, Burr, 257–58, 262, 264, 268

MacIntosh, William, 131, 136–37

McKinley, President William, 164, 244, 277

Maclagen, Dr. J. T., 321–22, 324

McNab, Reuben, 265, 310

McNeil, Hammond, 336

Maggie: A Girl of the Streets, 40, 59–60, 77, 125, 134, 138, 147, 294, 297, 335
    Library of Congress copyright, 59
    plot and characters, 54
    praise for, 116, 134
    reviews, 100, 153–54
    Roosevelt and, 161
    SC's hatred of, 150, 151
    SC's private printing of, 58–60, 84
    toned down and republished, 153

Maine (U.S. battleship), 243–44

Main-Travelled Roads (Garland), 40

Malaria, 275, 308

"Man and Some Others, A," 152, 161, 234

"Man in the White Hat, The," 208

"Manacled," 308

Marblehead (U.S. warship), 251, 252

"Marines Signaling Under Fire at Guantanamo," 253, 286, 333

Marriott-Watson, H. B., 316

Marshall, Edward, 76, 92, 119, 167, 186, 246, 257, 310
    praise for *Red Badge*, 127–28
    with Rough Riders, 258–59
    wounded at Las Guásimas, 259

Martí, José, 173

Mason, A. E. W., 298, 300–301, 312, 326
    at Christmas party, 315, 316–18
    and SC's last illness, 323

Mattison, Harriet, 27

Maxwell, Colonel Joseph E., 262

May, Phil, 56–57

Meldrum, David, 287–88, 289

Mencken, H. L., 129

"Men in the Storm, The," 79–80

Methodist church, 4–5, 13, 77

Methuen (publisher), 294, 305, 319, 321

Mexico, 105, 111–15, 121, 139
    SC and *pistoleros*, 113–14, 192
    SC's reports and fables, 126, 231

Mexico City, 112

Michelson, Charles, 173, 195, 275–78
    and SC's farewell to "El Dog," 277–78
    SC as "frail white ribbon," 274–75
    SC and taking of Juana Diaz, 277

Miles, General Nelson, 276

Millet, Frank D., 69

Mills, Althie, 286–87, 289

Minneapolis Tribune, 94

Monster, The (novella), 222, 239, 240, 241, 245
    American rights to, 223
    evaluation, plot, and characters, 215–19
    McClure's rejection, *Harper's* acceptance, 224, 236, 239, 249
    payment for, 297
    praised, 279, 333
    SC's enthusiasm for, 284

Monster and Other Stories, The, 239, 318, 320

Montgomery, C. B. (ship's steward), 180, 182, 184–85, 187

Morgan, J. P., 324

Morrison and Nightingale (law firm), 295

Mosquito Inlet lighthouse, 179–80, 183

"Mr. Binks' Day Off," 89

Munroe, Hersey, 46–48

Munroe, Lily Brandon, 246, 273, 274, 280
    as character in story, 61, 138
    remembering SC, 47–48, 334
    romance (1892), 46–48, 149–50
    SC's letters to, 61–62, 77, 81–82, 125

Munsey's Magazine, 122

Murphy, Captain Edward, 177–85
    and "Open Boat," 191
    sinking of *Commodore*, 181–85
    on SC's "grit," 187

Murphy, Vinton, 175

"Mystery of Heroism, A," 121–22

"Narrow Escape of the Three Friends," 249

Nebraska, 101–3, 106

"Nebraska's Bitter Fight for Life," 102–3

Nebraska State Journal, 94, 101–2, 102, 126

New Orleans, 107

New Orleans Picayune, 130

New Orleans Times-Democrat, 101, 278

New Realism, 40–41, 82, 134
New York Advertiser, 126
New York City, 143, 150. *See also* Clark,
    Dora, affair of
    Bowery and Lower East Side, 42, 45,
       73–74, 84, 93, 120, 138, 197
    Park Row, 45
    Police Department and Roosevelt,
       160–62
    Red Badge reviews, 134
    slums and immigrants, 52–55
    Tenderloin district, 155, 160, 163–64,
       169, 175
    and tuberculosis, 272
New York Daily Tribune, 237
New Yorker, The, 333
New York Herald, 17, 223, 246, 247, 249
New York Journal, 157–59, 164, 213, 246,
    257, 267, 274, 283, 320
    attack on *New York World,* 270
    Cora's dispatches from Greece, 200
    correspondents covering war in Greece,
       201
    on Dora Clark court case, 165–67
    "Irish Notes" published, 222
    SC asks to cover Boer War, 319–20
    SC sent to cover Puerto Rican
       campaign, 271
    SC's debts to, 222, 286
    SC's expense account cut, 280
    on SC's hiding in Havana, 282
New York Press, 76, 84, 92, 127–28, 152, 166,
    220, 222, 223
    Red Badge in Sunday edition, 94–95
    SC's pieces published (1894), 93, 94
New York Recorder, 129
New York Sun, 45
New York Times, 40, 45, 128, 165, 166, 197,
    213, 238
    Civil War story, 68
    on Frederic's death, 287
    review of *Active Service,* 314
    review of *George's Mother,* 153
    on sinking of *Commodore,* 187
New York Tribune, 22, 45, 52, 166, 332
    "Great Bugs" story, 36
    JOUAM parade story, 49–51
    review of *Black Riders,* 122

    review of *Maggie,* 154
    review of *Red Badge,* 127
    SC's summer reports, 25–29, 39–40, 41,
       48, 53
    SC as Syracuse correspondent, 33
New York (U. S. flagship), 247–48, 250,
    257
New York World, 45, 101, 166, 173, 187, 256
    payments to SC, 223
    SC in Cuba as war correspondent, 246,
       250
    on SC's part in ship disaster, 187–88
    SC's payment refused, 270–71
Newell, Peter, 279
Newgarden, George J., 265
Nigger of the Narcissus, The (Conrad), 232,
    233
Niver, Fred, 186
No Enemy (But Himself) (Hubbard), 138
Norau, Max, 129
Norris, Frank, 247, 248
Norris, John, 270–71
"Novelist Crane a Hard Man to Scare,"
    164
Noxon, Frank, 35, 59, 70, 136

"Occurrence at Owl Creek Bridge"
    (Bierce), 194
Ocean Grove, 11, 17, 25. *See also* Asbury
    Park/Ocean Grove
O'Connor, James, 166
"Octopush, The," 43
Oliver, Arthur, 48–49, 51
Omaha World Herald, 101
"Ominous Baby, An," 72, 84
"One Dash — Horses," 113, 147
O'Neill, "Bucky," 266
"Open Boat, The," 181, 182, 195, 196,
    234, 236, 238
    excellence of, 190, 321, 333
    payment for, 297
    in *Scribner's,* 211
    writing of, 190–92
Open Boat and Other Stories, The, 297
"Opium's Varied Dreams," 164
Orange Blossoms regiment, 64
O'Ruddy, The (Crane-Barr), 336. *See also*
    Irish romance

Oxenbridge, Sir Goddard, 292, 316
Oxted, England, 213, 291–92

"Pace of Youth, The," 61, 63, 285
Paine, Ralph, 51, 177, 247, 249, 251–52, 255
Paris, 212, 307, 321
Parker, Commissioner Andrew D., 160–61
Parker, Henry, 336
Parker, Judge Alton B., 302
Parker, Walter, 278–79
Parkin, Thomas, 319
Parodies
    of *Black Riders*, 123, 129
    of *Red Badge*, 154
    of theatrical melodramas, 76
    of war dispatches, 212
Pawling, Sidney, 139, 197, 229, 230
Pease, Edward, 214
Pease, Margery, 214, 318
Peaslee, Clarence Loomis, 32–35, 107
Peck, George (grandfather), 6, 10–12
Peck, Henry Thurston, 117
Peck, Jesse Truesdale (great-uncle), 5, 11, 14, 31
Peck, Wilbur F. (uncle), 11, 14
Peel, William, 200
Pendennis Club, 52–54, 55, 59–60, 62, 65
Pennington Seminary, 21–22
Pennsylvania coal mine, 59, 87–89
Pettie, Robert B., 101
Pharsala, Greece, 202
Philadelphia Press, 84, 94, 247, 249, 270
    Red Badge praised, 95, 101, 127
Philistine magazine, 122–24, 130, 152, 238
Philistine Society banquet, 131–37, 141, 681
Phillips, John, 138–39, 224, 238
Pictures of War, 269, 297
Pierce, Jennie, 27, 150
Pike, Charley, 120
Pike County, Pennsylvania, 89–91, 126
Pike County Puzzle, The, 90–91
Pinker, James B., 288, 289, 291–92, 294, 314
    appealed to for money, 307, 318–19, 320–21, 322–23, 328, 336

and Cranes' financial problems, 308–9
    takes control of SC's work, 305
    as guarantor for SC's debts, 294–95
    "Upturned Face" sent to, 309
Place de la Constitution, Athens, 200–201
Plant, Alfred D., 294, 321, 324
Political novel, 149–51
Ponce, Puerto Rico, 275, 276–77
Port Jervis, New York, 12, 64, 89, 196, 224, 324, 328
    lynching of black man, 46
    and *The Monster*, 216–17
Port Jervis Evening Gazette, 46
    SC writing for, 162
Port Jervis Union, 16, 90, 217
"Price of the Harness, The," 288, 310
    excellence of, 333
    plot and characters, 283–84
Prince of Wales, 293
Princess Aline (Davis), 128
Prostitutes, SC and, 81
Ptolemy, Adoni, 145, 240, 243
Ptolemy brothers, 213, 214, 302
Puck, 76, 121
Puerto Rican campaign, 274, 275–77
Pugh, Edwin, 306, 316
Pulitzer, Joseph, 244, 270, 324

Quick, Sergeant John H., 254

Raught, John Willard, 89
Ravensbrook house, 213, 214, 233, 240, 243
    creditors, 245, 291
    rent due, 282, 295
"Realistic Pen Picture, A," 94
"Recollections of a Private" (Goss), 68
Recollections of a Private Soldier in the Army of the Potomac (Wilkeson), 68
Red Badge of Courage, The, 86, 89, 117, 118, 124, 150, 153, 197, 211, 222, 261, 277, 294, 320. *See also* Fleming, Henry
    and *Century's* Civil War series, 63–65
    compared with *Sebastopol*, 68–69, 71n
    and "The Coward" (CGS), 68
    Davis's praise for, 198
    dialect, use of, 85, 86
    English sales of, 332

evaluation of, 65–66, 71
final transcription, 73, 74–75
Garland's editing of, 85
and *McClure's Magazine*, 87
mortgaging of, 294–95
origin of title, 86
page proofs, 126
parodied, 154
regarded as SC's only masterpiece, 333
religious imagery, 69–71
reviews, 95, 127–29, 134, 154
revisions, 83, 85–86
Roosevelt and, 161
sales of, 297
SC on, 65, 83, 105, 107, 143, 154, 191, 143
success of, 138, 140
serialization (December 1894), 94–95
writing of, and excerpts, 65–71
"*Red Badge* of Hysteria, The" (review), 154
Red Cross, English, 206
Reeves, Earl, 27
"Regulars Get No Glory," 270
Reid, Whitelaw, 50–51
"Reluctant Voyagers, The," 72, 190–91, 320
Remington, Frederic, 262
Republican Party, 51
Revolutionary War novel, 305, 319
Reynolds, Paul Revere, 196, 238, 240, 249, 251, 297, 319
    Cuban poems and stories sent to, 280, 282, 283–84
    end of relationship, 305
    inferior work submitted to, 294
    money advance on unsold work, 322
    requests payments from publishers, 236–37, 239, 282, 286, 287, 293–94
    as SC's literary agent, 222–23
Richards, Grant, 289
Riis, Jacob, 52–53, 54, 86, 160
Ritchie, Edith, 307, 315, 317, 325
    on Cora and SC's love for each other, 311–12
Rojo, Paul F., 187
Roosevelt, Theodore, 42, 293
    and Hare's defense of SC, 334–35
    impression of SC, 163, 198
    as New York police commissioner, 159–61
    with Rough Riders, 257–60, 263–64, 266
Rough Riders
    "gallant blunder" at Las Guásimas, 257–60
    at San Juan Hill, 261–66
Roycroft Press, 123, 136
Ruedy, Mathilde, 176–77, 198, 202, 213, 220, 240, 243, 286, 302, 305

"Sailing Day Scenes," 89
St. Marina (Greek ambulance ship), 207–8
Sampson, Rear Admiral William T., 246, 247–48, 250, 251, 257
"Sampson Inspects Harbor at Mariel," 248
San Antonio, Texas, 109–11
San Francisco Argonaut, 211, 314
San Francisco Examiner, 94
San Juan Hill, battle of, 262–68, 270, 283
    soldiers' illnesses, 275
    wounded and dying soldiers, 263–66
Santiago, Cuba, 250, 268, 286
    campaign, 256–58
Saturday Review (English), 219, 222
Schley, Commodore Winfield Scott, 250
Scott-Stokes, John, 251, 289, 292, 294–95
    accepts Irish novel, 319
    Revolutionary War novel promised to, 305
    and SC's requests for money, 308
Scovel, Sylvester, 173, 177, 246, 248, 250, 261, 264, 268, 270
    on Cora and SC in Greece, 207
    on cowardice of Seventy-first Regiment, 270
    letters to, 220–21, 224, 236, 244–45
    with SC at Santiago, 256–57
Scribner's, 54, 87, 245, 294
    "Open Boat" published, 196, 211
Seaman, Elizabeth Cochran, 101
Seaside Summer School of Pedagogy, 22, 40
Sebastopol (Tolstoy), 68–69, 71, 267, 310

Seitz, Don C., 270–71
Selene, Gertrude, 81
Senger, Louis "Lew," 38, 41, 43, 58, 64,
    101, 133, 135, 142
  camping with SC, 89
  on SC after shipwreck, 190
Senger, Walter, 135
Seven Seas, The (Kipling), 174
Seventy-first New York Volunteer
    Regiment, 270
Shafter, General William R., 257
Shaw, Albert, 62
Shaw, George Bernard, 213
Sheridan, Clare, 292, 301–2
Siboney, Cuba, 257, 294
Sims, Chancellor Charles N., 34
Skinner, Dr. Ernest B., 325
Smith, Bragdon, 26
Smith, Ernest G., 3, 30–31
Smith, Harry B., 130
Smith, Johnston (SC's pseudonym), 59
Smolenski, General Constantine, 203,
    205, 208
Social Evolution (Kidd), 128–29
Soldiers, wounded and dying, 206, 208–9,
    263–66, 268–69, 310
"Some Hints for Play-Makers," 76
Spanish-American War. *See also* San Juan
    Hill, battle of
  battles, 251–69
  beginnings, 243–45
  and Cuban independence, 246–48
  defeat of Spain, Puerto Rican
    campaign, 275–77
  field conditions, 260–61
  Mauser bullets, 258, 276
  SC's horses, 256, 265, 277, 278
  SC on wounded, 263–66, 268–69
  stories, 283–84, 286, 310, 335
  wood-dove calls, 258, 276
Sponge (SC's dog), 233, 325
"Spotted Sprinter, The" (parody), 123
"Squire's Madness, The," 308
S.S.T. Girlum society, 27, 27n
Stangé, Emile, 81
Stanley, Henry M., Jr., 28
Starrett, Vincent, 334
Steffens, Lincoln, 160

"Stephen Crane's English Years: The
    Legend Corrected" (Stronks), 297n
Stevens, Ashton, 334
Stevens, Wallace, 332
Stevenson, Robert Louis, 81, 301
Stewart, Captain Donald, 176, 207, 212,
    291, 336
Stokes, Jack, 243
Stronks, James B., 297n
Sudan, 224
Sullivan County tales, 38–39, 82, 83, 125,
    191
  and characters in *Maggie*, 55
  excerpts and analysis, 43–44
  "man alone in universe" theme, 43, 61
Swinburne, Algernon Charles, 213
Syracuse Daily Standard, 36
Syracuse Herald, 36, 57
Syracuse University, 31–37, 332–33, 337

Taber, Henry Persons, 123, 131, 136
Talmage, Thomas DeWitt, 54
Tammany Hall, 160
Taylor, Annie, 325
Taylor, Cora, 186, 217, 278
  Amy Leslie's lawsuit and, 239–40
  appeals to Pinker for money, 307,
    318–19, 322–23, 328, 336
  at Brede Place, 298–304, 311–12
  Christmas house party (1899), 315–18
  efforts to bring SC home from Havana,
    287–90
  in Greece at the front, 200–202,
    205–208
  in Jacksonville, 174, 176, 336
  and Kate Lyon's children, 286–89,
    302–3
  letters to Scovel, 224
  in London with SC, 198–99
  love for SC, 176–77, 188–89, 190,
    288–89, 300, 337
  marriage to McNeil, 336
  physical appearance, background, and
    personality, 175–76
  SC's apparent abandonment of, 245,
    251, 282–86
  after SC's death, 331–32, 335–36
  and SC's health, 272, 274, 305